KU-014-929

TAKEN FOR A RIDE

75

£8.00

RC
451
.4
.A5
.MEA

SOCIAL STUDIES
LIBRARY
45, WELLINGTON SQUARE,
OXFORD.

WITHDRAWN

SOCIAL STUDIES
LIBRARY,
SOCIAL STUDIES C TRE, GE OFF ST
OXFORD. OX1 2RL

WITHDRAWN

MICHAEL MEACHER

Taken for a Ride

SPECIAL RESIDENTIAL HOMES FOR

CONFUSED OLD PEOPLE:

A STUDY OF SEPARATISM IN

SOCIAL POLICY

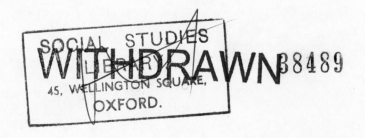

SOCIAL STUDIES
LIBRARY
45, WELLINGTON SQUARE,
OXFORD.
WITHDRAWN 38489

LONGMAN

SOCIAL STUDIES
WITHDRAWN
SOCIAL STUDIES CENTRE, GEORGE ST
OXFORD. OX1 2RL

LONGMAN GROUP LIMITED

LONDON

Associated companies, branches and representatives
throughout the world

© Michael Meacher 1972

All rights reserved. No part of this publication may be reproduced,
stored in a retrieval system, or transmitted in any form or by any
means, electronic, mechanical, photocopying, recording, or otherwise, without the prior permission of the Copyright owner.

First published 1972

ISBN 0 582 12701 7

WITHDRAWN

Printed in Great Britain by
Western Printing Services Ltd, Bristol

WITHDRAWN

Contents

Contents

Contents

Contents

Contents

Acknowledgements

We are grateful to the following for permission to reproduce copyright material:

A. Bigot for the table from *The Staffordshire Local Authority, Homes for old People and some General Characteristics of their Residents*, stencilled, Keele University: September, 1967, p. 19; The British Journal of Psychiatry for 'Problems arising from a study of mental patients over the age of sixty years' by F. Post, *J. Ment. Sci.* 1944, 90, 559, Table VII and 563, Table X and for Table II from 'Old Age Mental Disorders in Newcastle-Upon-Tyne, Part I, A Study of Prevalence' by D. W. K. Kay et al., *Brit J. Pschiat.*, 1964, 110, 150; British Medical Journal for 'Community needs of elderly psychiatric patients' by C. Colwell and F. Post, *Brit. Med. Jl.*, 1959, ii, 216, 22nd August, Table IV; British Medical Association for P. L. Parsons, 'Mental health of Swansea's old folk', *Brit. J. Prev. Soc. Med.*, 1965, 19(i), 44., Z. Stein and M. Susser, 'Widowhood and mental illness', *Brit. J. Prev. Soc. Med.*, 1969, 23, 108, Table II and T. McKeown and K. W. Cross, 'Responsibilities of hospitals and local authorities for elderly persons', *Brit. J. Prev. Soc. Med.*, 23, 36 and 38, Tables I and II; S. Karger, Basel, for M. Roth and D. W. K. Kay, 'Social, medical and personality factors associated with vulnerability of psychiatric breakdown in old age', *Gerontologia Clinica*, 1962, 4, 147–60; The Lancet for G. Wigley, 'Community services for mentally infirm old people" *Lancet*, 1968, ii, 963, 2nd November, and J. Williamson et. al., 'Old age and its implications for the general practitioner service', *Lancet*, 1964, i, 1117–20, 23rd May, Table V; Her Majesty's Stationery Office for an extract from the *Registrar-General's Statistical Review of England and Wales 1960, Supplement on Mental Health 1964* and Table from the same; Pergamon Press Ltd, for 'The Social and Medical Circumstances of Old People Admitted to a Psychiatric Hospital' by J. Connolly from *Medical Officer*, 10th August, 1962, 99; The Psychiatric Quarterly for B. Malzberg, 'Expectation of psychoses with cerebral arteriosclerosis in New York State: 1920, 1930 and 1940,' *Psychiat. Quart.* 1945, 19, 130; Routledge & Kegan Paul Ltd for an extract from Chapter 3 of *Old People in Hospital* by S. Benson and P. Townsend (forthcoming) and Tavistock Publications Ltd for a table from *Pyschological Illness* by E. J. R. Primrose.

Part I

INTRODUCTION

I

Aims of the study

We appear to be on the brink of a new departure in institutional care. Hitherto old people who showed signs of confusion have normally been placed either in ordinary residential homes for the aged or more particularly in the chronic wards of psychiatric hospitals or geriatric units. Recently, however, as a result of the 1959 Mental Health Act with its community emphasis and the Hospital Plan of 1962 with its proposal for a drastic reduction in the number of mental hospital beds,[1] an increasing number of local authorities are turning to the idea of special homes for confused old people.

The avowed aim behind this trend is to provide a setting where displays of confused behaviour would not cause irritation to other residents, as it is felt would be the case in ordinary welfare homes. On the other hand, it is widely regarded as undesirable to place confused old people, at least those 'mildly' confused, in a psychiatric hospital where their condition might be aggravated by association with gross mental illness.

Certainly there is evidence to support the former claim that confused action may cause considerable annoyance in ordinary residential homes. In one, for example, a woman who shared a bedroom with one other resident, got up in the night on one occasion, emptied the contents of her handbag into her bed and later took off all the blankets and strewed them on her neighbour's bed. Her companion, woken up three times, partly by the lights being switched on and off, was becoming overwrought when the matron arrived. Another woman in a different home on many occasions repeatedly took four pennies one by one out of a small tin box she kept in her handbag and then replaced them in the same methodical manner, with the accompanying metallic clinking sounds. Many of her companions did not seem to take any notice, but one of them confessed privately later: 'I try not to notice, but it drives me crazy. I try not to look at her.'

Such instances could be multiplied. But it is equally important to ask how far such disturbances are counterbalanced by possible

3

positive factors. Are the confused, for example, more integrated in the life of the home? Do rational residents tend to offer more assistance to the confused out of sympathy for their condition? Are the confused more likely to be involved in the main highways of conversation criss-crossing through each room as a result of living with predominantly rational companions?

About the second assumption – that a psychiatric ward constitutes an unwholesome environment for persons with senile confusion – it is less easy to reach any provable conclusions. Certainly, lengthy observation of two mental hospital wards showed that patients admitted on a diagnosis of arteriosclerosis or senile dementia displayed abnormally disorganized behaviour. There was almost no preoccupation with preserving one's own seat, as was so noticeable in the welfare homes. There was much greater restlessness and wandering of an apparently aimless kind. And speech, to an inordinate degree, represented the abrupt and fragmentary public expression of seemingly incoherent thoughts.

Nevertheless, whether this degree of disorganization reflected the number of severely mentally ill patients who shared the ward cannot be established by this study. Other factors may have been responsible, such as the lack of regular contact with any rational persons besides staff, or merely the fact that only the more severely confused were admitted in the first place.

Even if it is accepted that a chronic psychiatric ward is an unsuitable setting for old people with persistent confusion, it is not necessarily clear that a residential home reserved exclusively or mainly for confused old people would be manifestly more suitable. Perhaps this is best illustrated by a close look at a resident of one of these separatist homes who was interviewed in the course of this survey:

Miss Tangley is a very neatly dressed, rather plump woman who looks much younger than her seventy-four years. She had spent most of her working life in a bank, but now has lived for nearly ten years in the home where I met her.

She began her interview by saying, quite spontaneously, that she was looking for her friend, Mrs Carson, but found that she was in bed. 'Funny little thing she is – older than me, but she doesn't look it.' (In fact this was markedly untrue.) 'Nice little thing. She makes her mind up not to do something and won't do it.' Throughout the rest of the interview she kept returning on the slightest pretext to this friend of hers. 'I'm London born and bred. Mrs Carson, she pops in to see me when I'm in London or we go out together. She's sort of in my charge. I remember this place well – been here a few times. Not recently. I've stayed here with my own people, and we used to stay down here, mother, father, brother, sister.' When I then asked her where she was therefore living now, she replied: 'I've forgotten my address. We've taken a smaller house. Only three of us.'

She used this type of confabulation extensively to explain her present situation. When asked about the home and the people in it, she usually pleaded ignorance: 'I don't know her [the matron]. I've never been down this part. We've only just come, haven't we? I don't know the goings on.' Or she was at pains to emphasize the amenability of the company: 'I can assure you they're all nice people, you know. All quiet, or I wouldn't have come away with any of them. Quite elderly, aren't they, some of them? I'd *hate* a quarrel.' Above all, she stressed the transitory and voluntary nature of her stay: 'My people wanted me to [come here], and they said if you don't like it, we'll pick you up.'

Chiefly her conversation kept reverting to her central view of herself as the main economic support of her family. 'I'm still at ... What am I doing now? Oh yes, I've got to find a job. Long time since I left home, but mother likes me at home. I look after my mother and sister, but at the moment I'm out of work. I forget now what I was doing ..., I must get home, Mother couldn't spare me for long.'

She revealed the eager loquacity of the lonely person, and like many such persons she told her favourite stories with relish. 'Father wasn't strict, so Mother had to be. I once heard Mother say: "You must give him [the son] a thrashing, dear." But Father said: "No, I can't, dear." ... Father'll come and fetch me home. He's a darling. Mother has to do all the punishing. Unusual, isn't it?' But the story which through endless repetition had made her notorious among her companions concerned her engagement which she never tired of saying she broke off because she was still needed to look after the family.

It was this garrulity on well-charted subjects which offended other residents, and despite an equable and warm personality, she tended to be boycotted. This did not prevent her, however, from

5

usually being the first to engage visitors or new residents in conversation, but what soon antagonized even the unwary was her failure to react to any of her partner's cues in dialogue and her systematic restriction to a limited range of responses.

What bothered the staff were the consequences of her forgetfulness. When she made her daily complaint: 'Can you tell me where I sleep tonight? They tell me I'm sleeping here, but I've never slept here before', or 'You've moved my bed [untrue], but you never told me,' sometimes they did not know whether to laugh or cry.

Miss Tangley is perhaps the kind of person with a moderate degree of confusion who has led administrators to believe there is a new role for special homes in providing 'an environment suited to the needs and capabilities [of confused old people] out of competition with their mentally fitter companions on the one hand, and unassociated with gross mental illness on the other' (Andrews and Insley, 1962, p. 94). A similar conclusion has been drawn from concern about the best deployment of scarce psychiatric staff:

'There is a need for accommodation for demented patients who require some degree of restraint, but who do not require all the services of a mental hospital. Their needs could be met largely by nurses trained in geriatrics if the nurse in charge had psychiatric training' (Connolly, 1962, p. 100). Again the same plea has been made on grounds of the misuse of psychiatric beds (Enoch, 1963).[2]

Nevertheless, is it automatically clear that what Miss Tangley requires is a specialized form of residential care? Certainly her somewhat repetitive talk, her forgetfulness, the spatio-temporal dislocation of her ideas, her delusions and her inattentiveness to others' interests in conversation did seem trying at times to certain residents, though she did not display some of the severer signs of confusion like verbal incoherence, day or night wandering or incontinence. But would such characteristics seem less trying to residents in separatist homes than to those in ordinary ones? For there is no reason to suppose that the condition of the former necessarily impedes their capacity to react or the sensitiveness of their feelings.[3] Moreover, is it in Miss Tangley's own interest that she be segregated in a special home with others largely like herself? And might not some of the 'confused' behaviour, so far from being the irreversible consequence of organic deterioration, actually be a logical response to a very perplexing environment where regular contact with normal people in a balanced community was almost entirely lost? As Townsend (1962, p. 383) has put it, an increasingly rigorous classification of persons by age, handicap, and even sex 'may be clinically appropriate or administratively convenient, because specialists and trained personnel are scarce and equipment is expensive, but it may not assist the creation of real communities and may make the patients or residents psychologically more insecure'.

The object of this study, therefore, has been to compare the experiences of confused old people, together with the reactions of their rational companions and of the staff, in special homes where they form a majority or substantial minority of the residents, with their experiences in ordinary homes where they form only a small minority. At the outset a number of specific questions were posed for examination.

1. *Conversation.* Are the confused integrated in the normal frameworks of conversational exchange? If some are excluded, do the rational accept those whose speech is sometimes slightly irrelevant, but whose general meaning is apparent, whilst those whose train of thought is incoherent are boycotted? And if so, do the latter talk between themselves, or are they completely isolated?

2. *Activities.* Do the confused join in social activities, or what restrictions are put on their roles, rights and privileges because of their condition?

3. *Reaction.* What kinds of confused behaviour arouse irritation, how many feel this, how strong are such feelings, and what adjustments are made to tolerate such disturbances? Conversely, how far do the rational residents give assistance to the confused to compensate for any of their handicaps?

4. *Visiting.* How far do the confused manage to retain their contacts with the outside world?

5. *Adjustment.* How do the confused accommodate to feelings of impotence and inadequacy, and how do any defensive mechanisms they may employ affect their relations with other residents and staff?

6. *Staff.* If staff have to devote more time and care to the confused, does this arouse jealousy among rational residents? Alternatively, are staff authoritarian towards the confused because of the

strain of managing persistent incontinence or wandering, or because the temptation to manhandle confused residents with a deteriorated capacity to respond to requests or instructions is greater in a separatist home where fewer rational residents may be watching?

The answers to all these questions must then be compared between ordinary and separatist homes to see if any significant differences appear.

METHODS

Ideally, a study comparing the consequences between placing confused old people in ordinary residential homes and segregating them in special homes would proceed by isolating two matched samples, one of whom was being sent to the former environment and one to the latter, and then examining their relative experiences. The rigour of this approach, however, is unattainable in practice. For, chiefly, 'confusion' is so complex a phenomenon, and so heterogeneous in its manifestation, that it scarcely permits a finely graded calibration of individuals on a unidimensional scale. For variations in verbal incoherence, to take only one example, are often differences of type rather than of degree. Moreover, different forms of confusion, like physical wandering and verbal incoherence, involve such amorphous and varied concepts that they can be only very loosely applied to individuals in a graded manner. In other words, the precise matching of persons on the basis of a variable like 'confusion', except in the crudest sense, is almost impossibly difficult.

Secondly, there are the practical problems of actually obtaining a rating of confusion. Should this be carried out in the first week after admission to a home? But then because of the novelty of the experience, the break with a familiar past and the insecurity of temporarily feeling unsettled, disorientation is abnormally exaggerated. Should the rating therefore be carried out after a reasonable interval has elapsed following admission, say three months later? This would almost certainly be better, but it still faces the problem that at least some measure of the confusion, as it is estimated, probably *already* reflects the consequences of living in the institution.[4] The other possibility therefore is to carry out the rating immediately prior to entry to the home. This is perhaps the best solution from the point of view of accuracy of rating, but it means

8

that the total population of a home would not be rated until there had been a complete turnover of residents. Also, the problems of collecting the information where there was a wide catchment area for the home would be immense.

Thirdly, even if confusion could be measured in discrete intervals on a satisfactory scale, and even if a reliable rating could be obtained, there still remains an insuperable obstacle to measuring the exact effect of alternative social settings on the growth of an individual's confusion. For without recurrent pathological tests it is impossible to establish with any precision how far a measurable increase in confusion may be due to organic deterioration rather than to environmental influence.

And fourthly, there are anyway a number of other important variables, like the authoritarianism of the staff and the degree of encouragement given to activities, which may affect the extent of confused behaviour, but which cannot be satisfactorily controlled in the real situation.

For these reasons the bias of this study is impressionistic. It is based on a cross-sectional observation of each home at a particular point in time. No attempt was made scientifically to gauge the relative effect of different types of institutions by repeating tests at predetermined intervals of time. For quite apart from the problems of evaluation already mentioned, such an approach would categorize into unrealistic uniformities the inherent individuality which was so marked among the characters of this survey.

It was decided instead, having identified the 'confused' in terms of criteria of social dysfunction, to examine in both kinds of home the reaction of other residents to them and in the light of this their own relationships, activities and attitudes. To this extent the correlation of certain factors with either type of home was noted, but no certainty that the environment was necessarily the cause could be established.

First, three homes were selected from a list of eleven special residential homes supplied by the Ministry of Health. One was chosen as a voluntary home with long experience of caring for the confused aged, another as a purpose-built local authority home, and the third as the recently added wing of a comparatively small public assistance institution. For the purposes of control, three Part III homes were also selected on the basis of differing sizes – they had 19, 38 and 80 beds respectively. Furthermore, of the

9

chronic geriatric wards of a local mental hospital, one men's ward and one women's ward were selected which contained the highest proportion of patients diagnosed as suffering from arteriosclerosis or senile dementia. The aim here was to try to discover what differences the complete absence of rational companions made to the social relationships and attitudes of the confused. Lastly, a very large former public assistance institution was chosen, and five units within it examined, in order to assess how far these establishments still provided a final retreat for mentally infirm persons considered unsuitable for the newer purpose-built local authority homes.[5] Altogether 329 old people were interviewed and information sought about their backgrounds.

For each person, matrons were asked to classify their mental state on a specially designed scale. The ten-item Mental Status Questionnaire (Kahn *et al.*, 1960, p. 326) and the Tooting Bec scale (Doust *et al.*, 1953, pp. 397-8) were both considered, but rejected because they emphasized cognitive impairment rather than social maladaptation.[6] Equally the face-hand test (Fink *et al.*, 1952, p. 48)[7] seemed attractive, being culture-free as an unlearned perceptual task (which the two previous scales were not) and usable with persons who have problems with verbal communication. But again it was rejected because as a test of cerebral dysfunction it was too obliquely related to social performance. Instead a nine-part classification[8] was devised, with a three-point scale for each item, and the characteristics rated were: verbal confusion, wandering and restlessness, disorientation of place, misperception of the environment, memory defect, suggestibility, fear and insecurity, fluctuation of mood, and blunting of emotion.

Details of the social background and physical handicaps of each resident were sought from matrons, together with the allocation (and possible transfer) of bedrooms and of dining room and sitting room seats. The medical history of each resident was also sought wherever possible by consultation of case records and of the medication prescribed.

Each resident was interviewed and asked sixteen questions. These concerned: an explanation of admission to the home, description of daily activities, feelings about jobs or hobbies within the home, attitude to freedom within the home, capacity to read and write, contact with the world outside, friends in the home, degree of communication with others in the home, relationships with staff and residents, insight into self-situation, satisfaction with the general arrangements of the home, adaptation to the home, loneliness, attitudes to visits from friends and relatives, and financial position and use of money. Where at least some of the responses seemed rational, a further series of questions were asked about reactions to the behaviour of other residents, and in particular whether the subject was disturbed by incoherent talk, night or day wandering, interference with property, aggressiveness, and untidy or dirty behaviour in other residents.

Also, the daily routine of each home was observed at length. I watched each resident for a half-hour period in the course of systematic and continuous observation each day between breakfast and supper, taking notes of significant behaviour as unobtrusively as possible. In fact it may be claimed as an innovation in methodology that for the first time an exhaustive inventory of conversational and behavioural data collected in non-experimental conditions has been quantified. Of course, the participant observer is vulnerable to the charge that he inhibits the actions of those he watches. Clearly this influence was apparent in the case of certain residents at certain times: one woman could be heard muttering under her breath: 'I do wish that man wouldn't come in – don't know what he's messing about there for.' But even for these the length of my stay in each home (usually two to three weeks) meant that thresholds of suspicion gradually subsided. Others rationalized my presence, as emerged from interviews where my role was interpreted as 'inspector' or more usually as 'doctor', and indeed so sure was one woman of this assumption that she began the interview by rolling down her stocking. For these at least my presence presumably did not constitute an embarrassing interference.

Lastly, two national surveys were carried out by postal questionnaire. One was sent to the Chief Welfare Officer or Medical Officer of Health of every local authority in England and Wales to discover whether any special residential unit exclusively or largely for the elderly mentally infirm existed for that area, or if not, whether any was planned.

Altogether, therefore, this study presents only a preliminary insight into the care of confused old people. The problem has been steadily growing, as the next chapter seeks to show, but it has been neglected too long as a field of study. Too little is yet known, for example, about local authority procedures for assessing the mental state of persons believed to be subject to confusion, and no attempt has yet been made to clarify the relative merits of a bewildering variety of admission policies pursued by different authorities. Furthermore, before a satisfactory policy can be evolved, the relationship between domiciliary provision and the various forms of institutional care needs to be examined in representative areas. To this extent the present study offers only a brief glimpse of one aspect of the problem, but it is a field where further and deeper analysis can produce very rewarding results.

NOTES

1. Cmnd 1604, para 17: 'By about 1975, only 1·8 beds per 1,000 population will be required (compared with the present figure of 3·3)', based on Tooth and Brooke (1961).

2. Enoch (1963, p. 1160) claims that 'mental hospitals have been used as dumping grounds' because of the inadequacy of suitable accommodation for the mentally disordered aged. Fine (1963, p. 717) claims that if, alternatively, elderly patients with mild degrees of confusion are held to be primarily the responsibility of the geriatric service, then the current number of geriatric beds (1·3 per 1,000 population) will be inadequate and the Porritt Committee's recommendation of 2 per 1,000 would be appropriate.

3. Indeed the evidence presented in chapter 9 strongly contends the opposite.

4. Thus Wing and Brown (1961, p. 859) state the classic problem of interpretation: 'Are the different social conditions under which the patients live responsible for the differences in their clinical condition in the three hospitals, or are there different processes of selection which ensure that more clinically disturbed patients accumulate in one hospital than in another?'

5. Townsend (1962, p. 74): 'We get some deteriorated residents from small homes . . . the sicker you are, the less you're offered.'

6. The capacity to answer such questions as: What is today's date? When were you born? Who is the Prime Minister? is hardly relevant to successful functioning in a home. Nor, similarly, is it really satisfactory, for example, to assess reactions to interview ploys like deliberately letting a book fall or to 'please take one peppermint' as a means of measuring schizophrenic deterioration (Baker and Thorpe, 1956).

7. The test consists of touching the patient simultaneously on the cheek and on the dorsum of the hand and asking him to indicate where he was touched.

8. Other useful scales consulted were: (i) The Crichton Royal Geriatric Behavioural Scale (Robinson, 1960).

(ii) Psychiatric Rating Scales (Wittenborn, 1955).

(iii) A rating scale for appraising the behavioural adjustment of elderly brain-damaged patients (Bourestom and Iverson, 1965).

(iv) The Parkside Behavioural Rating Scale (1957), though the accumulation of details on this scale plus the occasional artificial fusion of different dimensions well shows the problem of demarcating gradations.

(v) Singer, Low and Zobel (1951).

Part II

THE
EXISTING FRAMEWORK:
DEFINITIONS
AND DESCRIPTION

2

The development of care

In order to understand the nature and function of existing residential care for the confused aged, it is necessary first to outline how the present services have evolved. This chapter therefore gives a brief sketch of their development and seeks to show reasons why the need for services for these persons, whether in the community or institutionally, can be expected to grow in future.

HISTORICAL DEVELOPMENT

Before the Mental Health Act of 1959, the Lunacy and Mental Treatment Acts provided the framework for the care of the senile confused. Originally it was never intended that the county asylum, later the mental hospital, should receive patients showing mild mental decay in old age. Such persons were regarded as properly cared for in the workhouses[1] or workhouse infirmaries, and their successors the public assistance institutions and the chronic wards of municipal and county hospitals. How confused old people fared in the general mixed workhouse at the turn of the century and what impact they had on the other residents is not explicitly recorded. A hint, however, may be gleaned from the following passage in one of the annual reports of the Local Government Board about 'senile imbeciles':

> I am sorry to say that in all but six of the workhouses in my district imbeciles mix freely with the other workhouse inmates. Many of them are mischievous, noisy, or physically offensive. In some instances, even if their bodily ailment is very slight, they sleep in the sick wards in order that they may come under the supervision of the nurses, and they frequently disturb other patients at night. By day they are a source of much irritation and annoyance, and in a small workhouse I have known the lives of a number of old men made seriously uncomfortable by a mischievous idiot for whom no place could be found in any asylum.

... A good many are often found useful in the laundry and other domestic work of the institution, but I do not think this consideration ought to outweigh what may almost be characterized as the cruelty of requiring sane persons to associate, by day and by night, with gibbering idiots (Preston-Thomas, 1901).

The criteria for admission laid down under the Lunacy and Mental Treatment Acts were designed to establish only that the patient was 'of unsound mind and a proper person to be taken charge of and detained for care and treatment'.[2] No distinction was drawn between different forms of care. This led to what the Royal Commission on the Law relating to Mental Illness and Mental Deficiency (Cmnd 169, 1957) considered to be 'an abuse of compulsory powers'. For

a judicial order for the admission of a patient to a mental hospital is usually considered mandatory, in the sense that the hospitals feel obliged to admit any patient when an order has been made unless there are quite exceptional difficulties in doing so. ... As a result, at a time (after 1948) of general shortage of accommodation, greater pressure can now be brought to bear on mental hospitals to admit a patient, provided he is 'of unsound mind', than on other hospitals or residential homes. There is some evidence that in some areas at any rate this has contributed to a tendency to use the compulsory powers contained in the Lunacy Acts to admit to mental hospitals patients who, though mentally ill or infirm, are not necessarily in need of the special facilities of a mental hospital.[3]

These were persons who, the Report contended, 'could be equally well cared for in a geriatric or chronic sick hospital or in an old persons' home'.[4] As a result it was concluded that the extent to which mental hospitals were used for social welfare purposes may actually have increased since 1948.[5]

To enable old people with failing mental powers to be given proper care and attention without undesirable and unnecessary 'certification', the Royal Commission considered a suggestion[6] that the compulsory powers contained in section 47[7] of the National Assistance Act 1948, should be used to effect the compulsory admission of senile patients to hospitals or welfare homes. But it preferred instead to recommend merely that there should be no mandatory order for admission to mental hospitals even when compulsory powers were used,[8] and in general that a wider range of residential and other services should be developed for elderly patients.

More specifically the Commission contemplated the establishment of some sort of specialized accommodation:

There is at present a clear need for more residential accommodation, of the type which should be provided by the local authorities, for persons suffering from a degree of mental infirmity which is manageable in such a home and which does not require care or treatment under specialist medical supervision. Some would be suitable for general old people's homes, but *it might be preferable for others to be in special homes.*[9] [Author's emphasis.] Many old people could be protected from further mental deterioration if they could be given the security and attention provided in this sort of home early enough, and might then not need to be admitted to hospital. Similar residential care is needed for elderly patients who have been in hospital and have reached the stage at which they would be discharged if they had relatives able to give them a home and a certain amount of supervision (Cmnd 169, para 628).

This immediately raises the question of guidelines for defining who is or is not 'suitable' for a special home and what degree of mental infirmity is or is not 'manageable' in such surroundings. On this issue the Commission drew a blank, since it made no empirical analysis of any homes with a significant proportion of confused residents. Attention was only given to establishing a division of responsibility between hospitals and local authorities, and for this the Commission was content to quote the judgment of the Committee of Enquiry into the Cost of the National Health Service (1956). Welfare authorities were to undertake the 'care of the infirm (including the senile) who may need help in dressing, toilet, etc., and may need to live on the ground floor because they cannot manage stairs, and may spend part of the day in bed',[10] whilst hospitals were to be responsible for the 'care of the senile confused or disturbed patient who is, owing to his mental condition, unfit to live a normal community life in a welfare home'. Unfortunately, what behaviour or condition rendered a person 'unfit to live a normal community life' was not specified. All that the Commission would commit themselves to was a belief in the efficacy of psychogeriatric assessment procedures. 'If it is doubtful whether an elderly person suffering from some degree of mental infirmity or confusion is suitable for a local authority home, or whether he or she needs hospital treatment, it is probably better that he or she should go to a psychiatric or geriatric hospital, at least for a period of observation, provided that this does not result in his having to remain there indefinitely' (Cmnd 169, para 629).

With the criteria for eligibility to special residential homes never satisfactorily examined,[11] the passing of the Mental Health Act in 1959 was greeted with apprehension in some quarters that mental hospitals might try to discharge old people who had been in-patients for many years into welfare homes. For, quite apart from shortages of accommodation produced by the closing of old and obsolete institutions and the upgrading of infirmaries to hospitals dealing mainly with acute illness, the mental hospitals had been forced before 1959 to accept on a three-day order many patients whose mental state was secondary to physical illness. Once these patients gained admission to a mental hospital, it was 'often extraordinarily difficult, if not impossible' (H. B. Kidd, 1963a, p. 442), to arrange their discharge or transfer, and so the real needs in terms of accommodation for the elderly were masked by the overcrowding of the mental hospitals.

In the event, however, the fear of an excessive number of transfers of mental patients to welfare homes has proved largely ill-founded. Indeed the overcrowding of many mental hospitals with elderly mentally infirm patients has continued unabated.[12] An investigation of 153 consecutive admissions of old people to a psychiatric hospital during the first six months of full operation of the Mental Health Act showed that six months from their admission only three had been discharged to welfare homes (Connolly *et al.*, 1964, p. 196); one of the three was suffering from affective disorder, another from late paraphrenia, and the third from arteriosclerotic psychosis. Furthermore, other means were found to reduce the number of in-patients in mental hospitals, including the month-in/month-out system,[13] day care, boarding out and community support. Whitehead (1965), illustrates the use of these in describing the evolution of a psychogeriatric unit at Severalls Hospital, Colchester, Essex.

THE PRESENT NEED FOR RESIDENTIAL CARE

In fact, the demand for residential accomodation for the confused aged following the extension of local health and welfare authority powers[14] under the 1959 Act has been variously calculated. One official estimate, for example, considered by some to be conservative, concluded that, of all patients over sixty-four in psychiatric hospitals in three hospital regions in 1954, about 25 per cent, representing some 10,000 in the country as a whole, 'were of a type suitable for care elsewhere, of whom about half might be suitable for old people's homes and half for chronic sick hospitals' (Min. of Health, 1957a, p. 226). Similarly a psychiatrist wrote in 1963 that 'no more than 15 per cent of the total number of mentally disturbed aged patients requiring institutionalization [*sic*] could be suitably accommodated in special local authority hostels' (Fine, 1963, p. 557).

By contrast, in a study of the 335 patients over sixty-five in a particular psychiatric hospital in Wales in 1961, it was judged that only nineteen, or 5·7 per cent, could be considered suitable for a special residential unit for 'senile wanderers' (Andrews and Insley, 1962, p. 96). They did add, however, that the small figures were mainly because long-stay elderly patients quickly became institutionalized and transfer to another environment was thought unwise. But they felt that from those recently admitted 'a steady stream of candidates' would be found for a special home. Andrews and Insley quote a private analysis undertaken over several years in Kent of all the applications for residential accommodation under the local authority, which suggested that 6 per cent of all applicants would be 'more suitable in a special type home' (W. E. Allison, 1961, personal communication). A further indication of the limited requirement for special welfare accommodation for the mentally confused elderly is provided by a questionnaire sent by the British Geriatrics Society to its members. This concluded that in eighteen geriatric units, out of a total of 1,846 elderly patients with mental disturbance, only 136, or 7·3 per cent, were considered to be suitable for care in a welfare home (National Corporation for the Care of Old People, 1963, p. 7). In close accord with this is the result of another study quoted by the 1957 Report of the Ministry of Health: it was estimated in April 1957 that of the elderly mental patients in the hospitals of the South-West Metropolitan Region about 5·6 per cent were suitable for welfare accommodation.[15]

Since the criteria lying behind these various estimates are not explicit, it is difficult to determine their relative validity. One can perhaps only conclude that of the approximately 60,000 old people in psychiatric hospitals and nursing homes (P. Townsend and Wedderburn, 1965, p. 23), a number between 3,500 (5·7 per cent) and 7.500 (12·5 per cent) might more suitably be accommodated in welfare homes or specialized residential units, and possibly another 8,500 (7·3 per cent) of the 115,000 old people in other (geriatric) hospitals and nursing homes. An idea of the extra demand which this could place on residential services can be gained from the fact that these figures would require the provision of additional beds to the extent of about an eighth of the existing total welfare accommodation in Great Britain.

But quite apart from confused old people in psychiatric hospitals or geriatric units, another source of demand for new or additional residential accommodation for these persons arises from the gradual closure of the former public assistance institutions. For of Chief Welfare Officers and Medical Officers of Health in England and Wales who, in answer to the specialized accommodation questionnaire, stated that a specialized unit had already been built or was intended, a third declared that this policy was motivated by the closure or expected closure of a former public assistance institution in their area. Now these institutions still contain nearly half the residents accommodated by local authority residential services for the handicapped and aged. (P. Townsend, 1962, p. 63, gives a figure of 49·7 per cent for 1 January 1960.) Some of the 34,780 persons resident in former PAIs in 1960 (*ibid.*, p. 43) will, of course, already have been transferred, but a large majority still remain to be moved, many in the latter half of the current local authority ten-year health and welfare plans. Since, then, a sizeable proportion of the aged remaining in the old institutions are mentally infirm,[16] it can be assumed that the gradual replacement of these buildings will generate a considerable demand for alternative residential accommodation, whether of a specialized nature or not. Nevertheless, however great or small the real demand for such accommodation, the initial reaction of local authorities to their new powers was cautious. By the end of 1961 only four hostels for the ambulant elderly confused had been provided by them.[17]

So far the discussion has been confined to patients known to be mentally disturbed already in hospitals or other institutions. But what proportion of the total population of pensionable age are confused to the extent that they may need care in a home, though not in need of specialist nursing care in a hospital? In fact a number of studies have been made of the prevalence of the main psychiatric syndromes of old age in various communities. The most detailed British study to date has been that undertaken by Kay, Beamish and Roth in Newcastle upon Tyne in 1960 (Kay *et al.*, 1964, p. 152). They interviewed a random sample of 309 persons aged over sixty-five and living at home, and where they found evidence of progressive mental deterioration, characterized by disorientation and failure of memory and intellect (provided this was not due to specific causes such as neoplasms, chronic intoxications or cerebrovascular disease), they made a diagnosis of 'senile brain syndrome'; where they found impairment of memory or intellect in subjects who gave a history of a stroke or of recent epileptiform seizures or confusional episodes, or who showed focal signs indicative of cerebrovascular disease, they diagnosed an 'arteriosclerotic brain syndrome'. On this basis they found that 4·2 per cent of the sample were suffering from a senile brain syndrome, with severe deterioration among 1.3 per cent of them, whilst 3·9 per cent were subject to an arteriosclerotic brain syndrome, with severe deterioration in the case of 2.6 per cent of them. Amazingly enough, their total of 3·9 per cent of old people living at home with severe mental deterioration from senile or arteriosclerotic psychoses was actually six times the proportion they found in a similar condition under institutional care.[18] They also found that a further 5·7 per cent of old people living at home suffered from a mild form of mental deterioration.

This evidence corresponds quite closely with other data. A British study in 1961 of a random sample of 228 persons in Swansea over the age of sixty-five estimated that 4·4 per cent were 'demented'.[19] An American survey of a large population of 1,592 persons aged sixty-five or over in various census tracts in Syracuse, New York, similarly found that 4·5 per cent of those living at home had a certifiable degree of illness due to psychoses of ageing (Gruenberg, 1961). Again, a Scottish survey presents evidence from which a figure of 5·5 per cent can be inferred (Mayer-Gross, 1948), and other data from abroad is largely consistent.[20]

We may therefore assume that of the 5,825,000 people aged sixty-five or over living in private households in Britain (P. Townsend and Wedderburn, 1965, p. 23), perhaps 300,000 (5 per cent) are suffering from severe mental deterioration.[21] and possibly between a further 600,000 to 900,000 persons from some milder form of mental impairment.[22] This immediately raises the question of whether they are being adequately cared for in their present situation, and indeed if so, as to whether some at least of those at present in psychiatric hospitals and geriatric units but not requiring specialized nursing care might not be enabled to maintain themselves, with the help of certain services, within the community rather than be transferred to a specialized residential unit for the 'ambulant elderly confused' or 'senile wanderers'. Unfortunately, no systematic study has yet been made of how elderly confused people manage in private households,[23] or how their families manage, or of what domiciliary services are or are not provided to ease their problems. Until such data has been produced on sufficient scale, it is impossible to calculate with any precision how large is the latent demand for residential care among this particular group of the elderly population.

THE CHANGING CONCEPT OF THE RESIDENTIAL HOME

Hitherto in discussing the need for residential care no attempt has been made to delineate possible differences of role between ordinary welfare homes and specialized units. Now this question has arisen only partly because since the Mental Health Act efforts have been made to seek residential care for many old people who had in the past been, or would otherwise now be, admitted to a psychiatric hospital or geriatric unit.[24] It has also arisen because of changes in the age and health of residents admitted to residential care in the customary manner as in need of 'proper care and attention' under the 1948 Act. For the average age on admission has been rising;[25] for the 137 persons admitted to the ordinary welfare homes in this study, it was 78·8 years. This may be related to data from Sweden about the average age of onset of senile dementia. A survey of 377 patients admitted to two large mental hospitals in Stockholm found that the mean age for men was 73·4 years and for women 75·3 years, with a mean age for first hospitalization for this condition at 76.4 years for men and 78·4 years for women, and a mean age at death of 78·5 years for men and 80·5 years for women (Larsson *et al.*, 1963, p. 219ff.). A rising age of persons admitted to residential care, together with an increasing longevity of existing residents, may therefore imply the likelihood of an increasing incidence of mental infirmity among the population of ordinary welfare homes.

This assumption seems to be confirmed by Ministry of Health statistics of the number of the elderly mentally handicapped in postwar residential homes which show a substantial increase (of 163 per cent) in absolute numbers since 1958 (Table 2.1).[26] However, as a proportion of the total number of 'aged' persons in postwar residential homes, the increase, though steady, has been the smaller one of 84 per cent over the past decade. Throughout England and Wales about one-seventh of aged persons in postwar residential care are now judged 'mentally handicapped' (or 'mentally disordered', defined as 'persons with an impairment of mental capacity in any form'). It is likely that the proportion is rather higher in the remaining former public assistance institutions,[27] but unfortunately Ministry of Health reports do not include details of prewar establishments used for residential accommodation.

Now admissions to residential homes for the elderly naturally reflect demographic changes amongst the elderly population in general, and trends in the latter may be expected to put further strain on the role of welfare homes as originally envisaged by the National Assistance Act in 1948. For not only is the proportion of old people to the rest of the population growing,[28] as is well known, but the higher age groups among old people are increasing proportionately faster than the lower ones, as Table 2.2 shows. For women this is already the case, and it will probably become true for men also within the next twenty years.

These estimates have significant implications for the likely incidence of mental infirmity among old people within the foreseeable future. For a recent study, taking a large national sample of old people in Britain, measured the proportion who could be judged 'illucid'. 'Illucid' was determined on the basis of the interviewer's observation and was defined as 'only at times or with considerable difficulty capable of organizing thoughts in lucid speech or any other form for the purpose of social communication'. Using this approach they estimated that of those aged 70–9, 5·1 per cent were illucid, whilst of those 80 or over the proportion rose to 9·2 per cent (Shanas, *et al.*, 1968). Now 'failure to communicate adequately' is not quite the same as 'confusion', but the figures do suggest that

Table 2.1

Elderly mentally handicapped persons in residential homes in England and Wales
(Annual Reports of Ministry of Health)

Year (31 December)	Sex	Post-war local authority homes with			Premises used as hospitals	Voluntary accommodation	Total	Index of absolute increase (1958 = 100)	Proportion of total number of aged in residential care (%)
		Less than 35 beds	35–70 beds	more than 70 beds					
1958	M	123	266	797	391	22	1,599	100	7·9
	F	528	762	1,719	744	117	3,870	100	
1962	M	183	486	896	347	25	1,937	121	8·2
	F	679	1,464	1,748	582	139	4,612	119	
1965	M	209	795	990	233	29	2,256	141	8·8
	F	830	2,397	1,895	368	142	5,632	146	
1967	M] F	(30 or under beds) 1,143	(31–70 beds) 6,037	2,699	1,276*	230	11,385	208	11·9
1970		1,321	9,141	2,738	839	370	14,409	263	14·5

* This figure is taken from all joint-user premises shared with hospitals, whether in the possession of a local authority or a hospital.

24

mental infirmity can be expected to occur most often amongst the oldest age groups.[29] This is confirmed by the evidence of Larsson *et al.* (1963) who found, in a large study of senile dementia already quoted, that a marked rise in the aggregate morbidity risk occurred with age. The risk was calculated at 1·7 per cent up to the age of 70, 5·2 per cent up to 75, and 10·8 per cent up to 80. Since the higher age groups are increasing disproportionately fast, the problem of management of persons with this handicap in welfare homes can only become more acute.

Table 2·2

Expected increases in the population of England and Wales aged 65 and over between 1961 and 2001*

Year	65–74 M	(%)	F	75–84 M	(%)	F	85+ M	(%)	F
1961	100	(1,419)	100 (2,102)	100	(594)	100 (1,081)	100	(90)	100 (212)
1971	125		115	104		117	112		137
1981	137		124	132		138	117		163
1991	138		110	146		151	154		200
2201	134		111	150		140	168		223

* G.R.O., Census 1961, England and Wales, pp. 28–9, and the Registrar General's *Statistical Review of England and Wales* for 1966, part II, p. 8. The figures in brackets are thousands.

This conclusion is further buttressed by reference to physiological factors. For it is known that some of the symptoms of mental confusion are direct consequences of senescence. It has been shown, by Bedford (1959, p. 186) for example, that cerebral circulation tends to become impaired in old age, and the brain is therefore more vulnerable in the elderly to the effects of anoxia[30] and of disease in other systems (Himwich, 1951). For firstly each and every one of the organs and systems of the body is directly concerned in cerebral cellular metabolism, and a disturbance of function of any may lead to adverse cerebral and mental effects. Secondly, in old age derangement of function of all organs, and hence of the brain, occurs more readily because their 'reserve' is lowered as a result of tissue and cellular ageing effects and of damage done by previous disease. Thirdly, with advancing years episodes of illness, especially infections of the respiratory and urinary tracts, tend to occur with increasing frequency, each episode carrying the hazard of cerebral metabolic or structural disturbances and mental confusion. These facts mean that the rise, both absolutely and relatively, in the number of old people in Britain must involve a substantial increase in the incidence of mental infirmity, though as Bedford is careful to point out, 'senile confusion' is by no means a necessarily irreversible condition, but rather 'means no more than that "this old person is ill" . . . It is not a diagnosis, but only a symptom of almost any disease within the whole field of medicine' (Bedford, 1959). (This is further discussed below, p. 39).

What do all these trends therefore imply for the role of residential homes for the elderly? It was foreseen as early as 1955 that their original role was changing, when the Minister of Health referred in circular 3 to 'the increasing difficulty of looking after the old people now that an increasing proportion of those needing admission will be the very infirm'. Reference has already been made to the unsatisfactory attempt, incorporated in circular 14 in 1957, to distinguish between hospital and local authority responsibilities by imputing to the latter 'the care of the senile confused or disturbed patient who is, owing to his mental condition, unfit to live a normal community life in a welfare home'. In circular 15 in 1962, the emphasis was reversed when it was declared that 'a patient should not be . . . admitted to hopsital without a clear-cut decision that he needs . . . such treatment, investigation or nursing care as only admission to hospital can provide'. Finally, in a memorandum accompanying circular 18 in 1965 the Minister prescribed that local authorities should be responsible for 'people with temporary or continuing confusion of mind, but who do not need psychiatric nursing care'. It also added that 'some incontinent residents may also be manageable in a residential home'.

This makes a picture very different from that envisaged in 1948 of homes for the elderly, and the various different strands intermingled within this developing policy have all tended to operate in the same direction. On the institutional side, the gradual clearance of the old workhouses after the abolition of the Poor Law has necessitated the residential accommodation in smaller homes of an unusually high proportion of both mentally and physically frail old people, while the extension of local health and welfare authority powers under the 1959 Mental Health Act has increased the number of mentally handicapped persons now cared for in homes for the elderly. On the residential side, the rise in the age of old people on admission from the community, reflecting the increased longevity of the elderly population at large, with the further vulnerability to mental and physical deterioration that this implies, has had the same effect.

In the face of these changes a number of local authorities have concluded that special residential units are desirable for confused old people, to permit them, as a number of local authority proponents of such schemes have claimed, 'to live in an environment suited to their special needs and capabilities'. Such specialized provision was first experimentally tried in the mid-1950s,[31] though for a time these sporadic schemes were confined to a few innovatory authorities. Recently the pace of this trend has considerably quickened, encouraged as it has been by Ministry advice.[32] How many local authorities then have made this choice, and what sort of special units are now being planned?

SPECIAL UNITS, EXISTING AND PLANNED

To discover how far the trend towards separatist accommodation had proceeded, a questionnaire was sent in November 1967 to every Medical Officer of Health or Chief Welfare Officer in England and Wales. From the 148 replies received,[33] it is apparent that thirty-seven local authorities,[34] or 25 per cent, already possessed 'a special unit (or units) exclusively or largely for the elderly mentally infirm'.[35] A further five such units were run by voluntary bodies or privately, and this may well be an underestimate.[36] In addition, sixty-four local authorities, or 43 per cent, have made definite plans to provide such accommodation for the future, as Table 2.3 shows. Altogether this constitutes, within eight years of the passing of the Mental Health Act, a substantial commitment to the concept of separatist residential care for the elderly mentally infirm, but even these figures understate the coverage. For half the local authorities which already possessed a special unit had no further plans to extend this form of care, so that a total of eighty-three authorities, or 56 per cent, either had already reserved accommodation for the elderly mentally infirm, or had definite plans specifically to do so in the near future.

Furthermore, the number of special units already existing or planned is 171, which represents a mean of 2·1 per local authority.[37] The number of beds planned to be in use in these units by 1972, where local authorities have made a definite decision on this question, totals approximately 4,365. For these authorities this indicates a mean provision of about fifty-seven beds in some form of

Table 2.3

Numbers of local authorities, voluntary associations and private agencies which have established, or are planning, specialized accommodation exclusively or largely for the elderly mentally infirm, in England and Wales

Local authority areas	Local authorities which have already established special units	Voluntary Asscns. known to have already established special units	Private Agencies known to have already established special units	Local Authorities which have planned special units for the future*
County Councils	19	2	1	28
County Boroughs	16	1	0	23
Metropolitan Boroughs	2	1	0	13
TOTAL	37	4	1	64

* As at November 1967.

segregated accommodation, whether a separate home or a separate wing of a home, for mentally infirm old people by 1972. (The scatter around this mean point is substantial, as might be expected. Cheshire, for example, intends to devote fourteen different units to this purpose by 1972, involving a total of 173 beds. But consideration of these differences is postponed until the fuller discussion of local authority policy in Chapter 10.)

Among local authorities providing such accommodation by 1972, considerable variation is apparent in the scale of the provision in relation to the population aged 65 and over, as Table 2.4 shows. At one extreme is Merthyr Tydfil which intends to offer 6·2 places per 1,000 of its elderly population estimated at only 7,400 in 1972. At the other extreme lie sixty-three authorities which have so far made no preparations for this form of care at all by 1972, while a further twelve authorities intend to provide only 0·5 places, or less, per 1,000. The median provision will be 1·1 places. In general,

Table 2.4 illustrates that the larger the size of the elderly population the smaller the extent of this type of provision. It might be thought that this pattern reflects the fact that the larger authorities may not yet have had time to implement plans sanctioned and encouraged by the Mental Health Act. But if the relative number of beds in ordinary homes for the elderly provides a reliable comparative guide, it remains true that provision is typically rather greater among the smaller authorities.

Table 2.4

Estimated local authority provision in England and Wales for the elderly mentally infirm in 1972

Local authorities listed by rank order of population aged 65 and over	Number of beds in ordinary homes for the elderly per 1,000 population aged 65 and over	Number of special units for the elderly mentally infirm	Number of beds in special units for the elderly mentally infirm	Number of beds in special units for the elderly mentally infirm per 1,000 population aged 65 and over
1 London	22·8	?? 27	?? 620	??0·7
2 Lancashire	17·4	NA	NA	NA
3 Kent	15·7	5	259	0·9
4 Essex	17·6	3	56	0·6
5 Surrey	18·0	3	75	0·3
6 Yorkshire – West Riding	17·7	1	30	0·1
7 Birmingham	16·7	NR	NR	NR
8 Cheshire	17·2	14	173	1·3
9 Staffordshire	17·2	3	109	0·9
10 Hampshire	14·3	3	108	0·9
11 Durham	13·5	—	—	—
12 Hertfordshire	15·4	1	24	0·2
13 Devon	14·2	2	70	0·7
14 Derbyshire	18·3	1+	13+	0·1+
15 Somerset	14·4	—	—	—
16 Glamorganshire	24·1	3	111	0·9
17 Liverpool	19·8	—	—	—
18 Sussex East	19·8	4	141	1·7
19 Sussex West	13·6	1	31	0·4
20 Warwickshire	23·1	—	—	—
21 Manchester	79·1	3	121	1·5
22 Nottinghamshire	15·2	2	82	1·1
23 Gloucestershire	18·3	3	*	*
24 Buckinghamshire	13·4	2	20–25	0·3

Table 2.4 (*contd.*)

Local authorities listed by rank order of population aged 65 and over	Number of beds in ordinary homes for the elderly per 1,000 population aged 65 and over	Number of special units for the elderly mentally infirm	Number of beds in special units for the elderly mentally infirm	Number of beds in special units for the elderly mentally infirm per 1,000 population aged 65 and over
25 Sheffield	18·4	2	16	0·2
26 Norfolk	19·8	1	35	0·5
27 Leeds	42·3	1	26	0·4
28 Bristol	17·3	3	105	1·6
29 Worcestershire	13·5	2	80	1·2
30 Dorset	17·8	3	108	1·7
31 Northumberland	15·5	—	—	—
32 Wiltshire	12·2	NR	NR	NR
33 Berkshire	16·2	—	—	—
34 Leicestershire	17·7	2	60	1·1
35 Yorkshire – North Riding	23·3	1	30	0·5
36 Cornwall	19·3	? 11	? 170	? 3·1
37 Bedfordshire	20·1	3	110	2·1
38 Lincolnshire – Lindsey	16·0	? 4	*	*
39 Northamptonshire	18·8	NR	NR	NR
40 Salop	21·0	—	—	—
41 Cambridgeshire (and Isle of Ely)	20·6	1	45	1·0
42 Monmouthshire	20·8	—	—	—
43 Suffolk – East	13·1	1	35	0·8
44 Portsmouth	19·0	? 1	*	*
45 Bradford	23·1	4	160	3·9
46 Nottingham	17·7	NR	NR	NR
47 Bournemouth	25·3	—	—	—
48 Leicester	33·4	—	—	—
49 Yorkshire – East Riding	14·5	1	35	1·0
50 Coventry	28·8	—	—	—
51 Southend	21·9	1+	25+	0·7+
52 Southampton	21·7	1	30	0·9
53 Kingston upon Hull	31·2	3	110	3·2
54 Brighton	26·7	1	35	1·0
55 Newcastle upon Tyne	25·1	? 3	? 105	? 3·1
56 Cardiff	21·7	—	—	—
57 Stoke-on-Trent	20·9	—	—	—
58 Oxfordshire	30·0	1	35	1·1
59 Cumberland	18·4	—	—	—

Table 2.4 (*contd.*)

Local authorities listed by rank order of population aged 65 and over	Number of beds in ordinary homes for the elderly per 1,000 population aged 65 and over	Number of special units for the elderly mentally infirm	Number of beds in special units for the elderly mentally infirm	Number of beds in special units for the elderly mentally infirm per 1,000 population aged 65 and over
60 Blackpool	12·7	1	30	1·0
61 Plymouth	15·2	NR	NR	NR
62 Denbighshire	15·8	1	30	1·1
63 Sunderland	27·4	2	70	3·1
64 Swansea	18·4	1	35	1·5
65 Wolverhampton	20·7	—	—	—
66 Suffolk – West	22·1	—	—	—
67 Carmarthenshire	22·5	1	35	1·6
68 Bolton	18·0	2	100	4·5
69 Huntingdonshire (& Peterborough)	26·2	—	—	—
70 Reading	18·1	NR	NR	NR
71 Caernarvonshire	22·8	1	6–8	0·3
72 Flintshire	17·5	1	26	1·2
73 Lincolnshire – Kesteven	23·4	? 3	*	*
74 Stockport	25·5	2	75	3·7
75 Norwich	27·4	NR	NR	NR
76 Herefordshire	20·6	1+	10+	0·5+
77 Oxford	31·0	—	—	—
78 Ipswich	26·7	—	—	—
79 Isle of Wight	16·2	—	—	—
80 Huddersfield	36·3	? 4	*	*
81 Birkenhead	16·4	NR	NR	NR
82 Derby	23·4	—	—	—
83 Hastings	21·8	1	50	2·9
84 Salford	28·9	NR	NR	NR
85 Middlesbrough	42·5	—	—	—
86 Southport	22·3	1	30	1·8
87 Northampton	21·5	—	—	—
88 Walsall	16·7	—	—	—
89 Blackburn	30·8	—	—	—
90 Wallasey	23·4	—	—	—
91 Lincolnshire – Holland	25·1	1	40	2·5
92 Eastbourne	18·6	—	—	—
93 Oldham	28·6	1	31	2·0
94 Preston	26·2	1+	40+	2·7+
95 Bath	23·4	NR	NR	NR

Table 2.4 (*contd.*)

Local authorities listed by rank order of population aged 65 and over	Number of beds in ordinary homes for the elderly per 1,000 population aged 65 and over	Number of special units for the elderly mentally infirm	Number of beds in special units for the elderly mentally infirm	Number of beds in special units for the elderly mentally infirm per 1,000 population aged 65 and over
96 Halifax	22·6	—	—	—
97 York	32·8	—	—	—
98 South Shields	29·8	—	—	—
99 Newport (Monmouthshire)	27·3	—	—	—
100 Grimsby	23·3	—	—	—
101 Pembrokeshire	18·9	1	35	2·7
102 Exeter	34·1	1	36	2·8
103 Rochdale	22·3	—	—	—
104 St. Helens	28·9	—	—	—
105 Lincoln	22·9	—	—	—
106 West Bromwich	24·9	1	39	3·4
107 Darlington	25·4	—	—	—
108 Gateshead	35·0	NR	NR	NR
109 Burnley	27·8	—	—	—
110 Rotherham	36·1	1	38	3·5
111 Westmorland	23·7	—	—	—
112 Worcester	28·1	NR	NR	NR
113 Doncaster	27·7	NR	NR	NR
114 Bury	34·9	1	34	3·4
115 Cardiganshire	27·6	1	34	3·5
116 Great Yarmouth	31·1	1	20	2·1
117 Wigan	25·4	—	—	—
118 Carlisle	22·0	1	23	2·5
119 Chester	27·2	—	—	—
120 Warley	19·0	—	—	—
121 Tynemouth	21·7	—	—	—
122 West Hartlepool	24·3	—	—	—
123 Anglesey	16·8	1	20	2·3
124 Gloucester	30·2	—	—	—
125 Barrow	25·3	1	25	2·8
126 Bootle	22·8	NR	NR	NR
127 Breconshire	23·1	NR	NR	NR
128 Warrington	29·1	—	—	—
129 Wakefield	27·8	—	—	—
130 Dudley	21·0	1	12	1·5
131 Barnsley	33·1	? 1	*	*
132 Merthyr Tydfil	26·0	2	46	6·2
133 Dewsbury	40·4	—	—	—

Table 2.4 (*contd.*)

Local authorities listed by rank order of population aged 65 and over	Number of beds in ordinary homes for the elderly per 1,000 population aged 65 and over	Number of special units for the elderly mentally infirm	Number of beds in special units for the elderly mentally infirm	Number of beds in special units for the elderly mentally infirm per 1,000 population aged 65 and over
134 Burton upon Trent	27·7	NR	NR	NR
135 Montgomeryshire	36·1	—	—	—
136 Merioneth	25·7	—	—	—
137 Canterbury	14·1	—	—	—
138 Rutland	15·3	—	—	—
139 Radnorshire	19·2	—	—	—

NOTES

Note. 1972 population projections from *Health and Welfare: the development of community care*, HMSO, 1963, Cmnd 1973, pp. 52–362.

'Special units' include wings of homes, which are regarded as individual entities, even if only a minority of the total establishment.

'London' represents (before 1965 when Cmnd 1973 was compiled) the LCC, Middlesex, East Ham, West Ham and Croydon, and also (after 1965 when the specialized accommodation questionnaire was sent out) the thirty-two metropolitan boroughs. It has been used as the only convenient means of comparing data relating to both before and after the London Reorganization of Government Act. However, a list of special units provided by statutory and voluntary authorities in England and Wales is given on pp. 371–5.

Bedfordshire includes Luton, Warwickshire includes Solihull, the Isles of Scilly are omitted, and Warley replaces Smethwick.

Key

? – it is unclear how many special units will have been built by 1972, but an average expectation has been taken.

?? – the figures have been calculated as precisely as possible, but the nature of the data makes a wide margin of error unavoidable.

+ – at least this number, and probably more, special units will have been built by 1972.

NR – no return made.

* – not yet decided.

— – no special units already established or planned.

NA – not applicable: some separation, but not systematic.

What can be said with certainty, however, is that the rate of growth in the establishment of segregated units of accommodation for confused old people is currently quickening. Table 2.5 reveals that the number in the present quinquennium 1966–70 is more than double that of the preceding one. Present plans for the succeeding quinquennium 1971–75, however, show a slight drop. But it is reasonable to expect, in view of the likelihood of some further plans yet to be formulated and others yet to be clarified, that any reduction will in the event prove marginal or even be transformed into an increase.

Table 2.5

Establishment of special residential units for the elderly mentally infirm in England and Wales by date and size

Date of estab-lishment	Special residential units with number of beds						TOTAL
	10 or less	11–20	21–30	31–40	41–50	51 and over	
1955–60	—	—	1	2	—	—	3
1961–65	1	4	8	13	5	1	32
1966–70	13	18	6	24	2	3	66
1971–75	4	9	12	19	5	—	49
Total up to 1975	18	31	27	58	12	4	150

Note. A wing of a home is again counted as an individual entity. Units are excluded where either the date or the number of beds had not been decided by November 1967, which means that the extent of future provision is somewhat understated.

Lastly, the size of these special units is clearly smaller than the great majority of ordinary homes for the elderly. P. Townsend (1962, p. 44) has shown that 11 per cent of residents living in postwar local authority homes, whether purpose-built or adapted, were in large homes of over sixty beds. Only two of the 150 residential units for the elderly mentally infirm surveyed in this study were found to contain over sixty beds, and both these were subdivided into largely self-contained parts. Nevertheless a large number of the units were larger than the size prescribed by government policy. For in 1962 the Ministry of Health recommended[38] that 'where a large proportion of residents will be mentally infirm or a home is planned specially for the elderly mentally disordered, it should not be for more than 35 residents. If it is necessary to exceed this figure, the residents' accommodation should be planned in self-contained units.' However, forty-five of the special units in this survey, or 30 per cent, contained more than thirty-five beds, whilst a further twenty units, or 13 per cent, reached the ceiling figure. Also, table 2.5 shows no shift over a period of twenty years towards the idea of a smaller home. Throughout this period two-fifths of the units established remained of medium size with 30–40 beds.[39]

The considerable recent increase in the accommodation provided specifically for the elderly mentally infirm can therefore be seen as symptomatic of the growing postwar trend towards more narrowly classified forms of residential care. As such, it at once raises important issues of judgment. On what basis are old people assessed as being suitable for such accommodation? Do special homes of this kind draw their residents direct from the community or from ordinary welfare homes? If from the latter, what sort of confused behaviour is regarded as unacceptable in an ordinary home? And above all, from the point of view of the welfare of the confused person himself (or more usually herself), how much does he or she benefit or lose from integration in an ordinary home, and conversely what adjustments are required as a result of segregation?

Now an answer to all these questions entails a clarification of the concept of 'confusion' or 'mental infirmity', and this will be attempted in the next chapter.

NOTES

1. Under Section 24 of the Lunacy Act 1890.
2. For instance, section 28(3) of the Lunacy Act 1890.
3. *Report on the Law Relating to Mental Illness* (Cmnd 169, para 259). In fact this was already a widespread practice before 1948. 'During the wartime years, the mental hospitals have admitted a very large number of patients with senile dementia, many of them of the simple dementing type who have no real need for special psychiatric treatment', though overcrowding was often as much as 25 per cent over the already inadequate peacetime accommodation (Dax and Reitman, 1946, p. 736). It was suggested at this time, that infirmaries were wanted where 'the simple dementing type of seniles' could be looked after.
4. Though long-stay psychiatric annexes already cared for 'elderly patients suffering from mental disorder pronounced enough to need nursing attention under psychiatric direction but not requiring the type of active treatment which can only be provided in a fully equipped mental hospital', Cmnd 169, para 226. Such annexes were administered either in conjunction with a mental hospital, or with a geriatric or chronic sick hospital, or were independent units.
5. *Ibid.*, para 596.
6. *Ibid.*, para 319.
7. This permitted, subject to certain conditions, the compulsory removal to hospital or elsewhere of 'persons who (a) are suffering from grave chronic disease or, being

aged, infirm or physically incapacitated, are living in insanitary conditions, and (b) are unable to devote to themselves, and are not receiving from other persons, proper care and attention.' Indeed the senile demented were one of those groups for whom residential homes were envisaged by the 1947 Nuffield Foundation Report (Rowntree, 1947, para 155), and by 1949, when the first statistics became available, over a third of residents were classified as 'physically or mentally infirm', and less than half of the residents were designated 'aged but not materially handicapped' (Ministry of Health, *Annual Report for 1949*, Appendix xi).

8. Cmnd 169, paras 381–3.

9. A sentiment vaguely echoed, but again not systematically explained, by the Seebohm Committee (1968, para 308): 'Suitable accommodation [for the mentally infirm aged] is essential but, at present, seldom available.'

10. The Commission also believed (Cmnd 169, para 631) that local authorities should provide temporary residential care for mentally infirm elderly people who normally live with their relatives, either to enable the relatives to take a holiday or at other times when illness or other difficulty makes it necessary to relieve the relatives temporarily of the responsibility of looking after them.

11. The British Geriatrics Society suggested, but without supporting evidence, that local authorities should provide residential homes for physically fit or frail ambulant patients with simple dementia, who do not have a marked tendency to wander, who do not have aggressive outbursts when properly handled and who are rarely or never incontinent (National Corporation for the Care of Old People, 1964, p. 8).

12. Thus Emery (1965, p. 643), speaking about Brookwood Hospital, Woking, Surrey, where 300 beds are specifically set aside for 'senile women patients', states that the fifty-bed admission ward 'is forced to extend hospitality to 18 women over 70, who are not likely to vacate their beds by discharge or transfer for many weeks. The inevitable result is demoralization of the staff and a serious reduction in the usefulness of the ward as the active treatment unit for younger women, for which purpose it was designed.'

13. Or any similar variation in time, for instance, six weeks in/six weeks out (Delargy, *Lancet*, 1957, i, p. 418).

14. Sections 6 and 8 of the Mental Health Act extend the functions of local authorities under the National Health Service Act 1946 and the National Assistance Act 1948 (sections 21, 1a and 2) so as to cover the care and after-care, including the provision of residential accommodation of persons who are or have been suffering from mental disorder – 'mental disorder' being defined by section 4(1) as meaning 'mental illness, arrested or incomplete development of mind, psychopathic disorder, and any other disorder or disability of mind.' Accommodation provided under part II of the 1959 Act is, of course, quite different from the 'residential homes for mentally disordered persons' sanctioned under section 19 of the Act. The latter are defined as establishments, other than mental nursing homes, the role or main object of which is to provide accommodation for persons suffering from mental disorder. But such homes, of which there were 142 registered with local authorities on 31 December 1967, are intended for mentally ill, subnormal and severely subnormal persons, and are not primarily designed for the elderly mentally confused (letter from Ministry of Health, 27 July 1967). However, implicit in this division is the problem of distinguishing between senile dementia and other mental illnesses, which a number of witnesses to the Royal Commission on the Law relating to Mental Illness and Mental Deficiency felt unable to resolve satisfactorily (Minutes of Evidence, Questions 54–5, 691–2, 1009–10, 1023–8, 2580–6).

15. To be more precise, 20 per cent (2,242) were considered fit to live elsewhere and of this group 14·3 per cent, it is said, could have been cared for at home if relatives and friends willing and able to take care of them could have been found), 42·4 per cent were considered suitable for chronic sick hospitals, 27·8 per cent for welfare accommo-

dation, and 15·5 per cent might have been placed in hostel accommodation, presumably within the hospital service.

16. See further, chapter 10.

17. *Lancet* editorial, 'Care of the elderly confused patient', 15 September 1962.

18. Of the sixty-one persons they found in institutions with senile or arteriosclerotic dementia, it is significant that they were distributed eleven in mental hospitals, twenty-one in geriatric wards and twenty-nine in welfare homes (Kay *et al.*, 1964).

19. Parsons (1965, p. 45), believes that Sheldon's (1948) finding, from a random sample of the elderly living at home in Wolverhampton in 1945, that only 1 per cent were demented, was an underestimate because of his lack of psychiatric experience.

20. Certain general practitioner studies have produced comparable results. A Norwegian study found a prevalence rate of 2·5 per cent (Bremer, 1951), and another Scottish survey estimated 3·6 per cent (Primrose, 1962). Both these surveys were undertaken by doctors personally acquainted with most of their patients. Also, a very thorough investigation of an entire Swedish rural population involving 443 persons over sixty found a rate of 5·0 per cent (Essen-Møller, 1956). Lastly, the most recent estimate of the prevalence of 'severe dementia' among a sample of 978 old people aged sixty-five and over is 3·1 per cent (Nielsen, 1963). By contrast, however, Tsung-yi Lin (1953, p. 329) summarizes data from a number of large-scale population studies which show rates varying from 0·2 to 2·3 per cent, though his estimate corrected for age expectancies would yield double these figures.

21. Of an organic type, as opposed to a further proportion of old people suffering from the major functional disorders, whom Kay *et al.* (1964, p. 153) estimated at 2·4 per cent in Newcastle upon Tyne.

22. Sheldon (1948) found 11·2 per cent of his subjects 'mildly impaired', while Essen-Møller (1956) found slightly less (10·8 per cent) and Nielsen (1963) rather more (15·4 per cent).

23. The two most recent British studies (Townsend and Wedderburn, 1965, and Tunstall, 1966) did not separately categorize old people who were confused. And Parsons (1965), who did isolate senile psychotics in his sample of the aged in Swansea did not examine the social provision made for them.

24. As a chief welfare officer replied to the specialized accommodation questionnaire: 'We have been increasingly concerned at the numbers of elderly mentally infirm who were requiring permanent residential care. After due enquiry and obtaining psychiatric opinions, these residents were considered to be rightfully the responsibility of this department. [But] we felt that there was a limit to the number of such residents who could be absorbed into normal accommodation.'

25. Another chief welfare officer wrote: 'With an increasing proportion of our applicants for part III accommodation being over 75, this problem of infirmity and mild senile dementia is on the increase.'

26. It is unfortunately impossible to trace the proportion of mentally handicapped persons in part III accommodation before 1958 because in previous *Annual Reports* of the Ministry of Health no division is made between physically and mentally handicapped persons and no distinction is observed between those in these categories who were 'elderly' and those who were not. But in general these figures must be treated with considerable caution, both because the classification of 'mentally handicapped' depended on the subjective judgments of matrons and superintendents of homes without any validation of interpersonal reliability of assessment, and because the method of analysis required by the Ministry is unsystematic. The categories into which residents are to be divided – 'not materially handicapped', 'blind', 'deaf', 'epileptic', 'others physically handicapped', and 'mentally handicapped' – are not mutually exclusive. Since there is such extensive overlapping of mental and physical illness in the 'multiple pathology' of disorder in the aged, there must be a sizeable proportion of residents

who are eligible for inclusion both in the category of 'mentally handicapped' and one or more of those of physical handicap. In such cases it is presumably arbitrary where matrons have included such residents. Certainly I was told by one superintendent that he enumerated former mental hospital patients under the category of 'mentally handicapped' just because of the source of admission, irrespective of their behaviour. Also it is possible, of course, that increased acquaintance with mental handicap over recent years has made matrons more conscious of registering it than formerly.

27. See pages 20–1 and chapter 10.

28. The proportion of the population of England and Wales aged sixty-five and over has risen from 4·7 per cent in 1901 to 11·9 per cent in 1961 (Registrar General).

29. Though Townsend (1962, p. 268), discussing the 92 persons (17 per cent) who were judged mentally impaired out of his sample of 530 from the 173 homes and institutions in England and Wales which he visited, notes that 'although there were proportionately more men and women in their eighties and nineties than in their sixties and seventies displaying signs of mental disorder, the differences were small and not statistically significant'.

30. The supply of oxygen to the brain is dependent on the state of the heart, the lungs, the blood and the blood vessels; the composition of the respiratory gases; the integrity of various homoeostatic mechanisms (Bedford, 1956a, p. 1063; 1956b, p. 614; and 1957, p. 505).

31. The National Association of Mental Health, for example, registered Parnham, an adapted mansion near Beaminster, Dorset, on 1 December 1955, as 'a home for old ladies suffering from mental infirmity but not requiring mental hospital treatment' (Royal Commission on the Law relating to Mental Illness ..., 1955, *Minutes of Evidence*, 28th day, p. 1154, para 4). Also a few local authorities like Kent were beginning various forms of specialized provision about the same time.

32. The Ministry of Health memorandum to local and hospital authorities of 15 September 1965 stated that 'While endeavouring as far as is reasonable and practicable to accommodate in (ordinary residential) homes people with physical handicaps, difficult personalities or confusion of mind, [the object of the local authority should be] to provide separate small homes, normally of not more than 35 places, for people with special needs, including elderly mentally infirm people who are found to be so disturbed that they cannot suitably live with other residents.'

33. Which represented an 86·1 per cent response rate.

34. If the number of such local authorities is 'corrected' to take account of the shortfall in replies to the questionnaire, it would be forty-three.

35. A list of these units is given in Table 2.4, pp. 30–3.

36. In some cases the questionnaire was not completed with regard to voluntary and private provision, and in other cases these details were explicitly stated to be 'not known'.

37. Excluding authorities which made no return to the questionnaire, but including those where no special unit already existed or was planned.

38. Local Authority Building Note, no. 2, *Residential Accommodation for the Elderly*.

39. It should be added that at least one local authority had observationally tested the significance of the thirty-five bed ceiling by permitting only a gradual increase in the number of residents admitted after the opening of a new home. Despite the effort to discover whether at a certain stage a further increase might adversely affect the morale or behaviour of the various groups in the home, it was reported to me that no obvious change was apparent at any particular point even though the final total of residents was nearly fifty.

3

What is 'confusion'?

Perhaps the single most important point to clarify concerning the concept of 'senile confusion' is that it is not a diagnosis. It is only a symptom which can occur in the course of a very wide variety of diseases and conditions, both mental and physical. The reason why disease in old people is so often complicated by 'mental confusion' is 'because the many adverse consequences of old age itself – structural, functional, psychological and environmental – enhance the extreme vulnerability of the brain at any age to hypoxia, bio-chemical derangements, and the effects of disordered function in other systems' (Bedford, 1959b, p. 185).

But apart from a lowered margin of reserve, old people are also predisposed to other conditions, such as arteriosclerosis, anaemia, diminished renal function, and borderline malnutrition and dehydra-tion, any of which may generate a confusional state even maniacal in character (Berk, 1958, p. 334). Furthermore, once old people have to stay in bed, the rapid development of loaded bowel and bladder, incontinence, dehydration, bedsores, terminal broncho-pneumonia or urinary infection must be anticipated (Nobbs, 1960, p. 888), and any of these conditions create a proneness to a period of confusion.[1]

THEORIES OF SENILE DEMENTIA

In view, therefore, of the fact that mental confusion may be quite transitory in duration provided its precipitating cause is found and can be remedied, what significance should be attached to the notion of 'senile dementia'? One medical authority, regarding the latter as a clinically distinct entity, has argued that it is an appropriate diagnosis where an old person has suffered a 'deterioration in total personality and mentality' (Bedford, 1959b, p. 185). Others, whilst accepting the validity of the concept, have stressed the similarity of its manifesta-tion to that of other unrelated disorders. 'A vast range of intra- and extra-cranial events, from congestive heart failure to bronchial

39

carcinoma, may masquerade as simple dementia' (Robinson, 1965, p. 192). And more explicitly, 'malnutrition, cancer, pulmonary infections and cardiovascular failure all can give a clinical picture easily misdiagnosed as senile psychosis'.[2] Yet others have stressed that as a descriptive term it is valueless. It 'implies a fixed state or steady deterioration with hopeless outlook. It gives no indication of needs that may vary from day to day; and it suffers the same drawback as cerebral arteriosclerosis, a pathological speculation of little value during life' (Parnell, 1965, p. 757).

In the absence of any generally agreed medical precision, it is perhaps not surprising that its predominant significance has come to be seen as a social one. 'Senile dementia is a term presently debased and loosely used, it seems, to indicate "difficult" behaviour in one whose intellectual powers are waning' (Robinson, 1965, p. 201). It is only taking the argument one step further to suggest that the term is merely a medical expression of despair applied to socially isolated old people for whom nobody will accept responsibility.

The key to the concept of senile dementia, if it has any independent reality, must lie in the degree of deviation from the 'natural history' of normal senescence. Now various attempts have been made to establish a significant differentiation. The chief of these is based on clinical criteria checked against post-mortem evidence. Thus one review of 300 persons in the course of terminal illness yielded a 75 per cent pathological correlation between predicted and actual findings for both senile and arteriosclerotic psychosis (Corsellis, 1962).[3] But this has not been corroborated in other investigations, which have revealed a marked discrepancy between the severity of mental disorganization seen in cases of dementia and the extent of brain damage (Rothschild, 1956).[4] One study, for example, concluded that there was no straightforward relationship between the degree of organic brain damage found at autopsy and age, orientation or level of intellectual functioning as measured by the Wechsler Adult Intelligence scale (Epstein *et al.*, 1963). Some researchers have therefore concluded, from reviewing the literature, that 'no good correlation exists between the degree, distribution and character of various abnormal changes and the age and state of neuro-function of the individual' (Wolf, 1959). In reaction against a purist neuropathological explanation,[5] they have tended to turn to the more subtle influences of personality and adaptive powers interwoven in various complex manners. Thus it has been hypothesized that the extent of psychosis might be considered in terms of the interaction of brain pathology, the emotional response to organic and functional changes and to the diseases of ageing, the degree of abnormality of the underlying personality, the degree of interpersonal conflict, and the accumulated traumata of living (Kassel, 1957).

Secondly, psychometric techniques have been used to indicate that dementia was not an inevitable stage in the normal ageing process, but was characterized by qualitatively different and measurable factors. The derivation of these techniques lies in Babcock's observation that in cases of senile dementia reasoning ability, as assessed by non-verbal tests, tended to decline while vocabulary was maintained (Babcock, 1930). Thus the ratio between the scores on non-verbal and verbal tests was believed to provide an index of deterioration. However, one investigator found that while vocabulary was preserved among normal old people and depressives, among patients with senile dementia on the other hand a decline in verbal performance was apparent, which became increasingly obvious as age advanced (Orme, 1957, pp. 408–13). Further studies found that those sub-tests showing the greatest decline due to normal ageing were not necessarily those most able to differentiate dementia (Botwinick and Birren, 1951a, pp. 365–8).[6] From this the conclusion has been drawn that it can be demonstrated by psychological tests that senile dementia is independent of normal senescent decline and probably superimposed on it (Dorken, 1954, pp. 187–94). Once again, however, the evidence is conflicting. Raven, in a review of 106 consecutive admissions to Crichton Royal Geriatric Unit, found that the patients functioned intellectually very much like normal healthy old people (Raven, 1959). He regarded dementia rather as the progressive impairment of processes by which an individual adapts to the present situation in relation to his own past and the future objectives he sets himself, and he suggested this impairment could be divided into definite stages. Such a construct is inevitably arbitrary in the demarcation of stages and not all cases, or even a majority, may adhere precisely to the model, but at least it indicates that a process of dementing is not necessarily qualitatively distinct from normal senescent decline rather than a distortion of it, even if a gross one in some instances.

Thirdly, attempts have been made to locate the existence of

dementia, and to measure its degree, by reference to abnormal electroencephalogram readings. One study revealed that a slowing alpha rhythm became more obvious in the presence of demonstrable arteriosclerosis (Obrist *et al.*, 1961), whilst other investigators have shown a quantitative relationship between the degree of slowing and the severity of intellectual impairment in a group of fifty organic psychiatric patients (McAdam and Robinson, 1956).[7] Nevertheless, these results have not gone unchallenged. In particular, EEG readings have been regarded with some caution. One survey concluded that 'a definitely normal EEG in our experience ruled out the presence of important brain changes, while an abnormal report would draw attention to the need for further careful diagnostic assessment' (Pampiglione and Post, 1958). Others have cast doubt on the reliability even of the former conclusion. Thus a study of 274 patients aged between sixty and seventy-nine who were examined over a three-year period, whilst confirming that EEG abnormality was more likely in the presence of dementia, also found that its incidence was often irregular in this respect (Turton and Warren, 1960, p. 1499). For where dementia was judged definitely to be absent, there were still a considerable number of abnormal EEGs, and where there was no clinical doubt about dementia, still a number of normal EEGs were registered. Furthermore, there was little correlation between clinical estimate of the degree of dementia and EEG abnormality, except where dementia was gross and obvious and also no correction between change in the degree of dementia and EEG change. Lastly, the proportion of EEG abnormality in patients suffering from schizophrenia, senile paranoid psychosis and affective psychosis was similar to that of a group of normals of the same age, and no EEG abnormality could be said to be characteristic of any particular type of dementia in this series.

Attempts to demonstrate the existence of a discrete condition of senile dementia by reference to neuropathological changes, psychometric tests and EEG readings have, therefore, produced very mixed results. But what is significant about these various attempts is that they all assume that there is a definable state which is known and that the problem lies rather in matching a symptomatology to it. It is assumed to be known because it is recognizable by certain marked characteristics of social behaviour. Any satisfactory causal theory of senile dementia must therefore be elucidated in terms of factors which can be predictively related to such behaviour. Moreover, in the face of the conflicting evidence concerning symptoms, a psychiatrist has been led to summarize the position thus: 'The most likely explanation of the phenomena of what we call senile dementia is to be looked for in terms of causes which accelerate, perhaps grossly, normal cerebral ageing' (Robinson, 1965, p. 202).

Now some theorists have postulated that these effects derive from a genetic causation (Larsson et al., p. 222ff.). A Swedish study of 377 persons with a definite diagnosis of senile dementia, together with 2,675 members of their families yielded the result that the morbidity risk for senile dementia among siblings of patients was 4·3 times the corresponding risk in the general population. From this it was concluded rather oddly that 'the evidence obtained concerning important hereditary factors in the aetiology of senile dementia does not exclude the possibility that senile dementia is sometimes conditioned by exogenous factors, but presumably by factors that are connected with the physiological process of ageing and not with the socio-medical environment'. In accordance with this approach the main inference was drawn that 'it cannot be excluded that senile dementia in certain individuals is caused by multifactorial inheritance or exogenous factors, but most probably senile dementia is mainly conditioned by a major gene, inherited as a monohybrid autosomal dominant'.[8] However, apart from the fact that this deduction is admitted to be very hypothetical, it also appears to be countered by other internal evidence presented in the study. Firstly, it was also found that while there were comparatively low morbidity risks up to the age of ninety among relatives, the marked rise in the risk beyond that age was equally apparent among non-relatives. Secondly, the wide spread of senile dementia through the whole population would seem to argue against a precise genetic causation. Furthermore, the significantly higher incidence of demented behaviour among siblings can just as reasonably be explained by sociocultural factors which can normally be expected to link family members in their effects more closely than persons chosen at random. And finally, a genetic cause would presumably operate on social behaviour through the medium of pathological changes and the poor correlation of these latter with overt behaviour would therefore cast some doubt on a posited cause of this kind.[9]

In contrast to a genetic theory, it is much more plausible to emphasize the importance of related social factors. Unfortunately, however, the social background of persons afflicted with dementia in old age has been sadly neglected,[10] and this area must have high priority for future research. Various pieces of existing data already indicate that this field could yield rich deposits of new and relevant information. A study of 100 consecutive female admissions over sixty-five to a mental hospital, for example, has shown that those diagnosed with senile or arteriosclerotic dementia had been living alone to a disproportionate extent (Morris, 1962, p. 802), whereas fifty-eight of the 100 were judged demented, twenty-two of the thirty-two who had been living alone were in this group.[11] It has been noted that rejection by the spouse was frequently indicated in the social histories of old people admitted to a geriatric unit in a mental hospital (A. J. Whitehead, personal communication). Furthermore, a psychiatrist has noted that

> the organic factor [in mental deterioration in the elderly] was found to be relatively less important than the environmental conditions, the general state of physical nutrition and health, and the inter-personal and social relationships of the patient. The attitude of relatives and neighbours or the degree of isolation of the old person living in solitude can be important factors and far outweigh the effect of the organic cerebral changes. . . . The symptoms of nocturnal restlessness, wandering and incontinence are usually reactive and not organic in origin, and are usually occasioned by the feeling of not being wanted which was caused by a loss of the desire on the part of the relatives to continue to care for the old person (Macmillan, 1962, pp. 740–1).

Similarly, another writer has suggested that

> bouts of excitement and confusion, even incontinence, may be due to the resentments and frustrations of being old or in hospital and to a fear of dying. . . . To understand the emotional processes of the ageing mind is never easy, but it must be done if we are to avoid labelling patients 'senile' or 'demented' when they are in fact reacting within the limits of normal for their age (Kemp, 1962, ii, 515).

In line with this, there is evidence that a severe reduction in social roles may be related to the development of dementia.[12] One study indicated that maintaining an old person in a maximum number of roles might make an important contribution to preventing senility.[13]

Some confirmation of this has been provided by another study which showed that day attendance at an occupational therapy department was of considerable benefit to mildly deteriorated old people with senile behaviour disorders who were thereby enabled to continue living at home longer than expected (Cosin and Mort, n.d.). It has also been suggested that people differ in their capacity to compensate for cerebral deterioration, and it has been demonstrated that outgoing personalities who remain actively engaged in the business of life tend to be better preserved mentally in old age than others (Pressey and Simcoe, 1950, p. 168).

The evidence does not, however, yet amount to more than pointers. We do not yet know in what ways isolation, loneliness, lack of affection and alienation may accelerate or distort the process of ageing, though by analogy the dramatic effect of an adverse social or emotional environment on development and behaviour in children[14] suggests that the impact of such factors may be substantial.

What is clear, however, is that any satisfactory explanation of senile dementia must fit into an acceptable general theory of ageing. Now social scientists have elaborated various patterns of adjustment whereby individuals accept the loss of familiar roles and socialize themselves to new roles in ageing. Thus Reichard, Livson and Petersen have suggested that the process can be categorized by five fairly distinct types of adjustment (Reichard *et al.*, 1962), three of them successful and two not, while Cumming and Henry propose a theory of 'disengagement' whereby reduced social interaction gradually blunts sensitivity to the accepted norms of behaviour, which itself tends to diminish further social interaction, and so on (Cumming and Henry, 1961). It is not surprising, in view of the extreme complexity in the patterns of 'normal' ageing that no simple model yet devised can give adequate meaning to the full variety of conditions seen in old age. For, firstly, personality requirements differ sufficiently between individuals so that while for one person comparative isolation after retirement may represent disaster, for another it may hold the freedom for which he has always craved. Secondly, there is a need to distinguish between the voluntary and gradual relinquishment of functions and the enforced and sudden deprivation of a role resulting, for example, from widowhood or caused by such unwelcome happenings as illness or a fall into poverty. Above all, it is necessary to see adjustment in old age not only as a process of disengagement *from* society, but also as an attempted compensation for this withdrawal by relating *to* society in new and satisfying ways. This may be demonstrated as a desire to maintain emotional family relations and may lead to a system of 'functional flexibility' (Rosenmayr and Kockeis, 1963, p. 423), instances of which were so strikingly documented by Townsend in Bethnal Green. Or it may be revealed in a predilection for reminiscing about the past which, so far from being a stubborn old-fashionedness, is better interpreted as a positive effort by the old person to integrate his views of his past with his new position (Birren, 1963, p. 276). Or, most importantly for the present study, the objective of compensation may be implied by behaviour which would conventionally be regarded as abnormal. We do not yet know enough about the mechanisms by which the widowed, the chronically sick, the lonely and the housebound counteract their disadvantage in old age. But what is asserted here and elaborated later (Chapter 9) is that very often behaviour which is too readily interpreted as the inevitable consequences of organic mental deterioration should properly be seen as a conscious attempt at reintegration rather than dismissed as a socially functionless aberration. Senile dementia should not be regarded as a pathological condition, but rather as an attempted adaptation, executed with varying degrees of ingenuity and meeting with varying degrees of success, to an environment which is inauspicious in terms of the needs of the pre-existing personality pattern, which has already itself been moulded by the steady accretion of earlier experiences which cumulatively tend to strengthen or weaken the reaction on each subsequent occasion to adverse or alien surroundings.

CLASSIFICATION OF MENTAL INFIRMITY

If this discussion, as it is developed later, therefore indicates that the forms of behaviour associated with senile dementia provide the key to its understanding rather than occur as its mindless and haphazard result, then it remains to construct a categorization of these phenomena. As one psychiatrist has said:

> To diagnose the majority of elderly people as dements (under a strict definition of mental deterioration) is nonsense and humiliating, misleading and hurtful. Psychiatrists have long recognized that in practice no sharp line can be drawn between senile

dementia on the one hand and the normal mentality in old age on the other: the one merges imperceptibly with the other, and the diagnosis is made on social rather than on psychological grounds. Broadly, if the aged individual fits into his customary surroundings he is usually, and rightly, considered to be 'normal' (Bedford, 1959b, ii, 185).

In similar vein another psychiatrist has insisted that the diagnosis should be made in terms of social competence, namely whether a person is sensible, continent, ambulant or wandering, since this kind of description would indicate the appropriate social arrangements (Parnell, 1965, ii, p. 1123).

The classification of mental infirmity adopted here is based on six dimensions: verbal confusion, physical wandering and restlessness, disorientation of person or situation, disorientation of place, 'anormic' behaviour, and memory defect. It should be stressed at once that these criteria are derived from observations of relevant behaviour, irrespective of any considerations of aetiology discussed in the preceding section. The aim is solely to provide a means of comparison of how persons presenting with similar symptoms experience different environments.

Before the analysis is begun, however, it is first necessary to enter a few general caveats:

1. The behaviour of confused old people observed in residential homes may have been partly induced by separation from their own homes and families. This is after all the converse of the situation pictured by one writer whereby in accustomed surroundings the old person with a considerable degree of dementia 'by deeply engrained habit and training produces the appropriate phrase or action automatically, and maintains himself quite adequately in his environment provided that no unusual or excessive demands are made on him' (Bedford, 1959b, ii, 185). Equally, as already hinted in Chapter 1, confused behaviour is also doubtless influenced by the actual social organization of the welfare home.

2. Different groups of persons in contact with confused old people emphasize different aspects of confusion relevant to the nature of the contact. Thus nurses and psychiatrists tend to stress the inability to appreciate and follow simple instructions, while visiting friends and relatives are more concerned about the inability to identify people and to remember shared events. Moreover, the

incapacity to marshal ideas and to digest complex thoughts in a rational order may only be apparent from prompting, and in such cases it may be judged that verbal abilities are sufficient at least for a reasonably satisfactory social exchange.

3. Confusion may be subject to a degree of periodicity with long or short, occasional or frequent lucid intervals.

> In one home a widow of eighty-six who was normally perfectly rational and incisive in her conversation was subject to occasional minor strokes which caused temporary confusional states. She was sporadically disoriented in time and might be incontinent for a short period.

4. It is only likely that whilst mentally confused persons may recognize the relevance of some questions, others may seem as crazy to them as their answers sometimes appear to a rational observer. Thus even very confused and incoherent residents could respond to questions of such stark and searching simplicity as: Are you lonely? Or to questions about matters which concerned them deeply:

> A woman of poor personal appearance who throughout much of her interview remained mute or made unrecognizable sounds, whilst continually wandering round the room, could neverthe-less reply accurately on certain topics:
>
> 'Is there any possibility of your going back to a home of your own?'
> 'Yes.'
> 'Where?'
> 'In the same place as before.'

Other suggestions, however, were met with quizzical curiosity:

> 'Do you want to stay here indefinitely?'
> 'That's a really funny thing to say. If I got courting and wanted to leave here . . .'
> (from a widower of eighty-five whose replies were frequently disconnected and irrelevant).

In marginal cases this can generate a belief that the old person is 'putting it on'.[15] An interesting parallel is afforded by the temporary influence of changes in blood supply on vision. 'It is not uncommon for an old person who is known to have poor eyesight to complain suddenly of a complete blurring of vision, so that momentarily they cannot read a book or see the television, yet an hour later they may comment on the presence of a crumb on the carpet or a spot on a dress or suit.' Presumably a number of statements, super-ficially confused, conceal such understandable bewilderment. Puzzling actions, too, could be seen as somewhat bizarre even to the confused mind. A man of ninety-four whose most earnestly expressed intention was to return immediately to Lancashire to resume work in the mills could nevertheless remark to Matron about my activities in the home 'He must be mad coming in here and writing every day.'

5. The problem of marginality inevitably arises when arbitrary demarcation lines have to be drawn for classificatory purposes in what are essentially continuous rather than discrete phenomena. Most obviously this occurs where a person shows faint or sporadic signs of a particular type of behaviour, but not enough to fit easily into the category. In such cases persons are allocated to those group-ings whose characteristics they *predominantly* reveal. Related to this is the problem of exhibiting the range of behaviour enclosed within any category and of distinguishing between the person who typifies this characteristic and the person who only intermittently reveals it.

More specifically the problem of marginality occurs with the question of the operationalization of the concept of confusion itself. Does the manifestation of any single one of the six chosen elements merit the title of confused? Or should gross memory defect, in the absence of any of the other components, be considered a necessary, though not a sufficient, condition for fulfilment of the conceptual requirements?

6. Various extraneous factors may give a false impression of confusion. The consequences of partial deafness offer one obvious example:

'Have you got a comfortable bed here?'
'I've never had a bear here.'

Again:

'Do you drive a car?'
'Do you mean if I have a horse?' (misheard 'cart' for 'car').

'You must know if you drive a car.'
'I don't know if I did.'

Or the same result may derive from unrecognized spatial disorientation. A woman who had clearly entered the wrong room complained: 'They've turned my room out and put in a sick bay.' Now, such mistakes would immediately be recognized for what they are in a normally rational person, but in a person whose rationality has already been discounted, the easier explanation may not be rejected. To this extent the ascription of confusion may be a self-reinforcing process.

With these reservations an analysis of confused behaviour must now be presented.

Verbal confusion

This is divisible into two main types, incoherent speech and tangential speech.

1. INCOHERENT SPEECH

This is chiefly characterized by the lack of development of recognizable ideas, and it may occur in a number of forms. Some of these forms may be identified as follows:

(a) *Fragmentary verbalization of private thoughts*[16]

Here, even if an apparently rational statement has been initiated, it tails off, whether through thought blockage or for other reasons, before enough words have been publicly expressed for the sense to be assumed.

'Is there any job you would like to do or help with?'
'I have . . .'
'Is there anything else you would like to do, such as a hobby, to keep yourself occupied?'
[No answer]
'Are you free to do what you like in this home?'
'I have . . .'
'Is your sight reasonably good?'
'And that . . . and that . . .'
'Can you read and write?'

'Yes.'
'Do you ever want to write a letter?'
[No answer]
'Or make a 'phone call?'
'I have . . .'
'Are you free to do what you like here?'
'What's it about . . . what a funny thing . . . it's the same thing as . . .'

A number of those who exhibited this characteristic only publicly verbalized their thoughts when prompted out of their private reveries by, for example, an unexpected noise. One such person, disturbed on a particular occasion, immediately muttered '. . . boys, those behind them', then lapsed into silence again.

(b) Neologisms
This may take the form either of definite word invention:

'Do you write letters?'
'Gutty, that's also . . . stutty.'

'Do you get enough food here?'
'Nuts?'
'Enough.'
'Oh yes, nutsfed, nutsfeet.'
(Where the tendency has been engendered partly by deafness)

'Do you know of any other homes?'
'Well, distinctly I am not after frost* her.'

A woman who had pulled the handle of a lavatory cistern, but could not make it work, exclaimed, 'It won't ackle.'
Or it may take the form of using existing words whose meaning is entirely inappropriate in the context:

'Are you going to do a shoot? Are the shoot undone?'
'All right? Good?'

'Do the other residents show bad manners?'
'No, they're very good on the whole. Exceptions come like this under headings. If you have a good curving soaping and put it through people who can, . . .'

* denotes the apparent transliteration of the sound.

Here words carry a meaning which is entirely private to the speaker (word façade). It should be added that these examples are, of course, quite different from dysarthric formations:

> matchbox – patchbox: pigeon – didgeon: chimney – chilney: half-crown – half-kine.

(c) Verbal restriction

This may be shown by a massive limitation of vocabulary within a very narrow range of words.

> A woman who had been removed by an attendant from the fireplace where she was fiddling with the fireguard cried out: 'Don't, don't, don't, go and go, go . . . go . . . go . . .'

The same effect may be seen in severe dysphasia.[17] An effort to break out into new expressions is often marked by neologisms and perseveration:

> 'What do you do in the morning?'
> 'Yes, well, um, weighty,* well, not, not, not . . .'

Perhaps also under this heading should be included the incomprehensible mutterings which regularly mark incoherent speech.

An analysis of this kind perhaps gives a too clinical, abstract and lop-sided picture of actual people. What, therefore, were the general characteristics of persons with incoherent speech?

> Mrs Tetley opened the interview spontaneously by remarking that 'the tennis has gone off, isn't it naughty of them?' Then she declared that she was not happy, and then at once denied it.
>
> She was a widow of seventy-four with a mobile, wrinkled face and because she suffered from oral dyskinesia, working her mouth with her endlessly active tongue, her cheeks alternately pouted and then deflated as she blew the air from her mouth in loud puffs. Never still for long, she kept getting up and drifting away in mid-sentence and wandering round the room, occasionally breaking wind loudly, though showing no embarrassment and not even appearing to notice. When I spoke to her, she would approach me again because she seemed to have a repeated desire to grasp my arm, as if to assure herself of my reality and interest. Although these moments attracted her interest, they clearly seemed rather an interruption to the reminiscings of her private

* denotes the apparent transliteration of sound.

consciousness than a genuine commitment to dialogue. This was particularly shown by her occasional abrupt surges of seemingly misplaced emotion, which were exacerbated by her nominal defect. Asked if she spoke much to the residents, she replied, 'I don't know, don't understand about that. No (almost angrily), why do you the whole time put ... put ...?' Her dress was neglected, and stains of dried food were visible on her cardigan and skirt, while one of her stockings persistently dropped down her leg. She was also incontinent and from time to time pulled at her skirt under her bottom and at the front. While I was staying at this home it happened that one of Mrs Tetley's two sons visited her, and though it was doubtful if she recognized him, she clearly enjoyed his attentions. She took his arm as he followed her wanderings and frequently responded to his efforts to re-capture her memory. Usually her replies were too laconic or too irrelevant to understand their meaning, but he was not deterred.

2. TANGENTIAL SPEECH

This is defined as speech in which the use of words is mainly appropriate and the ideas are broadly intelligible, but the whole statement is irrelevant to the context.

While it was decided that intelligibility and contextual relevance were the key considerations in assessing speech for the purpose of this study, it should nevertheless be made clear that other criteria can be and have been devised. Allison, for example, opted to differentiate confused speech according to the readiness of its flow rather than its appropriateness to the situation (Allison, 1962, p. 135ff.). Thus he makes three main distinctions between patients:

(*a*) those who were entirely speechless, neither attempting spontaneous conversation nor trying to reply to questions;

(*b*) those who showed little or no spontaneous talk, but attempted to answer questions or take part in conversation initiated by others;

(*c*) those who showed no inhibition of spontaneous talk and responded readily to questions.

This does, however, seem a rather subjective form of division since readiness to speak may well be a function, not so much of inherent mental infirmity, as of the structuring of the environment. But Allison goes on to define different elements present in his third category which approximate more closely to the approach adopted in this study. Such patients, he suggests, ramble on, often almost incessantly, with the 'push of talk' interspersed with confabulation and nominal or grammatical and syntactical defects, so that incoherence or jargon aphasia results. These latter two concepts are differentiated by the degree of the speaker's apparent purposefulness. The utterances of the incoherent patient are difficult to follow because of the tendency to leave sentences unfinished, the lack of pattern in the association of ideas and the liberal introduction of irrelevant material, but he shows no concern about the responses of his listener or his surroundings. In terms of linguistical techniques, the rudiments or 'instrumentalities' of speech are not lost, but expressive difficulties are more apparent in the conceptualization of thought. In jargon aphasia, on the other hand, the rudiments of speech are lost, but conceptual thought is much less disturbed. The patient seems to know what he wants to say, and indeed is exasperated when he is not understood,[18] but periphrasis, mispronouncements and neologisms turn his speech into gibberish. This distinction is certainly useful in so far as the speaker's expectations of response clearly affect his social relationships, but it is still only obliquely related to the crucial point of language as a precise means of communication.

Relevance was therefore retained as the key determinant once the intelligibility of speech was guaranteed. On this basis manifestations of tangential speech can perhaps be divided into six main types:

(a) *Skewing of responses to a preconceived framework of ideas*
The speaker takes his cue from one or more significant words uttered by his respondent and imaginatively twists his answer in the direction of his underlying interests.

One woman kept reverting to three main topics – her religion, looking after her household, and the work she once did outside her home:

'How do you come to be here?'

'We go out together, we used to go to Sunday school, the real school, yes.'

'What do you do in the morning?'

'Go . . . [she plays with a box on the table] . . . [inaudible] . . . doing the clothes, go to the boiler, wash them up. I've got four children. I live on top of . . .'

'And what do you do in the afternoon?'

'Washing the dishes and cleaning up the boots, and putting things straight, and things like doing now, walls, cleaning up with the ball.'

'And in the evening?'

'Not much ... [inaudible] this is my hair [she takes some hairpins from her hair], then we put them in.'

'Would you like to help with any job here?'

'We go in the ... 5 o'clock ... cleaning up, clean them up.'

'Do you have any hobby?'

'We go to church, church in the evenings. We sometimes go to church.'

'Do you have a close friend here?'

'My sister, two or three of them, my home. We go to places to go out in the evenings.'

'Do you talk much to other residents?'

'Sometimes I'm late ... twenty past eight. I'm not an assistant, I'm ... [inaudible]

'Do you talk much to the attendants?'

'When they come, we all go out together.'

'Or to matron?'

'Yes, we were bound to do that. Got to do what they tell us.'

'Of the staff and residents, who do you like most?'

'I like my mother and my little children.'

'Do you think you did the right thing in coming here?'

'The girl that was here ... is the one that ... I [inaudible] ... is the one who keeps this table clean. I go out and wash for people and clean up the beds in their homes.'

Sometimes the point of tangent was supplied by purely adventitious stimuli:

'Are any of them bad-mannered?'

'No, the other ones would mix them up [at this point a dog suddenly barked outside the room] because a dog's barking under the door.'

Often it was the last word which was taken up, as though the rest of the sentence could not be retained:

'Are there any personal possessions of yours which you would like to have with you here?'

'Who comes in and out of here? I can only say, if they crop up, I'll let you know perhaps.'

At other times, however, it is quite clear from the content of the reply that the question has been understood:

'Do you read or write much?'
'I look to have a good look at books, and Good Lord I do shorthand, or rather you can't go in for those different things without writing. I like to please people I'm chatting to. I'm rather fond of all those things which get you about.'

Where the underlying interest is too vaguely indicated, an answer could appear as the stringing together of seemingly disconnected ideas:

'How do you come to be here?'
'I'm staying with a friend, and she takes all the sacks which I don't take for myself. I was staying with this man, he was very nice – I don't in the least know how it came about – I should go and ask somebody who expected nothing or practically nothing. I think she must have come. Do ask. I shall ask, 'cos it makes a difference to me. Anyway my friend is very friendly and anxious we should.'

Often the cue for the tangent was the lacuna induced by persistent failure to recall the crucial word necessary to complete the sense of the statement:

'Is there any job you'd like in the home?'
'I couldn't say because I don't know who are the people . . . who would come to their . . . They came and gave to the grey sheck,* sheek, in the late afternoon. The friend who lives with them was going to take up that . . . I'm always sorry for the white ones who didn't get the same . . .'
'Didn't get the same?'
'No, didn't see it.'

Sometimes the take-up of the sentence after a pause could have comic effects:

'Who do you like most in this home?'
'Well, I think I like my own. . . .'

* denotes the apparent transliteration of the sound.

'What?'
'People in the water department.'

But more usually it involved a reversion to a focus of emotional concern:

'Have you any suggestions for making this home a better place to live in?'
'We were going ... [emphatic but unintelligible syllables] and my father was a Christian.'

(b) Perseveration

Key words are repeated irrespective of changing reference points and from the divergence between the meaning of the words used and the inflection with which the words are spoken it is clear that the words conceal an indefinitely extensible range of ideas.[19]

A woman who in the middle of her interview suddenly exclaimed, like an echo from the past, 'Clothworkers' company. Mincing Lane, root and branch may it flourish for ever', constantly perseverated with the words 'telly' and 'clothworkers':

'Are you free to do what you like in this home?'
'In some respects, but not others ... they go straight off, the clothworkers ... the telly itself might go. These tellies get all on one side and not on the other [picking up a sheet of paper with writing down one side] and here's my telly [feeling her apron] ... Sometimes I have it tellified, sometimes I don't trouble. The clothworkers put the telly on.'

The most extreme example of this tendency was seen in the case of another woman whose speech was entirely limited [as a result of cerebrovascular accidents, according to the medical record] to endless repetition of the same phrase, 'Plushy place, on the days and the days and the days of old', ocasionally intermixed with 'Scott wobbling, wobbling Tom', which were references to her deceased husband and son. But her expressive, agitated gesticulations in the air with her hand, together with her varied vocal inflections as she moved her first finger to either side of the base of her nose and tapped her head with her hand in three places, indicated her earnest desire to communicate, if only she could find the right words.

A variation of this type of speech was the persistent reiteration of a single phrase or sentence, perhaps picked up from an overheard conversation, over a period of time, possibly several minutes, before it was replaced by another phrase or sentence which was then treated in the same way.

A widow, who at her interview showed herself capable of expressing independent ideas, would nevertheless sometimes latch on to a phrase spoken in her presence and intone it endlessly. Thus one night when she was being put to bed and was particularly talkative, she was asked to keep quiet or she would 'wake the baby', at which she launched into repeating over and over again 'navy baby, navy baby, navy baby . . .'

(c) Dysfunctional word and idea association

Here various difficulties are encountered in finding the right word, and the devices used to circumvent these nominal defects impede rational communication.[20] The commonest form of this tendency was periphrasis or circumlocution:

A bee – a fly with a sting in its bottom.
A calendar – it dates.

But it also occurred as an executive defect or failure to verbalize accurately through alliteration or phonetic similarity:

Work – 'I can't see your walk, what you're writing.'
Trouble – 'I've never had any tunnels with people.'
   'Tunnels?'
   'Tumbles.'
Comfortable – 'Have you got a comfortable bed?
     'Yes, I've got a com . . . com . . . cup of tea.'
Permanently – 'Do you want to stay here permanently?'
     'Yes, herbertly.'[21]

Some examples of functional word substitution, or paraphasia, were also found:

Wheelchair – spring wheel,

– and similarly with neologisms:

penny – sixen
diary – rare paw book.[22]

Another instance of verbal dysfunction was the simple re-adoption of others' words without regard to the sense:

> A woman, asked a problematic question, replied –
> 'It's very difficult to say.'
> 'Can you try?'
> 'It's very trying.'

Lastly, the obvious point should be made that it is not always possible to trace what kind of association lies behind certain bizarre utterances. How, for example, should one explain:

> 'Do you feel other residents are bad-mannered?'
> 'Yes.'
> 'How?'
> 'In a white, white, white, wild tree.'

These three preceding types of linguistic phenomena constitute the chief manifestations of tangential speech, but brief mention should be made of two other variant forms.

(d) Non-referential statements

This speech type was shown at its most extreme when the speaker initiated a spontaneous utterance without apparent connection to any feature of the situation:

> A woman, waking suddenly from sleep after lunch, exclaimed
> 'Yes, I think I ought to.'

Another, while wandering round the room, momentarily broke into an anguished cry, recalling her husband by name:

> 'Oh, Oliver, why do you . . . do you . . . do you . . . ?'

More usually, however, this tendency was illustrated by constant and inexplicit pronominal usage, which made it particularly difficult to follow rapid movements of thought:

> A woman who often lapsed into a lengthy monologue of reminiscence at one point said –
> 'There's a fair one . . . is that the one who goes there? . . . White one she is . . .'
> Another person at her interview suddenly remarked animatedly –
> 'They're coming out again . . .'

Where only the context seemed to indicate that she meant that I had started writing again.

(e) Internal inconsistency of meaning

Here two statements are conjoined which are logically inconsistent, at least implicitly.

'Yes, I don't like to sit here with nobody with me; I like to be by myself.'

'Now that you're here, do you want to stay here permanently?'
'When I'm eighty, I'll come here.'
'How old are you?'
'Eighty.'

'Is your sight reasonably good?'
'I don't know, so seldom I'm . . . my mother's daughter.'
'What about her?'
'Oh she died long before. I could ask her when she comes along here.'

Some caution, however, is needed here against a pedantically excessive attention to logical defect. For some technical inconsistencies occurring within the same stream of dialogue are after all not really so divergent. The following were two examples which were recorded:

'I'm not a great talker. . . . I like to speak to people, like to be sociable.'
'I like nobody. . . . I don't dislike people.'

Nevertheless some statements do provide clear evidence of confused patterns of thought:

A woman who had been making a rag doll during an occupational therapy session held up the finished product, which led one of her neighbours to remark –
'I didn't know you could do that; I'd have had more respect for you if I'd known you could do that.'
To which the doll-maker replied with concern –
'She had more respect for me than for the doll!'

These, therefore, are the main types of tangential speech. But of course it should be remembered that the foregoing analysis necessarily distracts from the fact that a single piece of speech may contain several of these types simultaneously:

> On one occasion I was sitting at the side of a room as the residents returned from lunch. One of them who was in an excited mood came up to me and exclaimed –
> 'Will you wear your glasses? [I already had them on.]
> 'Better not, I might trample them on the ground. What are you now?'
> 'What am I?'
> 'A snort, a snorty laugh ... today's September 1st. [It was in fact March 22nd.] ... tomorrow we're going to foregather, I gather.'

Perhaps this should be interpreted as follows:

1.	Wear ... trample ...	Tangential (*e*): she presumably meant – will you take your glasses off?
2.	A snort, snorty laugh	Incoherent (*b*): neologism.
3.	Laugh ... today's September 1st.	Tangential (*a*): the pause induces the change of subject.
4.	Foregather, I gather	Tangential (*c*): homoioteleuton.

Once again, given that these constitute the various linguistic deviations observed within the category of tangential speech, what personal characteristics typified those who demonstrated this form of speech, and in particular how were they different from those whose utterances were classified as incoherent?

Mrs Sawbury, despite the mild arthritis that caused her to spend most of the day hunched up in a wheelchair, had a radiant face and a spirit that was positively uplifting. Aged eighty-nine and married, she had been brought into residential care because when her husband was taken to hospital, she was reluctant to stay in their bungalow, despite the considerable help that their plight had attracted from neighbours. Asked about her activities in the home during the daytime, she replied: 'If anyone comes and wants something, I do my best to give it, and please myself. None of us is perfect, God bless us, and go and see if all is clean and nice, and be happy.' And in the afternoon and evening? 'Just sit here, talk to Queenie. She always comes to see us, "Is there anything you want, Mum?" Then go to bed early. They all come home early in the evening. We're pleased to see them and make sure they're well. He's very hard-working, Dad, now – my sweetheart, yes, we've never had a cross word. God bless them, they've never been any trouble to me, thank God.' And at these recollections a small tear began to roll down her cheek. But despite her sudden invocations of the deity ('Take up your cross, the Saviour said, and we've all been confirmed') and her constant reassurances about the happiness of her family, she retained an earthy awareness of her situation quite alien to the incoherent. On one occasion she remarked abruptly: 'Well, I reckon this is a cold room, matey. I wouldn't like to come here to retire.' And again, 'They'd be the first to help, they're better off, they've got good pensions – all the others who live here, all our helpers here. We're only post office veterans' [her husband had been a post-man]. She had never identified with the home and when somebody came into her lounge [whom she would not be able to recognize because she was nearly blind], she would often call out 'Well, time for me to go home', and turning to a neighbour, 'Have they come for me?' When once I questioned her about this and asked, 'But who is it?', she replied, 'Don't know. Known him for years, he's my friend.' On one occasion she was told that somebody was looking for her, and wandering with uncertain steps into the hall she encountered a male resident sitting there. When she enquired after the person trying to find her, he replied in a loud, gruff voice which she could not understand. Politely repeating her question, she was again met by an incomprehensible rebuff, and she broke down and sobbed. Nor did her neighbours in the lounge appreciate her needs. They regarded her with a mixture of amusement and tolerant scepticism. Once when Mrs Sawbury broke a silence with the exclamation, 'How beautiful Doris is!', one neighbour sagely nodded her head, 'You can't enjoy, can you, dear?', whilst another more outright said, 'No, I don't know what you're talking about', and the first added, 'She's only half awake half the time.' It is certainly true that there were times when she misperceived the situation. On one of my visits I was told that she had the previous night placed her faeces in her handbag and had clawed some of it in her hair. But throughout her loneliness and frustrations she was always sustained by her faith. Her parting words at her interview were: 'We can't expect to live much longer, can we? No, I thank God [she began to cry] for all his mercies . . . none of us is perfect . . . the Lord is our Shepherd . . . had so many friends, never had a cross word with any of them, isn't that lovely?'

Now a lengthy discussion had been devoted to confusion which is of a verbal kind because the capacity for rational or semi-rational communication is the immediate touchstone of social acceptability. But the analysis must now shift, briefly, to the five remaining dimensions of confused behaviour.

Physical restlessness

This is manifested in two main ways – physical wandering, whether by day or night or both, and restless fiddling.

I. PHYSICAL WANDERING

This is defined as locomotion to an abnormal degree which is not accounted for by any functional responsibility. It was observed as being distinguishable in two main forms, according to whether the movement appeared aimless or directed. Unfortunately, this method of classification omits whether the wandering was frequent or only occasional. But it was felt that the character of the activity was more indicative of the nature of confused behaviour than the degree of its persistence.

(a) Aimless wandering

This is characterized as locomotion with no obvious purpose and to no apparent destination. It usually took the form of a compulsive activity:

A single woman of eighty-six wandered incessantly till sheer exhaustion forced her to relax temporarily in a chair on a couch. When questioned as to her reason for this, she could give no explanation of her behaviour. Even a brief conversation with her visitors, whom she liked very much, could not be completed before she rose to her feet and wandered away. She walked slowly, occasionally flapping the air with her arms as though to balance herself, rather like a swimming action. She did not confine herself to the lounge, but often wandered at large outside the home, and was active at night as well.

63

The aimless wanderers were as perplexed by the seemingly involuntary nature of their behaviour as others were,[23] and would either sidestep an explanation:

'Where are you going?'
'I don't know – before I come back?'
'Yes.'
'I'll let you know then, when I come back.'

Or would offer a rationalization:

A woman who kept getting up and staggering uncertainly from chair to chair justified this with the frequent declaration, 'I'd like to get away now.'

(b) Directed wandering

This is differentiated from aimless wandering by the fact that it is carried out less haphazardly, with an apparently clearer idea of direction, but is still different from 'going for a walk' because there is nevertheless no apparent sense of destination. It also lacked any compulsive element.

In one home the hall, the dining room and an adjacent corridor provided a circuit round which three or four of the residents could regularly be found travelling, with varying degrees of purposefulness, for most of each day. In another home the same function was served by the layout of pathways and lawns in front of the home which provided a route uncomplicated by any marked changes of level.

Where the movement did not follow a circuit, it was sometimes the channel through which a deluded person would play out their thoughts:

A man who sporadically gave vent to his florid fantasies about the war and his delusions of grandeur about himself chose to declaim his imaginary exploits as he paced up and down the length of the hallway.

A resident who had previously been a Shakespearean actress occasionally indulged her distinctively prolix but empty homilies as she wandered earnestly from room to room.

Lastly, if these vignettes have not already made it clear, it should be added that directed wandering excludes the phenomenon whereby new residents, whose pre-existing disorientation is accentuated by an unfamiliar environment, are constantly motivated by insecurity and bewilderment to get up and go and peer round doors to satisfy their curiosity.

2. RESTLESS FIDDLING

This denotes a reluctance to be still for long and a readiness to play with surrounding objects to an abnormal degree beyond the reasonable requirements of handling for a specific purpose. Its commonest manifestation was the tendency to fiddle with one's clothes or a button:

> A woman who was nearly blind sat in her chair all day incessantly smoothing out the ruffles of her skirt and running her hands up and down her legs. Such an excess of energetic activity could not reasonably be ascribed to a mere concern over her personal appearance.

The habit of playing with one's clothes, however, should be differentiated from the tendency gradually to roll up or even finally remove a garment, like a skirt. The affront to social proprieties which this latter involves marks it as a qualitatively distinct process, and it is therefore listed instead within the category of 'anormic' behaviour. Another common manifestation of restless fiddling was the tendency to take hold of and fiddle with whatever object happened to be within reach at that moment.

> During an interview the hands of one resident kept darting out and roaming over a succession of articles. First she played with a little box that happened to be lying on the table, then she extracted a hairpin from her hair and began to fiddle with that.

> A man was in the habit of extracting bits of torn paper from the waste paper basket and fiddling with them inanely for minutes on end.

> Another resident was inclined to grasp nearby objects, like a cushion, and inspect them with a minute inquisitiveness. This childlike fascination with ordinary articles seemed to arise from an apparent loss of understanding of the purpose for which the object was designed. Similarly, another resident was entranced by the holes of the fireguard.

Sometimes the fiddling was performed with the aid of an instrument:

> A woman, whose fingers were frequently straying over and toying with any articles within reach, on one occasion began to fiddle with a postcard using a knife until after a time she had gradually cut up chunks of it into little pieces.

Another form of this phenomenon was the habit of shifting nearby objects, however minutely, till they conformed to some inscrutable inner sense of orderliness:

> A woman who in the words of one of her neighbours 'liked to push the chairs on either side of her this way or that' earned the title of 'furniture remover' for her predilection.

> Another woman devoted more than an hour after every meal meticulously replacing the cutlery and tableware in an exactly precise position in the drawers and cupboards.

Lastly, there was the uneasy bodily restlessness of the person who could never relax:

> One man sat listlessly all day, obsessively twiddling his thumbs, as he disinterestedly gazed at his hands or generally to the front.

> A woman who rarely engaged in conversation spent most of her time obsessively chewing her fingers, whilst sporadically her face gave a slight nervous twitch from side to side.

> Similarly another woman constantly scratched her leg until a severe sore developed which had to be protected from her picking by a dressing.

Any of these characteristics, of course, could be, and often were, combined with physical wandering.

> A woman who was a constant aimless wanderer was particularly inclined to stripping beds and then partially remaking them, in the course of which she would sit on the edge of the bed and fiddle with the sheets and other objects to hand with an intense, singleminded curiosity which resented any interference.

Disorientation of person or situation

This is defined as an apparently mistaken perception of one's own or others' role or situation. However, what may at a superficial level be regarded as a gross delusion cannot be properly interpreted except in the context of the dynamics of institutional life, and a discussion of the significance of residents' claims about their situation is reserved until chapter 9 after the social system of the homes has been examined. Nevertheless, because certain declarations of confused residents cast a *prima facie* doubt on their rationality, a brief categorization of these statements should be given here in purely descriptive terms since they unquestionably contribute to the general picture of confusion.

Perhaps the commonest claim was that of maintaining a heavy burden of household duties:

A woman who could scarcely rise from her chair insisted, 'I keep the place clean, have all the beds to do upstairs and downstairs. The staff just give me enough for housekeeping.'

Others took the line that the residents were dependent on them for their care:

A man of eighty-five who never moved from his chair all day except to ask where the lavatory was, declared, 'That's why I'm not unhappy. I generally go to help them in a quiet way. Though I've got to speak for myself, I think I've done a lot for the patients.'

Others again spoke of themselves in the context of childhood:

'I must talk to mother about . . . [and beckoning to the side of the home] . . . my parents live over there.'

Some claimed they were not resident at all:

'I'm not living here – I go away.'

Others stated they were merely taking a temporary holiday:

'I'm just here because my mother put her foot down and said you must rest.'

Or from thoughtfulness to relatives:

'I'm just staying here with some friends, to save my people taking me home.'

Or they declared that they only happened to be there because they had just arrived:

67

A woman who had been resident over five years said, 'It's the first day I come here.'

Whilst many anticipated an almost immediate departure:

'I'm going back to London tomorrow.'

Yet others insisted that they wielded power over their companions by issuing instructions to the staff·

A woman of eighty referred to the staff as 'those people with whom I board', whilst declaring modestly, 'I'm only a young person who supervises one or two persons in a home.'

Not that all their assertions were equally grandiose. Some were self-deprecating:

'It would be out of place for me to talk to persons much more important than myself – not etiquette.'

Or they saw themselves as cruelly persecuted:

'You're flung in this damn place simply to make a misery for ever. I suppose they hate me because they're all so different from me. . . . I suppose they kill people here, don't they?'

Or they excused their presence by alleging chicanery:

'I came here through wickedness. There was a man at Lincoln College, and they had to send an R.A.F. police control [*sic*] and Sir Malcolm Sargent and his girl friend, and they brought them back.'

Now these examples do not provide an exhaustive catalogue of the frameworks of ideas by which confused old people interpret reality. They are merely designed to give an impression of their conceptual world as it is occasionally revealed in glimpses in the course of speech. A fuller classification, together with a theoretical explanation, will be attempted later.

Disorientation of place

Orientation refers to a person's awareness of his or her own spatial and temporal relations with other persons and the external physical environment. Correct orientation implies also the ability to recall at least some past experience and the capacity to register fresh data.[24]

In this study only spatial disorientation was measured and temporal relations were omitted. For of all the various forms of the latter – awareness of the length of stay, precision in stating age, knowledge of the weekday or month or year, perception of the time of day – none seemed relevant to the question of social adaptation.[25] Anyway, even if a resident were somewhat temporally disoriented, it would not create problems when staff take the decisions and tell residents what to do and when to do it.

Spatial disorientation was assessed on the basis of the author's personal observation supplemented by the matron's judgment. A person was regarded as moderately disoriented if he sometimes misidentified persons and surroundings, but could find his way about to the toilet, bed, etc.:

> In one home which was a converted four-storey hotel a woman who could normally find her way without any difficulty was occasionally found by the matron wandering about in the corridors and rooms one storey below her actual bedroom. Certainly the complicated layout of the home and the similarity of the design of each storey rendered residents vulnerable to such mistakes.

A person was considered severely disoriented if he did not know where he was and could not find his way about:

> When she wanted to go to the lavatory, a woman who had been resident in her home for over a year merely stood up and called to a member of staff, 'Where is it?'

> Another woman, who had been resident two years, on various occasions climbed into the wrong bed, and because she used to wander into the wrong bedroom she was frequently accused of interfering with other people's property.

Anormic behaviour

This category combines phenomena of a more varied kind than any other. On a denotative basis it is defined as either the use of objects or the manifestation of behaviour or the reiteration of certain activities in a manner which is not sanctioned by the conventional social norms. To embrace these different types of action the rather ugly term 'anormic' behaviour was coined because no existing word seemed to offer the required emphasis. 'Abnormal' signifies a quantitative rather than a qualitative deviation from the norm, while 'anormic' is esconced in the literature with implications of social isolation and non-integration in the general social structure which were clearly inappropriate here (see, for example, Srole, 1956; Clinard, ed., 1964; G. Rose, 1966; Bell, 1957).

I. NON-CONVENTIONAL USE OF OBJECTS

Here objects are used or manipulated for a purpose or in a manner for which they were not primarily intended but where such action is not necessarily dictated by an ulterior motive aiming at a more satisfying adaptation to an institutional milieu.[26]

One example was the substitution for one object of another which was functionally similar:

A conical hat in a cupboard in the hall of one home was found on one occasion to have been used as a commode. Similarly, the shape and design of a pillared cupola in the garden apparently led one wanderer to believe that it constituted a toilet, while another requisitioned a hand basin as a urinal at night time in place of a lavatory pan.

Another resident occasionally poured cornflakes into her teacup along with the tealeaves and then proceeded to eat them from this novel receptacle.

One woman was seen to use an old piece of paper to blow her nose, whilst another regularly pulled up her skirt for this purpose.

Another resident was constantly mobile through her insatiable desire to explore and probe with her fingers, and her restless fiddling encompassed anything she could seize or unloose, whether fireguards, shoelaces, glasses or books, to retain which she would if necessary resort to force when the owners tried to retain them. On one occasion, however, she was observed to place a circular Dunlopillo cushion carefully into position, then to draw a knife with a smoothing motion over its upper surface, and finally to place another cushion of similar shape equally carefully on top. Presumably memories of household duties, and of making sponge cakes in particular, still engrossed her.

Another example was hoarding:

One resident regularly stored food and sometimes hair in her handbag. Another had been known to keep her faeces there. Another who enjoyed frequent walks was in the habit of collecting leaves which she would either show off for interest in the lounge or hide away in her bedroom, to be discovered in a withered and emaciated heap some weeks later. Again, a number of residents in one home had developed the practice of removing toilet paper from the roll, folding it up neatly leaf by leaf and packing it tightly in wads in their handbags. Yet another resident indulged in the jackdaw habit of removing at lunchtime the materials which others had been using in occupational therapy sessions and concealing them under the cushion of her chair.

Lastly, there was the tendency, in apparent ignorance of the true purpose of an object, to divert its use, often in a spirit of inquisitive fascination, to some other quite different purpose:

A man who had been diffidently eyeing a large square walking frame equipped with castors at each corner, but who was obviously puzzled by its function, finally sated his curiosity by jumping on to the framework and launching himself into a ride down the centre of the tiled room.

A woman who had clearly lost an awareness of the purpose of toilet paper used to sit in the lavatory entranced by the pleasure of screwing up pieces of toilet paper into a ball and flicking them into the air.

Another woman who was given a sweet merely held it admiringly in the palm of her hand as though it were a jewel or trinket, until her exasperated benefactor was finally prompted to exclaim, 'Well, aren't you going to *eat* it?'

Conversely, another resident was reported as having eaten shoe polish.[27]

2. NON-CONVENTIONAL BEHAVIOUR

This is defined as behaviour which is unreasonably deviant from the accepted social norms, but which has clearly not been calculated to procure personal advantage. Much of this behaviour related to dress. Either clothing was put on in the wrong order and underclothes were worn on the outside:

One woman occasionally tried to put on her petticoat over her skirt, while another was observed trying to pull down her petticoat and fold it back up again over her skirt. Another resident on one occasion put on three pairs of knickers.

Or certain clothing was removed:

> Over a period of an hour a woman slowly rolled up her skirt and petticoat, unwinding them a bit as she went and then again rolling them up further, till her thighs were exposed and an attendant pulled down her skirt again. No doubt clothing was also removed partly out of discomfort, and certain residents took off every piece of clothing altogether.[28]

Or the conventional proprieties concerning dress were not adhered to:

> One woman openly lifted up her skirt in order to adjust her suspenders, whilst another on one occasion climbed into bed fully clothed and wearing her shoes, and a third wandered out on to the lawn one evening clad in her nightdress. Yet another woman was reported to have come down to breakfast once with only a frock on.

Apart from oddities in the wearing of clothes, non-conventional behaviour also related to the conventions of toileting:

> A man wishing to urinate when in a room full of residents sitting round the walls, merely turned his back on a throng of others standing in the centre, undid his fly buttons and urinated on to a piece of paper which happened to be lying on a nearby table.

> A woman, wishing to pass a motion when seated with others in the lounge, one afternoon, removed all her clothes and squatted down in a corner of the room.

And to the conventions of speech:

> A woman was reported to have been in the habit of getting to her feet at various times during the day and loudly proclaiming her religious convictions to her seated companions. When the attendants tried to stop this religious preaching, she refused to be calmed and only became more vehement still.

> Another woman was often inclined, when her neighbour was holding up a newspaper to read, to chant out loud the main headlines in an uncomprehending monotone.

3. NON-FUNCTIONAL REITERATIVE ACTIVITIES

By this is meant the persistent repetition of actions where this constant reiteration is not required by any extra-personal function. Much of this behaviour, which falls into no obvious pattern of classification, may be seen as the extension through time of a form of restless fiddling. It is then the repetitiveness together with the apparent inanity of the act which constitute the additional essential attributes:

A man of ninety-nine who was particularly shaky on his feet used to spend most of his day sitting on a chair behind the door of the men's toilet, striking matches endlessly one after another, letting them burn out, dropping the charred remains on to the floor, and then picking them all up again and replacing them in the box.

Another man spent much of his time repeating a set of actions whereby he took out his wallet from his waistcoat pocket, extracted letters and photographs from the wallet, looked at them for a few moments, replaced them, then removed his pocket watch, checked its time against the clock on the mantelpiece which had long since stopped, asked his neighbours whether the clock was going, and finally put back his watch.

Reiterated action was also exhibited in regard to the person's own body:

One woman at sporadic intervals kept clapping her hands, often accompanied by loud protestations seemingly unrelated to the situation. The more she was rebuked by her irritated neighbours, the more insistently she carried on her practice. Another woman similarly kept slapping her arm, her knee and even her cheek.

And also in regard to the person's own clothing:

A woman who remained seated all day but watched every happening in the room with a hawklike eye channelled her energy into obsessively picking hairs off her cardigan or alternatively picking at the cardigan itself.

Lastly non-functional reiterative activity was found in the field of speech. Included here in particular is the person who asks the same question over and over again, as though never satisfied however often the answer is given. A more extreme example, however, is the constant repetition of the same phrase several times without a break:

> The words of a woman who illustrated this habit were recorded over a fifteen-minute period as follows. As some residents left the room, she began 'Oh he's going away now ...' (repeated 4 times), then 'Going at it ...' (20–30 times), then 'There's a boy sitting there in blue ...' (referring to a woman sitting nearby in a blue dressing gown), then 'Sweet sitting on his mother's knee ...' (10–15 times). At this point several residents told her to stop, but she persisted, 'All right I won't talk so much ...' (30 times), then as she gazed out of the window, 'Look at the hill, the window's wide open ...' (10 times), then 'The other one knocking as hard as he can ...' (20–30 times), then 'The other one knocking with eyes in his nose ...' (at least 50 times).

These three types of non-conventional activity therefore together illustrate the variability and eccentricity of 'anormic' behaviour. A caution, should be given. None of these pieces of behaviour which have been recorded should be treated in isolation. Many are clearly related to the pathology of an institutional existence and are therefore inseparable from the latter's dynamics, as will be shown later.

Memory defect

Allison (1962, pp. 125–30) claims that memory defect may be analysed on four different dimensions:

1. Inability to sort former events into their proper sequence (temporal disorientation).
2. Inability to remember the spatial relationships of previously well-known places (loss of topographical memory).
3. Inability to remember names (nominal amnesia).
4. Failure to use memory as a tool (amnesic indifference).

What this analysis implies is how variegated but essential is the requirement of memory as an underlying factor in the successful performance of many simple but wide-ranging functions.[29] It indicates how pervasive are the consequences which at a secondary level reflect memory failure, whether it be inability to follow a planned routine, paranoid accusations of stealing or interference with others' property, inability to sustain a lengthy dialogue, or reversion to a stereotyped response to certain situations. Nevertheless, it was felt, with an eye to the question of social adaptation, that the components of Allison's framework should be distributed in other categories on a behavioural basis. By the same token, whilst memory defect may be related to various manifestations of the confusional syndrome, it is not taken per se as sufficient evidence of the existence of confusion.

Under temporal disorientation Allison includes such cases as where the person does not know when he had his last meal,[30] when is the time to stop or start work, when a change of clothing is due, or when to get up or go to bed. But as has already been stated (p. 69), in a situation where staff give instructions about the details of the routine and residents are subject to regimentation for the fulfilment of a prepared schedule, such considerations seem hardly relevant to the problem of social adjustment and they are therefore omitted for this analysis.

With regard to topographical memory, Allison maintains that the tendency for some old people to get lost out of doors and to be found wandering in the streets is explicable by an illusion of unfamiliarity arising from perseveration. In other words, persons with this form of memory defect cannot reorient themselves because of the persistence of former scenes in their minds. In this study, behaviour of such kind is discussed as disorientation of place.

Allison's third component, nominal amnesia, is certainly relevant to social adjustment in that it clearly makes the maintenance of prolonged dialogue very difficult:

'What do you think of the sleeping arrangements here?'
'On perfect. We've got a . . . what do you call it? . . . big thing . . . trying to work it out . . . no, I can't think of anything.'

But here it is discussed, together with the devices intended to circumvent it, as a form of tangential speech.

Lastly, the fourth component, amnesic indifference, may appear in various forms, and in the particular guises of confabulation and overdependence on a dominant or stereotyped idea, it is treated here as a specialized example of 'diplomatic adjustment' (see chapter 9).

For these reasons a simple pragmatic scale was devised to measure memory impairment as it affected the capacity of residents to execute a preconceived course of action, whether designed by themselves or required by the instructions of staff. On this basis moderate memory defect was defined as a state of mind where a person occasionally forgot what he had just been doing and what results his actions had had:

> A woman whose actions normally showed her memory remained intact, having been asked on one occasion to have a bath, turned on all the taps to run in the water, but then having walked away paid no further attention to the matter till the overflow warned attendants to intervene.

Severe memory defect was attributed where a person seemed to have completely forgotten everything he had done:

> A man who could recall nothing of his past and who could give no information about the other residents except for the single delusional idea that he helped them, remarked once about his own forgetfulness, 'Funny thing, I can't think of things when I want to. ... That's a bit of a tease; I'm going soft, I suppose. ... 'Course my memory for various things has got weak on account of age. ... I don't remember a lot of detailed things.' In fact he could not be relied on to carry out any instruction which required any degree of memory retention beyond the immediate situation.

In summary, then, a theory of confused behaviour, where the confusion cannot be ascribed to remediable physical causes,[31] has been presented in terms of social adjustment. On this theoretical basis confused behaviour has been analysed on six dimensions – verbal confusion, physical restlessness, disorientation of person or situation, disorientation of place, anormic behaviour and memory defect. We now return to the six homes which form the scene of this study in order to discuss the numbers of confused old people in different types of residential settings together with their social backgrounds and physical incapacities.

NOTES

1. Flint and Richards (1956, p. 1537) in an examination of 242 elderly people, found that aetiological factors of confusion included cerebral disease in eighty-two cases, heart-failure fifty-three, pulmonary disease forty-six, and uraemia twenty-six. The remainder were anaemia hepatic failure, avitaminosis, endocrine disorders, drugs, cancer, injuries

and miscellaneous infections. The cause of confusion in half their cases was extra-cerebral.

2. *Geriatrics*, Jan. 1960, p. 82.

3. Further, Freyhan *et al.* (1951, p. 449) concluded that the psychoses are 'probably the result' of a significant reduction in cerebral oxygen utilization on the basis of increased cerebrovascular resistance and diminished cerebral blood flow. A confirmatory study (Doust *et al.*, 1953, p. 395) added that a correlation had been found between the *intensity* of the anoxaemia and the *degree* of the accompanying dementia throughout a sample of eighty-nine aged hospitalized patients whose illness represented a continuum of clinical senile dementia, and stated further that a statistically significant correlation existed between oximetric level and intelligence.

4. In fact Rothschild (1937, 1941) had already produced evidence of the unsatisfactory nature of clinico-pathological correlates in dementia, based on post-mortem examination of cerebral damage.

5. The search for physical cause nevertheless continues. Another theory, for example, has been propounded that some cases of senile dementia are determined by a chronic cerebral ischaemia due to occlusion of one or both carotid channels. This condition has been found even where the intra-cranial cerebral vessels themselves were virtually free of arteriosclerosis and it has been suggested that the blocking of the left internal carotid artery, the main supply of the dominant hemisphere, is especially related to the development of dementia (Fisher, 1951, p. 6). However, it remains difficult to reconcile the theory with the well-documented observation that, despite pronounced clinical symptoms, post-mortem examination commonly shows little evidence of cerebral damage.

6. Botwinick and Birren (1951b) further elaborated a comparison of indices used for estimating intellectual deterioration in the elderly.

7. Similar relationships have been reported by Robinson (1955); Mundy-Castle *et al.* (1954); and Weiner and Schuster (1956).

8. The authors do try to take account of the range of manifestations in senile dementia by pointing out that, apart from Huntington's chorea, studies on essential tremor and torsion dystonia have given clear evidence of the existence of monohybrid dominant diseases with great variability of age at onset and symptomatology.

9. One of the authors of this study, Sjögren (1964, p. 52), suggests in another survey that disturbances of processes in the glia cells may be significant in the pathogenesis of senile brain atrophy.

10. This is rather surprising when such typical characteristics of senile dementia as growing egocentricity, apparent shallowness of emotional response, increasing rigidity, and growing irritability and bad temper clearly portend a social reaction.

11. It should be added, however, that a similar study by Connolly (1962, p. 99) did not confirm this result. He found that of 153 consecutive admissions, forty-two patients had previously been living alone, and within this sub-group senile and arteriosclerotic psychotics formed approximately the same proportion as they did in the series as a whole.

12. It is interesting in this regard to note that the dominance of the grandmother in working-class life in London, as against the tragedy which retirement often represented for her husband, was due in large part to the maintenance of an independent role into old age through the provision of mutual services between the grandmother and her daughter (P. Townsend, 1957).

13. Albrecht (1951, p. 386) found that 'non-senile' personality patterns were associated with the following social factors: active social roles, especially having a family, but not depending only on family members and relatives for social life; association with other people in groups and individual relationships; interest in a variety of activities; interest in the future; marriage; middle-class status; and continued work. Senile patterns, on the other hand, were associated with the opposite.

14. The Plowden Report, *Children and their Primary Schools* (1967) i, p. 12, suggests that in child development there may be critical periods, or at least periods of maximum sensitivity, during which, if a certain stimulus is not received, behaviour may be drastically affected. Thus, for example, if in early infancy the baby 'expects' cuddling, as many psychologists believe, and does not receive it, he may after a while develop pathological behaviour, perhaps irreversibly so. Again, it has been shown from clinical experience of deaf children that the facility for discriminating speech sounds, and therefore for understanding speech and learning to speak, may diminish after early childhood (Loring, ed., 1965). On this basis it is a reasonable hypothesis that there may be crucial stages in the process of adaptation to retirement and old age when the absence of the required social support may drastically curtail the capacity to perform the conventional role. Also it is significant here that irritability and anger in response to frustration are common emotional characteristics among demented persons.

15. *Mental Frailty in the Elderly*, National Old People's Welfare Council, 1962.

16. Slotkin (1942, p. 345) discusses disconnected verbalization, which in extreme cases he calls 'word salads', but concludes rather curiously that it may serve a distractability purpose, to keep the mind off a complex of painful thoughts. In fact, it is the content and direction of much bizarre speech, rather than its intermittent scatter, which performs this function.

17. One woman whose speech was virtually confined to uttering 'yes' or 'no' would even draw in her breath in a sustained effort to produce new words, but in vain and would sink back into her accustomed expressions with a relaxed sigh.

18. Allison adds that the buoyancy of mood and self-confidence of all severely dysphasic patients who are uninhibited in spontaneous speech suggests an associated defect in auditory word recognition interfering with awareness of the defects. Moreover, Symonds (1953), in reviewing word-sound and word-meaning deafness, notes that patients' behaviour in such circumstances is so odd that one might think they were play-acting.

19. One is reminded in listening to such expressions of Lewis Carroll's dictum put into the mouth of Humpty Dumpty: 'Words are what I want them to mean.' The technique has also been dubbed 'abstract speaking' on the analogy of abstract painting, and it clearly bears affinities with Allison's jargon aphasia.

20. It is this tendency to which Kosmyryk (1967) in an article about her mentally infirm father, refers colloquially as 'getting the lines crossed'. She states that he used to get angry with frustration because 'he always knew what he wanted to say, but the words would never come out right', and only she could understand him from long practice.

21. Allison (1962, p. 18) also gives two interesting examples of homophonic word substitution: 'Tent – camp . . . no . . . hut . . . eh . . . trench . . . tent.' 'Fork – I couldn't use the claw at all . . . the clubs . . . aw, the hell, I can't find the word for it.'

22. Weinstein and Kahn (1952, p. 72) note that paraphasia, which only occurs in persons with diffuse cerebral lesions, is usually associated with other defects, especially euphoric mood, anosognosia (lack of recognition of illness) disorientation in place and time, and some ideomotor apraxia (different action performed to that intended).

23. The extent to which drugs may act as a causal agent here is discussed in chapter 8.

24. Allison (1962, pp. 173–200) classified disorientation as including (i) spatio-temporal disorientation, together with prosopagnosia (inability to recognize faces), (ii) more abstract disorientation at a propositional and conceptual level (which may be equated with 'disorientation of person or situation' in this study), and (iii) disturbances of corporeal awareness. This last was described, in the form of Gerstmann's syndrome, as embracing the inability to distinguish left-right, finger agnosia, the inability to write spontaneously and dyscalculia (the inability to count accurately).

Stengel (1944, p. 753) shows that constructional apraxia (the inability to construct objects from their component parts) is often associated with this syndrome.

25. With the exception of nocturnal disturbance which may be due to gross distortion of the time scale. Such behaviour has been classified under night wandering.

26. In other words, non-conventional use of objects does not necessarily constitute a 'secondary adjustment' as conceived by Goffman (1961). He defines, and illustrates by copious examples, 'secondary adjustment' as 'any habitual arrangement by which a member of an organization employs unauthorized means, or obtains unauthorized ends, or both, thus getting around the organization's assumptions as to what he should do and get and hence what he should be' (p. 189).

27. Coprophagia would also be included within this category of acts, but no instance was found in the homes visited.

28. It was the exception rather than the rule for this to be associated with sexual fantasies.

29. Allison (1962, p. 202) writes that since memory plays such an important part in perceiving and apprehending an object many types of agnosic and apraxic defect may be regarded as a specialized form of memory impairment. In this sense Kinnier Wilson has defined agnosia as 'the failure of intellectual recognition where there is integrity of primary identification', and apraxia as 'the inability to perform certain subjectively purposive movements or movement complexes with conservation of motility, of sensation and of co-ordination'.

30. And indeed a number of instances were found in the course of the present study where within minutes of completing a meal a confused resident claimed he had not eaten for a long time and asked when the meal he had just finished was to take place. Again, however, this should not perhaps be taken too literally in view of the common reference to food as a symbol of affection.

31. What Cosin *et al.* (1957, p. 195) call 'persistent senile confusion'.

4

The residents: the confused and
the rational

THE NUMBER OF CONFUSED RESIDENTS

Of the 260 residents in the three separatist and the three ordinary homes investigated, how many were confused in terms of the dimensions elucidated in the last chapter? As Table 4.1 shows, the proportion in the ordinary homes who showed at least some manifestation of confused behaviour was 16 per cent. In the separatist homes, which were specifically intended for the accommodation of confused residents, the proportion was surprisingly only 58 per cent. The reasons why more than two-fifths of the residents found in separatist homes were in no way confused will be examined later when admission policies are reviewed (in chapter 10). Here it will only be stressed that the proportion demonstrating at least some kind of confused behaviour varied considerably between the three homes, from 80 per cent in one to 47 per cent in another.

Comparison on the basis of whether residents display at least one component of confused behaviour does not, however, give full weight to the relative distribution of such behaviour between the different kinds of homes. This is more adequately shown by the fact (presented in Table 4.2) that whereas only 4 per cent of the residents in the ordinary homes manifested four or more components of confused behaviour, the corresponding proportion in the separatist homes was 28 per cent. Moreover, the incidence of the most obtrusive forms of confusion – physical restlessness,[1] verbal confusion and anormic behaviour – is very much higher in the special homes. For while only a tenth of those in the ordinary homes displayed physical wandering or restless fiddling, a third did so in the special homes. None of those in the ordinary homes exhibited incoherent speech, and only a twentieth were tangential in their speech; in the separatist homes, by contrast, over a third were verbally confused. Furthermore, with regard to anormic behaviour,[2]

Table 4.1

Numbers of confused residents in three separatist and three ordinary residential homes

Type of confusion displayed	Number of residents in three separatist homes					Number of residents in ordinary homes				
	Home A	Home B	Home C	All homes	% in all homes	Home D	Home E	Home F	All homes	% in all homes
Verbal confusion:										
incoherent	4	1	1	6	4·9	0	0	0	0	0
tangential	18	13	6	37	30·1	1	5	1	7	5·1
Physical restlessness:										
aimless wandering	7	2	3	12	9·8	1	1	2	4	2·9
directed wandering	7	4	1	12	9·8	0	2	2	4	2·9
restless fiddling	15	6	7	28	22·8	0	4	1	5	3·7
Disorientation of person or situation	31	20	12	64	51·2	1	5	2	8	5·8
Disorientation of place:										
severe	10	8	10	28	22·8	1	6	0	7	5·1
moderate	16	7	2	25	20·3	0	2	7	9	6·6
Anormic behaviour:										
non-conventional use of objects	11	0	2	13	10·6	0	1	0	1	0·7
non-conventional behaviour	9	3	1	13	10·6	1	3	0	4	2·9
non-functional reiterative activity	7	2	3	12	9·8	0	3	0	3	2·2
Memory defect:										
severe	15	12	11	38	30·9	1	2	0	3	2·2
moderate	16	12	9	37	30·1	2	10	9	21	15·3
Total number of residents without any of the above symptoms (excluding memory defect)	8	25	19	52	42·3	18	67	30	115	84·0
Total number of residents	40	47	36	123	100	19	80	38	137	100

Table 4.2

Residents in three separatist and three ordinary residential homes by number of components of confused behaviour displayed* (excluding memory defect)

Number of components of confused behaviour displayed	Residents in separatist homes					Residents in ordinary homes				
	Home A	Home B	Home C	All homes	% in all homes	Home D	Home E	Home F	All homes	% in all homes
5	11	3	4	18	14·6	1	2	0	3	2·2
4	9	6	2	17	13·8	0	1	1	2	1·5
3	5	3	2	10	8·1	0	2	1	3	2·2
2	4	5	4	13	10·6	0	4	2	6	4·4
1	3	5	5	13	10·6		4	4	8	5·8
0	8	25	19	52	42·3	18	67	30	115	84·0
Total Residents	40	47	36	123	100·0	19	80	38	137	100·1

* Verbal confusion, physical restlessness, disorientation of person or situation, disorientation of place, and anormic behaviour.

which was often the most obtrusive characteristic of all, only one in seventeen in the ordinary homes revealed such tendencies, whilst more than a fifth did so in the special homes, and many of these showed both a greater variety and a more acute degree of normlessness in their behaviour than those similarly classified in the ordinary homes.[3] Thus a picture emerges of the latter as homes where a sizeable minority of confused old people are accommodated, but their symptoms of confusion tend to be mild in character and often single rather than multiple. The separatist homes, however, though containing on average a very large minority of residents who show no sign of confusion at all, nevertheless also accommodate persons whose confusion is extensive both in range of different types of behaviour and in degree of abnormality.

Given this distribution of confused residents between the homes,

Table 4.3

Degrees of relationship between the five components of behaviour* as measured by χ^2 tests

Components of confused behaviour	χ^2 values for relationships found with:				
	Verbal confusion	Physical restlessness	Disorientation of person/ situation	Disorientation of place	Anormic behaviour
Verbal confusion					
Physical restlessness	104				
Disorientation of person/ situation	123	99·9			
Disorientation of place	133	95·4	146		
Anormic behaviour	55·8	79·6	64·8	69·3	
	(df = 1; p = ·001 where χ^2 = 10·827)				

* Excluding memory defect on the grounds that it cannot alone be regarded as a symptom of confusion and anyway this deficiency is already largely covered by disorientation of place which Allison regards as a specialized form of memory impairment (see p. 75). The parameter for these tests therefore consists of ninety-three persons in both the separatist and ordinary homes.

how far were the confused distinguishable from the rational[4] by their social characteristics ? And was their mental infirmity paralleled by a corresponding physical infirmity? For this purpose it is necessary to link the five main dimensions already established into a single index.[5] This raises the further questions of how far the five dimensions are intercorrelated as elements of a cohesive concept, and if so, what internal weightings should be applied. Now Table 4.3 shows that the chance that for any pair of these five dimensions no relationship subsists between them is less than one in a thousand. Hence the mutual interrelationships of all the dimensions may be interpreted to mean that they are interchangeable parts of a single coherent concept of 'confusion'. If then the concept can be satisfactorily operationalized by means of these various dimensions, how should they be weighted on a numerical scale ? Now the factors which should have influence here would seem to be the degree of impact which each aspect of behaviour has on other residents, the amount of extra work they impose on staff, and the extent of psychological withdrawal which they imply for the resident himself. On this basis a scoring system was devised which is shown in Table 4.4.

Using this approach we can then rate degree of confusion on a unidimensional scale. If we regard a score of 7–14 as indicating severe confusion and a score of 1–6 as implying moderate confusion, then (as Table 4.5 demonstrates) a quarter of the residents in the separatist homes were severely confused and a third moderately so, whilst in the ordinary homes only an eighth were moderately confused and severe confusion was confined to only one in every twenty-seven residents.

How do these findings relate to other data concerning the incidence of mental infirmity among the elderly in ordinary homes ? Now reference has already been made to the fact that Ministry of Health statistics reveal that on 31 December 1967 about 11·9 per cent of all persons aged sixty-five and over in residential accommoda-in England and Wales were mentally handicapped.[6] Apart from this the evidence available is extremely fragmentary. A review in September 1967 of residents in homes for the elderly and handicapped in the London borough of Hounslow found that 11 per cent out of a total of 431 persons were 'senile dements', while another 11 per cent were described as 'psycho-geriatric'.[7] A similar review in Nottingham at the end of 1963 produced a total of 17 per cent of

Table 4.4

Scoring system for rating confusion in the elderly

Confused behaviour	Score per item	Maximum score per component
Verbal confusion:		
incoherent	4	
tangential	3	4
Physical restlessness:		
aimless wandering	3	
directed wandering	2	4
restless fiddling	1	
Disorientation of person/		
situation	1	1
Disorientation of place:		
severe	2	
moderate	1	2
Anormic behaviour:		
non-conventional use		
of objects	1	
non-conventional		
behaviour	1	3
non-functional reiterative		
activity	1	
TOTAL	—	14

Table 4.5

Distribution of residents in separatist and ordinary homes
by degree of confused behaviour

Degree of confusion	Score on confusional scale (inclusive)	Separatist homes (%)	Ordinary homes (%)
Severely confused	7–14	25·2	3·7
Moderately confused	1–6	32·5	12·4
Non-confused (rational)	0	42·3	84·0
TOTAL		100·0	100·1
Number		123	137

547 residents who were 'mentally confused'.[8] Again a comprehensive survey of the physical and mental health of 533 elderly residents in Cardiff in July 1967 indicated that whilst half enjoyed a 'good' mental state, 22·5 per cent were severely mentally confused and a further 13·3 per cent were mildly so. With regard to the remainder, 10·8 per cent were judged severely or chronically depressed, while 2·6 per cent were subject to 'irresponsible behaviour', by which was meant they would be a danger to themselves and others in, for example, handling gas or electricity. It was also found that 2·1 per cent showed a tendency to wander, 3·3 per cent demonstrated noisy behaviour and 9·3 per cent showed marked aggressiveness.[9] But this data should be treated with some caution since in each case the criteria used in making the classifications have not been made explicit, and there is also no guarantee of consistency between different persons making these assessments. One study, however, has met both these objections. Peter Townsend (1962, p. 268), using a consistent approach over his whole sample of 530 residents and stating his criteria[10] found 5 per cent were mentally impaired to a severe extent and a further 12 per cent moderately so. These results correspond strikingly with the findings of the present study.

THE NUMBER OF RESIDENTS WITH PSYCHIATRIC DISORDER

Lastly, before leaving a discussion of the numbers of the confused, how do the social criteria used here to elucidate confusion compare with normal clinical diagnoses?[11] For the residents in the three separatist homes the clinical diagnosis was obtained from the case records and checked against observation. The results of the comparison, given in Table 4.6, display the obvious overlap between confused behaviour as measured here and senile or arteriosclerotic psychosis (df $= 1$, $\chi^2 = 48\cdot7$, $p < \cdot001$), particularly amongst the more severely confused. Nevertheless, those whose behaviour shows only marginal symptoms of confusion form, as might be expected, a much more clinically heterogeneous group. But even of those with medium or high scores for confused behaviour a number also appeared quite different from the stereotype of senile psychosis:

Mr Gossthwaite was tangential in his speech, a directed wanderer, disoriented of situation, moderately disoriented of place, and

Table 4.6

Degree of confused behaviour of residents in separatist
homes by clinical diagnosis

Clinical diagnosis	Severely confused (%)	Moderately confused (%)	Non-confused (%)
Senile or arteriosclerotic psychosis	(90·3)	(67·5)	13·4
Paranoid psychosis, senile schizophrenia, or paraphrenia	(9·7)	(10)	9·6
Affective disorder	0	0	26·9
Subnormality	0	(12·5)	13·4
Neurosis	0	0	1·9
No psychiatric disorder	0	(10)	34·6
TOTAL	(100)	(100)	99·8
Number	31	40	52

moderately defective in memory (confusional score 7). At his
interview, however, he was smartly dressed, confident in manner,
articulate in expression and revealed a fluent flow of ideas. Aged
68, and separated from and rejected by his wife, he had spent
two years in the special home where I met him, but before that
had been confined for 21 years in the nearby mental hospital.
When I asked him how he came to be in the home, he replied:
'I had the sleeping treatment at Clingthorpes [Hospital] in 1942
after shell shock. Then they came to see me four or five days after
that, along with Jerry, fired at us on the gasworks, missed the
cylinder by fifteen inches. The next one dropped on the primrose
shelter and the sergeant's family. That's how I happened to be in
Laspar [the site of the hospital]. Went home after that, threshed
the corn, carried fourteen tons on my back – I carried some of it.
Then I went to Clingthorpes Hospital in '42, till I came here two
years ago. Epileptics, I used to shave their heads.' This passage
reveals many of his prominent characteristics: a capacity for
grandiose confabulation; an obsession with death, destruction
and impending doom; a meticulous concern for trivial detail; and
an exaggerated love of intellectualizing at the expense of emotional superficiality. On occasion he would stride up and down
the hallway of the home declaiming his horrific delusions about
war, in short, sudden snatches: '... Take the person there, not

much to say about the end, but when you get there, you'll know
... tie them to their graves on two rifles ... been inside the
Gezer Pyramid, been in the Holy Sepulchre, been in the Mosque
of Omar, been on the top of the Russian Mosque on the Mount
of Olives, 272 steps, looking over the Dead Sea ... we went up
Suez in two barges ... been at County Hall and writing out special
reports ... Ghurkas there before, and the Turks killing prisoners
by stripping them, tying them to olive trees and firing at them.'
Furthermore, his extravagant sense of danger was transposed to
the home itself: 'Everything's full of electricity – the bathroom
upstairs – no lightning conductors, nor with the 'phones buzzing
all the time, and the shaft under the floor ...' At least in part
these grandiose expositions of his experiences were a reaction
against what he regarded as the stigma of his incarceration. He
wrote once to his sister-in-law that 'all this must stop' and that
being in hospital had ruined his life. On another occasion he stated
that the *Daily Mail* a year previously had carried a reference to
him and that he 'would have gone out of the country incognito if
the authorities had wanted it'. Within the home, however, Mr
Gossthwaite had achieved what the staff considered a satisfactory
adjustment: he mowed the lawn for the gardener, helped to shave
and bath the other male residents, and retained enough independence to go on betting sprees into the nearby town. Apart
from his constant shoulder tic and his occasional bizarre utterances
he did not appear noticeably abnormal in any respect.

It should also be noted that only a third of the rational (or non-
confused) were free of psychiatric disorder. An eighth were diagnosed as suffering from senile or arteriosclerotic psychosis and
another quarter from affective disorder, chiefly depression. Two of
the latter provide illustrations of how varied were the conditions
of rational residents:

Mrs Howlett spent every day strapped into a geriatric chair and
was very often to be seen with her head on her crooked elbow
slumped over the tray which was locked into the chair. She only
rarely uttered any words and when she did so, they were expressed
in a slow and very indistinct drawl. Yet when an effort was made
to communicate with her, she showed she could think logically
and construct short, rational sentences. Her husband had died of
cancer three years previously, as a result of which she became

very depressed (as the case record makes clear), lived an isolated life and refused to mix. Her son and his wife, however, built two rooms on to her bungalow at their own expense and came to look after her. But because she still proved very trying and had lost interest in herself, the daughter-in-law soon collapsed under the strain and was forced to return to her parents' home to recuperate. Since the son was also subject to bouts of depression, Mrs Howlett was admitted informally to the nearby mental hospital where she appeared restless and confused, continually wandering around in an aimless manner and demanding constant attention from the nursing staff.

After five months, having become more settled and 'co-operative', she was transferred to the special home where I interviewed her. The medication originally prescribed for her was continued, and whether or not this had become responsible for her languid torpor, her slurred speech and the disfigurement of her oral dyskinesia, she was certainly now pathetically unable to secure the attention she craved for. When once at morning teatime she seemed to be requesting a biscuit, a neighbour, who was also rational, brusquely dismissed her plea with the stern retort, 'Joanna, I don't know what you say.' At another time when she clearly wanted to be helped to walk because her buttocks were sore from her incontinence, two attendants rather abruptly passed on, seeming not to understand.

Miss Ackerton declared quickly that she did very little now because she had 'put all her eggs in one basket', spending over forty years as a military nurse and rising, she proclaimed proudly to the rank of Lieutenant-Colonel in the Royal Army Nursing Corps. Now a quiet, introspective, bespectacled woman of 73 who had never married, she confessed to a nagging sense of frustration and purposelessness. 'Sometimes I feel mad – can't knit, can't read, and Mrs Ossett makes awful noises in the evening. When you're old, you're so useless. I've led such a life of activity and doing things for people. I feel such a useless wretch now. I can't help it. I loved my life. I feel I've got to stick it, feel I can't die. I want to, just because I'm no use to anybody. Old soldiers never die – they only fade away.' As she said this, her weak voice trembled and cracked, and she swallowed hard as though on the verge of tears. She insisted she liked outside contacts, but these had become very rare now. For example, since she came from York, where she used to help cleaning in the cathedral after retirement, she still liked to send money for flowers to adorn the altar. She also corresponded about three times a year, with an old nursing friend in London, but apart from these haphazard links she 'did not have a friend in the world except Mrs Quentin'. 'She and I,' Miss Ackerton assured me, 'are devoted to one another,' but unfortunately it was clear that the emotional dependence was all on one side. Mrs Quentin tolerated her amicably enough and they shared a bedroom and could often be seen on walks arm in arm, but being a stronger and more assertive character, Mrs Quentin grew noticeably tired of her companion's attentiveness at times. Perhaps the ultimate unreliability even of this her last remaining friend had not escaped Miss Ackerton because a few months before my arrival at this special home she had a hysterical fit. Suddenly, and for no obvious reason she insisted she could not walk and kept crumpling up. She was found on the floor several times, was 'severely nervous and jumpy' (in the words of her case file) and said she could not see. She seemed no longer able to control either her speech or movement when called upon to make any effort to help herself. She would only declare that she had lost all confidence in herself and that she felt completely 'degraded'. The doctor could find no physical cause to explain this behaviour, but after a few days she gradually recovered her balance. Possibly the breakdown occurred because her fears had been aroused at the time that Mrs Quentin might desert her to go and live with her daughter, and certainly Miss Ackerton, whilst having again achieved a superficial façade of stability, is still prone to moods of depression.

The two sketches give an impression of the inherent dissimilarity among those conventionally summarized beneath the title of 'rational'. To complete the picture, further case studies will be presented at the end of the chapter to illustrate the scale of mental impairment at various points and to demonstrate the interplay between mental impairment and social background, inhibitions on mobility and personal care, and physical handicap.

THE SOCIAL BACKGROUND AND PHYSICAL
HANDICAPS OF THE CONFUSED

How far does a link exist between mental infirmity in the aged and social deprivation on the one hand and physical incapacity on the other? Firstly, Table 4.7 shows that significantly more of the ninety-three confused residents in the separatist and ordinary homes were women (df = 1, $\chi^2 = 8\cdot2$, p<·01), whilst Table 4.8 reveals that proportionately more of the confused were widows, but not significantly so (df = 1, $\chi^2 = 3\cdot51$, p>·05). A test was also made to discover whether, among the widowed, the confused represented to a significant degree those without children, but the result was negative. Of the widowed who were confused 73 per cent had children, against 76 per cent of the widowed who were rational. To this extent the confused did not appear to come from unusual family backgrounds, though the quality and frequency of family relationships prior to admission could not be measured. Nor did age significantly differentiate the confused, though again proportionately rather more (as Table 4.9 shows) were found in the highest age group, composed of those aged 85 and over, than was the case with the rational (df = 1, $\chi^2 = 1\cdot26$, p>·05). Social class, however, provided a decisive division[12] and indicated that confusion was not associated with low social ranking. Where socio-economic data could be collected, it was found that confused residents were preponderantly middle class (df = 1, $\chi^2 = 33\cdot9$, p<·001), three-fifths of them belonging to the professional and managerial classes compared to less than a quarter among the rational, as Table 4.10 illustrates.

Mental confusion does not therefore seem to be correlated with

Table 4.7

Degree of confused behaviour by sex

Sex		Severely confused (%)	Moderately confused (%)	Non-confused (%)
Male		(5·6)	21·0	31·2
Female		(94·4)	79·0	68·8
	TOTAL	(100)	100	100
	Number	36	57	167

Table 4.8
Degree of confused behaviour by marital status

Marital status	Severely confused (%)	Moderately confused (%)	Non-confused (%)
Single	(22·2)	31·5	34·2
Married	(2·8)	0	6·6
Widowed/separated	(75·1)	68·5	59·4
TOTAL	(100·1)	100·0	100·2
Number	36	57	167

Table 4.9
Degree of confused behaviour by age

Age	Severely confused (%)	Moderately confused (%)	Non-confused (%)
74 or under	(27·8)	10·6	28·2
75–84	(41·7)	50·8	43·2
85 or over	(30·6)	38·6	28·8
TOTAL	(100·1)	100·0	100·2
Number	36	57	167

Table 4.10
Confused behaviour by social class

Social class (Registrar General's classification)	Severely or moderately confused (%)	Non-confused (%)
Professional and managerial (middle class, RG I, II)	59·6	23·8
Skilled, semi-skilled and unskilled manual (working class, RG III, IV, V)	40·4	76·3
TOTAL	100·0	100·1
Number*	52	80

* Information regarding the social class of residents was obtainable for only just over half the total sample.

social deprivation. Is it associated with physical disability? Certainly confused behaviour was found to be linked with limitation in mobility (df = 1, χ^2 = 16·8, p<·001). The criterion was whether a person was able, even if with difficulty, to move beyond the bed, the chair, the room and the building without the aid of another person. On this basis, none was bedfast, but while only a ninth of the rational were limited in their mobility, nearly a third of the confused were subject to such limitations, as Table 4.11

Table 4.11
Degree of confused behaviour by limitations in
mobility

Mobility limited to	Severely confused (%)	Moderately confused (%)	Non-confused (%)
Chair	(8·3)	1·8	6·0
Room	(8·3)	3·5	0
Building	(25·0)	19·3	4·8
Unlimited	(58·4)	75·3	89·3
TOTAL	(100·0)	99·9	100·1
	36	57	167

indicates. Further, as might be expected, the confused revealed an incapacity to undertake the tasks of personal care without assistance to a significantly greater degree than their rational companions (Table 4.12). This applied to the tasks of dressing and washing (df = 1, χ^2 = 55·2, p<·001) as well as bathing (df = 1, χ^2 = 6·95, p<·01),

Table 4.12
Degree of confused behaviour by incapacity for
personal care

Inability to	Severely confused (%)	Moderately confused (%)	Non-confused (%)
Dress self	(83·4)	38·5	12·6
Wash self	(80·6)	40·3	11·4
Bath self	(90·7)	77·0	67·8
Feed self	(11·1)	0	1·8
Number	36	57	167

though perhaps the absolute figures are somewhat inflated in reflecting the anxiety of matrons to require the participation of attendants for fear of accidents even where this was not strictly necessary.

The only physical handicaps, however, with which confused behaviour was significantly correlated were impaired hearing (df = 1, $\chi^2 = 8\cdot49$, p$<\cdot$01) and incontinence (df = 1, $\chi^2 = 26\cdot2$, p$<\cdot001$). The latter association may be explained partly on a physiological level, but also partly on a social basis. Continence depends on the inhibition of the reflex arc which is established when the bladder reaches a certain stage of distension, and this process can be damaged by cerebral atrophy or arteriosclerosis. But as mentioned earlier, incontinence may also reflect acute unhappiness and a sense of rejection. The association with defective hearing raises the important question as to whether in some cases at least an impression of confusion, conveyed especially by tangential speech, is generated by the consequences of selective deafness.

It is known, for example, that though old people may adapt themselves to the voices of constant companions, the unfamiliar inflections of a visitor can throw them off balance and even cause acute confusion.[13] Again, old people may accustom themselves to conversation taking place which does not concern them, but if some word or sound breaks through to their consciousness, they may suddenly initiate speech, perhaps vehemently, yet without their remarks having any real bearing on the previous dialogue.

No relationship was found between confused behaviour and the other physical disabilities noted (Table 4.13). Rather more of the rational had defective sight (25·3 per cent as compared with 21·1 per cent). Similarly, the proportion of crippled residents was much higher among the rational (17·4 per cent compared to only 4·3 per cent of the confused), but still not significantly so (df = 1, $\chi^2 = 2\cdot37$, p$>\cdot05$). Two other factors were also taken into account. Impaired speech was defined as sufficient impediment, such as resulted particularly from hemiplegia, in the physical production of words as to make comprehension difficult. Oral dyskinesia denoted the incessant pushing of the tongue round the mouth, pouting out the lips and constantly mobilizing the jaws to open and close.[14] Neither of these conditions related significantly with confused behaviour.[15] Altogether, substantially more of the confused revealed at least one type of physical disability (72·2 per cent of the severely confused and 63·2 per cent of those with moderate confusion, as

Table 4.13

Degree of confused behaviour by physical handicap

Physical handicap	Severely confused (%)	Moderately confused (%)	Non-confused (%)
Defective sight blind	(8·3)	1·8	4·8
poor sight	(8·3)	19·3	20·4
Defective hearing deaf	(5·6)	7·0	9·0
poor hearing	(36·1)	24·5	10·2
Impaired speech	(13·9)	7·0	8·4
Oral dyskinesia	(13·9)	3·5	5·4
Crippled	(2·8)	5·3	17·4
Incontinence wetting and soiling*	(47·3)	7·0	5·4
wetting only	(5·6)	17·5	4·2
Number	36	57	167

* This includes two persons with carcinoma of the rectum who occasionally soiled but did not wet.

Table 4.14

Correlation of various social and physical factors with confused behaviour at the ·05 level of significance

| Social and physical factors | Type of correlation | | |
	Positive (+)	Nil (o)	Negative (—)
Female sex	+		
Widowhood		o	
Widowhood with children		o	
Age eighty-five and over		o	
Working-class			—
Limitation in mobility	+		
Inability for dressing and washing	+		
Personal care: bathing	+		
Defective sight		o	
Defective hearing	+		
Impaired speech		o	
Oral dyskinesia		o	
Muscular dysfunction (crippled)		o	
Incontinence	+		
Physical disability (conjunction of preceding six items)		o	

compared with only 55·0 per cent of the rational), though the differences were not significant (df = 1, χ^2 = 3·33, p > ·05).

Finally, a comprehensive picture of the relationship of each of the social and physical factors considered is summarized in Table 4.14. Four brief sketches are now appended to illustrate the interplay of these various factors at different points on the scale of confused behaviour (Table 4.15).

MISS MCGINKLE was perhaps the most confused resident in the special home in which she lived, but unlike many confused old people she was energetic, talkative, vivacious in manner and radiated charm from her twinkling eyes. Smartly dressed as befitted one formerly employed in the fashion business, she equally revealed, beneath the puzzling disarray of her actions, an acute sensitivity in her personal relations. 'He gives me a beautiful smile, but he dosen't mean it,' she once made reference to me half provocatively, half regretfully. Lacking the attention of any close relative and rarely visited, she had 'adopted' another resident who was also an aimless wanderer and channelled all her repressed protective and affectionate instincts on to this friend whom she once spoke of as her 'elder sister'. She would drag off her companion to ramble on 'walks' round the home, insist on fetching her a chair even when it was not wanted, and was seen more than once to wake her up with an earnest plea to accompany her: 'I want you to come down,' and when the request was not met, 'Oh my dear, I *so* want you.' Her friend seemed too disoriented to be either appreciative of or irritated by these endeavours, but the staff, with perhaps a misplaced desire to safeguard her privacy, were frequently telling Miss McGinkle to leave her alone. Whether as a result of her rebuffs she felt persecuted is a matter for conjecture, but she certainly felt lonely and unhappy. Originally found unconscious on the floor of her bungalow after a fall, she had been moved into a geriatric unit, assessed as suffering from cerebrovascular degeneration and arteriosclerosis, and then transferred to the special home, but had often wandered back to her own house after she was first admitted. Now thwarted in her efforts to form a close and stable friendship, she was increasingly turning to her childhood as the only reliable haven of affection left to her. When I asked her how she came to be in the home, she replied: 'I don't know. I wondered from the train why they've taken it over. I don't know what the trouble is. But I'm off tonight, I'm going to see my mother. She was great to me,' and tears began to glisten in her eyes. Again, later, 'I would be with my mother –

Table 4.15
Four case studies

Name	Marital status	Age	Occupation (class)	Nearest relatives	No. of visits received	Limitation of mobility	Incapacity for personal care	Physical disabilities	Confusional characteristics	Confusion score
Miss McGinkle	Single	88	Clothes buyer (RG II)	Cousin	Less than once a month	No limitation	Cannot dress, wash or bath self	Wetting and soiling	Tangential speech, aimless wandering, restless fiddling, disorientation of person, severe disorientation of place, severe memory defect, non-conventional behaviour, and non-function reiteration	12
Mrs Bridgewood	Widowed	89	Civil Servant (husband) (RG I)	No near relative, only 'friend'	None	No limitation	Cannot dress, wash or bath self	Wetting, soiling, deaf, oral dyskinesia	Tangential speech, restless fiddling, disorientation of person, severe disorientation of place, severe memory defect, non-conventional use of objects	8

Table 4.15 (*contd.*)

Name	Marital status	Age	Occupation (class)	Nearest relatives	No. of visits received	Limitation of mobility	Incapacity for personal care	Physical disabilities	Confusional characteristics	Confusion score
Mrs Glenville	Widowed	78	Worked in Naval Intelligence in the War (RG I)	Son	None	Limited to building	Cannot dress, wash or bath self	Wetting and soiling	Aimless wandering, disorientation of person, moderate disorientation of place, severe memory defect	5
Mrs Wilks	Single	87	Not known (? working class)	Nephew	Once a year	Limited to room	Cannot dress, wash or bath self	Poor hearing, impaired speech	Restless fiddling	1

that's the one I want to be with, take her to the service. Father's in the choir.' Constant remarks muttered sotto voce at moments of frustration revealed the same restless uneasiness. 'If I had more money, I would go anywhere'; 'I'm too poorly to do anything'; 'I get very tired very often'; 'I don't know what I'm doing'; 'I can't sleep. I don't mind what I do. I'm very sad in my mind.' Nor was her search for affection aided by her confused loquacity and regression to childhood. Rather it produced a critical, bewildered or jocular reaction which only sharpened her need for withdrawal. She often read aloud uncomprehendingly from the newspaper headlines and for this was sharply reprimanded by a neighbour who was herself confused. Rational residents on the other hand usually regarded her with a mixture of paternalistic rebuke and tolerant amusement, especially when she wandered off down the drive, an event for which a number specially watched in order to warn the staff. The attendants also regarded her with a certain whimsical petulance – 'If she goes on wandering away like that, I'll smack her bottom' – and their light-hearted indifference to her more deep-seated needs could spark off her occasional flashes of anger. Once, after being repeatedly told to keep quiet, she exclaimed 'Cut your mouth out, you don't know what you're talking about,' and again, with some insight, 'We're not such fools as what they think.' On another occasion, when forced to leave the gallery round which she was walking, she retorted in exasperation, 'That cursed woman downstairs, she'll get it one day – she'll get it *three* times as much.'

MRS BRIDGEWOOD presented a real puzzle: was her tangential speech artfully contrived to deflect the prying question and to conceal her loss of memory, or was it merely the accidental excrescence of mindless thinking? The Matron inclined to the former view, remarking that she was deaf except when she needed to hear, but other staff were doubtful. Mrs Bridgewood was a stocky, heavy-boned woman, who, though still ambulant, could no longer move easily and spent most of every day sitting squarely on an upright chair. Her concern for her personal appearance had recently deteriorated, and she attended the interview with her stockings half rolled down and half fallen down her legs. Very quickly in the ensuing dialogue she assumed her traditional style of defensive sallies. When I began by asking what she normally did in the morning, she replied, 'Ah, now we're going to dip . . . oh you've got to go in the morning have you? Penetrating questions were countered with aplomb:

> 'Do you have a close friend in this home?'
> 'No, I don't get the gist of it.'

The question was repeated.

She was silent for a moment, then abruptly asked, 'Do you ever take your teeth out?'

In other words, one personal question justifies another.

She seemed to be able to 'utilize' her confusion for the purpose of diplomatic evasion, sometimes with a faint ring of mocking derision:

> 'Do you think you did the right thing entering this home?'
> 'It's a good thing to have, a round of questions, isn't it? . . . That wasn't far out, was it?'
> 'What?'
> 'What I said before. If it is, reverse it, and I'll bring it back.'

Another tactic of this woman with her puckish sense of humour was the abrupt insertion of capriciously irrelevant material: for instance, in the midst of discussion about writing letters, 'That's a pretty cup and saucer, nice-shaped cup.' But why should her confusion be interpreted as an exercise in deadpan, noncommittal ambiguity? Because the good sense of most of her comments, despite the tortuous innuendos, indicated she clearly understood the gist of the dialogue. For instance:

> 'Would you like to leave if your family or friends could take you home again?'
> 'Well, it's a thing for the persons themselves, isn't it?'
> 'Is there any possibility of your going back to a home of your own?'
> 'Oh, I see what you mean. There's a question there. Bit of a do. I don't think it's very nice'.
> 'Is there any other home you would prefer to be in?'
> 'No, well, I don't really treat that like that. I remember this from my younger days. I thought it useful to come, at least for a time.'

In her social relations Mrs Bridgewood had always been some-what paranoid since her husband's death eleven years previously, and had for a short spell been admitted to mental hospital as a certified patient with a diagnosis of cerebral arteriosclerosis. In the special home to which she was transferred she appeared at first (according to the case file) very garrulous, and on one occasion invited a few of the other residents to return to Northampton with her as companions. She also spent much of her time in the garden, and frequently walked down to the nearby village with another resident whom she had particularly befriended. Recently, however, interest in this friendship had noticeably waned, and she now idled away the hours with habits like sitting in the lavatory rolling up the tissues in her hands and flicking the paper balls into the air. Never visited, her remaining contact with the outside world, after the premature death of her only daughter, was the house she still owned. When the Official Solicitor, acting as her Receiver, wrote to her and asked if she wished to sell it or relet, Mrs Bridgewood refused emphatically to contemplate a sale and requested a relet, at a higher rent if possible.

MRS GLENVILLE, despite a medium confusion score of 5, clearly retained an excellent insight into her deteriorating powers. More than once in the course of her interview, she insisted 'I don't know what I'm talking about' and in the context of answering questions apologized profusely ' 'Fraid I'm a very bad person for this sort of thing,' and 'You must think me an idiot,' and again 'I can't get the word I want, I'm *awfully* bad. Nobody could be worse than I am.' Yet her speech was always logically constructed, even if the sentiments she expressed were not always entirely rational. Her excessive concern over social conventions and her fears about her failing capacities to conform were shown both by her acute recognition of the disruption which certain other residents caused and by her solicitude over her own appearance. She kept pulling up her stockings and regretting 'they won't stay [up]', even when they were. Only in her aimless wandering as she lurched compulsively from chair to chair was her confusion im-mediately observable. The effort was obviously intense as she staggered a few paces forward up the room before sinking down panting into a chair. 'You see, everything's such a bother.' But she would be up again in a moment, 'I'd like to get away now,' though she was also ready to admit: 'Don't know where I'm going.' Her whole personality seemed rigid, both in her slow and methodical way of speaking and in her stiff gait, and indeed her rigidity seemed designed to shield her partial loss of awareness. 'I have meals, but I never know when I'm having them,' and later, 'I don't really know anything about anybody here, don't get much chance to see them. . . . No, I'm not with them at all.' In place of this memory loss she had inserted various protective fantasies. 'I can get around to domestic things, but not much more.' And again, 'I don't have meals here, I go back home for them,' Later when I asked about the sleeping arrangements in the home she insisted doggedly 'You still haven't got it. I . . . what shall I say? . . . go home at night.' When asked, therefore, what sort of place she was in, she replied 'I haven't had a chance to think about it. I didn't know what I was coming here for . . . I don't want to live in any home.' Certainly Mrs Glenville espoused little interest in the other residents and struck a rather isolated figure. Once when the matron came in, she claimed she had never seen her about.

MR WILKS, apart from restless fiddling, showed no obvious signs of confusion. It was entirely on other grounds that he was notorious in the home as a 'character'. He always wore a cloth cap at a rakish angle, even deliberately pulling it crooked when attendants straightened it for him. When he closed his eyes for his afternoon nap, he was accustomed to indulge himself in an orgy of singing, usually tunelessly, at the top of his voice. Nevertheless, for all his extravert uninhibitedness, he possessed little opportunity for social participation. The four men with whom he shared one of the male day-rooms comprised one who was stone deaf, another who was given to repetitive questioning, a third who was said to be subnormal and inclined to dribble, and a fourth, the only one who was even moderately confused, who was always fascinating himself with any nearby object he could obtain to fiddle with. Mr Wilks himself, according to the case record, was mentally deficient and also had a history of epilepsy, though he had had no fit for ten years. Before entering the home he had lived with his married nephew until the latter's wife could no longer cope and he had then been admitted for a short stay in a mental hospital. At his interview it was clear that it was not mental confusion, but physical handicap, which constituted his real dilemma. Following a stroke, his speech was markedly slurred and he was inclined to make grunting or sighing sounds which were not easily interpreted. Besides dysarthria deafness, he also, at the age of eighty-seven, could only move slowly and with great difficulty. His handling of objects too was clumsy, and I once observed him swearing lustily when he dropped the urine bottle he was obliged to use.

These short sketches give some impression of the range and variability of confused behaviour. The next chapter turns to the other aspect of the preparatory analysis – the environmental contrast between ordinary and special homes.

NOTES

1. This refers throughout only to restlessness during the daytime. Data concerning the incidence of nocturnal disturbance was collected in only one of the separatist homes where it was found that two-thirds of the severly confused were night wanderers, including half persistently so, three-quarters of the moderately confused were active at night (though only one persistently), and only one of the twenty-five rational.

2. The figures for anormic behaviour are probably an understatement inasmuch as, unlike each of the other factors, they could not be exhaustively discovered from interviews and systematic observation and depended to some extent on the reporting by staff of unique events in the past.

3. Also there was considerable over-determination of this characteristic in separatist homes. Whereas over a third of residents in these homes revealed more than one of the three components of anormic behaviour, none of those similarly classified in the ordinary homes did so.

4. This designation derives purely from the absence of any of the confusional characteristics discussed in Chapter 3 and is not intended to reflect on their inherent rationality or otherwise.

5. The alternative procedure of analysing social background and physical incapacity according to categories of confused behaviour would clearly be invalid in view of the extensive overlap between the categories. One would be ascribing attributes to attributes rather than to persons uniquely classed in mutually exclusive groups.

6. Ministry of Health (1968), *Annual Report 1967* (cf. Table 2.1).

7. Letter from the Chief Welfare Officer, 23 November 1967.

8. Letter from the Chief Welfare Officer, 20 August 1965.

9. Letter from the Assistant Medical Officer of Health, 23 November 1967.

10. Townsend makes clear that one main question was asked to ascertain mental infirmity: 'Was the person mentally capable of organizing personal services for himself – such as finding his way to the W.C., remembering where to find articles of clothing, managing electric switches and gas taps, keeping clothing and household goods in order – irrespective of any *physical* infirmity?' A supplementary question was also used: 'Was the person capable of organizing his thoughts in coherent speech and/or writing, so that he could communicate adequately with other members of society, irrespective of any physical incapacity?'

11. Apart from the intrinsic purpose, this would enable the results of a clinical study

of a sample of seventy-three residents in welfare homes to be brought into perspective with the methods of classification used here. Kay *et al.* (1962, pp. 181–2) found that a third of their welfare home residents were mentally normal, 29 per cent showed evidence of developed and 11 per cent of milder forms of senile or arteriosclerotic dementia, 4 per cent suffered from other kinds of psychosis, 11 per cent from minor emotional disorders, and 10 per cent showed one or other of a miscellaneous group of conditions, such as lifelong mental subnormality, epilepsy, character disorder or mental confusion associated with serious physical illness.

12. In this respect the evidence diverged from that produced by P. Townsend (1962, p. 268) who found that the greater proportion of his middle-class sample displaying signs of mental impairment (20 per cent as compared to 15 per cent of his working-class sample) was not statistically significant.

13. *Mental Frailty in the Elderly*, National Old People's Welfare Council, 1962.

14. Since saliva was often gathered by this process, it often also involved the gradual but steady dribbling of large drops from the mouth.

15. The correlations were as follows: with impaired speech df $= 1$, $\chi^2 = 0.12$, $p > .05$, and with oral dyskinesia df $= 1$, $\chi^2 = 0.47$, $p > .05$.

5

The homes and the routine

It has already been shown that the essential difference between separatist and ordinary homes for the aged lies in the fact that while the former on average contain a majority of residents, albeit a small one, who exhibit confused behaviour in one or more forms, only a sixth of residents in the latter show similar characteristics. Furthermore, comparison has been made between the confused in the two types of home, and it has been established that the confusion of those in the specialized homes tends to be both grosser in degree and composite in type. We now consider, secondly, whether the rational differ in any noticeable respects between the two types of home.

DIFFERENCES BETWEEN RATIONAL RESIDENTS IN THE TWO KINDS OF HOME

The application of similar techniques of analysis to those used in the preceding chapter yields the following picture of the social and physical data concerning residents in the separatist homes. A significant proportion, as revealed by Table 5.1, were women (df = 1, $\chi^2 = 6{\cdot}70$, p$<{\cdot}$01), though this conclusion is limited by the fact that one of the three separatist homes admitted only women and by the finding previously mentioned that confused behaviour correlated significantly with female sex. Paradoxically, however, contrary to the tendency for the confused to be widowed and to be found among the older age groups, the separatist homes displayed the opposite trend: in comparison with the ordinary homes, their residents tended to be younger (Table 5.3, df = 1, $\chi^2 = 2{\cdot}27$, p$>{\cdot}$05) and of single marital status (Table 5.2, df = 1, $\chi^2 = 4{\cdot}25$, p$<{\cdot}$05). In other words, while the distribution in age and marital status of confused residents in both types of home was similar, the rational in the separatist homes were disproportionately younger and unmarried compared to their counterparts in the ordinary homes.[1]

This suggests that those rational persons are admitted to separatist homes who are least protected by family ties and by relatives who might complain on their behalf about the activities of other residents.[2] It was also found that there was a significant proportion of middle-class residents in the separatist homes, as illustrated by Table 5.4 (df = 1, χ^2 = 12·3, p<·001), but this can be ascribed to the fact that the residence fees of one home effectually excluded any person without substantial private savings.

In terms of physical handicap, rather more residents in the separatist homes were at least partially limited in their mobility, but not significantly so (Table 5.5, df = 1, χ^2 = 2·37, p>·05). However, the differences in capacity for personal care were significant: two-fifths of those in the separatist homes could not dress or wash themselves without assistance, in contrast to only a seventh in the ordinary homes (Table 5.6, df = 1, χ^2 = 23·3, p<·001). But this balance was unexpectedly reversed in regard to bathing. Significantly more of the residents in the ordinary homes needed some assistance

Table 5.1

Distribution of residents in separatist
and ordinary homes by sex

Sex		Separatist homes (%)	Ordinary homes (%)
Male		21·1	29·2
Female		78·9	70·8
	TOTAL	100	100
	Number	123	137

Table 5.2

Distribution of residents in separatist and ordinary
homes by marital status

Marital status		Separatist homes (%)	Ordinary homes (%)
Single		38·2	26·3
Married		1·6	7·3
Widowed/separated		60·2	66·4
	TOTAL	100·0	100·0
	Number	123	137

Table 5.3

Distribution of residents in separatist and ordinary homes by age

Age	Separatist homes (%)	Ordinary homes (%)
74 or under	28·5	20·4
75–84	43·9	45·3
85 or over	27·6	34·3
TOTAL	100·0	100·0
Number	123	137

Table 5.4

Distribution of residents in separatist and ordinary homes by social class

Social class (Registrar General's classification)	Separatist homes (%)	Ordinary homes (%)	Ordinary homes (Townsend)*
Professional and managerial (middle class, RG I & II)	51·4	21·7	19·8
Skilled, semi-skilled and unskilled manual (working class, RG III, IV, V)	48·7	78·3	80·2
TOTAL	100·1	100·0	100·0
Number	72	60	6,007

* Since the proportion of residents in the three ordinary homes in this study concerning whom social class data could be collected was rather small (44 per cent), this information has been supplemented by similar data gathered by Townsend (1962) from his sample of 173 institutions and homes for the elderly in England and Wales. The figures given here have been deduced from those given in his p. 55, table 15.

in bathing (Table 5.6, df = 1, $\chi^2 = 6·74$, p < ·01). This must reflect at least partly the comparatively younger age grouping of the rational in the separatist homes; for whereas less than a fifth of the rational in the ordinary homes could bath themselves without assistance, more than half of the rational in the separatist homes were able to. But the difference may also reflect that the contrast presented by their confused neighbours in the specialized homes seemed to justify giving the rational particular privileges.

Again, bearing in mind the relationship, as elucidated in the

Table 5.5

Distribution of residents in separatist and ordinary
homes by limitations in mobility

Mobility limited to		Separatist homes (%)	Ordinary homes (%)
Chair		3·3	7·3
Room		4·1	0
Building		14·6	7·3
Unlimited		78·0	85·4
	TOTAL	100·0	100·0
	Number	123	137

Table 5.6

Distribution of residents in separatist and ordinary
homes by incapacity for personal care

Inability to		Separatist homes (%)	Ordinary homes (%)
Dress self		42·3	15·3
Wash self		41·5	14·6
Bath self		61·8	83·2
Feed self		4·1	1·5
	Number	123	137

preceding chapter, between confusion and the specific physical handicaps listed in Table 5.7, it was in accordance with expectations that significantly more of the residents in the ordinary homes were found to have defective sight (df = 1, $\chi^2 = 7\cdot66$, p < ·01) and that proportionately more were crippled (df = 1, $\chi^2 = 2\cdot96$, p > ·05). By contrast, however, the fact that residents in the separatist homes tended significantly to exhibit impaired speech (df = 1, $\chi^2 = 5\cdot01$, p < ·05) and oral dyskinesia (df = 1, $\chi^2 = 5\cdot25$, p < ·05), when neither of these conditions correlated significantly with confusion, indicated that the rational in the special homes were disproportionately afflicted by these characteristics in comparison with the non-confused in the ordinary homes. In fact, both conditions were three times more prevalent among the former than among the latter. Conversely, while both defective hearing and incontinence have been shown to be significantly related to confusion, neither of these impairments was found to a significant degree among residents in the special homes. And indeed, as this result would indicate, the incidence of defective hearing was almost twice as high among the rational in the ordinary homes as amongst their counterparts in the separatist homes, though no such disparity existed in regard to incontinence.

Table 5.7

Distribution of residents in separatist and ordinary homes by physical handicap

Physical handicap		Separatist homes (%)	Ordinary homes (%)
Defective sight	Blind	3·3	5·8
	Poor sight	12·2	24·1
Defective hearing	Deaf	9·8	6·6
	Poor hearing	16·3	17·5
Impaired speech		13·0	5·1
Oral dyskinesia		9·8	2·9
Crippled		8·9	16·1
Incontinence	Wetting and soiling	14·6	8·8
	Wetting only	7·3	7·3
	Number	123	137

Table 5.8

Correlation of various social and physical factors with residence in a separatist home at the ·05 level of significance

Social and physical factors	Type of correlation		
	Positive (+)	*Nil (o)*	*Negative (—)*
Female sex	+		
Unmarried status	+		
Age under seventy-five		o	
Working class			—*
Limitation in mobility		o	
Inability in personal care: dressing and washing	+		
bathing			—
Defective sight			—
Defective hearing		o	
Impaired speech	+		
Oral dyskinesia	+		
Muscular dysfunction (crippled)		o	
Incontinence		o	

* But this is explained in the text as a special case.

An overall picture therefore emerges, from a comparison of Tables 4.14 and 5.8 of the different use that is made of specialized and ordinary welfare homes in accommodating old people who are rational. Those admitted to the former tend to be younger, and therefore partly are less likely to be crippled or to suffer from deficiencies in speech or hearing, but nevertheless tend to exhibit characteristics, in particular impaired speech and oral dyskinesia, which do not directly spring from confusion, but may be closely associated with it by those responsible for admissions. Rational residents in the special homes also tend to be unmarried, which suggests that their vulnerability may be at least partly responsible for their segregation, and in this context it should perhaps be noted that the separatist homes also contain a significantly high proportion of residents of allegedly subnormal intelligence ($df = 1$, $\chi^2 = 5\cdot25$, $p < \cdot05$).[3]

DESCRIPTION AND LOCATION OF THE SPECIAL HOMES

The policy implications of this distribution of both confused and rational persons with particular characteristics between the separatist and ordinary homes will be examined when the different institutional functions are discussed in chapter 10. At this point the preparatory analysis must be completed by a brief reference to variations in the physical environment and daily routine between the alternative residential settings. Now the method of selection of the homes has already been indicated (above, p. 9), but it is clearly not possible to generalize about significant differences between two groups of three homes each. A brief description will therefore be given of each of the separatist homes, though with certain details changed to avoid identification, and the result can be compared with the picture of ordinary welfare homes for the aged already provided elsewhere at much greater length (notably by P. Townsend, 1962, chs 4–7).

NORTHROP HALL, situated in the rolling Sussex countryside, was a large old manor house set in its own terraced lawns and lying on the outskirts of a small village. Though modernized and now centrally heated, it still retained its traditional atmosphere of ornate elegance and its long drive seemed to act as a cordon sanitaire which isolated the timeless routine of the house and kept it blithely unconcerned by the village life nearby. The buildings had an intricate design, complicated by many changes of level and abounding in short, twisting corridors. Moreover, the narrow grilled windows gave the passageways and even some of the rooms a foreboding air, almost of mystery, like one of the sombre country houses standing as a gaunt sentinel at the unravelling of one of Hardy's novels. Many of the rooms were massive, capped by lofty, engraved ceilings and appropriately entitled 'the Queen Anne bedroom', 'the Jacobean ante-room', etc. The house had been tastefully decorated throughout, a number of wooden tiled floors had been renovated and a sense of noble splendour was imparted by the beautiful, embossed and panelled woodwork. One room in particular, which was immaculately furnished, was reserved for the quarterly meetings of the Friends of Northrop Hall – mostly local gentry, retired military and rural councillors – and for other important visitors. The residents themselves spent each day in three capacious rooms, one of which seemed once to have served as the baronial banqueting hall, where the seated and motionless figures could often be observed as if frozen into the landscape like ageless statuary. But despite the substantial expenditure on modernized furnishing and heating, the three storeys were not connected by a lift, lavatories were sometimes available only at some inconvenient distance, and there were few handrails along the maze of corridors and almost no devices to assist in lifting for bathing or toileting. When one particularly heavy resident of seventeen stone found herself embedded in the bath on one occasion, the matron told me she had been obliged to call in her husband to heave her out by *force majeure*.

ASTON. By contrast, Aston was characterized by an architecturally open plan which aimed to afford staff the fullest opportunity for supervision. Purpose-built only a few years previously to take mentally infirm old people from throughout the county, it lacked formal dayrooms and seating was partly provided by clusters of chairs in small bays opening off the main hallway, while glazed partitions were designed to offer an appearance of privacy without hampering staff observation. But supervision was chiefly facilitated, the building being L-shaped and two-storeyed, by the construction of a gallery offering access to the bedrooms upstairs which was visible throughout its length from the ground floor and also by the building of a staff room on the upper floor at the crook of the L spanning both passageways leading from it underneath. Also the matron's room at the top end of the L had a square spy-glass in it so that she could survey the entrance and upper hallway. Furthermore, corridors were kept to a minimum in order to discourage wandering out of curiosity or bewilderment, though wandering did still take place on the circuit provided by the hallways beneath and the long gallery above which were connected by staircases at either end. The home itself was sited near the edge of the residential area of a medium-sized town, within walking distance for the fully ambulant of the shopping centre. Its most immediate neighbour, however, set beside the adjoining lawn, was a junior training centre for subnormal children. The buildings were cast in a modern 'functional' style, with huge bay windows to admit maximum light and French windows to give immediate access to the lawns from several points, though during my three-week visit in the summer these were never opened. The sole enclosed rooms, apart from bedrooms, toilets and staff quarters, were reserved for specialist purposes – occupational therapy, watching television, medical examination or laundry – and even meals were taken in part of the open central areas. Some attempt had also been made to generate interest by having a few chickens and rabbits kept at the rear of the premises, together with a parrot in a cage near the entrance and an aquarium to the side of the main hallway.

BLANCHEFIELDS was a recently added annexe at the back of a comparatively small former public assistance institution. The main residential blocks formed diameters, perpendicular to each other, of a circular area the perimeter of which had gradually been filled by further administrative buildings accessory to the life of the institution. Blanchefields completed the circle to the rear. It was built of red brick, the freshness of which contrasted sharply with the drab monotony of the surrounding buildings in the front. To the rear the outlook lay over a small lawn to the prefabricated bungalows which had been constructed for the temporary homeless. The dayrooms in the annexe were all small and compact, with the chairs set round the walls, and a small glass conservatory had been set at either end of the building. Each room was connected by a passage running the length of the building at the front. The bedrooms were mostly on an upper floor which was reached by a staircase, though a lift had recently been installed in the central core of the main buildings to the front. Most of the formal dayrooms had a television set, though much of the decorations and furnishings were of very moderate or even inferior quality. A new kitchen with modern equipment had been installed not long before, and it was exhibited to me with great pride by the superintendent and matron, but all 140 residents continued to eat in the two tightly-packed adjoining rooms.

The three special homes selected, therefore, presented considerable contrasts, though no conclusions can be drawn about the typicality of any of them. The only general comment which can be

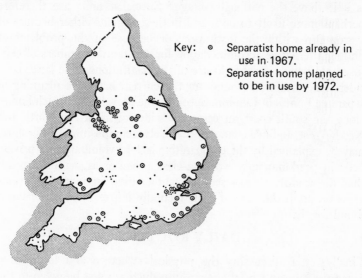

Key: ⊙ Separatist home already in use in 1967.
      • Separatist home planned to be in use by 1972.

FIG. 1. *Geographical distribution of known separatist homes for old people in England and Wales*

(both those currently in use and those planned for construction by 1972)

made from the data available concerns the geographical distribution of the separatist homes. From the replies submitted by 86 per cent of the Chief Welfare Officers and Medical Officers of Health in

England and Wales, the spread in the provision of these homes, both those already in use in 1967 and those planned to be in use by 1972, is mapped on page 113. This reveals that the provision of specialized homes has so far chiefly centred in the North-West and North Midlands, though planning for such homes in the near future is concentrated rather in the South-East, particularly in London and along the south coast. Other parts of the country, on the other hand, especially the North, Wales, East Anglia and the South-West have made little or no separatist provision up to now, nor have they formulated such proposals to any substantial degree for the future.

How are these variations to be explained? Firstly, the areas where separatism has crystallized partly reflect the pattern of local authority retention of the former public assistance institutions. For in areas like the West Riding and London these are known to offer a proportion of local authority accommodation for the elderly that is well above the national average.[4] Specialist units are therefore perhaps more likely to be found in these regions either because of segregation within the institutions or because of the problems of finding alternative accommodation for substantial numbers of confused old people on the closure of the institutions. The latter consideration certainly accounts for the current extensive planning of separatist homes in London. Secondly the prevalence of such homes along the south coast, in certain seaside towns in the North and North-West, and in a county with the class composition of Cheshire, may be explained by the comparative lack of voluntary and private beds in predominantly working-class urban areas, with the result that the middle classes seek accommodation in more salubrious areas or, as in the case of their mentally infirm members, have it found for them.

DAILY ROUTINE

Finally, after discussing the physical structure and location of separatist homes, a brief general introduction must be given to the routine life of the homes, aspects of which will be examined later in detail to illustrate the different experiences of confused and rational residents (see chapter 7).

The day centred round the mealtimes. Breakfast was fixed at 8.30–9.00 a.m., a cup of tea might be provided at 10.30–11.00 a.m., lunch was served at 12.15–1.00 p.m., then tea at 4.00–4.30 p.m., after which the residents would retire to bed, or be put to bed, at varying intervals between 5.00–10.00 p.m., though a cup of cocoa and a biscuit might be provided for those still up at about 8.00 p.m. One woman, a rational resident in one of the special homes, talked spontaneously about the daily round thus:

'It's an aimless life. I was never cut out just to sit down and do nothing, so I help by putting out the plates on the trolley and handing out food. When I do knitting, I've just done squares, but I could do more ambitious things if she [the occupational therapist] came more. I'd like more books – these are old books here – I must walk to Bampton [the nearby town] to join the county library, but I'm frightened to walk alone. I need companionship, but when once I suggested it to Mrs Mawson, she said she preferred to "go it alone" . . .

'I'm rather hard-pushed for space, and I'd like more drawers, though I've got my own mattress, my own dressing table and my own bureau. We get enough food, but it's not satisfying, and it's very institutional in quality – not enough variety. The washing arrangements are abominable – I have an old-fashioned basin and the plunger doesn't keep in the water. I have my laundry done in my home town by my friend. . . . I want more wool to do more knitting – don't like sewing, but I do it to pass the time away. I always go to concerts, but there aren't enough of them . . . The sides of the baths we use are too high, so I need an attendant to help me in and out – I always fear I'll get giddy. . . . I get up at 8.00, but I'd like to get up later. And I go to bed at about 8.45 in the evening, but only because the night nurses want to give out the tablets and hot drinks then. Yes, I could take them at 10 o'clock, but still I like to escape these people and take the tablets and get off to sleep and forget everything.'

This passage, collated from different sections of a single interview, strikes many ambivalent chords which were frequently echoed by others – a tacit admission of functionlessness combined with a fierce resistance against accepting it, a sense of isolation and a desire for more social occasions mixed with a feeling of abhorrence towards certain of her fellow-residents, and a generalized discontent with an institutional existence sometimes rationalized by a casuistry of reproach towards the details of her surroundings. But above everything else lies the pall of hours to be lived through with no obvious satisfactory purpose left. A majority of residents spent most of each day sitting disinterestedly in their chosen chairs, intermittently dozing or gazing listlessly at the moving figures of attendants hurrying about their work. A few, particularly subnormal residents, gave themselves over to household chores with energy and persistence, but many others preferred the temporary oblivion of sleep, whether slumped in their chairs or retiring perhaps every afternoon to lie on their beds with the eiderdown pulled over them. What social interaction did take place seemed necessarily trivialized. This is illustrated by the following extract from an ordinary home, taken at random from hundreds of such annotations of thirty-minute observation periods collected in the course of this investigation:

The room contains twelve persons, excluding myself. Three spend the half hour dozing, one reads a book, another a paper, whilst another half-heartedly attends to a book between periods of shutting her eyes. One resident knits, another sews, and the remainder sit quietly in their chairs, doing nothing except watching. As the half-hour begins, at 3.00 p.m., Mrs Lathers is telling Mrs Spenley about the woman who disturbs her nights. After two minutes' description, Mrs Spenley goes out into the corridor to try to identify the unnamed woman, but in vain, and she returns three minutes later to resume the conversation for a further three minutes. Mrs Lathers indignantly declares that 'the woman used to crawl all over the floor and jog my arm at night'. Meanwhile Mrs Gambrill, who normally sits like a ramrod staring fixedly to the front, has been searching in various bags round her chair and finally takes out a pair of spectacles and puts them on. Having now moved to her usual seat, Mrs Spenley immediately engages her blind neighbour in a brief exchange: 'That clock's still wrong.' 'It's stopped'; which is true. Mrs Spenley then quickly harangues her patient listener about the liver she disliked at dinner today. Silence, for six minutes, the atmosphere being palpably heavy and sluggish. However, Mrs Gambrill has taken off her spectacles, replaced them in a bag and started eating part of a banana she has taken from a paper wrapping in her handbag. Mrs Duggleby asks her neighbour what the time is, then says she'll go upstairs to get her laundry ready. She rises unsteadily to her feet and slowly crosses the room. Silence again. A long drowsy silence of nine minutes, only broken by the odd noise – a man walking down the passage outside, the raised voice of a clamorous resident echoing from the next room, the rattling of newspaper pages being turned. Miss Ness, who is blind, finally calls out: 'What time is it, Mrs Westney, please?' Mrs Westney, intent on sewing, does not hear. 'Asleep!' Miss Ness muses. Another return to silence. Mrs Cawthorn, who sits by the window sporadically muttering disconnected interjections about passers-by, suddenly repeats the odd comment to herself: 'There he goes!' One resident, then another, visible through the open door, stumps along the corridor outside. Mrs Gambrill props up her head against the back of her chair with a blanket and closes her eyes. A couple of residents remark disapprovingly on Mrs Cawthorn's reveries. The clock strikes 3.30 and another half-hour has passed.

Inevitably this brief sketch of a typical scene in mid-afternoon can only be impressionist. We still require answers to fundamental questions about the social relationships of residents within the routinized life of alternative residential settings. How do the rational react to the confused, and vice versa? How much conversation or activity do they share with each other, in comparison with their dealings with others like themselves? What is the balance of power between confused and rational residents, in the light of the distribution of freedoms and privileges? How do they compare in contacts maintained with the external world? Above all, do confused and rational residents seem happy or dissatisfied? And do any differences that are detected in their varying network of relationships seem to derive from the contrasted kinds of homes they occupy? Now that part I of this book has identified the characters and depicted the residential backgrounds, it is the aim of part II to tackle these problems.

NOTES

1. A sixth of the confused residents in both types of home were aged under seventy-five, but whereas only a fifth of the rational residents in the ordinary homes were of this age, almost half of the rational residents in the separatist homes fell within this group. Similarly, whilst under a third of the confused residents in both types of home were single, and only slightly more than a third of the rational residents in the ordinary homes, more than a half of the rational residents in the separatist homes had never married.

2. This point will be more fully explored in Chapter 10.

3. The average proportion in the three homes, 9·8 per cent, was largely influenced by the fact that in one home over a fifth of the residents were declared subnormal.

4. P. Townsend (1962, p. 47) indicates that a national average of 51 per cent of local authority accommodation was in former public assistance institutions in 1960, but in the West Riding the proportion was between 80–90 per cent and in London 74 per cent.

Part III

THE SOCIAL RELATIONS OF THE CONFUSED IN RESIDENTIAL CARE

6

Reaction : the response of other residents to confusion

The social relations of the residents will be examined first in terms of the attitudes that the rational in particular, but also the confused, had developed towards confused behaviour. The consequences of these attitudes will then be described in the light of various dimensions of everyday life in the homes. Finally the mechanisms of adjustment are discussed by which the confused protect themselves in the face of these experiences.[1] In each case the topic will be treated separately for special as opposed to ordinary homes, to point up the effects of residential differences. This chapter will be devoted to the initial item, the attitudinal response of both rational and confused residents to confusion, and statements of disparagement, to which a majority of comment was directed, will be weighed against expressions of sympathy. In both cases the comments will be explored in isolation from their source, after which those offering the comments will be surveyed.

CRITICISMS

How did complaints about confused behaviour differ between separatist and ordinary homes? Each person interviewed was asked if he or she was perturbed by any residents exhibiting incoherent talk, any form of nocturnal disturbance, day wandering, interference with others' property, aggressive or violent behaviour, or offensive eating, dress or toileting habits. The replies compared in Table 6.1 show that those in the separatist homes were relatively much more concerned about day wandering and interference with their possessions. Residents in the ordinary homes, on the other hand, whilst being much less likely to offer any criticism at all, were nevertheless relatively more worried about disturbance at night and offensive toilet habits. Incoherent talk attracted more criticism than any other kind of behaviour, but there were no significant differences in the reaction between special and ordinary homes. Each of the main criticisms will now be examined in turn.

Table 6.1

Frequency of criticisms of confused behaviour by rational and confused residents according to type of home

Criticism made of others' behaviour	Residents making criticism	Frequency of criticism in :	
		Separatist home (%)	Ordinary homes (%)
Incoherent talk	confused	12·7	(9·1)
	rational	42·2	40·0
Night wandering or night disturbance	confused	7·1	(22·8)
	rational	23·0	25·2
Day wandering	confused	4·2	0
	rational	42·2	14·8
Interference with others' property	confused	5·6	(4·6)
	rational	17·3	8·7
Aggressive or violent behaviour	confused	1·4	(4·6)
	rational	11·5	13·1
Offensive eating habits	confused	1·4	0
	rational	5·8	6·1
Offensive dress habits	confused	1·4	0
	rational	0	4·4
Offensive toilet habits	confused	1·4	(9·1)
	rational	3·8	11·3
No criticism made	confused	22·6	(50·0)
	rational	21·1	36·5
Too incoherent to give valid answer at interview	confused	45·1	(18·2)
	rational	3·8	0
Refused interview or not available for interview, or too deaf	confused	12·7	0
	rational	9·6	3·5
TOTAL*	confused	115·6	(118·4)
	rational	180·3	163·6
Number of residents	confused	71	22
	rational	52	115

* The totals do not add up to 100 per cent because some residents made more than one criticism.

Incoherent talk

At the interview each person was asked: 'Do you find, when you talk to other residents, that some of them talk nonsensically and cannot give you a rational or sensible reply?' This evoked a strong response, but prolonged observation showed that in practice criticism crystallized around a very few residents whose dialogue

generated disturbance by its repetitiveness rather than by its
incoherence. The repetition might take an inane form, as in the
case of the woman whose verbal communication was virtually
restricted to the sole phrase: 'Plushy place, oh for the days and the
days and the days of old.'

On one occasion another resident first told her angrily to 'Shut
up!' when she repeated this phrase several times, but when this
failed to stop her, she resorted to physical coercion by tightly
squeezing her arm, in order to intimidate her into silence. This
failed too. Reversing her tactics, she then tried to ignore the
culprit, telling the others with a contemptuous gesture, 'Leave
her alone'. But all to no avail, and the critic blustered in desperation: 'I shall say "You're crazy" every time you say "Days of
old".' This she in fact did for several minutes, but with no effect.
Finally throwing all propriety to the winds, she yelled at her
tormentor that she was a filthy woman who didn't change her
clothes. Stung by this accusation, but still clinging hopelessly to
her single phrase, the perseverator, who was in fact very clean in
her habits, beseechingly refuted this slander by unravelling her
petticoat for all to see.

A variant on the reiteration of a single phrase was the habit of
grasping a particular sentence caught in the process of conversation
and playing the sentiment back in a seemingly endless stream of
repetition before taking hold of another phrase and giving it similar
treatment. This, too, generated first an aggressive, then a despairing,
reaction. Again, the repetition of fixated words, the indiscriminate
application of which rendered them meaningless, drew angry
protest:

A woman, for whom the universal substantive was 'telly' and
the universal agent was 'the cloth workers', was frequently
reprimanded. 'Oh it's no good talking about that sort of tripe,' a
neighbour said on one occasion and when the reproach had no
effect she became very cross, blurting out [she was confused
herself]: 'What are you doing shaping your lips for like that?
Surely you've got enough sense to answer . . . holding your lips
together like that and waggling your gums.' A pause, and then the
'telly' muttering recommenced. 'Don't you start that again, we

don't want to know; gets on your nerves, keep talking about that,' another companion complained. When the speaker, however, unable to perceive the cause of the disturbance, persisted, a third neighbour shouted: 'Oh be quiet, you silly old woman; yap, yap, yap about the telly. Drive us all potty before you've finished.' The situation was by now unusually inflamed, and another resident slapped the offender's hand, while a fifth yelled out: 'Oh sit down for God's sake.'

Inane repetition of words, phrases or sentences, which was anyway confined to the separatist homes, was rare even in them. Alternatively, however, repetition might take a rational form. Complaints against this were more subdued. A man who kept asking about the time, a woman who chattered on tirelessly about fantasies of her youth, and another woman who constantly asked if a bed was available for her each night were endured with a ruffled patience through which the repressed aggravation sporadically erupted.

But apart from repetition, incoherent talk was criticized when it appeared as haphazard prattle, though only if uttered obtrusively, which again was uncommon. One typical example was recorded in a separatist home:

Miss Iredale, an aimless wanderer with tangential speech, was sitting in a group of four chairs with a rational companion who was sewing and two others who were occasionally tangential in their speech, Mrs Appleby and Miss Meir.

MISS IREDALE: Lovely shape (*referring to Miss Waterhouse's embroidery*).

MISS WATERHOUSE: Yes, 'tis.

MISS IREDALE (*with a sigh*): I shall be very happy when I have to . . .

MRS APPLEBY: Shut up!

MISS IREDALE (*looking to the side and leaning back*): Makes you smart . . . don't smile . . . look at what I've got there, look at my arm.

MISS MEIR: You can't read or write, only yap, yap.

MRS APPLEBY: Shut up!

MISS IREDALE: Put me in the laundry . . . go to the laundry and have a jolly good laundry.

MISS WATERHOUSE *laughs, but the others are unamused.*

MISS IREDALE: He's[2] annoyed one day and full of life the next.

MISS MEIR: I think you're a freak.

MISS IREDALE: What's that? What does she say?

MISS WATERHOUSE: You're a freak of nature.

MISS IREDALE: What are you? Man? Woman? . . . She has three sheets and she's reading three times. She reads that, reads that and reads that.

MRS APPLEBY: Shut up!

MISS IREDALE [*carrying on without a break*]: My mother said to me, 'I don't like that dress.' So she got me one.

MRS APPLEBY [*firmly*]: Shut up!

MISS WATERHOUSE [*with soothing paternalism*]: You go down into dinner now.

MISS IREDALE: He likes a good dinner.

MRS APPLEBY: Shut up!

MISS IREDALE: I'm very particular. I like to see people eating nicely. She wouldn't like that.

MRS METCALFE [*from across the room*]: I can't understand what she's saying, can you?

MISS IREDALE: Don't know what they're doing . . . new motor . . . [*A short pause*].

MISS MEIR: Nice evening now.

MISS IREDALE: Good, glad she has . . . next to last, very nice indeed [*addressing Miss Waterhouse about her embroidery*]. . . . got tremendous length.

MRS APPLEBY: Shut up!

MISS IREDALE [*angrily*]: I'm not talking to you, I'm talking to somebody else . . . I don't think it's at all a nice lamp.

MISS WATERHOUSE: Dinner now.

MISS IREDALE: I shall have a think for a few minutes. If any-one's dirty, I won't go in there . . . I'd have thought they'd go to school in their own place. I've got plenty of chalk . . . I shall have to get you a fringe [*catching sight of me with my hair falling over my forehead*] . . . I'm going away then. Will you come with me? What are you going to do with the little ones?

Miss Waterhouse talks about her embroidery.

MISS IREDALE: He's going to be the first page.

MRS APPLEBY: Shut up!

MISS IREDALE: Did she say 'Shut up!' To me? [*incredulous*].

With the important exception of the voluble and extravert Miss Iredale and the instances of repetitive phraseology already quoted, however, the irritations of irrational talk rarely obtruded into the public forum within the homes. If a confused person did utter a fragmentary or distorted comment, it was almost always quietly to themselves or to an immediate neighbour, or sufficiently infrequently to remain tolerable. The almost incessant mutterings, like a perpetual buzz, of a resident with tangential speech produced no evident reaction except once when a rational neighbour nearby remarked testily: 'That woman gets on your nerves, doesn't she? Like the clapping of a mill – enough to drive you crazy.' Again, nobody objected to a person who never herself initiated conversation with anyone, but on one occasion, revolving her religious memories through her mind, repeated in a slow drawl: 'In the name of the Father, Son and Holy Ghost, the Lord be with you. . . . Morning service is ended . . . Amen.' The bizarre trivialities frequently poured into the ear of her mentally subnormal neighbour by a schizophrenic did not cause affront. And the disconnected verbalizations of private thoughts thrown out by an incoherent resident at various times did not seem to trouble anyone.

All these examples have been drawn from the separatist homes. In the ordinary homes, obtrusive incoherence was not found and the odd tangential remark occasionally expressed publicly was readily brushed aside with a curt note of dismissal.

Nocturnal disturbance

The question was asked: 'Do any residents disturb your sleep at night by coming into your room, getting up in the middle of the night, talking, opening drawers, etc.?' It was this aspect of confused behaviour which raised the most outspoken comments over a wide range of opinion in both separatist and ordinary homes. In contrast to the case with irrational talk, criticism concentrated on certain well-remembered incidents. Thus a woman in one of the special homes who shared a bedroom with a night wanderer stated:

> Miss Aubrey talks after lights out, then wants the lights on to go to the cupboard. She also goes to my drawers as she can't remember where her things are, and says she's going home, but can't find the key to the house. But not so much now. I was once in a

bedroom with someone who was much more of a nuisance, who got up and bumped into me in the middle of the night, and took my things about once every two months and I couldn't get them back. She used to put them in a drawer or on the landing. But then I moved, and she died. I once complained about her, but not about Miss Aubrey – she's not so bad. . . . She [her former companion] used to put on the lights and tried to dress herself in the middle of the night, till the staff took her clothes away from her. Once she went out in the night with only a nightdress on and without any footwear, in the garden for an hour, and she couldn't be found.

Objectors were divided between those who were disturbed by residents mistakenly entering their bedroom through getting lost, especially on return from the lavatory and those who shared a room with a regular wanderer. The latter had usually accepted the likelihood of a certain degree of disturbance, and only remonstrated if wakened frequently over a short span of nights or repeatedly during a single night. It was instances of the latter which aroused the greatest irritation:

On one occasion Mrs Nomish got up in the night, emptied the contents of her handbag into her bed and later took off all the blankets from her bed and put them on her neighbour's bed. Her companion, woken up three times at diminishing intervals, partly by the lights being switched on and off, was becoming overwrought when the matron arrived.

If occasional disturbance at night by a disoriented bedroom companion was an accepted hazard in the separatist homes, intrusion into one's bedroom in the ordinary homes by a person unknown in the dark, whilst perhaps rare and irregular, nevertheless generated real fear because of its unexpectedness and unpredictability. A blind woman in one of the ordinary homes said:

'The door frequently opened at night, like the man who'd been to the toilet and couldn't find his way back. Once a cold hand came up the pillow and over my face, and then went away.' [Again] 'a woman tried to get into my bed and said, "If you don't let me come in, I'll wet it." And she did. I'd only been there a week. It's rather a shock. You feel afraid.'[3]

Another single woman recalled past episodes with a shudder:

'One man came in at night and wanted the toilet. Also a woman who was a new resident. It scared the life out of me. Didn't know where her bedroom was. And another man, before he died, came in asking if I was his wife and tried to get into bed with me. It put the wind up me and I trembled from head to foot all over.'

But attitudes to the occasional interruption in the ordinary homes varied, from stark rejection on the one hand, usually because interference with sleep was felt to be intolerable:

One old woman who came in that day came into my bedroom at 2 a.m. and asked, 'Is my son in here?' And I said, 'No, he's not, clear off and go and find him.' And she came in twice again that night.

A newly arrived resident who was a disoriented wanderer and subject to dramatic hallucinations created havoc among her two rational bedroom companions when her shouting fits on one occasion woke them five times in the course of a single night. They were reduced to tears of impotent desperation, and could not be assuaged till the matron agreed to transfer the offender to another bedroom.

to bemused tolerance:

'I have Plowright in my bedroom. He's nutty but harmless – he dresses at night. The other night he got up, started walking about, opened drawers, put on his pyjama jacket, then another pair of pyjamas. Then he fiddled with a large shirt, put one sleeve round his neck, and another he put his leg in. So I told him it was 1 a.m., and he asked if it was one in the morning or night.'

and to understanding sympathy at the other extreme: 'I put it down to the mentality of the person – they can't help it.' 'I know they're ill or sick, poor things,' and at least some got out of bed to help.

'The woman I sleep with, she disturbs me, wakes me up and keeps on messing my things about and switches the light on and off. She's mentally affected and very restless. She used to mess about with my flannel, but not after I told her. She thought it was hers. Sometimes she's better than others. She don't disturb me every night. I know the woman can't help it. I have no ill-will towards her. I help her – I tell her what clothes to put on, put them on for her, and have to tell her where to wash.'

Thus the commonest response to disturbance at night in both separatist and ordinary homes was 'not annoyed unless it happens often', though the unanticipated and, at the time, frightening nature of irregular nightly intrusions, particularly in the ordinary homes, could cause a fearful alarm. Generally, however, apart from episodes of repeated interference with sleep on a single night, a tolerant understanding prevailed.

Physical restlessness

The third question which was asked of each of the residents was: 'Do any of them disturb your peace and quiet during the day by wandering about or being restless?' In the ordinary homes, day wandering did not constitute a major source of complaint because even the few aimless wanderers were not normally mobile. In the special homes, however, the rational objected strongly to those whose peregrinations were both aimless and unceasing, partly because their wanderings frequently penetrated the sanctum of their privacy in a separate room and partly because, in contrast to the directed wanderers, their movements seemed so haphazard and uncertain. In one of the special homes, where daytime wandering was particularly obtrusive, three of the aimless wanderers were constantly being shouted at, but to no avail, because they clearly could not understand how they were causing irritation. Their critics were confined mainly to four residents, including one woman who was herself restricted by laconic bursts of tangential speech and in her exasperation used to stick out her foot to trip up wanderers or give them a hard kick on their bottoms. Nevertheless, the more usual reaction, even in the separatist homes, was one of acceptance, albeit reluctant: 'I don't take much notice of it. I feel like this [spreadeagling her flattened palms outwards] – they can't help it.' 'She [a wanderer] *would* irritate me if I gave way to it, but you get accustomed to it in this sort of place. It's bound to be.'

Restless fiddling did not normally occasion any marked reaction unless it took the form of a compulsive habit, in which case interference could provoke violent recriminations.

Mrs Normanton got up and crossed the room to an unoccupied chair. She spent a few moments fingering the loose threads, then returned to her own chair and tried to play with the headcloth draped over the back of it. The woman in the next seat, however, took offence at this, and cried out: 'Leave that alone!' and stretched out her arms so as physically to restrain the culprit. But Mrs Normanton pushed her hand away angrily, retorting: 'Leave me alone.' 'No, that's my business,' snapped the other, but Mrs Normanton continued unabashed to run her fingertips over the fabric of her chair and an adjoining one. She failed to grasp hold of any object, however, and her neighbour remarked bad-temperedly 'See, you can't do anything. You wait till my husband gets home tonight.'

But such outbursts were rare, and restless fiddling was commonly ignored or it attracted only the odd testy comment: 'She's always fiddling about with her apron and getting up and sitting down and fidgeting. I said to her: "For goodness sake, stop it! It makes my nerves bad." '

Physical restlessness during the daytime did not therefore create much noticeable disturbance in the ordinary homes. In the separatist homes, however, a very small minority caused severe aggravation, unwittingly, by the aimlessness and persistence of their wandering or by their interference with privacy, whilst a similar number annoyed residents by their habit of constant fiddling, especially when it involved the seizure of others' belongings or a reproach led to a violent response. Both these latter phenomena will now be discussed further as separate items of criticism.

Interference with others' possessions

Each person was asked: 'Do any of the residents interfere with your property – not deliberately, but through perhaps forgetting what belongs to them, they might take something which belongs to you?' The replies showed that almost nobody harboured feelings of outrage about this. Rather what few comments were made on the subject were delivered in a spirit of faintly irritated dismissal.

Everybody liked her when she first came, but now she's just a nuisance. She *will* pick the flowers off the stalks, play with the rubbish in the hearth and pick up people's things.

Occasional loss of one's possessions seemed to be tolerated without undue ire, even in the separatist homes where it happened most often, largely because such unwitting interference was seen as a venial misdemeanour of old age:

> I get tired of residents who take books from the sitting room and it's not easy to get them back. They can't help it, but when they get old, they get batty. I only hope I don't get like that.

Moreover, the inability to locate one's possessions often left an uneasy sensation of one's own forgetfulness rather than the chicanery of others. 'I do lose things, but I think it's my own fault for not putting things where I can find them.' If an object were mislaid, however, a few, particularly those who were very marginally confused, were apt to project the blame on to well-established scapegoats. 'If Mrs Rumbleton loses anything, she always accuses others of having taken it, and she rifles other people's drawers in their bedroom.' Sometimes the implicit censure of others appeared a rather facile device to explain ill-understood changes that had nevertheless been administratively sanctioned:

> I've missed small things. When I went up to my case, it used to be mauve, but now it seems to be blue. But I don't take much notice of it.

From the projection of blame it was only a small step to a gullible suspicion.

> Somebody came into my bedroom and said, 'Oh, you back here again so early.' Pilfering, not stealing. But I had nothing in the larder anyway. I've lost a lot of things.

At the extreme was the habit of engaging in paranoid accusations:

> Mrs Welson was notorious for her malicious slanders. Once on a coach trip, after quarrelling with the others, she shouted to the driver with animus 'They're all jailbirds – don't attend to them.' And when one of them remonstrated with her, she added, 'Don't listen to her – she kicked a woman downstairs at the last home she was in.' On numerous occasions she had called Mrs Povie, her particular enemy, a thief and accused her and another of taking soap from her wardrobe. Mrs Povie, coarse and aggressive though she herself appeared, was reduced to tears and complained to

matron about the allegation. But when matron suggested to Mrs Welson she might be mistaken, she retaliated vehemently: 'I don't tell lies. I'm not ninety-four for nothing.'

In the ordinary homes, therefore, interference with possessions was regarded as a pardonable, even if occasionally exasperating, offence. In the separatist homes it was usually lightly dismissed, except where retrieval might involve violent reprisals, as will be discussed next. More commonly it was merely used as a convenient cloak to divert attention from the person's own failing powers of memory.

Aggressive or violent behaviour

The general question was put to each interviewee: 'Would you say that any of the residents are aggressive, liable to pick quarrels, or frighten you?' The answers were not necessarily concerned with specifically confused behaviour, but in fact the few precise comments made on this topic were actually directed at three or four particular individuals, all of whom were confused.

One of these was a small woman with an aquiline face inflamed by a running sore at the edge of one of her eyes which gave her face a fierce, embattled look. She frequently wandered into a room which the rational residents had tried to reserve for themselves and would then fiddle intently with any object which attracted her attention, whether the fireguard or the pom-pom of the slipper of a seated resident. When confronted with a firm rebuke, she used to stare at the protester without speaking and then resume her activity, or else physically assail her opponent. 'She stands in front of the fire, turns the waste-paper basket upside down, and when you try to lead her away she fights.' 'She's been up in my bedroom three times and I tried to get her down, but I couldn't. She can be vicious – she's hit my glasses.' 'She comes up and grabs you and almost pulls you down. She clings on and looks quite wild.' Only one resident was strong and determined enough to frogmarch her out of the room by force at times of trouble.

Apart from this unique case, complaints centred round odd incidents where certain residents were alleged to have used their sticks as a weapon.

I dislike the one who holds my hands. She's very strong and I'm frightened of her. She uses her stick. Once when my husband was being taken to the meal-room in his wheelchair, one wheel touched Mrs Laughton's leg and she swore and hit him.

However, such isolated occurrences underline the rarity of this form of offence, and apart from the single instance of the individual in one of the special homes who was prone to occasional acts of violence, in neither type of home was the fear of aggression or physical attacks a significant factor.

Offensive eating, dress or toilet habits

Residents were asked, 'Do you find any of them neglect their person, or become untidy, unclean or dirty in any way?' The replies indicated that feelings were most strongly aroused against incontinence, that little concern was shown about improprieties of dress, and that objections about eating habits, while sometimes appearing trivial, met with the distaste normally reserved even for small infringements of a strict code of conventions.

Complaints about manners at table, though not exclusively directed at confused residents, did usually involve them rather than the rational. At a general level, disapproval was shown at any over-eager hastiness: 'Some wait for the meal bell and like to be first, and take the food as if they'd never had any. Greediness!' and at incorrect procedures: 'She uses a dessert spoon when she ought to use a knife and fork.' More specificially, certain idiosyncrasies were greeted with aversion, even sometimes disgust:

One dips her bread and butter in the marmalade jar, and another, who we call 'rabbit', munches toast with both her hands and takes out her false teeth.

One at our table couldn't get the sugar, so she put marmalade on her porridge, and they're always shouting at Mrs Garbutt because she throws food in the fireplace.

Nevertheless, condemnation of indelicate table manners was doubtless reduced because in one of the separatist homes the six messiest eaters were segregated at mealtimes from the main dining hall. Anyway, similar remarks of disapprobation were voiced also about a few rational residents in the ordinary homes:

'She's not very clean at table. She dips bread into her tea, pulls food from her mouth and puts it on her plate. My stomach's upset by this. I won't say she's dirty, but she's not particular. She takes food off my plate and leaves one with too little for breakfast. It shouldn't be allowed – she should be put somewhere else. You lose your appetite for food.'

Very little censure was passed about irregularities of dress. This was chiefly because improprieties, like donning underclothes externally, only rarely escaped the immediate attention of staff or sympathetic residents, though where, for instance, a woman did come down to breakfast wearing a petticoat over her jumper, it contributed to her being ostracized as someone who was 'a bit touched in the head'. What did cause some displeasure was the failure to adhere to certain conventional standards of appearance. 'Pull your stockings up. Damn lazy! If you can't pull them up, you must be a damn brute.' And the practice of a man who was incontinent through hemiplegia and used to leave his fly-buttons undone evoked some irritated gossip. Probably the protesters did not appreciate the handicaps where, for example, a confused resident had her suspender belt removed, and a man could not easily do up buttons. No comments, however, so far as could be observed, were made about the stains caused by food which had spilled down cardigans and skirts and when caked hard had discoloured areas of clothing. In general, the attitude was one of indifference:

Some have their stockings and knickers down and can't do their own hair. I don't worry much. They just look rather untidy. Objections to incontinence came chiefly from the ordinary homes.

One rational resident, who was unusually articulate, remarked:

I can see and smell the incontinence – offensive! Others perhaps can't see when they go to the toilet, and urinate outside the pan. But I'm squeamish!

Reactions were normally limited, however, to those immediately affected by constant close contact with the offending person, chiefly bedroom companions. Very few residents were severely incontinent during the day so as to cause offence even to neighbours, since regular toileting by the staff seemed effective in obviating mishaps. Only one episode was reported where residents had strongly expostulated to staff: after a very confused woman had twice soaked her chair within a brief period of time, two of her companions protested openly to staff and two others privately because the smell was said to permeate both the dining room and the sole sitting room in use. In general, resentment was only expressed forcibly against those who were believed to mess the lavatory unnecessarily by careless use and against those who, it was felt, did not bother to walk to the toilet because of laziness. Some allowance was conceded by most for those regarded as physically incapable of achieving continence, and a few enterprising individuals accepted the inevitable with stoic dignity: 'Some are weak in the bladder – rather unpleasant – but I keep a bottle of eau de cologne in my bag and put it up my nose.' Apart from actual incontinence, the odd complaint was also alleged against a coarse lack of inhibition:

Another old lady had obsessions about the toilet, and once in the sitting room she thought she *was* in the toilet, and she pulled up her clothes around her waist and pulled down her knickers – in the lounge.

In summary, therefore, disapproval of eating, dress or toilet habits was by no means exclusively alleged against confused residents, and to this extent, in the absence of extenuating circumstances frequently conceded in cases of confusion, they sometimes attracted a critical acerbity, particularly in the ordinary homes, which seemed out of proportion to the offence.

ANORMIC ACTIVITIES

Nothing was asked specifically about reactions to anormic behaviour partly because it formed a residual and somewhat artificial category and partly because this area of experience was already substantially covered by the preceding questions. Nevertheless, the disapproval shown towards certain anormic activities was noted in the course of observation of the daily routine, as well as being spontaneously raised at interview.

Non-conventional use of objects[4] caused no apparent disturbance because it was rarely obtrusive, whilst non-conventional behaviour,[4] apart from encroachments of dress and toilet conventions already mentioned, appeared aggravating chiefly in terms of the persistent uncomprehending prattle of ill-digested sentiments:

A woman who would frequently catch others' phrases or seize on the printed word and repeat them out of context, had on one occasion been loudly publicizing her thoughts in this vein for a few minutes, when she read a newspaper headline held up by a neighbour: 'Mr Wilson in censure debate storm.' 'Don't know if I have a storm or not', she loudly interjected, 'I think I have a storm.' The patience of her companions was by now wearing thin, and one retorted angrily, 'Keep still! Shut up!' When this failed singularly to stem any of the effervescence being ceaselessly poured out a number of others joined in to subdue the flow: 'Read to yourself. What do you want to read it all out for?' 'If we all did that, a pretty row there'd be.'

Otherwise, aggravation chiefly centred round the noisy reiteration of what appeared inane activities. A blind and confused resident who kept withdrawing four pennies from a tin, letting them slip down her wrist into her palm and then replacing them one by one in the tin, induced a rational neighbour to remark irritably: 'I try not to notice, but it drives me crazy. I try not to look at her.' Again, a woman who had developed the habit of continually chewing her fingers caused a nearby resident to snap at her: 'Makes me *sick*. Do you feel hungry?' Above all, inexplicable hand-clapping at irregular intervals aroused the fiercest indignation. One such incident observed was recorded as follows:

Mrs Ironside was a strong-willed woman of seventy-eight, with snow-white hair and whiskery face, and her hawk-like nose, piercing eye and venomous tongue transformed her, when challenged, into a redoubtable antagonist. Her tendency to indulge in spasms of hand-clapping invariably instigated a commotion. On this occasion she began in one of the dayrooms during a sleepy period after lunch.

MRS CHOLMLEY: Oh shut up!
MRS GRATTON: I think I'll cut her hand off.
Mrs Ironside claps her hands again.
MRS CHOLMLEY [*emphatically*]: Shut up!
MRS IRONSIDE: What's wrong with you? [*and she claps again*]
MRS CHOLMLEY: Stop it. You ruin it for everyone.
MRS GRATTON: You're right there.

MRS IRONSIDE *claps her hands again, pauses, then again lightly then lightly, several times, then once loudly.*

MRS CHOLMLEY [*screeching*]: Shut up, you maniac.

MRS GRATTON: Yes, you're right.

MRS IRONSIDE *stands up, then sits down again, then claps once more.*

MRS CHOLMLEY: Stop it!

MRS GRATTON: Yes, you're right.

MRS IRONSIDE: Stopping it again, are you? Well, stop it and stick it up your arse.

MRS CHOLMLEY [*in utter disgust*]: Dirty, filthy creature.

MRS WHYATT: She doesn't know what she says.

MRS CHOLMLEY: Well, it's about time she did learn – dirty, foul-mouthed beast.

Significantly enough, even here it was the obscenity rather than the eccentricity which produced the final outburst.

As would be expected, therefore, complaints about anormic activities were concentrated heavily in the separatist homes where the great majority of such behaviour was found. In the ordinary homes, the display of inanely repetitive habits, though rare and of a much less overtly disturbing nature, nevertheless generated a disproportionately petulant response.

THE GRAVITY OF CRITICISM

Given this range of expressed disapproval, how vehemently were the various complaints launched? In particular, were certain forms of confused behaviour, even if regarded critically, nevertheless excused with sympathetic tolerance, while others provoked intractable opposition? Above all, how did the experience of confused behaviour affect the acceptance of confused residents in separatist and ordinary homes?

In order to test the intensity of feeling about the various activities of confused residents which were censured, each resident was asked: 'Of all the things that other residents do, what disturbs you most?' More than four-fifths of those who answered this question, among both confused and rational residents and in both separatist and ordinary homes, proffered no outstanding complaint to which they would attach particular significance as having caused them excessive

Table 6.2

**Major objection to confused behaviour as stated by
rational and confused residents according to type of home**

Single main objection	Residents making criticism	Proportion of residents making objection in:	
		Separatist homes (%)	Ordinary homes (%)
Incoherent talk	confused	0	(4·5)
	rational	1·9	1·7
Night wandering or night disturbance	confused	2·8	0
	rational	5·8	5·2
Day wandering	confused	0	0
	rational	1·9	1·7
Interference with others' property	confused	1·4	0
	rational	0	0·9
Aggressive or violent behaviour	confused	0	0
	rational	0	0·9
Offensive eating, dress or toilet habits	confused	0	0
	rational	0	2·6
A major objection not included above	confused	1·4	(4·5)
	rational	0	3·5
No major objection	confused	36·4	(72·7)
	rational	76·9	80·0
Too incoherent to give valid answer at interview	confused	45·1	(18·2)
	rational	3·8	0
Refused interview, or not available for interview, or too deaf	confused	12·7	0
	rational	9·6	3·5
TOTAL	confused	99·8	(99·9)
	rational	99·9	100·0
Number of residents	confused	71	22
	rational	52	115

worry, as Table 6.2 reveals. The only objection which even a twentieth of the rational regarded as justifying especial emphasis was their distress at being disturbed at night, while as many residents or more were perplexed by sources of irritation entirely unrelated to confusion,[5] such as gossip and backbiting, as by incoherent talk or day wandering. Moreover, of the 204 residents giving an opinion on this issue, interference with possessions and aggressive or violent behaviour were each mentioned by only one person, and offensive eating habits by only three, as a major complaint. Even more significantly, Table 6.3 indicates that fully half the residents, even in the separatist homes, declared they had not observed any confused behaviour. Each person interviewed was asked: 'Have you noticed

if any of the residents are confused or "funny in the head"?' Of
those giving a coherent reply to this question, seven-ninths of the
confused in the ordinary homes stated that they had not, as did half
of the rational, whilst in the separatist homes the corresponding
proportions were only very slightly less, three-quarters of the confused returning a negative answer and two-fifths of the rational.[6]

These figures convey a much greater tolerance, not to say disregard, of confused behaviour than is often imagined in local
authority policy-making circles.[7] However, doubts may be cast on
the validity of this data on the grounds that at interviews people may
be inhibited in expressing their real opinions, especially if adverse,
about the behaviour of their companions, either out of a spirit of
generosity or through fear of the consequences, however firm the
assurance of confidentiality.[8]

Table 6.3

**Recognition of confused behaviour by rational and
confused residents according to type of home**

Recognition of confused behaviour	*Mental status of respondent*	*Separatist homes* (%)	*Ordinary homes* (%)
Have recognized confused	confused	10·5	(18·2)
behaviour	rational	51·9	48·7
Have not recognized confused	confused	31·5	(63·6)
behaviour	rational	34·6	47·9
Too incoherent to give valid	confused	45·1	(18·2)
answer at interview	rational	3·8	0
Refused interview, or not available	confused	12·7	0
for interview, or too deaf	rational	9·6	3·5
TOTAL	confused	99·8	(100·0)
	rational	99·9	100·1
Number of residents	confused	71	22
	rational	52	115

Alternatively it may be argued that old people may underestimate
their antagonism through being forgetful of the relevant incidents[9]
and that their spontaneous reactions as seen in the course of prolonged observation of the normal routine would constitute a better
guide to their true feelings. How far, therefore, were the interview
statements confirmed or belied by observations?

Undoubtedly, a very small minority of confused persons did
cause real outrage. Apart from isolated and largely irregular episodes
like a severe attack of incontinence, these were those who publicly

demonstrated some irrational activity which was either inanely repetitive, like persistent hand-clapping or tiresomely reiterated utterances, or which destructively intruded into others' peace and quiet, like interruption of sleep at night or interference with possessions by persons notorious for unpredictable aggression. Only some 9 per cent of those in the separatist homes and 1·5 per cent in the ordinary homes could be said to fall in this category, not all of them being amongst the most confused. However, even about this nucleus who could on occasion cause real distress and provoke retaliation, very few actual complaints were made to staff. Even in the separatist homes with the highest proportion of confused residents (80 per cent) where 43 per cent were severely confused,[10] only five protests could be traced as having been raised with staff over recent years – a record which, if not necessarily indicating ready acquiescence, does not suggest irrepressible dissatisfaction either.

Apart from this core of contentious behaviour, attitudes to confusion tended to follow four distinct lines. Firstly, persons displaying irrational activity might be met by a rejection which made no pretence at insight: 'I think to myself "You stupid ass!" If they should say anything, I would say "That's my affair; shut your mouth!" ' Such instant antagonism, however, was rare, and much more common was an attitude of indifference where any potential hostility had been tempered by the insulation of likely offenders. 'Some are a bit odd and funny, talk to themselves, but it doesn't disturb me, not in the least. If you know they're that way, you don't answer them and they won't bore you stiff.' 'No effect on me. I let it go in one ear and out the other.' Thirdly, tolerance was granted, but only grudgingly. This response was typified by a woman who complained bitterly of the constantly reiterative utterances of two residents: 'They nearly drive me mad . . . but one can't do anything, must be tolerant, and just keep away.' Lastly, tolerance was combined with a sympathetic understanding. One particularly dignified example was a firm assurance: 'I make every allowance for their senile condition.' But this aspect of the reaction is developed more fully later.

If this represented the spectrum of attitudes, what views were held about a proper place for the confused? Overwhelmingly favoured was a policy of segregation. 'What's wrong is that they mix the perfectly sane with those of mixed mentality.' 'They should be graded like with like.' 'I feel they can't help it, but they should be put in Abbey Towers [the local mental hospital].' Sometimes the desire for dissociation was rationalized: 'They create a lot of work for the staff, so they can't do the job properly.' 'She should be somewhere where she could be properly looked after.' It was on these grounds that a specialized allocation was occasionally recommended whereby the 'mental' ones would be discharged to an 'asylum', the cripples into hospital and the blind into a blind home. Very few recognized the drawbacks of segregation, and even if they did, the reaction was ambivalent. A rational resident in an ordinary home philosophically reflected: 'If you put them apart, it would be a stigma to the relatives, but if you put them together, they'll sink to the lowest level.' By contrast, however, a minority of residents did oppose segregation. 'Two are a bit touched in the head, but they're quiet. They don't talk to anyone ... Not bad enough to be sent away.' And another rational resident in this ordinary home, referring to the same person who was tangential in speech, an aimless wanderer, incontinent and liable to disturb at night through disorientation, quietly concluded: 'She should stay here, as long as she's no harm.' Alternatively, a number of residents countered with a remark of ambivalent resignation: 'Must put up with them; it's not up to you to want them to be moved away.'

Lastly, how far were these attitudes particularly associated with either separatist or ordinary homes? And how far was the severity of criticism linked with the grossness of the confused behaviour seen in a home? Now the weight of criticism was certainly greater in the separatist homes, but less than proportionately greater in the light of the amount and degree of confused activity found in them. This suggests two hypotheses. Firstly, between homes, overall, the sharpness of the criticism is related to the degree of deviation from an approximately even balance in the numbers of rational and confused. Thus, in the ordinary homes where the confused formed a small minority of 16 per cent, they tended to be exposed to criticism because of the uniqueness of their behaviour. In one of the separatist homes, on the other hand, where they constituted a substantial majority of 80 per cent the irregularities of their actions seemed so dominant that the rational manifested the strength of their feelings of rejection publicly by retreating into defensive isolation. It was only in the other two special homes, where 47 per cent of the residents were confused, that their behaviour seemed neither remarkable by its rarity nor overwhelming by its ubiquitousness, so that relative to the extent of manifestations of confusion criticism was least harsh. Secondly, within the homes, a further hypothesis may be conjoined with this: that severity of disapproval is a product chiefly of both the frequency of the offending behaviour and the proximity of the offending person. It was quite common for a resident to mention a source of complaint, and then immediately add that he or she was not annoyed unless it happened *often*. Equally typical after a short catalogue of objections was the rider: 'They don't get under my skin unless I'm in close contact with them.'

Certainly other factors did also influence the general reaction to confused behaviour, especially the attitudes of staff. The matron and superintendent of one ordinary home strongly sided with the 'right' of the rational to be left in peace without disturbance by the confused, while in another ordinary home the matron met a complaint about an incontinent bedroom companion with the rebuke: 'Don't be fussy, they can't all be like you.' Also important was acclimatization to the values of the home: 'It doesn't worry me now. The real knock was when I first came.' Familiarity with the confused produced its own adjustment of expectations: 'Only one misbehaves at my table, but I've got used to it now. I don't take much notice.' Moreover, the layout pattern of the home, in the opportunities it offered for privacy, and the positioning of the chairs, in that their arrangement into small groups insulated the general atmosphere from irruptions of confused activity, also affected the level of toleration. Nevertheless, the frequency and proximity of the offensive action remain the crucial variables, and it was particularly noticeable that aberrant, rather than specifically confused, behaviour frequently proved a sharper focus for discontent, if it was more proximate. This tendency will now be examined more fully.

THE RELATIVITY OF CRITICISM

The full significance of the criticisms made of confused actions can only be properly seen in the light of a few further associated factors. These are now considered in turn.

Disapproval unrelated to confusion

Many residents, and indeed a majority in the ordinary homes, declared themselves less distressed by confused behaviour than by disagreements, often deep-seated and bitter, interwoven into the daily web of ordinary relationships within the home. Such matters included gossiping abuse and rudeness, disputes about having windows open or shut, quarrelsomeness, personality conflicts about persons 'laying down the law', garrulity ('I think, "Put another record on"'), compulsive hypochondriacal complaints, coarse or obscene language (' "Bloody sod!" and all the rest – if you heard that man cursing at night, it would turn your blood'), greediness ('She eats all my bread and butter, not just her ration'), snobbishness ('giving herself airs'), lack of gentility,[11] toadying to staff, loss of privacy, lying ('I sometimes think, "Oh *bother you*," when she doesn't speak the plain truth') and hyper-critical fault-finding. The singling out of a few individuals on each of these points prompted both retaliation and defensive explanations from the more articulate of those attacked. 'I feel I'm not one of them; I feel alone.' 'They're always trying to make out I'm doing something wrong, when I'm not . . . they take what you say the wrong way.' In fact, those who were subjected to this tacit subtle persecution were more positively isolated even than the confused, who were often ignored rather than explicitly rejected.

While confused behaviour was usually accorded a spontaneous allusion as a matter of concern, it was also often relegated, especially in the ordinary homes, to the level of an afterthought.

'There's a man with a terrible Cockney voice. "I've never been to Blackpool," he says, "but I've seen the tower lit up when I come up the Channel!" It gets you down if you've got nerves. He said when he first came that he'd been in the Australian Army, but being a military man I asked him in what part, and he didn't know. He's full of fantasies – said he'd been to Canada and seen the Heights of Abraham! Others give him the bird, but he likes it. It dries him up for five minutes, but he's thick-skinned and goes on again, on and on. You sometimes have to get out. Some others are a little bit upstairs – senile decay, but I don't find it disturbing.'

They're all right. One or two funny ones. One who hits with her stick as easily as anything. Amy [Turtle] plays with four pennies all the time and closes and opens her bag all the time. I'm not very tolerant, yet she's clearly not right in the head, so I can't blame her. And Jane – I keep out of her way. She belongs to the other room, and if somebody tells her off, she swears at them. The fact that people are so different, queer – that's what irks me, after living alone. I only wish they didn't have the TV on so loud. One has a hearing aid, but won't wear it. Yet the TV is turned on so loud, when she says she can't hear it. It's *wrong!* Some are inclined to pick quarrels. Aggressive, "You should be so-and-so." You could soon pick a quarrel if you answered them. One is always going to the matron, "I've lost so-and-so, and I know who's taken it." And another is the same. You can't believe what they say. She said she'd been to Kirford and back, but she'd not been out long enough. And people who get up and walk about and are not steady themselves get me het up . . . Mrs Turtle wipes her nose on her frock, which irritates me – not used to it. But I mustn't let it irritate me. Mrs Sawbridge is dirty, always looks like a ragamuffin – laces always undone and dirty apron. But it's very easy to criticize when you've nothing else to do. Three or four in my room shout at Amy to sit down, and say these people should be in hospital, not here. I'm always afraid of interfering – never know how they're going to respond.'

These two extracts show clearly how sharply the perfunctory references to the idiosyncrasies of confused residents contrast with powerful animosities directed against the rival assertiveness of rational companions.[12]

Varying norms

About the same proportion of residents mentioned incoherent talk as a source of disturbance in the ordinary homes as in the separatist (p. 122 above), yet the proportion of residents who displayed this characteristic was seven times greater in the separatist homes (p. 81). From this it is clear that inter-home comparisons do not reflect the reaction to a consistent standard, but rather to the differential norms of each individual environment. In the ordinary homes, where confusion was not always pervasive enough in its impact to offer an adequate frame of reference, complaints of 'nonsense' talked by other residents, for example, might mean no more than a dislike of what they said. Similarly, the terminology more accurately reserved for the confused was not infrequently used, particularly in the ordinary homes, to express displeasure at even marginal peccadillos of rational neighbours. 'Arkwright is a nuisance – asks all sort of silly questions and fiddles with her front. She and Ebbs want to know all your business, and they talk a lot of rot. All funny up top.' The description 'mental' was readily used, on seemingly trivial or even non-existent criteria, to vilify an opponent. Criticisms of confused behaviour, therefore, were in no sense an absolute response, but rather were determined by expectations moulded by experience of the traditional conventions of the home. This has important implications for social policy.

Double standards

A varying criterion was not only applied between homes, but also between rational and confused residents within the same home for similar behaviour:

> In one of the special homes a woman (confusional score 4) who constantly reiterated a single phrase produced paroxysms of enraged frustration among her involuntary listeners, while a rational woman in the same room who broke into little agitated shouts when the TV was on, disjointing the flow of the sound track, was tolerated sympathetically: 'She's ninety-three and deaf, and one must make allowances for her.'

> Again, a woman in another separatist home (confusional score 12) who read aloud newspaper headlines uncomprehendingly was bitterly rebuked, yet a rational resident in the same home who laa-laa-ed hopelessly out of tune with some background radio music was ignored, though the disharmony was positively hurtful to the ear.

This suggests a threshold point up to which personal eccentricities were excused, but beyond which the attribution of 'mental' instability prejudiced every judgment.

Misplacement

Not only were the confused sometimes treated with inconsistent harshness, they might also be conveniently selected for automatic blame where the real cause of a disturbance was not immediately obvious:

Miss Kee in one of the separatist homes was subjected to instant reproof tantamount to persecution. On a typical occasion when the sound commentary on TV was interfering with a resident's concentration, she was told crossly: 'Somebody reading? Who is it? [then addressing Miss Kee] Shut up!'

Apart from the crystallization of censure on to certain marked individuals, or scapegoating, by which the confused were penalized, they were also liable to derision when occasionally they retaliated, but themselves misdirected the attack.

A rational but euphoric resident who had launched into a seemingly endless stream of monologue was increasingly irritating a confused neighbour. However, when finally the speaker happened to declare that she did not think another person in the room would survive long, and this person replied, it was the latter rather than the former whom the confused resident assailed for talking.

But once again, rational residents in a similar situation of displaced anger were leniently overlooked:

A woman[13] who had grown more and more perturbed by my presence over my three-week stay in this separatist home finally rounded on me during the last day. Hardening her jaw, she hissed at me: 'I despise you. I resent the way you mother me and Mrs Keitch [turning sideways to face her innocent and startled victim] – the way she looks into my affairs. I know you better than you know yourself' [with a self-satisfied smugness]. Mrs Keitch, recovering quickly from this unprovoked onslaught, assented quietly, 'Yes,' and turned to give me a knowing smile.

Identification with mental illness

Another factor which influenced the reaction to the confused was the assimilation of their condition by others, particularly in the ordinary homes, to that of former psychiatric patients. In a typical remark about an aimless wanderer who was disoriented and tangential in speech, a rational resident concluded: 'They shouldn't put these feeble-minded [*sic*] people with others – they should be put in a mental home.' This tacit association necessarily implicated the confused in the stigma attaching to those who had been admitted from psychiatric hospitals. This stigma was utilized for two main purposes. It was used to denigrate a personal opponent: 'Lady

Kingston!' remarked one resident about another in contemptuously scornful tones, 'and her husband's been in Connaught (mental hospital) too.' Secondly, it was employed as a means of strengthening self-assurance by downgrading others: thus a man who protected his insecurity behind a façade of hauteur reduced a new resident to tears with the public aside, "Course you know where she comes from – she's funny.'

Both these tactics were brought into operation against the confused. The former explains why a policy of segregation and removal to mental hospital was so widely supported for confused persons. The latter was particularly favoured by certain subnormal residents who were anyhow praeternaturally anxious to reinforce their self-esteem by eliciting praise and gratitude from staff for the domestic chores they so readily undertook. A mystified disdain for the oddities of the confused was therefore an obvious extra handle with which to confirm their own acceptance within the establishment. 'Thank God I've got sense and don't do it,' said one characteristically about a wanderer.

The analysis has so far been confined to the content, gravity and relativity of the criticisms made about confused behaviour. It remains now to examine the source of the criticisms.

THE CRITICS

Was disapproval of confused activities limited largely to the rational? Were criticisms evenly distributed or concentrated among a few individuals? What kind of irritation chiefly perturbed rational as against confused residents?

It has sometimes been alleged that the mentally infirm should be put together because they are too demented to be affected by each other's abnormal behaviour. Table 6.1 demonstrates that this is false. Of those interviewed and able to give a coherent answer, three-quarters of the rational in the special homes offered some criticism of confused behaviour, but so also did half of the confused residents; in the ordinary homes the critics embraced three-fifths of the rational, but also a quarter of the confused. Also many instances were recorded, and some have already been quoted, where confused residents took offence at the aberrant activities of their companions and retaliated either verbally or physically. Indeed, the severity of the censure expressed by some of the moderately confused against their companions may have reflected their gathering unease at their own deterioration and their need to assert their failing rationality. For their hypercriticism was often masked by a placid self-image: 'I've not had a cross word with any of them'; 'I'm not one to look for trouble.'

Nevertheless it is true that, where disapproval was expressed, the confused were more likely to offer a single criticism, whilst the rational tendered multiple complaints. This applied to both separatist and ordinary homes, as Table 6.1 also reveals. Furthermore the multiple criticisms, both among the confused and the rational, tended to be concentrated among a few persons rather than evenly spread among all. And observation confirmed that it was these same individuals who repeatedly vented their indignation whenever a cause for offence arose, while others generally registered an indifferent or apathetic acceptance of the fact.

Lastly, how did the total perspective of residential companions differ between separatist and ordinary homes? Two examples illustrate the variation of concern. A woman in one of the special homes sketched her feelings thus:

'I lie down in the afternoon to escape all these people. Mrs Hanwell bullies one – she gets hold of one and gets you in her grip. Mrs Ganley's always going in and out, in and out. But she doesn't mean any harm. Mrs Wraith once used to wear my clothes – took them from my cupboard – a long time ago, though even now she takes things out of rooms. And there's Miss Turton. She wakes Miss Gilchrist up in the middle of the night and says she's going home, but can't find the key to her house. And when I first came here, I shared a room with two sisters who put on hats in the middle of the night, and got into the wrong end of the bed. I'd like to go to another home where people are not so funny. But I suppose as long as they don't come into our room and don't annoy us too much, which they don't really, I don't mind. If I can get out in the day, I'm hardly disturbed at all. But lots of them say, "They shouldn't be here." And I say to my friend, "Let's go into the garden and escape from all the loonies." '

By contrast a man in one of the ordinary homes unravelled his institutional portrait with rather different emphases:

'A number here are mentally defective, from Silberton [the local psychiatric hospital]. They can't be companionable. You talk to them and they merely laugh, so you don't try again. Two in my lounge are like that. One is childish in manner, and says, "Is there any more post today?" But she's asked this many times before. And a new one – you can't make her understand what you want, but she never misses an observation outside the window. She keeps rearranging the flowers. Annoying if somebody brings flowers and somebody else messes them about. But what gets me most is that cripples don't try to help themselves in any way. And table manners. At my table one woman has rotten habits. She reaches for things without asking and spills things. She says it's a bother to ask people, and I say, No! She picks sardines off toast with her fingers and puts them on bread and butter, and pushes the plate away. And Mrs Drange every day: "Will you send someone to help me down?" at mealtimes and when it's time for bed. I remonstrated with the staff about it, but they say, "She's old, she can't help it." I wipe these things out like a black-board. I wouldn't ask to be shifted from my table for another to endure it. I'd rather stick it out.'

These extracts suggest that whilst a sense of imposition was equally powerful in the ordinary homes, it was concerned there with comparatively minor irregularities of behaviour and did not engender the desire to escape which continuous over-exposure to a whole range of confused misdemeanours was liable to produce in the separatist homes.

Hitherto, the discussion in this chapter has centred on adverse reactions to the confused. In order to restore balance to the picture, therefore, the nature and extent of favourable attitudes must now be examined.

SYMPATHY

In what form was sympathy for the confused exhibited and how far did it counteract the criticisms? Who were the sympathizers?

Where tolerance was shown towards confused residents, it was occasionally manifested as a qualified acceptance, but more usually as an indifference which fell far short of integration, or even as a support for their segregation on the ostensible grounds of their self-interest. The last attitude was epitomized by a judgment on an aimless wanderer who was incontinent and tangential in speech:

'She didn't annoy me at all in any way. I was sorry for her. But they want putting somewhere where they'll be well looked after. She didn't know what she was doing.'

Tolerance was most commonly displayed, however, as a cool acquiescence in the presence of the confused based more on an absence of repudiation than real acknowledgement. Sometimes it depended on an appreciation of diminished responsibility: 'Things which might be objectionable are bound to happen to them when they're old, but it's not their fault. It's not done deliberately.' 'They've got no memory – would help if they had.' And in general, many seemed anxious on occasion to plead extenuating circumstances for the confused: 'Poor soul, she doesn't know where she's going.' 'They can't help it, poor things.' In most such cases, however, the implications of such feelings were limited: 'I *don't* feel they can help behaving as they do, and I feel *sorry* for them, but I feel no responsibility for them.' It was often a case of sympathy at a distance: 'They do wander about and don't know where things are. I pity them, I'm sorry for them. But I don't sit in the same room with them. It would upset me then perhaps.' Expressed more negatively, this approach grudgingly acceded rights to the confused so long as they were exercised elsewhere:

I don't like certain of the patients. I keep out of the way – mental cases here. There are many admissions on the mental side – not fair! The mental ones can't feed themselves properly and use their fingers. I didn't know the sort of place it was, or I wouldn't have come. If I could see a more comfortable place, I'd consider going. Though of course I fully realize it's not their fault, and they must have *some* place to come to.

Alternatively, tolerance took the form of bemused onlooking:

When a disoriented resident in one of the separatist homes began to exclaim excitedly about the 'pinky-green tellies' outside the window, a rational neighbour leant towards me with a knowing wink, 'You'll remember this. We do see life here.'

A man in another of the special homes took the attitude, 'A large part here are not normal, and if they can't understand me, I just shrug my shoulders.' When once an attendant was bringing a persistent wanderer back up the drive to the home, he smiled wistfully, 'You'll have to have a ball and chain put on you,' with a protectiveness and affectionate rebuke.

The strongest motivation for sympathy, however, was a realization that the ravages of age were unpredictable.

Too many who're 'funny' here. We should be very thankful we're not like them. I hope I never am like that [nearly weeping]. You have to show kindness, show you're not bad. You can't blame them if they don't know what they do.

A few residents, on the other hand, did transpose a tolerance of the confused into a relationship of equal acceptance, even if the dependence in terms of need was one-sided. Such examples as occurred will be discussed in the next chapter. Here, however, it should be added that the sense of equality could sometimes be blurred by an element of condescension.

Me myself, I'm philosophical. It would have a greater effect on others than on me. I accept it. I'm more or less a humanitarian. I have sympathy. I help them, like I write an address on a letter for them. And once when I was going to the toilet at night, I found a woman who was lost and told her to return to her room next time by turning on her light and leaving the door open.

Sympathy, whether positive in the form of acceptance or with resignation at the level of more tolerance, was spontaneously accorded to confused residents much more often in the ordinary than in the separatist homes. Within the latter a sympathetic reaction was more forthcoming in the house built on an open plan without formal dayrooms[14] than in the others. Also, hardly any of the confused in either type of home commented favourably on companions with similar behavour.

SUMMARY OF DIFFERENT REACTIONS TO CONFUSION ACCORDING TO TYPE OF HOME

What conclusions can therefore be drawn from the foregoing analysis of the variations in critical or sympathetic reactions to confused behaviour between separatist and ordinary homes? The results can be most usefully listed as follows:

1. In the separatist homes irritation was chiefly expressed about

day wandering and interference with possessions, while in the ordinary homes, where the level of criticism was anyway relatively much lower, aggravation centred chiefly on night disturbance and incontinence.

2. The only incoherent talk which caused serious disturbance occurred in the separatist homes in the form either of a constant inane repetition of fixed words or sentences, or as a loud publicizing of uncomprehended phrases. But both these phenomena were rare.

3. Only some 9 per cent of the residents in the separatist homes and 1·5 per cent in the ordinary homes displayed confused behaviour of a kind which did, at least occasionally, cause real outrage.

4. Of those interviewed and able to supply a coherent answer, four-fifths of residents in both types of home abstained from suggesting that any criticism merited special emphasis, and in the ordinary homes more gave as a major objection behaviour unrelated to confusion than any of the aspects of confusion itself.

5. Very few complaints were actually made to staff in either type of home about confused behaviour, even in the special home where over two-fifths were severely confused.

6. Relative to the amount and degree of confused activity in a home, it seemed that criticism, together with support for a policy of segregation, was found least where confused and rational residents approximately balanced each other in number, whereas the presence of only a few confused persons (in the ordinary homes) exposed them to censure because they appeared exceptional, whilst an over-whelming predominance of confused persons (in one of the special homes) made their rational companions feel unduly threatened.

7. Apart from this factor, the severity of criticism seemed to depend chiefly, in both types of home, on proximity to the offensive action and its frequency of occurrence, especially in the case of interruption of sleep at night. But the attitude of staff, the gradual adjustment of expectations and the opportunity for privacy also governed the sharpness of the critical reaction.

8. A majority in the ordinary homes and a substantial minority in the separatist homes indicated they were less irritated by confused behaviour than by other sources of complaint, a whole range of which were mentioned, particularly gossiping.

9. The discrepancy between the quantity of criticisms and the relative incidence of the behaviour complained of between the specialized and ordinary homes suggests that the reaction was

determined less by a consistent comparative standard than by expectations adjusted to the norm of a particular environment.

10. It seemed more likely in the separatist homes, where confused behaviour appeared so pervasive, that confused residents would be subject to semi-automatic blame over certain misdemeanours rather than given the benefit of an excuse, and that such an environment made certain individuals particularly prone to being scapegoated.

11. The quantity of criticisms of confused behaviour was similar in both types of home as between the rational and confused critics, in each case the rational being more likely to express multiple criticisms.

12. Sympathy for confused residents, whether as positive acceptance or mere tolerance, was spontaneously expressed much more commonly in the ordinary homes.

In view, therefore, of the distribution and nature of critical or sympathetic attitudes towards confused persons in both separatist and ordinary homes, how were these reactions translated into the flow of activities and relationships within the daily routine of life in either type of home? This forms the subject of the next two chapters.

NOTES

1. It is, of course, appreciated that this framework of exposition separates in deductive order what is in fact a simultaneous and continuous process of mutually interacting elements. Thus the nature of the relations actually observed in a home at any time both depends on the predetermined opinions and attitudes of the participants and itself helps either to reinforce or alter those attitudes for the future. The scheme used here has nevertheless been adopted because of its logical convenience.

2. It was not uncommon for persons with confused speech to use the inappropriate sex pronoun.

3. It must certainly be admitted that allegations of this kind require independent verification which it was often difficult, if not impossible, to obtain. In the absence of such confirmation, it was problematic to decide what evidence should be given to claims like that made by one particular rational resident in one of the specialized homes: 'One of them empties her chamber pot out of the window at night, and I'm always frightened that somebody may be walking around underneath.'

4. In the sense that these concepts have been operationalized in this study (pp 69-72).

5. In a typical response in one of the ordinary homes a woman said she was annoyed most by bad table manners, complaints about the food when it was very good, and the use of the toilet by ladies with the door open.

6. It might be thought that these high proportions of residents declaring they had not noticed any confused behaviour in their homes indicated they could not have understood the meaning of the question. But this is hardly likely when this particular question immediately followed six others which detailed each of the main facets of

confusion. Also, the figures are confirmed by their close similarity to the corresponding proportions of those who answered all six of these questions negatively – in the ordinary homes two-thirds of the confused and one-third of the rational, and in the separatist homes half of the confused and a quarter of the rational.

7. For example, one superintendent declared his view that: 'I fully believe that the more sensible residents find living with the more confused is extremely trying. At our home the average age is eighty plus and at this age it cannot be too easy to understand the difficulties and confusion of others, and I would venture an opinion that they find this behaviour extremely trying and irritating.'

8. Some justification for this view is afforded by the unquestionable suggestibility of some residents. The following conversation, for example, was recorded with one particularly tractable woman:

'Would you say you're indifferent to these things you've complained of?'
'Yes.'
'Or do you mind a bit, but not much?'
'Yes, you've taken the words out of my mouth.'
'Or do you get pretty irritated by it?'
'Yes, I do get irritated by it.'
'Or do you find it intolerable?'
'Yes, I find it intolerable, to tell you the truth.'

9. One woman, who herself had a confusional score of 7, insisted at interview that 'I've never had a wrong word with any of them', yet was observed to be the most relentless and nagging critic of a confused neighbour, censuring her roundly even for nonexistent acts.

10. With a confusional score of 7 or more points (on the scale given on p. 85).

11. 'It's the "mixed grille" that causes trouble here. Such a different class – though I'm not a snob. Some come from Stancliffe (the local mental hospital), some from the streets.' 'They shouldn't put people who've had their own home with others who've had no family, which makes you consider others the pigs they are, some of them.'

12. The question ostensibly at issue might sometimes appear trifling. Characteristically, a woman in one of the ordinary homes complained of incoherent talk, nocturnal disturbance, day wandering and offensive toilet habits, but admitted she was disturbed most 'only when I *know* something and they keep contradicting me when I know I'm right, for instance about wild flowers,' and she named her main antagonist.

13. She had a confusional score of 1, being disoriented in regard to her person and situation (having recently informed the matron that a helicopter was soon due to take her back to Exeter), but in general her rationality was not held in doubt by her companions.

14. It is, of course, only hypothetical that the architectural structure was the main factor in influencing the atmosphere of greater tolerance.

7

Rejection and deprivation: the loneliness of the confused

The previous chapter has indicated that whilst a sense of outraged repudiation was only very rarely felt towards confused residents, even in the separatist homes, nevertheless an attitude of tolerant or merely apathetic disregard was pervasive in both types of homes, alleviated only by occasional snatches of sympathetic concern, especially in the ordinary homes. In the light of this pattern, how far did indifference inhibit the integration of the confused within the weft of daily contacts in either kind of home? In particular, how far did they play a part in the conversational networks and how much did they participate in communal activities? To what extent were they isolated by the structuring of arrangements within the home or from contacts with the outside world? These questions will be examined in this chapter, and the next will be devoted to the role allocated to confused residents in the distribution of rights and privileges.

CONVERSATION

How should integration be measured in a home? How should the level of morale be assessed between alternative types of home? So far, no study has attempted to collect quantifiable evidence to calibrate the quality of social life between different institutions.[1] For the purposes of this survey, therefore, a number of indices were constructed to form a measure of integration, and they are combined on a single scale at the end of chapter 8. All are based on observable criteria and exclude socio-psychological measures of subjective satisfaction or sense of involvement which have limited utility with mentally infirm old people.

The first of these indices concerns involvement in conversation and the differential participation of the confused and rational will be explored in terms of the quantity, quality and purpose of talk, the varied conjunctions of conversational partners and the range of factors determining access for the confused to the networks of dialogue.

Degree of conversational involvement

In order to provide an action frame of reference for an empirical analysis of integration, a pattern of systematic observation was undertaken in each of the homes. For successive periods of half an hour some time between breakfast and supper, excluding mealtimes, the activities and conversation of each resident in turn, together with the relevant behaviour of those immediately surrounding or from time to time in contact with the person in question, were noted and concurrently recorded on sheets of paper divided into sixty half-minute periods. No tape-recording was used. Methodologically it can be argued that my presence watching across the room and taking occasional notes may have distorted the flow of inter-action that I was seeking to ascertain as unobtrusively as possible, but it has already been suggested (p. 11 above) that the regularity of my attendance quickly diminished any initial curiosities.

The data thus collected, having been scored by counting the half-minute[2] periods in which any conversation or activity took place, did not *prima facie* bear out the hypothesis that the confused were comparatively isolated. Firstly, the degree of apathy varied less than might have been expected. It was operationally defined as time spent sitting in a chair, with eyes open or closed, or lying on a bed, whether asleep or awake, but not indulging in any of a set of activities exhaustively listed, including conversation. On this basis, the confused in the separatist homes were only marginally more apathetic than the rational, though in the ordinary homes the apathy of the confused was significantly greater (Table 7.1), nearly seven-tenths of their time during the day being devoted to complete inactivity. Secondly, the confused in the special homes actually spent slightly more of their time in conversation than did the rational, though in the ordinary homes it was again the confused who appeared unduly isolated, less than one-twenty-fifth of their time being expended in talking (Table 7.1). Thirdly, the plotting of the amount of conversation undertaken by the confused, compared to the rational, against the proportion they formed of the total number of residents in each of the homes (Figure 2) yielded similar results. In each of the separatist homes the confused obtained

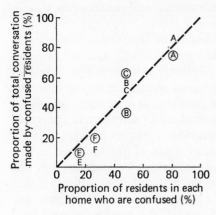

Note:
A...F Conversation index of confused residents
Ⓐ...Ⓕ Activity index of confused residents
A,B,C – Separatist Homes
E,F – Ordinary Homes
(Home D is omitted as no conversation or activity was recorded for the single confused person in it.)
'Confusion' entails one of the five components listed in ch. 3, excluding memory defect.
The broken-line diagonal denotes parity participation of the confused with the rational: points below the diagonal mean the confused get less than their share, and points above it mean they get more.

FIG. 2. Degree of conversational (and activity) participation of confused residents in relation to their numbers in each of the separatist and ordinary homes

Table 7.1

Indices of time use by confused and rational residents
in separatist and ordinary homes

Occupation of time	Residents of separatist homes (%)			Residents of ordinary homes (%)	
	Severely confused	Moderately confused	Rational	Severely confused and moderately confused	Rational
Conversation*	13·2	9·2	7·7	3·6	12·0
Activity †	40·2	39·1	47·1	29·1	45·6
Neither conversation nor activity	49·8	55·2	48·9	69·0	46·7
TOTAL ‡	103·2	103·5	103·7	101·7	104·3
Number of minutes of observation	1305	1660	2455	638	2985

* 'Conversation' here includes muttering to oneself as well as dialogue with other residents and staff.

† 'Activity' here includes all forms of action apart from sitting on a chair or lying on a bed, namely standing, wandering, (purposive) walking, knitting, fiddling with clothes or nearby objects, going to the toilet, eating, being led or helped by attendants, helping another resident, watching television, reading, personal care, cleaning or tidying up, smoking, looking for objects, doing a job for staff, giving or taking an article, etc.

‡ The proportions total more than 100 per cent because of the occasional overlap of conversation and activity in half-minute periods in which both took place.

marginally more than parity in conversational participation, though substantially less than an equivalent share in the ordinary homes.

Nevertheless, the implicit crudity in representing the data in terms of monolithic half-minute periods wholly ascribed to either activity or inactivity doubtless distorts the more flexible subtleties of interaction. Perhaps a more accurate impression may be gained by categorizing the conversational involvement of residents simply on the basis of the experience accumulated by lengthy and systematic observation. This approach provides a rather different picture. Firstly, more than half as many again of the confused in the separatist homes were judged reticent in comparison with the rational, while the proportion of the confused in the ordinary homes who were less than normally conversational was three times that of the rational (Table 7.2). Secondly, the regular conversational networks depicted in Figs. 3 and 4 reveal that whilst less than a third of the confused were integrated within a recurrent communication pattern, three-fifths of the rational were involved thus. In the ordinary homes the discrepancy was greater still: in comparison with a third of the confused who were embraced within such a framework, more than two-thirds of the rational were included. Furthermore, even this divergence understates the domination of conversation by the rational in both types of home, since many of them regularly used multiple conversational connections with others, while the confused enjoyed only single connections.

Table 7.2

Degree of conversational participation of confused and rational residents according to type of home

	Residents of separatist homes (%)			Residents of ordinary homes (%)	
Degree of conversational participation	Severely confused	Moderately confused	Rational	Severely and moderately confused	Rational
Talkative	(19·4)	(7·5)	7·7	(4·6)	4·3
Normally conversational	(35·5)	(55·0)	67·3	(40·9)	77·4
Reticent	(45·1)	(37·5)	25·0	(54·5)	18·3
TOTAL	(100·0)	(100·0)	100·0	(100·0)	100·0
Number	31	40	52	22	115

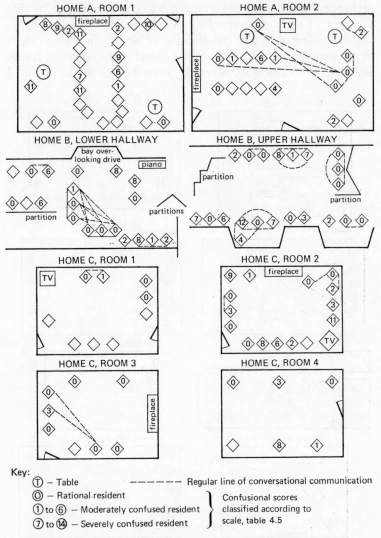

FIG. 3. Regular conversational networks in the separatist homes

How can the contrasting impression conveyed by this latter evidence be reconciled with the first set of data? Perhaps two main considerations are relevant here. Firstly, a sizeable proportion of the utterances of the confused represented, not the conventional exchange of sentiments, but a tendency to undirected garrulity that was part of the symptomatology of the confusion itself. This is largely confirmed by the classification of almost three times more of the severely confused than of the rational in the separatist homes as 'talkative' (Table 7.2). Secondly, even if some of the confused

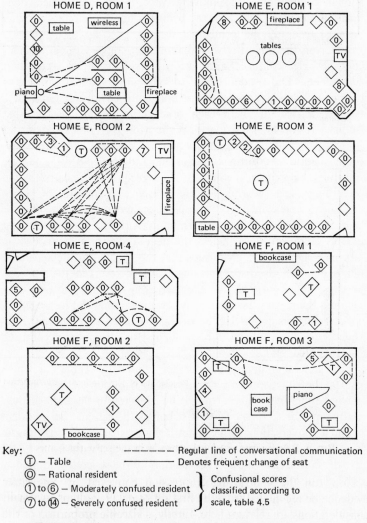

Key:
- ⓣ — Table
- ⓞ — Rational resident
- ① to ⑥ — Moderately confused resident
- ⑦ to ⑭ — Severely confused resident

--------- Regular line of conversational communication
————— Denotes frequent change of seat

} Confusional scores classified according to scale, table 4.5

FIG. 4. Regular conversational networks in the ordinary homes

residents did not indulge in loquacity, the fragmented and tangential nature of much of their dialogue, whilst scoring in the undifferentiated system of compilation adopted in this study, did not encourage their absorption into regular channels of communication. We can conclude, therefore, that the evidence presents a consistent picture of the confused in both types of homes, compared to their rational companions, as enjoying very much diminished conversational contact, which in the ordinary homes amounts to what can most accurately be termed ostracism.

But given the quantitative differences in conversational engagement between confused and rational residents, who were their respondents? Did residents tend to seek conversational partners at their own level of rationality, or did confused and rational alike share their dialogue with each other randomly? The fact that confused residents, particularly in the ordinary homes, fall so far short of parity of access to the regular networks of communication would suggest the former conclusion, and indeed this is largely confirmed by statistical analysis. The recipients of conversation were categorized according to the presence or absence of verbal rationality, and whilst the groups of tangential and incoherent residents are not entirely co-terminous with the moderately and severely confused, nevertheless the degree of overlap is extensive. On this basis Table 7.3 indicates that the rational in the separatist homes to a wholly disproportionate degree reserved their speech for those non-confused like themselves, while the confused distributed their conversation fairly evenly among both tangential and rational residents. In the ordinary homes the rational overwhelmingly constituted the respondents for rational and confused residents alike.

This general impression is further refined by Table 7.4 which reveals the divergence of the actual distribution of respondents among residents from what might be expected in the light of their relative numbers. In the separatist homes the rational devoted half as much conversational time again beyond a balanced weighting to other rational residents, but less than a quarter of that due to the verbally confused. On the other hand, both the severely and moderately confused devoted more than a proper share of their conversation to tangential and incoherent residents, but in markedly different degrees. The severely confused still devoted a majority of their attention to their rational companions and gave less than a quarter of the time appropriate (numerically speaking) to those whose speech was incoherent. The moderately confused, however,

Table 7.3
Distribution of conversational respondents of confused and rational residents according to type of home

Conversational respondents	Residents in conversation in separatist homes (%)			Residents in conversation in ordinary homes (%)	
	Severely confused	Moderately confused	Rational	Severely and moderately confused	Rational
Rational residents	27·3	27·6	60·2	(83·0)	76·4
Tangential residents	25·2	43·7	5·5	(1·9)	0·4
Incoherent residents	0·6	3·3	0	none	none
Staff	8·1	19·4	12·0	(9·4)	16·4
Self (muttering)	38·8	6·0	22·3	(5·7)	6·8
TOTAL	100·0	100·0	100·0	(100·0)	100·0
Number of minutes	173	153	190	23	357

Table 7.4
Distribution of conversational respondents among residential companions of confused and rational residents, in relation to proportion of companions by degree of verbal confusion, and according to type of home

Conversat'al respondents among residential companions	Respond'ts as % of total residents in separatist homes	Residents in conversation in separatist homes (%)			Respond'ts as % of total residents in ordinary homes	Residents in conversation in ordinary homes (%)	
		Severely confused	Moderately confused	Rational		Severely and moderately confused	Rational
Rational residents	65·0	51·4	37·0	91·6	94·9	(97·8)	99·4
Tangential residents	30·1	47·5	58·5	8·4	5·1	(2·2)	0·6
Incoherent residents	4·9	1·1	4·5	0	0	none	none
TOTAL	100·0	100·0	100·0	100·0	100·0	(100·0)	100·0
Number of minutes	(123 residents)	102	114	125	(137 residents)	20	265

were the group most favourable to tangential and incoherent residents, alone allotting a due share of their conversation to the latter and almost double that due to the former. With regard to the ordinary homes, it is difficult to obtain meaningful results since the paucity of confused residents usually meant they had little alternative but to accept a rational conversational partner. Even so the severely and moderately confused devoted almost half the appropriate conversational share to tangential residents, while the rational devoted less than a sixth.

If then in both types of homes the rational kept very much to themselves and the confused were comparatively withdrawn from conversational contact, what role did the staff play in the conversational network? Did they, for example, try to compensate the confused for their isolation by engaging them in discussion as often as their duties permitted? The evidence of Table 7.3 is somewhat equivocal on this point. For the rational in the special homes devoted half as much again of their conversation to the staff compared to the severely confused, but this is still very much less than the proportion which the moderately confused spent in talking to staff. In the ordinary homes the rational gave relatively almost double the amount of conversational time to speaking with staff in comparison with the severely and moderately confused. It seems doubtful therefore whether attendants and other staff can be construed as playing in either kind of home an active role in favour of remedying the conversational insularity of the confused. The evidence points rather towards their giving greater attention to rational residents because of the more rewarding response, and this is borne out by the admission of the matron of one of the separatist homes, in reference to the rational: 'I do devote more time to those who seem to benefit from it.'

One last piece of evidence serves to highlight the insularity of the confused in the separatist homes. While confused and rational alike in the ordinary homes spent a sixteenth of their conversation muttering to themselves, as did the moderately confused in the specialist homes, the rational residents in the latter devoted more than a fifth of their talking to monologue and the severely confused nearly two-fifths. Now engaging oneself in conversation may reflect, for the severely confused, partly the nature of their condition and partly a response to rejection, but in the case of rational residents it presumably suggests a preference even for self-denial of company in conscious repudiation of dialogue with persons of dubious rationality.

It may be argued, however, that evidence of the conversational restriction of the confused largely to other confused residents is weakened by the finding that half of the confused in the separatist homes[3] who were involved in the main channels of communication were linked to rational respondents (Fig. 2). But this apparent inconsistency is explained by the presence of negative as well as positive conversational ties. A few of the confused residents were subject to a recurrent theme of critical or pejorative remarks from their rational neighbours, and the existence of these links should clearly not be interpreted as alternative sources of conversational satisfaction. In general, however, it raises the wider question of the need to qualify the extent of conversation interaction by reference to its varying nature and purpose. This is discussed next.

The quality and purpose of conversational exchanges

Dialogue among rational residents was typically of markedly different construction and function from that which their confused companions pursued. For the former, conversation was often of a parochial nature, and any incident outside the ordinary routine, however trivial – for instance if a person tripped slightly on entry to the room – could provoke earnest discussion for a time. Clock-watching, too, was a constant preoccupation. In general, much of the exchange among the rational can be summarized as comprising those felicitous enquiries of courtesy that maintain the basic infrastructure of social relationships at their most superficial level. This attitude to conversation was reflected in the strong sense of self-sufficiency which most retained:

'I sit down quiet, and if they ask me anything, I'll answer, but I'm not a talkative person. I don't want to know their business.'
'How do you get on with the people who share your bedroom?'
'All right. They don't say anthing to me and I don't say anything to them.'

'They're all very nice if I speak to them, but they're all strangers to me.' [A woman who had been resident over a year.]

Indeed the formation of any close contact with fellow-residents was sometimes positively rejected on the grounds that it might constitute interference: 'I just pass the time of day with them, not a lot. I don't want to know others' business.' But although conversation among the rational typically was not used as a channel for the fostering of any depth of relationship, it was certainly characterized by an implicit acceptance of a fragment of reality governed by the conventions of residential life and knowledge of routine occurrences and the personalities involved.

The dialogue of the severely confused, however, was not necessarily fettered by the realistic constraints of plausibility, but neither were these necessarily germane to its central purpose. For this was less the exchange of relevant information than the use of the spoken word, irrespective of content, to establish and maintain social contacts as a defence against loneliness and rejection. Thus two confused residents were heard on one occasion, for example, to be discussing the shipwreck of the parents of one of them on their way to Tasmania, but the other was quite unperturbed by the improbability of the topic. Similarly it was typical to find confused residents conversing together at cross-purposes with each other about entirely unrelated subjects – though this is admittedly a conversational practice by no means limited to confused old people. However, it is true that even among those characterized by tangential speech, wandering tendencies and anormic behaviour, sufficient recollection of conventional proprieties survived to form the basis of a shared joke – that social event most clearly highlighting linguistic command.

> As a wanderer (confusional score 9) pursued her peregrinations across the room, another verbally confused resident (confusional score 8) patted her on the bottom as she passed, at which the wanderer turned round and scolded her jocularly, 'Oh you naughty woman!'

> When a disoriented resident started picking hairs off her cardigan, her marginally confused neighbour sardonically quipped: 'Moulting? Fleas?', and her friend laughed.

Nevertheless, in the absence of a constant check against escape into private worlds of fantasy imposed by at least a minimum of rational respondents, dialogue between exclusively confused residents could take on haphazard, transient and highly individualistic forms. This can be best illustrated, together with the accompanying breakdown of social organization, by an extended extract from notes of a continuous period of observation early one afternoon in one of the separatist homes:

As Mrs Heworden (confusional score 6) moved away from the corridor of chairs in the centre of the room, her seat was at once taken by Miss Leal (confusional score 11) who happened to have arrived at this point in her wanderings. Within seconds, however, Miss Leal had moved on again. Mrs Blissett (score 8) murmurs her complaint that 'her legs are going funny again', and her neighbour, Miss Flixton (score 1) gets up and walks away, her seat being occupied momentarily by Mrs Petty (score 12) before resuming her passage round the room. Mrs Longbottom (score 8) now moves in front of the fire and fiddles with the fireguard, while Mrs Hannan (score 9) also in the process of wandering (the sixth at this moment in a room of seventeen people), talks briefly to an attendant who has just entered. Meanwhile Mrs Capper, who despite her confusional score of 10 retained a sharp residual insight, comments aloud to herself on the curious behaviour of her companions. An attendant has now entered the room and encourages Miss Flixton, who had temporarily re-occupied a chair, to move into the next room to make way for the wanderer Mrs Petty to sit down, in the absence of sufficient chairs for all. It is now 1.20 p.m.

Suddenly Mrs Allingly (score 4) launches into the repetitive refrain she habitually employs, and is sharply reprimanded by her neighbour Mrs Watters (score 7): 'Don't be so silly even if you can't help it.' The culprit nevertheless persists and Mrs Capper, assuming her usual superintending role, reinforces the reproof with a sharp 'Shut up!' The altercation abruptly brings the dozing Mrs O'Neill (score 9) to life: 'Time? Time? . . . Left, right, left', tapping the wrist of her neighbour as she speaks; 'Big time, time for dancing . . . better not that my house be thought disrespectable.' She continues mumbling incoherently, mentioning 'holidays' which is perhaps a reminiscence of her life as a headmaster's wife, then adds: 'Robert, what do I call him? What does Mama call him? . . . Darling . . .' Meanwhile Miss Campleman (score 10) addresses her neighbour Mrs Rawdon (score 8): 'If you say to me . . .' But she doesn't finish the sentence and Mrs Rawdon looks round at her, uncomprehending. Mrs Longbottom is also heard to add her own private thoughts: 'Ought to know after a little time.' Simultaneously Mrs O'Neill has launched into a further stream of monologue: 'The birds are very intelligent. They know what to do and how to get it. Food.' Then turning to the person who happened to be seated beside this point in her wanderings, she remarked eagerly, pursuing her association of ideas: 'The tuck shop. Have you seen the tuck shop? Like it?' 'All right,' nods a nearby listener, Mrs Longbottom, fittingly. With the burble of her talk jarring some-what with the repetitive chorus of Mrs Allingby, Mrs O'Neill continues unabashed to serenade a resident who does not reply: 'We had a most amazing game.' The antiphony is maintained by Mrs Longbottom along her own independent line of thought: 'We'll have to be polite.' Again Mrs O'Neill: 'Do you think it's all right? First Sunday in the month. Ask Mama, perhaps she'll know.' She then suddenly lifts her skirt to expose a stain on her slip. 'How did I spill tea on that? Or perhaps it isn't tea?' She does not pursue the insight. Mrs Longbottom breaks in once more: 'The teachers don't want to sit down at once. Make it better for him [the observer]. Nobody minds much.' Mrs O'Neill stands by the observer, chattering all the time and referring to herself as 'Green'. 'You write so close,' she observes, 'your eyes will fall out. What eye colour do you call my eyes? Blue?'

At this point Mrs O'Neill approaches Mrs Pickles (con-fusional score 5) as the latter is nodding off. She accosts her rather abruptly: 'Want to rest? Can I give you company?' Apparently returning to the previous cue, Mrs Pickles remarks wearily: 'There's nothing wrong with my eyes.' Unabashed and propelled by a strong push of talk, Mrs O'Neill rushes on: 'I shall say I don't like Mrs . . . Mrs . . .', as she extracts the wedding ring off Mrs Pickles's finger. 'Mrs . . .', her companion replies, 'one is an engagement ring and the other is a wedding ring. Yes, it's getting light.' Returning to the ring, Mrs O'Neill rattles on jerkily: 'Nice, strong. I've got one now. I must have a look at the bedroom inside, to see if they've put it in the drawer. Don't want to drop it somewhere. I was using it all the time.' The time is now 1.30 p.m.

Meanwhile Miss Campleman has been muttering repetitively to herself. Mrs O'Neil, still blossoming in her outburst of garrulity, now approaches the observer: 'Poor chap, they do give you a lot to do. Show me your work when it's finished, all neatly

primed, primmed and pronged.' Mrs Longbottom mutters something into her breath, while Miss Campleman echoes loudly across
the room: 'I think ... I think ... I think ...' Simultaneously
Mrs Rawdon makes faces as though she is surprised by the
conversation.

Miss Flixton now re-enters the room and immediately plies
Mrs Reay (confusional score 2) with questions about the where-
abouts of the stick she has mislaid, as though she suspected that
the other's stick was her own. Two attendants lead in Mrs
Hannan and put her in a chair, but she soon rises and resumes
her wandering. One of the attendants then brings Miss Vose
(confusional score 11) to her feet, and puts down in her place
Mrs O'Neill who is promptly addressed by Mrs Hannan who
has reached this point in her circuit of the room: 'It's a place for
walking through, I think.' Miss Campleman, who has been
mumbling rhythmically throughout as she pulls at the nightdress
under her nightgown, from time to time raises her voice: 'It'll be
all right, among my own people. I've got to make them like it.
Do it quietly.' Continuing with what may be reflections on her
former career, as the matron of a residential home, she suddenly
says: 'I'd better get on with the second post.' She then takes hold
of a skein of wool lying nearby and her neighbour, Mrs Rawdon,
strikes up a dialogue: 'Have I got it?' Miss Campleman: 'Got it?
That's right.' Mrs Rawdon: 'Oh you are strong.' Miss Campleman, perhaps mishearing: 'Making love?' Mrs Rawdon: '*You're*
making love.' Miss Campleman, certainly now mishearing: 'No,
I can't make it last. Could you put one finger there and another
there?' She holds up the wool for Mrs Rawdon, who replies: 'I
don't mind.' Miss Campleman, again misunderstanding: 'No,
they're not dyed. Wish they were. Nothing to go down there
really. Tuck it away. Don't let it go.' Mrs Rawdon, imitating:
'Don't let it go.'

Meanwhile Mrs Griffin (confusional score 9) has entered the
room and sat down on a chair by one of the side tables. Three
residents have been wandering about the room almost continuously and Mrs Capper, in apparent reference to them,
mutters sotto voce: 'They want chucking out.' Miss Campleman,
reverting to a private monologue announces: 'It's a half-way
home, I think.' Memories of her matron's experience still flicker.
Mrs Griffin addresses Miss Leal as she proceeds with her inter-

minable peregrinations: 'Would you like to sit here?' 'Yes,' Miss
Leal replies, but wanders on just the same. 'I thought perhaps my
sister was here,' remarks Mrs Griffin wistfully. Mrs Hannan
has now entered the room again, clad in a dressing-gown, and
she advances on Mrs Griffin. 'Can you tell me where my clothes
are?' 'I haven't got them,' replies Mrs Griffin rather non-
chalantly; 'what sort of clothes?' 'I think the clothes I want to
put on,' comes the answer. She then importunes Miss Vose for
her clothes, but the latter is asleep, so she moves on to Mrs
Capper. Weary and bewildered, she confides in Mrs O'Neill:
'I've got no clothes on me except my night-gown.' 'No, not coming
off,' responds Mrs Rawdon, quizzically. It is now 1.40 p.m.

As the wanderers still wander and Miss Campleman still mum-
bles incoherently in the background, Mrs Hannan pursues her
fruitless search. 'I don't know where my clothes are. I can't find
anything here.' Mrs Griffin asks her tentatively: 'You won't be
cold, will you?' 'Not that, I want my knickers,' moans Mrs
Hannan. Undaunted, Mrs Griffin turns her question to Miss
Leal who is approaching: 'You're not cold, are you dear?' At this
point Mrs Blissett returns to the room and joins the refrain about
lost clothes: 'Is there no one to look to me? Little bit here, little
bit there. No clothes to put on. Wish I could find the police. I've
no proper clothes or anything.' Suddenly Mrs Reay's stick falls
to the floor with a crash and Mrs Capper picks it up for her. Mrs
Blissett persists with her lament: 'I've got one stocking on one
leg and one shoe on another, and nothing more. I wish the police
were here.'

These seemingly fortuitous, bizarre and unpredictable exchanges
were confined to the sole sitting room covered by this study which
was occupied almost exclusively by residents who were severely
confused. How did the confused 'make out' in conversation when
they sat with rational neighbours and yet were often rejected by
them, as has been shown?

Different conversational 'fits'

It was particularly noticeable that where confused residents regularly talked with rational neighbours, it was often within the

compass of one of a number of dyadic or occasionally triadic relationships each of which was uniquely constituted. In one separatist home, for example, one group was composed of a garrulous schizophrenic and a laconic subnormal resident of low intelligence. In another pair, a woman who was rational but deaf sat next to a confused resident whose loquacity was diffuse and irregular, but the exclusiveness of their disabilities enabled them to converse at cross-purposes with each other without irritation to either. In a third case, a rational resident sat between two severely confused persons who constantly quarrelled and devoted her soothing powers to pacifying their animosities. How far such instances of 'happy juxtaposition' were the result of deliberate staff policy aimed to minimize social conflict is not clear, though some of the staff did occasionally claim credit for this.

Nor were such pairings confined to the contingencies of the seating distribution. A rational but severely incapacitated resident, for example, in one of the special homes regularly walked each day with the aid of his crutches down the hallway to talk to a severely confused woman, perhaps because he was flattered by her deference and apparent readiness to listen without interruption to his interminable sporting reminiscences. Again, an exuberant but very confused woman who was sometimes taunted by residents and attendants alike for her comic extravagances found solace and acceptance from the handyman and the newspaper vendor on his daily round. These 'fits', however, were exceptions rather than the rule, and we must still ask why in general the rational tended to reject the confused for conversational purposes.

Conversational reactions of rational residents to the confused

One factor which may have contributed towards the ostracism of the confused is the state of their dress, together with any lingering smell of incontinence if they were thus prone. Table 7.5 shows that poor personal appearance, marked by foodstains on clothes, slipping stockings, disordered neckwear or similar characteristics, was strongly associated with confused behaviour, particularly if severe. But whilst the rational presented a significantly better personal appearance (as judged by the author) than the confused in both kinds of home, it also reveals that the confused in the ordinary homes were much more likely to offer a 'good' appearance than their counterparts in the separatist homes,[4] and this may have contributed towards their greater degree of integration.

Table 7.5

The state of personal appearance of confused and rational residents in specialist and ordinary homes

| State of personal appearance | Residents of separatist homes (%) | | | Residents in ordinary homes (%) | |
	Severely confused	Moderately confused	Rational	Severely and moderately confused	Rational
Good	(16·1)	(52·5)	71·2	(68·1)	83·5
Indifferent	(32·2)	(40·0)	23·1	(27·3)	16·5
Poor	(51·7)	(7·5)	5·7	(4·6)	0
TOTAL	(100·0)	(100·0)	100·0	(100·0)	100·0
Number	31	40	52	22	115

The main reason, however, adduced by rational residents in the special homes for their repudiation of the confused was the alleged conversational ineptitude of the latter: 'I don't talk very much to the other residents as a lot of them are senile, and they've got to understand you.' 'You know pretty well – if they don't read, there's not much to talk about.' At best, experience of the conversational jerkiness and tangentiality of the confused produced a feeling of unsympathetic tolerance: 'If they talk to me, I talk to them. But there isn't one you could make a friend of. They're too stupid. One said at 1.20 p.m. today, having just had dinner, "Have we had dinner?" ' Or it could cause a desire, even among the sympathetic, to escape from the confused: 'Lot who shouldn't be here. But they can't help it. I try to shake them off by saying I must have a wash before tea.' At worst it could generate an angry resentment at being confined with a despised group:

'Nobody can talk in my room. They seem to be imbeciles – even children could do better. I'm a sane person; I like to talk about politics. It's driving me melancholy mad. Nobody to talk to. Only sane ones to talk to are the attendants. Matron's very nice, but I don't suppose I've had half an hour's conversation with her since I've been here. Only talk to the underlings and they can't help you. Anyway I think matrons in all homes don't like us to be too friendly with staff.'

171

'Mrs Shaughnessey's about the only one who you can talk to, and she takes me to the toilet [the speaker was blind]. As for one in the room – the language! Never heard such filthy language, and another woman's not quite so bad. Why should I, a sane person, sit with a lot of mad people? How can I be moved? My son is an estate manager, and my daughter teaches at the Polytechnic, so you can see we're not used to this sort of life.'

'Thank God I've got all my faculties. To me it's like being in prison. The others do tell Mrs Allnough to be quiet and shut up, but they've not got the intellect to complain. I got bored in the other home [she had recently been transferred to this separatist home], but it wasn't like living in solitary confinement here, with all the gibberish. Though there's a danger that if all the intelligent were put together, they may backbite. Scandal.

'But them [the confused], they should be removed. They're making others mad. They should be segregated in their own home, and they should be kept in one room to themselves, not be mixed up. I blame those who put them here.'

'I told one old lady who had lost her memory: "You have amnesia. You should listen to songs on TV. There might be old ones, and perhaps your memory will come back." She loved me for talking to her.'

Lastly, given this repudiation of the confused, how far was it promoted by the structural arrangements of the chairs room by room and by the allocation of residents to them throughout the home?

Seating patterns as an influence on communications

How far was the conversational involvement of the confused enhanced or retarded by a varying numerical balance between them and rational residents in any room? And to what extent did the positioning of confused residents in each room affect their participation in any exchange of dialogue? Or were other factors more important in this respect?

Now Figs. 3 and 4 illustrate that the balance per room between confused and rational residents varied from 13 : 1 to 1 : 6 respectively in the separatist homes and from 4 : 17 to 1 : 18 respectively in the ordinary homes. Apart from the unique instance of a sitting room in one of the special homes where the confused formed an overwhelming majority, there was no clear evidence that any particular proportion of confused residents in a room either stimulated or impeded conversation. Only in this single case where informal efforts were made to preserve the strict demarcation of their territory from the rest of the home were the confused denied at least the casual greetings of rational companions as they daily moved around the home. More important in this context than the precise numerical weighting seemed to be the degree of personality extraversion or otherwise of residents, whether confused or not, the pervasiveness of processes of institutionalization, and the impression cumulatively created by disconnected replies from any individual. In the last respect, where only occasional irrelevancies or non-sequiturs were introduced, conversation was generally tolerated, and persons whose speech exhibited this limited faultiness did initiate dialogue and were not ignored by others. Where, however, the syllables uttered were meaningless or speech was abruptly halted at a crucial referential noun, or where sentences degenerated into repetition before the meaning could become clear, such persons were likely to be isolated. Others ignored them and they themselves hardly ever introduced any conversational exchange.

It is not only the distribution of confused residents *between* rooms, but their location *within* rooms which may have affected their access to the main channels of communication. Were they evenly distributed round the rooms, or were the seats they occupied in an isolated position, or were they bunched into groups? Again, Figs. 2 and 3 reveal a definite tendency, particularly in the separatist homes, for confused residents to be located either at the end of a line of chairs or on the edge of conversational groupings. How far the staff were responsible for their isolation, whether through their informal allocation of seating at first admission or through guiding confused residents who were also blind or arthritic to their chairs, is not clear and is re-examined later (see p. 188, 'Structured isolation'). Certainly the dominant positions commanding a view of whatever activities were happening tended to be monopolized by rational residents, and, moreover, a place at the extremity of a row of chairs minimized opportunities for participation because conversation usually followed a linear pattern round the walls of the room.

The first index of integration, therefore, conversational participation, reveals the confused as comparatively isolated, especially in the separatist homes, though able to compensate to some extent through the formation of a mutually satisfactory combination with certain other handicapped individuals. In general, speech was used by them, irrespective of its precise rationality, to maintain social contacts, though such an exclusive attitude to conversation was alien to most rational residents and invited rejection by them, which was facilitated by the locational extrusion of the confused to the edges of the room.

COMMUNAL ACTIVITIES

The second index of integration takes account chiefly of friendship and activity groupings within the home. Now it has already been shown in Table 7.1 how extensive is the inactivity of both confused and rational residents in both types of home, in terms of time spent during the day merely sitting on a chair or resting on a bed. In this sense the confused in the separatist homes were inactive for three-fifths of the day and the confused in the ordinary homes even more so (seven-tenths), whilst inactivity among rational residents was less, though only slightly so in the special homes (53 per cent and 54 per cent respectively). Of the time that was in fact devoted to some form of activity, however, Table 7.6 reveals that, apart from wandering and fiddling which are components in the pathology of confusion itself, the main significant differences between the rational and the confused in the separatist homes lay in the greater emphasis the former gave to reading, personal care and smoking. In the ordinary homes, on the other hand, the rational spent more time in particular on reading and watching television, while the confused were significantly more occupied in toileting, personal care and 'cleaning and tidying up'. These latter two categories encapsulate a rather heterogeneous range of activities and do not therefore disqualify the general conclusion that not only is the extent of activity of confused residents in both types of home more restricted than that of their rational companions, but the ambit of what activity they do indulge in is more circumscribed and mainly generated by the peculiarity of their condition. It is within this general framework of activities that this section will examine in particular the pattern of friendships, the giving of mutual assistance between residents and the distribution of pastimes and communal leisure activities.

Table 7.6

Nature and distribution of activities of confused and
rational residents according to type of home

	Residents of separatist homes (%)			Residents of ordinary homes (%)	
Nature of activity	Severely confused	Moderately confused	Rational	Severely and moderately confused	Rational
Knitting sewing[1]	13·3	4·8	11·5	0	8·1
reading[2]	4·4	17·8	31·4	31·0	40·9
walking[3]	14·7	17·7	14·4	22·2	18·8
standing	4·2	3·4	6·1	5·7	2·4
wandering	27·7	0·3	0	0	0
being led or helped by an attendant	2·7	0·6	0·3	0	0·1
helping another resident[4]	0·4	1·1	0·5	0·3	0·5
fiddling with clothes or nearby object[5]	13·3	17·7	5·3	2·1	0·1
eating[6]	2·7	5·2	1·4	0	3·8
watching television	8·8	8·1	7·8	7·7	14·0
in toilet	4·4	10·3	3·6	11·8	3·9
looking for objects[7]	0	7·7	2·7	2·8	1·2
personal care[8]	1·0	1·4	6·1	5·9	0·9
cleaning and tidying up[9]	0	0·5	0·1	10·2	0·3
smoking[10]	0·6	2·8	6·8	0	3·0
giving or taking an article	0·4	0·5	0·9	0·3	0·1
doing a job for staff	1·4	0·1	1·1	0	1·9
TOTAL	100·0	100·0	100·0	100·0	100·0
number of minutes of observation	525	649	1156	186	903

1. Includes the manufacture of objects in the course of occupational therapy. 2. Includes also occasional writing. 3. Defined as purposive movement from one place to another (including getting up and sitting down), where the aim and destination are reasonably clear (as opposed to wandering). 4. In particular guiding, or fetching an article for, another resident. 5. Includes also such miscellaneous activities as sucking or biting fingers, playing with a parrot, etc. 6. Includes the preparation of food, for example, cutting up an apple; excludes all organized meals. 7. Particularly in pockets, handbags and drawers. 8. Includes cleaning nails, combing hair, nose blowing, cleaning or putting on spectacles, washing or having a bath, powdering the face, dressing, removing hairs from clothes, spitting, etc. 9. In particular clearing away personal effects. 10. Includes preparing a pipe.

Friendship patterns

If friendship is measured by the tendency to seek out a particular person or persons for regular social contact, how far were confused residents united by friendship ties in comparison with their rational companions? Were such pairs composed exclusively of either confused or rational persons, or did they mix? And in what ways was friendship chiefly expressed?

On the basis of the definition adopted, in the separatist homes some 11 per cent of the confused residents and 35 per cent of the rational seemed to be involved in definite friendship ties, while in the ordinary homes only some 5 per cent of the confused and 26 per cent of the rational appeared to have such links. Also, interestingly, among the confused residents who had friends, the severely confused were disproportionately represented.

Even more significant than the much smaller proportion of confused residents bound by friendship links in both types of home was the composition of these pairs. Of the five friendship groupings in which confused persons were involved in the specialist homes,[5] three embraced solely residents who were confused. In both the other cases the confused person involved had a confusional score of only 1, and in one of these instances the confused resident was a member of a closely interlocking group of six persons.

How was friendship manifested between a pair where one or both were confused? The nature of the relationship was of two markedly different kinds. Where both friends were severely confused it was noticeable that a strong attachment could materialize despite the apparent failure of one or both to appreciate some of the subtler and profounder nuances of the bond:

A woman of eighty-one who was a directed wanderer, disoriented both of person and place, tangential in speech and liable to certain forms of anormic behaviour, was befriended on arrival by another woman of seventy-six who was a spinster. The latter desperately wanted affection and sought to express this in a direct sexual fashion. Her confused partner responded – and indeed their nightly embraces earned them the title of 'lovebirds' – but she appeared wholly ignorant of the significance of the sexual advances made to her, and when after a short time her amorous companion died, she exhibited no obvious sign of grief.

In another separatist home a woman of eighty-eight who was tangential in speech, liable to restless fiddling and aimless wandering, disoriented of both person and place, and occasionally anormic in behaviour had befriended, or more accurately 'adopted', another woman with an approximately similar confusional profile. But their personalities were entirely contrasted, the latter being reticent, vague and discursive in manner, while the former appeared voluble and forcefully, though affectionately, direct. The more active partner frequently seemed to cosset her friend with her importunities, tugging at her arm to induce her to walk with her, undeterred by her coolness and reluctance: 'Come on now. I've got to go now. Be a sport. Come on now.' At other times she interpreted her friend's vacancy as a specific call on her maternal protectiveness, eagerly pulling her companion towards a spare seat, 'I've found you a chair', or assuming she was hungry, 'I'll take you up [to the table]'. In spite of the lack of reciprocation and despite warnings by staff not to badger her innocent and long-suffering friend, she continued to seek out her company, to walk on her arm and sporadically to pour out her pent-up feelings of devotion and tenderness, however distorted and unintended the outcome.

Where one of the friends was only marginally confused the relationship took a more formal and verbalized form. But if such attachments lacked some of the more florid features of relationships between the more severely confused, they also appeared to lack some of their warmth and underlying tenderness. Thus a woman with a confusional score of 1 who was constantly found in the company of a rational neighbour spoke endearingly of the latter: 'I have a friend I sit with upstairs – she's quite a mother to me,' yet no indication was observed of the kind of intimacy which often persisted between pairs of rational friends, like holding hands or kissing a farewell. It was the lopsided direction of dependency between a confused and rational couple which rendered their friendship less one of egalitarian reciprocity than of a helping relation with predetermined roles of donor and recipient. Perhaps it was this lack of active mutuality which robbed such partnerships of a true sense of amity.

Why were the rational so unforthcoming towards friendship with confused neighbours? It was not as if rational residents did not desire more companionship. Remarks made by them included such typical sentiments as: 'I've lost all the people I knew. Not got a soul now. I've got people, but they don't care anything about one, don't care if I live or die.' 'I like the companionship of other people. I like to think we're all one community.' But many had resigned themselves to a limited social ambience: 'I'd like some more company, but as it is, I'm quite used to it.' Partly such insularity derived from passivity:

'How easily do you get to know the other residents?'
'Depends on them pretty much.'
'Do you discuss problems with them?'
'Not much. If they begin it. But I'm pretty Scotch. I'd probably not say very much.'

And passivity might be rationalized as a preference for privacy: 'I only know a few of them. That's enough. I don't want to know more. I'm not anxious to know people's arrangements or business.' Or even as a fear of a meretricious reputation: 'I don't associate. When I'm with people, I like to be introduced to them. You see, I don't know who this person is or who that. If a man talks to Matron, next thing they say is he's going with Matron or pursuing her, and I keep away from her for that reason.' Or passivity might merely reflect a feeling of security within the general company: 'They all like me, and call me Little Miss Brussel Sprout.'

Very few spontaneous comments, however, were offered about the company of confused persons. Only in the separatist home where the great majority were confused did they generate a reaction of escapism: 'I often go upstairs with Mrs Lorne after lunch and discuss funny things, and she says "Let's go out into the garden to escape from all the loonies".' In general it was the prevailing wisdom of almost all the staff that confused persons were accepted by others if they became so in the course of residence in the home, but not if they were admitted in an already deranged mental state. While the research procedures adopted in this study did not permit this theory to be properly checked, it did seem, from observation both of those very recently admitted with some degree of confusion and of those who had deteriorated since admission, that such a view was unduly mechanistic and over-simplified. Far more important as a touchstone of acceptability was the exact nature of the confusion and its capacity for disturbance, as outlined in the preceding chapter. Beyond a quite early stage in the process of decline the integration of those whose behaviour was characterized by interference with possessions, nocturnal disturbances, repetitive talk or incontinence became problematic irrespective of whether such symptoms began to be manifested before or after admission.

Assistance between residents

But if such excursions into real friendship across the boundaries of confusion were rare, did rational residents alternatively establish ephemeral links with their confused neighbours by the occasional service or act of physical assistance? Conversely, how far and in what ways did the confused offer such help to the rational or to others like themselves?

The support offered by the rational to confused residents seemed in both types of home to be of a somewhat random and unsystematic nature. In the separatist homes, for example, a rational man from time to time offered a match and struck it for a pipe-smoking disoriented neighbour, who gratefully replied 'Mark it up on the slate', even though the donor was well aware that his beneficiary never sucked hard enought to get the pipe alight and then requested help all over again. A hypomanic woman who was nevertheless ranked as rational on the criteria adopted here often led into meals a severely confused neighbour as well as two blind members of her dayroom; on another occasion, when a confused resident wanted a comb after a bath, she combed her hair for her, eliciting the remark that she reminded her beneficiary of her mother. A woman who was marginally confused in her speech and afflicted by a myxoedematous tardiness was meticulously attended to, not to say fussed over, by rational neighbours, one of whom would tie on her bib at mealtimes, whilst another would put her walking frame to one side and later return it to her, and a third would virtually combat the attendants against hurrying her up. Again, a severely confused resident, whose behaviour was characterized chiefly by restlessness, disorientation and tangential speech, was assisted with dressing each morning by her placid rational bedroom companion, who also made the beds for both of them. Such instances as these are, of course, selective, but they do illustrate the highly particularistic nature of such acts of assistance, their focus on the more moderately confused and their limitation to certain individuals.

It is obviously difficult to quantify the incidence of such help between different homes, though a matron in one of the separatist homes was of a strong impression that residents in an ordinary home where she previously worked were much more ready to assist each other. Careful observation supported this view as a comment on relations between exclusively rational residents in the ordinary homes, but their assistance to the confused in these homes did not seem more frequent or of a markedly different character. Two restless, disoriented and tangential residents were brought cups of mid-morning tea by an obsessive but obliging rational member of their lounge, who also gave his arm to bring back a mildly deluded resident from tea, carrying her bag for her. An aimless wanderer who was aged ninety-nine and unsteady on his feet was occasionally guided to a chair by a considerate rational companion. An incipient wanderer used to be reminded by her rational neighbour about changing her glasses whenever she embarked on a walk. A disoriented and blind woman was redirected by a shout from a rational resident in another lounge when she groped her way down a corridor in the wrong direction. Also noticeable was greater assistance than in the separatist homes to those with problems in eating, though accompanied also by more criticism of the wayward habits of some of those who ate badly.

What cannot be deduced from the citation of isolated examples, however, is whether such acts of assistance were irregular and coincidental or whether they constituted significant components within the mesh of social life in a home. Some impression of the social function of various types of supportive help can be gauged from these extracts from one half-hour period of observation in a room of one of the ordinary homes which contained four confused and seventeen rational residents:

Mrs Beulay (o)[6] cuts the fingernails of a temporary holiday resident, Mrs Travers (o). Mrs de Witt (o) drops her glasses and her neighbour, Miss Lossock (o), picks them up. Soon after Mr Hardcastle (o) gets up from his seat and takes over a newspaper to Mrs Beulay who is still talking to Mrs Travers. General conversation now ensues, and then when the tea bell has sounded Mr Wyke (1), known alike for his joviality and compulsiveness, goes out to get tea for three, asking Mrs Montfellier (8) as he passes if she would like a cup as well. Meanwhile Mrs de Witt has been upstairs to fetch a watch from a bedroom drawer for

Mrs Beulay. Mrs Redding (o) has been fishing out some cake from a cellophane bag she keeps under her chair, and offers a slice to Mr Hardcastle on his return, after he has distributed the cups. Mrs Redding then offers a piece of cake to Mr Potts (o) sitting nearby, who declines, but not to Mrs Grimes (8), his neighbour. After a while Mr Hardcastle gets up again and collects the cups, including Mrs Montfellier's which has been removed by her neighbour (o) presumably because she is both blind and severely confused. Mrs Beulay now winds up Mrs Travers's watch. Shortly afterwards Mr Tipping (o) arrives from the shops with tissues he has purchased for Mrs Beulay, and since he is on his feet the severely arthritic Mrs Ewing asks him to fetch two magazines lying on a table in the centre of the room, which he does for her. Mrs Beulay now gives Mr Tipping a letter to post when he next goes out, and as he leaves the room, she calls out to him by his first name and asks him to buy some paper handkerchiefs for her neighbour, Mrs Travers, who has just intimated to her that she would like a box of them, too. Mr Hardcastle then wonders aloud if Mrs Travers would like to have the box posted, and amid some laughter Mrs Beulay explains that it is not meant for posting.

While this excerpt is untypical in the number of incidents of personal service concentrated into a single half-hour, it nevertheless accurately reflects the manner in which confused residents (all but the most marginally so), though not ignored, are left willy nilly at the fringes of the social network.

If then rational residents, whilst not usually dissociating themselves from formalized assistance to their confused companions, did not utilize such services as a means towards achieving integration either, did the confused endeavour to establish such links between themselves through the medium of mutual help? Certainly the confused were generous in their support of each other, but again such acts of assistance appeared as discrete events rather than integral parts in a continuous and complex pattern of interaction. In the separatist homes, for instance, an active but disoriented man of ninety-four hurried across the room to help a severely confused woman get to her feet when she found difficulty in rising from her chair. An affectionate but very confused woman (confusional score 12) stooped to tie up a shoelace of a mildly confused neighbour, seeming unperturbed by the latter's ungrateful blank incomprehension. A moderately disoriented woman massaged the hand of a confused companion for some minutes when the latter complained that it ached, though apparently acting out her frustrated aspirations to a maternal role rather than affording obvious material assistance. In the ordinary homes, however, there were too few confused residents in too little contact with each other for any firm conclusions to be drawn in this respect.

Thirdly, even if the rational were somewhat disinclined, was there any evidence that confused residents took the opportunity through the performance of services to win acceptance by their rational companions? What limited data was discoverable on this question suggested partly that they did not, and could not, co-ordinate such systematic efforts, and partly that the rational might treat such overtures with a rebuff. Thus in the separatist homes a disoriented woman with disorganized speech patterns who on one occasion helped a rational neighbour put on her cardigan, when asked to do so, did not otherwise share a close relationship with her. Again, a mildly disoriented woman who more than once, despite her age of eighty-one, came across the room to help a sixty-nine-year-old rational resident who was crippled rise from her chair, did not normally participate in the constant interaction of the social group of which her beneficiary was a member. And in one of the ordinary homes a woman whose gross delusions and speech irrelevancies were superimposed on a very affectionate personality was observed once to offer to take out a chair for some card-playing rational companions, but was rejected and later rebuked for 'trying to do things she can't, like opening the door for you' (which she certainly could do). Again, a mildly disoriented woman whose speech was subject to spasmodic thought block frequently accompanied an aphasic hemiplegiac to the lift at bed time, and at meals often cut up food for a semiparalysed neighbour, was implicitly selecting the isolated for her attentions rather than establishment figures.

We may conclude, therefore, that while the help given to the confused by rational residents reflected the latter's feeling that they should not be excluded from the network of ordinary courtesies, neither such acts nor the reciprocal efforts of the confused themselves served to insinuate them into the mainstream of social life within the home. In fact remarks made by rational residents about offers of assistance revealed an interesting variety of attitudes to the confused. Such help might be dismissed on the grounds that it was rather the function of attendants: 'No (I don't feel any sense of responsibility for them), as one can always get a nurse, if they do anything wrong or become aggressive.' Or help was construed in a narrow sense: 'They've got no memory. If they could help it, they would. I'm a bit sorry, but don't seem able to help them. It's not as if they asked me to write a letter for them which I certainly would. There are nurses here, aren't there?' Or refusal might be rationalized as preservation of the self-respect of the confused: 'They might resent it. You don't want them to think that you think they're funny.' Indeed a definite distinction was drawn between physical handicap and mental disability. A rational resident in one of the ordinary homes, for example, who referred to confused companions as 'deranged' and clearly regarded them as beyond the reach of personal services, nevertheless was very attentive to the needs of two blind neighbours at table. It was perhaps symptomatic of the same approach that when rational residents did actually give assistance to confused persons, their manner was sometimes rather brusque and authoritarian. A woman distributing the mid-morning tea, for instance, finding that a severely confused resident neglected the offer, administered the cup to her with the impatient injunction, 'Come on, *drink* it'.

Pastimes and leisure activities

Lastly, did the patterns of interaction so far described prevail also in the distribution of pastimes, particularly those demanding joint participation? Table 7.7 demonstrates that in both types of home the confused were more than twice as likely as the rational to indulge in no specific recreation, and in the separatist homes more than three-quarters of the severely confused spent their days wholly unoccupied in this respect. In virtually none of the pastimes did a greater proportion of confused residents participate than of the rational in either kind of home.[7]

Both the confused and the rational admitted they were frustrated by the inactivity. In the separatist homes, for example, rational residents made spontaneous comments such as: 'I used to do drawing, but they don't do much drawing here.' 'The only thing I miss is the absence of anyone to play cards – I love a game of solo occasionally.' 'I did a lot of singing in the Wesley choir', meaning

that she no longer had any opportunity to express her capabilities.
Or the responsibility for apathy might be projected on to staff: 'I
wouldn't mind if they asked me anything, and I could do it.'
Confused residents too appeared equally perplexed by the lack of
occupation, though they might also be inexplicit in suggesting a
remedy: 'I'd like to do lots of things. What? I don't rightly know.'
'Better if I'd stayed in my own place. I'd be better occupied. I've
not settled down. I go out each day. I don't think I'm ill enough to
come in. Others have had a family and need a rest more. The others
think me restless, but they just sit down.' 'I'd like to go for more
walks if I could find someone [to walk with].'

Table 7.7

**Recreational pursuits of confused and rational
residents in separatist and ordinary homes**

Regular recreational pursuits	Residents of separatist homes (%)			Residents of ordinary homes (%)	
	Severely confused	Moderately confused	Rational	Severely and moderately confused	Rational
Reading	(3)	(28)	38	(23)	31
Knitting or sewing	(16)	(18)	21	(5)	16
Watching TV	(10)	(23)	37	(14)	29
Walking *	(6)	(5)	23	(27)	36
Domestic chores †	(3)	0	6	(14)	3
Caring for animals, birds, pets	0	0	6	0	1
Gardening	(3)	0	0	0	1
No recreational pursuit	(77)	(55)	29	(55)	24
TOTAL ‡	(118)	(129)	160	(138)	141
Number	31	40	52	22	115

* Excludes wandering.

† Comprising housework and washing up, and excluding lighter tasks such as laying or clearing tables.

‡ The totals exceed 100 per cent since many residents pursued more than a single pastime.

This picture, based on lengthy observation of six homes, forms a
puzzling contrast to the ideals expressed by matrons interviewed in
the course of another study:

Rejection and deprivation: the loneliness of the confused

The widely experienced matrons of two homes caring exclusively for the mentally confused were virtually unanimous on general principles when they were consulted. . . . There is general agreement that one of the best insurances against a restless night is a reasonably active and interesting day. . . . A daily walk, or mild pottering in the garden if an old lady is physically up to it, helps to work off their energy. The homes have discovered that even people who are rather noticeably astray can enjoy doing handwork of various kinds, and produce quite creditable specimens, but few of them are capable of persevering at this kind of activity unless they are in a group with somebody to help and encourage them. 'Handwork' is a term that can be used widely. It can imply knitting blanket-squares or making felt rabbits; equally it may mean unravelling a pile of wool for an old lady who would otherwise be worrying her scarf or her bedcover to bits.

All these things the matrons encouraged, even to the extent of allowing their charges to take mild risks, which they felt were to be preferred to the frustration and hopelessness produced by constantly checking and forbidding them. Both set great store on the personal appearance of the old ladies, agreeing that feminine vanity was a valuable aid in maintaining self-respect. Nice clothes were encouraged and soft, becoming colours preferred to black and slate-grey. There were regular visits to the hairdresser, with the full flattering routine of a cup of tea and biscuits under the drier and picture magazines to look at. One of the Homes arranged sessions for removing facial hair for those who needed it. The underlying idea is that a normal appearance, normal surroundings and, as far as possible, a normal routine, are aids to normal behaviour (Roberts, 1961, pp. 14–15).

Apart from the issue of the degree of permissiveness granted to confused residents, which is discussed in the next chapter, how far is this impression of organized group activities validated by examination of the actual routine?

Occupational therapy was confined to two of the separatist homes, none being arranged in any of the ordinary homes. The sessions in one case were two mornings a week, in the other three afternoons a week,[8] and whilst the therapy was usually presented with vigour, its impact tended to be ephemerally dramatic rather than long-lastingly integrative:

Mrs Littlewoode, the therapist, revelled in a flamboyant and effusive manner, commending herself on her arrival, sometimes accompanied by her daughter, with an affectionate if somewhat artificial endearment to various residents as she passed through. She then dispensed materials for knitting or sewing or for the making of small ornamental objects, spending the rest of her two-and-a-half hours slowly touring round the assembled groups, with between a quarter of a minute to two minutes encouraging, admiring or cajoling each individual, till she departed with equal flourish at the end. Certainly her presence stimulated and enlivened with temporary sparkle a routine otherwise heavily encumbered with apathy, but her forceful middle-class self-confidence contrived to be rather a focus of activity than a catalyst. Interest was essentially directed at *her* at the moment of each confrontation, and it abated after her departure as abruptly as it had been aroused. Not that these shortlived tonic experiences were not much appreciated in their duration by the residents. But she did not possess either the skill or the persistence to draw out the more confused who did not, or could not, respond to her instant glamour. When, for example, she asked one such person if she wanted to knit and the latter merely stared back blankly, she quickly picked up a weekly magazine, placed it open on the person's lap and began to turn the pages, but still eliciting no response, she gave up and moved on to the next resident. To this extent she was more successful at enthusing the already active rather than uncoiling the bewildered loneliness of the confused.

No doubt the transitory influence of the occupational therapy[9] sessions should also be partly ascribed to the artificiality of the commitment, which did not escape the confused. One said: 'I do crochet, but I've nothing to make,' another was stated to be capable of doing beautiful embroidery except when she 'gets it into her head she's going home', whilst a third was declared to be 'excellent at making woollen balls, but sometimes just stares at her hands', presumably recognizing that the need was neither genuine nor urgent. In one of the separatist homes a group of half a dozen rational residents monopolized the manufacture of the sole article – embroidered needle cases – which the makers were found later actually to use.

If, then, organized work therapy had only a shortlived effect in arousing interest, did spontaneous joint ventures between the residents themselves more successfully engage the voluntary participation of the confused? Now another study found that social activities like tea-parties, newspaper readings or discussion groups did not increase the interpersonal contacts of confused persons 'who tended only to withdraw from participation unless approached personally' (Cosin *et al.*, 1958, p. 36). Also when combined with rational patients in mixed groups they were found to be 'consistently less happy than those in the homogeneous group', possibly because the rational became 'irritated by the remarks and behaviour of their confused companions, and tended to "snub" or "repress" them on occasions' (*ibid.*, p. 38). Though the declaiming of newspaper head-lines, for example, was vigorously rebutted in the separatist homes (see p. 136), the present study did not confirm this latter finding so much as the more subtle process whereby the participation of the confused was effectively neutralized as a mere ritual. Thus in two of the special homes a few of the confused together with a number of the rational bought newspapers from a vendor on his daily visit or had them delivered, but they were not brought into the subsequent interchange of papers between rational residents, partly because some of the latter placed papers they had finished with under the cushions of their chairs and only other rational residents seemed to know where to look. Further, some of the confused who took newspapers tended to look at them mechanically, perhaps partly because sporadic discussion of daily topics was circumscribed within small networks of rational residents. Again, though some of the confused joined in television viewing in the early evening, it was typical that one who had poor hearing and repeated the complaint 'Can't hear a thing, still it's a change', was not enlightened, and comments about puzzling or stimulating programmes were confined to the rational viewers present.

More straightforwardly, confused residents tended to be simply excluded from joint activities. In the ordinary homes it was observed that only one attended one of the regular religious services, photo-graphs passed round for gossip and edibles offered to neighbours tended to miss them out, books borrowed from a residents' library did not attract their support, and the occasional games of cards or dominoes did not bring them into wider social circulation. Indeed when on one occasion a rigid though intelligent ex-psychiatric patient, who did not, however, score on the confusional rating, was drawn into a game of cards with some rational players by an attendant, but was soon induced by an undercurrent of criticism to get up and abandon the game, her traducers commented sardonically: 'They shouldn't say they can play cards when they can't.' Possibly similar treatment would have been meted out to any confused residents who had been artificially drawn into activities otherwise dominated by rational residents. In the separatist homes, on the other hand, whilst the opportunity for joint recreation between the confused and the rational was diminished in one case by physical segregation and in another by institutional apathy, in the third home where open planning facilitated easier contact at least a minimum flow of communication was preserved between moderately confused and rational residents through the exchange of newspapers or sweets and accompaniment in walking.

The analysis has, therefore, confirmed the failure of the confused to be involved in a proportional share of the conversational networks by demonstrating that in both separatist and ordinary homes neither the friendship patterns, nor the framework of assistance between residents, nor the distribution of recreational pursuits adequately integrated confused residents within the social life of the homes. The next section will consider how far this isolation can be attributed to the structure of arrangements imposed by staff.

STRUCTURED ISOLATION

The various systems of allocating residents gave the staff great power in influencing the degree of integration or otherwise in a home. Such systems included the assignment of seating, bedroom and dining places, together with control over transfers made for whatever reason, and segregation of residents on other criteria, such as sex. These will now be considered in turn, bearing in mind the effect of staff procedures on the attitudes and behaviour of rational residents.

Seating

Staff influence over the placing of residents was important in that it constituted a partial limiting factor not only of access to conversational exchange, but also of the range of visual stimulation,[10] the leadership and control structure of the various rooms and the opportunity for establishing friendship relations. However, system-

atic and direct staff pressure in allocating seats could be traced in
only one home:

> In one of the separatist homes, in which 43 per cent of the
> residents were severely confused and 38 per cent moderately so,
> the staff appeared ready to assume, and to give priority to their
> assumption in practice, that the remainder who were rational
> would be more contented together in a room to themselves. The
> matron declared she had no intention to isolate any persons, but
> also that she pursued a general policy of putting together persons
> who might be expected to 'get along', which willy-nilly produced
> the disclaimed result. Whilst staff insisted that all new residents
> were free to sit where they liked, they did also show those who
> were rational on arrival into the room traditionally reserved for
> such persons, and the latter in fact tended only to leave this room
> if and when they gradually deteriorated. Five instances were
> recorded of still living residents, now all ranked as severely
> confused, whose mental impairment had caused their removal to
> the adjoining room. Nor had the other residents' complaints
> instigated the transfer, since I was told that they had only pro-
> tested about one beforehand. Only one of the rational residents
> had taken her seat on arrival in the adjoining room occupied almost
> wholly by the confused, but she had soon yielded to staff sug-
> gestions that she might prefer the other sitting room.

In this way a funnel was operated not only to channel confused
old people into special homes, but also within those homes into
separated territories. And once the demarcations were established,
several justifications easily secured their maintenance. When once
an incontinent wanderer was found sitting in the preserve of the
rational, an attendant quickly ushered her out with the remark,
'We don't want these chairs marked'; it did not occur to her
instead to fetch in one of the protective rubber sheets. Similarly,
if on a certain occasion not enough chairs were available, for
example at tea-time when a few came in for the daily ritual from
the next room, or for television viewing (since this room alone had
a set), it was generally the most confused residents who were led
out to make way.

Furthermore, this pattern of internal separatism was to be
extended. In order to prevent the rational being disturbed by
wanderers, and also to avoid the time-consuming energy in getting

confused residents upstairs to bed in a home without a lift, the sitting-room hitherto occupied by the rational on the ground floor was to be turned into a bedroom for the eight most confused residents, while the rational were to be elevated to the privacy of a daily routine on the first floor.

Though only in this special home were such efforts made to preserve the territorial inviolability of the rational, in another the staff policy in distributing residents had spawned some curious non-communities:

In this home two sun-lounges were reserved, one for men and one for women, for those, whether confused, anti-social or generally problematic, who were not considered suitable for the ordinary sitting rooms.

In the sun-lounge for men were housed five individuals. One was stone deaf and consequently often aggressive whenever he suspected (incorrectly) that he was being ridiculed. Another, who was acromegalic, was inclined to dribble and suffered from an impairment in speech formation. Another, a subnormal, was afflicted with slurred speech and restricted movement from a stroke and was notorious for his abrupt launchings into loud singing of his rather limited repertoire. A fourth, who was slightly disoriented and liable to repetitive questioning, could nevertheless with his wry jokes act the life and soul of the party if given his cue by attendants for a set piece. The fifth, who alone was severely confused, spent his time either staring into space or diffidently exploring ordinary objects nearby with minute curiosity. Needless to say, this collection of disparate individuals did not coalesce into a natural group, and careful observation revealed hardly any significant interaction between them at all.

In the other sun-lounge there was only one person. Her never-ending mumbling seemed at first incomprehensible, but the change in manner and content of her monologue soon showed how acutely aware she was of others present. But instead of being encouraged by constant human contact to develop a more recognizable means of communication, she was permanently isolated as being irreversibly confused. Her need for activity, channelled into the incessant restless fiddling of her hands which she had turned against herself by scratching her back and making it raw, was now inhibited by gloves which were bound on at the wrists.

No such techniques of separatism appeared to operate in the ordinary homes. Here matrons declared that factors influencing the allocation of seats included such considerations as nearness to windows – a prime source of wrangling, proximity to the toilet, and the need to avoid congestion at meal-times from too many wheel-chairs being required in any single room. Such guidelines did not specifically affect the confused.

Lastly, how far did staff policies of seating segregation for the confused exacerbate their isolation by seeming to legitimate their rejection? Such a question is difficult to evaluate precisely, but it certainly did appear that automatic and unthinking repudiation of confused persons was largely confined to the two special homes where marked seating divisions were implemented and to one of the ordinary homes where the staff sided unabashedly with the rational against a confused resident. The evidence is drawn from the accumulation of a wide range of indicative remarks and incidents in these particular homes:

I asked a well-institutionalized and self-confident subnormal woman: 'Do they [confused residents] interfere with your privacy?' She replied: 'Not really. I prevent them getting into the kitchen when I'm working there by blocking the door.'

A rational woman said: 'I don't like the deranged people here, so I go out when I can into the garden.'

A rational resident in one of the separatist homes showed her intense disdain for the other members of her sitting room, two-thirds of whom were confused, by pulling her chair away from the wall, turning it round so that she sat with her back to the others, and conversing solely with her blind but rational neighbour in the corner.

When a woman who was incontinent as well as disoriented and tangential in speech came in from the day hospital where she had spent the day, a rational resident, who was sitting in her usual chair next to the one normally occupied by the new arrival, rather pointedly rose to her feet and moved to a chair on the opposite side of the room.

Such instances were not uncommon where the environment seemed to afford an official sanction for rebuffing 'deranged' behaviour. Of course, it may be argued that rational persons, particularly in the special homes where four-fifths were confused, felt psychologically overawed at the imbalance which appeared as a challenge and a threat to their sanity and so naturally welcomed the opportunity to band together for their own mutual reassurance, regardless of the nostrums of staff. But this is a static view of the integrative process, and whilst a weighting of four confused to every rational resident may be considered unwise, territorial segregation is bound to polarize attitudes and actions and to generate unhelpful stereotypes. Conversely, territorial flexibility might have created greater understanding and enabled a less rigid means to be found for handling abnormal behaviour than the drastic solution of physical isolation.

Bedroom and dining-room allocations

Even if the distribution of seats in the special homes seemed designed to secure a degree of separatism, the statistics offer at least a prima facie impression that the bedroom allocations were intended to achieve a measure of integration. For Table 7.8 reveals that in the special homes a fifth of the severely confused and more than a third of the moderately confused shared rooms with at least one rational resident, while in the ordinary homes every one of the confused who did not possess a single room had at least one rational bedroom companion. Even this very modest degree of mixing needs some qualification. In four two-bedded rooms a rational resident shared with a person who was only very marginally confused (score 1–2). Again, one very confused woman, for example, shared with two rational residents, but one was subnormal, while the other had a history of extreme negative self-pity and never spoke a word to her companions. In the ordinary homes, too, there was a tendency for confused persons to be placed with rational residents who were either physically disabled or aggressive and anti-social. Thus in one home the single confused resident was allotted a room with a companion who was deaf and nearly blind and whose irritability had caused her transfer from many other bedrooms. In another home a severely confused woman shared with two rational residents who were disabled, one stone deaf and crippled with arthritis, the other a hemiplegiac who had become over-sensitized to every behavioural irregularity of her neighbour and seemed to regard her more as an unpredictable hazard than a potential companion. Similarly in the third of the ordinary homes one of the mildly confused residents was given a room with an ex-psychiatric patient who, though ranked as rational, appeared excessively rigid and depressed in manner.

Table 7.8

Intermixing of confused and rational residents in
bedroom allocations in separatist and ordinary homes

Bedroom partners	Residents of separatist homes (%)			Residents of ordinary homes (%)	
	Severely confused	Moderately confused	Rational	Severely and moderately confused	Rational
Shared with rational resident(s) only	(15)	(18)	(48)	(59)	66
Shared with confused resident(s) only	(69)	(46)	(30)	(0)	7
Shared with both rational and confused residents	(4)	(18)	(7)	(18)	11
Had single room	(12)	(18)	(15)	(23)	15
TOTAL	100	100	100	100	99
Number*	26	28	33	22	115

* Data concerning bedroom allocations could not be obtained from one of the separatist homes.

Integration would therefore be rather a misnomer as a description of policy in allocating bedrooms, especially in the separatist homes where seven-tenths of the severely confused and nearly half of the moderately confused shared exclusively with others similarly handicapped. Rather than being influenced by the opportunities for involving confused residents in potential friendships, matrons tended to be motivated by the advantage which confused persons presented as bedroom companions of rational residents who were problematic or difficult, in that they were unlikely to protest about the latters' provocations. Admittedly, these arrangements cemented a friendship between two pairs of confused persons which persisted during the daytime. But overwhelmingly the result in the special homes was one of division.

This effect was accentuated by two further trends. Firstly, the confused in both types of home tended to be placed in the larger bedrooms where opportunities for privacy were reduced. Table 7.9 indicates that half the confused in the separatist homes slept in rooms of four or more beds (including in one case ten, all confused, in one large dormitory who were the frailest members of the home), while in the ordinary homes significantly more of the confused occupied three- or four-bedded rooms. Secondly, confused residents, again in both kinds of home, were put to bed at a much earlier hour than their rational companions, and so lost the opportunity to enjoy the evening's entertainment. Thus Table 7.10 demonstrates that in the separatist homes 74 per cent of the severely confused and 40 per cent of the moderately confused, but only 17 per cent of the rational, were in bed before 7.15 p.m., while in the ordinary homes three-quarters of the confused, but only half of the rational, were in bed before 8.15 p.m. The significance of these differences lay not only in the forfeiture of television viewing by the confused, but more importantly their deprivation of contact with staff at the one point in the day when many attendants relaxed and conversed at length with residents.

Table 7.9
Bedroom sizes occupied by confused and rational
residents in separatist and ordinary homes

Bedroom sizes	Residents of separatist homes (%)			Residents of ordinary homes (%)	
	Severely confused	Moderately confused	Rational	Severely and moderately confused	Rational
5 or more beds	(27)	(11)	(0)	(0)	0
4 beds	(27)	(39)	(18)	(10)	6
3 beds	(12)	(4)	(6)	(38)	21
2 beds	(23)	(29)	(61)	(29)	56
Single room	(12)	(18)	(15)	(24)	17
TOTAL	101	101	100	101	100
Number*	26	28	33	21	97

* Data concerning the allocation of bedrooms could not be obtained from one of the separatist homes and one of the ordinary homes.

Table 7.10

Times of going to bed of confused and rational
residents in separatist and ordinary homes

Times of going to bed (p.m.)	Residents of separatist homes (%)			Residents of ordinary homes (%)	
	Severely confused	*Moderately confused*	*Rational*	*Severely and moderately confused*	*Rational*
Before 5.15	(0)	(0)	2	(14)	10
5.15–6.15	(42)	(15)	0	(5)	3
6.15–7.15	(32)	(25)	15	(5)	4
7.15–8.15	(16)	(20)	27	(54)	37
8.15–9.15	(6)	(35)	37	(9)	38
9.15–10.15	(3)	(5)	15	(0)	4
After 10.15	(0)	(0)	4	(14)	4
TOTAL	99	100	100	101	100
Number	31	40	52	22	115

For meals the disposition of residents at table was similar in its extent of intermingling confused with rational to their distribution between bedrooms. For in the separatist homes nearly half of the severely confused and two-thirds of the moderately confused had at least one rational resident at their table, while in the ordinary homes such an arrangement applied in every case, as Table 7.11 reveals. Nevertheless an elaborate hierarchy of segregation persisted in the separatist homes:

In one home the six confused residents with the poorest eating habits had originally been grouped together on one table in the single dining-room. The matron then had the table moved into the hall, away from the others, and finally into one of the sitting rooms, so that the six ate and spent the day in the same place. Apart from these six, there were a further four confused residents who were given their food each sitting in their usual daytime seats. One was treated in this way because she was too frail to walk easily, another because she protested vehemently against super-fluous movement, the third owing to her endless wandering preoccupation, and the last because of the severe osteo-arthritis of her knees. Also, two small tables had been laid aside in the main dining hall for two residents whose behaviour at meals was considered offensive by the others. One, who suffered from

Table 7.11

Dining table companions of confused and rational
residents in separatist and ordinary homes

Dining table companions	Residents of separatist homes (%)			Residents of ordinary homes (%)	
	Severely confused	Moderately confused	Rational	Severely and moderately confused	Rational
Shared with rational resident(s) only	(0)	(18)	(12)	(57)	51
Shared with confused resident(s) only	(50)	(25)	(18)	(0)	2
Shared with both rational and confused residents	(46)	(50)	(64)	(43)	47
Had table to self	(4)	(7)	(6)	(0)	0
TOTAL	100	100	100	100	100
*Number**	26	28	33	21	97

* Data concerning dining table allocations could not be obtained from one of the separatist homes and one of the ordinary homes.

extremely repetitive speech, had previously been called a 'pig' by a rational companion at her table because she spat food from her mouth, while the other, who was rational, had been found to kick neighbours under the table if they annoyed her.

In this home, therefore, a hierarchy had been established whereby only the confused with 'suitable' eating habits shared with the rational at dining table, and confused residents with eating habits of which the rational were likely to disapprove tended to be put rather with others like themselves in the dining-room, while those with the most socially unacceptable eating habits were taken out of the room altogether. In one of the other separatist homes, too, this segregation was paralleled by the practice of allocating those residents with the poorest eating habits to a separate and partly hidden alcove adjoining the main dining room. In the third home only two residents were detached from the main body at mealtimes and fed while strapped in geriatric chairs, one because she was disoriented, restless and incoherent, and the other due to the inhibiting effects of accumulated medication. Otherwise a real effort had been made to bring together confused and rational residents at meals, though even here some curious combinations emerged. At one table, for example, were grouped an active and garrulous schizophrenic, a reserved and unassertive subnormal, a rational woman who had been reduced to inert lethargy and rigidity by drugs, and a blind and delusional resident who usually appeared anxiously consumed in restless fiddling.

How far did the physical juxtaposition of confused and rational residents at the dining table facilitate conversation? Careful observation in the special home with a great majority of confused residents suggested such arrangements had little impact. For at the three tables where a couple of rational residents shared with confused neighbours, they tended to monopolize the conversation between themselves, while at the two tables where a single rational resident had three confused dining partners, one of the two was thoroughly inward-turning and withdrawn and the other directed her conversation to another rational resident at an adjoining table.

Lastly, did transfers of residents as arranged by matrons between bedroom and dining room allocations influence the pattern of integration in either kind of home? Such transfers were much more common in the separatist homes. In one of these homes, for example, five-sixths of the severely confused had been moved to a different bedroom at least once, and also half of the moderately confused, though none of the rational. Similarly, two-thirds of the severely confused had been transferred at least once to another dining-table position, together with a fifth of the moderately confused, though again none of the rational. In the ordinary homes, on the other hand, only a quarter of the confused and rational residents alike had been reallocated bedrooms, and only one of the twenty-two confused together with an eleventh of the rational had had their place at table changed. What did such transfers indicate? In the special homes they chiefly reflected either complaints by the rational about the irregular behaviour of confused bedroom partners or the wish of staff to have confused residents brought nearer to the night duty room as their condition deteriorated. In the ordinary homes, by contrast, such changes were normally provoked by personality conflicts between the rational or by the need to accommodate new residents with special disability problems. Exchanges of residents between tables were usually designed to ease interpersonal tensions, though on one occasion the matron in one of the separatist homes observed that a certain person 'is being moved to the table with the more confused ladies since she carries on no conversation'. The meaning of transfers, therefore, in so far as they affected the confused, was negative: those most disapproved of were shifted till they were found companions, whether confused or rational, who were sufficiently unassertive to accept them.

Segregation by sex

Finally, the acutest form of structured isolation was divestment of normal social contact between the sexes. In one of the separatist homes only women were admitted and in another the dayrooms were exclusively reserved either for men or for women, though none of the ordinary homes was restrictive in this respect.[11] Though these policies did not specifically touch on confused persons, it must have been to their bewilderment and frustration in particular that the regulations contributed. For sexual restrictions form a prototype of depersonalization:

> It is no libel on very devoted people that a few years ago the ideal of an old folks home or a mental hospital was not the jail as it really is, but the administrator's idea of a good jail – orderly, adjusted, tidy, full of contented old people praising God at church parade and, as it were, getting lost between times. . . . Introduce sex, and you somehow introduce disorder and danger. . . . It makes people people, and people are what we do not want in our institution – they are untidy, vocal, feeling and onymous (Comfort, 1967).

To this extent sexual deprivation may be seen as having weighed most heavily on those facing segregation in other respects. The evidence on this point, however, was ambivalent:

> In the single-sex special home a disoriented and incoherent wanderer was sharply sensitive to my presence, tending to follow me around until she could secure an opportunity to sit beside me. Being only able to hum and to utter one or two simple words, she sought continually to win my affection by humming and laa-ing a certain few tunes, breaking out into ingenuous laughter whenever I turned and smiled at her. But such attention was not confined

to the confused. One of the rational residents, a divorced woman of sixty-nine, was equally compelling. 'I'd like male company,' she confided on one occasion, and 'Come up and see me in my bath,' on another. Nor were such desires for freer heterosexual company limited to single-sex institutions. In the more open special homes a rational resident, who was a recovered schizophrenic, remarked darkly: 'I don't know that we can do what we like – we can't meet men. Not that I want to make myself a prostitute.'

CONTACT WITH THE OUTSIDE WORLD

Lastly, did this manifold segregation of the confused within the structuring of the internal routine, particularly in the special homes, extend to their relations with the outside world?

Visits received

In fact, the experience of the confused in receiving visits from relatives or friends depended less on their mental state than on the type of home they were resident in. For perhaps no single factor differentiated the separatist from the ordinary homes more than did the visiting pattern. Whereas more than half the confused and nearly two-thirds of the rational in the ordinary homes were paid weekly visits, the corresponding proportion in the separatist homes was a mere 2 per cent for the rational and only 4 per cent for the severely confused and 8 per cent for the moderately confused (Table 7.12). Conversely, whilst no residents in the ordinary homes who did have visits paid to them were visited less than once a month, in the separatist homes more than two-thirds of the severely confused and nearly half of the moderately confused and rational residents were in this position.

How are these very large discrepancies in visiting patterns between the two kinds of home to be explained? Firstly, because there are still comparatively few separatist homes, their catchment areas tend to be very much wider than in the case of ordinary homes. Of the three studied here, two drew their residents from throughout the counties in which they were situated, and the third, a voluntary home, accepted persons on a national basis, including Scotland, and did not in fact take a resident from its own county till it had been

Table 7.12

Frequency of visiting of confused and rational
residents in separatist and ordinary homes

Frequency of visits received	Residents of separatist homes (%)			Residents of ordinary homes (%)	
	Severely confused	*Moderately confused*	*Rational*	*Severely and moderately confused*	*Rational*
Never	(14)	(29)	(35)	(27)	17
Less than once per month	(71)	(45)	(42)	(0)	0
At least once a month, but less than once a week	(11)	(18)	(21)	(18)	20
At least once a week	(4)	(8)	(2)	(55)	63
TOTAL	100	100	100	100	100
*Number**	28	38	48	22	115

* Data on visiting could not be obtained concerning nine residents at one of the separatist homes.

functioning for nine years. For this reason more than a third of the confused and a tenth of the rational in the separatist homes were now more than a hundred miles distant from their nearest relative, yet this applied to none of the confused and only 4 per cent of the rational in the ordinary homes (Table 7.13).

Secondly, visitors were predominantly the children of residents, and significantly fewer of those in the separatist homes had a child (Table 7.14). Also, rather more of the residents in these homes had no close relative alive.

Thirdly, Table 7.15 demonstrates, taking a stay of more than two years as an index of chronicity,[12] that a much higher proportion of those in the separatist homes are longer-term residents and that such persons are likely to have either no visits at all or only very seldom.

Fourthly, it may be conjectured that the image of separatist homes discouraged visitors. Such considerations cannot, of course, be quantified, but some prima facie evidence tended to substantiate this hypothesis:

At the separatist home where four-fifths of the residents were ranked confused, I was told that one visitor's friend had been

Table 7.13

Distance from residential home of nearest relative of confused and rational residents of separatist and ordinary homes

Distance from residential home of nearest relative	Residents of separatist homes (%)			Residents of ordinary homes (%)	
	Severely confused	Moderately confused	Rational	Severely and moderately confused	Rational
Less than 5 miles	(11)	(12)	(15)	(15)	28
5–20 miles	(19)	(24)	(41)	(62)	26
21–100 miles	(30)	(18)	(15)	(23)	35
More than 100 miles	(33)	(40)	(11)	(0)	4
No close relative	(7)	(6)	(17)	(0)	7
TOTAL	100	100	99	100	100
*Number**	27	33	46	13	72

* Data concerning the place of residence of the nearest relative could not be obtained in the case of seventeen residents of the separatist homes and fifty-two of those in the ordinary homes.

Table 7.14

Nearest relative of confused and rational residents in separatist and ordinary homes

Nearest relative (including step relation) in order of priority	Residents of separatist homes (%)			Residents of ordinary homes (%)	
	Severely confused	Moderately confused	Rational	Severely and moderately confused	Rational
Spouse	(3)	(0)	4	(5)	8
Child	(52)	(45)	35	(62)	56
Brother/sister	(36)	(30)	33	(19)	18
Nephew/niece	(3)	(20)	13	(14)	14
No close relative	(6)	(5)	15	(0)	5
TOTAL	100	100	100	100	101
*Number**	31	40	52	21	108

* Data on relatives could not be discovered concerning eight residents in one of the ordinary homes.

diffident about the prospect of mixing with confused persons and and would not pass beyond the hallway at the entrance. Another

Table 7.15

Frequency of visits received by confused and rational
residents in separatist and ordinary homes according
to their length of stay

	Residents of separatist homes (%)				Residents of ordinary homes (%)			
	Confused		Rational		Confused		Rational	
Frequency of visits received	resi-dent <2 yrs	resi-dent >2 yrs	resi-dent <2 yrs	resi-dent >2 yrs	resi-dent <2 yrs	resi-dent >2 yrs	resi-dent <2 yrs	resi-dent >2 yrs
Never	(14)	(27)	(24)	(48)	(7)	(50)	0	(40)
Less than once per month	(45)	(70)	(52)	(26)	(7)	(0)	2	(0)
At least once per month, but less than once a week	(24)	(3)	(20)	(26)	(29)	(0)	23	(13)
At least once per per week	(17)	(0)	(4)	(0)	(57)	(50)	75	(47)
TOTAL	100	100	100	100	100	100	100	100
Number*	29	37	25	23	14	8	68	47

* Data on frequency of visits could not be secured concerning nine residents of one of the separatist homes.

resident (who was rational) declared that her daughter's husband on a visit felt disturbed by the confused because he was unsure what they would say to him and asked to sit alone in the panelled room specially reserved for guests. Again, another person's daughter stated that she found visits to this home very distressing and always asked her husband to accompany her. Another visitor was said to have asserted: 'Would drive me crackers if I lived here.' And the son of yet another woman, who had been resident over three years without a visit, had been more than once invited, but each time declined on the grounds that he 'could not bring himself to visit'. On the other hand, in one of the ordinary homes the attitude of visitors to the confused was one of tolerance and sympathy. A rational resident declared: 'They feel sorry for them. I've pointed them out, and they [the visitors] think I'm fortunate to be so well.'

The evidence, therefore, tentative though it is, suggests that a heavy concentration of confused old people in a home may generate a deterrent stereotype in the minds of potential visitors based on anxiety or fear of unpredictable reactions. If so, the belief in the 'oddity' of persons in the separatist homes may become a self-fulfilling expectation. For the relative isolation from visitors will provide scant opportunity to disprove the attribution of stigma.

Given the comparative infrequency of visiting to the separatist homes, does this overall picture conceal a substantially different experience of confused and rational residents *within* either type of home? Table 7.12 demonstrates that in the separatist homes, though the confused were rather less likely than the rational to receive no visits at all, they were also much more likely, particularly the severely confused, to be visited only very rarely. Furthermore, rational residents in the special homes were five times more likely to have either no visits or only very occasional visits than their counterparts in the ordinary homes. This means that in the separatist homes not only did the confused tend themselves to have fewer persons from outside bringing news to see them, but also they enjoyed less opportunity for contact with people visiting their rational companions.

At least two factors explain this comparative deprivation of confused residents in the separatist homes. Firstly, they were more than three times more likely than their rational neighbours to have their nearest relative living over a hundred miles away (Table 7.13), though significantly more of them as compared to the rational did have a child (Table 7.14). Secondly, 56 per cent of the confused in the specialized homes, in comparison with 48 per cent of the rational, had been resident over two years,[13] and Table 7.15 indicates that for both confused and rational alike such long-term residents were twice as likely to receive no visits at all, and in the case of the confused, more than half as likely again to be visited only very occasionally. It may also be argued that the deteriorating mental condition of a close relative may have seemed too distressing to some visitors and deterred them from returning. But no direct evidence was found to support this supposition.

What are the implications of this detachment from the outside world for residents of separatist homes, especially the confused? Above all, it represented the enforced relinquishment of the contacts which had solely, or chiefly, afforded a frail hold over reality. To an extent this was deliberately encouraged as a matter of policy. Thus at one of the special homes relatives of persons at admission were officially advised to leave some time before the first visit so that the old person could 'settle down'.[14] Even so, for many of the confused their memories of family life continued to provide an oasis of stability which largely explains their frequent preoccupation with the past, though this was sometimes mistakenly interpreted as a sign of senility.

> In one of the separatist homes one disoriented old man spontaneously treated every visitor who came to a showing of the small collection of family photographs which he kept in a wallet in his inner coat pocket. He usually accompanied this viewing by a recital of his full name, the day of his birth (accurately stated according to the records), the village where he was born and grew up, and the first jobs he had as a boy tradesman. Even when sharing a sitting room with only his three or four regular companions, he continued many times throughout the day silently to extract photographs, postcards and family letters from his wallet, to survey them one by one, and then to return them to their place of safe keeping.

For the severely confused, however, even visits from their children, if sufficiently irregular, might yield only a temporary breakthrough from the enveloping world of delusion:

> A woman in one of the separatist homes who was incoherent in speech, disoriented, an aimless wanderer and afflicted with a severe memory defect was visited about four times a year by either of her two sons. On one occasion when a son arrived, her eyes, normally other-worldly with self-involvement, instantly lit up as though she recognized him. But within a little she had resumed her wanderings, at one point actually coming back and sitting beside him and confiding in a slow and almost furtive manner, 'I don't think I know you.'

Only regular contact with visitors from outside fostered a continued interest in the wider community and an expectation of a possible return to it. As a former psychiatric patient in one of the separatist homes expressed it: 'I don't mind if they (relatives or friends) don't visit, as if they come, I want to go back with them.'

Secondly, and extremely importantly, visits, as symbols of the persisting attention of relatives, represented to residents the appreciation that they were still wanted within an intimate and exclusive family circle.

There was no shortage of evidence, particularly from the ordinary homes, to indicate that many residents were possessed of an inordinate pride in their families. One particular scene may be recorded here. The daughter of a rational resident in one of the ordinary homes brought in her newly born baby to show to her mother. The latter was overjoyed to take the child in her arms and carried it round the room for each of her companions to admire, almost tearful with emotion and repeating 'bless his heart' in endless benediction. Others, aware of their dependence on visitors might express their gratitude in almost apologetic tones – 'So glad you were able to spare the time to come' – but the sense of a confidential and special bond was unmistakable.

If therefore, as has been argued (pp. 43–6), some degree of social rejection plays a role in the development of a demented condition in old age, then the persistence, for confused persons now segregated in a special home, of this comparative lack of a close and intimate link with relatives outside must have been peculiarly devastating. In fact, so vital was the craving for acceptance within the family that the failure to receive visits that might have been expected could produce rationalizations to exonerate relatives from any suggestion of indifference:

'My niece comes every Wednesday, and I'm content if she doesn't come oftener because she's got a husband to attend to.' (In fact her niece visited only very seldom.)

There are rules which must be carried out. You can't have people coming all hours of the day. Though sometimes when you're a bit down, you feel as if: why don't they come?'

'My brother's now got a house and invited me to stay there. But he had lumbago, so I couldn't go. But I'll probably stay with him soon.' [A single woman who had not once during five years of residence been visited by her brother who had, as an alternative, paid for her to be taken out monthly by the WVS.]

'They won't come and see me as I don't go and see them as much as I used to.' [A single man of seventy-six with a sister living some two miles away who had never been visited in two years.]

'They come oftener than when I was up Crowfield' [a psychiatric hospital]. 'They couldn't afford it.' [A widow who had previously attempted suicide and who was occasionally visited by a daughter living about twenty-five miles away admitted reluctantly, when pressed as to whether she would wish her relatives to come more, that she would like them to.]

'My daughter and her husband have pals in their own age. They like it that way. Elderly people have had their fun. I don't want to upset their pleasures. But sometimes I wish they were nearer . . . I'd like to see my daughter, but I don't want to bother her.'

'I don't want to worry anybody.' [A single woman who had never been visited throughout more than two years by her sister who was living in the same town.]

Significantly, all these comments were made by rational or only marginally confused residents in the separatist homes. The more severely confused residents in these homes were equally concerned to assure themselves of being wanted and to protect their self-respect by various justificatory devices, but the means they employed was of a more fantasied and florid nature, as will be argued in Chapter 9.

Thirdly, the comparative absence of visitors to residents in the separatist homes meant a certain loss of protection and a deprivation of an important feeling of implicit reliance on an external source of support. Again, the import of such security is best seen in the light of its operation in the ordinary homes. For only here were relatives found to have complained when an elderly member of the family suffered an alleged affront as a resident:

In one case when two women quarrelled and one slapped the other's face, the latter complained to her son who immediately tried to have his mother's assailant removed by the police. Again, when a woman gruffly told her bedroom companion to pull herself together, the latter's daughter remonstrated with the matron because her mother was arthritic and in no fit condition, and sought the complainant's transfer to another bedroom. And another resident's children lodged a protest on the grounds that their mother had to sit next to an incontinent and disoriented neighbour, though this was the sole instance discovered of such a complaint. Both these protégées were rational. Interestingly enough, in view of the former example, when a severely confused resident was struck in similar circumstances, no protest was forthcoming from her family.

In the separatist homes intervention by relatives was infrequent, and instances recorded were confined to rational residents and covered such typical matters as requesting a certain bedroom with particular facilities.

More generally, the proximity of relatives gave a sense of support, and regrets expressed by residents of the separatist homes about the remoteness of their families may be seen at least partly as a recognition of the loss of access to this safeguard. A number of rational residents, after commenting on life in the home, ended resignedly: 'But I wish my family (or friends) were living nearer.' Again, the severely confused, less inhibited by the constraints of rational expectation, expressed their desires more straightforwardly: 'He's sure to come home for me – my brother and my son.' But such a reaction, in contradiction of experience, represented rather a pathological indication of the converse need.

Lastly, a lack of visitors involved a loss of those personal services which they often performed for elderly members of the family living away from home. Examples were found, in the case of rational residents in the separatist homes, where relatives, especially a daughter, took away and laundered clothes, bought new clothes and sent them through the post, and brought in wool as a supply for embroidery. One such resident, who was hurt that she had never been invited by her daughter to stay for a holiday, nevertheless declared her gratitude for the valuable help rendered:

'She's been a very, very good girl since I've been here. I don't lack for anything. She takes my clothes in the winter and brings spring clothes in the spring – useful when the clothes get dusty in the winter without a wardrobe. And because my bedroom lacks a wardrobe, she also made a curtain rail to hide the clothes.'

Yet no instance was discovered where confused residents in the separatist homes received such external services.

Excursions into the community

If then the comparative absence of visitors to residents in the separatist homes, particularly the confused, had serious implications, not only for their material support and protection, but also for their psychological wellbeing, was some compensation secured through more frequent excursions into the nearby community or repeated invitations to stay with relatives? In fact, once again the evidence pointed to a compounding rather than a balancing of deprivation for confused residents in the separatist homes. They were less likely than those in the ordinary homes, whether confused or rational, to indulge in walking outside the home and somewhat less likely than their rational companions in the separatist homes to make visits to friends or relatives outside, though such visits were anyway extremely few (Table 7.16). With regard to membership of clubs in the community, it was, with one exception,[15] only the occasional rational resident who attended. Similarly, those from time to time offered a ride in a private car by one of the staff, like those sometimes taken to church by the occupational therapist at one of the special homes, were, so far as could be traced, rational residents to a disproportionate degree.[16] Again, telephonic contact with friends or relatives outside, though sparsely used, was almost monopolized by the rational, and it was a rational hemiplegiac who complained in one of the ordinary homes: 'They don't let you use the office 'phone, and there's no other. I miss the 'phone more than anything.'

Table 7.16

Proportion of confused and rational residents in separatist and ordinary homes making visits into the outside community

Type of excursion	Residents of separatist homes (%)			Residents of ordinary homes (%)	
	Severely confused	Moderately confused	Rational	Severely and moderately confused	Rational
Walking outside the home	(13)	(23)	15	(23)	36
Visits to friends or relatives*	(0)	(3)	6	n.a.	n.a.
No outside excursion at all	(87)	(74)	83	n.a.	n.a.
TOTAL†	100	100	104	100	100
Number	31	40	52	22	115

* Information of visits paid to friends or relatives was not collected concerning residents in the ordinary homes.

† Some totals exceed 100 per cent since certain individuals both walked outside the home *and* visited friends or relatives.

This insulation from the external community which inevitably circumscribed the range of interests and activities of the confused,[17] had several roots. Above all, matrons nursed a fear that certain residents, particularly the confused, if given an unrestricted opportunity to explore beyond the bounds of the home, might come to physical harm. Nor were such anxieties unfounded:

The grounds of one old institution visited, situated as it was in the suburbs of a large town, were adjacent to a trunk road always extremely busy with traffic, and though the annexe for the confused was built at the furthest point from the road, accidents had nevertheless occurred. One woman in particular, I was told, had been in the habit of stepping straight out from the kerb to cross the road with the sole warning of a white handkerchief which she waved above her head, until one day this brief signal proved inadequate and she fractured her femur.

But even in the absence of actual physical danger, staff constantly feared that the charges for whom they were responsible might wander and absent-mindedly become lost. At one separatist home in particular this had happened not infrequently, and police on a number of occasions had had to be called in for a wide-ranging search. One typical instance involved a severely confused woman who, while returning by bus from shopping in the nearby town, had failed to get off at the appropriate stop with her mildly confused companion and was later found wandering through the streets of the next town on the route, blissfully oblivious of the worry she had caused. Attempts had therefore been made (with mixed success) to introduce a rule that certain residents should not leave the grounds of the home without the prior permission of the matron, and a gate had been locked at the end of the terrace.

What gave further point to these apprehensions of staff, it may be surmised, was the anxiety lest the distorted impression of reality which some confused persons cherished should tempt them to undertake expeditions regarded as beyond their powers:

A moderately deluded woman of seventy-seven in one of the separatist homes held to the yearning to pay a final visit to her brother over a hundred miles away. 'I want to get down to Bromley for a week. I'd like to get to my brother. He can't live long. Go to London Bridge Station.' Similarly, another disoriented woman of eighty-six constantly spoke of her desire and intention to return from rural surroundings to the large city where she had hitherto spent her life. Above all, it had once been discovered in one of the special homes that a severely confused woman of eighty-five had invited a few of the other residents to return with her to her house.

Of course the balance between regulations to protect residents from their own whimsicalness and those symbolizing an apparently authoritarian restrictiveness is a fine one. It may then be equally argued that the inclination to escape is more a product of the process of segregation than a characteristic inherent in the psychology of confusion.

Secondly, staff may have felt inhibited by the anticipation of embarrassments or misunderstandings which confused residents might unwittingly generate in public:

A woman who through a cerebrovascular catastrophe was now limited to a very restricted repertoire of phrases was on one occasion taken out on a summer bus trip from the home and in the course of the day whilst crossing a road addressed a policeman with one of her few sentences: 'You're a nice husband.' However, owing to dysphasic distortions, the sentiment actually appeared more like: 'You're a nice saucepot.' More seriously, confused residents might present a false impression of their situation, with distressing consequences. One mildly deluded woman in one of the ordinary homes was notorious among her companions for her occasional wild and unprovoked outbursts, which were accordingly discounted. But outside in the market-place her allegations that residents were contained by a ball and chain and subjected to other barbarities provoked a furore. Her listeners in the street returned with her to the home to challenge the warden, and their ire was only assuaged when he permitted them to make their own examination of the premises. Whether this incident arose from pure delusion or from mischief with malice intent was open to doubt. Certainly, no evidence was found in this survey of mis-apprehensions caused by moderately or severely confused resi-dents, whilst evidence was indeed found of accusations of staff cruelty and malevolent misreporting of dialogue by rational residents which may well have been designed to secure removal from the home on the demands of sympathetic and outraged relatives.

There was therefore little solid reason in this respect for staff to limit the access of confused persons to the wider community, and indeed too tight a restraint on outside contacts could breed in the surrounding area reckless and alarmist rumours about activities within the home which were totally unfounded.[18] This was illustrated by the hostility at first aroused when the warden of one of the separatist homes, on taking up his appointment, opened the buildings and grounds to the public for visits.

A third reason why residents in the separatist homes had comparatively little contact with the outside world was that some of the rational felt shame at being associated with the confused:

A rational resident at one of the separatist homes who admitted that 'being shut up here is not good' and complained that she had never been out on a car trip at all since her admission except with her daughter and friend, felt that her relations with the outside must be carefully controlled. She would not let her daughter come into the home, nor would she herself travel out with the other residents. 'I'm afraid that my daughter would think worse of me for being here with people like them [the confused], and I won't go out in the bus with them in case I'm seen with them.'

Similarly, another rational resident in the same home who had no next of kin and was wholly restricted in external contacts to business letters to her solicitor and a brief correspondence with her few friends at religious festivals, also remarked: 'I don't like to go out with all these people – the barmy ones – though they're all right privately. I don't want more outings with more people, but I'd like more outings privately.'

Such sentiments were, however, confined to the separatist home where nearly half the residents were severely confused. Assertions like: 'We don't want visitors; we don't want them to know we've come to this,' which were occasionally voiced in the ordinary as well as the separatist homes, were probably motivated at least as much by anxiety at the functionless apathy of residential life as by concern at the proximity of the confused.

SUMMARY

This chapter has revealed, in terms of conversational patterns, communal activities and friendship relations, the structuring of routine arrangements and contacts with the outside world, the failure of the confused to gain equal acceptance with the rational in residential life. Within small margins of variation the pattern was similar in each sphere of the social network. In most respects this applied to both types of home. In fact, the main contrast between the different environments was not necessarily between separatist and ordinary homes as such, but between those homes which permitted undiscriminatory intermingling of confused and rational residents and those which fostered segregation in every facet of the regime. In other words, from the point of view of integration, the precise numerical balance between the confused and the rational was subordinate to the degree of openness or restrictiveness of the administration. The only exception appeared to be where persons whose confused behaviour took a systematically bizarre or florid form constituted at least a sizeable minority. In such cases the evidence tentatively suggested that a defensive and rejecting pathology might be likely to develop within the coterie of rational residents who felt threatened.

NOTES

1. 'Sociometric techniques could be used, for instance, to measure the degree to which homes had become communities', but so far 'there is no sociometric data on service quality available for study'; Davies (1968, p. 39).

2. Since a half-minute period was counted positively, however brief the duration of conversation or activity within it, the scoring system is obviously geared to over-estimating the degree of conversational and physical activity of residents.

3. Since only five of the confused in the ordinary homes were thus integrated, the numbers were too small there to justify comparisons.

4. How far such variations reflect merely differences in staff concern about their residents' appearance in either kind of home is considered in chapter 8.

5. The numbers are too small for any conclusions to be drawn among friendship mixes between confused and rational residents in the ordinary homes.

6. The figures in brackets after each name denote the rationality (o) – confusion (1–14) score.

7. The only exceptions were the single confused man in one of the special homes who helped with gardening and the three confused residents in the ordinary homes who undertook domestic chores of various kinds. But both cases may merely be quirks of the very small numbers involved.

8. Though the prospectus rather misleadingly claimed that 'Occupational therapy is part of the daily routine and there is a well-planned programme of indoor and outdoor social activities throughout the year.'

9. This is corroborated by the results of a pilot experiment in which the performance

of thirteen confused old people at two-hour occupational thereapy sessions three days a week was tested against that of thirteen controls. It was found that 'these forms of treatment might stimulate patients while they were actually applied, but that their effect on the patients' state in between treatment sessions might be negligible' (Cosin *et al.*, 1958, p. 26).

10. Both confused and rational residents in certain positions in the small rooms of one of the separatist homes, for example, insisted: 'We don't want the door closed. I like to hear and see people, don't you?' Otherwise, they complained they felt 'boxed in'.

11. P. Townsend (1962, p. 140) found that 35 per cent of the postwar homes in England and Wales housed men or women only.

12. This is a conventional yardstick used also, for instance, by Brown (1960, p. 414).

13. Other studies have discovered a positive relationship between lack of visitors to persons in their first two months after admission to an institution and their subsequent chronicity. One study, for example, found that in one psychiatric hospital 83 per cent of the non-visited schizophrenic patients were still retained two years after admission, compared to only 25 per cent of the visited patients with this disorder. Also, two-thirds of the non-visited patients had either no known relatives or none living in the London area where the hospital was situated (Brown, 1959, p. 1300). Unfortunately, data concerning the frequency of visiting of residents in this survey in their first two months after admission could not be obtained.

14. Goffman (1961, p. 15) defines the initial deprivation of visititors as a typical instrument in the process of disidentification and mortification. 'In many total institutions the privilege of having visitors or of visiting away from the establishment is completely withheld at first, ensuring a deep initial break with past roles and an appreciation of role dispossession.' As illustrations, he instances initial visiting restrictions in military academies, mental hospitals and for domestic servants newly ensconced in country houses.

15. Who had a confusional score of only 1, being slightly disoriented spatially.

16. However, the regular summer bus rides organized to take residents into the surrounding country from one of the separatist homes included confused and rational persons alike.

17. Such interests could extend widely, if given a free rein. One former psychiatric patient in one of the separatist homes, for example, had developed a proclivity for horse-racing, and in the course of my visit once made a winning of £2 13s. on a 4s. bet.

18. Suspicions of strait-jackets, padded cells and other mechanical contraptions of restraint showed that the new separatist home was readily identified publicly with the old asylum.

8

Rights and privileges: the powerlessness of the confused

The final dimension by which the experience of confused and rational residents will be compared in the two types of home is the distribution of rights and privileges, the social expression of the gradations of opportunity and power. Now access to power is perhaps the single most important variable determining a hierarchic stratification of individuals. This chapter will therefore explore in depth the nature of the restrictions imposed on, or the concessions allotted to, confused residents, the patterns of staff attitudes and techniques of control, and finally the psychological and social implications for the confused of administrative procedures of segregation.

RIGHTS, REGULATIONS AND RESTRICTIONS FOR RESIDENTS

First the comparative restrictiveness of the two kinds of home will be examined. Then within both these environments the differential staff treatment of confused and rational residents will be considered, in terms of privileges on the one hand and loss of particular rights on the other. Finally, the supposition will be reviewed that in separatist homes superfluous restraints on rational residents might be necessitated for the sake of ensuring the safety and security of their confused companions.

The homes: comparative restrictiveness

It might be hypothesized that a belief in the diminished responsibility frequently attributed to the confused by staff would lead to greater restraints in the residential life of the separatist homes where a much higher proportion of the residents were confused. Some attempt to give numerical weighting to this issue was made through the construction of an inventory of twenty-three items covering all aspects of the routine, and each item was scored according to the degree of choice permitted (Table 8.1). This approach did not fully confirm the hypothesis. It revealed rather that while the ordinary homes were much more homogeneous in affording a considerable degree of freedom to their residents, a separatist home could nevertheless be organized on equally permissive lines (Table 8.2).[1] Another of the special homes, however,

Table 8.1

Scoring system for the assessment of the restrictiveness
of residential life

Topic	Item	Score		
		2	1	0
1. Clothing	(a) Do residents have access to stored private clothing?	All residents	Some residents	None
	(b) Do residents decide what they are to wear each day?	All residents	Some residents	Staff
2. Bedtimes	(a) By what time are a majority of residents in bed?	After 8 p.m.	Before 8 p.m.	Before 7 p.m.
	(b) When are residents first called in the morning to get up?	After 8 a.m.	7–8 a.m.	Before 7 a.m.
3. Meals	(a) Can meals be had at other than normal times for any reason?	—	Yes	No
	(b) Is alternative food provided if residents reject an item on the menu?	—	Yes	No
	(c) Can residents leave the mealtable before all have finished?	—	Yes	No
4. Help to staff	(a) Are opportunities given to residents to help staff with various small jobs?	Extensive opportunities	Limited opportunities	No
	(b) Are residents encouraged to help staff?	—	Yes	No
5. Letter-writing	Do residents write their own letters, or do staff write letters for them?	All residents write their own letters	Most residents write their own letters, but some have letters written for them by staff	Almost all residents have letters written for them by staff

215

Table 8·1 (*contd.*)

Topic	Item	Score		
		2	1	0
6. Recreation	(*a*) Are the residents allowed to turn the TV on/off and to change the programmes?	All residents	A few residents	None
	(*b*) Can the residents spend their time privately in their bedrooms during the day?	—	Yes	No
	(*c*) Are the residents permitted to smoke where they like?	Anywhere	In restricted places only	Only under express staff super-vision
7. Visits	(*a*) What are the visiting hours?	—	More than 5 hours per day	Less than 5 hours per day
	(*b*) Can residents see their visitors privately?	In their own room	In the visitors' room	No
	(*c*) How many outings a year are arranged on average?	7 or more	3–6	2 or less
	(*d*) Can residents leave the grounds of the home during the day without permission of staff?	All residents	Some residents	None
8. Pocket money	Are edibles and household articles, etc., brought round regularly for sale to the residents?	—	Yes	No
9. Self-care	(*a*) Can residents choose when they have a bath (within reasonable limits)?	All residents	A few residents	None
	(*b*) Can residents make their own bed if they wish?	All residents	A few residents	None
	(*c*) Are residents encouraged to choose their own doctor?	—	Yes	No
	(*d*) Where there is a lift, are residents permitted to operate it themselves?	—	Yes	No
	(*e*) Can residents use the kitchen to make a sand-wich, drink, etc.?	—	Yes	No

Table 8.2
A comparison of the restrictiveness of residential life in separatist and ordinary homes

Topic (according to table 8.1)		Score (according to Table 8.1)						
		Separatist homes			Ordinary homes			Maximum score possible
		Home A	Home B	Home C	Home D	Home E	Home F	
1.	(a)	1	1	1	2	2	2	2
	(b)	1	1	0	2	2	2	2
2.	(a)	0	1	1	2	1	2	2
	(b)	0	0	0	1	0	1	2
3.	(a)	1	1	0	0	1	0	1
	(b)	1	1	0	1	1	1	1
	(c)	1	1	0	1	1	1	1
4.	(a)	1	1	0	1	1	1	2
	(b)	0	1	0	0	0	0	1
5.	—	0	1	0	1	1	2	2
6.	(a)	1	1	0	1	1	1	2
	(b)	1	1	0	1	1	0	1
	(c)	1	1	0	1	1	1	2
7.	(a)	1	1	0	1	1	1	1
	(b)	1	2	0	0	1	1	2
	(c)	2	0	0	0	1	1	2
	(d)	1	2	1	1	1	2	2
8.	—	0	1	0	0	0	1	1
9.	(a)	1	1	0	2	1	1	2
	(b)	1	1	0	1	1	1	2
	(c)	0	1	0	1	1	0	1
	(d)	n.a.	n.a.	n.a.	n.a.	1	1	1
	(e)	0	1	0	0	0	0	1
	TOTAL	16	22	3	20	21	23	36

Key: total score 30 or above: almost complete freedom,
20–29 : substantial freedom, but some restrictions,
10–19 : moderately restrictive, but some choice,
1–9 : very restrictive, with little or no freedom or choice.

Table 8.3
Scoring system for assessing authoritarian/permissive
attitudes of care attendants

Questions	*Possible answers*				
Would you say whether you agree or disagree, and whether you feel either way strongly, that a good matron:	*Strongly agree*	*Agree*	*Un-certain*	*Disagree*	*Strongly disagree*
1. Is anxious to suppress behaviour which may disturb the other residents?	ZZ	Z	X	Y	YY
2. Encourages the residents to be active to express their feelings?	YY	Y	X	Z	ZZ
3. Spends as much time as possible with the residents?	YY	Y	X	Z	ZZ
4. Discourages fuss?	ZZ	Z	X	Y	YY
5. Is careful to give her residents every opportunity to take their own decisions?	YY	Y	X	Z	ZZ
6. Disciplines her staff to obey her without question?	ZZ	Z	X	Y	YY
7. Knows all the residents personally and maintains a close relationship with them?	YY	Y	X	Z	ZZ
8. Encourages her staff to tell her criticisms if they feel them?	YY	Y	X	Z	ZZ
9. Is careful to show no favouritism?	ZZ	Z	X	Y	YY
10. Thinks that rules are essential to ensure the smooth running of the home?	ZZ	Z	X	Y	YY
11. Relieves her residents of as much responsibility as she can (e.g. in spending pocket money)?	ZZ	Z	X	Y	YY
12. Does not get involved with the residents?	ZZ	Z	X	Y	YY
13. Encourages visitors to come at any time?	YY	Y	X	Z	ZZ
14. Encourages residents to make complaints to her if they feel them?	YY	Y	X	Z	ZZ
15. Minimizes the rules?	YY	Y	X	Z	ZZ

Score: Each Z scored 1 mark for authoritarianism and each Y scored 1 mark for permissiveness; X indicates an uncertain reaction.
The range of possible scores therefore lay between Authoritarianism: 30 + Permissiveness: 0 on the one hand, to Authoritariansim: 0 + Permissiveness: 30 on the other.

was revealed as excessively restrictive, and the variation in the scores indicated that other factors besides sheerly the proportion of confused residents might be more influential in circumscribing various freedoms. Observation suggested that the personality and attitudes of the superintendent or matron might be predominant here, and this is perhaps supported by the application of an authoritarianism scale devised for this study (Table 8.3) which established a markedly different constellation of attitudes between attendants in two of the separatist homes (Fig. 5) corresponding roughly to the polarities of their restrictiveness scores.

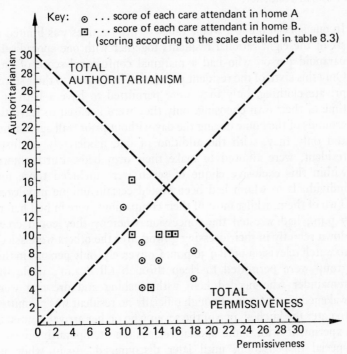

FIG. 5. Authoritarianism-permissiveness scores of the care attendants of two separatist homes

The residents

PRIVILEGES AND CONCESSIONS

Given that the separatist homes, with one major exception, were not noticeably more repressive of individual liberties or initiatives, how were such privileges and restrictions as existed for the residents distributed between the rational and the confused in either kind of home? First, the allotment of privileges will be examined, in terms of both the discriminatory concentration of certain rights on selected individuals and the limitation of opportunities to assist staff, together with the implications for the internal status dynamics within the home. The converse reaction of those correspondingly deprived will then be considered in the light of the social and psychological effects.

Overwhelmingly in the separatist homes privileges were centred on rational residents:

In one special home a whole range of prerogatives was limited to six of the eight rational residents together with one sporadically paranoid person who had a marginal confusional score of one. Only this sixth of the resident population had access to their stored private clothing, only they were permitted to have a bath at a time of their own choosing, only they were licensed to leave the grounds of the home during the day without prior staff agreement, and only they, with the addition of one moderately confused resident, were allowed to make their own beds. Furthermore, within this exclusive clique of seven were included those few individuals in whom had been vested certain unique privileges. Two of them, whilst most of their companions were in bed before 7 p.m., had wrested the concession whereby they could creep down secretly in their dressing gowns after the others were asleep to watch television until 9.30 p.m. Conversely, only persons in this group were permitted to sleep through till 8 a.m., while the remainder who needed help with washing and dressing were wakened about 6 a.m. Though officially no resident was permitted to enter the kitchen, one of the seven who on her arrival wanted to experiment with some special recipes was temporarily given a special dispensation, until later discouraged. Again while no precise stipulation actually forbade smoking, this right was in fact exercised by only two persons, both members of this group. Nor did any prohibition exist on handling the television, though informally custody was acknowledged to have passed to two of the seven, one of whom held the chief responsibility and summoned the warden whenever flickering on the screen could not be stopped. With regard to money, only one person actually frequented the local bank, though a few others occasionally wrote out their own cheques, again all being members of this group. Nor could it be construed as coincidental that the most dominant person among the seven had been allocated the only double bedroom in the home which contained a basin that had been decorously curtained off in a recess, a prize which enabled her, as she proudly proclaimed, 'to organize my routine in the morning in my own time and way', yet without loss of privacy.

A similar convergence of privileges on the coterie of rational residents was paralleled in one of the other separatist homes, though in the third the automatic staff categorization of all as 'elderly mentally infirm', despite representation across the whole spectrum from full rationality to complete confusion, resulted in universal subjection to unvariegated regimentation. In the ordinary homes, on the other hand, separation between confused and rational residents on this dimension should be interpreted not so much as the confinement of prerogatives to the latter, since as a majority they symbolized the norm, as the withdrawal of rights from the former, and this will be examined later.

Confused residents in the separatist homes, in contrast to their companions, were afforded very few, if any, special sanctions. Their incidental remarks included such comments as: 'There was a bit of a bust-up about washing my clothes. I wasn't allowed to do it. Yet I like washing my nylon stockings.' 'I like weeding, but I've no permission to do it.' 'I've got a diploma for cooking, but they seem to like to do their own cooking.' 'You aren't allowed to use the phone, I understand.' 'I sometimes want other clothes, but I can't get them.' Again, cross-checking with the case records yielded further hints of the retraction by confused residents of their former way of life: one severely confused woman, for instance, was attested as particularly enjoying smoking, but in the course of a fortnight's visit to the home was not seen to smoke once. Even where concessions were offered to the mildly confused, as by the readiness of the handyman in one of the special homes to shop for them as well as their rational neighbours, such an overture stopped short of those confused persons whose articulation appeared indistinct or whose meaning seemed incoherent. Similarly other examples of acquiescence in the wishes of the confused might be more realistically regarded as techniques of management than as genuine concessions: when a severely confused woman, whose mental and physical state required that she occupy a multi-bedded room for the sake of easier supervision, insisted on having the light on in her room at night, while her companions wanted it off, the staff compromised by tying a piece of matting or cloth round the light. It should finally be added, however, that this loss of privileges, while preponderantly applying to the confused, did also embrace a few of the more passive rational residents, though in such cases resentment was more likely to be expressed: 'I'm not allowed to wash my own clothes. I've offered, but they say: "There are people here to do it." Yet some do their own washing, like Mrs Geekie, and the staff don't mind.'

One type of privilege deserves special discussion – the opportunity to assist staff. For not only did it offer a rewarding and self-evidently useful function, but the implicit intimacy with staff served to elevate the status of the person in question, a consequence studiously pursued particularly by certain subnormal residents. Conversely, the deprivation of such an opportunity to perform at least some services in reciprocation of staff care undermined the sense of independence and self-respect. In fact, in the separatist homes staff readiness to accept help from residents was very much limited to a minority of the more assertive persons among the rational:

In one of the special homes three rational residents regularly ran messages and shopped in the adjoining town for staff, while another daily undertook housework like sweeping the floors, dusting the staircases, laying the cloths and napkins on the tables and changing them on Sundays. Two always collected up the cups and saucers after morning tea, while a third was in the habit of making tea and washing up afterwards for the dozen or so residents still up at 8 p.m. At least two women frequently did small serving jobs for the staff, and one of the men was observed on one occasion repairing the lining of his coat with needle and thread. Another woman, who had recently been admitted from a cottage where she had lived alone with her sister for years, conscientiously checked at night-time that all the windows on the ground floor, including the kitchens and bathrooms, were fully closed and locked. Yet another three of the rational held themselves responsible for looking after one of the parrots in the home and fed the livestock. Of a further pair, one played the piano for the weekly religious service, while the other gave out the hymn books.

In contrast, the only assistance undertaken by the other half of the resident population who were confused was the occasional drying of dishes in the kitchen irregularly performed by one mildly confused woman, together with the work of a former psychiatric patient. The latter bathed other male residents and shaved them with an electric razor when the official male attendant was absent or off duty, he mowed the lawns and raked the grass, tended the plants in the greenhouse and watered the flowers with a can, and sharpened knives and scythes on the hone in the tool cupboard. However, his maverick record cannot be taken as representative of general experience of the confused, since anyway his usual behaviour indicated a psychiatric abnormality only indirectly presenting as confusion.

As with the distribution of privileges already illustrated, this pattern of the monopolization of the available roles in assisting staff by the rational was reproduced in one of the other separatist homes, though in the third again the rational were indiscriminately subdued by the pervasive apathy and no significant degree of help was either expected from or provided by any of the residents. In the ordinary homes a handful of rational residents pursued a vigorous routine of laying tables, washing and drying up after meals, posting letters, making beds and other similar functions, but a more usual attitude was one of indifference: 'I've come here to rest – my working days are over.'

Now two observations put these differences into perspective. Firstly, as a proportion of the total number of the rational in each home, those assisting staff were far more numerous in the separatist establishments, which seemed to suggest how anxiously the rational in these latter homes sought the implicit familiarity with staff[2] as a means of elevating their status in dissociation from their confused companions. This interpretation is perhaps reinforced by the further observation that those rational residents in the special homes who did not avail themselves of these opportunities gave as their explanation not indifference, but positive rejection of the idea: 'I don't think they expect the patients [*sic*] to do their own washing . . . I'm not going to do it. The servants what's here could work a jolly lot harder than they do. They seem to have a jolly good time here.' 'You're not supposed to interfere with the staff.' 'I don't have to wash anything. The attendants don't want you messing around.' One mark, therefore, of the division in the separatist homes between confused and rational residents was that all the rational tended to assist staff who did not feel positively inhibited by the prospect, while only those of the confused tended to give such help whose will had not been undermined by the constant discouragements imposed.

Predictably, matrons in the separatist homes justified their reluctance to accept assistance from the confused on the grounds of their unreliability in quality and persistence of work:

'Staff never ask for help. But Mrs Jilkes (confusional score 9) does ask to wash up, and sometimes she's allowed to dry the dishes. Mrs Stabler (score 2) also sometimes dries the dishes, but she dries what's dried and leaves the wet dishes wet. Miss Scarcroft (score 7) also helps in the kitchen, but she's muddled too. It delays the staff, the residents are so muddled. Some do put the dishes on the trolley after a meal, including Mrs Cockerill (score 0) who always says her plate's clean and needn't be washed.' Mrs Stabler, referred to here, avowed real eagerness at her interview to assist staff with various chores. 'I help to make my bed, look after my room, and do my hankies and underclothes myself. I like sewing or mending for the staff, if they'll give me something to do. I always try to get something to do, like sewing [she wore a thimble on her finger during the interview]. But I do no cooking – I used to like doing cooking. I always say, if you've got mending to do, for goodness sake give it to me.'

The matron was less enthusiastic about Mrs Stabler's offer. 'She wanted to help "the Master" [as she calls him] very much, so eventually I gave her a frayed tie of my husband's to sew round the edge. But she made a terrible mess of it.'

Nevertheless, the lack of encouragement towards independence in *some* activities could, and did, lead to a loss of initiative in others where limited opportunities really were available, for instance in making beds.

RESTRICTIONS AND LOSS OF RIGHTS

But the leit-motiv of confused residents in their attitude to rights was not so much the lack of specific privileges as the sheer weight of restrictions. Sometimes the expression was disordered:

An eighty-six-year-old widow (confusional score 6) who was

tangential in speech and disoriented both of person and situation, when asked how satisfied she felt about clothing, replied: 'Not much, and they haven't treated me, some of these, put me in proper, and the girls always rush, and I always feel I'm not going to be put in, and they talk to me and say: "Don't take no notice of her." Sit there as though they're going to . . .'

Sometimes the sentiment was all too blunt:

A widow of seventy-six in one of the separatist homes (score 7) who was tangential in speech and a disoriented wanderer, speaking about the furnishings in her room, declared: 'There must be certain ideas and plans. Put down "what the people in authority want".' Similarily a mildly disoriented man of eighty-six (score 2): 'No, I'm not free – got to do what whose hospital it is.'

Or angry feelings, normally repressed below the surface in conversation, might suddenly well up, uncontrolled, in a revealing flash:

A disoriented woman of eighty-seven (score 3) was speaking about her resignation to institutional life: 'No, I only do just what they ask me, though I've been a very energetic person in years gone by. . . . You can't go and order a great joint, not all that, you have to have what you can get. Oh arsehole, I don't kick up a fuss about nothing.'

Such indicators were, however, necessarily fragmentary since in the nature of their condition the confused were unable themselves explicitly to articulate their whole situation. Hazardous though it is to argue by analogy, a fuller picture of the feelings of confused residents can perhaps be deduced from the comparable statements of some of their handicapped rational companions. To illustrate their significance, these statements should be evaluated against the backcloth of the reaction of a typical non-handicapped resident in one of the separatist homes:

I'm pleased with everything in the home. I like the way the staff address you – no 'Come here you!' They treat you as decent, responsible persons. They call you 'residents', not 'inmates', and avoid the smack of charity which I should resent.

The assertions of rational but disabled residents present a sharp contrast:

A blind woman declared: 'You can't express your own opinion, go to Matron and say "I don't like it being done this way". They can say to me: "You do it like this", and I have to. I've lived too long on this earth as my own mistress and I don't like it. My husband used to leave me with all to do with the home.'

A subnormal resident declared: 'We have to go where they put us. We have to do what we're told, don't we? Though they let me go outside when I want.'

A woman who had superficially been reduced to automaton rigidities in her behaviour by excess medication, and was treated accordingly by staff, noted succinctly: 'I don't like the rules – must do a certain thing at a certain time.'

A woman who, though rational, was usually isolated in a corner of the day quarters in one of the special homes, confessed: 'One nurse I don't like here. Anything I do is wrong. But I don't take no notice. I wouldn't mind if I didn't see her again. She treats me as if I'm a bit of dirt. When she's on at me, I wish I could let out at her, but I keep quiet, and then you think about it. I keep quiet, so that that nurse won't say: "You said this or that".'

A blind resident hinted unwittingly at the predicament of the marginally confused where staff might suspect a simulation of dependence: 'The nurses are a little bit jealous with me. They have to help me a lot, and they think I'm putting it on.' Equally she revealed some of the persisting resentment at attributions of helplessness: 'I feel that I can't get used to needing somebody to take me to the lavatory.'

Now of course all these extracts are mere straws in the wind, but there was no reason to believe that they were not widely representative of a deadening sense of powerlessness among those residents discounted by staff as relatively incapable.[3] One last quotation deserves to be given since it aptly depicts at greater length the dilemma of the resident noted in the case records as afflicted with senile psychosis, but as yet without symptoms overt enough to score on the confusional scale, and therefore still articulate enough to analyse her situation at what is clinically regarded as the pre-confusional stage:

'I don't like homes – want a room somewhere. I don't feel the same as if in my own home. There's nothing to do. They've got maids to do all. You're not allowed to help anyone infirm or old, like Mrs Guthrie. . . . You're free to a certain extent, but I must say that going out to tea once, I didn't tell them and they nearly called the police. And they wanted to wash a dress of mine, but it's always been dry-cleaned, so I didn't let them wash it, as it would have shrunk and I've lost six blouses – don't know where they've gone. And another thing I don't like is that the keys are taken away and you can't lock the doors. How they talk to me if you do anything wrong. One or two of them are nice, but they seem to order one about. All nice in a certain way if you do what they want. But I don't see much of them. They seem to rule the place, no doubt about that. I don't like it when you have to do what you're told.'

Must it not therefore be assumed that such feelings, as the gradual encroachment of symptoms of confusion is taken to imply increasing dependence and helplessness, can only intensify at later stages of the syndrome?

If this was the general reaction of confused residents, particularly in the separatist homes, to the structure of decision-making they experienced, we must next ask how far the specific application of this restrictiveness justified such attitudes. The tenure of rights and opportunity for self-determination will be briefly explored in terms of control over decisions relating to place of residence, activities, money, clothing, medical consultation, protest, privacy and territorial integrity.

(a) Place of residence

Two separate issues must be distinguished here. Firstly, how far did residents feel they played a sufficient part in the decision to admit them? And secondly, how far were they satisfied that they had secured self-determination, or at least adequate consultation, concerning their residence for the future? On either count there was little evidence of proper explanation,[4] but there were marked differences in attitudes between the rational and the confused.

Of the rational residents in the separatist homes, those who felt most aggrieved about the circumstances of their admission were, almost without exception, either subnormal (or officially classed as such) or former psychiatric patients, and their feelings ranged from resignation to resentment. Typical comments of passive acquiescence included:

> 'I liked it on my own. But they don't think I should live by myself. Personally speaking, I should have liked to have stayed in my own place. But if it's for my own welfare, I suppose it's best for me.'

> 'I've got to live here for the time being. I didn't come here: I was brought here by the welfare officer. I sometimes think about lodgings, and I'll wait till somebody comes along and moves me.'

More common, however, was an indignation,[5] whether latent or still impassioned:

> 'I was in lodgings, got out quickly, came here. But my life's not in homes. I like to be alone and looking after myself and the children – two young men and two girls, all married, but no room to take their mother. I don't like it here. I want a room to myself. The others aren't right – lacking in brains. They brought me here against my wish. The doctor said I shouldn't be in a home: "You should rather live on your own and get a nurse to look after you".'

> 'They come there to our home – police, doctors – and heaved us right out of it, me first to [a mental hospital]. My husband was put into [a home] – the workhouse I call it – then taken to [a hospital]. A cover to get us out of our home. Nay, we've been crucified. They came and took us out, with policemen, the welfare lot. Dr Lightfoot [the psychiatrist] said: "You're not well enough to look after your husband," and I said "I am." A pile of thieves – they couldn't have treated us worse. On 12 July last they came and took us away against our will. I only found out I was at (the mental hospital) the day after I was put there when they told me so. Our house was cleared out, and they sent us the bill for the rent while we were out – £11. I would have gone to court about it, but my husband didn't want that, so we paid.'

The issue at stake here is not whether such admission procedures, either by force[6] or more subtle pressures, were or were not justified by the real interests of the person concerned, but whether enough explanation was offered to win willing cooperation, allay understandable apprehensions and avoid an impression of benevolent, or even malevolent, paternalism.

Interviews with the confused, among whom the dominant response was one of sheer bewilderment, suggested that in their case these dangers were fully substantiated. Asked how they came to be in the home, their mystification was unmistakable, even if expressed in garbled form:

A widow who was severely disoriented of place (confusional score 2): 'Nobody asked me. I was just brought. I feel shut in here. You're buried alive here. Can't go out much, can you? What home am I in?'

A former midwife of eighty-four, who had been resident nine months, and was disoriented and tangential in speech (score 4): 'I wish I did know. I haven't the foggiest idea. I was working . . . I wasn't able to concentrate because I'd got things down to . . . Money, want to be independent. I didn't want to beg through the Poor Law.'

A widower of eighty-six who was severely disoriented spatially (score 5): 'They brought me here in a great big van, and I knew no more about it than you did.'

A single woman of eighty-eight who had been resident over a year and was a grossly disoriented wanderer and very discursive in her speech patterns (score 12): 'I don't know. I wondered [wandered?] from the train why they've taken it over. I don't know what the trouble is.'

Similarly, subnormal residents in the separatist homes were not regarded as capable of participating in decisions, even fundamental ones, about their future. One stated laconically: 'I had no more idea I was coming here than a born baby.' Another, who had only very recently been admitted, confessed similar puzzlement: 'I really don't know how it came about really. It seemed to come quick.' Both literally and metaphorically the confused, and those few others seen as equally unable to profit from explanation, were *taken for a ride*. (This process bears close affinities with the 'betrayal funnel' pictured by Goffman, 1961, ch. 2.) Repeatedly evidence was found that they had been unceremoniously dumped in a new and bewildering environment, having been told some disingenuous tale to elicit their preferred cooperation.

Secondly, how far did residents feel secure and in control concerning their future? Again, it was the former psychiatric patients, who rated zero on the confusional scale but whose history was never discounted, who felt their vulnerability, most clearly: 'I don't know how long I'll be here. The authorities – doctors – can transfer you to another place at any time.' 'I want to go back to my home, but Priviter (the Chief Welfare Officer) said it wouldn't be suitable for me.' A similar sense of utter powerlessness seemed to pervade the confused, though the direct evidence was more fragmentary. Typically, a woman of eighty-five in one of the separatist homes who was severely disoriented, tangential in speech and addicted to anormic fiddling and repetitiveness (score 10), when asked if she wished to stay there, hinted darkly: 'I think I should, but I can't do it. They've got other plans.'

(b) Activities

Loss of opportunity for activity was very widely felt in both kinds of home. Such characteristic comments were made by rational residents in the separatist homes as: 'Life is getting very boring really. Not much to do, just looking out of the window.' 'Boredom – that's what I complain of. I'm sick of sitting in this chair hour after hour. There's nothing to cheer you up here. All you hear is moaning and groaning. You're just a cog in the machine. You lose your own individuality. You might just as well have a number and finish with it. Rather a fatalistic way of looking at it, I know.' A psychiatrist's report on one such person read: 'She does feel depressed since she is not doing anything for anyone and she is full of fears. She is kept in one room with seven people and does not seem to occupy herself in any way.' Occasionally, when rational residents permitted themselves to expand at greater length on their feelings, they unveiled a sense of functionlessness and lack of organized purpose which seemed tantamount to anomie:

'I don't do anything. It's not a life I'm used to. I'm used to housework. I used to go to bed about 11 p.m., but now there's nothing to stop up for. It's no good asking if you can do something since they don't listen to you.'
'Have you asked somebody?'
'Not been here long [she had been resident two years]: I don't know who to ask. I'm prevented from going out: they come

round here and tell us when we can go out. It's normally too cold, they say . . . I've nobody to write to. I'm quite stranded really. Don't know where I am.'

Even the rational felt that any opportunity for initiative had been effectively pre-empted by staff: 'I'm tired sitting. Never sat down so long. I'd *like* to do lots of jobs. At Fernway [from which she had been transferred] they offered me to wash up a few plates. I do feel bored.' Almost all residents answered the interview question 'Is there any job you would like to do or help with?' by reciting what jobs, if any, they already did, implying that they did not regard a change of routine as really practical.

Confused residents in the separatist homes were equally afflicted by a sense of the pointlessness of it all: 'You sit around here all the bloody day and get nothing done' (a forthright man with a confusional score of 3). But with the more resigned, a suppliant's gratitude for every minor offering, however customary or insignificant, was also apparent: 'Still, it [television] makes a bit of a change, you know. We've got to do something, haven't we?' (a woman with score 7). Above all, their reaction was permeated by a feeling of alienation from any activity which could not only enrich their own self-respect, but perhaps also gratify others. 'I used to say "I wish there were no work", but now by God I wish there were more' (a woman with score 3). 'Almost every day I feel I must do something. . . . My governor saw me and said: "Miss Rehoe, you're doing my job when I ought to"' (a very confused but ebullient woman with score 12, expressing tangentially a wish fulfilment?).

(c) Money

Residents in the separatist homes had very little chance to exercise purchasing power. This was partly because in only one of these homes was a weekly trolley brought round containing food and various personal articles for sale. But chiefly it arose because the other two special homes, in contrast to the practice of the ordinary homes, did not dispense the pocket-money component of the pension. Nor, of course, did they distribute pension books which, though administratively inconvenient, would alone have obviated the impression that the pocket-money was a charitable concession rather than a deserved remainder after board and loding charges had been duly handed over. Instead, where the Court of Protection[7] had not already removed financial control over a person's assets, pocket-money in these two homes was retained by the warden on the understanding that it could be claimed whenever it was needed.

These arrangements led to some paradoxical results. Firstly, not only the confused, but even some of the rational did not appreciate that they had current income or indeed any money at all at their disposal: 'Not had a penny since I've been here. I've got no money, except I'd saved £40 to bury me when I die' (a blind but rational woman, resident three months). 'No pocket-money; that's absolutely gone, out of the question' (a confused woman, score 12, resident over a year). Alternatively, residents seriously underestimated the amount of money available to them: one man, for example, who was only very marginally confused (score 2) thought he received 2s. 6d. every third week, instead of the actual sum of 16s. each week. Sometimes this ignorance was curiously rationalized: 'I did have a pension, but since I've been here, not a halfpenny. They tell me I'm not old enough yet' (a rational man of eighty-five, resident two years).

Secondly, however earnest or ingenious the efforts to avoid it, procedures designed to reintroduce some element of consumer choice in purchasing inevitably became tainted with paternalism. In one of the separatist homes, even in the case of the rational, the matron, having asked residents what they wanted, herself effected the purchase rather than enabling visits to be made to the shops by the persons concerned. Even this fundamental request about shopping wants was ignored in another home where staff, having decided that a resident needed a particular article or its replacement, merely counted out the money involved in the person's presence to give reality to the explanation. It is perhaps no surprise that for many this procedure carried little but ritual significance: 'I hold the money on my hand and the man takes it. I don't know what he does with the money' (a man of eighty-five, score 4). Sometimes, again, the matron simply made the purchase she felt the resident required and then without consultation deducted the cost from the balance on the person's account. One woman (score 8) who was subjected to this service commented: 'We can't go out and go where we want. We're under control. What you want, if she hasn't got it, you can't have it.' Another said: 'I get no pocket-money. Staff get things from the shops. But I'd like it, to buy cigarettes with. I used to smoke five a day' (she was never seen to smoke during a three-week visit).

Thirdly, and more insidiously, not only did these arrangements minimize administrative complications for the wardens, but the application of power of attorney did seem dubiously justified in terms of the mental state of certain residents. This is a topic which deserves closer study. It was noticeable, however, that such beneficial legal powers might be used to execute transactions which in marginal cases of confusion could be construed as psychologically ultra vires, and that to avoid the consequent emotional upset recourse might be had to dissimulation. Thus in the case of a woman, for example, who was only slightly disoriented and given to the occasional localized and innocuous delusion (score 3), the Court of Protection, in whom her affairs had been vested, sold her bungalow, but she was not told, so that whenever she spoke of returning to it, which was frequently, she had to be constantly dissuaded by one artificial device after another. This raises the general issue: at what point are the gains of a benevolent paternalism in terms of administrative protection outweighed by the losses in terms of psychological disfranchisement? This survey can do no more than indicate that certain data suggested that the procedures for transfer of overriding legal jurisdiction to a third party should be re-examined, particularly the framework for reviews and appeals.

(d) Clothing

It was a regular practice to keep clothes in locked drawers 'to save excess washing if they're likely to keep changing'. But this restriction was less inhibiting than the practice of attendants, in the case of confused residents and also many of the rational, in determining each morning and at bathtimes which clothes should be worn. The only systematic attempt discovered to reverse this arrogation of power on behalf of a confused resident was made by the daughter of one of the latter who wrote to the matron:

'Mother sleeps well if she has her daily paper, her handbag, spectacles, hot bottle and a lot of bedclothes and a glass of water. She wears three vests – Celanese next to her skin, then a Jaeger wool one, and an Aertex one with a lace top on the outside. She wears two pairs of pants, lock-knit underneath and a wool one on top; also corsets, but she doesn't wear a petticoat except under her pink dress and her summer ones. She also forgets to exchange her underclothes except when soiled. She makes endless notes in her room on a memo book, but when she's worried, it's best to tear it up and she quickly forgets. She tends to take her nail-brush, etc., from the bathroom to her own room and is then worried and apologetic when she discovers she has done so.'

But so far from such superfluous cosseting proving effective, the convenience of staff was paramount to the point where some confused residents in one of the separatist homes were kept in night-dresses and dressing gowns all day because of the intractable problems of dressing and undressing them, while others were given night attire after a bath in the early afternoon, causing a few to complain bitterly that they had lost their underwear.

The other main feeling voiced by confused residents in the special homes about clothing was a sense of impotence about securing necessary replacements: 'I've a change of jacket, but it's not big enough. Even the trousers are becoming too dilapidated, and the other clothes aren't respectable enough to come out in' (a man of ninety-three, score 3). 'I've lost my handbag, but I'd like another one. I miss it very much. I don't know if the staff would give me one if I asked for one' (a woman of eighty-one, score 2). 'I was measured for a pair of trousers more than once, and never saw them again' (a man of ninety-four, score 2). Presumably the more seriously confused residents felt even more frustrated about the difficulties of securing new clothes since they were the poorest dressed members of the separatist homes (Table 7.5, p. 171), but direct evidence was not available. Possibly matrons felt that expenditure on new clothes for the severely confused was not justified when they might be so quickly spoiled by incontinence or food stains or alternatively that they would not be appreciated by the wearers.

(e) *Medical consultation*

Little evidence could be assembled on this important subject, but the implications of the limited data were disquieting. In only one of the separatist homes were residents encouraged to choose (or retain) their own doctor, but more important were the problems confused residents encountered in communicating the genuineness and urgency of their complaints to staff as requiring a doctor's visit:

A woman of eighty-eight who was disoriented, tangential in speech and subject to excessive fiddling (score 8) complained at the time of my visit of sharp pains in her back. The staff were openly suspicious of the reality of this alleged indisposition and assured her somewhat flippantly that she would soon be better. At her interview she protested bitterly at this indifference: 'I wish the doctor would come – pain in my back and all over. I want to go somewhere where somebody knows more about my back. My back is a misery. I'd like a change now. I'd like to go to Furleigh Hospital and see what they can do.' Despite her pleas and periodical groaning, the matron did not finally call the doctor till several days had elapsed.

A similar dependence on the judgment of attendants was indicated concerning the care of feet in another of the separatist homes where it was regular practice for the chiropodist to see all new residents and thereafter only at six-monthly intervals unless staff who saw the old person at the weekly bath detected a need for an intermediate visit. Again, of those found to have poor hearing, the confused were more likely not to have been equipped with a hearing aid, whilst one slightly disoriented woman (score 2) declared, quite spontaneously at her interview, her unmet wish to attend an oculist's for an eye-test. She also commented that her hair had been cut too short and straight and that she wanted hairpins. In fact the only person who had her hair shampooed professionally in the nearby town was rational. Since no comprehensive enquiry was made about medical or welfare aids, these citations doubtless represent no more than odd examples, but they do suggest some of the powerlessness the confused felt to secure satisfaction concerning their health anxieties or even their more idiosyncratic inclinations: 'I think when you get to this age, you're a helpless, sorry creature. When I get a very bad cold, I like to take a cup of hot milk. But I don't get this now . . .' (a woman of eighty-one, score 3).

(f) Protest

If confused residents tended to be subject to more restrictive regulations and to view their situation as more circumscribed, how far did they, or could they, protest? In fact, in accordance with the isolation which was repeatedly pinpointed in the preceding chapter as their dominant social characteristic, virtually none of the very few complaints made in the separatist homes emanated from the confused. Their overwhelming response, if not of apathy, involved some pattern of withdrawal,[8] intermingled perhaps with various inarticulate techniques of resistance to physical handling.[9] However, when they did wish to express a grievance, they faced a twofold problem, first of making their attitude intelligible and second, more difficult, of getting it taken seriously rather than dismissed as yet another manifestation and proof of a disordered mind. Evidence of failure on both these counts was recorded:

> A woman who was judged rational at interview, but who was treated similarly to the confused because she had become so incapacitated by drugs and her voice so slurred, was habitually enclosed within the confines of a geriatric chair. Partly because of her incontinence and partly for the sake of daily exercise, she periodically expostulated against her captivity, but was either blandly ignored or reprimanded for her incomprehensibility.

> A single woman of eighty-eight who was notorious for her constant wandering and echolalia (score 12) was frequently stung by the rebukes of attendants, but compounded her misery by retaliating with a misplaced word or phrase which produced an unintended comic effect. Provoked on one occasion, for example, she endeavoured to silence her opponent with the thrust 'Go to the laundry and have a jolly good laundry'. At another time she lashed back at an adversary 'Leave me. You think I'm wonderful. Well, I'm not.'

One can only imagine that the failure to create the requisite impact in publicizing disaffection, let alone a response of indifference or even ridicule, must have enhanced the sense of alienation and bewilderment of the confused and promoted further the 'solution' of withdrawal.

(g) *Privacy*

Aggravation was widespread in the separatist homes, among both rational and confused residents alike, at the lack of security offered for personal possessions. 'You can't lock the drawers because you've got no key. Yet Mrs Shewring [conspicuous for her wandering and interference with others' property] goes to my drawers in the bedroom, and I've got money in them.' Equally strongly resented was the general loss of privacy and self-determination engendered by institutional regulations, and this grievance was particularly voiced by rational persons admitted through reason of social emergencies or transferred because of unpalatable behaviour in other homes:

'I want a bed-sitting room in lodgings so that I can lie down when I like. But you're restricted here: "What are you doing up there? Come down!"'

'I don't like it here. The officers are inclined to be bossy. I come into my room each day [where the solitary window faced a high blank wall immediately opposite about five feet away] to have tea, out of the way, and *then* they won't leave me alone. I'm fed up with them. I only swear at them, that's all [laughing]. I don't like it – I like to be free. As long as they leave me alone, I'm all right.'

By comparison, in both these matters, protection of possessions and freedom from regimentation, the ordinary homes were much less exposed to criticism. The chief aspect of residential life, however, where loss of privacy uniquely affected the confused lay in the censorship of letters. In one of the separatist homes the process of supervision had reached the point where control over the exchange of letters, even in the case of those only very mildly confused, had been virtually appropriated in entirety by the warden: when letters addressed to residents from their relatives were received, he not only read them, but replied to them of his own accord without consultation of the person concerned, so that relatives soon wrote to him direct.

(h) Territorial rights

Of all the rights and conventions which in practice defined the hierarchic status of the confused, none highlighted their weakness so clearly as the conflicts over territorial acquisition. Many studies in the field of ethnology (e.g. Ardrey, 1967) have emphasized control over territory as a critical power variable, and the concept has already been fruitfully applied to the seating arrangements in a welfare home for the aged (Lipman, 1967). The latter study found that, though a number of other seats remained empty, each old person clung to 'their' seat despite all hindrances which included inability to see the television screen and on one occasion almost unendurable heat. In the present survey it was clear that especially in the separatist homes pernickety regard to precise seating dispositions performed the dual function, not only of translating the rights of the self into concrete form, but also of protecting an ordered environment against the haphazard encroachments of the confused. Indeed it was the most signal characteristic of rooms dominated by confused residents that seats were exchanged in apparent randomness without any underlying thread of consistent ownership.

Whilst this phenomenon was most commonly observed in the form of rational residents ejecting wanderers from chairs to which they drifted, it also shed light on the internal ranking system within the homes that subnormal rational residents did on occasion similarly repel their confused companions. For the relation was an asymmetric one in that the confused never conversely asserted such rights against any of their rational neighbours, even when occasionally justified. Furthermore, it represented perhaps one touchstone of psychological integration within the social order of the home when a confused resident, as was sometimes seen, exerted the claim of territorial integrity against another who was also confused.

SUPERFLUOUS RESTRAINTS ON THE RATIONAL ?

The preceding discussion has assembled a comprehensive catalogue of elements illustrating the relative powerlessness and depressed status of the confused. It has indicated, particularly in the separatist homes where the evidence was most pronounced, that the sense of restrictiveness found to pervade the thoughts of many of the confused was borne out by verifiable criteria over a wide range of facets of residential life. It now remains to ask one final question in this part of the enquiry: how far, especially in the separatist homes which had been designed specifically for the care of the confused, were the rights of rational residents circumscribed, or their freedoms impeded, by policies aimed primarily to secure the safety or welfare of the confused?

In one of the special homes the superintendent insisted on regarding all the residents as 'elderly mentally infirm', irrespective of their widely varying mental state, as partly corroborated by the finding that an actual majority, on the scale of confusion adopted

here, could be categorized as rational. This indiscriminate stereotyping engendered an undifferentiating application of the set of
regulations, and the ensuing universal apathy was taken to
substantiate the 'accuracy' of the original stereotype. Examples
of restraints which seemed needlessly imposed on rational residents
included a prohibition on handling the television – a large notice
was stuck to it saying NOT TO BE TOUCHED BY RESIDENTS
IN ANY CIRCUMSTANCES, the retention of all pension monies in
supervised accounts, the refusal to permit the private holding of
cigarettes for fear of unattended smoking at leisure, and the
withdrawal of instruments for knitting or sewing. A number of
rational residents commented spontaneously on these rules. One
blind woman, for example, said: 'I'd like to do knitting, but the
scissors and needles have been taken away from me. I had a
thimble and a self-threading needle. I've asked for them back,
but the matron says others might get the scissors. ... I like
smoking, and one man resident said he'd get me cigarettes, but
now he's been told he mustn't do this.' Similarly, rational
residents felt bewildered and affronted at being discouraged from
helping staff. 'I'd like to peel the potatoes, and wouldn't mind
other jobs, but I'm afraid of doing something wrong. The
attendants nag at me.' 'I could help to darn stockings—I'd like
to do this. But I'm not sure they'd like me to do a job.'

This alignment of the rational with the confused, with the consequent sense of unjustified deprivation among the former, was not,
however, replicated in the other separatist homes. In these, greater
implicit reliance was placed in the exercise of informal social controls
by the rational over their confused companions.[10] In conjunction
with evidence presented earlier in this chapter about the assignment
of privileges, this suggested a tentative typology of the distribution
of power between confused and rational residents in separatist
homes (Table 8.4) whereby the more authoritarian the regime, the
less the differential favouring of the rational in terms of rights and
opportunities and the greater their superfluous subjection to
vicarious regulations.

In the ordinary homes indications of this phenomenon were
tenuous:

A semi-paralysed woman who shared a bedroom with a severely
confused resident had been in the habit of summoning attendants

Table 8.4

**Typology of the distribution of power between confused
and rational residents in separatist homes according to
the degree of restrictiveness of the regime**

| | Nature of treatment in: | |
Type of resident	Relatively permissive environment (score 15–25)*	Authoritarian environment (score 0–10)*
Rational	privileged	subject to undifferentiated restrictions
Confused	comparatively under-privileged, but subject to little positive restrictiveness	subject to strong and pervasive restrictions

* According to the scoring of restrictiveness in Table 8.2, p. 217.

by the bedside bell system whenever her companion manifested, as she did frequently, any eccentric behaviour. The staff, irritated at what they considered unnecessary calls, forbade her to ring the bell except in dire emergencies, so that she then complained of feeling vulnerable because of her physical handicap: 'When they go out, I can't get them back.'

But such contingent impediments of the rational in these homes were exceptional.

STAFF ATTITUDES AND PATTERNS OF CONTROL

So far the survey of the locus of power and distribution of rights in the separatist homes has been confined to an examination of the differential experience of the residents over a range of specific issues, and the activities of staff have appeared as incidental to this theme. Now these will be scrutinized in their own right for the light they throw on the routine functioning and authority structures of homes geared to the care of the confused. The difficulties of managing old people with disordered perceptions, the various patterns in the exercise of control, the techniques of adjustment to staff authority developed by the confused will be successively examined.

First, however, how did staffing complements vary between the separatist and ordinary homes? Two comparative indices were adopted, relating to night care and day care respectively. The former comprised the ratio per night attendant of residents who were incontinent together with those who persistently wandered at night. The latter sought to weight the differential degree of care required by the confused by counting residents according to their confusional score, the rational being numbered for this purpose one each. On this basis only one of the separatist homes seemed deficient in night staffing in comparison with the ordinary homes, though for day care, while the unadjusted staff : resident ratio appeared to favour the former, the weighted ratio, which probably approximated much more closely to the true burden of care, revealed them as relatively seriously understaffed (Table 8.5). This comparative

Table 8.5

Ratio of night and day staffing complements to numbers and kinds of confused residents in separatist and ordinary homes

Ratio components	*Separatist homes*			*Ordinary homes*		
	Home A	*Home B*	*Home C*	*Home D*	*Home E*	*Home F*
Number of duty attendants* per night	2	1	1	0	2	1
Number of residents who persistently wandered at night	10	4	5	1	4	2
Number of incontinent residents	15	6	6	2	14	8
1. Ratio of night wanderers plus incontinents per night attendant	12·5	10	11	—	9	10
Number of duty attendants* per day	7	7	6	2	10	5
Total number of residents	40	47	36	19	80	38
2. Ratio of number of residents per day attendant	5·7	6·7	6·0	9·5	8·0	7·6
Total score of residents†	222	136	99	28	119	54
3. Ratio of total residents' scores per day attendant	31·7	19·4	16·5	14·0	11·9	10·8

* Excluding the matron on call.

† Scoring in accordance with the confusional scale (1–14) adopted in this study (Table 4.4, p. 85), and rational residents for this purpose each counting 1.

shortage of care staff in the special homes, in the light of the greater demands made on them, forms a crucial background for an examination of staff handling and attitudes towards the confused.

The social relations of the confused in residential care

Difficulties of management

PROBLEMS OF STAFF HANDLING OF THE CONFUSED

A Chief Welfare Officer outlined the particular problems involved in the care of the confused in a large institution thus:

Of the 113 residents, twenty are regularly incontinent both of urine and faeces, fourteen more are frequently incontinent of urine and nine of faeces, and forty-five more are occasionally incontinent of urine and nine of faeces. Incontinence in one form or another, therefore, affects ninety-seven of the 113 residents. The amount of care and attention needed to deal with persons who are either incontinent or have a tendency to incontinence from stresses such as coughing requires thirty of the residents at least to be taken regularly to the toilet and have all their needs attended to while they are there. A number of other residents need to be taken regularly to the toilet because severe physical handicap prevents them making their own way unaided. Regular two-hourly attention is necessary in a large number of cases to avoid or mitigate the effects of incontinence, but the daily average number of articles that has to be dealt with after being soiled by excreta is ninety-five nightdresses, fifty knickers, a minimum of twenty dresses and 100 drawsheets.

About one-third of the residents require assistance at meal-times, some having to be fed, with about one-sixth needing their food to be cut up for them, and have epilepsy as a concomitant disease. Thirty of the residents have such an extent of mental degeneration that they wander as they do not know where they are. Since no power of restraint can be exercised, constant supervision is needed, but even so, one resident has been killed and another injured in road accidents. (Private communication, August 1964.)

Besides the more obvious tasks of dealing with incontinence, feeding and forestalling physical danger, staff also faced several other subtler problems. Firstly, non-cooperation in functions like dressing, undressing and bathing, whether through deliberate resistance[11] or sheer misunderstanding on the part of the confused, caused a vast expenditure of time, as well as sometimes loss of patience, over comparatively simple procedures. For this reason the most seriously

242

confused in one separatist home were woken an hour and a half before the remainder of the residents to allow for this contingency, while at least three of the very confused were often left all day in night clothes and dressing gowns to circumvent repeated conflicts. Other instances of the failure to secure the anticipated or desired behaviour in various contexts from the confused also entailed considerable extra work for staff. Thus in the special homes residents known to be incontinent were regularly toileted once or twice each night, but some who omitted to utilize the opportunity promptly urinated within minutes of returning to bed.[12] Again, residents who combined physical disability with mental confusion presented peculiar problems, like the obese woman of seventeen stone (confusional score 6), who either could not or would not get up out of her bath and had to be lifted out by force majeure by the matron's husband.

Secondly, various aspects of anormic behaviour created unexpected difficulties. Examples like the screwing up of endless strips of toilet paper, the requisition of repositories unintended for toilet use, the hoarding of dirty tins and leaves in the bedroom, and eating eccentricities like mixing cornflakes with tea-leaves in a cup, all necessitated constant and close supervision by staff, as well as readiness to face the obloquy of those who resented intrusion into their idiosyncrasies.

Thirdly, some characteristics of confusion led to unwitting interference by disoriented residents in the execution of routine staff duties. The most striking instance here was the practice of persistent wanderers, especially those who incessantly traversed a fixed circuit, in obstructing the efforts of attendants to wash or polish floors.

Fourthly, though rather exceptionally, there was the hazard involved in handling residents whose misapprehensions might be reflected in violence rather than aimless passivity. An attendant in one of the separatist homes recalled, for instance, that once in bathing a confused but very aggressive woman, she had slipped on the wet floor, at which the other immediately grabbed her stick lying nearby and would have struck her had she not herself then slipped in a pool of water.

It must, however, be added that staff difficulties in managing residents were not exclusively, or even mainly, concerned with the confused, particularly in the ordinary homes. Some of the rational were equally stubborn or evasive about aspects of the routine they disliked – 'Really sick of this place I am, bath, bath, bath.' Indeed their oversights, like leaving bath taps running (in one case causing severe flooding), their complaints, like the articulate protests of blind residents left forgotten in the toilet, and their personal antipathies, like an obsessive preoccupation with the foibles of others at table and a mischief-making propensity to set attendants one against another, were far more wearing and time-consuming to staff efforts at appeasement.

THE PRESSURE FOR CLOSE SUPERVISION OF THE CONFUSED

It has already been indicated that one particular management problem for staff, their fear of accidents to the confused for whom they were responsible, was one important reason inhibiting the latter's contact with the outside world. The same fear also led staff, especially in the separatist homes, to restrict freedom for the confused, and thus diminish their power, in other directions. Cigarettes, for example, were only permitted to be smoked in one special home under the rigorous eye of an attendant specially detailed to watch. Residents therefore had to wait till they were *given* cigarettes, then also wait for a light ('Wish they'd come in and bring me a light . . . Oh, come on Mrs Doings and bring me a match'), and then were obliged to smoke them at once so that they could be strictly supervised and the butts taken away at the end. Otherwise cigarettes were simply removed: 'Mr Geece brought me twenty cigarettes before Xmas, but I was only allowed to smoke two, and then the rest were taken away. And I had to leave my pipe behind' (a mildly disoriented man, score 4). Any exchange of edibles between residents was suspected: on one occasion when one gave another a piece of chocolate, attendants who witnessed the offer through a window rushed in to check the nature of the present. In another separatist home efforts were made to keep a careful watch on the kitchen for fear that wanderers might inadvertently scald or burn themselves, ever since one confused woman strayed in and collapsed over the hot-plate. Again, bed-making by the confused was discouraged, not only because beds might not then receive a proper airing, but, as one matron put it: 'If a flea were brought in and beds not stripped, just straightened, it could go through the home.'

STAFF ATTITUDES TO THE CARE OF THE CONFUSED

This last example – of an over-protectiveness buttressed by a rationalization – suggests perhaps that tight supervision of confused residents might reflect more the peculiarity of staff attitudes towards them than the reality of their supposed incapacities. It raises several questions. How did staff conceptualize the implications of mental confusion? What was their occupational background and motivation? How did their feelings affect their job? What qualities did they regard as necessary or desirable for their work? What views did they hold about the overall problem of how the care of confused old people should be organized? These topics will be explored for the light they cast on the actual operation of patterns of control in the homes.

Ideas about the meaning of confusion held by attendants, none of whom had received training in the condition and care of the confused,[13] tended towards two main emphases. One stressed their inherent helplessness: 'They're really like children when all's said to be done. You must treat them like children – must take them to the toilet and wash their hands.' This view centred on those whose previous occupation had been entirely external to the field of the welfare services, for instance, cinema usherette, café owner, chemist's assistant and cleaner, and whose attraction to their present job did not lie chiefly in its intrinsic social service satisfactions. A similar approach was revealed by the superintendent of one of the separatist homes, who explained that a rota system for staff operated between the main establishment and the annexe for the confused whereby no attendant was ever required to work for more than a three week period in the latter: 'That's about as much as we think staff can take with the elderly mentally infirm at any one time.' Again, matrons in the special homes grossly over-estimated the degree of confusion of some of their residents in comparison with the rating the latter received on the confusional scale adopted in this study.[14] The other main view held about the confused focused rather on their wider human needs, irrespective of their limitations:

'They want company, paying them attention, even asking them how they are, trying to prevent them feeling they're put in here out of the way. Joke with them. I talk to them a lot when putting them in bed and at bath-time. Most talk their heads off in the bath. They've got you on your own for a while, even if they talk nonsense. . . . Some can be independent, don't like being helped if they think you're helping them because they're frail.'

These different concepts of the confused were reflected in varying approaches to their care. All staff interviewed in each of the homes showed concern for satisfying the basic health and physical welfare needs of confused residents, but little recognition was apparent of their social needs for self-expression.[15] One type of staff perspective in the separatist homes adopted a model of benevolent custody:

'If one's troublesome, you coax her out of the room with the others and put her to lie down in her own room. A kind word does a great deal, though you can't get to know them really. On entry, you watch them closely lest they go home and lead them back when they go to the door till they settle down after a week or so.'

Another type of staff reaction approximated to detached repudiation, partly perhaps from the insecurities aroused by constant harrowing contact with confusional deterioration:

'Incontinence – it's a shock that you too could be like it – animal. Hurt more than dislike. I sometimes wonder over dripping beds: *why* do I do it? I don't know . . . I won't allow myself to like them a lot, for fear of favouritism, and can look after them better, and danger if they died – you might crack up. You'd suffer with them, and then you couldn't nurse them. . . . I get a personal tiredness, not physically, but mentally. If I'm annoyed, I go off to the linen cupboard [i.e. I turn my back on it] and then I recover and do the job.'

'You certainly have to be firm though kind. I don't think I could work with mental defectives – it'd be too depressing.'

The third sort of approach embraced those who were positively motivated:

'I like old people, have a great respect for them. But I feel sorry too for them – some are dumped here. I hate to think of my own mother like this.'

This group was the most likely to exhibit the occupational qualities of patience and good humour which were almost universally considered requisite, but even they were discouraged by frustrated efforts to form relationships[16] with residents:

'I'm attached to some more than others, but with others you never seem to get anywhere, however you try.'

Despite these varying approaches, there was widespread agreement implicitly, particularly in the separatist homes, in the virtues of pliancy and a placid institutionalism among residents. A typical staff remark, 'She's no trouble,' was offered as a compliment. The case records emphasized qualities like 'quiet', 'docile', 'clean', which were conducive to manageability, not to say malleability. Some attendants characteristically expressed a preference for looking after the confused on the grounds that they were more amenable to instructions ('It's easier to get things done by them') and would not, for instance, grumble about being given certain clothes to wear after a bath. Similarly, staff misgivings centred less on the isolation and erosion of self-determination[17] of the majority of residents than on the intractability of a small minority.

'Bathing is worst, when the bathroom's hot and you're perspiring, when they won't help you to get their clothes off.'
'We have to get them all undressed, all those horrible large ones, especially Mrs Trybley. Oh she's awful, we have to push and shove her.'
'The more lucid are less trouble. You have to do everything for the others.'[18]
'I object most strongly to having to launder the soiled night-dresses and sheets in the morning after a whole night.'
'I only dislike it when they don't want baths and may physically resist and push you away.'
'I get angry when some night wanderers continually get up after they're put to bed, even when the staff want to go.'

The frustrations and irritations involved in handling confused residents produced almost undivided support for their segregation among staff in both types of home. 'There are twelve incontinents – it's wrong for them to be in the same place as the ones more able.' A matron in one of the special homes said: 'It's more difficult to nurse the confused and the non-confused. Better for them to be segregated because it's painful for the non-confused to look at the others. It worries them that one day they'll be like this. So it's better for them to be segregated *within* the home.' Even more blatantly a warden argued: 'The elderly mentally infirm would be better by themselves since then they wouldn't annoy others if they interfered with other mentally infirm old people.' This patent subordination of the interests of the confused was defended by a superintendent in another way: 'If the confused are in a minority, they get a rougher time from the others. They don't like being organized, which would occur more in an ordinary home.' Advocacy for extending segregation was therefore chiefly found among staff of the special homes where the processes of separatism had already reached considerable dimensions, but hostility to integration was also widespread among staff of the other homes. A National Old People's Welfare Council's conference for matrons detected 'considerable resistance to the idea of caring for mentally infirm residents in ordinary homes':

> The matrons reacted to much of the course with hostility. Their reactions were not objective. Much discussion was concerned with trivialities and they seemed unwilling to come to grips with the subject matter of the course. Many of them expressed a marked sense of grievance against welfare officers, general practitioners, committee members, etc. ... There is no doubt that some matrons feel they are now being asked to shoulder responsibilities which are too great and which they never expected to have to undertake ...
>
> If matrons are to care for mentally infirm residents, it is essential that they should have good support from the hospital and domiciliary psychiatric services. This was thought to include full and frank reports on residents before admission; access to medical help from both general practitioners and consultants; help from the appropriate social workers; someone with whom matrons can talk over their difficulties; and the guarantee that, if necessary, mentally disturbed residents will, at the appropriate time, be admitted to specialized accommodation ... (Shaw and Stevens, 1964).

Given then this background of staff attitudes, what patterns could be delineated in the network of authority relations in either kind of home?

Staff authority patterns

Before the various formats adopted in the exercise of authority are discussed, the range of sanctions collectively comprising the system of social controls must first be illustrated, with particular attention to those operated in respect of the confused.

TECHNIQUES OF CONTROL

(a) Discriminatory deprivation

Staff regulation of the supply of desiderata like cigarettes offered an obvious opportunity to exert pressure by threatening or carrying out their removal.[19] But the only instance found of this type of sanction being applied specifically to the confused involved the removal of clothes from night wanderers. As a symptom-oriented approach, however, this policy was predictably ineffective and those concerned persisted in wandering out of the building clad only in a nightdress and without footwear.

(b) Physical constraints

The main means of containment consisted of 'geriatric' chairs, with hand-rest trays clipped into the back of the seat, and 'cot-beds' with raised sides. One of the separatist homes contained three of the former in constant use, and each of these homes reserved one of the latter, usually in a sick bay, for sporadic service. Since residents occupying geriatric chairs were still alleged to be in danger of falling out, they were also confined by a belt fastened across their body and buckled to the seat. This further restriction of bodily movement made it awkward to turn round and thereby difficult to draw attention by facial gesture where the chair had been parked, as was usually the case, in front of the rest of the company. Neither of these mechanical restraints, however, were found in the ordinary homes.

(c) Drugs

The list of medications used in two of the separatist homes, contrasted with those employed in one of the ordinary homes (Table 8.6), reveals that though the proportion of residents regularly receiving drugs was no higher in the former,[20] the proportion in these homes nevertheless who were being regularly administered with tranquillizers was significantly greater.[21] The importance of this finding is demonstrated by research which has indicated, not only that very large numbers of elderly demented patients are receiving tranquillizers unnecessarily,[22] but that the sustained administration of such drugs as paraldehyde, barbituric acid derivatives and the phenothiazines may positively induce toxic side-

Table 8.6

**Day and night medications administered in two
separatist homes and one ordinary home**

Medical Function	Drug	Separatist home A (total residents: 40)		Separatist home B (total residents: 47)		Ordinary home (total residents: 80)	
		No. of residents receiving drug (% in bracket)	Total No.* of daily drug units administered	No. of residents receiving drug (% in bracket)	Total No.* of daily drug units administered	No. of residents receiving drug (% in bracket)	Total No.* of daily drug units administered
(a) Sedatives and tranquillizers	Largactil (25mg)	3 (8)	7	6 (12)	16		
	,, (50mg)	4 (10)	7				
	,, (100mg)	2 (5)	2			2 (3)	2
	Phenobarbitone (½g)	4 (10)	13	3 (6)	8	5 (6)	10
	Sparine	2 (5)	7			2 (3)	4
	Stelazine	2 (5)	5	1 (2)	1		
	Librium	1 (3)	3			1 (1)	3
	Seconal	3 (8)	5				
	Melleril	1 (3)	2				
	Sodium Amytal	2 (5)	4	3 (6)	3	5 (6)	5
	Soneryl	2 (5)	3	2 (4)	2	4 (5)	7
	Amargyl			3 (6)	7		
	Welldorm			4 (8)	4	4 (5)	4

Table 8.6 (*contd.*)

Medical Function	Drug	Separatist home A (total residents: 40)		Separatist home B (total residents: 47)		Ordinary home (total residents: 80)	
		No. of residents receiving drug (% in bracket)	Total No.* of daily drug units administered	No. of residents receiving drug (% in bracket)	Total No.* of daily drug units administered	No. of residents receiving drug (% in bracket)	Total No.* of daily drug units administered
	Theogardenal			1 (2)	2		
	Fentazin			3 (6)	11	4 (5)	20
	Beplete			1 (2)	3		
	Serenace			1 (2)	3		
	Mist. Pot. Brom.					1 (1)	1
	Scorbital					1 (1)	3
	Sodium Barbitone					1 (1)	1
(b) Cardiac reactants	Digoxin			6 (12)	10	1 (1)	2
	Trinitrini			2 (4)	2		
	Abicol			1 (2)	2		
	Cedilanid			2 (4)	3		
	Digitalis (Folio)			1 (2)	1	5 (6)	14
	Sustac					1 (1)	1
	Peritrate S.A.					1 (1)	3
	Lanoxin					2 (3)	2
(c) Hypnotics	Syrup Chloral	6 (15)	8				
	Mist. Chloral			1 (2)	1		
	Carbrital			1 (2)	1	2 (3)	2

Table 8.6 (*contd.*)

Medical Function	Drug	Separatist home A (total residents: 40)		Separatist home B (total residents: 47)		Ordinary home (total residents: 80)	
		No. of residents receiving drug (% in bracket)	Total No.* of daily drug units administered	No. of residents receiving drug (% in bracket)	Total No.* of daily drug units administered	No. of residents receiving drug (% in bracket)	Total No.* of daily drug units administered
	Medomin			1 (2)	1		
	Tuinal			1 (2)	1		
	Sonalgin					4 (5)	4
(d) Diuretics and anti-diuretics	Navidrex					1 (1)	1
	Navidrex-K			5 (10)	7		
	Nephril	1 (3)	1				
	Lasix			1 (2)	1		
	Aprinox			1 (2)	2	2 (3)	2
	Bendrofluozide					6 (8)	6
	Neo Naclex					1 (1)	1
	Neo Naclex-K					1 (1)	1
	Saluric					1 (1)	1
	Hydrosaluric					2 (3)	2
	Hydrosaluric-K					1 (1)	1
	Dytide					1 (1)	1
(e) Bronchial spasm relaxants	Choledyl			2 (4)	3		
	Franol			1 (2)	2	5 (6)	12
	Franol-Plus					1 (1)	1
	Theodrox et Phenobarbitone					1 (1)	2

Table 8.6 (*contd.*)

Medical Function	Drug	Separatist home A (total residents: 40)		Separatist home B (total residents: 47)		Ordinary home (total residents: 80)	
		No. of residents receiving drug (% in bracket)	Total No.* of daily drug units administered	No. of residents receiving drug (% in bracket)	Total No.* of daily drug units administered	No. of residents receiving drug (% in bracket)	Total No.* of daily drug units administered
(*f*) Analgesics and anti-pyretics	Panadol			2 (4)	5	1 (1)	3
	Paracetamol			2 (4)	2	2 (3)	2
	Prednisone					2 (3)	4
	Prednisolone			1 (2)	3		
	Butazolodin			1 (2)	6	3 (4)	9
	Hypon					1 (1)	3
	Aspirin					4 (5)	6
	Codeine Co.					1 (1)	3
	Lobak					1 (1)	5
	Paynocil					1 (1)	3
(*g*) Anti-depressives	Parstelin			1 (2)	1		
	Amphetamine			1 (2)	1		
	Tofranil			1 (2)	3		
	Nardil					1 (1)	3
(*h*) Vascular reactants	Serpasil-Esidrex			1 (2)	3		
	Equivert			1 (2)	3		
	Mycardol					2 (3)	6
	Serpasil					1 (1)	3
	Vasculit					1 (1)	2

Table 8.6 (*contd.*)

Medical Function	Drug	Separatist home A (total residents: 40)		Separatist home B (total residents: 47)		Ordinary home (total residents: 80)	
		No. of residents receiving drug (% in bracket)	Total No.* of daily drug units administered	No. of residents receiving drug (% in bracket)	Total No.* of daily drug units administered	No. of residents receiving drug (% in bracket)	Total No.* of daily drug units administered
	Aldomet					1 (1)	2
	Rauwiloid					1 (1)	1
(*i*) Antacids	Taka-Diastase	1 (3)	3				
	Mist. Mag. Trisil			1 (2)	1	2 (3)	8
	Magnesium Carbonate					1 (1)	2
	Neutradonna					1 (1)	3
(*j*) Rigidity tremor controllers	Artane	4 (10)	13			1 (1)	3
	Disipal			1 (2)	2	1 (1)	3

* Where a drug was administered PRN (as necessary), 1 unit was counted.
Note: Certain other drugs administered in only a very few cases – gastro-intestinal sedatives, anti-hystamines, iron preparations, anti-nauseants, vitamin preparations, sulphonamides, aperients, expectorants/cough suppressants, and thyroid preparations – are excluded from the list.

effects[23] and possibly even itself generate confusion. However, the consequences of polypharmacine and the dangers arising from an injudicious use of sedatives and tranquillizers will be discussed later.[24] Here it will only be said that not only did the daily application of sedatives constitute the single most potent handling device in regular use, but also sporadically the most cogent instrument for controlling the eruption of the occasional acute behavioural disturbance, however caused.

(*d*) *Physical force*

Where staff required cooperation in movement, rather than simply quiescence in the interests of control, and where they could not procure the desired response either properly or quickly enough, their ultimate resort lay in the employment of superior strength to achieve the intended action through physical manipulation. One incident observed will illustrate the exercise of this sanction:

A well-preserved, ambulant woman of eighty-six (confusional score 6), whose constant mumbling soliloquies about her childhood experiences concealed a hawklike shrewdness of observation concerning movements around her, was approached by an attendant, a large, well-built woman, in her usual seat and asked to come for a bath. She demurred. The attendant persisted with the wheedling comment: 'See, it's only a matter of getting out of the chair.' But the old person was not deceived and countered immediately: 'No, it isn't.' The attendant began to lose patience, and when the other's speech started to ramble, she grasped her tightly under the armpits, lifted her bodily from the chair and frogmarched her off down the corridor, despite her confused protests, to the bathroom.

(e) Simulatory manipulation

Besides the powerful physical restraints so far mentioned, staff also had recourse to other devices of a more subtle nature. One of these involved the deliberate utilization of the known fantasies of certain residents, or the deliberate taking advantage of their known weaknesses, especially forgetfulness, to secure a certain objective. Examples included giving a woman sheets to fold when she had an obsession with stripping beds as part of her desire to play a useful role which staff saw as misplaced; allaying the impulse of a confused resident to return home by telling her that her son needed her house when she was known to believe that she had only left to make way temporarily for him; and leaving residents alone provisionally who were required for bathing if they offered undue resistance, on the grounds that at a request later the same day or the next day they would have forgotten and acquiesce readily.

The ethics of this type of paternalistic manipulation did not seem to be questioned, nor the possibility that a resident, though confused, might detect the subterfuge. In fact some attendants clearly saw this ruse as a legitimate tactic in a constant battle by no means one-sided:

'I very often lie to make their minds easier. But it taxes the mind to outwit them – and they win. They're crafty!'

(f) Ridicule

Another subtler means of applying pressure, though in a rather negative and diffuse manner, lay in the use of ridicule to inhibit undesired actions, even if its employment in some cases was scarcely calculated. It seemed to be applied chiefly in admonishing wanderers. Sometimes it operated through the belittling humiliation of an offender in front of other residents: 'I'll smack her bottom', loudly exclaimed an attendant in mock derision as a woman (confusional score 12) was being brought back who was constantly wandering away beyond the grounds of the home. Sometimes the effect was generated through staff making public play of a confused resident's own exposure of his or her eccentricities or incoherence: when, for example, a confused woman kept trying to solicit the attention of another who was dozing and an attendant intervened to protect the latter's privacy, the former, finding her misplaced affections thwarted, protested strongly in a garbled fashion with unintended comic results, at which other residents nearby broke into laughter at her discomfiture as she was forcibly removed. This sanction only appeared to be utilized, however, in the separatist homes.

(g) Segregation

Two further instruments of control remained to staff, both involving the physical displacement of the resident, either internally within the home as a mode of segregation or, more drastically, through transfer to another establishment. The operation of the former technique of control has already been extensively described in Chapter 7,[25] and its employment could be varied to secure the isolation of even a single individual (p. 190). It was for these reasons that the matron of one of the special homes strongly supported the possibilities inherent in a home of larger size which thus permitted greater manoeuvrability.

(h) Transfer

In the ordinary homes the threat of transfer constituted par excellence the ultimate deterrent when it involved, as it often did, removal to a former public assistance institution which still retained an aura of less eligibility[26] and might itself fulfil the role of the separatist home for the locality.

When a marginally confused but aggressive woman (score 1) persistently subjected a fellow-resident to verbal attack on the fabricated pretext that he was an ex-convict and even complained to the police about his presence, she was only finally curbed when her victim threatened to take legal proceedings against her and the matron intervened to warn that if she did not cease, she would be recommended for transfer to the local former PAI. She then ostensibly yielded, though not without launching the occasional surreptitious accusation and transfering her main assault to another victim.

Similarly for the special homes, transfer meant removal to a psychiatric unit with its implicit stigma. Consideration of the use of these procedures is, however, reserved till later (see Chapter 10).

PATTERNS OF CARE

Corresponding to this range of sanctions was an equally variegated categorization of patterns of staff care. The following analysis is not intended to offer an exhaustive typology, but rather to highlight those facets relevant to the distribution of power within each establishment.

(a) Authoritarianism

Staff emphasis on manageability combined with a conviction of the helplessness of the confused, as already illustrated, naturally tended to produce an exercise of authority and expectation of compliance untrammelled by the need for consultation, especially in the separatist homes. This was revealed chiefly through the sharpness of staff instructions to the inarticulate, their interpretation of resistance as unwarranted aggressiveness, their reservation of social distance and their emphasis on an external appearance of orderliness. Underlying all these practices was an over-readiness to deal with the symptom regardless of the cause.

Several incidents witnessed in the special homes exhibited an approach characterized by tart injunctions. 'Sit down there!' to a confused woman brought back from the toilet. 'Stand up straight!' to two residents strapped in geriatric chairs. 'Take that off!' to a woman who eventually gathered that she was required to undress in the middle of the day so that her corsets and knickers could be changed. 'You sit down and just be quiet!' to a wanderer who was making no noise or disturbance at all.

Resistance to these snap orders was neither tolerated nor understood. Rejection of the pervasive ethos of submissiveness came chiefly from rational residents, particularly men, whose antisocial and idiosyncractic behaviour had previously caused their transfer to a separatist home,[27] but it was also occasionally displayed by the more spirited of the confused residents, though its significance was not appreciated:

> A wanderer, rebuked for drifting beyond certain permitted boundaries, refused to take heed and proceeded unabashed on her chosen route. Asked imperatively 'Why don't you go and sit down?' she replied 'I sit down all day.' Unmoved, the attendant persisted in her demands that she should return to her seat, till finally the latter reluctantly submitted, though only after revenging herself on her persecutor with abusive name-calling, 'Dirty pig!'

The maintenance of social distance from residents was manifested especially by the conscious preference of staff to confine conversation very largely within their own ranks in such free moments from work as they enjoyed during duty hours. Only in the ordinary homes were attendants observed sometimes to watch television or to play cards with residents in the evening. In the separatist homes, by contrast, a few attendants sustained a rather boisterous relationship with certain confused residents, but the attachment appeared to make little impact because of its obviously episodal and artificial character.

Also occasionally noticeable in the separatist homes was a staff predilection for orderliness, even if this introduced custodial overtones of suppression. A sudden and unexpected visit by a doctor, for instance, generated a rushed inspection of the residents to tidy up any slovenliness of dress and to silence one in particular who was singing loudly in a manic state.

(b) Impetuous manhandling

Sporadically in the separatist homes authoritarianism spilled over into actual staff violence. Such eruptions, even if infrequent, are perhaps inevitable in residential establishments for the elderly where staffing schedules are typified by worker shortage and hence excessive workloads, long hours of duty and the need to deal with an unusually high incidence of disturbed behaviour. Furthermore the built-in tendency towards residents' long-term physical and mental deterioration undermines the prestige of the work and thus exacerbates recruitment and turnover problems. Certainly these hazards have received widespread adverse publicity from the exposures of recent reports.[28]

Data already presented has demonstrated the staffing shortage, on a weighted basis, in the separatist homes (Table 8.5), and at least in one such home exceptionally long, but fewer, shifts of twelve hours[29] were opted for by married women staff, despite the likely decline in care standards caused by tiredness, because they offered longer unbroken periods of time-off. But apart from pressure of work and the effects of exhaustion, it may also be surmised that the comparative lack of rational observers in the special homes might undermine staff inhibitions against rougher or less sensitive handling of the confused at times of frustration because of their vague or slow reactions.

Certainly a number of incidents in the special homes, both related and personally observed, attest the force of these pressures. One attendant had recently been dismissed for physically maltreating residents, and severe handling was privately alleged at interview by a few of the confused. 'She [an attendant] keeps you on the run. She's rough. I'm terrified when she gives me a bath. She plonks me down. I've had so many falls I'm frightened. Some of the nurses are very hot-tempered. There's one who comes on night duty and says "Shut up!" I could have boxed her ears. . . . If anything goes wrong, I'm blamed for it. I'm blamed for everything. One of the nurses said "You're a liar!" But I'm not a liar and I don't like being called a liar. One day she gave me such a crack on the head that ever since I've had pains in my head.' 'The night nurse bruised my legs, pulled at the beads round my neck and shoved me backwards and forwards.' 'The staff are really *hard* on those who can't look after themselves, and that's what I dread being here for – being shouted at' (a woman who had written several complaints about staff to County Hall). But though rough handling was also personally witnessed,[30] more commonly seen were impetuous actions of inconsiderateness towards those least able to complain:

A woman who was strapped into a geriatric chair kept complaining in incoherent syllables about her sore bottom. Eventually the matron asked two attendants somewhat casually to give her a walk if they happened to have ten minutes spare. For some considerable time nothing was done until finally the attendants, approaching the seated figure from behind as she lay slumped over her tray, suddenly tilted back the chair without warning, jerking her violently from her private reveries, and wheeled it out, slanting her body backwards at an angle over the rear casters.

Or insensitivity could take the form of lack of sympathy and a preference to regard an inability to conform as stubbornness:

Mrs Garrett, a moderately confused woman of eighty-eight who before had been satisfactorily tractable, suddenly lapsed inexplicably into a state of disoriented apathy, accompanied by some complaints of physical pain. In one of a series of similar small episodes during the day she began to cry out: 'Oh my back! Oh my! Whatever shall I do? Oh my!' A rational resident sitting nearby asked: 'Whatever's wrong with you?' An attendant came in, but was called back by another outside the room. Mrs Garret cried out again 'Oh my! Oh . . .!' and another rational companion went out to fetch an attendant, who duly appeared. 'What's the matter, Gran? You'll be better after dinner and tea.' Mrs Garret groaned again, and tried to explain what was wrong, but the attendant insisted: 'You've been pampered all along and now we haven't time. We have all these others here.' Mrs Garret replied, incoherently.

Later, while being brought from the medical examination room, she appeared to dither and her legs dragged between two attendants who were supporting her. The matron who was also accompanying her commanded her to 'Lift your head up! Lift your feet up!' When Mrs Garret weepily exclaimed she was afraid of falling, the matron countered: 'Tell us why you can't walk. There must be a reason. You could walk yesterday. Why not now?' Mrs Garret was silent and sad. The attendants, releasing her from their grip, let her slip, with the matron's agreement, to the floor. 'Do you like it down there?' asked the matron. No reply. After a pause the attendants pulled her up on to a nearby seat and told her to move on when she was ready. 'Why can't you stand up straight? Why can't you walk now? You walked an hour ago.

Yours legs are all right – it's in your mind,' persisted the matron. Mrs Garret was brought to her feet again, and the matron instructed her afresh as the party moved off: 'Head up! Feet up! One, two; one, two . . .' Mrs Garret, however, still stumbled. 'You can't walk – you're bent at the knees,' declared the matron, and an attendant added menacingly: 'If you don't walk, Grannie, I'll leave you on the floor. I *mean* it.' Finally, when all the threats proved of no avail, Mrs Garret was placed in a wheelchair and transported to her chair, her foot tapping on the floor as it trailed limply over the edge of the footrest.

Again, later the same day when a rational resident proffered her arm to Mrs Garret as a support to reach the toilet, a passing attendant, still presuming she was 'playing up', voiced strong disapproval: 'You can do that by yourself. You're being lazy.'

(c) Paternalism

Another form of authoritarianism was also noticeable in staff dealings with the confused, subtler but perhaps equally damaging, being more insidious and more pervasive. Particularly in the separatist homes, staff readily adopted a role of overprotectiveness or benevolent custodianship. Not only did this consist of a systematic underestimation of the capabilities of the confused and non-confused alike in self-determination and self-expression over a whole range of facets of residential life[31] – restrictive staff judgments like 'We prefer her not to go out alone as she's so forgetful', 'She *could* cut her fingernails and toenails, but she would be dangerous with scissors' were typical – but also it involved, more seriously, a somewhat cavalier disregard of complaints and an enforced inclusion in 'suitable' innocuous activities as and when made available. Thus the action of a rational resident in one of the special homes in regularly protecting and helping a marginally confused companion, protesting persistently she was abused and shouted at by staff through impatience at her abnormally slow movements, was readily dismissed by the matron on the grounds that it was 'common in old people's homes for a spinster to fasten on to a cripple and slave for her, and this was what the cripple wanted'. Also, while staff restrictions and physical constraints severely limited the scope of possible activities for the confused and handicapped, strenuous efforts were made, conversely, to initiate an artificial commitment to more manageable habits:

A woman in one of the separatist homes confined to a geriatric chair, who had been reduced to extreme torpor by excess medication but whom the interview revealed as both rational and observant, spent most of each day drooped over the closely incarcerating bonds of her seat. On one occasion, an attendant, seeing her leaning awkwardly out of her chair, pulled her body upright, placed her hands on the tray in front, and asked her if she wanted anything to look at. When she only stared in reply, the attendant fetched a nearby women's magazine, put it on her tray and with the comment: 'Food, that's in your line,' turned to the cookery page. Despite these endeavours, however, the resident continued to stare ahead and paid no attention whatever to the magazine.

Indeed the superficiality of such exercises in paternalistic badgering was repeatedly demonstrated by casual incidents:

Seeing a confused companion knitting with materials recently distributed, another resident who was also slightly confused asked: 'What's it going to be?' 'I don't know,' came the nonchalant reply, 'something useful.'

(d) Delegated custodial power

In addition to the wide array of sanctions commanded by staff and the authoritarian structuring of relationships with residents which was so marked a feature of the separatist homes, a further means of control was brought into operation through informal collusion between the management requirements of staff and the psychological needs of certain residents, usually (though not exclusively) rational, to establish a position of dominance over their companions. This control was exercised through the latter's arrogating to themselves, with the tacit connivance of the attendants, certain functions of superintendence which were chiefly directed towards the aberrations of the confused.

This supervision took various forms. Perhaps the chief one constituted private warnings against prohibited or disapproved actions, especially of day wanderers: 'Leave those alone; they've nothing to do with you' (to a wanderer who seemed about to take a cup from the table). 'Sit down, stay sitting down and don't get up!' (to a disoriented woman walking down the path from the entrance of the separatist unit). 'You're not supposed to do that. Don't come here again' (to a wanderer trying to entice a reluctant companion to accompany her). 'Don't you pull that down. They won't get it back' (one confused woman to another who was fiddling with a fireguard).

Another form of superintendence involved notifying staff of those who had transgressed the conventionally accepted limits of personal freedom. Again this functioned chiefly as a restraint on the excesses of wanderers. In one separatist home at least half a dozen rational residents kept regular watch on the drive and reported to staff accordingly.

A third type of supervision comprised the giving of positive instructions to those of wayward or aimless habits. Thus a severely confused woman who had transferred some clothes from a bedroom to the sitting room was persuaded to return them, disoriented wanderers were led to one of the few vacant chairs left unclaimed in the normal seating distribution, and directions were sometimes administered as to dress propriety, if somewhat peremptorily ('Pull up your stockings! Damn lazy!' 'Jane, put your glasses straight!').

A fourth aspect of delegated custodianship was the actual physical enforcement of order. Restless fiddlers were forcibly escorted from the room. A confused woman who seemed about to drift away was roughly told 'What are you going to do? Sit down!' and pulled back into her chair. A quarrel in which a wanderer had seized the newspaper of a slightly disoriented neighbour was settled by the third party intervention of a rational resident who took charge of the newspaper. And a wanderer who had walked out into the gardens in the late afternoon clad only in a nightdress and barefooted was duly marched back into the house.

Lastly, a few of the rational in the separatist homes had usurped the responsibility for the organization of certain parts of the daily routine, and for this purpose they exercised a quasi-authority not only over the recipients of such services,[32] but also over the small group of acolytes who assisted in the execution of these duties. Such functions included the arrangements for the distribution of mid-afternoon tea, gathering in residents for supper (including in one instance the abrupt pulling out of the electric plug controlling the television to enforce attention to the command 'Everybody out!') and inspecting and correcting the daily handiwork of companions in sewing and embroidery.

This self-appropriation of power, however, sometimes proceeded further than either staff or other residents felt justified:

Mrs Gamblin was a tall, wiry, rational woman of seventy, strongly built for her age, subject to periodic bouts of depression for which she compensated by holding domineering sway in this special home over rational and confused alike. A woman, for example, who was given to an excessively stereotyped repetition of phraseology she regularly sought to stop by wagging a firm finger of admonition at her, but if in vain, she led her out of the room. It was Mrs Gamblin who bodily pulled outside the door one notoriously restless and violent fiddler, Mrs Retberg (score 12), whenever the latter pestered one of her companions. 'I'm not afraid of Retberg. I can deal with her. But the majority are afraid of her. She tries to hurt, but I'm on my guard, though one day she kicked me twice. Mrs Ingerstone (score 1) *loathes* her and shouts at her "Go away! Go away!" Then I have to take Retberg out and hold the door closed when she pushes on the other side. The worst incident was when Miss Ramm (score 6) was in the sitting room and asked: "Can you get me a meal?" and I said "You've *had* a meal." And she snatched the glasses from my face, and I was afraid she might snap them, but I over-powered her.' Even the matron confided that she had been 'frightened' on one occasion to approach Mrs Gamblin to ask her to do a particular service.

Nevertheless she exercised her power with avowedly benevolent intentions. 'Mrs Thaughey's quite attached to me, and I try to help her, but she cries if I pull her up for anything. But once when I told her off very firmly, she was very upset, so I kissed her.' 'I'm only disappointed with Mrs Farquhar (score 5). Matron said "You may be able to help her a lot, Mrs Gamblin." But I don't know her background. If *I* knew her background, *I* could help, though not the others.' She also saw herself as sanctioned by, and working in conjunction with, the attendants. 'I enlist the help of the staff to keep Retberg out.' 'I was put up to it by the staff that somebody had closed the windows at lunchtime which I'd opened.' 'Staff like to feel I have to pour tea for a full quota, so they bring some into our room for me.'

This usurpation of power did not, however, escape resentment from all quarters. One attendant accused her of putting herself 'on a pedestal', another elevated her with jocular irony: 'Oh soon you'll be one of the staff,' while a third told her angrily: 'You've no *right* to take someone out of the room.' One mildly confused resident complained openly to staff about her overbearing interference, while another confessed privately: 'I don't like the head of the TV room. If I rattle the newspaper or speak, she comes down and makes an awful fuss.' Some of the rational residents even spoke of her with loathing for the subservience she extracted from them.

Possibly the sharpness of this authority figure reflected in part the unspoken need for insulation from the confused behaviour of such pervasiveness and severity in this particular home, where more than two-fifths of the residents were judged severely confused. For in the other two separatist homes and even more so in the ordinary homes supervision of the irregularities of the confused was less intense, less frequent and less focused round the dominance of any individual, while in the one special home each of the sitting-rooms contained its own well-established control agent. Two of these persons, interestingly enough, were themselves confused. Yet one (score 10), despite her situational disorientation, directed wandering and tangentiality of speech, kept a searching and inquisitive eye on every move in her room, commanding wanderers to sit down again, reproving women who revealed too much in pulling up their stockings and enquiring about the progress of companions' knitting.

(e) Infantilizing practices

Closely allied to authoritarian handling techniques was a tendency to ignore the subtleties of respect and to override the rights normally predicated of relationships between adults. Again this dimension of social control, which was particularly distinctive towards the confused, was manifested in various guises.

Firstly, certain residents, especially the severely confused, were implicitly treated as though utterly unable to perform even the simplest basic tasks of self-care. Instead of their being politely informed of dress improprieties, for example, and left to undertake their own adjustments privately, stockings which were drooping down were publicly pulled up by attendants, skirts which had ruckled up were pulled down, and feeders were tied on, all without consultation or permission.

Secondly, some confused residents were encouraged by childish endearments which demeaned their status as grown persons. Attendants were observed to use on various occasions such belittling blandishments as: 'Big girl now!' in composing a skirt that had been rolled up; 'You are a good girl today!' to a very severely confused and talkative woman who had obediently accepted a drink after being told to 'stop jawing' as she was being put to bed.

Thirdly, the more seriously confused were sometimes subjected to techniques of puerile socialization, on the apparent assumption that they were incapable of responding to verbal incentives. Several times when a confused person performed some socially disapproved action, like blowing her nose on a petticoat or skirt or picking up some small abandoned object from the floor, a bystander, whether staff or resident, reacted by slapping the person's hand, together with some equally humiliating remonstrance, like 'Dirty! Dirty!'

Another mortifying habit, adopted particularly by the immediate neighbours of an incoherent resident, was the disregarding of the latter's direct speech and a switch without warning to discussion of its intelligibility or otherwise with third person references to the original speaker as though absent or deaf. Typically, when a woman who was strapped into a geriatric chair pleaded in slurred but recognizable tones 'I want to get up', one rational neighbour remarked to another 'What does she say?' and the other replied unconcernedly 'Goodness knows.' Alternatively a third party would answer a question addressed to a confused person, as though the latter were unable themselves to express an opinion: 'Are you tired sitting down, Mary?' 'She won't tell you what's wrong.'

Fifthly, some of the confused were humiliated by being obliged to make certain ritualistic responses in order to obtain a favour. A woman who was being offered a biscuit by her neighbour, for example, found gratitude extorted from her by the sharp reminder: 'What do you say?'

Yet another method of handling which degraded the status of the confused was the frequent staff habit of initiating action to achieve a desired movement of a resident without explanation of the objective which would be necessary to gain voluntary cooperation. Thus for toileting or at mealtimes some confused persons were regularly pulled to their feet or signalled to rise without indication of the purpose, as though their capacity to appreciate and respond to oral requests were non-existent.

A further humbling facet of imbalance in staff relationships with certain residents was the one-way use of first names, especially in diminutive form, when correspondingly even the surnames of attendants were known only to a very small minority of rational residents. The use of 'Sammy', 'Minnie', 'Sarah', or similar appellations in addressing confused and also subnormal persons imparted to them an ornamental precocity normally reserved for tame pets or feeble and innocuous humans.

Lastly, another approach which debased those to whom it was applied, chiefly wanderers, was the automatic and entirely un-provoked anticipation on encounter that certain persons spelt trouble. Characteristic of this attitude was the casual remark of an attendant on seeing a wanderer calmly seated: 'Hallo, don't you go off!'

All these infantilizing practices amply fulfilled the staff dictum that 'sometimes you must treat them like children'. In view, therefore, of the accumulated evidence of the varied operation of authoritarian procedures, we must now ask how residents of the separatist homes, especially the confused, reacted to the denial of their opportunity for self-determination and, even more, to their tacit deprivation of many of the attributes of adult status.

Responses of the confused to authority

Quite apart from the more pervasive and insidious long-term effects on residents' behaviour induced by staff attitudes and techniques of control as elucidated, some of the confused, chiefly in the separatist homes, did utilize more immediate measures of retaliation to reassert their autonomy. No doubt such actions should not be directly construed as calculated efforts to redress an imputa-tion of powerlessness, but equally it would be a mistake wholly to disregard the repercussions on the power relations between staff and residents which the latter's resistance, however spontaneous or sporadic, inevitably generated. Whether then as overt acts of deliberate defiance or merely unpremeditated responses to sudden frustration, reactions ranged from violent piques of rage to a systematic silent intattentiveness to instructions.

The most constant focus of opposition among the confused in

the special homes lay in the routine operations of dressing, undressing and bathing. Table 8.7 demonstrates that in the separatist

Table 8.7

Numbers of confused and rational residents in one separatist home who resisted staff handling in the routine of daily care

Routine care function resisted	Severely confused residents	Moderately confused residents	Rational residents
Bathing	6	5	2
Dressing/undressing	9	6	0
Toileting	4	1	0
Number	17	15	8

home with the highest proportion of confused residents, half of these regularly resisted staff handling in dressing and undressing them, a third rebelled against being bathed, and a quarter of the more severely confused obstructed their being toileted, in contrast to little or no hindrance to these functions by the rational. Some staff saw residents' antagonism as deliberate thwarting:

They cling when you're dressing or undressing them. It's frustrating. You feel obstructed – have to rush, but can't. Incontinence one can understand the reason for, so you can put up with it. But in dressing it's just non-cooperation.

Yet the temptation to take countermeasures was felt to be blocked:

'The worst thing is getting heavy people out of bed. Mrs Bilberry, for example, hates it and screams, but she's incontinent and you can't leave her as she'll get sores on her back.' 'Mrs Riccall's heavy and quite strong and she stiffens up. She's scared about everything and won't be interfered with. It needs three or four of us to handle her to get her dressed. But we mustn't talk roughly to her because of the shock of her husband's death.'

Certainly in one men's geriatric ward in a mental hospital male nurses were observed to resort to armlocks from behind against fractious patients who resisted undressing, but no comparison could be made with procedures in the residential homes since personal access could not be obtained to these aspects of the daily routine.

Now interpretation of residents' motivation in this context is necessarily hypothetical, and doubtless their behaviour reflected multi-factorial influences. Thus resistance to dressing and bathing may have indicated a dislike of being badgered in the absence of personal control over the daily schedule, or in the more confused sheer puzzlement about the function of clothes, or hostility to being bothered with trying tasks (a mildly disoriented and otherwise apathetic woman referred in screeching tones to the bath as 'this hell-hole'), or resentment at interference with privacy, or antagonism to strong-armed and tactless handling methods, or indeed any compound of these. Similarly incontinence may have represented merely an involuntary physiological reflex, or the physical expression of emotional bewilderment and social isolation, or a taxing act of defiance, or a mixture of these elements. However, other actions could be more safely construed as emanating chiefly from an urge for retaliation.

A severely confused woman (score 9) stuffed cotton wool down her ear till it became excoriated and the matron had to prise it out with forceps. Later the resident asked for more cotton wool and when this was refused, she became furious and stuffed a toffee paper down her ear instead.

Concerning another very confused woman (score 12) who was also very refractory, an attendant commented: 'She's artful. She'll go to other rooms, open drawers and wake people. And she'll go where the staff aren't. She used to be the one who hid behind the doors and hid in the folds of the screen in the hall, and though she was said not to be able to walk well, she could even run when she wanted to. You can put her on the toilet and even sit with her, and then put her back in bed, but she then gets out and does it on the carpet. . . . She'll really try to *hurt* with a blow, if one is trying to get her to do what she doesn't want. If you're dressing her, she'll kick, so you step back, but then she walks off. So you need one member of staff in front to hold her wrists and one behind.'

Another very confused resident (score 12) who was constantly harassed by staff for her wandering proclivities and her habit of importuning others for affection was on one such occasion told to leave a companion alone. She protested, but her tangential expression made the nearby attendants laugh, at which she exploded in anger: 'You think you're it, leave me alone. I'm going to report you as soon as . . .' But finding that words failed her again, she resorted to the only means left to get herself taken seriously and struck the nearest attendant squarely on the shoulder.

Other actions of the confused might appear to be of more dubious or more complex purpose, but could plausibly be argued to contain defiance as a principal component of intention. Self-mutilation by scratching one's back raw, stripping off clothes sometimes to the point of nakedness, and physical wandering as an avenue for escapism, all of which were found, might be understood at least partly in this light. All such actions, however, were only too likely to be interpreted by staff as requiring even more stringent measures of restraint on the individuals concerned for the sake of their own safety and protection. But occasionally resistance was 'successful'. The four residents in one separatist home, for instance, including three severely confused, who were most recalcitrant towards the daily ordeal of dressing and undressing were permitted to sit through the day in their nightclothes and dressing gowns.

As the examples have amply illustrated, obstinate and retaliatory behaviour centred disproportionately on the severely confused, and hence was scarcely found in the ordinary homes. This may be explained partly by the fact that the rational and those only slightly confused were more readily understood by staff and other residents and so could achieve satisfaction through more conventional means, and partly that they were more able to invoke outside contacts, whether relatives or welfare officials, to their protection. But above all the contumaciousness of the severely confused may reflect their utterly perplexity at their social experiences and their emotional desolation. Indeed this prompts the question as to whether confusion might actually not possess any independent existential validity, but rather represent a collective ascription of mental derangement to a heterogeneous range of refractory behaviour.

THE SOCIAL AND PSYCHOLOGICAL IMPLICATIONS OF SEGREGATION, ISOLATION AND POWERLESSNESS

How far then is it true, not that the confused exhibited defiant or 'difficult' behaviour, but rather that it was only through the medium of their defiance and nonconformity that their alleged confusion was recognized? This question poses both an empirical problem and an analytical problem. Empirically, did the cumulative extent of social deprivation among the confused, both in frequency and severity, rationally 'explain' such rebellious behaviour? To this the argument of the present chapter, together with the preceding one, has suggested a positive answer. But secondly, analytically, whatever the magnitude of social deprivation of the confused, was their intractableness a reaction to an unduly repressive environment, or rather were the regulations and restraints tightened only in response to dangerously aberrant or idiosyncratic behaviour? This latter question introduces the classic dilemma of determining cause and effect in a dynamic process described by a series of static cross-sectional analyses, when in fact the two components involved may each successively have occupied cause and effect positions in a mutually reinforcing spiral. However, again, the argument of the two present chapters has repeatedly demonstrated that the administrative procedures and social dispositions, for the confused at least, were restrictive to a degree far beyond that minimally required for the purpose of secure handling and residents' protection. For a more satisfactory explanation of these administrative rigidities, we must look to the social and psychological implications of residential separatism.

Above all the act of segregating certain individuals in special institutions implicitly designated all those thus selected as exhibiting at least one common attribute, and the identification of this quality as 'mental infirmity' or 'confusion' tended automatically to determine the character of the system of care irrespective of the actual possession or non-possession of particular powers and capacities by each individual. For segregation *per se* seemed to indicate something amiss about those segregated – that they were not in every respect fully human or normal – and this underlying premise readily provided a psychological justification for any irregularity of treatment or insensitivity of care. Symbolic of this tendency was the action of the superintendent of one of the separatist homes, in reviewing a room containing some confused residents, when he loudly pronounced upon their incapacities in their presence as though they were unhearing or unfeeling, and when later he promptly excused the absence of choice for them as irrelevant on the grounds that they were 'EMI' as though this were some inanimate substance. Thus a process which might originally emanate from the correct recognition of the diminution or total extinction of certain specific powers could structurally engender, despite the sincere personal efforts of many devoted care staff, an unintended generalized depersonalization of the individuals concerned.

In more particular ways, too, staff thinking and actions were influenced by the fact of separatism. Since the special homes were intended for 'confused' or 'mentally infirm' persons, any quirk of behaviour, regardless of its likely cause, was readily ascribed to 'confusion'. The initial restlessness and bewilderment immediately after entry, for instance, was interpreted as the product of a mental state justifying admission rather than as at least partly reflecting the dispossession and mortification procedures (Goffman, 1961, p. 14ff) inevitably accompanying admission. Psychological explanations were adduced to project the deficiencies of the environment on to individuals. Thus those who were uncooperative and occasionally abusive because they were clearly unhappy in unaffectionate surroundings were judged 'insensitive to the feelings of others'. Similarly, out of many revealing entries in the case records, a woman in one of the separatist homes who insisted, whenever staff turned off the basin light or heater she left on in her bedroom, on coming back upstairs and turning them on again, was seen not as expressing the right to self-determination, however much its explanation in this case might be verbally discouraged, but as 'throwing a tantrum' from which 'she recovered next week'. Again matrons tended to overemphasize personality inadequacies, independently of the constraints imposed by the environment, which conflicted with the management ideal of acquiescence. Residents who resisted apathy, for example, were regarded as 'overactive', 'always wanting to be doing' or 'fidgety, not happy being still for long'. 'Difficult' persons were labelled as manifesting a 'rigid routine', whether or not their recalcitrance might be understandable, or as 'seeking attention'.

Above all, in one of those self-fulfilling prophecies which so tragically distinguished the career of the confused in residential institutions, staff unwittingly could, by the administration of excessive medication and the use of various physical restraints, manufacture the conditions conducive to this type of personalized explanation. For the adoption of mechanical restraints like geriatric chairs or cot-beds and the employment of pre-emptive strategems like removing the clothes of a night wanderer merely exacerbated, as symptom-oriented rather than cause-removing approaches, the underlying pathologies and compelled resort to alternative, possibly bizarre (anormic) behaviour which then validated the diagnosis of mental derangement or confusion. In no area was this process more insidious than in that of medication. A quarter of the residents in one separatist home were regularly receiving barbiturates (Table 8.8),[33] yet most workers in geriatrics now recognize that they tend

Table 8.8

Numbers of confused and rational residents regularly receiving sedatives, including specifically barbiturates in two separatist homes and one ordinary home

Drug type	Residents of separatist home A		Residents of separatist home B		Residents of ordinary home	
	Confused	Rational	Confused	Rational	Confused	Rational
Sedatives	16	3	12	10	3	23
Barbiturates*	8	2	4	4	0	15
TOTAL Residents	32	8	22	25	13	67

* Including Phenobarbitone, Sodium Amytal, Seconal, Soneryl and Sodium Barbitone.

to produce depression in the morning if used as a night sedative and certainly increase confusion during the day, as well as appearing to play a part in making incontinence more common, while the administration of phenobarbitone during the day would certainly contribute towards producing confusion. Furthermore, polypharmacine is known to induce other pathological conditions, including irreversible oral dyskinesia, with which 14 per cent of the severely confused were afflicted, drug-induced Parkinsonism, akathisia (Haase and Janssen, 1965, pp. 65, 121),[34] and possibly also a disturbing loss of dream-sleep.[35] Thus the injudicious use of drugs,[36] ostensibly required for medical purposes, could inadvertently supply an *ex post facto* vindication for the original decision to segregate in a special home. One case may be quoted in striking illustration of this process:

Miss Mowbray on entering the separatist home appeared an agile and sprightly figure for her eighty-eight years. Initially she used her nimbleness to assist in various domestic tasks, expecially laying tables, but since she was regarded as overactive, she was placed on a heavy treatment of Serenace. Over time she was reduced to a state of almost helpless flaccidity, and was now strapped into a geriatric chair all day except when carried between two attendants to the meal-table or the toilet with her legs dangling impotently on the floor. She was treated by staff as though she were utterly incapable of performing even the simplest function for herself, for her fixated stare, her awkward movements from the loss of muscular flexibility in her hands and her continuous excessive salivation with regular dribbling streaking her dress certainly gave an impression of abnormality. Yet at her interview, though she thought and spoke slowly, read the questions laboriously and answered laconically with a ponderous heaviness, she was nevertheless clearly rational and percipient of her surroundings. But significantly, in assessing her incapacities, not only did the matron regard them as endogenous rather than as a product of her highly circumscribed environment, but she also appeared to see her lethargy as a sign of other, entirely unrelated disabilities. Thus she was judged to be 'disinterested in social contacts' and to suffer from 'complete disorientation' though she was held fast in a geriatric chair facing the window and with its back to the rest of the company so that conversation was only possible with a neighbour, also in a geriatric chair, who was disjointedly fragmentary in speech (score 8). She was considered to 'ramble incoherently', though she scarcely ever spoke and was rational when she did so, and to be 'unable to communicate verbally what she meant or wanted' when the existence of this ability was merely concealed by her main barrier of deafness. She was regarded as 'insensitive to others', though it was not clear how this could have been shown, and to be 'indifferent to visitors', though she had not had any for a long time. Lastly she was also stated to be 'completely forgetful' and described as 'never perceiving the existing situation realistically', though the interview provided positive evidence to the contrary.

Apart from the frustrating staff habit of ascribing all abnormalities to a uniform cause loosely identified as 'mental infirmity' – an umbrella concept in practice capable of almost indefinite extension – other procedures and policies, equally deriving from the presumption that residents of separatist homes were confused, may be seen as unwittingly conspiring to *create* confusion and thus artificially to uphold the presumption. Some of these have already been described, such as the various infantilizing practices[37] observed and the custom of 'dumping' residents in their new home without explanation, after eliciting their cooperation by the fiction that they were being merely 'taken for a ride', and then using tranquillizers to subdue their initial restless disturbance. Further customs with similar implications, such as the use of ritualized questions,[38] have been noted by other writers, and the aggregation of certain administrative procedures and social patterns in residential or hospital life, all of which[39] have been shown to be present for the confused in both separatist and ordinary homes, has been conceptualized as the distinct pathological syndrome of 'institutional neurosis'.

But above all the whole analysis of the present two chapters derives its force from the fact that the relatively very low level of social integration achieved by the confused (as quantitatively measured on four separate dimensions by Table 8.10, using scales set out in Table 8.9), together with their widespread loss of independent self-determination and almost total alienation from power

Table 8.9

A measure of the social integration of confused residents in residential homes for the aged

Sphere	Source of data	Indices		Score
I. Conversation	Table 7.1 (page 157) & figure 4 (p. 160)	(a) Proportion of time spent in conversation: More than 125% of proportion of time spent thus by the rational		4
		100–125%	,,	3
		75– 99%	,,	2
		50– 74%	,,	I
		Less than 50%	,,	o
	Figures 2 & 3 (pp. 157 & 159)	(b) Inclusion within a regular conversational network: More than 125% of proportion of the rational thus included		4
		100–125%	,,	3
		75– 99%	,,	2
		50–74%	,,	I
		Less than 50%	,,	o

Table 8.9 (*contd.*)

Sphere	Source of data	Indices	Score
2. Activities	Table 7.1 (p. 157)	(*a*) Proportion of time spent in some form of activity: More than 125% of proportion of time spent thus by the rational	4
		100–125% ,,	3
		75– 99% ,,	2
		50– 74% ,,	1
		Less than 50% ,,	0
	Table 7.7 (p. 184)	(*b*) Devotion to some regular recreational pursuit: More than 125% of proportion of the rational thus devoted	4
		100–125% ,,	3
		75– 99% ,,	2
		50– 74% ,,	1
		Less than 50% ,,	0
3. Contact with friends in home or relatives outside	p. 176	(*a*) Involvement in definite friendship ties within the home: More than 125% of proportion of the rational thus involved	4
		100–125% ,,	3
		75– 99% ,,	2
		50– 74% ,,	1
		Less than 50% ,,	0
	Table 7.12 (p. 200)	(*b*) Visits received at least as often as once per month: More than 125% of proportion of the rational thus visited	4
		100–125% ,,	3
		75– 99% ,,	2
		50– 74% ,,	1
		Less than 50% ,,	0
4. Residential arrangements	Table 7.8 (p. 193)	(*a*) Bedroom shared with at least one rational resident: More than 125% of proportion of the rational thus allocated	4
		100–125% ,,	3
		75– 99% ,,	2
		50– 74% ..	1
		Less than 50%	0
	Table 7.11 (p. 196)	(*b*) Dining table shared wih at least on rational resident: More than 125% of proportion of the rational thus allocated	4
		100–125% ,,	3
		75– 99% ,,	2
		50– 74% ,,	1
		Less than 50% ,,	0

and influence, produced a situation in which the need for restrictive and authoritarian handling became a self-fulfilling prophecy. For whilst the close supervision of confused persons for some purposes (for example, smoking) is clearly warranted, the institutional

Table 8.10

The differential degree of social integration of confused residents in three separatist homes as opposed to two* ordinary homes (scoring system as stated in Table 8.9)

Sphere		Separatist homes			Ordinary homes		Parity of Integration score
		Home A	Home B	Home C	Home E	Home F	
1. Conversation	(a)	2	4	4	0	1	3
	(b)	0	2	1	1	2	3
2. Activities	(a)	2	1	3	0	2	3
	(b)	1	0	0	0	2	3
3. Contact with friends in home and relatives outside	(a)	0	0	0	0	0	3
	(b)	2	4	2	2	2	3
4. Residential arrangements	(a)	0	2	n.a.	3	3	3
	(b)	2	2	n.a.	3	3	3
TOTAL		9	15	10+	9	15	24

* The third ordinary home could not be included as it contained only one confused resident.

regulation of decision-making can become so overpowering and the range and depth of relationships so confined – and these two chapters argue that for confused residents this point has been reached – as to produce such apathy that they are regarded as systematically incapable of taking any initiative or forming any normal relationship. Indeed it may be true that once the opportunity for at least some minimal daily exercise of discretion is regularly removed, the will to make and carry through any judgments at all is ultimately undermined. Now the socio-psychological assessments by matrons of their residents indicate that blunting of emotion, especially complete apathy, was significantly more frequent among the confused and staff remarks like 'They don't ask for anything but an easy chair, and don't want anything if they don't ask for it. They require little of life now', and 'Sometimes they just want to sit; if they want to talk to you, they will', illustrate the dangers of an over-literal interpretation of this condition. Alternatively, if they reacted with withdrawal or aggression – and similar assessments reveal that significantly more of the confused manifested these tendencies than the rational in both the separatist and ordinary homes – then such behaviour would be constructed as confirming suspicions of their mental instability or social abnormality. Furthermore, beyond a hypothetical threshold point of acceptance, even straightforward efforts at relating with their companions by the confused might be liable to perverse misapprehensions. Typical of such incidents was the following:

> A severely confused and blind woman of ninety who was afflicted with partial deafness, feeling some objects on the seat beside her, asked innocently: 'Anyone know whose slippers these are?' One of her rational neighbours then got to her feet and removed the slippers to another chair with the comment to her friend: 'I've put them out of her reach.' But even in addition to this entirely unprovoked repudiation of a perfectly innocuous question, all the rational residents within earshot then broke into unreflecting mirth when their blind companion, obviously mishearing the last word spoken, replied perplexedly: 'I don't want any meat.'

Such cruel and unaccountable treatment, though inadvertently delivered, must have driven the confused, if regularly repeated, deeper into feelings of loneliness, mistrust and helplessness, and by reducing the incentive to act normally, have generated or reinforced the shift towards irregular activity which then initiated the vicious circle whereby the irregularity, greeted with rejection, was likely to be exacerbated, thus inviting even stronger disavowal. Equally this self-intensifying process may be construed as an isolationist spiral in which a person, once identified as eccentric or 'confused', is increasingly ignored and then in seeking to adjust to growing isolation has recourse to the limited avenues of self-expression left which, being probably of an unusual or 'anormic' nature, then supply a 'logical' justification for even firmer rejection.

How can the devastating impact of this process be measured? As a gauge of the pathology consequent upon subjection to segregation and powerlessness, matrons' assessments of the comparative psychological susceptibility of the confused are perhaps too flat and indirect, and must be supplemented by more personal illustrations of the crushing loss of self-identity which could be unwittingly inflicted:

A widow of eighty-two, who was a persistent wanderer and tangential speaker (score 8) in a separatist home, was still able to detect, through the confused mists of her disorientation, that her bearings were hopelessly adrift. 'I don't know who I am or what I am. So far gone as that. Haven't the faintest idea what I'm doing here. I don't know whether I'm here or there, that's the feeling. I keep wondering now what's going to come to me. I don't know where I'm going to live.'

Perhaps the extreme example of personal anomie was that of another widow, aged seventy-seven, in another special home whose desperate feelings of utter abandonment were fed into jagged and disjointed sentences and actions of unpredictable violence. 'They don't care about me. They bugger about about my father and mother. They don't care if I don't eat. I've got nothing. [She claps, slaps and bangs her hands continually.] I wish to God they'd take the bloody papers away from here. [She slaps her hands.] I can't hit it, I haven't . . . There's no-one here. Oh for Christ's sake [becoming anxious and distressed], I won't want to get outside. I want to get inside. What can I do? Where can I go? Only that boy will let me have any.'
'Who?'
'That, him, sitting with you. [Three was nobody with me.] Makes me bloody mad to think there are such bloody people about. [Slaps her hands again.] What can I do for them? [Continually wanders about very restlessly.] Got a mental gadget. Oh Christ Almighty [her voice rising to crescendo], I don't want to lose them. They've taken it all from me. I've got a blasted bit of paper. I've got no one else to help me. . . . Dear, oh dear, I wish I were in my own home. Yes, he comes down here sometimes. Look at that – only a pinch of cupboard. God help me, let me go home. I won't make a mess, I'll only come to the window . . . I'll have to go and get it, Oh God help me, I don't get anything to eat. Look here, I want to get it home. Oh by God Almighty [her voice rising in anguish again], let me get out of here. Oh let me go home and drown my bloody self.'

Indeed such an agonized pitch of despair may have been more

pervasive than it appeared since such sentiments could only be explicitly recognized when communicated verbally, and in the case of others insights were concealed by their unwillingness or inability to articulate.

But however the reality of this process is most effectively pictured, the fundamental point for the theory enunciated here is that 'confusion' is seen less as an endogenous condition than as a system of 'logical' adjustments to a mystifyingly insecure and alarming environment. Certainly this still leaves certain theoretical problems unresolved. In particular, if the very process of dissociation and impoverishment of decision-making itself generates 'confusional' behaviour, on what basis were the persons exhibiting this reaction selected for segregation in the first place? In other words, if an at least partially administrative explanation is promulgated for confusion, how is the vicious circle initiated? To a degree this objection is met, as already indicated, by the psychological implications of residential separatism which made the presumption of mental infirmity universally applicable.[40] But at a deeper level the dilemma may be removed by a theory of old age which hinges on the social appropriateness of the reaction developed in the face of the growth of physical disability, the weakening of sensory acuities and the deprivation of hitherto crucial social and economic roles. This reaction may be a 'successful' (socially acceptable) one, or it may involve behaviour which in certain contexts is interpreted as 'eccentric'. Now the construction initially placed on the gradual manifestation of these adjustment techniques may prove to be critical for influencing their future development. For a response which stresses their oddity or peculiarity may feed back to the elderly person a self-image which successively, as the process of adjustment gathers momentum alongside the increase in physical handicap or deterioration, demands revaluation of the approach adopted to meet the range of new problems confronting him. However, each further setback in a sequence of repudiation may enlarge the difficulties of regaining the normality of mutual acceptance, and at some hypothetical threshold point, the precise location of which in a notional process is systematically undefinable, the old person comes to be regarded as more than merely eccentric.[41] From this point the administrative consequences of the 'confusion' label naturally flow, and these will be explored further in Part IV. First, however, how far does an empirical analysis of the observed manifestations of 'confusion' substantiate the theoretical function here ascribed to them as mechanisms, however ostensibly irrational their conception, to assist adaptation to bewildering and unsatisfying surroundings? The following chapter will seek to answer this question.

NOTES

1. It should be said, in regard to the scoring, that where a discrepancy was found to exist between what was theoretically permitted by the regulations, formal or informal, and what actually happened in practice, the item was evaluated with the latter in mind.

2. In a few cases it led to conversation with some attendants on a first name basis.

3. This observation applies exclusively to the hierarchic framework of decision-making, particulary in the separatist homes, and is not incompatible with individual feelings of gratitude to attendants *as persons*. Thus an extremely lethargic woman (confusional score 5) who rebelled violently against being bathed could also show her sincere appreciation of staff by the remark at her interview: 'Nobody could be better than they are to me.'

4. See further, P. Townsend (1962, p. 237).

5. It should, however, be made clear that such resentment was not confined to the separatist homes. A woman in one of the ordinary homes said, for example: 'I was in hospital, then had the shock of my life when put here. Thought I was going home – they never actually said so. It was a shock to find men and women, some deranged, all living together, when you're used to a quiet country life in a cottage.'

6. The couple in the last example were removed under section 47 of the National Assistance Act 1948.

7. The Court of Protection, an office of the Supreme Court, is responsible under section VIII of the Mental Health Act 1959 for the protection and management of the property and affairs of persons judged incapable, because of mental disorder, of managing and administering their own. The court's jurisdiction runs whether or not such persons are compulsorily detained and whether they are residing in their own homes or elsewhere.

8. This is elaborated in chapter 9.

9. See, 'Responses of the confused to authority' p. 267.

10. This is explored below, see 'Patterns of care: (*d*) Delegated custodial power' p. 262.

11. This reaction is examined below, see 'Responses of the confused to authority', p. 267.

12. Also one woman used regularly to get out of bed, wrap herself in blankets and wet them through.

13. One matron had attended a course on the care of the mentally infirm resident organized by the National Old People's Welfare Council at Guildford in February 1964.

14. Instances include two residents elsewhere described (pp. 88 and 273) who were regarded as seriously confused but categorized as rational in terms of the criteria of this study and whose undoubted irregularities of behaviour were caused, or exacerbated, by the social and medical treatment they received. The assumption that lay behind these staff assessments – that admission is prima facie evidence that a resident must be the kind of person the institution was established to handle – is not, of course, confined to separatist homes for confused old people (see Goffman, *Asylums*). In this study the

same tendency was illustrated by the over-estimate by matrons in the ordinary homes of the *physical* incapacity and mobility limitations of their residents.

15. At least in the separatist homes. Possibly one reason why the confused in the ordinary homes exhibited a 'better' personal appearance than those with equivalent behaviour in the specialized homes (Table 7.5, p. 171) is that staff in the former, where normal conventions of dress propriety still predominated, took care over the odd dress irregularities of the few confused, while in the latter such abnormalities had become too frequent for staff to bother.

16. In none of the homes were attendants given access to the case records, though almost all felt that 'reading the past they can't tell you' would offer perspective and increase understanding.

17. Many of the staff in the separatist homes clearly felt that the exercise of choice by the confused was impractical and the issue therefore irrelevant. One matron pointed the moral, in illustrating the existence of an alternative menu, by the almost proverbial tale of the resident who refused to eat rabbit, but on one occasion the option specially prepared for her by the cook was accidentally passed to somebody else and she ate the rabbit without complaint.

18. Though for some staff, far from being a burden, this eminently satisfied their psychological needs: 'I love it. The old people are so dependent on us. I prefer the [confused] because they need more help.'

19. Thus a rational resident in one of the separatist homes who broke the prohibition against smoking in bedrooms had his cigarettes removed, but clearly the sanction was susceptible to wider application.

20. 60 per cent and 70 per cent in the two separatist homes, and 61 per cent in the ordinary home.

21. 50 per cent and 47 per cent in the two separatist homes and 32 per cent in the ordinary home.

22. Barton and Hurst (1966, pp. 989–90): their double-blind trial suggested that about 80 per cent of elderly demented patients were being tranquillized unnecessarily.

23. For example, D. B. Robinson (1959, p. 41) found that the prolonged administration of chlorpromazine (largactil) produced a significant lowering of the level of functioning.

24. See below 'The social and psychological implications of segregation . . .', p. 270.

25. See 'Structured isolation', p. 188.

26. This is paralleled in other residential systems hierarchically ranked by degree of authoritarianism where one, or a very small minority, of institutions occupied a notoriously deterrent position, e.g. Portland in the Borstal system.

27. The partial function of separatist homes as a repository for those expelled from ordinary residential homes is discussed in chapter 10.

28. *Sans Everything*, edited for Aid for the Elderly in Government Institutions (AEGIS) by B. Robb, June 1967. These allegations of ill-treatment and cruelty to elderly patients in seven hospitals were somewhat unconvincingly dismissed as mainly 'totally unfounded or grossly exaggerated' by independent committees of enquiry set up under hospital boards (though not under the Ministry of Health): *Findings and Recommendations Following Enquiries into Allegations Concerning the Care of Elderly Patients in Certain Hospitals*, Cmnd 3687, HMSO, 9 July 1968. Similar charges, including beatings, were later repeated in an enquiry for the Welsh Board of Health into the condition and treatment of patients at Ely Mental Hospital, Cardiff, March 1969, and also in the form of four independent allegations of maltreatment of patients at South Ockenden (Essex) mental hospital (*Sunday Times*, 6 April 1969). These cumulative indictments prompted the appointment of special Ministry investigators and consideration of an independent health commissioner or ombudsman (finally appointed in March 1972 following the Whittingham Hospital Report).

29. Three twelve-hour shifts rather than four nine-hour shifts to fulfil a weekly quota of thirty-six hours.

30. See above 'Techniques of control, (*d*) Physical force,' p. 254.

31. See above 'The residents. Restrictions and loss of rights', p. 224.

32. This power could be abused. A recovered schizophrenic in one of the separatist homes, for example, who shopped for her companions was suspected of exploiting her confused beneficiaries by taking a cut on the side when she returned the change.

33. This assumes, of course, that they actually took them rather than disposing of them without swallowing them. In fact various studies of tablet-taking have shown that between 30 per cent and 70 per cent of patients in different series did not take tablets as prescribed.

34. Akathisia is a syndrome reported by Bing of a chamberlain at the court of Napoleon III, suffering from Parkinson's disease, who despite the rules of etiquette, could not sit still and was continuously on the move.

35. Luce and Segal (1967), report that there is now considerable evidence that the barbiturates, tranquillizers and amphetamines can all reduce the amount of REM (rapid eye movement) sleep which is known to be associated with dreaming, and that the reduction of REM sleep produces irritability, forgetfulness, poor concentration and obscure feelings of uneasiness.

36. Several factors contributed towards this rashness, including the expectations of residents and their relatives for medicines, the anticipations of the care staff, doctors unacquainted with the latest pharmaceutical developments and the lack of adequate supervision of medical treatment.

37. One such practice, for instance, the humiliatingly public pulling up of drooping stockings had in some cases been predetermined by the staff policy of removing suspender belts.

38. 'Questions may be accompanied by simultaneous searching by the staff which physically discloses the facts, making these verbal questions superfluous' (Goffman, 1961, p. 45).

39. Loss of contact with the outside world; enforced idleness; authoritarianism of medical and nursing staff; loss of personal friends, possessions and personal events; indiscriminate use of drugs; poor ward atmosphere; and loss of prospects outside the institution: Barton (1959). Another analysis, in a different context of the determination pathological behaviour by the institutional framework is provided by Cicourel and Kitsuse (1963).

40. However, it can be countered that this merely pushes the argument one stage back by requiring an explanation of the original selection for a separatist home. That persons were frequently chosen thus on other than strictly medical grounds of assessment is demonstrated in chapters 10 and 11.

41. A similar theory of 'secondary deviation' has been suggested by Edwin Lemert to describe the state which results from the interaction of an individual's primary deviation (e.g. stuttering or the first criminal offence) and the modes of social control in a particular society (the way in which other people react to the deviation): Lemert (1967). A parallel thesis is provided by the 'drift' theory of adolescent delinquency which argues that the original delinquent act is not in itself important. It largely comes from bad judgment and the inability to foresee consequences in a complex social situation. But it is then reinforced by group loyalties and also by the reactions of authority, and the potential deviant has to meet the situation thus created by rejecting the stigma (rationalization), accepting it (identifying himself as delinquent), or by withdrawal.

9

Adjustments: mechanisms of defence adopted by the confused

If the claim is to be substantiated that confusional behaviour represented a series of 'logical' adjustments to a distressing environment rather than the irrational excrescence of a deranged mind, then *a fortiori* it must also be shown that confused persons were capable of registering the significance of events around them and of responding to them in an interpretative manner. This question will be discussed first. Secondly, how far did the confused in reality regard their environment as distressing? Their own statements concerning their satisfactions and dissatisfactions will then be debated, together with evidence of the degree and nature of their alienation and unmet need for affection. Finally, a functional typology of confused behaviour will be analysed.

AWARENESS OF THE ENVIRONMENT AMONG CONFUSED PERSONS

Sensibility to the social atmosphere was demonstrated by confused residents chiefly in their perception of their own or others' loss of sensory powers or mental altertness, in their own humour and their recognition of others' facetiousness, in their ability and readiness to respond to incentives and conversely their distress at being hurt (or at seeing others hurt) by neglect or rejection, and in their general capacity to identify the subtle significances of social events. Often, however, these insights seemed only to represent flashes of lucidity or understanding since they were combined in certain individuals with much behaviour otherwise considered abnormal. This suggests that if 'confusion' is viewed as a socially unacceptable technique of adaptation, at least the disordered nature of the adjustment was tempered by a structural framework of conceptual normality retained in varying degrees intact.

Many confused residents recognized their own failing powers of memory: 'That's a bit of a tease. I'm going soft, I suppose. 'Course

my memory for various things has got weak on account of age'
(man, aged eighty-five, score 6). 'I've found out I sometimes wander
at night, but I have no recollection. In fact my memory's clear
gone. Any funny in the head? Only myself!' (woman, aged ninety-
one, score 5). 'I've got . . . I can't think of any words now. I'm
dotty' (woman, aged seventy-five, score 9). 'You must think me an
idiot' (a woman, aged eighty-four, score 5, embarrassed at her
inability to answer certain questions). Some also appreciated the
degree of their deterioration, though their explanation of its
aetiology might seem dramatized:[1] 'I had a terrible illness – done
me up, finished me. I've lost my speech proper – made a proper
dummy of me' (woman, aged eighty-eight, score 8). Those with
only moderate disabilities indicated how painful was their sensitivity to their ailing capacities by their efforts to conceal them: 'My
memory's going, but I don't let people know' (woman, aged eighty-
one, score 2). Nor were the insights of some confused residents,
even of those more seriously affected, into the behavioural irregularities of their companions any less: 'Some of them are very funny. I
don't know why they're funny. They're trying to . . .' (woman, aged
eighty-six, score 6). 'I don't know what you're talking about' (one
aimless wanderer with tangential speech, score 9, to another, score
12). And by their conniving looks or winks to the observer, or by
their self-adoption of an informal role of social control in their
respective dayrooms, some confused persons, even those at other
times appearing seriously disoriented and restless, revealed their
familiar awareness of others' abnormalities.

Another hallmark of insight into social situations is a capacity for
humour, and this too was readily displayed by a few of the confused:

A widower of ninety-three who was disoriented and inclined
towards repetitive questioning and playing with his watch (score
3) also revealed a marked propensity for wit. 'You've seen me
before, but not me behind' he joked at his interview, and later
turning over a note from his daughter which he regularly with-
drew from his waistcoat pocket with the quip, 'What's this, one
of my love letters?' he wrote on the back: Dear Sir,
John Thomas Plaxton
Good Luck to
Every Body
J. T. Plaxton.

Indeed his very repetition could be seen merely as an unvarying effort to enliven the torpid atmosphere by provoking an exchange as a cue for some rather forced merriment. One conversation, for example, with a rational companion (RC) ran as follows:

JTP: [*glancing at the clock on the mantelpiece long stopped registering 8.10*] Coming up to 9. What do you make the time? Nine?

RC: No, 6.

JTP: Lot of laughing bloody apes, aren't they? [*he winks across at me*].
[*Then to me*] You don't know my name?

RC: Plaxton.

JTP: Gonna fatten you up for Xmas! Got anything in your bag to give away? [*Pause*] You don't know my name, do you?

With small modifications this dialogue was repeated several times at sporadic intervals.

An attendant added similar comments: 'It's difficult to get Plaxton up. "All right where I am." Burst of wit. "Can I stay here? Can I have a bedmate?" And he laughs like mad. He sings in bed: "There'll come a time one day when we'll all pass away".'

The wit of some other confused residents was no less bluff. When I asked one severely disoriented woman (score 3), for instance, if I could sit on the chair next to her, she replied brusquely: 'Yes, it's your bottom. I'm very rude, aren't I?' Similarly when I asked an aimless wanderer, aged ninety-nine (score 6), whether he spoke much to the matron, he replied knowingly: 'No, I don't do any courting.' Again, even seriously confused persons could acknowledge the jocular taunts of others. Thus an aimless wanderer with markedly tangential speech and personal disorientation (score 12), accosted by an attendant when once she sat by me, 'Are you making up to your boy-friend again. You're artful,' retorted briskly: 'Good thing somebody's artful,' with an aside to me 'She pulls my leg.'

Thirdly, confused residents exhibited an acute consciousness of their social surroundings by their capacity, and eager readiness, to respond to a personal interest taken in them. It has been shown that even brain-damaged, poorly educated persons with disturbed orientation, memory and desire can make use of supportive personal relationships (Kahn *et al.*, 1962, p. 241). Experiments with a 'small-group assignment' technique by other researchers, in which each nursing assistant was allotted the primary responsibility for the physical and emotional needs of a limited number of patients, also produced considerable improvement, chiefly in personal mood, whilst intellectual deterioration remained unchanged, among a group of forty-eight patients a quarter of whom were judged 'inaccessible to any meaningful personal interaction' (Silver *et al.*, 1963, p. 33).[2]

Other studies, moreover, have demonstrated the positive capacity of elderly confused patients to respond to occupational incentives (Cosin *et al.*, 1958, p. 24), analogously to the abundant weight of evidence in support of the influence of social stimulation on the mentally subnormal, the mentally ill and other institutionalized groups (Gordon *et al.*, 1955, p. 371; Wadsworth *et al.*, 1961, p. 593; Wing and Freudenberg, 1962). Conversely, exposure to negative attitudes and rejecting behaviour could produce in confused persons a sense of deep hurt:

A single woman of eighty-eight who as an aimless wanderer with disoriented movements and tangential speech (score 12) enjoyed a notorious reputation for flightiness and volatility because of her rambling escapades and the unintentionally comic impression of some of her verbal outbursts, nevertheless also revealed, in a multiplicity of incidents, an extreme sensitivity to the nuances of others' reactions to her. On one occasion when she asked her rational neighbour who was reading a newspaper, 'Do you like my collar?' and the latter merely muttered 'Yes' without looking up, she showed her resentment at being fobbed off: 'You can hear too much sometimes.' At another time when one particularly relentless persecutor was irritatedly instructing her to 'Keep still!' even when she was not restless, her plaintive response 'Me again?' disclosed how painful was her awareness of such harassment, and when her traducer was finally led away by attendants for other reasons, how complete her satisfaction: 'Very nice, very nice indeed!' Her pained asides, too, illustrated perspicacity amid bewilderment: 'Nobody knows how tired I get. First one shirty, then another. I feel absolutely worn out. I don't know what to do. . . . Somebody here, I don't know what her name is . . . I don't want to clear out. I want to go away. I'm tired of it.'

Nor was recognition of social distress confined to insight into the self-situation. A woman, for example, who was handicapped by severe disorientation, anormic activity and verbal tangentiality (score 8) could still feel for a rational companion crying silently about her corns, having been unsympathetically dismissed by an attendant 'Don't cry, it won't help,' and still express her solidarity with passion: 'Poor old girl, she's crying. Poor old girl, don't cry!'

Lastly, confused residents displayed their consciousness of the environment by their capacity accurately to interpret the subtleties of social conventions and events.[3] This was most apparent in regard to clothing. Thus a woman who seemed so disoriented and restless as to be confined to a cot-bed with raised sides (aged eighty-eight, score 8) nevertheless immediately understood the significance of the dog-collar worn by the clergyman who had been summoned: 'They only bring them when you're going to die.' A man who appeared extremely lethargic, ate meals by himself in his room upstairs and (according to an attendant) was 'inclined not to notice others present' (aged eighty-three, score 8) still had the dress sense to remark: 'Must clean up myself.' A woman who was blind and appeared introverted as well as confused (aged eighty-six, score 8) declared: 'I can't afford more [clothes], but I'd like more.' Even when expressions seemed enigmatically disordered, the same concern for propriety showed through: asked whether she possessed a hearing aid, a woman with evasively tangential speech and anormic tendencies (aged eighty-nine, score 8) replied, 'I foget whether . . . I can always get one when I want it. I don't like to be without what I'm asked about. It shows some neglect.' Moreover, a whole series of incidents illustrated the percipience over a wide range of nuances of social behaviour which many confused residents still retained. Examples included a display of loyal discreetness: 'You can't run them down behind their back – they respect you and you must respect them' (man, aged ninety-three, score 3); a sense of price realism: 'You can't get a good suit of clothes for £20 – lot of money to spend for at most five years' (man, aged eighty-six, score 2); a wary (and justified) suspicion of strangers, demonstrated by a number of severely confused residents who were acutely vigilant of my presence as a daily observer and distrusted my purpose; and a marked reaction to proximate physical indignities, exemplified by a blind and severely disoriented woman who introvertedly laughed aloud at her private jokes (aged eighty-three, score 8) but could still reveal her strong repugnance of the loose coughing of her rational neighbour by her angry facial contortions.

Of course all these quoted instances cannot be generalized as of universal application. Perhaps no more than a small minority of the confused residents of this study could be included in this context, yet there is no reason to doubt that the coverage of relevant incidents adventitiously witnessed in the course of a brief period of observation would have been broadened to the point of embracing most, if not all, of the confused if recording techniques were sufficiently sustained and ubiquitous. What this data does prove, however – and this alone is required by the central argument of this chapter – is that the manifestation of confused behaviour was not incompatible with a searching insight into the significance of perceived social phenomena.

ALIENATION

Having established the integrity of their powers of judgment, we must now try to determine the overall assessment by the confused of their residential environments in order to gauge the pressure to achieve some redeeming adjustment. An immediate difficulty, however, lies in conceptualizing their level of satisfaction or otherwise when their verbal summaries were so obviously influenced by considerations of expediency, feelings of loyalty, uncertainty of the consequences of honesty, inhibiting beliefs in the absence of residential alternatives, or sheer inarticulateness, forgetfulness or misunderstanding. Two examples, drawn from interviews with rational residents and thus obviating the further complications entailed for the confused in communicating experience, may serve to illustrate this problem:

'They [the residents] gossip. They're jealous of one another. And I don't like it that people can go into my room when I'm not there. You can't lock anything up. I've seen things turned over and I've lost a lot of things . . . We need more lavatories – one for the people upstairs. They put the light on, and it wakes you up, and they wet over the toilet floor. . . . Mrs Carlston uses her fingers at table, and Mrs Kittenberg – she's rather dirty, smells! Mrs Alleyn's objectionable too – she *will* try to lay down the law. And two have been in mental hospital, and I don't think they should come here . . . But nothing disturbs me. I take no notice of it. I'm not sensitive. I like it here.'

When I asked Mrs Leggbottom if she wanted to stay in the

(separatist) home permanently, she merely bent down and pulled at her apron and stockings. Later she confided she would like to go to her daughter, but 'They don't always want you, and it's lovely to have everything done for you here.'

'But better if you could do it yourself?'

'Yes, but that word "if" is what counts.'

'Could you look after yourself if you went home?'

'Yes, but I'd need help in the bedroom.'

'Would your daughter do it?'

'That's the thing. She's very good, do anything for you. But that's not everything, is it? She's got such a lot to do.'

Throughout the interview Mrs Leggbottom persisted in her circumspect approach, but then suddenly at one point, out of context, exclaimed: 'I wish my daughter would come to take me back.' A few days later as I was passing her seat, she caught my arm and appealed to me to write to her, taking my name and address.

More indirect approaches therefore seemed advisable in assessing degree of satisfaction, whether the greater trustworthiness of spontaneous statements or theoretical constructs like the ratio of confused residents who exhibited disorientation of person to the total number of the confused. The latter method which is dependent on the interpretation of situational or personal disorientation as an adaptive mechanism to substitute for an unacceptable reality,[4] would produce a picture whereby 89 per cent of the seventy-one confused in the separatist homes and 36 per cent of the twenty-two confused in the ordinary homes found their actual situation intolerable enough to require some compensatory device.[5] On the basis of the former measure, 38 per cent of thirty-nine confused residents in two of the separatist homes, together with 50 per cent of forty-four rational residents, spontaneously mentioned in the course of interview a desire to leave the home, whilst only 5 per cent of the confused out of this limited sample and a mere 2 per cent of the rational volunteered a positive wish to remain.

Now the evidence of both these indices in suggesting an overall judgment of deep dissatisfaction among a high proportion of the confused and rational alike in the separatist homes was buttressed by a wide range of unsolicited opinions at interview which were similarly pointed. The most commonly expressed feeling was a begrudging admission of the need to remain because no alternative accommodation was available: 'Have to stay here. I've got nowhere else to go.' 'I'd love to leave if I could get somebody to look after me. People don't look after the old nowadays.' In many minds reservations concerning residential life were reluctantly outweighed by anxiety about becoming a burden to relatives: 'I feel I might become an incubus, and old people *do* become an incubus, with the best will in the world.' 'No, I don't think I could get on with 'em [her family]. All right for a month or two. I'd like to live with one person, me and she. Don't know that I want to stay here all my life.' Others again, particularly the confused or the physically handicapped, stressed that residential life was just not comparable to one's own private home: 'I'll have to stay here now, but if I could manage with a small two-roomed cottage, I might. There's no place like home' (a woman, aged seventy-nine, confusional score 7). 'I shouldn't have come here – last place I'd have chosen. Welfare homes aren't suitable for me. I'd like my own home and my own room' (a woman, aged eighty-seven, score 1). 'I sometimes get homesick. Can't expect to come into one of these places and be treated as if I were at home, where there are a lot to look after' (a rational but blind woman, aged eighty-eight).

For the more seriously confused, dissatisfaction revealed itself in images of their situation highlighting coercion or incarceration, with the consequent desire to escape:

Miss Slater, a rather old-fashioned though punctilious spinster of eighty-four in one of the special homes who was disoriented and mildly tangential in her speech (score 4) recalled at her interview: 'I was a matron in the '14–18 War – took Ann with me, my maid. She's been with me twenty-nine years, hanging on for me till I'm freed. And I was visited by my mother and father the day before who're distressed I'm still here.'
'Would you like to leave then?'
'That's a hard question.' Tears began to well up in her eyes and she seemed very moved. 'I'd love to go back to my own home. A fisherman's wife at Yarmouth said, "It would be lovely if you could be back." I've got my own house. Ann's looking after it. This is the only home I've been in, and it's not treated as a home like that – you're just one of the family. They haven't been agitating and wanting me out . . . I'm homesick and go to bed very early

and cry myself to sleep.' She began to weep softly. Later in the day she came up to me and said: 'I've changed my mind. I'd like to go back home. . . . You needn't be so wished [miserable]. I'm wished too. I guess I disturb them. I get a fit of the blues. But I've had letters from Canon Sleight and other influential people, and they say "We'll fight and fight till you're free."'

Such feelings of detainment naturally gave rise to manoeuvres aimed at escape. At a more prosaic level, this development might take the form of a strongly urged plea to leave to resume employment. 'I want to get to the road home. I can soon find work. I'd sooner live with my friends because they know one another' (a man, aged ninety-four, marginally disoriented, score 2, who had formerly been a textile worker in Oldham and was now resident in a separatist home on the south coast). 'I should like to get out in time because if I get out, I can get my living on my painting' (a rational man of seventy-six, a retired boilermaker, who proudly displayed his high-quality crayon paintings which he kept in his wallet). The more seriously confused, however, could resort to more elaborate strategies, however unconsciously directed:

The following three-week episode was extracted from the medical records of one of the separatist homes:

1 Nov. Mrs Tribble (the widow of a headmaster, aged seventy-five, who was rated with confusional score 9 when seen six months after these events) did not get to sleep till 12.15 a.m. She was found at 11 p.m. with her suitcase open and many articles of clothing strewn about the room. She stated 'she was packing ready for my visit to Durham'. Persuaded to leave it till morning.

2 Nov. Very confused all day. Says she expects her sister-in-law to fetch her to take her to Durham to a 'tennis weekend'. Told that possibly she got the dates mixed.

4 Nov. Still wants to play tennis. Difficult to convince that not going to Durham.

5 Nov. Packed again to go by train to play 'hockey'. Very confused, very tired, but eating well.

6 Nov. Visited by daughter (who had been summoned) who said she's too old for tennis. She seems rather deflated by this, but very good about it.

12 Nov. Asks where her husband is. When told that he died long

ago, she denied it and said he was away at school teaching.

14 Nov. Deflated and depressed when her daughter visits again and tells her that her husband has been dead twenty-five years.

15 Nov. Still thinks an escort is coming to take her away at the weekend. Seen by g.p. who says she is to have Largactil 50 gr b.d., Tofranil 1 tab. t.d.s. and Artane 1 tab. t.d.s., Largactil to be discontinued after one week. Wandered in the early night. Unsteady walking. Fell outside bathroom door and slightly bruised her upper left eye. Quiet till 3 a.m., when found getting up for breakfast.

16 Nov. Showed very strong Parkinsonian symptoms: was moving to and fro across the sitting-room and then went on her hands and knees picking things off the floor. G.p. instructed that Tofranil tablets be stopped at once, and to have Largactil 100 gr b.d., and Syrup Choral at night. Very restless and getting in and out of bed till 6 p.m., talking complete gibberish all the time.

17 Nov. Woke 5 a.m., and talked continuously since waking – mostly gibberish. Asleep for most of the day, but very confused.

18 Nov. Missing clock found in her bed and torch taken to pieces three times!

19 Nov. Complains continually of pain in her back and seems to have hallucinations: talks of seeing cats walking round the room. Seen by g.p. about her back – rheumatism? Ovaltine and biscuits given nocte. Continually talking when awake. Put on commode with no result. Restless, picks at bedclothes.

20 Nov. In bed most of the day, though getting up at 6 p.m. Takes very little food. Very unsteady and lethargic.

21 Nov. Extremely sore mouth with white patches on roof.

22 Nov. Very confused and very frail. Cannot dress or undress. Finds it very difficult to feed herself, especially with fluids. Mouth still very inflamed.

23 Nov. Looks very ill. Has to be dressed and undressed, fed and toileted. Mouth a little better.

24 Nov. Dressed at 11.15 a.m., very frail and very slow. Had to be fed with supper: says she is not hungry.

25 Nov. Much better today. Takes meals well, less confused and asks to watch TV.

Whatever precise interpretation is sought for the precipitation of confusional 'attacks' of this kind, the analysis of the preceding two chapters suggests that the cumulative affront to social identity arising from segregation, isolation and decision-making impotence must represent a major contributory factor.

As serious indicators of distress as escapist withdrawal, though less dramatic, were the manifold symptoms of emotional insecurity which aggregatively, in terms of their extensiveness in the separatist homes and occasional bizarreness, appeared to determine a state of mind tantamount to alienation.[6] The range of evidence, which collectively forms a vital backcloth to the psychodynamics of adjustment, will be summarized under the headings successively of insecurity, shallowness of relationships and unrequited affection.

Firstly, a wide variety of confusional habits may be construed as stemming from the common root of insecurity. One such characteristic, which ostensibly provided confirmation of tangential speech, was a persisting and earnest recollection of the past when the old person once enjoyed positive and definite roles and life made 'sense'.[7] The following passage, from an interview with a moderately confused woman of eighty-six (score 6), vividly demonstrates not only a moving nostalgia for past experiences and for relationships lost and not replaced, but also a perplexed and uncertain mingling of past and present:

Mrs Peggs soliloquized about her childhood when her father ran a mission in East London: 'They all know me. I'm the one who used to be there. But they've all gone away without my bothering about . . . I was there this morning – must have been asleep. Everything is gone of mine . . . Now it's a funny thing, I went into there, I looked at the watches and balls and it's very same as we had before, and I'm wondering if it's the same place. I've met with people, and I've written or go with some people, and I went there one day, and they said, You by the post near the door (?), and I thought it was the other place. It wasn't . . . My mother's gone, everyone's gone too, because my mother was a great woman, and she used to put the children out right opposite the Mission. I can't think what I'm going to do now. But only just now I found out it's not in the proper place. So many Jews there. In fact

I went there in the First Work [War?]. .... They've got a place there, one place, and the same sort of thing. But I'm just about finished. It's my head, and feet too. I'm sorry when I found it was gone, and we'd been sitting in the other place.'

Other confused residents in the separatist homes displayed a similar hankering after past security, whether in the form of a satisfying role, as in resurrecting the status of being constantly consulted as a midwife, or of personal impact, as in constantly reiterating the story of how breaking off an engagement caused a fiancé to die of a broken heart.

Another symptom of insecurity was persistent restlessness. The channelling of bewilderment by the confused into aimless wandering is strikingly demonstrated by two extracts from the records of a psychiatric hospital to which certain residents were transferred from one of the separatist homes investigated in this study:

Mr Roggan, a widower of seventy-four, came to feel that his son and daughter-in-law, with whom he had been living, did not want to have anything to do with him after he began to develop senile psychosis, following a fall downstairs and the onset of pneumonia. He began to wander away from his home and was admitted to Brightside (the separatist home).

He continued, however, his habit of wandering away and becoming lost. When he was found, he would say that he did not know where he was living, that he had walked all day from a distant spot, and that his children did not want him. It was impossible to keep him in Brightside because the doors and gates were open all the time and there was no barrier to prevent his access to the roads outside. When transferred to mental hospital he was unable to give an account of himself, stating that 'since my wife died, I've been on the road for three years'.

After her mental deterioration began, Mrs Mettam developed odd ideas that somebody was spying on her and at one time thought her husband was somebody else and intent on killing her. This period culminated in a 'brainstorm' after which, at the age of sixty-eight, she was admitted to Brightside. But she still became increasingly confused and for some time before her eventual transfer eight months later refused to eat some of her meals. It was often extremely difficult to get her to take her tablets (from a paranoid fear of being poisoned?). She was extremely restless and would not sit down, even at mealtimes. When admitted to hospital, she claimed she was little more than thirty years old, and a fortnight later was still very restless, continually wandering about aimlessly and drifting out of the ward.

Other evidence observed in this study plentifully corroborated this link between insecurity and restlessness among the confused, sometimes in indirect or cryptic form: one persistent wanderer, for example, commented significantly, 'I'm looking for a place to put a bed, and I haven't even got a bed.' The same conclusion was pointed up by the converse observation that 'ownership' of a chair meant stability,[8] since it has already been shown that one practical consequence of confused behaviour in the separatist homes was loss of territorial rights.[9] The insecurity generated by being pushed from pillar to post was sharply reflected in such plaintive questions, often repeated daily by the confused, as: 'Am I going to stop here tonight?' (a widower of ninety-three, score 3, who had been resident over a year). 'Can you tell me where I sleep tonight? I've never slept here before' (a single woman of seventy-four, score 6, who had been resident $8\frac{1}{2}$ years).

Yet another sign of insecurity was an irrepressible tendency to hoarding, and this again was very widely observed among confused residents. One woman (score 6) hoarded sewing materials under the cushions of her chair, another (score 10) habitually secreted knitting needles in her bed, a third (score 2) was exceptionally anxious (unjustifiably) about the retention of her monetary resources,[10] a fourth (score 9) accumulated food in her handbag, and a fifth (score 4) regularly collected leaves from the garden and stored them in her handbag, which she then often hid among or under her clothes or at the bottom of drawers or under pillows.[11] Nor was this aspect of insecurity confined to the confused in the separatist homes. Several behavioural traits observed among rational residents in these establishments hinted at the same pathology:

> One unmarried woman of eighty-seven, for example, who scored as rational demonstrated her lack of security in a wide variety of ways. She hid objects to deny their use to others – on one occasion she was seen murmuring contentedly to herself as she privately noted the position of some magazines lying on a shelf half hidden by her couch 'so that the others can't get at them'. She constantly

talked to herself, though when asked to stop, regularly denied it. She spoke of her family as famous (they owned some landed property in Scotland) and was inordinately proud of her age. Her unconcern, even contempt, for her fellow residents she displayed by kicking under the meal-table any who incurred her annoyance, while her eagerness to win the favour of staff was illustrated by her habit, when she brought over her plate after a meal, of insisting 'there's no need to wash this up'.

A second facet of alienation and relational breakdown which confused residents in the separatist homes manifested to an intense degree was shallowness of social ties, often in conjunction with an overt sense of rejection. Frequently remarks were passed like: 'I don't know anybody about here. I'm no good for anything now' (a widow of eighty-eight, score 6, who had been resident four years). 'No, I don't see them [other residents] much to talk to' (a widow of seventy-five, score 9, resident over two years, who shared a sitting room with twenty companions). 'I don't really know anything about anybody [here]. I don't really get much chance to see them' (a widow of seventy-five, score 5, resident nearly a year, who shared a dayroom with many severely confused neighbours). Another indicator was the very frequent use of circumlocutory descriptions, in the absence of knowledge of surnames, to refer to persons with whom daily contact had been experienced even for years: 'The woman who . . .' 'Lady, I like your dress.'

Occasionally protection was sought against a hurtful isolationism by the obverse technique of cavalier dismissal of others:

'Very big place here: don't see much of the other residents. Not interested in them actually. I've knocked around the world too much to be interested in these locals. Don't take much notice. Half of these are old women [she herself was eighty-three]. I've got nothing in common with them. They're quite pleasant and nice.' She then recited a rhyme she remembered from a tombstone (a widow, score 4, resident nearly four years).

More commonly, however, the tenuousness of relationships was registered as bewildering and stultifying:

A woman who was only mildly disoriented but restless and very agitated (score 3) when interviewed some eleven weeks after transfer from an ordinary home because of nocturnal wandering, confessed to her utter perplexity about the intentions and actions of her companions: 'To tell you the truth, I don't know what's wrong with them all. I don't understand their behaviour. For some reason they're sending me to [Coventry?]. I don't know why, I'm usually popular. They're pilfering. They've pilfered everything – biscuits, all the little things. They go through my things and help themselves, I'm missing things. Details, not big things, but things that you want. Two were very jolly last night, but today I'm missing bits of things. They don't understand me, and I don't understand them – young people [she herself was eighty-six]. I've worked hard all my life, and now I feel I'm tired. There's not much I can do. I wish the end would come. I've outlived myself, or if you like to say, I've lived too long. When you lose your faculties, you begin to feel life isn't worth living, and the sooner the end comes, the better for all parties. I just feel I want to go to sleep.'

But the most startling characteristic of confused residents' view of their relationships in the separatist homes was the extraordinary paradox of subjective isolation in the midst of company. Halmos has summarized this situation in a manner which may well represent for the severely confused their reality-image: 'He is shut up amidst the fellow-members of his community into a cubicle where he is engaged in a lifelong conversation with himself' (Halmos, 1952, p. xv). In this study this reaction was verbalized chiefly by the moderately confused:

A widow of eighty-seven (score 1), who had been resident a year declared: 'I'm a stranger here. I've never felt at home here. They've never trusted me here. They say "a silent tongue shows a wise head." You have to be very careful. It's not easy to make friends when you're old. I'm penned in. No *real* company. Not [people] with the same taste. I feel like a lone wolf.'

In some of the more seriously confused the touch of paranoic estrangement which this last quotation reveals was developed into a crushing sense of self-abasement:

'They don't seem to know I'm here. They don't know I'm talking to you. They don't seem to take any notice of me. . . . They regard me as someone not to be listened to. I'm the last to be consulted if they want to change a room' (a spinster of eighty, score 6).

A similar interpretation should perhaps be placed on some of the more enigmatic statements of the severely confused, for example: 'What do you do in the evening?' 'Sit in the coal cellar . . . I know I'm old; do you want to cut me or shoot me?' (a widow of seventy-five, score 9).

A third sign of alienation among confused residents in the separatist homes was a desperate hunger for affection which, when unsatisfied, could find alternative expression in verbal or behavioural form whimsical enough to earn the title of 'confused' for its author. Most directly, the frustration of this craving for affection found issue in a promiscuous desire for physical contact, with or without undertones of sexual fantasy:

Several of the confused in the special home where they heavily predominated took advantage of my presence to establish a physical contact normally denied them. One, for example, pointedly linked her arm in mine whilst walking to the interview room, another leant towards me at interview and seemed to be trying to rub up against me, and a third, who was severely dysarthric in speech and effectively could only communicate through laughing and facial gesture (score 11), persistently followed me round during my stay, always seeking a seat as close as possible to mine. Kissing, as well as blowing kisses, was frequent between female residents, though not confined to the separatist homes nor to the confused.

In the case of a few of the confused in the specialized homes the sexual implications were more pronounced. One woman, who was incoherent and an aimless wanderer (score 12), on roaming late one evening into the bedroom of the superintendent, quickly hopped into bed in the unoccupied place beside him. A moderately confused single woman of seventy-six whom the medical records described as obviously very neglected and living unaided on her own before admission developed a strong and overt sexual interest in a severely confused female companion and threatened to become aggressive if parted from her 'lover' at night. Another moderately disoriented woman (score 2) with marked delusions – she claimed 'a big fly four inches across, with blue wings and black body, a bird, made a hole three-quarters of an inch in my leg, deep down into the muscle', and complained of 'doodles crawling through my skull' which at one time she thought were depriving her of her voice – also stated significantly, though with incongruity of affect (for she smiled as she said it), that 'macaroni men are following me'.

Less direct, though pointed enough, as a sublimation of an unsatisfied longing for affection was an inordinate eagerness for food. Some of the confused in the separatist homes exhibited this by the voracity with which they swallowed enormous mouthfuls of food, and others by their ill-tempered impatience and churlish dismissal of delay: 'Well now, bloody well hurry up!' (a disoriented and tangential, but normally quiescent, woman of seventy-nine, score 6, when the matron once appeared slow at serving). Another manifestation of deprived affection was the expectation, frequently voiced by confused residents in the special homes, though without any experience to grant it plausibility, that food was about to be denied them: 'I don't suppose we'll get any tea today.' Or, equally frequently, the disavowal that food had been provided earlier in the day: 'I've had no lunch, and nobody cares for me, though I care for them.' One disoriented and tangential hoarder (score 6) projected her cry for affection on to a third party by knocking on the sitting room door and begging food for 'a starving friend'.

Recalling dead relatives was also widely observed – again almost uniquely – among confused persons in the separatist homes, and this may be reasonably construed as their seeking from the past an affection now denied to them by their present environment. Sometimes the name of a husband, sister or son was summoned up aloud in the midst of otherwise private reveries, sometimes case reports made comments like 'she talks of her family often with great affection', and sometimes there was an outright denial of the fact of death of a spouse. A wanderer of seventy-one (score 10), for example, who had been informed that her husband had died, did not seem unduly disturbed by the news at the time, but next day came to matron and disaverred his death, while a wanderer who occupied her time initially after admission peering round doors and corners declared she was looking for her husband. Even the content of confabulation could imply a similar intent: 'First when I came I had a different room; I had a husband with me, but I don't think they were anxious to have a double bed' (a widow of seventy-five, score 9, whose husband had died long before her admission). The same propensity to seek solace from deceased relatives, especially parents, was exhibited by the habit of locking dialogue on to such memories, however disconnected the logic, and elaborating them irrespective of context:

'Can you tell me how you come to be here?'
'All my folks come from here. I was surprised this afternoon. I went to leave my mother's place, East London. My mother died, and she was in . . . what was this place. When we went into the . . . mother,[12] listen for the car coming, singing like the rest of them. My mother was a proper young woman, and the gentleman he was come from prison, no, in the country. Then it all fell down. She came from Cambridge, and came along and had a fine man, and we all grew up. The boys used to go, all sorts of jobs near the top of the place, now getting on uncomfortable, as all go from us . . .' (a widow of eighty-six, score 6).

Perhaps best of all the significance of the invocation of loved relatives is revealed by the generalized ambivalence in relationships which the loss of reliance on them generated:

A rational woman of seventy-six in one of the separatist homes confided at her interview: 'The girls [attendants] aren't very nice to me. I like it here, but not the residents. The other residents are very off-handed – and my sons are very off-hand to me. My son is going to sell my home. I don't think I want to leave – don't think they'd want to take me home. I often feel lonely. But my sons are very nice. The girls aren't very nice to me. I don't care for them, but still! The residents are queer people. I don't like them much. They disparage me. They're always discussing things together. I don't like the way they talk to me, and I think it's disgusting the way they speak. Bad manners.'

Yet another aspect of the search for affection was the various techniques utilized by confused residents in the separatist homes to attract attention, even if the message was not usually understood. One such device involved the request for assistance in tasks which could be satisfactorily accomplished without external help, such as lighting a pipe, or the asking of questions, often repetitively, to which the questioner already knew the answer, for example:

'Can I stay here tonight?' 'What shall I do next?' 'Have you got somebody called Wynneck here?' (asked by a widower of ninety-three, score 3, named Wynneck).

Another device, indiscriminately directed, was the practice of loud singing in tones of abandon, or persistent laa-ing, a habit developed by one aphasic and incoherent woman (score 11). Another tactic observed comprised the exploitation of the requirement on staff to perform certain routine care functions for the infirm by the deliberate withholding of cooperation until the unusual opportunity to extract conversation and solicitude from staff had been maximized. Perhaps even limited physical violence, such as striking the shoulder of an attendant, should be seen in this context as a mechanism to draw attention, especially if used by an otherwise placid incoherent resident, when all the normal avenues of approach appear closed. More subtly, a whole range of other actions seemed motivated by the calculation of the indirect achievement of sympathy or attention. Thus a woman who regularly returned her pension quota to the matron equally regularly complained a little later that it had been taken, while another resident who tore up a towel to send a face flannel as a present to her daughter could be plausibly regarded as making a desperate appeal to the last source of affection left to her.

ADAPTATION

As a prolegomenon to the psychodynamics of confusion, we have seen that confused residents in the separatist homes manifested firstly an awareness of their environment involving a consciousness of the social significance of events around them, and secondly, on a wide scale, an overall feeling of dissatisfaction, even despair, culminating in intense emotional insecurity and craving for affection. These reactions were not, of course, confined wholly to the confused, but their concentration among those designated 'confused' in the special homes was truly distinctive and remarkable. We must therefore imperatively ask how these persons managed to salvage, or construct, an acceptable Weltanschauung out of the wreckage of a world which had apparently lost its meaning and affection. For on the answer to this question hinges our judgment of the nature of 'confusion'.

Careful analysis of the variegated verbal and behavioural traits

Table 9.1

Schema of adjustment mechanisms utilized chiefly by
confused residents in the separatist homes

Functional level of adjustment	Functional direction	Purpose	Type
strategic	positive (inventive)	Compensation (compatible with institution)	1. insistent claim as to performing household duties. 2. delusions of grandeur, associations with the famous, notions of ownership, supervisory function 3. resumption of lost roles 4. dissimulatory presentation of virtuous or altruistic image 5. rationalized explanation of presence
		dissociation from institution	1. regression to childhood 2. belief in imminent departure or temporary stay, avowal of residence in hotel 3. presumption that still living in private household
	negative	externalized projection	paranoia
		escape	withdrawal, self-involvement
tactical	positive (defensive)	rationalization of 'confused' behaviour	1. protection against tangential speech 2. protection against wandering 3. protection against disorientation of situation: vide stratgeic adjustments (*supra*) 4. protection against disorientation of place 5. protection against anormic behaviour 6. protection against memory defect 7. protection against incontinence
		rationalization of social consequences of 'confused' behaviour	1. protection against isolation 2. protection against embarrassing questions 3. protection against powerlessness 4. protection against apathy

conveniently (though misleadingly, as we shall see) grouped under
the stereotyped abbreviation of 'confusion' suggested that these
traits served two fundamental purposes. Firstly, such traits might

comprise mechanisms of adjustment utilized, consciously or unwittingly, to promote self-protection against an accumulation of
painful experiences.[13] This may be termed the *strategic* function.
Secondly, these traits might supply a rationalization for behaviour,
conventionally judged abnormal, which had been generated by
other factors, such as insecurity, bewilderment or powerlessness.
This type of diplomatic defensiveness, which constitutes a second-
level adjustment, may be termed the *tactical* function. The ramifications of this analysis are elaborated in Table 9.1.[14]

STRATEGIC ADJUSTMENTS

Techniques of strategic adaptation appeared to be classifiable in two
main forms, each divisible into two subtypes. The central forms
differed in terms of their functional direction, one being judged
positive in an inventive sense (as opposed to the defensive purpose
of positive tactical adjustments) and the other *negative* in an escapist
or punitive sense. These will now be separately analysed. It is also
interesting to note that this analysis independently reached bears
close affinities with a breakdown of functional response among
elderly patients with chronic cerebral pathology as developed by
other researchers.

Strategic adjustments of a positive nature

Positive adaptation at a strategic level was also susceptible of a dual
classification. One class consisted of a set of *compensatory* notions
compatible with the framework of institutional life. Underlying
the other type of positive strategic adjustment was the basic aim of
dissociation from the institution. Once again each grouping will be
illustrated in turn.

POSITIVE STRATEGIC ADJUSTMENTS OFFERING
INSTITUTIONAL COMPENSATION

Five types of what we have termed positive strategic adjustment
behaviour were delineated which provided compensatory satisfaction
in a manner which was consonant with the fact, however unrealistic
the details, of the institutional framework within which the agents
were living. These five techniques for achieving recompense to
counterbalance a harsh reality will now be explored.

(a) Insistent claim as to the performance of household duties

One striking facet of compensatory manipulation employed by confused residents in the separatist homes, particularly those afflicted by physical infirmity or handicap, was their earnest declaration that they had onerous duties of housekeeping to uphold:

> A woman aged eighty-six (score 8) who was nearly blind and rarely moved from her chair asserted: 'I do hard work. I've got the house to do in the morning.' Another woman in the same home, aged seventy (score 3), who could only walk with difficulty even with two sticks, suggested she could help out with laying the table, clearing away, dusting and cleaning. She added that she did not talk much to the other residents because she had too much to do. A third woman, aged eighty-eight (score 9) who was ambulant enough but regarded as too confused to be allowed to perform any job within the home, stated: 'I keep the place clean, and have all the beds to do, upstairs and downstairs. Staff just give me enough for housekeeping. . . . Matron comes to me a lot. She has lots of jobs she asks me to help with.'

Apart from notional self-characterizations, some forms of anormic activity could also be regarded as disposed to the same end. Thus a persistent predilection to stripping beds (see above, p. 66) might be reasonably interpreted as a desire to help in the process of remaking beds, especially since the woman who most strikingly demonstrated this propensity (aged eighty-one, score 11) also indicated that she would like to press clothes for men and would like a hobby – 'I don't mind what sort.'

Protestations of hard work could also be made to serve the further purpose of enhancing relative status:

> A man who entered a special home at the age of eighty-three (score 1) and at the time of interview two years later was severely crippled, and scarcely mobile as well as suffering from impaired speech and oral dyskinesia avowed: 'Since I've been here, I've done two men's work when everybody else's done one. . . . I haven't been lazy since I've been here – I've done my bit. They call me all hours doing different jobs, night and day.'

Sometimes concern over household duties supplied the sole satisfaction of an on-going commitment. Thus a woman of eighty-one

(score 2) who was normally noticeably lethargic came to her interview worrying about 'the bread and meat', while another aged
eighty (score 6) interrupted an interview to offer me tea, but warned:
'I haven't made any more tea, darling, and I can't run round the
streets.'

Though usually the domestic duties appeared to be located within
the residential milieu, occasionally they seemed to be fused with
ideas of continuing responsibility for the person's private household and family:

> A widow of seventy-one (score 10), whose husband had died
> after her admission and who had been informed accordingly,
> declared that she normally shopped in the morning and, when-
> ever she was confronted with a probing question, that 'I haven't
> much time because I must return home to get a meal for my
> husband and family.'

> A widow of seventy-three (score 8) who was highly inarticulate
> in her speech could still convey this simple idea of personal
> care: 'Go ... [incomprehensible words] ... doing the clothes,
> go to the boilers, wash them up ... I've got four children. I
> live on top of ...'

(b) Delusions of grandeur

Perhaps the most obvious and effective psychological counter-
valence against feelings of intolerable humiliation is provided by
fantasies of grandeur, and indeed these were found in profusion
among the confused in the separatist homes. One interview in
particular, however, is worth quoting at length as an archetypal
illustration of the range, nature and proliferation of this central
kind of compensatory behaviour.

> Mrs Jones, a widow of seventy-six (score 7), possessed a sharp-
> featured face distinguished by an imposing Roman nose, penetrat-
> ing eyes and a running sore which she had scratched to unsightly
> proportions just below one cheekbone. 'I don't take time to
> think about myself', she began, 'but I'm not cut and dried about
> things. ... Morning is the clearing-off process, doing what I
> must do. I don't get up for breakfast. Usually I have work cut
> out for me in the morning. I work for animals, quite free of
> course. They come in in the morning. I'm well up in animals. I

understand them and they understand me. It's just that we must teach people to understand animals. In the afternoon I go out and find a peaceful spot away from the wear and tear. I like to do a bit of historical thinking, Shakespearean sometimes. I'm free to think, and that's the pleasure. Don't seem to be a great deal with life.'

'In the evening?'

'Not the workaday hours? Think a good deal, mix with people a bit.'

'Is there enough to keep you occupied?'

'More things to do what I want to do than I can do, but it's good to keep a lot of interesting things ahead of you. I'd be lost if I could catch them up, but I can't. Life is very wide to me. I can never catch up on myself.'

'Is there any job you would like to help with?'

'I usually think jobs are interfering. If you live as long as I think, you find you're not as necessary as you once thought. Probably people do the job better than you could. No desire for any company – we just jog along, shoulder to shoulder. Sometimes I pick up something from somebody else and sometimes they from me.'

'Is there anything else you'd like, such as a hobby, to keep yourself occupied?'

'I don't want hobbies. Life is fairly serious, and I don't mind it being serious – it's seriously interesting. They would probably lay on the wrong thing. They would either take me too seriously or not seriously enough. With myself I work out a happy medium.'

'Who owns this place then?'

'I don't know. Two or three families in it. I'm not sure.'

'Do you ever write letters?'

'I write each day. I write to Canada, America, Ireland, France – in French. My writing is always ahead of me. I never catch up with it. My life is a scattered life, dodging here and there. People want me to meet someone everywhere I go. There are a great many people in the world – many I don't know yet. I came to know them through other friends who do not live in this home. I appreciate my surroundings and they appreciate the fact that I do appreciate them. .... I perhaps talk to them more than they either know, only for information, perhaps historical information, only so far as can make me something interesting. I just go about talking to everybody about everything, and not very deeply. People with depth are boring. They make other people think, and people don't want to think. Life will unfold a great deal. I appreciate their company and any information they can give me, but I don't very often find anything interesting. If I do, I ask their permission to find out more and write it up a little bit; this place is not me at all.'

'What sort of place is you?'

'I knew you'd ask that, so I was getting ready for it. Wider scope and fewer people. Does that sound selfish? We do know such a lot of people. We don't *need* to know so many people. My throat's a bit off. I've got such a lot to think about. My mind's not vacant to take in other things, with thoughts to work out and thoughts to think about . . . I don't intend to stop here. When I can get all the information I can glean here, I'll pass on. I don't flatter myself they want me to "stick around", as they say. Doesn't cross my mind if I'll see them again or not see them again. I live entirely in the present with them.'

'Is there then any possibility of your going back to a home of your own?'

'Yes, I think there is. Would be very restful when I do. I'm living here, that's all – domiciled here – no idea of waiting here. Simply take it as I pass by – that suits me. That's the way I take most of life.'

'What about the meals here?'

'What meals I have are quite satisfactory. Lunch I have out, and might have dinner instead of lunch. Thus we make more time, if we don't want to be tied down – see more – have more time when we get home, have all night to eat it.'

'Recreation?'

'Oh yes [chuckling] I have indeed. I have to remember I'm here to work and not just to play.'

'Do you discuss any problems with either the staff or the residents?'

'No, I have a great name for minding my own business, so I get on with people. No reason to discuss. When a reason comes up, we'll discuss it, and then let it go at that. No intention of stopping here any great length of time. Just a place of repose, so that I can write. Home belongs to other people quite definitely.'

'What money do you get?'

'I get petty cash from my father – father's money.'

'Is your father still alive then?'

'Yes, but he doesn't seem to bother much. We know we could get it if we wanted. We seem to have enough allowed us.'

'How do you get on with the staff?'

'You mean the people with whom I board. I'll just say I manage my own affairs by myself. . . . If there's smoking a lot – I don't mean ordinary smoking – I don't like the girls smoking. I don't like it if she's doing it on purpose. I don't know her name.'

'Are any of them here confused?'

'I don't see enough of them. I hardly see anything of them. I'm not one to look for trouble. I look to life clear of trouble rather than picking it out, all the time. That's the only peaceful way to live.'

'Do the other residents disturb you at all?'

'I think if they did it, I should be very disturbed, if they started talking to people on the second command. Because I've got the first command. The second command is more what second people have charge of.'

'Do any of the residents talk nonsense?'

'Never think about it. Let that go. If I took it one way, they'll take it as an insult, and if I took it the other way, they'll take it as an insult. How will I let you go?'

As the interview ended, she rose and left, but continued as she walked upstairs: 'That woman's in a hurry to get her little girl fixed up. There's a grandchild. Life's full of grandchildren. That last question worried me. I don't want people to think I meddle in their affairs.'

This single passage crystallizes several of the positive responses to the classic dilemma of powerlessness, and its analysis as a proto-type should be noted. The central theme is one of temporary lodging ('no intention . . . length of time') in a hotel ('people with whom I board') to assist with the work of writing ('here to work, not just to play', and 'place of repose so that I can write'). But the main rationale is fused with at least two other variants – a state of some financial dependence on her father ('I get petty cash from my father', despite her age of seventy-six) and a self-ascription of authority ('I've got the first command') – though none of these notions is logically consistent with the others. Apart from these explicit protective devices, several other threads are woven into the fabric of the dialogue which help to restore dignity and self-respect, including claims of heavy work ('work cut out for me in the morning'), philanthropic endeavour ('work for animals, quite free of course'), self-projection as a wide-ranging thinker ('such a lot to think about . . . thoughts to think about'), haughty aloofness from ordinary mortals ('peaceful spot away from the wear and tear'), international correspondence with linguistic command ('write to Canada . . . in French'), ubiquitous acclaim ('people want me to meet someone everywhere I go'), insatiable pressure of interests ('more things to do . . . catch up on myself'), unrepentant use of people for interest value ('perhaps talk to them . . . make me something interesting'), conversational manipulation ('what sort of place . . . getting ready for it') and presentation of an easy-going and placid image ('I'm not one to look for trouble', when she was observed to be unusually cantankerous). Above all, pervading the whole extract is the language of grandiloquent fustian, designed as a stylistic vehicle for personal exaltation while recalling her past as a Shakespearean actress.

Other confused residents employed yet further devices to convey a grandiose façade. One such mechanism was the asseveration of ownership of the institution: 'Well, it's my place. I don't really see why I should share with other people. I didn't invite them here'[15] (a widow aged eighty-two, score 8) – a remark tinged also with the pathology of hoarding as a symbol of the craving for affection. Again, another woman (aged eighty-nine, score 8), asked if she discussed any problems with the other residents, replied: 'Well, I haven't been spoken to by them. If it was against the rules, I shouldn't have them.' A third woman, on the assumption that she owned the home, treated the warden as a gardener and asked who paid him.

Another device to achieve personal elevation was the claim of association with famous people:

A widow (aged eighty-seven, score 1) living in Cambridge who had answered an advertisement in a distant town for lodgings let at seven guineas a week and had been transferred to the separatist home after she had travelled down and the dismayed proprietor discovered she was dependent solely on her retirement pension of just over £2 a week without further resources, declared:

'I came here through chicanery – a man at King's College and they had to send an R.A.F. control [*sic*] and Sir Malcolm Sargent and his girl friend and brought them back.[16] Matron got it into her head that I wanted somebody her daughter wanted to have. But I expect to leave soon. It depends on my friends and solicitor in Cambridge – I've been here fifty years. My solicitor's got rooms for me.' She also expressed the confident expectation that a helicopter was soon due to transport her back to Cambridge, and in general announced: 'I would have been a national celebrity, but my duty was with my mother and father.'

A rather different kind of pretentious connection with the notable, even the exotic, is supplied by the bromide reminiscences and prophecies of disaster expounded by a former psychiatric patient in one of the special homes[17] ('I would have gone out of the country incognito if the authorities had wanted it').

Another artifice of self-exaltation was the vaunting of extraordinary personal powers. Thus a woman (aged seventy-four, score 3) who had fallen on to a radiator and burnt her face when nobody quickly pulled her off, but later claimed she was burnt by the pressure of steam as she walked by a train, also earnestly alleged: 'I give people power from my eyes. I look into blind men's eyes and make them see. I emanate powers from my head, like a growth', and to prove her point, she told me at her interview to shut my eyes and asked if I could see the backs of my eyes.

Lastly, the well-documented association between paranoia and notions of grandeur was again confirmed in this study.

A former psychiatric patient with a history of paraphrenia, aged eighty-one (score 1) translated a disdainful loftiness into action by keeping strictly to himself throughout the day in his first-floor bedroom and by exercising himself, apart from occasional walks outside, only along an upper gallery overlooking the hallway where the other residents sat. 'They abuse me and tell tales about me, two men do – not very nice. I haven't done any harm since I've been here or before I came here. I don't like some of the men. One said my father was a fisherman, which is a lie. My father was a farmer all his life, and a church-warden. They like to pick a quarrel with me, some of them. They want to get me out of here. . . . My father and all of us are well-to-do people, so I don't mix with *common* people of either sex, never have or shall throughout my whole life. I'm not going to ruin my character just to do so either.'

Sometimes those with paranoid susceptibilities made outright claims of superintendent responsibilities, though in an incongruously self-effacing manner:

'I'm only a young person who supervises one or two persons in a home – very small fare. I get a certain amount of money – payment for what I do. . . . But they regard me as someone not to be listened to. I'm the last to be consulted if they want to change a room' (a woman aged eighty, score 6, many of whose actions demonstrated a damaging loss of affection).

At a more mundane level confused residents were not above openly advancing an expedient presumption of class superiority where other means to self-respect were unavailable:

'You shut your eyes a lot. What can you expect when they come from very poor houses and everything? Though there's nothing of the lodging-house type about it. . . . They're a different class, not the riff-raff. They're working people. You've got to make allowances for them when they don't know how to hold a knife and fork' (a single woman of eighty-four, score 4, who was formerly a matron).

(c) Resumption of lost roles

Another method of restoring downtrodden dignity and authority lay in the make-shift reversion to a previously held role which had offered satisfaction, status and security. For some this desirable transformation proved conveniently easy. Thus a former matron of a welfare home took it upon herself each night to check the windows and general arrangements in every room, while a former nurse, aged eighty-four (score 4), rubbing the wrist of another confused companion when the latter complained it hurt, intimated coaxingly:

'I do massage. This will drive the blood to its proper house. If anything worries you, foot or hand, don't worry the doctors. Come to me, why didn't you come before? . . . I shouldn't crush your knees too much or you'll get varicose veins. Tomorrow or to-night, whichever you like, I'll do a little more massage.'

For others the attempt to translate a return to past roles into positive form was attended by few opportunities for direct expression and the consequent effort at make-do might be readily misinterpreted. Anormic behaviour, such as going through the motions of apparently making a cake with the aid of Dunlopillo cushions (as described in chapter 3, p. 70), or cutting up a sheet with scissors or tearing up a dress, all of which confused residents in the separatist homes, were observed to do, was perhaps the best means open to act out a desire to engage in cooking and dressmaking respectively when the proper facilities were not made available. In other cases the purpose could only be guessed at. Thus a similar aid was possibly being supplied by a daily newspaper at which a widow (aged eighty-three, score 5 and very lethargic), who had previously been the wife of an MP, gazed uncomprehendingly each day with ritualistic obdurateness.

For others again recognition that they saw themselves at least in some sense resuming past roles depended on their own verbalization. This might be explicit, as in the case of a woman (aged eighty-three, score 4) who had previously worked as a clothes designer and once remarked to the matron: 'I like your skirt, and I notice these things as I'm a fashion artist.' Or it might be implicit. A woman, for example, who had once been matron of a home (now aged eighty-five, score 10, and tangential and highly repetitive in speech, as well as almost always confined to her chair or bed), appeared to be envisaging her former employment when she replied to a question about her relations with the staff: 'Pretty well, I think – don't take much trouble to make it go wrong. I take a lot of trouble to make it go right.' A former midwife (score 4) seemed to rationalize her presence by regarding the female attendants as requiring her professional attention: 'I don't do any nursing now. I feel it's better for the time being. But these girls – their mother is away. I was asked to come and came.' Again, the widow of a headmaster (aged seventy-five, score 9) with a capacity for mental reification at will, insisted 'Course we have a chapel here' and 'I've got my bicycle here', asked people what they thought of the tuck-shop, and called the interviewer 'boy' and told him not to tease her or she would raise the matter with Uncle Meyrick (her husband?). In the same vein a former nurse (score 4) contended: 'We *are* the staff. . . . If I'm lonely, I put on my clothes and go and see any old patients.'

(*d*) *Dissimulatory presentation of virtuous image*

A more direct and abrupt technique of psychological recompense in the face of environment-induced apathy or cantankerousness was the self-ascription of a generous or altruistic character, where observation did not substantiate the claim or even suggested the contrary.

A widower of eighty-five (score 6), a former builder's foreman, who had been admitted to the special home after being frequently found wandering by the police, and who now appeared never to leave his chair throughout the day except to visit the WC (after regularly having to enquire where it was) or for meals, nevertheless asserted proudly: 'That's why I'm not unhappy. I generally go to help them in a quiet way. Though I've got to speak for myself, I think I've done a lot for the patients [*sic*]. I've had numerous letters from patients when they leave, thanking me. I don't like to boast, but I think I've helped by the affection I've gained. Means nothing to me. I think I've had a few knowledge of kindnesses. I was very weak when I came to hospital and I think I've taught others. I can understand some of them better than the officials really, because I've been one of them. . . . I help a little in checking them up. I expect they know that. I don't let them disturb, and if they did, I'd put a check on it right away, and I think I've done a bit of good in that way. . . . I've got a name for doing odd little jobs for the boys which they can't do. I know I've been a great help to others weaker than myself, though I don't shout about it. . . . I make myself at home. I don't divulge on it. I think I know when I'm worried too much, and I put a downer on it. If you're all right yourself and not too strict in any way – I don't think I spoil the boys in any way. If I hear of anything, I'd put a spoke in, of course. It's home from home for me, and I think others could make it, if they tried hard. So I think I'm helpful like that. I definitely make the best of things, though I'm not an habitual talker about myself. Plenty of it – "whiners" I call them.'

Apart from the central theme, this passage also reveals many other facets commonly predicated of this countervailing device. There is a marked attempt to convey impressiveness by the ponderousness, almost pomposity, of the language, in obvious incongruity with the sentence content. There are strands of grandeur, not only in the effort at imposing style, but in the hint of supervisory authority and in the indirect promotion of a deflated ego by reproaches to others for their alleged querulousness. Also present is a distinct repetitiveness of the main sentiment, and one that is employed irrespective of changing context and fresh questions. This kind of stereotyped defensive manoeuvre – a calculated perseveration – reached its apogee in the hands of a woman (aged eighty-two, score 7) who reiterated almost verbatim fourteen times in the course of a single interview, in response to questions on every subject: 'No, I'm very happy here. I don't think I've had a wrong word with any of them', though she was observed to be the most unrelenting persecutor in the home of certain other residents more confused than herself. Indeed a façade of amenability in plain antinomy to the facts was the thread underlying almost every manifestation of this mechanism. 'I see Jesus Christ and he says "Follow me" and I *do*. "In my house there are many mansions; if it were not so, I would have told you. Follow me." Some jeer at me, but I don't mind' (a widow of ninety-five, score 1, who was notorious for her destructive and hurtful outbursts – 'All jailbirds here!' 'You bugger, you should be in hell!') 'Course I'm a very agreeable person. I never look for the faults of people. I look for the best side' (a woman of eighty-six, score 2, with an inexorably critical tongue for the wayward habits of confused companions).

(e) *Rationalized explanation of presence*

Where a more specific recompensing notion was not employed and yet the stigma of rejection and impotence required some socially acceptable explanation, recourse was usually had to some kind of rationalization to warrant the existing predicament. The function of this manoeuvre was most clearly highlighted where the reality obstinately obtruded only to be consciously rejected in favour of the fantasy:

A widow of seventy-seven (score 7), whose early days after her admission were marked by nocturnal hallucinatory notions of maggots and ants assailing her and by paranoic accusations of being poisoned, justified her presence thus: 'I live in Beverley Gardens, Plymouth, and I'm here for a stay away from housework. I've come to rest, and I'll go back to the flat when I want to.

Just staying here as I might be at the seaside. I'm quite able to pay – no anxiety about that. I like hotel life.' But then she added rather nervously: 'This is a hotel, isn't it?' When asked if she noticed if any of the residents were 'funny in the head', she replied: 'No, not so far. I hope that none were off their head, or like that. I'd hate to be in a place where I was disturbed at night. I'd *hate* it.' But then timorously and fearfully: 'Is this a sort of asylum?' Finally she fortified herself against the oddities of others by assuming herself the home was indeed a hotel, so they couldn't be demented. 'I would be very worried if I found the others were mad here.'

The particular apologia employed here, that of residence in a hotel, is discussed later in the wider context of a belief in the likelihood of imminent departure,[18] but there it can be seen as forming part of the category of defensive notions built round a respectable alternative to selection for a home for confused old people. The other institution mainly utilized for this purpose was a hospital. For a physical explanation lacked the degrading overtones of a dubious psychiatric one. 'I broke my leg, otherwise I wouldn't be here.' 'I was in Bury St Edmunds at the time, when I got a paper from . . . I sort of sprained my leg' (a widow of eighty-seven, score 3, where the case record gave as the reason for her admission: 'her daughter couldn't cope with her cantankerous and abusive mother'). 'This is a hospital, not a home. I'm a patient here on the ward' (a woman of eighty-one, score 2, who was indeed suspected of having a carcinoma of the stomach). 'I was a widow living alone, had a heart attack, and had to go to the infirmary, then sent by the doctor to Pinewood (mental hospital) waiting to come here' (a woman of seventy-five with a background of paraphrenia).

The advantage of a hotel lay not only in its social respectability, but more particularly in the fact that voluntary initiative was retained over entry and departure, and this claim was sedulously fostered in a generalized form. 'After I left work, I walked the roads back to mother, then came here' (a subnormal man of eighty-five, score 4, who had spent thirty years in a mental hospital after violently attacking his mother, but now alleged his age was twenty-seven). 'I had to sell my house; didn't want to stay there any longer.' 'I lost my mother and father, and there was nothing else for me but to come here.' Some put an honourable gloss on an equivocal history by implying that control of their personal destiny was only obstructed by the contingencies of misfortune:

'I became ill and had to leave my home in Boroughbridge when it was pulled down. So I went to High View, but didn't like it. It's a mental home – lots of old women with dolls and prams. I shouldn't be there by rights. I wanted to go into a Salvation Army home, as I was a member of it at Boroughbridge, but I couldn't get in. I come from a good family and can't understand their ways' (a subnormal woman of seventy-one).

As an acceptable substitute for personal initiative in explaining entry, it could be excused as at the behest of relatives. 'I was in Great Oakes (mental hospital) more than five years. My grandson wanted me to come here as he lived in Todderton [the nearby town].' The influence of relatives could also, however, be seen as malevolent: 'Well, I've got to get here and stop here for a little while, I want to let you know. My husband, he's a bugger – he won't let me go out.'

But the plea which most attracted confused residents in the separatist homes was an altruistic one. 'I'm just staying here with some friends, to save my people having to take me home' (a widow of eighty-six, score 2). 'I'm staying because my nephew wanted it, so I'd be free of chores' (an unmarried woman of eighty-one, score 1).

One final rationalization frequently espoused, by rational as well as confused residents, was the employment of 'sad tales'.[19]

'I was working at a china clay place down here, and I was transferred to here. I had some money to pick up. I hadn't been here above a day, it was gone. Somebody took the lot' (a widower of ninety-four, score 2, who had been on holiday when his daughter reneged on him, refusing to take him back, a shock which precipitated a skin eruption for which he was still treated).

'I've been in Innaston [mental hospital] thirty years with bad nerves. My husband paid for me there – cheapest place. I scrubbed the floors and walls, and got colds, and said I was tired of it. So I was brought here. I prefer this to Innaston. . . . Last summer I had Matron's baby out on the grass – sort of babysitter' (a widow of seventy-eight, rational, who had originally been admitted suffering from depression and melancholia associated with pregnancy).

'Most of the others [residents] have had some strokes or shell-shock. When we were young, we were put out in the sun' (a man of sixty-eight, score 7, obsessed by bizarre expectations of doom).

POSITIVE STRATEGIC ADJUSTMENTS FACILITATING DISSOCIATION FROM THE ENVIRONMENT

Three other types of compensatory device were also found which, unlike the five already analysed, seemed to be geared to achieve dissociation from the whole institutional association. These also must be discussed and illustrated.

(a) Regression to childhood

It is a well-understood phenomenon of old age that those who have become by degrees helpless and dependent should look back longingly to the days when they wielded influence and life still held a vital meaning. Not surprisingly, therefore, this device was frequently adopted by the confused, though carried to a further extreme commensurate with their greater sense of powerlessness and bewilderment. The wish received its simple fulfilment, and the tense was the present:

'I've got my mother and father and sister living here. I live with my mother now. I've been a very delicate girl' (a widow of ninety, score 6, who was never seen to engage in conversation and was often brusquely turned out of her chair).

'All my people are here. I'm not away from anyone, you know' (a widow of eighty-two, score 8, who also later declared: 'Don't know who I am or what I am – so far gone as that. Haven't the faintest idea what I'm doing here.')

Even where the blatant simplicity of these fantasies was missing, the same intention was clearly implicit in the return to childhood or youth. 'Some of my girlfriends have gone away. One or two have got married. I'm not quite sure how old I am' (a widow of eighty-one, score 9). Similarly, an eighty-two-year-old woman who had her hair plaited used regularly to ask that her hair be put down since her mother liked it (she insisted she was seventeen), while a man (aged ninety-three, score 3) who declared he went out occasionally insisted that he went round the town where in fact he spent his early years, now a hundred miles distant.

Perhaps the most favoured theme, however, was that of imminent departure back to mother – and significantly it was parents, especially the mother, with the focus of self-sacrificing dependability that maternal love represented, who were recalled rather than husband or children.

'I want to get back home to Mother's as soon as I can' (a single man of eighty-five, score 4).

'I've got my mummy and my daddy and my sisters to come and see me. . . . I want to go home to my mummy and daddy – don't know what mother would say!' (a widow of eighty-six, score 8, who was blind and often sat nodding her head to the side and gesticulating with her hands as she exclaimed repeatedly 'Poppa!').

'I'm off tonight. I'm going to see my mother. She was great to me. [Tears glistening in her eyes]. I'd be with my mother – that's the one I want to be with. Take her to the service: father's in the choir, I'd be glad to get out of here and go with mother. I feel the place is absolutely upside down' (a severely confused and much persecuted woman).

Again, overlapping with the dissociational genre assuming continued residence in one's private household[20] was the claim that one actually *was* at home with mother. 'My mum likes me to be at home, but I'm none too keen' (a widow of eighty-nine, score 8). 'I don't have anyone here. It's my ordinary, usual house. My parents see that I look after myself' (a widow of seventy-one, score 9). Even where the precise identification with the childhood home was not effected, comparison blurred the differences: 'At first when I started life, I didn't come here. I lived at Rosetta and I think this house is what Rosetta used to be' (a woman of eighty-one, score 9). 'Well, it's wonderful here because I think it's like the kirk [where she lived as a child], and I have to think, "Is this the same place?" ' (a widow of eighty-six, score 6).

Lastly, where no claim was made that mother was living there or that a return to mother was imminent, the remaining equally effective alternative was utilized – that mother was about to visit. 'I'm stiff with worry. Mother's coming down tonight, so I mustn't be too late to see the . . .' (an unmarried woman of eighty-eight, score 12, deeply sensitive, who often referred adoringly to her mother). 'My financé's coming to collect me' (significantly not her husband, as he later became – a widow of seventy-five, score 9).

(b) Temporary stay with departure impending

Perhaps the most obvious reaction to unhappy surroundings is a wish to depart. This wish many confused residents translated into an accomplished fact or at least an earnest intention. The most popular facility employed for this purpose was the assumption, whether overtly asserted or implicit, that the home was a hotel:

> Miss Doherty, an energetic and forceful woman for her eighty-one years (score 1), declared: 'I'm only here for a week – at least I think so. They don't provide anything but meals here. This is a hotel. You're not given anything. I'm rather surprised you should have such an idea. The others are all very normal. The maids[21] here – "nurses" they call them – are very pleasant. Don't know where they get them these days.' She emphasized the point by apologizing on one occasion 'Sorry, I've forgotten my purse' when she felt a tip was called for, and by insisting that the sharing of her room was an intrusion on her privacy: 'Somebody sleeps in my room in the afternoon, so I'm down here. Bad luck on me!' When her wish to pay for the occupational therapy materials she was given was politely ignored, she replied: 'All this time I've been here, I must owe you something. Well, I'll send you back a present [after I return home]'. Her aim of severance from the institutional reality, implicit in her protestation 'If everybody here worked, quite a lot would be done',[22] was made plain by her wish-fulfilment: 'I dreamt last night I was home. So disappointed to find I wan't.'

Alternatively, one particular aspect of hotel life, the opportunity for voluntary departure at one's own initiative, was sometimes stressed: 'I can go home when I like. I do go home two or three times a week' (a single woman of seventy-seven, score 1, who had never been on a visit outside the separatist home since her admission fifteen months previously).

Several other variations on this central theme were noted. 'I'm staying with a friend' (an unmarried woman of eighty-nine, score 11). 'Only staying here for a short while – here on holiday from Heron Cottage, Worcester' (a widow of eighty-three, score 4, who had been resident nearly four years). Sometimes the dissociative goal was even clearer: 'I'm not living here. I go away' (a widow of seventy-nine, score 6). 'I go home for meals and at night' (a widow of eighty, score 5). 'Course I'm not *living* here. I go home. Down the . . . Anywhere. I'm *not* going to live in this home' (a widow of eighty-three, score 8). 'I'm not a resident here. My home is where I've been out living. I'm only just passing through this place. I went home last night' (a widow of eighty-seven, score 3, who spoke also of 'the lady on the train with me today' and declared 'whatever I have I cook myself', presumably at home). And in accordance with the logical requirements of these allegations, temporariness was contended even to an extreme degree: 'I've only been here two or three days' (the widow of eighty-three). 'This is the first day I come here' (a French-born widow of eighty-six, score 8, resident nearly six years). 'We've only just come, I've never slept here before' (a single woman of seventy-four, score 6, resident over eight years).

A similar pretext to sustain the belief that residence was only ephemeral was the claim that the purpose was purely convalescence. 'I'm here till I feel well enough to go home' (a widow of seventy-four, score 3, who had been resident nearly three years). 'It gives mother a chance a little more to look after things. At present she won't let me do very much. We're always used to working together. Then she put her foot down and said, "You won't do anything till you're better." I had a general let-down. Just a little breakdown. But I'm better now' (a widow of seventy, score 3, resident over three years).

Yet another device to substantiate transitoriness was the expectation of marriage. 'I'm going to marry a Mr Hynard. Don't know when or where. But I'm preparing a trousseau for my bottom drawer' (a former psychiatric patient of seventy-seven, rational). 'I'm a widower, so I've got to go to my old family. They're nearly all married. I've got no proper home at present. Can I ask *you* a question: do you think a man of my age should get married?' (a man of eighty-six, score 2).

Finally, casting all subtlety aside, some confused residents in the separatist homes revealed their underlying purpose with blatant directness. 'I'm going back to London tomorrow' (a severely crippled woman of eighty-six, score 2). 'I'll have to go home now. I don't belong here' (a widow of eighty-eight, score 6). 'Where should I go to go home? It's too wet to walk home. I want to go now, you see, when it's light' (a woman of eighty-eight, score 9). Some went further and tried to take matters into their own hands. One woman repeatedly approached a male companion with the urgent request: 'Will you come up all quiet now and take me home?', while another resident (an unmarried woman of eighty, score 11) packed her cases, explaining 'I think I'll go back to my sister now.'[23] A blind woman of ninety (score 8) constantly harangued persons entering the room with the plea: 'Time for me to go home. Have you come for me?', while a desperately unsettled resident of seventy-seven (score 7) continually tried to elicit from staff 'the way to the ticket office'.

(c) *Presumption of still being at home*

Finally, many confused residents in the separatist homes achieved their object of dissociation from the fact of institutional life by the simple ruse of denying this fact.[24] They expressed surprise at being asked whether they wished to return home. 'Take me home? Home's here. I think I'm up to date with the rent and all' (a widow of eighty-two, score 7). Others made casual remarks in the course of questioning like 'My son and daughter are upstairs.' Sometimes the image of home and all its association was resurrected with refreshing directness:[25]

> A blind and incontinent woman of ninety (score 8), whose husband was chronically ill in hospital and who after nine months' residence was now thoroughly lonely and rejected by her neighbours, compensated by idealizing her home and transporting it into the present. 'They all come home early in the evening. We're pleased to see them and make sure they're well. We have the tea things to wash up, and we're very, very happy. The children are too, God bless them! Yes, this is *home* for us, dear one. I can cook, got enough money to live on, don't want for nothing. No, I wouldn't change. I'm happy, So is Daddy. Mr Sawbury – you must see him. He's sensible – I'm not.'

NEGATIVE STRATEGIC ADJUSTMENTS

All the eight adjustment techniques analysed so far possess the common characteristic that uncomfortable facts are evaded or mitigated by the projection of an alternative positive situation to which commitment has in varying degrees been transferred. Occasionally, however, the breakdown of psychological integration with reality appeared not to be accompanied by the substitution of any positive construct. Nevertheless the motive seemed still to consist basically of self-protection, even if conscious control was less in evidence, and for this reason the phenomenon is here classified as negative strategic adjustment. The two main instances of this genre observed among confused residents in the separatist homes, paranoia and withdrawal, will therefore now be examined.

PARANOIA

One mechanism by which the socially isolated were saved from having to explain and face up to their rebuff was by projection of the blame for their loneliness squarely on to the shoulders of some external agent. Sometimes the imputation of moral wickedness was pinned in generalized fashion on to the institution itself:

> Miss Willey, well-preserved in health for her age of seventy-five (score 9), spent most of the time each day in her chair engaged in secret conversation with herself and occasionally slapping her left arm, thigh or cheek with her right hand. 'I suppose they kill people here, don't they? You're flung in this damn place simply to make a misery for ever. This place should be pulled down. Wicked that they hurt people who come in. If people are going to hit and plot and kick you. They hate me, that's understood.' Yet this contrivance had its price, and her guilt at her accusations showed through when she was pressed, 'I didn't say people get hurt here,' and by her tantalizing anxiety about her own partial culpability: 'I suppose they hate me because they're all so different from me, because I don't want to be tied here. They don't take notice of me.'

The same underlying theme was taken up by other confused residents in other ways, for example: 'I don't suppose we'll get any food today' (a widow of eighty-seven, score 1). Hallucinations, too, could serve a similar purpose. Another woman (aged seventy-seven, score 7) complained of maggots and ants on the table and in the food, protested one night 'You're murdering me' when she was being given medicine (thinking it was poison?), and accused staff of raining powder from the ceiling on her. Alternatively, protection against the persistent frustration of valid aspirations to self-dignity might be sought in denial: 'I'm not very happy. I'm in an awkward position – can't do what I want to do. I'm only a minor person. It would be out of place to talk about persons much more important than myself. Not etiquette. I'm of no value at all.'

WITHDRAWAL

The other main type of strategic adjustment which was negatively oriented was the tendency towards an escapist withdrawal from reality. The concept is clearly capable of varying degrees of instantiation, and the partialness of the phenomenon has been well expounded by Laing.[26] Examples falling within this category have already been cited in other contexts,[27] mainly in regard to incoherence and anormic behaviour, but a discussion of their significance is left to the following section because it raises questions of the precise psychological status of adjustments.

Fact or fantasy?

Did the confused really credit their own strategic adjustment façades? The question is prompted by the existence of palpable *inconsistencies* in their claims and by some curious *misperceptions* so patently contrary to reality.

Inconsistencies were found in two main forms. Firstly, where two or more types of strategic adjustment were thrown together within a single individual's psychological framework, the overlapping implications did not always cohere.

Miss Tutty, a single woman of seventy-seven (score 2) with chest scoliosis and osteo-arthritis in one knee, prided herself on her supervision of others: 'I look after the person I sit with in the hall.' Though she could not physically help anyone, she nursed the feeling that her remarks were comforting to her neighbour even if they were not in fact appreciated or even understood. Later, however, she made clear that her superintendent responsibilities were cast rather wider and involved definite authority: 'I sent the patients to bed. I didn't speak to them. They knew I didn't like it.' But she was ready to acknowledge some limitation of her powers: 'I like cooking, but it's a very big order here. Don't think I could do it. Mr Thurleigh [the superintendent] doesn't give me work to do. I don't do the typing. We do the shopping. I pay for what I buy. I'd like to clean a room. I'd like to settle down and keep work going – knitting, big needles.' Already the image has shifted to that of temporary residence in a hotel, which at one point, she explicitly endorsed: 'That's all right, we *are* the guests, all right.' Nevertheless, the main focus lay on grandiose recompense for her recognizedly lowly position. On another occasion she showed me the picture of a woman in a *Reader's Digest* edition which she kept in her handbag, claimed it was Elsa Maxwell, and recounted how the latter wanted to marry her father, but he refused. She further alleged that her brother bored a hole into the earth to seek treasure underground, according to an article 'The mysterious money pit' in the same *Reader's Digest*, and ended by telling the story of how she met a man in Lewisham, where her niece lived, who took her to West Africa. On a rather different plane, as an attention-eliciting and dramatic, if also negative, device with perhaps a tinge of sexual fantasy, she protested that 'a man pulled out all my clothes and twisted the curtains – a murderer whom they tried to hang, but could not'.

Strands of several adaptational images are here intertwined, sometimes contrary or even contradictory and sometimes exaggerated or plainly unrealistic. Household duties ('We do the shopping. . . . I'd like to clean a room') are antithetic to supervisory authority ('I sent the patients to bed'), which itself is incompatible with the hotel idea ('We *are* the guests'), while each separately scarcely coheres with the more exotic delusions of grandeur, including paranoid ones.[28]

How should these conflicting dimensions be explained? The dilemma is partly resolved by seeing the integration of the *manifest* presentation of the adjustment façade as a matter of irrelevance for the confused. Since what really concerned them was the *latent* function here analysed as chiefly compensation within or dissociation from the institution, it is not surprising that, on the principle of *over-determination*,[29] their underlying purposes should be channelled into overt expression in a structured form not wholly susceptible of internal integration.

A second main form of inconsistency lay in the promulgation of details, even within the compass of a single adjustment façade, which were incompatible or at best uneasily co-existing. Such contradictions might, of course, simply reflect the failure to sustain an assertion under pressure:

'I only come once a week. I'm not forced to come. I've got a

good home and good husband. Don't know why I come [laughing]. No need to come. If you want to come for only a day or two, they let you go. My husband might come for me tomorrow.'
'What is this home then?'
'A home for those who haven't got a home' (a widow of seventy-seven, score 2).

Or they might represent a persistent ambivalent tension between the rigours of reality and the striving for a fantasied wish-fulfilment, a tension created partly by the need to conceal the embarrassing truth:

'We tuck in pretty early. Nothing to do here. . . . Got so many friends here. They take up so much of your time. We potter about, go to each other's homes and help there. Always find a job to do. My people are all handy and round about me, always coming to see me. So I'm never lonely . . . I'm sometimes lonely. I feel in the country I'm shut away from everybody. I dislike the lonely life here very much' (a crippled widow of eighty-six, score 2).

But more significantly, such incongruities in adjustment façades might be construed as indicating, not merely the indifference of their creators to the logical cohesion of the manifest content, but perhaps also the extent to which a limited withdrawal from reality permitted an at least partial breakdown in the system of causal relations, so implicitly contradictory are the insinuations:

'My nephew's a Navy man. It's through him I'm here, after I got the 'flu, for a week or a little longer. . . . I'm annoyed that Mrs Cleathon [another resident, aged seventy-one, score 10] spies on me in all her rooms. I come from Portsmouth and went to live at her guest house at Portsmouth. She wanted a man, and because I as a visitor got on very well with the man, she asked me to leave. She now has no friend and she's a bad lot. . . . I'm really lazing here – that's what I was meant to do. My nephew wanted me to come. He's paying for it. He's very kind, so that I don't have to do the chores . . . Please write to Oaklands [the name of her separatist home] as I left my handbag there on my last visit' (a single woman of eighty-one, score 1).

'I shall have to see where my people are. They're here, I suppose . . . My things are at home. I shall be home presently. No-one troubles about me. I go home as a rule. . . . My son and daughter are upstairs. . . . I don't belong here. I've got my own home' (a widow of eighty-eight, score 6).

Or withdrawal could license a convenient suspension of spatio-temporal restrictions:

A widow of eighty-eight (score 9) in the course of her interview nostalgically telescoped several periods of her life into one all-embracing present. 'I write once each week to my mother and father. . . . My parents live over there [beckoning to the side of the home] . . . Both I and my son can drive the car. . . . I've got plenty of friends here, like my sister Jessica. . . . If I want any money, my husband says to me "Do you want this darling?" '

If therefore withdrawal from reality is characterized as a gradual shift from a state in which concepts are more or less realistically aligned, through a piecemeal and disorganized phase of partial realism and partial fantasy, to one (perhaps never wholly realized) in which the delusional world achieves complete inner integration, then the degree of functional and constituent intactness of the adjustment notions propounded by the confused will serve as a measure of their psychological renunciation of their actual situation. Initially an awareness of the decline in one's own mental capacities and of the behavioural irregularities of others was evident (see pp. 284–5). Gradually this discernment is diminished, though the grasp on reality still persists in fragmentary form. Thus a woman who was deeply sensitive to her failure to memorize details to answer questions also insisted both that she slept and had her meals at her own house, and that 'I have meals here, but never know when I'm having them' (a widow of eighty, score 5). A resident who twisted every question about the home to fit her preconception that she was still living in her own household ended with the suggestion that I should consult her husband since 'he's sensible and I'm not' (a married woman of ninety, score 8, see p. 322). Another woman who confidently declared her belief that she was staying temporarily in a hotel could also ask nervously 'Is this a sort of asylum?' (a widow of seventy-seven, score 7, see p. 316). Similarly the recognition of others' deterioration and remoteness was miti-gated. A mildly disoriented woman, for example, who in accordance with her conviction of hotel life argued that the other residents were normal, repeatedly asked severely confused and even incoherent companions, whenever she lost her stick as she often did, if they knew where it was, seeming not to learn from the frustrating replies how to be more discriminatory in her future contacts. Again, conversational ineptness at this stage was overlooked.[30] When one speaker (score 6), for instance, complained that water had been thrown over her at night, the other (score 1) did not dismiss this as fantasy or a dream, but rather suggested it could hardly be so when there was no pump about. To a degree, however, these inconsistencies must be seen as necessitated by the logical requirements, even at a minimum level, of the strategic adjustment adopted, if self-deception, an integral part of the goal, was to be more than marginally successful.

The final stage in this process is reached when the adaptive façade assumes greater predominance than the claims of reality. In this study this point was found to be marked, not only by the comparatively unimpaired cohesiveness of the adjustment image, but also by a range of distinctive misperceptions of the immediate surroundings. Chiefly these concerned the weather:

'What a lovely evening . . . I suppose it's raining' (a woman of eighty-eight, score 9, speaking at 11.30 a.m.).

Or sexual misidentification:

'Miss, will you forget this?' (a woman of seventy-four, score 10, to a man of twenty-seven).
'There's a boy sitting there in blue' (a woman of eighty-nine, score 10, about another woman, aged sixty-five, sitting nearby in a blue dressing gown; on another occasion the speaker declared 'My name's Henry Johnson').
'They're nice boys' (a severely confused woman of seventy-six, referring to two very feminine girls of eight and eleven).

Or age miscalculation, to a grotesque degree:

'Her parents live at Todmorden. She's over twenty I think' (a woman of seventy-nine, score 7, seeking to identify a wanderer in the home).
'I was telling this young lady . . .' (a severely confused woman of seventy-eight in reference to a companion aged seventy-three).[31]

Sometimes quaint interpretations were constructed out of uncomplicated visual objects, indicating that remoter psychological associations had become superimposed on straightforward perceptions:

'Is it a cross made?' (a single woman of eighty-nine, score 11, whose father had been a clergyman, pointing at an empty fireplace). 'You mustn't push those sticks down' (a severely confused woman to another whose legs were rucking up the carpet). 'She's shivering from cold' (a woman of eighty-seven, score 1, quite inaccurately, concerning a companion, who immediately denied it, 'Not a bit of it'). 'She looks as though she's in a baby's pram' (a severely confused woman addressing another in reference to a third who was sitting on a couch without any apparent resemblance whatever to that claimed).

The analysis of this section can be summarized by reverting to the original question: how far did confused residents really believe in their own strategic adjustment façades? The answer is seen to be two-fold. In one sense they were committed to the functional objective of these techniques without particular concern for the precise logical consistency of the outer forms in which their needs were expressed. At another level, the partial realism retained at least in the initial stages of confusional deterioration indicated that the delusional exterior had not so much been assimilated as semi-deliberately utilized for determinate ends. Total absorption within the world created by the adaptational construct, which only occurred when a person's social outlook appeared so demoralizing as to necessitate psychological withdrawal, was more likely to produce an internally integrated set of beliefs, but only at the price of an increasingly capricious treatment of actual surroundings.

II TACTICAL DEFENSIVENESS

So far only that part of the function of adjustment behaviour has been discussed where a definite initiative has been taken to erect a notional haven as a compensatory substitute for an unendurably painful reality. The tactical use of adjustments, reactively inspired but equally important, must now be explored. The purpose remained self-protection, but here, more parochially, against either the acknowledged social disapproval or intolerance of confusional symptoms, or the undesirable social consequences of confusional manifestations.

Adjustment against social displeasure at confusion

The various devices developed by confused residents in the separatist homes to shield, explain or otherwise manipulate confused behaviour will be briefly examined in relation to each of the six broad symptoms of such behaviour, as analysed in Chapter 3, together with a frequent physical concomitant – incontinence.

INCOHERENT OR TANGENTIAL SPEECH

Speech characterized by irrelevancies or disordered logic may be regarded as one consequence of the mental disorganization induced by unnerving bewilderment and rejection, if not as a mark, in more extreme instances, of actual withdrawal into a world untrammelled by normal conversational conventions. Given its predetermined existence, it is difficult to avoid the conclusion, however, that it could be taken advantage of for ulterior ends.[32] It could, for example, be operated in the form of face-saving circumlocutions:

'What place is this here?'
'Rather hard to describe. One part's very important. Full of pastry and cuckoos. Then if it's done very badly, we go down and give them a hand and help them (a widow of eighty-five, score 10).

Neologisms,[33] too, had their use:

'Do you have enough to keep yourself occupied?'
'That's a siding affair' (a woman of sixty-nine, score 11, indicating by the correct grammatical syntax of her answer that she well understood the tenor of the question).

Equally, some dark sayings may be explicable by this means:

'Do you talk much to the attendants?'
'Yes, just depends if the burning bush is burning all night' (a severely confused resident who, as a former matron, prided herself on her handling capacities).

RESTLESSNESS AND WANDERING

It has already been suggested (p. 44) that nocturnal restlessness, wandering and incontinence usually reflect a sense of rejection, and again, given this pre-existing syndrome, attempts were occasionally made to conceal its social curiosity:

> A wanderer (aged eighty-four, score 5) who perpetually rose from her seat to stagger a few paces across the room to another seat[34] once justified her action to a severely confused companion with the simple explanation: 'I've just been round the corner.' 'Was anybody there?' 'No, just about three.'[35]
> Or, 'I've been on the road for three years' (see p. 295).

DISORIENTATION OF PERSON OR SITUATION
As classified in this study, this category is by definition entirely to be subsumed in this context since it has been demonstrated as identifiable with the strategic adjustment façades already elucidated.

DISORIENTATION OF PLACE
If spatial disorientation, similarly, is regarded as a reaction partly to the generalized felt disruption and loss of meaning of life and partly, more immediately, to unfamiliarity with a new, large home of often complex design, exculpation from what might otherwise be taken as a personal defect could be, and was, sought by means of projection, for instance: 'You've moved my bed, but you never told me' (see p. 6: a single woman of seventy-four, score 6, who could still never find her bedroom, even after nine years of residence).

ANORMIC BEHAVIOUR
Anormic activities have already been cited (p. 324) as par excellence exemplifying withdrawal, and to this extent, where contacts with reality appeared at their most tenuous, protective devices aimed at retaining social acceptability were clearly at a discount.

MEMORY DEFECT
Coping with a declining memory capacity is a common requirement in old age, but the ingenuities deployed by confused residents to minimize its ravages assumed almost the nature of an art.[36] At the simplest level, awkward problems were crudely deflected:

> 'Are there enough things laid on for you here to enjoy yourself?'
> ''Fraid I'll have to think. Wait for that till I know what to do'
> (a widow of seventy-nine, score 7).

Or any number of neutralizing mechanisms could be adopted for the abrupt termination of difficult passages in conversation: 'It's the usual thing'; 'Yes, that's about it'; 'I should think so'; 'They're all right'; 'That's a lot isn't it?'; 'Doesn't worry me'; 'Definitely something of that sort, yes, I know, very nice'; and many others. Or an affectation of unconcern might be broached by facial gesture: a man of eighty-five (score 4) reacted to recall dilemmas by looking down or away, sucking in breath and sniffing. More sophisticatedly, however, protective devices included sidestepping by a pretence of outraged surprise ('That's something to say to me!' a marginally confused woman of eighty); confabulation[37] ('Can't say how much pocket-money I get because it varies so much', a widow of eighty-eight, score 9, though the amount was always constant); expedient alibi ('I usually leave it till I get home', a widow of eighty-three, score 5, who had never left the home in six years); stereotyped block ('I don't think I've had a wrong word with any of them', repeated indiscriminately in the face of every probing question by a woman of eighty-two, score 7); sharp rebuttal ('I didn't put them [clothes] in . . . What do you do with them? They're all right', a widow of seventy-nine, score 6); and canny retreat:

'Didn't you like it?'
'Like what?'
'Doing what you just said you did?' (a woman of seventy-four, score 6).

Finally, nominal amnesia was met by the employment of paraphrase:[38]

Briefcase – 'nice covered one down there, and brown' (a widow of eighty-seven, score 9).
Bee – 'fly with a long behind which bites' (a woman of seventy-four, rational).

INCONTINENCE

As an unpleasant consequence, whether of social repudiation and hopelessness or of organic deterioration, incontinence required concealment or explanation, and indeed rationalizations were occasionally forthcoming from severely confused residents.[39] A woman of seventy-five (score 9), for instance, who on lifting her skirt noticed a stain on her slip, immediately remarked: 'How did I spill tea on that?' (adding thoughtfully, however 'or perhaps it isn't tea?')

Protection against the social consequences of confused behaviour

As important as the rationalization of actual confusional symptoms where these were likely to incur displeasure or exacerbate exclusion was protection against the devastating social consequences of confused behaviour, as expounded in the two preceding chapters. These outcomes, together with the rationalizations adopted for self-preservation against them, are here enumerated under four main headings – isolation, embarrassed humiliation, powerlessness and apathy.

ISOLATION

Strategically the first line of defence against the pains of isolation and rejection lay in the psychological erection of dissociative adjustment façades. But, more narrowly, confused residents were usually quick to take advantage of almost any interactional opportunity whatsoever that became available, even in the most circumscribed situation. Much of the muttering to themselves which some, especially the segregated and lonely,[40] engaged in proved, where the contents were discoverable, to be directed, rather like the disinterested and objective comments of a detached observer, towards wrestling to make sense of an obviously puzzling and disturbing environment. Conversational openings were also readily seized with others, though these tended to a disproportionate degree to be similarly confused companions,[41] and persistence in the face of the irrelevance of many replies indicated that the purpose was social exchange as an alleviation of personal insularity.[42]

The following conversation was recorded between two women in one of the separatist homes, one aged eighty-seven (score 3) and the other who was blind aged eighty-eight (score 1), in which for nearly half an hour they continued to externalize their private thoughts with little or no reference to feedback from the other:[43]

'That old lady [an aimless wanderer] comes from my home. One of my neighbour's nearly eighty.'
'Who?'

'My neighbours.'
'Oh. Some people live to be a hundred.'
'Lady on the train with me today's ninety.'
'Moving about.'
'On the train.'
'Not working?'
'Yes, walking.'
'No, that's not what I said.'
'Worth it?'
'How many brothers and sisters did you have?'
'Three brothers . . .'
'I had nine brothers and sisters.'
'Oh.'
'Four boys and . . .'
'That lady over there sat in my yard.'
'Four girls.'
'She must have a travel ticket.'
'Brought up with four boys.'
'Eh?'
'I was brought up like a carthorse.'
'You were?'
'The others were brought up like ladies.'
'Quarter past two, this clock.'
'Don't know.'
'Twenty minutes to two before that bus went.'
'I'm sure it's right.'
'That lady – she goes in my yard.'
'She'll miss you.'
'Yes, I'll miss her. I'll have to get another seat down here.'
'There's so much on the road today.'
'What bus did you come down on?'
'It's not all the driver's fault – it's the people who don't look where they're going.'
'She's a nice old girl, ninety, you know.'
'Why worry?'
'If I go out with her, I'll get a seat. Doesn't she look a nice old lady?'
'I've never seen her. Perhaps she's had an easier life.'
'She's lived alone. My daughter was very good to her when she first came that way.'

'Ah yes, you can't trust everybody.'
'No, you can't.'
'I've been good to others, too, and this is what I've come to.'
'No home of my own.'
'Chair's an old devil to sit on.'

The consequences of deafness, which occasionally added a dimension of bizarreness to an already eccentric conversational pattern,[44] were also overlooked, though they must have reinforced any sentiments held by the confused about the peculiarity of those around them:

A widow of eighty-six (score 8), sitting next to another woman of similar age and confusional score, suddenly initiated an exchange without apparent reference:

'Have I got it?'
'Got it? That's right.'
'Oh, you are strong.'
'Making love?'
'You're making love?'
'No, I can't make it last [misheard "love"?]. Could you put one finger there, and another there?' [holding up some cloth].
'I don't mind.'
'No, they're not dyed [misheard "mind"?] Wish they were. Nothing to go down there really. Take it away. Don't let it go.'
'Don't let it go' [echoing].

Apart from conversational manipulation, the whole array of attention seeking manoeuvres already described (p. 301) must also be included here.[45] Prominent among these was confabulation, even if as a technique it was not always well sustained.

A crippled widow of seventy (score 3), who normally sat by herself at the side of the room and rarely spoke to anybody, on one occasion told attendants she was pregnant; on another she explained to the warden that she had smelt arsenic in the lunch, but didn't want him to do anything about it since she knew it was only a prank of the nurses.

EMBARRASSING HUMILIATION

One of the hazards of segregation in a special home for the 'confused', where the causes might be overlooked and only the curiosity of the adaptive mechanisms perceived, was exposure to situations fraught with potential for personal embarrassment. Protection against one such situation, prying questions about admission, was sought by the construction of rationalized explanations of entry (see pp. 315–18). Defence mechanisms adopted against other searching probes displayed the same range of adroitness as that already illustrated in dissimulation of memory defect, and indeed similar considerations applied in both cases. Such devices included hedging by skilful footwork:

'Do you write letters much?'
'That's a funny thing to ask. If a chap's in trouble, and I owe a letter, I'll help him. I suppose I can write a letter as well as anything else' (a man of eighty-five, score 6).

Tantalizingly elusive logic:

'Are you free to do what you like in this home?'
'Free? I don't want to be tied up. I should imagine it's enough to sign, isn't it? Very likeable people. Don't want them all your life' (a widow of eighty-nine, score 8).

Utilization of fortuitous contingencies, real or imagined, as a diversionary tactic:

A woman of seventy (score 10) who found certain questions too pressing or direct took advantage of the superintendent's unexpected arrival: 'No, but the governor's come down. Would you like to see him?'
'Do you find you have enough to keep yourself occupied?'
'Nobody tells me, I don't know. Can't leave the baby outside talking' (a woman of seventy-five, score 9).

Shocked protest at interference:

'I'll go down the road and tell my husband somebody wants to know a lot. Besides, I haven't time as I have to cook a meal for my family' (a widow of seventy-one, score 10).

Deliberate insertion of irrelevant material for off-putting effect:[46]

A woman of eighty-eight (score 12) suddenly asked in the midst of questions at her interview:
'Are you in business? Do you take business in?'
'Well.'

'Then you must have things in your thoughts.'

She repeated this strategem sporadically throughout the interview. Cavalier dismissal of details, when statements were taken literally which were only intended for the comfort of self-assurance:

'My son suggested I come here. He's close, in touch with them all the time.'
'With whom?'
'People he's known and is in contact with. That's all right!' (a widow of eighty-three, score 6).
'It's my friend' (when somebody enters the room).
'Who is it?'
'Don't know. Known him for years. He's my friend' (a woman of ninety, score 8).

POWERLESSNESS

Refuge against the loss of self-determination could, once again, be sought in the appropriation of a suitable adjustment façade in some form of grandiose delusion.[47] But it is worth asking the much more subtle and pervasive question: how far did bewildered, unhappy and lonely residents, in order to gain affection, security or more stable relationships, live up to their reputation as being 'confused', 'mentally infirm', or 'mad', or to the consequential image of a pliant and submissive patient? In other contexts it has been shown that where a system allots persons to polarized positions of power, those allocated a grossly subordinate rank tend to play up to the expectations of the 'master'.[48] Certainly in the course of this study instances were found among the confused of an excessive urge to conform,[49] and the diplomacy of submissiveness was darkly insinuated:

'Are you free to do what you like in this home?'
'Must do what the authorities want you to do. Job of the circles. . . . Leave some money.'
'Who for?'
'For the owner of the turkey' (a severely confused woman, hinting at the tactfulness of bequests to those responsible for her care?)

APATHY

As in previous cases, the primary defence against enforced idleness was derived from the propagation of such strategic adjustment

337

façades as conviction in the performance of household duties and the resumption of lost roles.[50] More parochially, however, protection was sought not only obviously by an exaggerated pretence of activity:

'In the morning I go out for a walk, because the fresh air's good for you. In the afternoon I go out again and we walk as much as we can. And I go to chapel every Sunday' (a widow of seventy-nine, score 7, who rarely left her chair)

but more shrewdly by the smokescreen of tangentiality to conceal shame at the humiliating truth:[51]

'What do you do in the afternoon?'
'Well, I'm a bit fussy myself. I like to have it look nice, and then I can look forward to the next.'
'And in the evening?'
'Personally, I'm with them. I like them. Well, I had so many I didn't really think there were any I didn't like. Have you found any substitute you can put in its place? They *do* find them' (a widow of eighty-nine, score 8, who also was almost always sedentary).

Or by a clever suggestion that apathy represented normality anyway: 'When you get to an advanced age, as I am, you can sit around for quite a time without doing anything' (a single woman of eighty-seven, diagnosed as psychotic in type) a statement which incidentally rationalized the image of conformity.

III THEORETICAL IMPLICATIONS

Enough has been said to validate the original hypothesis[52] that rather than representing a purely adventitious outflow of meaningless gibberish and inexplicable behaviour, so-called confusional symptoms in fact constituted a series of skilful adjustments compensating chiefly for the painful experiences of isolation, impotence and hopelessness.[53] Moreover, the ingenuity of the various mechanisms of tactical defensiveness indicated that confused residents, so far from being of limited mentality, were in fact extraordinarily inventive and original, to a degree indeed far beyond the simplistic and ingenuous reactions of many ordinary persons in situations of equal challenge or embarrassment.[54] So rich and profuse were the veins of contrivance and fabrication, so overdetermined the precipitating impulses by creative compensatory material, that the manifest product, the strategic and tactical adjustment façades, appeared at times extravagant florid, inconsistent, even incoherent, or, as they have been typed by one writer, mischievous and irresponsible.[55]

If then the 'confused' were not really confused at all in the conventional sense, how did they come to receive such appellations as 'mentally infirm' or 'demented'? In other words, how did social phenomena of the kind expounded here assimilate some of the overtones of psychiatric illness and impel so many deep and searching investigations to detect a purely physical cause?[56]

Certainly the partial correlations that have been obtained between confused behaviour and cerebral change suggest that physiological factors may in some cases predispose an old person, under pressure of the decline in certain mental or physical capacities, to adopt a compensatory device of the type outlined in this chapter.[57] Nevertheless, the perversity of attachment among researchers, medical specialists and welfare workers alike to physical or psychiatric morbidity in positing an aetiology for confusion, and the inconsequentiality applied to overt social behaviour, do require some explanation. Perhaps the most plausible reason for this misdirected preoccupation should be sought by reference to the function served by attributing 'confusion' to an old person. Basically, by deflecting the focus away from their very real social needs (and incidentally, though no less significantly, distracting attention from the inadequacies of those actually or potentially responsible for their care, whether family, friends or the wider society in the context of a caring community), it sanctioned their removal to an institution.[58] For this purpose some at least of the normal paraphernalia of medical and psychiatric associations were required. But assimilation to the model of physical deterioration or psychological breakdown offered other 'advantages' besides the convenient liquidation of a chronic social problem. It meant not only that 'confused' persons were to be relieved of normal social duties, so that their status as self-determining individuals was justifiably held in abeyance, a situation from which the consequences of powerlessness explored in the preceding chapter naturally flowed.

Nor did it merely mean that they were incapable of helping themselves and must be cared for professionally, an interpretation which exonerated the family or those immediately in contact from direct responsibility. It meant also, since one aspect of the sick role is the obligation on the person in question, having sought competent medical help, to co-operate in the process of getting well (Susser and Watson, 1962, p. 293), that release from the institutional place of 'treatment' could not be contemplated until the symptoms were at least mitigated, if not eliminated. Yet for all the reasons outlined in Chapters 7 and 8 concerning isolation and rejection, the symptoms were all too likely instead to intensify, making permanent residence a virtual certainty. Finally, the incorporation of medical analogies into the conception of confusion even lent some support to the policy of segregation. For on the principle of the isolation of infected persons, any overdue exposure of normal people to the condition appeared to be an infringement of their right to freedom from 'contamination'.[59]

The social adaptational model of confusion propounded in this study on the other hand, contains very different implications. It sees the individual as the helpless victim of an inappropriate diagnosis of his needs, cast often without consultation, and even sometimes by deception, in a milieu which can only exacerbate his underlying deprivation.[60] The more ingenious the defensive strategems adopted for self-protection against an oppressive reality, the more the mistaken label of 'confusion' or 'derangement' becomes reinforced.[61] If in desperation the old person ultimately succumbs by a gradual but inexorable retreat into fantasy and total self-involvement, it is greeted as the final vindication of the original diagnosis.

Now one aspect of this model which should also be mentioned is that it throws doubt on theories of old age which purport to distinguish successful from unsuccessful adjustment (see e.g. Reichard *et al.*, 1962). Such teleological niceties are open to two main objections. Firstly, they are prone to value distortion in the interests of other groups in society, so that what is, within the circumstances, both an objectively efficient and a subjectively satisfying adjustment may still be regarded as unsuccessful because in significant respects it conflicts with a model predetermined to suit the advantage of rival groups, particularly younger generations. Secondly, even more seriously, emphasis on stochastic rather than normative factors places a wholly unwarranted focus on the fact of deterioration, leading to the final point of death, rather than on the vitality and ingenuity of the efforts made to overcome impediments both naturally and artificially imposed. Thus König has spoken of 'desocialization' and Cumming and Henry (1961) of 'disengagement' in old age (see also p. 45). One implication of the theory of social adjustments developed in this chapter is that, so far from divesting themselves of crucial roles, old people will seek, even in the most unpropitious situation, to engineer means to resurrect lost functions or to fabricate new ones necessary to retain power and self-respect. The central task of theories of old age should therefore, perhaps, rather be to elaborate the ramifications of the techniques utilized by the elderly to maximize these persisting goals in the face of successive and accumulating handicaps, whether, most obviously, from loss of economic opportunity after enforced retirement and from the partial decline of physical or mental capacities, or, more subtly, from competition with the young whose dependency is balanced by the prospects of later economic returns in a society where status is largely dependent on the market value of one's economic function, and from restrictive ideologies centred round the alleged inutility of the aged, whereby social priorities are gradually but systematically withdrawn.[62]

Finally, before leaving this chapter, we should also now briefly return in the light of its findings, to another of the central themes of this book – the functions and characteristics of separatist homes. Almost all the examples drawn to illustrate the theoretical framework of adjustment devices were derived from the special homes, certainly to a disproportionate degree even considering the much smaller number of confused residents in the ordinary homes. Moreover, a majority of the instances were extracted from the single separatist home where four-fifths of the residents were confused by the criteria enumerated in Chapter 3, including nearly half of the total severely confused. This suggests *prima facie*, in terms of the psychodynamics of institutions, that segregation within a specialized home largely restricted to persons with the same basic underlying social needs can only exacerbate their deprivation of normal acceptance, affection, stability, sense of meaningfulness, and assuredness of being wanted within a system of interlocking roles. It remains possible to argue that the separatist homes limited their admissions in the first instance to the more seriously confused, so that the concentration of adjustment behaviour within these establishments was only to be expected, though as between persons of similar confusional scores, adaptational façades adopted by residents in the special homes were more pronounced both in frequency and intensity than those espoused by residents of equivalent state in the ordinary homes. Issues of administrative function and procedure are therefore raised, and these form the subject of the next part of the book.

NOTES

1. Though see also below 'Positive strategic adjustments,' p. 304, rationalized explanations of one's presence in the home.

2. The basic tenet of this treatment method is stated as 'regarding each patient as a person with unique physical, mental and emotional problems, each worthy of individual attention and care by interested personnel'. After three months, of those with arterio-sclerosis four were judged moderately improved, and four slightly so; in eight no change was registered, and only two were moderately worse and one slightly so. Of those with senile brain disease, one had slightly improved and in three no change was reported. Of the total of six who became worse, all had 'severe, progressive, complicating medical illnesses' as well as 'organic brain disease with dementia'.

3. This conclusion is supported by matrons' observations recorded in another study. 'Both matrons were emphatic that even old ladies who scarcely knew where they were, or what century it was, let alone what day of the week, took the greatest pleasure in agreeable surroundings, whether in the form of pretty wallpapers and bright paint or beautiful gardens. They were extremely interested in food – a "surprise pudding" for lunch on Sunday was the event of the week at one of the Homes – and they greatly enjoyed outings, whether a drive in a friend's or relative's car or a trip down to the village café for mid-morning coffee and biscuits' (Roberts, 1961, p. 15).

4. See section 'Adaptation', p. 302.

5. This contrasts with the conclusion of another study, of fifty persons in a welfare home, that 'residents with a chronic brain syndrome (dementia) were capable of making a good social adjustment to the home, though others with functional psychiatric disorder (depression) were usually not. The authors noted that 'those with falling off of intellectual capacity can adjust to the institution environment with a sense of subjective satisfaction, and in accordance with the expectations of the institution milieu', from which it was curiously deduced that this was 'some indication that mildly demented persons are suitable for care in homes for the aged' (Walton *et al.*, 1964, p. 897).

6. Of the five operationalized definitions of 'alienation' accepted by Seeman as logically distinct usages, two would appear particularly to apply to confused residents in separatist welfare homes: (1) powerlessness: 'the expectancy or probability held by the individual that his own behaviour cannot determine the occurrences of the out-comes, or reinforcements, he seeks'; (2) normlessness: 'a high expectancy that socially unapproved behaviours are required to achieve given goals' (Seeman, 1959).

7. Birren (1963, p. 276) has noted the reconciliatory function of reminiscing: 'More than must a young person, the older individual must see and reconcile his past place in the world of people, places and things. He is under pressure to integrate his views of his past.' One central difficulty therefore for the confused persons reminiscing in an unsympathetic environment was the lack of interested persons skilled enough to interpret latent meanings.

8. 'The attachment to one particular place in the day-room, dining-room and dormitory symbolized a yearning for security in an insecure environment' (P. Townsend, 1962, p. 98). Chairs offered one private and inalienable possession in an otherwise public and communal world.

9. See pp. 237–8.

10. Though this is not, of course, a propensity limited to the confused.

11. The fact that she often later forgot the location of her handbag, which then led (according to the medical records) to 'accusations of dishonesty and wild confabulation', provides one more example of the self-fulfilling process whereby a neutral factor (insecurity) could produce a defensive reaction (hoarding) which in conjunction with normal impairments of age (growing forgetfulness) could then create a stereotyped label (confusion) leading to a reaction from others (rejection) which would reinforce the original condition (insecurity), and thus the spiral would continue.

12. An instance of perseveration.

13. Similar adaptive mechanisms, as developed by psychiatric patients, have been described by Goffman (1961, ch. 3).

14. Kennedy (1959, p. 78) also suggested a simple sevenfold classification of senescent decline: (1) dependent decline; (2) defensive limitation; (3) overcompensation; (4) retreat from reality; (5) projective decline; (6) maladaptation with psychosis; (7) maladaptation with psychoneurosis.

15. However, this kind of statement could also be interpreted as an instance of the dissociative adjustment implied by the presumption that one is still living in one's private household (see p. 322).

16. Further examples of this genre of rationalized explanations for one's presence in a home are discussed below, p. 315.

17. See p. 87.

18. See 'Temporary stay with departure impending', p. 320.

19. Goffman (1961, ch. 2, p. 151), illustrates the corresponding employment of this type of rationale particularly by convicts and prostitutes.

20. See 'Presumption of still being at home', p. 322 below.

21. Another woman (score 8) called them 'servants'.

22. Another woman (score 2) remarked in the same vein: 'They're all dreadfully lazy.'

23. Cf. the escapist 'attack' of Mrs Tribble, pp. 292–4.

24. Those severely disoriented following the bewilderment of recent admission – for example: 'There's only one person who occupies these rooms. It's my daughter's house and son-in-law's. Is this opposite the chapel? Don't know where I am. I came to live with my daughter at the end of these houses here, at the end of Crumblin Terrace' (a widow of eighty-two, score 8, admitted a fortnight previously) – are, of course, excluded from this category since they were exhibiting a reactive confusion rather than a strategic adjustment.

25. See the account of Mrs Sawbury, p. 61.

26. Laing has brilliantly argued that the patient-to-be is forced into a position where his true self has to be denied and a false, protective self created, and the better established the false self, the less integrated can the real self be: Laing, 1960, 1967; Laing and Cooper 1964.

27. e.g. non-referential tangential statements (pp. 59–60), bizarre and unpredictable monologue (p. 279), utilization of objects for unintended and usually socially disapproved purposes (pp. 70–1), and improper use of dress (pp. 71–2).

28. Cf. the inconsistencies prevalent in the account of Miss Tangley (pp. 4–6): presumption that still at home with domestic duties ('I look after my mother and sister', 'I go to the shops for mother'); hotel residence ('All quiet ladies here, you know, or I wouldn't have come away with any of them'); temporary stay ('My holiday here's

up – I must return to my room in London'); rationalized explanation of entry ('My people wanted me to come here'); regression to childhood ('Father'll come and fetch me – he's a darling'); age incongruities ('I've left off school now' – she was aged seventy-four); employment contradictions ('I want to get a good position when I return to London', 'at the moment I'm out at work'); incompatible accounts of her relationship to her parental home ('long time since I left home', 'must get home – Mother can't spare me'); irreconcilable attitudes to the separatist homes ('I remember this place well, been here a few times, not recently', 'never been to this place before'); and disorientation of time sequence ('Only just come, haven't we?' when she had been resident nearly ten years).

29. Cf. 'It thus seems plausible to suppose that in the dream-work a psychical force is operating which on the one hand strips the elements which have a high psychical value of their intensity, and on the other hand, by means of *overdetermination*, creates from elements of low psychical value new values which afterwards find their way into the dream-content. If that is so, a *transference* and *displacement* of psychical intensities occurs in the process of dream-formation, and it is as a result of these that the difference between the text of the dream-content and that of the dream-thoughts comes about', Freud (1900); trans. Strachey, 1952, pp. 308–9.

30. See also p. 165: the shipwreck on the voyage to Tasmania, and pp. 166–9 passim.

31. In view of parallel examples, this cannot be taken as merely part of the convention of polite tactfulness.

32. As has already been hinted in the case of Mrs Bridgewood (pp. 132–3).

33. See pp. 51–2.

34. See pp. 64–5.

35. This type of interpretation bears obvious affinities with the well-known phenomenon of post-hypnotic rationalization.

36. Of course, the perplexity was also at times dealt with by a straightforward apology: 'It's this old thing of mine – I can't remember how it started' (a widow of eighty-one, score 2), see also p. 285.

37. Confabulation was apt, however, to be betrayed, where it was overdone, by internal inconsistencies: 'I lost my mother – had a bungalow – flew to my son in Africa, then came here on my return as I had nowhere else to go. I didn't get on with my daughter-in-law. She got jealous, had a temper, led me a bit of a life. I used to live in Bayswater. I kept changing lodgings, had a big garden and couldn't look after it, and the others around didn't look after the garden. After my husband died, I lived alone, but I didn't like being alone at night, so I babysat, then went into a home. I stayed with friends in lodgings after I got back from Africa, then went into a home' (a widow of seventy-nine, score 2, displaying a garbled mixture of truth, distortion and invention).

38. See also p. 58.

39. Cf. the technique of externalized projection: 'Somebody poured cold water on me last night' (p. 328).

40. A widow of eighty-seven (score 9), for example, who had been totally isolated in a room by herself because of her continued 'gibberish', was found, from careful observation, to have interspersed throughout her monologue a series of interpretations about such limited novelties and changes in her surroundings as remained to her. She was particularly conscious of my presence and when once I had my head lowered and supported by my hand, she exchanged ideas with herself about my purpose and then when I finally moved, commented: 'I thought he was asleep.'

41. See pp. 161 and 163.

42. See p. 165.

43. This phenomenon is not, of course, confined to confused old people, but their manipulation of this technique was perhaps more systematic.

44. See also p. 49.

45. Many other 'indispositions', of course, afford similar prospects for gaining un-
wonted attention. In the case of children's asthma, for example, it has been found that a
significant element of its pathology was its potential as a means to control and modify
the mother's dominance. 'Whilst clearly no child would consciously will upon himself
such an incapacitating illness, a child's susceptibility to illness undoubtedly alters
according to his mood and the gains the illness situation affords him' (Burton, 1965).

46. See also p. 100.

47. See pp. 306–12.

48. Patterson (1967, p. 180), for example, describes the 'Quashee' slave personality
where the slave, partly to conceal his true feelings and partly in defiance of his master,
consciously or unconsciously lived up to the stereotype of fecklessness imposed on him.
A similar syndrome is analysed by Elkins (1959, ch 3) in relation to the 'Sambo' personality in North America.

49. See the examples on p. 225 ('I only do just what they ask me').

50. See pp. 305 and 312.

51. On the principle that tangential speech was itself an (albeit semi-involuntary)
protective reaction, its deliberate manipulation here for ulterior motives may be classified
as a second-level adjustment.

52. See pp. 6 and 271.

53. A similar approach has been developed in fictional form. Bailey (1967) relates
how a woman who loses her daughter from leukaemia and finds little affection or
contentment from her stepson's family to whom she temporarily moves, is sent to an
old people's home, a converted workhouse, where she is repulsed and humiliated by
the place and its people. She endeavours to derive solace from her fragmented memories,
but her only effective line of retreat lies finally in the adaptive efforts of her own
crumbling consciousness.

54. Though perhaps the ingenuity of the strategems adopted by the confused should
be seen as merely a logical extension by degree of the kind of adjustment which *most*
persons are obliged to resort to in old age.

55. Nesta Roberts (1961, p. 14) has written of confused persons in residential homes:
'Others may indulge in escapades which, if the cause were not sad and the results
embarrassing, would be comic. They are liable to order expensive goods to be delivered
from local shops, to spin fantasies to casual acquaintances, to believe that the local park
is their own garden and pick its flowers accordingly. One home catering for mentally
confused old ladies long remembered the evening when, after bedtime, one of the residents collected the false teeth of all her fellows from the bathroom tumblers where they
were soaking and hid them in her pillow case. Another engaged a housekeeper for a
large and entirely imaginary country house. A third ordered a great deal of household equipment – washing machines, vacuum cleaners and the like, in the names of other
residents, and presumably enjoyed herself greatly when representatives of the firms
concerned arrived at the home to demonstrate them. There is in this behaviour a good
deal of a child's sense of mischief, with a child's lack of responsibility.' So far from
imputing irresponsibility, the following interpretations, based on the theoretical framework unravelled in this chapter, might be offered: 'order expensive goods to be delivered . . . ordered a great deal of household equipment' – attention-seeking, possibly
also a crafty settling of past feuds; 'spin fantasies to casual acquaintances' – eliciting
of sympathy; 'believe that the local park is their own garden' – fantasies of grandeur
through extravagant claims of ownership; 'collected false teeth of all her fellows . . .
and hid them in her pillow case' – hoarding as a symbol of affectionlessness; 'engaged
a housekeeper for a large and entirely imaginary country house' – self-promise of
impending departure, and again delusions of grandeur.

56. See pp. 40–3, especially p. 43.

57. This process would bear similarities with certain theories of delinquent behaviour.

Eysenck (1964), for example, has postulated that inherited physical factors – particularly the tendency of the autonomic nervous system to mediate the establishment of conditioned responses well or poorly, together with emotionality, also inherited, which provides the drive by which conditioned habit systems are strongly or weakly expressed in action – predispose individuals differently (other things being equal, i.e. irrespective of the superimposed operation of social class and other considerations) to anti-social behaviour.

58. This approach to the confusional syndrome approximates to the conspiratorial model listed by Siegler and Osmond (1966, p. 1200) in their typology of explanatory theories of schizophrenia. This model 'focuses on the civil liberties aspects of mental illness. It notes that calling someone crazy is a good way of getting rid of him, and that the staff of a hospital may conspire with or co-operate with a family who wish to do this. This model notes that mentally ill behaviour can be defined in such a way that it will include the understandably frantic behaviour of someone who is not mentally ill, but who is trying to get out of a mental hospital. Certainly, many of the methods of treating mental patients have the effect of teaching them to behave in such bizarre ways that it is difficult to imagine that they could function outside hospital.' The conspiratorial model has similarities with the moral model, which stresses that unacceptable behaviour is that which violates the agreed mores of a society, in that both models emphasize that there is no illness and that it is the families, the staff and the society, rather than the patient, who are immoral. But whereas the moralists see society as benevolently paternalistic and wisely but firmly re-socializing deviant individuals (e.g. Glasser, 1965), the conspiratorialists see society as actually or potentially dangerous to the patient, whose actions are by no means irresponsibile or socially deviant.

59. See p. 248, for example.

60. A similar line of thought has been developed by Thomas Szasz in relation to schizophrenia. He has argued that mental illness as such does not exist, and that it is the individual's own prerogative to decide whether he wishes to alter his personality or behaviour. If he does, he should contract freely with a psychotherapist for treatment. Otherwise psychotherapy, where involuntary, can become a type of brainwashing. With this premise, Szasz (1963) fears that psychiatrists could acquire a position of social or political power through being professionally sanctioned to label eccentric, radical or other behaviour as 'sick' and to 'treat' it, armed with the laws covering insanity.

61. See p. 278.

62. Perhaps the most pointed aspect of this process has been the recent public discussion concerning non-resuscitation after cardiac arrest. 'Today we must decide whether senile patients, or those suffering from incurable diseases, who in the past would have been carried off by pneumonia, should be kept alive with antibiotics' (*Observer*, 24 September 1967). The issue was brought to public attention by a notice in Neasden Hospital forbidding resuscitation in the case of the very elderly (interpreted as those 'over sixty-five') and those with malignant disease or chronic disease of the kidneys or chest. A survey by the Royal College of Nursing among senior nurses at 152 hospitals revealed that other hospitals also observed an upper age limit (ranging from sixty to eighty, but chiefly the age of seventy) above which patients were not resuscitated, the criteria employed being malignant disease, terminal illness or 'serious handicap'. In such hospitals the consultant usually decided on resuscitation policy as each person was admitted, and then either the ward sister was informed, or the patient's notes were marked with a red or green star or NTBR (not to be resuscitated). When the Minister of Health, however, consulted doctors and heart specialists on this question, they advised that 'no patient should be excluded from consideration for resuscitation by reason of age or diagnostic classification alone and without regard to all the individual circumstances'.

Part IV

FUNCTION AND POLICY

10

The functions of the separatist homes

In order to determine the functions of the separatist homes, and before we analyse local authority practices as revealed by the national survey, we must first briefly answer certain questions about procedures operated in these homes. In particular, what were the main sources of admission, in what proportions were they used, and what were the main reasons in each category? What assessment techniques were employed, and with what success? And to what extent were certain persons admitted to the special homes found on experience to be unsuitably placed? In such cases, how frequently were transfers made, and what kinds of behaviour among residents prompted these moves?

ADMISSIONS

Analysis of the admission statistics (Table 10.1) revealed pre-

Table 10.1

**Sources of admission of confused and rational residents
in separatist and ordinary homes**

Source of admission	Residents of separatist homes (%)			Residents of ordinary homes (%)	
	Severely confused	Moderately confused	Rational	Severely and moderately confused	Rational
Psychiatric hospital	(19)	(20)	29	(9)	5
General hospital	(6)	(10)	4	(5)	7
Residential home	(19)	(28)	35	(41)	23
Private household	(55)	(43)	33	(45)	65
TOTAL	(99)	(101)	101	(100)	100
Number	31	40	52	22	115

eminently that the separatist homes recruited their residents to a significantly greater degree than their ordinary counterparts from psychiatric hospitals,[1] and at the same time rather less from the wider community.[2] Independent analyses of admission data in the case of other separatist homes (Table 10.2) reinforce this conclusion. Secondly, *within* the separatist homes it was the rational rather than the confused residents who produced these differences. For while only a third of the former were drawn from private households, compared to nearly half of the latter, almost a further third of the confused were admitted from psychiatric hospitals, as opposed to only a fifth of the rational.

A more far-reaching picture, however, of the function of separatist homes within the overall institutional framework can be gleaned from an analysis over time of 'through-flow'. The admission and discharge system of one of the specialist homes was therefore analysed (Table 10.3) for the whole four-year period since its

Table 10.2

Comparative sources of admission of different separatist homes

Source of admission	*Separatist homes in the present study* %	*Llanerch hostel Bridgend, Glam.*[1] %	*Greenmount House Bolton*[2] %	*Hartley House Cranbrook, Kent*[3] %
Mental hospital (including psychiatric unit of general hospital)	24	(30)	45	50
General hospital (geriatric unit)	7	—	8	15
Part III Welfare Accommodation	28	(57)	9	10
Private households (own or relatives' home)	41	(12)	37	20
TOTAL	100	(99)	99	95[4]
Number	123	33	66	108

Sources
1. Jones and Milne (1966, p. 159).
2. Nicholas and Johnson, 22 Oct. (1966).
3. Written communication from Dr A. Elliott, County Medical Officer, Kent, concerning a home for 108 women with varying degrees of physical and mental infirmity.
4. The remaining 5 per cent were composed of (i) emergency admissions arising from eviction by a landlord or homelessness; (ii) emergency admissions after rejection by a relative which rendered the old person homeless; (iii) admission of occasional itinerants who come into the county and lack any fixed address; and (iv) compulsory admissions on court application under section 47 of the National Assistance Act 1948.

The functions of the separatist homes

Table 10.3

Throughflow in a separatist home: the destination at discharge of all residents of one separatist home over a consecutive four-year period (from date of opening) by sources of admission

Year	Destination at discharge*	Sources of admission					Total
		Psy-chiatric hospital	General (Ordinary) hospital	residential home	Private house-hold	Un-classified	
1	Psychiatric hospital	1	2	2	2	1	8
	General hospital	0	2	4	0	5	11
	Private household	0	0	0	28	2	30
	Death	4	9	4	5	8	30
	Still resident at end of 4-yr period	4	1	5	4	0	14
	(Ordinary) residential home	0	0	1	0	0	1
	TOTAL	9	14	16	39	16	94
2	Psychiatric hospital	0	0	0	0	0	0
	General hospital	0	2	0	3	0	5
	Private household	0	0	0	3	0	3
	Death	3	3	0	5	1	12
	Still resident at end of 4-yr period	3	1	1	2	0	7
	(Ordinary) residential home	0	0	1	0	0	1
	TOTAL	6	6	2	13	1	28
3	Psychiatric hospital	0	0	0	1	0	1
	General hospital	0	2	0	0	0	2
	Private household	0	4	0	1	0	5
	Death	0	6	0	1	2	9
	Still resident at end of 4-yr period	3	2	1	1	5	12
	(Ordinary) residential home	0	0	0	0	0	0
	TOTAL	3	14	1	4	7	29
4	Psychiatric hospital	0	0	0	0	0	0
	General hospital	0	0	0	1	0	1
	Private household	0	1	0	1	0	2
	Death	1	3	0	1	1	6
	Still resident at end of 4-yr period	0	9	0	2	0	11
	(Ordinary) residential home	0	0	0	2	1	3
	TOTAL	1	13	0	7	2	23
	Four-year total	19	47	19	63	26	174

* Where a resident died almost immediately after transfer to a general (acute) hospital, the destination at discharge has been counted as 'death'.

opening. This revealed that referrals from psychiatric units and ordinary residential homes, which originally accounted for more than a quarter of admissions, dwindled to only 4 per cent after four years, and that whilst the proportion admitted directly from private households dropped slightly, the number admitted via the psychogeriatric assessment unit at the local general hospital rose steadily from a seventh to more than half. Similarly, plotting the shifts in the distribution of destinations at discharge indicated an increasingly stabilized population oriented probably more towards exchange, where this still occurred, within the local authority residential system than with the psychiatric services.[3] For after the first year transfers to a mental hospital virtually ceased, while transfers to other residential homes showed signs of a marginal rise, albeit on very small numbers. The overall impression, therefore, is that, for this particular separatist home at least, the function was less concerned with a regular interchange with suitable psychiatric patients than with a selective filtering of the elderly bound for residential accommodation.

A further dimension of the latent role of separatist homes can be derived from investigation of the social profile of the residents in

Table 10.4

Social characteristics of all residents admitted to one separatist home over a consecutive four-year period (from date of opening)· by source of admission

	Sources of admission					
Social characteristics	Psy-chiatric hospital (%)	General hospital (%)	(Ordinary) residential home (%)	Private house-hold (%)	Un-classified (%)	Total (%)
(a) Sex						
Men	(20)	(24)	(30)	24	(26)	25
Women	(80)	(76)	(70)	76	(74)	75
TOTAL	(100)	(100)	(100)	100	(100)	100
Number	19	47	19	63	26	174
(b) Marital status						
Single	(33)	(28)	(32)	(18)	(23)	25
Married	(7)	(8)	(5)	(23)	(0)	10
Widowed, separated, divorced	(60)	(65)	(63)	(60)	(77)	65
TOTAL	(100)	(101)	(100)	(101)	(100)	100
Number	15	40	19	40	22	136

(Unclassified 38)

Table 10.4 (*contd.*)

	Sources of admission					
Social characteristics	Psy-chiatric hospital (%)	General (Ordinary) hospital (%)	Private residential home (%)	house-hold (%)	Un-classified (%)	Total (%)
(c) *Age*						
74 or less	(45)	(18)	(13)	19	(17)	20
75–84	(45)	(60)	(50)	46	(57)	52
85 or over	(10)	(22)	(38)	35	(27)	28
TOTAL	(100)	(100)	(101)	100	(101)	100
Number	19	47	19	63	26	174
(d) *Nearest relative* (in descending order)						
Husband/wife	(11)	(7)	(5)	(18)	(12)	11
Son/daughter (incl. adopted)	(16)	(36)	(32)	(42)	(32)	34
Brother/sister	(32)	(29)	(26)	(16)	(28)	25
Nephew/niece	(21)	(11)	(26)	(22)	(20)	19
Other	(21)	(11)	(5)	(2)	(8)	8
No relative (incl. friend only)	(0)	(7)	(5)	(0)	(0)	3
TOTAL	(101)	(101)	(99)	(100)	(100)	100
Number	19	45	19	45	25	153
(Unclassified 21)						
(e) *Distance of nearest relative*						
Less than 5 miles	(26)	(30)	(29)	54	(38)	39
5–20 miles	(53)	(48)	(24)	26	(38)	37
21–100 miles	(16)	(13)	(12)	10	(10)	12
Over 100 miles	(5)	(9)	(35)	10	(14)	12
TOTAL	(100)	(100)	(100)	100	(100)	100
Number	19	46	17	50	21	153
(Unclassified 21)						

relation to their source of admission. Table 10.4 shows that the special home analysed here recruited three distinct types of resident. From the community it drew particularly the married and more elderly person, three-fifths of them with a spouse or child still living very near. The residents admitted from mental hospital, on the other hand, tended to be unmarried women from the younger age ranges without any close relative to rely on, consanguineally or geographically, while those transferred from other residential homes were usually single persons of greater age dependent especially on a brother's or sister's children living at a considerable distance. Given then the different kinds of persons drawn from various sources, what were the main reasons for their admission with which it was felt separatist homes could most suitably cope?

Identification of the causes of admission presented a number of methodological problems, quite apart from the scantiness of information in some of the medical reports and case records. Firstly, the categories of explanation adopted (Table 10.5) are not mutually exclusive: for example, relatives might be unable or unwilling to offer further care (2(i)) because of the old person's physical disability (5(i)–(iii)), confusional symptoms (3(i)–(iii)) or 'aggressive, unsociable or difficult behaviour' (2(ii)). In such cases, primacy was allotted to the factor precipitating admission rather than to the predisposing behaviour. Secondly, several mutually reinforcing factors may have been operating simultaneously. Here priority was given to that element which seemed in each case to have been most disturbing and to have proved decisive in securing admission. Thirdly, the recorded data was often inexplicit. An impression was quickly formed of an over-ready attribution of 'mental deterioration' or 'memory loss', but it was sometimes difficult to decide whether this acted as shorthand for a range of socially disturbing symptoms or whether it merely constituted a convenient formula appropriate for entry to one of these homes.

Nevertheless, within these limitations, a number of important conclusions emerge. First, almost a half (45 per cent) of total admissions resulted from social causes, whether socially distressing behaviour or inadequate supportive care, and only a third were brought about by direct confusional or psychiatric symptoms. The remaining 17 per cent of admissions were due to the transfer of subnormal elderly persons, usually highly institutionalized, from mental hospitals or part III accommodation (particularly former public assistance institutions), to various forms of physical disability, and in two cases, that of a husband and a sister, to joining a near relative already admitted for other reasons. Secondly, the distinctive intake from each source characterizes the differing functions that separatist homes present to each of the transmitting agencies. Thus two-fifths of those drawn from psychiatric units were suffering from paranoia or depression (often residually, though still subject to moderate or severe tranquillization), a third from general hospitals displayed confusional or dementing symptoms, a third from other residential accommodation manifested aggressive or disturbing behaviour, and two-fifths from private households were proving

Table 10.5

Reasons for admission of residents to the separatist homes. by source of admission

Reason for admission	Source of admission				
	Mental hospital	General hospital*	Part III accommodation	Private household	Total
1. Lack of supportive care	(8)	(11)	(16)	17	15
(i) Danger of causing harm to self	(4)	(0)	(3)	5	4
(ii) Lack of adequate self-care	(4)	(11)	(0)	7	5
(iii) Loss of home†	(0)	(0)	(13)	5	6
2. Social disturbance	(11)	(11)	(35)	40	30
(i) Relative cannot or will not undertake further care	(7)	(11)	(0)	38	19
(ii) Aggressive, unsociable or 'difficult' behaviour	(4)	(0)	(35)	2	11
3. Confusional or dementing symptoms	(15)	(33)	(10)	15	14
(i) Gross confusion	(4)	(11)	(0)	4	3
(ii) Gross memory loss or disorientation	(4)	(22)	(0)	2	3
(iii) Wandering or restlessness	(7)	(0)	(10)	9	8
4. Psychiatric illness	(54)	(11)	(10)	5	18
(i) Paranoid delusions	(29)	(11)	(0)	0	7
(ii) Depression	(14)	(0)	(0)	5	6
(iii) Residual mental symptoms	(11)	(0)	(10)	0	5
5. Physical disability	(0)	(22)	(9)	7	7
(i) Illness (stroke)	(0)	(0)	(3)	5	3
(ii) Incontinence	(0)	(11)	(3)	0	2
(iii) Frailty, liability to falls, arthritis, etc.	(0)	(11)	(3)	2	2
6. Subnormality	(14)	(0)	(16)	2	8
7. Joining relative already in residence	(0)	(0)	(3)	2	2
8. Unclassified	(0)	(11)	(0)	11	6
TOTAL	(102)	(99)	(99)	99	100
Number	28	9	31	55	123

* Persons admitted from private households via a hospital assessment unit are classified here under the former rather than the latter source.

† Loss of home includes refusal by a landlord to accept a tenant back following a stay in hospital, the closing down of a residential home and request for transfer from a residential home, and the removal of a propping relative or neighbour.

beyond the management capabilities of their relatives. For each of these groups the separatist homes offered, within limits, a terminal point in the process of shift of responsibility for an insoluble problem. Thirdly, the access route to these homes was often oblique. Sometimes irregular means were used to secure immediate disposal of a problem, with little regard for the consequences of misplacement:

Mr Whelbrough, a droll yet perspicacious man of ninety-one, had for some years been staying with his daughter of sixty-eight. But owing to exhibitionist and otherwise problematic behaviour, one example of which quoted in the case notes was that of undressing whenever anyone called at the house, his daughter 'was now on the verge of a breakdown'. Since an earlier application by the W.V.S. had succeeded only in having Mr Whelbrough's name put on the waiting list for residential accommodation by the Welfare Department, to no further avail over $3\frac{1}{2}$ months, the daughter's GP decided to have her father admitted to the local mental hospital as a psychiatric emergency 'in order to give the daughter a break'. The psychiatric unit, however, soon discovered the truth: 'Time has now proved Mr Whelbrough's admission was for social reasons, as he has no psychiatric illness and is a very well-preserved man who looks after himself completely and shows no physical abnormalities.' Six months later he was therefore moved to Part III accommodation where, however, he remained for less than fifty days. The Welfare Department records note that he wandered from room to room and chair to chair, that he smoked in the dining room and 'spat about the place', and that he insisted on using the female staff WC or the visitors' WC, though he had been shown the residents' WC on several occasions, and if prevented, he urinated in the wash hand basin. He was therefore again transferred, this time to the annexe of a former public assistance institution at the other side of the county from his daughter's home.

Fourthly, the separatist homes frequently acted as the final refuge after a temporary catastrophe, such as a bout of incontinence, a cerebrovascular accident or the development of paranoid delusions, had interrupted an adequate adjustment to old age by a spell of hospitalization. Instead of returning to the community after recovery, such persons often found themselves transferred to a special home:

Miss Ruskett, a sprightly and energetic woman of eighty-one with considerable insight, was admitted to a separatist home where on interview a year later she received a confusional rating of 1. According to the brief medical report, 'she sustained a compound fracture of the right tibia and fibula in a road accident. She is now ambulant, but very disorientated in mind. Pleasant and cooperative, she shows relatively minimal signs of senile deterioration, especially an impairment of memory for recent events, though she remembers remote events well.'

It remains to explore in rather greater depth the role of the separatist homes within the interplay of forces controlling the residential network between the community and ordinary or special welfare homes. Within this area what particular kinds of behaviour determined admission to the latter?

Admission from the community

Admission from private households occurred primarily when a system of social homoeostasis was suddenly snapped by an accident, or by evidence causing definite fear of a threat to safety to the elderly person, particularly if living alone, or where adjustment was abruptly shaken by the removal of a propping relative. Case-records indicated that accidents might be from wandering near a busy trunk road:

She incessantly wanders from the house into the road, gets up all hours of the night and needs constant watching (single woman, aged seventy-seven, score 1).

Or unacceptable risks might be involved regarding fire or gas:

Her son, who lives next door to his mother, says that in the past he has several times discovered used matches and candles, etc. down her bed, and he is petrified she will one day set fire to herself and the house. He and his (second) wife are not in a position to have his mother to live with them as he has a very small basement flat. Also, he has had an operation for a hiatus hernia and has three times been to Hinksley (mental hospital) for ECT (widow, aged ninety, score 6).

Since retirement she has lived alone in a small flatlet. Faulty memory caused her to leave gas taps on without firing the jets (single woman, aged eighty-five, score 10).

357

Alternatively, a relative, especially a daughter, who had been providing crucial support, might no longer be available because of the accumulated effects of strain ('the doctor has ordered her daughter to have a complete rest'), or because of the consequences of employment ('there has been much friction between her and her stepdaughter who is now beginning employment and is afraid to leave Mrs L alone all day',[4] or sometimes because the relative gradually developed a commitment to another family member felt to have prior rights to care:

> Her sister now has their aged mother handicapped with arthritis to look after, and she feels she can no longer look after Mrs W who tends to wander at night or has bouts of incontinence of urine and faeces (widow, aged seventy-nine, score 7).
>
> Her niece has asked us to take Mrs P into part III before 7 March when her married daughter comes to stop with her (the niece), and asks us to let her remain in part III this summer. I feel this may well become permanent (widow, aged eighty-two, score 1).

Equally the propping relative might herself become disabled or indisposed:

> The sister with whom she had been living had a right leg amputation and is still in hospital. Miss S is senile, forgetful, anxious, deaf and has osteoarthritis of the cervical spine, so she cannot be allowed to care for herself.
>
> Temporary part III accommodation was therefore arranged, from which she was soon transferred to the separatist home.

Secondly, admission from private households might be precipitated by behaviour for various reasons regarded as unacceptable by relatives or neighbours. It might arouse feelings of irritation:

> The strains in her right shoulder and wrist and the long-standing ulcer in her eyelid give her an obsession to demand immediate treatment. At home she repeated things, for example even if a third time she had repeated a news item in the paper in fifteen minutes, she still insisted that her son and his wife listen. Now after a stay of two years the son's wife is thoroughly exhausted (widow, aged seventy-eight, score 12).
>
> She tends to be slightly emotional, moves things about in the house and tends to use furniture for the wrong purposes. She

wanders at night a bit, and tends to think sometimes that her sister is against her when she tries to control her, ... She requires a certain amount of constant supervision [*sic*] (single woman, aged eighty, score 11).

Sometimes the indignation seemed implausibly associated with confusion:

She is fully ambulant, not incontinent, very confused, but able to hold a conversation. She seems pleasant and her home is very clean and tidy. ... But was referred by the District Welfare Officer because she was becoming a nuisance to her neighbours. She went around the estate at night knocking on people's doors for no reason whatever [*sic*] since there is a warden in charge of the estate from whom she could get attention through the call-bell system (widow, aged eighty-two, score 7).

Or unaided responsibility for an ageing mother, perhaps with a mild proneness to disorientation and wandering, might gradually prove too worrying in the context of the competitive demands of the wider household: 'She is perfectly manageable and biddable though clearly a great strain in a normal family including young children, owing to the amount of observation needed' (widow, aged seventy-one, score 10). Or too wearisome:

She became more depressed than usual about a year ago when her husband was taken ill (he later died). Lately she has had memory difficulties, continually losing her glasses. She continually asks where her things are and cannot bear to be left alone. On 23 October her daughter-in-law collapsed and could cope no further (widow, aged eighty-two, score 0).

The third main reason for admission lay in deficiencies in self-care. Only rarely, however, was a section 47[5] removal contemplated:

District Welfare Officer's[6] report: 'She and her husband had lived in isolation. He was eccentric to an unreasonable degree and reluctant to agree to meals on wheels, and both had malnutrition. I was only able to enter the house last week and found it reasonably clean and tidy downstairs, but upstairs was very bad indeed. ... (later). The husband was found dead this morning and the body was removed by the police. Mrs C was too confused to realize her predicament. If she had refused to come into part III, Dr A would have taken her under section 47.'

Psychiatrist's report: 'She was rambling, incoherent, suspicious and filled with persecutory delusions. She accused her brother of not only breaking into her place and robbing her, but of committing crimes too horrible to talk about. Her clothes were verminous and she herself very neglected, and the house was found to contain no food whatsoever. Through the confusion which accompanies her deterioration, there is a real risk that she might have a fatal accident from her own disability. Once I found her in her house late at night, in darkness, with a box of matches strewn over the floor and an open can of paraffin beside her. At another time she was found wandering around the streets late at night, in winter, without shoes on her feet. She was also once found by her doctor lying on the kitchen floor shouting "Murder! Murder!" She thought various people, especially her relatives, were trying to kill her and that they had chained her up in a cage, and she could still "see" the people around the room.'

More commonly incapacity for self-care was attributed without dramatic symptoms. Typically case-records contained comments like: 'Her chief symptom is a fairly severe defect of recent memory, though she has a fairly good insight into this', 'she tended to leave doors and windows open and could not be relied upon to do anything at all in the house'.

Admission from ordinary residential homes

The intake from other welfare homes embraced a rather different category of persons. Admissions here were rather of those who scored only marginally, if at all, on the confusional scale,[7] but whose behaviour was seen basically as antisocial and disruptive, however much such epithets might be concealed behind the terminology of mental infirmity. Two characteristic reports from previous establishments ran as follows:

He is very pleasant to meet, but can be very stubborn and difficult to handle. He has spasms of violence and is determined to do as he wants. He has no idea of time and often refuses to get out of bed, and sometimes refuses to take his boots off. His wanderings at night are disturbing and upsetting to the other residents (widower, aged eighty-six, score 2).

The residents at Bridwall wanted her removed as she was a very heavy smoker and stole other residents' cigarettes, and kept asking Matron for a cigarette five minutes after she had been given one. She also kept dropping lighted cigarettes and holes were found in some chairs. She frequently wetted her bed and sometimes left puddles in the bedroom and toilet, and the matron had to clean the walls for incontinence. Once she slipped in a puddle she made and bruised her left leg (widow, aged seventy-nine, score 2).

The signs were unmistakable that not only did the separatist homes fail to select their residents purely on strict medical criteria of confusion or mental infirmity, but that with the demise of the public assistance institution, they had at least in part appropriated the unofficial function of the latter in acting as a final repository for aggressive behaviour among the aged:

She is difficult and aggressive and refuses to have medical treatment. She does not like going to bed at the proper time, and is frequently incontinent and a messy feeder. She smokes in bed and disturbs her room-mates by eating biscuits at night. But not a proper case for a geriatric unit or for psychiatric treatment. Possibly a transfer to a *rather less select welfare home* (widow, aged eighty-three, score 0). (My italics.)

He bolts his food – institutional type – and even splutters it over the table if he chokes. In view of his habits he would only be suitable for admission to P— (the separatist home where he was later interviewed) (single man, aged seventy-seven, score 0).

Similarly for indelicate conduct and dirty habits:[8]

Miss Roskoff, a retired housekeeper of sixty-nine, had been diagnosed manic – depressive psychotic before she returned to part III accommodation after a spell in hospital. She was described as alternatively 'very boisterous, and sometimes irritable and uncooperative, and a series of incidents concerning refusal to wash or undress at night, wandering propensities and sexual aberrations finally culminated in an outburst when 'she was discovered on the main staircase interfering with a male resident whose trousers and pants had fallen down. When asked to go away, she stormed to the bedroom and started throwing things around, tying her clothing together with crepe bandages, saying she was going away.' A few weeks later she was moved to a nearby special home.

Mr Royle, a widower of eighty-three, had entered an ordinary residential home because in a recent stroke he had burnt his legs and he had also left gas taps on accidentally, so that his sister-in-law felt unable to manage him further. In the home, however, 'he was found urinating in a grating in the kitchen and also rummaging through another resident's wardrobe. He was a constant wanderer, too, quite lost at various times of day. He urinated in his boots, tipping some of the contents out of a window, and also over the flower troughs at the front entrance and on the road at the front.' Within eleven months he had been transferred to a separatist home.

Mr Oundle, a widower of ninety-three, had been cared for by his daughter, and then went to live with his son, but after some friction the latter turned him out. In part III accommodation his condition quickly deteriorated. 'Incontinent day and night, he used foul language [which he didn't seem aware of] and finally started to undress in the lounge and use the corner of the room as a toilet.' He was soon transferred.

Admission of the non-confused

Why were rational residents admitted to separatist homes? Apart from the fortuitous location of bed vacancies,[9] which equally accounted for the placing of some severely confused persons in ordinary homes, it has already been indicated that offensive or unsociable behaviour could play a major role. Such considerations could even become exclusive determinants:

Her daughter, who is arthritic, can't cope since her mother is very cantankerous and abusive, and enjoys being stubborn, rude and objectionable (widow, aged eighty-seven).

And occasionally a cryptic note in the case record prompted at least a suspicion that separatist homes afforded an all too convenient solution for riddance of a persisting problem:

Her cousin, Lady Benton, is anxious to move her to St John's (special home). Lady Benton says Miss Machin has always been difficult and sometimes odd and rather aggressive. Her mother died in a mental hospital when Miss Machin was still a child, her maternal uncle was psychotic and her paternal aunt died in a mental hospital' (single woman, aged eighty-seven).

Frequently also a history of violent behaviour was recorded, now controlled by heavy sedation:

Mr Sporle had been in a psychiatric hospital with a diagnosis of recurrent hypomania seven times in the last thirty years. Between these intervals he had resided in part III accommodation where he was described, despite losing a leg in a road accident in 1938, as 'very strong and threatening to the other residents'. Several times he had been referred for psychiatric treatment after striking other men on the head (unmarried man, aged sixty-two).

Mrs Weale lived with her son and daughter-in-law for five years, but was very depressed. She had brainstorms, and from short temper and frustration at her blindness and helplessness had one episode at home when she smashed the furniture. She then attended a regular psychiatric clinic, before admission to part III for two days, then for in-patient psychiatric treatment for a month and finally transfer to the separatist home (widow, aged eighty-eight).

A further explanation in a minority of cases seemed to be the imposition of ageing effects on lifelong traits of abnormality or eccentricity. 'She suffers from a senile character change superadded to her long-standing neurotic personality with elements of hysteria', wrote a psychiatrist about a widow of seventy-six. Another widow of seventy-four was described by her GP as suffering from 'senile depressive illness with a marked hypochondriasis. She has been a great and continual nuisance to this practice for some years. She will not take any medication for her numerous complaints, so one has given up trying.'

Summary

It is doubtless hazardous to draw any definite conclusions about the role of separatist homes from such a small sample of admissions. Difficulties of generalization are emphasized when each of the three special homes studied was characterized by a distinctive intake pattern and the inclusion of other such homes might have some-what modified for the picture. For one of the separatist homes in this survey was marked particularly by its preponderant acceptance of paranoics and depressives from mental hospitals, another (the annexe of a former public assistance institution) of those rejected as anti-social and aggressive by ordinary residential homes, and the third, which was nearest to the national part III admission pattern, by its number of 'social emergencies'.[10] However, it remains funda-mentally true that, not only did two of the homes contain residents slightly under half of whom scored on the confusional rating, but that the basic function of these homes seemed less a creative one of providing an integrated environment for the confused than the residual one of comprising an entrepot for the socially rejected. The other main conclusion to be drawn from the data derives from the almost total absence of mention in the case records of any statutory or voluntary assistance compensating for or supplementing relatives' efforts to support an elderly person in the community prior to admission. The following example is typical:

> 'Mrs Rayburn is hypertensive, subject to minor blackouts and falling over, and is diagnosed arteriosclerotic. Yet nobody is available to keep an eye on her. The neighbour undertakes some household work and general supervision through the day, while her daughter from B writes her occasionally [nineteen miles away]. Otherwise her unmarried son with whom she lives copes, but he is away early morning till late evening at work.'

Repeatedly the case notes gave cause to wonder whether an extended home-help service, especially night sitting-in aid, might not have provided an adequate and much more satisfactory framework for continued life in the community amongst family members, at least for rather longer, than the eventual actual dénouement. But such evidence as exists about the community care of those diagnosed with senile or arteriosclerotic psychosis will be reviewed in the next chapter. Here we must now turn to examine what limits must be placed on the residuum function of separatist homes by an analysis of the pattern of transfers from them.

TRANSFERS

Apart from removal to an acute hospital because of physical illness, residents of specialist homes might be transferred to ordinary homes or back to the community or to psychiatric hospital. Now Table 10.6 indicates that moves to the first two were not common, amount-

Table 10.6

Extent of transfer to private households and to ordinary welfare homes from two separatist homes

Transfer to	Hartley House, Cranbrook, Kent (over 5 years)*	Home D in this study (see Table 10.3) (over 3 years)†
Ordinary welfare homes	10	4
Private households	41	10
Total number of departures	288	50
Full bed complement at any one time	108	47

* Source: Andrews and Insley (1962, p. 98).
† Excluding the first year when a large number of short-term holiday admissions was made while the main body of intended residents was deliberately built up only gradually.

ing to only between a seventh and a quarter of total departures (including death), and some of these were merely inevitable temporary misplacements on grounds of social emergency. What then can be gleaned from transfers to psychiatric hospital[11] about the functional division between the two types of establishment?

Detailed written records explaining the background behind transfers over the previous three years could be obtained only from one of the separatist homes, though some supplementary material was gained from the other two. From a total of thirteen case histories it emerged that at least four basic clusters of symptoms could be construed as cause for rejection and removal. The mean length of stay in these cases was fourteen weeks, ranging between four days and one year, though five of them stayed for less than six weeks.

Mania

The first of these factors (three cases) was the obstreporous manifestations of hypomania. Such disturbances might typically represent the manic stage of a manic-depressive psychosis:

Miss Tolkien, in the course of the twenty years prior to her admission to the separatist residential home at the age of fifty-nine, had already nine times had in-patient psychiatric treatment for her recurrent bouts of mania. On more than one occasion a social worker had recorded that she had tried to persuade her to buy adequate cooking and heating facilities. For 'she needs daily supervision short of coming into hospital, which she would never do voluntarily. She keeps herself clean and tidy, but lacks nutrition and warmth.' And again, 'she has antagonized almost everybody by her garrulous agitated behaviour, but she still appeals for help, though she hasn't sufficient insight to accept it when it's offered.' Once when discovered by the social worker in bed with no heat or food in the cottage, she was admitted to the special home as a social emergency till she could be properly settled again, but over a period of six weeks her 'psychopathic behaviour upset the whole home'. Two further periods of hospitalization followed soon after, one on account of 'agitation, agoraphobia and sleep disturbance', and the other when 'after accosting people in her home town and alarming them with swearing and bad language, she was admitted to H [mental hospital] very manic, talking almost non-stop, shouting and at times laughing uncontrollably, overactive, euphoric, singing and shouting at the top of her voice, and uncooperative, abusive and difficult'.

Or the noisy recriminations of paranoia:

Mrs Heall, a widow of seventy-four, believing that there was some 'device' in operation to end her life prematurely, frequently became very excitable, expressing various religiose ideas and paranoid delusions. She regularly 'preached' to the other residents and according to the matron 'was inclined to become sometimes a little aggressive. Though other residents were afraid of her when she was having one of her bad bouts, she was never violent, though sometimes she seemed very near to hitting out'. In her letter requesting a transfer the matron added: 'Mrs Heall is a quite friendly person between her bouts of shouting and recriminations to all and sundry, but the bouts have become more frequent lately and last longer. It is impossible to get her bathed regularly and she washes herself in a small bowl in her own room. We are not able to get her underwear to wash, and she herself does her washing at night, drying things on the radiator. Then whenever she shuts herself in her room, she stuffs on all kinds of things she gets into the home somehow. She is also diabetic, but it is impossible to keep her to a diet.'

Again, noisy agitated behaviour might take the form of loud and constantly reiterated demands for medication which 'could only be calmed by colossal doses of largactyl'.

Violence

A second major cause for discharge from the separatist homes (two cases) lay in eruptions of physical violence.[12] This might take the form of hitting out at regular neighbours, like a bedroom companion, and perhaps also at staff, or at least threatening them with a stick: 'She is demanding, peevish, abusive and spiteful with other residents, though perfectly charming and plausible with those in authority' (a widow of seventy-five who stayed three months).

Extreme restlessness

Another unacceptable aspect of behaviour, of which four instances were recorded, was gross wandering and especially persistent nocturnal restlessness. One typical case record read: 'She is very difficult, wandering all the time, has to be fed, continually demands attention, and is up at night and wanders around' (a widow, aged eighty-two). Such excessive restlessness might be the result of cataclysmic feelings of rejection:

Mr Rissall, a retired and widowed labourer of seventy-four, had been living next door to his son, but became convinced that his son and daughter-in-law did not want anything to do with him and began to wander away from his home. Admitted to the separatist home, he still continued to wander and became lost, and when found he would say that he didn't know where he was living, that he had walked all day from Land's End and that his children did not want him: 'Since my wife died, I've been on the road for three years.' It was impossible to keep him in the home as the doors and gates were open all the time, so after six weeks he was discharged to psychiatric hospital.

Or from the development of paranoid beliefs:

Mrs Gritton, aged sixty-nine, 'had odd ideas somebody was spying on her and at one time thought her husband was somebody else and intent on killing her'. After admission, following a 'brainstorm', the matron's report continued, 'she became increasingly confused, and for some time now has refused to eat some of her meals. It is often extremely difficult to get her to take her tablets, and she is extremely restless, wandering about aimlessly, and will not sit down, even at meal-times.'

Or even as a result of extreme financial anxieties: 'when the subject of money and payment was first broached, she began wandering away, has not returned for meals and has not said where she was going, so that she has been brought back by the police, GPs and others, and the staff of the home also have to go out looking for her'.

Stripping

The final factor which in another four cases produced outright rejection was the public removal of clothing. This might consist of the development of a preoccupation with stripping naked during the daytime in a dayroom or in the grounds of a home prior to using odd corners as a toilet. Or it might represent the culmination of a period of agitated restlessness:

> Following a stroke and admission to an acute hospital with a fractured skull caused by a fall, Mr O'Deahy, a retired boiler-maker aged sixty-eight, was later transferred to the special home where he displayed extreme restlessness. 'He did not sleep at night and on the second evening refused either to go to his room or to undress till about 5 a.m., when he undressed and had a bowel opening in the middle of the lounge. He was extremely aggressive, using bad language, and refusing either to be coaxed or directed to his room. Largactil 100 mgs was given on advice from N. Hospital, but had no effect.' After four days he was transferred to psychiatric hospital where thirteen days later he died.

In summary, however, these examples of various behavioural excesses, whilst imposing some restrictions[13] on the potential even of segregationist residential policies, do not collectively amount to a significant diminution of the positive functions of separatist homes as already alluded to.

THE ROLE AND ORGANIZATION OF SEPARATIST HOMES IN LOCAL AUTHORITY POLICY-MAKING

Reference has already been made to one central function of separatist homes:

1. They act as a repository for anti-social or aggressive behaviour, and thus insulate small ordinary homes from the disruptions of non-conformism either by a system of transfer or even by a threat of transfer where matrons deliberately made known their power to offer recommendations to the supervisory committee.[14]

Other implicit functions are also attributable:

2. They enable former public assistance institutions, where these still exist, to be gradually phased out through their being available for the rehousing of the more 'difficult' residents, so often at present accommodated in the older, large institutions,[15] and thus preserve the class exclusiveness[16] of the newer local authority home.

3. They enable local authorities to promote their status through the establishment of homes with a quasi-medical function.

4. They offer an alternative residential-type care for old people, especially depressives, originally admitted to psychiatric hospital[17] who later manifest only mild or residual symptoms. 'They would not have been able to return directly from hospital to normal life, and had there been no accommodation for them in the intermediate stage, they would probably have had to remain in the large but overcrowded hospital' (Hill, 1961, p. 94).

5. They divert pressure that would otherwise build up for admission to psychiatric or geriatric hospital beds. As one Chief Welfare Officer wrote: 'For many years, and certainly since the passing of the Mental Health Act, it has been virtually impossible to admit an old person to a mental hospital for treatment. . . . Geriatric hospitals will not freely admit cases of senile confusion uncomplicated by other illnesses requiring treatment and it therefore remains for part III accommodation to cope increasingly with the problem.' In Lancashire, since it was estimated that in 1959 some twenty-four men and twenty-one women were admitted to hospital through alleged mental disorder, but 'in the final assessment of the hospital authorities were not deemed to require more than hostel care', it was decided to provide in the next four years ultimately 200 places in special welfare hostels 'for those mentally disordered elderly people who do not need hospital care,

but whose disability is too great for them to mix with aged persons in an ordinary old people's hostel' (Gawne, 1961, p. 14).

6. They provide a haven especially for those rational old people who have lost contact with their families and therefore lack the protection of external support (see p. 110 and Table 10.2).

On the basis of the performance by separatist homes of at least these six functions, whether consciously determined or not, we must now explore the organization and deployment of these homes within the local authority residential framework of those areas where they have so far been established (a list of which with some of their main characteristics, is attached in Table 10.7). And where they do not yet exist, in what alternative ways is the care of the confused elderly handled? For this purpose a postal survey of every sixteenth residential home for old people in Great Britain[18] was conducted, and a postal questionnaire was also sent to the Chief Welfare Officers or Medical Officers of Health of every county, county borough and metropolitan borough in England and Wales.[19]

Most strikingly, the surveys revealed that complete segregation or complete integration represented polarized policies pursued unvaryingly by only a minority of authorities. Most rather, by a mixture of administrative devices, occupied places along what appeared as an intervening continuum. Indeed the evidence suggested that a segregation-integration typology could be constructed as follows:

1. External segregation of units according to the mental infirmity (or social unsuitability) status of their residents, together with an internal grading of residents by similar criteria. This occurred occasionally where a former institution had become developed for the particular accommodation of the confused.

2. Homogeneous segregation within a special home, either adapted or purpose-built.

3. Partial segregation (strong sense): a wing of a part III home, whether purpose-built or adapted, with lounges, bedrooms and dining halls separate from the main block.

4. Partial segregation (weak sense): a wing of a part III home in which at least some facilities, such as a dining room, are shared with the main block.

5. Partial integration: a general policy of allotting the mentally infirm to ordinary homes, subject to a reserve procedure of transferring especially 'difficult cases' to a particular home.

Table 10.7

Separatist homes provided by statutory and voluntary authorities in England and Wales for the elderly mentally infirm, 1968

Authority	Total number of beds per authority	Controlling committee	Name of home	Residents Men	Women	Date of opening (as home specifically for the elderly mentally infirm)	Other information (purpose-built/adapted)
1. County Councils							
Anglesey	21	Health	Llys-y-Gwynt, Holyhead		21	1967	adapted
Bedfordshire	75	Health	Rivermead, Halsey Rd, Kempston, nr Bedford		35	April 1964	purpose-built
			Ridgeway Ave, Dunstable		40	1969?	purpose-built
Buckingham	10	Health	Meadowlands, Cressex Rd, High Wycombe		10	1964	purpose-built wing
Cardigan	34	Health	Bryntirion, Tregaron	—	34	1960	adapted part III home plus new purpose-built wing opened 1965
Cheshire	108	Health and welfare	Hill Bark, Frankly	9	33	Sept. 1964	adapted
			Earls Court, Macclesfield	4	7	Nov. 1966	purpose-built with wing adapted for elderly mentally infirm
			The Sycamores, Hyde	—	11	May 1967	,,
			Elm House, Nantwich	2	9	Feb. 1967	,,
			Wellcroft, Gatley	—	11	March 1967	,,
			Wealstone, Upton	—	11	Sept. 1966	,,
			The Hawthorns, Wilmslow	—	11	March 1966	,,
			Milton House, Alsager	12		Jan. 1969?	,,
Cornwall	48	Health and welfare	The Green, Drump Rd, Redruth	37	11	April 1963	part of thirty-six-bed home
Derbyshire	13	Welfare	Clay Cross Hall		13	1966	purpose-built

Table 10.7 (contd.)

Authority	Total number of beds per authority	Controlling committee	Name of home	Residents Men	Residents Women	Date of opening (as home specifically for the elderly mentally infirm)	Other information (purpose-built/adapted)
Devon	70	Welfare	Parkers Barn, Totnes	35		July 1966	
			St Michael's, Honiton	35		Oct. 1965	purpose-built
Dorset	36	Health	Bourne House, Parkstone	8	28		detached infirmary block of former institution
Essex	58	Welfare	St Albright's, Stanway, nr Colchester	14	34	July 1963	adapted wing
			Tyrells, Thundersley	—	10		
Flintshire	26	Welfare	Carr Holm, Bastion Rd, Prestatyn	—	26	1963	adapted
Glamorgan	75	Welfare	Llanerch, Bridgend	16	19	Nov. 1964	purpose-built
			Garffwysfa, Neath	8	30	Aug. 1966	purpose-built
Hampshire	36	Welfare					
Hereford	10	Health and welfare	Holmer Hall, nr Hereford		10		wing added to existing home home of thirty-two beds
Kent	259	Health and welfare	Hartley House, Cranbrook	—	108	1957?	adapted former institution in nine self-contained units
			Honeyfield, Hextable	—	80	1966?	purpose-built, in four self-contained units
			Pembury Grange, Sandown Park, Tunbridge Wells	—	40	March 1964	converted
			Willow House, Medway Homes, Rochester		22		nine houses under group management
Lincs. (Holland)	40	Health	South Field House, Spalding		40	Jan. 1968	purpose-built
Nottinghamshire	82	Welfare			82	1963	two separate wings of adapted part III home (forty-four and thirty-eight beds)

Table 10.7 (contd.)

Authority	Total number of beds per authority	Controlling committee	Name of home	Residents Men	Residents Women	Date of opening (as home specifically for the elderly mentally infirm)	Other information (purpose-built/adapted)
Oxford	35	Health and welfare	Orchard House, Littlemore	10	25	1964	purpose-built
Pembroke	35	Health	Prendergast, Haverfordwest		35	Sept. 1968	purpose-built
Stafford	69	Health	Hillport House, Newcastle-under-Lyme		40	Feb. 1965	purpose-built
			Summerhill Grange, Kingswinford		29	March 1965	adapted
Suffolk (East)	35	Health	Adair Lodge, Church Walk, Aldeburgh		35	1963	converted
Sussex (East)	70	Health and welfare	Hillcrest, Portslade,	—	35	Jan. 1965	purpose-built
			57 Harebeating Drive, Hailsham	6	36	March 1966	purpose-built
Sussex (West)	31	Welfare			31	April 1968	adapted
Wiltshire	30	Health			30	1969 ?	
2. County Boroughs							
Bath	21	Health	Springfield, Entry Hill		21		
Bolton	50	Health	Greenmount House, Chorley New Road		50	Dec. 1963	purpose-built
Blackpool	31	Health	Rydal Lodge, Ferguson Road		31	April 1966	purpose-built
Bradford	30	Welfare	The Park, Rooley Lane		30		two wards of former PAI
Bristol	35	Health and welfare	Petherton, Petherton Rd, Hengrove		46	Jan. 1968	purpose-built
Bury	34	Welfare	Beach Grove Hostel, Chesham Rd	34	35	April 1963	adapted
Carlisle	23				23	1960	adapted

373

Table 10.7 (contd.)

Authority	Total number of beds per authority	Controlling committee	Name of home	Residents Men	Women	Date of opening (as home specifically for the elderly mentally infirm)	Other information (purpose-built/adapted)
Dudley	21	Welfare	Diddale, Lightwood Rd, Sedgley New Bradley Hall, Kingswinford Lawnwood House, Dudley Wood		21		
Eastbourne	10	Welfare	St Anthony's Court		10		
Hastings	50	Health	Mount Denys, The Ridge		50	Jan. 1967	purpose-built
Kingston-upon-Hull	35	Welfare	Catherine Ellis Home, Ashton Close		35		purpose-built
Leeds	36	Health and welfare	Springvale, Stainbeck Lane, Leeds 7 East Leeds Hostel, Leeds 9 Armley Grange Hostel, Leeds 12		26 10	Feb. 1965	converted
Manchester	61	Welfare	The Dell, Gorton Weylands, Baguley	— —	40 41	1963 1965	purpose-built purpose-built
Merthyr Tydfil	15	Health	Sandbrook House		16	Dec. 1961	a wing of a former hospital
Oldham	31	Welfare	Ford Lodge, Shore Ave, Milton		31	1955	adapted
Portsmouth	35	Health			35		
Sheffield	10	Welfare	Brookdale, Ainsdale		10	June 1967	unit in purpose-built home
Southport	30	Health			30		purpose-built
Stockport	30	Health			30	Jan. 1967	purpose-built
Tynemouth	12	Welfare	The Cedars, Morwick Rd, N. Shields		12		

374

Table 10.7 (contd)

Authority	Total number of beds per authority	Controlling committee	Name of home	Residents Men	Residents Women	Date of opening (as home specifically for the elderly mentally infirm)	Other information (purpose-built/adapted)
West Bromwich	27	Health and welfare	Warstone House, Salters Lane		27	Jan. 1964	purpose-built
Wolverhampton	81	Welfare			81		not specifically for mentally infirm
3. London Boroughs							
Barking	11		Alexandra House, Maitland Park Rd	11			wing of sixty-bed home
Camden	67				67		
Croydon	39	Health	Morland Home	39		Aug. 1955	adapted
Waltham Forest	60	Health and welfare	Heathcote, Chingford		60	1965	adapted
4. Voluntary Organizations							
Hill Homes	39	—	Gwendolen Sim, (Northolme), 22 Broadlands, London N6		39	1953	adapted
Jewish Welfare Board	16	—			16	1962	adapted
National Association for Mental Health	45	—	Parnham, Beaminster, Dorset	—	45	Dec. 1955	adapted
WVS	17	—	Woodbury, Surbiton, Surrey	—	17	Nov. 1962	Closed 1965

Source. G. Wigley (1968), Survey by the Mental Health group of the Society of Medical Officers of Health, together with a few additions.

6. Full residential integration, though combined with separatist facilities for the day care of the elderly mentally infirm living in the community.

7. Complete integration of residential and day care facilities.

At one end of this spectrum was the attempt to give topographical expression to a rigorous classification of need. Thus one authority had divided a former public assistance institution into nine parts, and the Chief Welfare Officer described the functional categorization in the following terms:

Group 1 (fourteen persons). All these residents are completely self-sufficient, requiring only minimal attention, and are quiet and very clean. All are quite active, though they do not mix in very well with each other and tend to isolate themselves. Some sedation by day is needed. There is no incontinence.

Group 2 (twelve persons). These are a little less able to fend for themselves, but require minimal attention personally and more attention to general standards of hygiene. All are fairly active. Sedation is required for most of them, though their behaviour pattern is reasonably good. There is no incontinence.

Group 3 (nineteen persons). These residents need bathing and supervision of personal hygiene. They require a lot of encouragement and initiative to help themselves, and as many show a low IQ it is necessary for staff to descend to this level in order to produce results and make universal understanding possible.

Group 4 (twelve persons). Apart from needing bathing and supervision of personal hygiene, supervision at mealtimes is essential to maintain a good standard of eating habits. But an amenable pattern of behaviour is attained by good relations with staff. There is a degree of incontinence. Sedation is needed. Few are very active or occupy themselves.

Group 5 (twelve persons). These are more regressed and all need constant help and supervision in every aspect of care. Most are inactive and incapable of occupation. Most present a degree of incontinence, but simple repetition can achieve a great deal, i.e. two-hourly potting, punctual meal-times and bed-times. Some wander and some have outbursts of aggression. The staff must be able to 'ramble incoherently' with the residents as needed, for this avoids frustration of these more regressed persons. To avoid outbursts it has been found that opportunism achieves more than rigid routine. Sedation is needed.

Group 6 (twelve persons). This is the most difficult group. All show paranoidal behaviour, with marked aggression to-wards each other and towards the staff. Most present a subsocial pattern of habits and a low standard of hygiene and dress: not incontinence as such, but very dirty habits. They are very noisy and argumentative people, and subject staff to abuse and even violence on rare occasions. Constant supervision is vital, as they collect and hoard all sorts of food and rubbish, and staff ingenuity is required to find all the hiding places! Heavy sedation is needed, together with very firm handling.

Group 7 (two sub-groups of six persons each). These are very frail, easily disturbed residents who cannot tolerate living in an atmosphere of stress. Most are incontinent, and need maximum care day and night, with sedation. Staff have to be gently persuasive as any emotional upheaval may trigger off a sudden regression, i.e. a suicidal attempt, anorexia, etc. Should any resident become disturbed, she must be removed immediately from this group so as to avoid a chain reaction of stress among the others.

Group 8 (nine persons). This group is reserved for those who become chronic sick, or those who are ill, or those who enter into their terminal illness. This alleviates any distress that ill people can cause by not being nursed in a special section. This week is often heavy and monotonous for staff, and in addition to routine care, feeding is another aspect that requires a lot of time and patience. Again staff must refrain from emotional involvement and adopt an attitude of detachment.

Group 9 (twelve persons). This floor houses our very regressed residents. All are incontinent, and need constant day and night care. They are unable to do anything much for themselves, and are mostly so senile that they are de-personalized and just sit and vegetate. They are completely unaware of time and space. No training in habits is possible and they remain unpredictable in mood and situations have to be coped with as and when they arise. Staff soon become adept at 'talking butterflies' with these residents, and carry on the most outlandish conversation with ease. Sedation is needed. During residence, regression will occur, and residents are gradually moved over a period of months or years from group to group, i.e. on admission 1, then 3, on to 8, and inevitably to 7.

By sharp contrast, at the other end of the spectrum, undifferentiating integration was pursued by almost three-quarters of local authorities, though less than three-fifths of this number (sixty authorities) intended to persist with this policy for the future.

Along the intervening continuum between complete segregation and full integration were grouped the majority of authorities. Only sixteen, or 11 per cent of those from whom the necessary information was collected, had built one or more special units for their mentally infirm elderly residents, but now intended to establish no further separatist accommodation. In almost every instance this was due to the belief that existing arrangements now satisfied immediate demand rather than a judgment that the experiment with separatism had proved unsuccessful. A further twenty (14 per cent) had built separatist units in the past and proposed to continue with this policy. But most, a total of forty-seven authorities (32 per cent), having previously integrated those elderly residents who were confused, were now turning, occasionally with uncertainty or reluctance, towards a policy of separatism. Combining the effects of these four trends as distinguished for individual authorities, as has been done in Table 10.8, reveals the weight of the movement towards segregation. Whereas 27 per cent of local authorities had already set up separatist units by November 1967, fully 47 per cent at that time were planning to do so in the near future. Also the mean number of special units for each of these authorities was rising marginally from 1·5 hitherto to 1·6 for the future.

Within this general trend, we must now examine the physical structure within which separatism has so far developed, and ask whether policy in this respect is changing. Table 10.8 also demonstrates that separatist homes (with frequently 33 or 36 beds, occasionally 45, and only rarely 60 or more) have hitherto been more popular

378

Table 10.8

Patterns of separatist provision, past and future, for the elderly mentally infirm in England and Wales, by the type of establishment

Form of separatist provision	Separatist units already established by November 1967				Separatist units planned for the future as at November 1967			
	No. of local authori-ties*	No. of separa-tist units	Units purpose-built	adapted	No. of local authori-ties*	No. of separa-tist units	Units purpose-built	adapted
Separatist home	29	41	23	18	47	69	67	2
Separatist wing (or otherwise segregated unit)	11	20	13	7	19	37	32	5
No separatism	108	—	—	—	74	—	—	—
TOTAL	148†	61	36	25	140‡	106	99	7

* Provision by voluntary or private organizations is included under those local authorities in whose areas such units were located.

† A total of twenty-four local authorities either refused to participate in the survey or did not reply.

‡ Eight local authorities either had made no decision for the future or provided information too vague for classification to be made.

than the creation, or adaptation, of separate wings to an ordinary home, though in future the balance is shifting slightly towards the latter,[20] together with, as might be expected, a movement almost totally towards purpose-built establishments. Preference for wings (with beds ranging from 6 to 20 in homes with a total 30 to 60 beds) was argued on four main counts:

1. that the confused can remain in their own locality rather than be moved to one large home serving the needs of the whole county, yet be accommodated without their presence causing distress to others in the home;

2. that they avoid the stigma which would otherwise attach to an establishment exclusively for the mentally infirm;

3. that separate units reserved for such groups as the mentally infirm or physically disabled permit the transfer where necessary of deteriorating residents to appropriately specialized care within the overall ambit of a single home;

4. that staff can be rotated and afforded the maximum time off from difficult work, and thus recruitment difficulties which might otherwise exist can be evaded.

Several even of those authorities committed in principle to integration indicated that their plans were keeping open the option of potential unit separatism:

There are, of course, elderly mentally infirm in all the eighteen old people's homes run by my Department. On the whole this arrangement has proved generally satisfactory and it is hoped that it will continue to be so because my Authority feels that to isolate mentally infirm and senile old people in special establishments is not in the best interests of the old people themselves or their relatives. . . . [however] the last three purpose-built homes have been so designed that a number of residents can be segregated from the others if so desired, and all future homes will contain this feature. So far, and the first of these homes was opened three years ago, the superintendents and matrons have not found it necessary to make use of this facility.

Equally, a few authorities with a segregationist bias which had previously built special homes were now turning to the idea of separate wings, though with opposite expectations of the result:

It is not now our purpose to build any further homes specially provided for confused and senile old people. The policy at the present time is to build homes of 48 beds each, preferably in most cases in four wings of twelve beds each with their own lounge, and that one of these wings shall be used for the confused and senile, another for the physically frail and the other two wings for what we might call the ordinary elderly people. My own guess is that within five to ten years' time all the beds will be occupied by either the mentally frail or the physically handicapped. We have built five of these tripartite homes up to the present, and we propose to continue to build at the rate of about two homes per year.

Further, authorities adopting the philosophy of separatist units tended to carry the policy to extensive lengths. One borough planned to adapt for the elderly mentally infirm four units of five, nine, ten and twelve beds respectively in mid-1968, and in addition to constructing a purpose-built home of thirty-five beds for this group in 1970–71, to insert a ten-bed unit for them in all future new homes. A county which had already established seven purpose-built homes of thirty-three or thirty-six beds, all containing a separate wing with a third of the beds reserved for mentally infirm residents, now for the next six years planned annually to build a new home with a total of thirty-six beds including a quarter for the mentally infirm.

The rationale for segregation, whether by home or within homes, was variously stated. The main division lay between those authorities seeking to channel off what were regarded as disruptive elements from ordinary homes – 'to keep these types away from the mentally alert because of the demoralizing influence imparted' – and those aiming rather to bridge the gap between psychiatric hospital and ordinary part III establishments – 'to provide accommodation for recovered aged mental patients who had no other home to which they could be discharged'. Some authorities implied a more passive motive, such as reaction to persistent pressure from psychiatric or geriatric consultants or from the local HMC, or even merely legislative prompting: 'built because of the duty placed on the local health authority by the Mental Health Act 1959 to expand community services and the most urgent need being residential care for the elderly mentally infirm'; 'to keep abreast of community need and the Hospital Plan rundown of beds'. Other authorities tacitly indicated considerable unease at the prospect of separatism.[21] Similarly, integrationists might be influenced, apart from inertia to change, simply by the paucity of the mentally infirm, especially in the case of smaller authorities, or positively by arguments of principle:

We are planning for a balanced community in each new home for the elderly.

I impress quite clearly on manageresses that only in extreme cases will I permit a transfer to be effected to a large establishment, and I remind them that by next year, if sites and loan sanctions are obtained, the last of the former Poor Law institutions will be closed, at which stage there will no longer be a so-called 'safety valve'.

We do not think that people should be put into separate compartments because of one or other special disability.

Among those authorities which had hitherto rejected separatism, however, the adoption of certain changes in practice could be detected for the purpose of accommodating the new demands being made on them. It was clear that most authorities normally tried to avoid admitting confused old people to homes where the staff-resident ratio was low and especially if no night staff could be procured; or where the superintendent and matron had no nursing qualifications; or where the small size of a home produced a fear of excessive disturbance, especially from wandering or persistent incontinence; or where the absence of a lift tended to restrict admission to the fitter and physically more ambulant and then by extension to the mentally more alert; or where the possibilities of segregation in emergency were less available. Consequently, except where authorities explicitly eschewed separatist classification, the confused tended to be concentrated in one or two larger establishments, especially the local former public assistance institution where still in use, with wards and dayrooms sometimes specifically reserved for this group and internally graded according to the mental status of their occupiers. Typically, one authority, for example, reported that of the seventy-one old people currently classified as mentally infirm in its area, forty were accommodated in a former institution and only twenty-six more in all its other six homes, while a further five were housed in voluntary homes. However, with the gradual demise of these institutions, many authorities were turning, whether in conjunction with the construction of separatist units or not, towards modified arrangements designed to cater for the elderly mentally infirm more flexibly within existing or new ordinary homes. One Chief Welfare Officer wrote:

> The size of homes has tended to increase so that the supervision for 24 hours a day can be provided economically, and it is now the Committee's policy to build new homes for approximately 60 residents in large communites of over 70,000 population, and smaller homes for approximately 40 residents in other areas. All new homes are equipped with lifts for the benefit of residents who find difficulty in climbing stairs, and lifts have also been installed in the majority of the older and smaller homes. Arrangements have been, or are being, made for the provision of night attendant staff in all the homes,[22] and all homes have some members of staff with either nursing qualifications or nursing experience.

Also mentioned by other authorities were such segregative devices as the judicious placing of curtaining, the possible reservation for senile residents of a particular floor in a planned multistorey block (vertical segregation), and even consideration of a consortium of neighbouring local authorities to provide a special home. The last development might be interpreted as the re-embodiment of the separatist function of the old institution now that capacious residential centres were no longer available to absorb the confused and the 'difficult' whilst at the same time such persons might form too tiny a minority within the jurisdiction of a single authority to warrant a specialized home for them alone.

But whatever variant to the theme of structural solutions to the separatist issue was adopted, perhaps the most influential element affecting the actual handling of the question and determining *de facto* the degree of integration or otherwise achieved was the attitude of the matron. Some matrons appreciated the responsibility in leadership which this entailed:

> I have always found that the sensible and rational ones will copy the attitude of staff towards the more helpless ones. The only exception seems to be those who have extremely dirty and offensive eating habits, and these they will not tolerate. ... I believe that, however confused the behaviour of the elderly becomes, they are only too well aware of rejection in a move to more suitable accommodation, and it instils into the remaining residents an ever-present fear that eventually it will happen to them.

Others, however, implicitly sided with what seemed the interests of the majority: 'The needs of the senile are greater, and therefore greater attention must be given. The active aged, being essentially egocentric, tend to resent this unequal care.' 'Several lounges are advisable, to keep the incontinent from the continent and the restless and noisy from the placid. A servery with a dining room each side would also be a great boon. Bad table manners and dirty habits often prevent the more sensitive ones from enjoying their food.' Where the aim was essentially the threat-oriented one, as often appeared the case, of avoiding friction in the home, whether separatist or otherwise, rather than the accent being on the challenge of developing relationships, opportunities for integration of the confused were obviously curtailed. And where residents were transferred on grounds of, typically, 'mental changes such that they are no longer acceptable', the absolute emphasis placed on the matron's subjective judgment seemed scarcely checked by confirmatory medical opinion standardizing the degree of confusion or social problem. Moreover, prior attention to the interests of the few who 'even abuse their fellows for quite harmless minor eccentricities' rather than to the feelings of the majority who 'are quite tolerant of or indifferent to the behaviour disorders of some' reflected the matron's power to elevate the interests of a few rational objectors over the unspoken needs of the inarticulate confused.

Corresponding to the support of many matrons for the separatist handling of the mentally infirm was the trust of a number of local authorities in the desirability, or even necessity, of care by psychiatrically trained staff. For the scarcity of such personnel strengthened the argument for concentration in a specialist unit, and preferably one sited near a psychiatric hospital in order to ease recruitment problems. On this basis local authorities commonly aimed at a staff ratio in their separatist units a third above the average in ordinary homes,[23] with at least the matron being a registered mental nurse or holding an RMPA certificate. Sometimes authorities also provided in-service training for their staff to include talks by a local consultant psychiatrist. Yet at the same time few special homes were registered under permissible mental health powers,[24] for reasons that were succinctly stated as follows:

1. inevitable local opposition at the creation of what was described by responsible people as a 'lunatic asylum';

2. distress to relatives because, in the completion of certain formalities, forms need to be used making reference to the Mental Health Act;

3. the extent of medical care and the relatively high cost of prescribing that has to be provided by general practitioners giving services under part IV of the NHS Act, which provokes requests for additional remuneration because they believe additional responsibilities exist for what they call 'mental work';

4. the difficulty sometimes of obtaining planning clearance on these grounds for homes for the elderly mentally infirm.

Similarly, admission procedures to separatist units appeared increasingly based on psychiatric referral or at least quasi-medical criteria, even if the latter also seemed to contain a strong social management component. Typically, 'each case is seen by a consultant psychiatrist before admission and the social background is supplied by a social worker, at present untrained'. At Llanerch separatist hostel in Bridgend, Glamorgan, information was sought, not only about the usual personal data, clinical diagnosis and a brief account of the mental and physical condition and current treatment, but also

> A profile of five behavioural items (incontinence, wandering, irresponsibility with fire or gas, noisiness and aggression) chosen because they so often present as obstacles to domiciliary care, comment on the social circumstances (general adequacy of care already given, interruption of employment of key relatives, and interference with the welfare of children at home), and finally the reason for requesting admission and the attitudes to this of the prospective resident and his family (Jones and Milne, 1966, p. 159).

On the other hand, the shift to separatism on explicit psychiatric criteria holds dangers which a few authorities did recognize. One hazard is that such specialist units could become assimilated to the role of the infirmary as attached to the older, larger homes, which the Royal Commission on the Law relating to Mental Illness and Mental Deficiency and Circular 14/57 were so anxious to prevent. One Chief Welfare Officer described the predicament as follows:

> Only if suffering from some other *treatable* conditions are cases considered for admission to either mental or geriatric hospitals, and this again is a question of degree. ... If admission to a geriatric hospital is required, this is invariably on an exchange basis and the incoming resident is almost without exception as difficult a problem as the one discharged. ... The danger from all this is that the old people, both senile and rational, might become subject to a standard of care much less than that to which they would ethically be entitled. A situation could arise where we are merely substituting the unsatisfactory conditions for the senile confused in mental hospitals with similar conditions in part III accommodation and, furthermore, without the assistance of adequate staff, medical and nursing facilities or legal safeguards.

Such questions raise the whole issue of the allocation of confused old people between alternative institutional placements and this we must now examine.

THE WIDER DISTRIBUTION OF THE ELDERLY MENTALLY INFIRM WITHIN THE TOTAL INSTITUTIONAL NEXUS

Despite their recent proliferation, separatist homes probably still account for only some 2–3 per cent of beds in residential accommodation for the elderly in Great Britain,[25] and perhaps also only some 3 per cent of beds occupied in all types of institutions by elderly persons reasonably identifiable with the mentally infirm. For of the 28·6 per cent of old people in institutions assessed by interviewers in a national survey as being 'not at all lucid' or only intermittently so (Benson and Townsend, *Old People in Long-Stay Institutions*, Chapter 3), a total of about 80,000 persons,[26] those accommodated in known separatist units (Table 10.7) number only some, 2,300.[27] Moreover, if account is taken of the fact that this present survey found only 47 per cent of the residents in the two local authority separatist homes investigated to be confused by the social criteria adopted, on this basis specialist residential units may be estimated to house only some 1·3 per cent of the confused elderly distributed in various types of institutional accommodation. Even of the 12,131 beds occupied by the 'elderly mentally handicapped' in residential accommodation in England and Wales on 31 December 1968,[28] separatist home beds in total accounted for less than a sixth. We must therefore first assemble such data as exists concerning the overall allocation of persons in this category between different residential and medical units before examining any underlying rationale.

Numerical distribution of the confused

The absence of any national survey embracing both institutional and community sources according to consistent criteria of mental infirmities means that a fragmentary picture must be built up from partial and non-interlocking data. Three main pieces of information seemed relevant. The first was a prevalence survey by Kay, Beamish and Roth based on psychiatric assessments of senile or arteriosclerotic dementia or other severe brain syndromes[29] among 517 old people in Newcastle upon Tyne in 1960–61 who were living in mental hospitals, geriatric wards, welfare homes or in private households (Table 10.9).

Table 10.9

Estimated total prevalence rates for senile and
arteriosclerotic dementia and other severe brain syndromes
per 1,000 population aged sixty-five years and over in
Newcastle upon Tyne, by place of residence

| Disorder | Persons living in institutions | | | | Persons living in private house-holds | Total |
	Mental hospitals	Geriatric wards	Welfare homes	All insti-tutions		
Senile dementia	1·5	1·4	1·3	4·2	12·9	17·1 ⎫
Arteriosclerotic						⎬ ± 11·0
dementia	0·8	1·3	0·4	2·5	25·9	28·4 ⎭
Other severe						
brain syndromes	0·2	0·4	0·2	0·8	9·7	10·5 ± 5·0
TOTAL	2·5	3·1	1·9	7·5	48·5	56·0
Number	21 (46)	62 (84)	125 (78)	208	309	517

Source. Extrapolated from figures given by Kay *et al.* (1964, Tables II, IV and V). The estimated population aged sixty-five and over in the five areas (electoral wards) samples in 1960 totalled 9,031. The symbol ± indicates the standard error. The authors admit that the standard errors of the calculated prevalence rates are relatively large owing to the small size of the domiciliary random sample, that forty-one residents of private homes who had originally been domiciled in the chosen areas could not be interviewed, that old people whose names were missing from the electoral register are omitted (though there were probably few of these), and that long-stay mental hospital patients admitted before 1957 are not included in the statistics (*ibid.*, p. 47).

* The actual numbers of the three institutional samples are supplemented by corrected estimates in brackets based on the known national ratio of the totals of old people in each of these three types of residence (Townsend and Wedderburn, *op. cit.*, p. 23, Table 1). The prevalence figures have been recalculated in line with the corrected totals.

Extrapolating from this small local sample on the basis of the total elderly population in Britain of 6·2 million (mid-1963) suggests that old people with these conditions in mental hospitals number approximately 15,500, in geriatric wards 19,200, in welfare homes 11,800, and in private households 300,700. Apart from demonstrating that some six or seven times more elderly persons with 'severe brain syndromes' are living in the community than in all institutions put together, the significance of which is left for discussion until the next chapter, these figures reveal a rather surprising distribution between institutions in that almost four-fifths as many old people with severe organic syndromes were found in welfare homes as in mental hospitals.

This dispersion is not corroborated by the second main source of evidence, a national social survey in 1962 of old people in long-stay institutions, undertaken by Benson and Townsend. This included a dual assessment of the sample of 1,102 persons aged sixty-five and over, both an interviewer rating of illucidity and a staff rating of mental impairment (Table 10.10). The former produced a picture whereby 16,100 elderly patients in psychiatric hospitals were judged 'not at all lucid', and similarly for 13,700 in non-psychiatric

Table 10.10

Lucidity and mental impairment assessments by interviewers and staff, of persons aged sixty-five and over living in three types of institution (1,102 persons)

	Residential homes	Non-psy-chiatric institutions†	Psychiatric hospitals	All institutions
	%	%	%	%
Lucidity* *(interviewer rating)*				
Complete	82·6	64·0	45·5	67·2
Intermittent	10·4	19·3	22·2	16·2
Not at all lucid	3·9	11·9	26·9	12·4
Interviewer unable to judge	3·0	4·8	5·4	4·2
TOTAL	100	100	100	100
Number	460	311	279	1050
(52 unclassifiable)				
Mental impairment‡ *(staff rating)*				
None	63·6	54·5	9·4	46·4
Some	28·9	29·6	46·5	33·8
Severe	6·9	14·5	43·4	18·9
Not known if any	0·6	1·5	0·7	0·9
TOTAL	100	100	100	100
Number	464	324	286	1074
(28 unclassifiable)				

Source. Benson and Townsend, *Old People in Long-Stay Institutions* (forthcoming) Chapter 3.

* Interviewers were required to record at the end of each interview whether they had found the elderly person capable of organizing thoughts in lucid speech (or other form) for the purposes of social communication.

† Non-psychiatric institutions comprised chronic sick hospitals together with private and voluntary hospitals and nursing homes.

‡ Staff were asked to assess mental impairment irrespective of possible effects on lucidity, for example in the case of those with a severe depressive illness or where phases of illucidity were found.

institutions and 4,100 in residential homes. In addition, the figures for those 'only intermittently lucid' were respectively 13,300, 22,200 and 10,900. The latter rating by staff furnished substantially higher all-round numbers which would seem to indicate either that mental impairment is a much more pervasive phenomenon than illucidity or, more probably, that staff tend perhaps to over-estimate the disability of residents or patients. Staff judged that 26,000 of elderly patients in psychiatric hospitals were 'severely' mentally impaired, 16,700 in non-psychiatric institutions and 7,200 in residential homes, while a further 27,900, 34,000 and 30,300 respectively were assessed as suffering from 'some' mental impairment. What is significant is that, despite the differences in the absolute figures yielded by these two types of appraisal, both offer a pattern by which psychiatric hospitals may be estimated to accommodate almost four times more old people, whether seen as completely illucid or severely mentally impaired, than residential homes.

The third source of data derives from a study by Bigot of 740 residents in local authority accommodation for the elderly in Staffordshire in 1966–67 (Table 10.11). This survey which was primarily concerned with analysing the incidence of apathy, also assessed the degree of mental confusion, though without any explicit statement of the conceptual criteria, among residents in pre-1948 accommodation as opposed to post-war adapted or purpose-built homes. On the basis of the disposition of the elderly residential population in England and Wales in 1960,[30] it indicates, if Staffordshire is representative of the national picture, that some 4,800 persons resident in former public assistance institutions might be judged 'permanently confused' and a further 1,800 'transitorily' so, while in adapted homes about 1,000 and 5,800 were respectively permanently and transitorily confused, and in purpose-built homes only about 170 and 800 respectively. These findings amply confirm the policy of placing confused old people in older establishments, the permanently and more seriously confused particularly in the former institutions and the transitorily and less severely confused particularly in adapted homes. Interestingly, the figures in Table 10.11 also reveal that not only were there more than half as many again female residents in the sample as male, but that, with the single exception of the transitorily confused in the former institutions, women were more than twice as likely to be ranked confused, at both permanent and transitory levels, than men.

Table 10.11

The incidence of mental confusion among 740 residents of different kinds of local authority accommodation for elderly in Staffordshire, by sex

Degree of mental stability	Former public assistance institutions			Adapted home			Purpose-built homes		
	M %	F %	Total %	M %	F %	Total %	M %	F %	Total %
Not confused	63·6	49·1	55·3	52·2	45·9	48·2	84·2	77·7	79·7
Transitorily confused*	9·3	4·0	6·2	8·9	28·3	21·3	7·0	15·4	12·8
Permanently confused	9·3	21·2	16·1	2·2	4·4	3·6	0	3·8	2·7
Not known	17·8	25·7	22·4	36·7	21·4	26·9	8·8	3·1	4·8
TOTAL	100·0	100·0	100·0	100·0	100·0	100·0	100·0	100·0	100·0
Number	129	175	304	90	159	249	57	130	187

Source. Bigot (1967, p. 19).

* For example, considered normal during the day, confused and disturbed at night.

Any attempt to construct a single composite picture out of all this divergent data is beset chiefly by the obstacle of independent and irreconcilable criteria of confusion, as well as by the difficulty in scaling degrees of this intangible concept. Further, none of the definitions adopted is comparable with the measures used in Chapter 3 of this report. One point of reasonable agreement, however, is that between the 15,000 rated as illucid (4,100 completely and 10,900 intermittently) by interviewers in the national survey of long-stay institutions and the 14,400 assessed as confused (6,000 permanently and 8,400 transitionally) in the Staffordshire project. Leaving aside the 'intermittent' and 'transitory' estimates as being even more subjectively uncertain, and accepting the lower end of the range for severe illucidity or confusion on the grounds that it adheres more closely with the projected national figure of 3,800 for the confused in ordinary homes as calculated in the present study, we may then add to this, on the basis of the four-to-one ratio agreed between private interviewers and staff for the distribution of the severely illucid or mentally impaired between psychiatric hospitals and residential homes, a total of some 16,000 severely confused old people in the former. This accords very closely with the prevalence figure in the psychiatric study for elderly patients in mental hospitals with severe organic syndromes, and also with the figure of 14,224 admissions to psychiatric hospitals in England and Wales in 1961 of persons with organic mental disorder (9 per cent of the total). An approximately similar figure is suggested for severely confused elderly patients in geriatric wards or nursing homes in view of the totals of 13,700, 16,700 and 19,200 offered by two of the surveys from the application of varied criteria. No doubt all the assumptions employed here could be challenged, but they are perhaps the most appropriate in the light of the extremely fragmentary and inchoate nature of the data. Therefore all that can be concluded is that very tentatively, if half the beds in known separatist units are occupied by residents with a marked degree of confusion,[31] then for every one such person in this accommodation there are perhaps three more in other residential homes (including four-fifths of them in former public assistance institutions), 14 more in psychiatric hospitals and 12–17 more in geriatric units. The relative numbers in private nursing homes or private residential homes are unfortunately not known, but could well be significant.

Another method of viewing the overall allocation of the confused is to examine what proportion they form of each type of institutional population. It has already been shown that Benson and Townsend's national study found 3·9 per cent of old people in residential homes were completely illucid, which compares closely with the 3·7 per cent assessed as severely confused in ordinary homes in this present report. Bigot, however, judged 8·5 per cent of his Staffordshire sample to be permanently confused, including 16·1 per cent of residents in former institutions (among whom were 21·2 per cent of the women), while Kay and Roth actually considered 29 per cent of a sample in welfare homes in Newcastle upon Tyne to be suffering from 'developed senile and arteriosclerotic dementia' and only a third to be mentally normal (Table 10.12).[32] The latter authors' figure of two-fifths in residential accommodation with either developed or milder dementia seems exceedingly high, yet on apparently consistent criteria they also similarly diagnosed 49 per cent of elderly patients in mental hospitals, which is quite compatible with the findings of a number of localized series (Table 10.12). This table, which demonstrates a range of estimates for organic cerebral conditions in various samples between 25 per cent and 59 per cent, suggests that the divergence between a staff rating of 43 per cent subject to severe mental impairment in psychiatric hospitals and an interviewer rating of 27 per cent as wholly illucid (Table 10.10) is not unbridgeably large. For geriatric units, a staff assessment of 14½ per cent as severely mentally impaired was close to an interviewer estimate of 12 per cent as completely illucid, though neither figure is compatible with the 42 per cent diagnosed as afflicted with developed forms of dementia (Table 10.13). In the community, Kay, Beamish and Roth (1962, p. 182), using the same criteria as in their institutional sample for their diagnosis of psychosis with disease of the brain, found an incidence of 4·3 per cent. (Comparison with other community data [Chapter 11], however, indicates that this estimate may be rather high.)

The net conclusion, therefore, from this variety of evidence must be that, again in the broadest terms, the concentration of the confused elderly in separatist residential establishments is perhaps as great as in psychiatric hospitals (though the association with mentally normal as opposed to mentally ill comparisons constitutes an obvious sharp difference), probably considerably greater than in geriatric units, and probably three times greater than in former public assistance institutions, quite apart from representing a

Table 10.12

Diagnosis of persons aged sixty-five and over admitted to psychiatric hospital in different series

Diagnosis	(1) Roth %	(2) Liddell et al. %	(3) Fish %	(4) Gibson %	(5) Connolly %	(6) Kidd %	(7) Mac-Millan %	(8) Herbert and Jacobson %	(9) Morris %	(10) Haider %	(11) Roth %	(12) Post %	(13) Wood-side %
Affective psychoses	49	54	42	45	28	34	21	56	31	26	54	37	29
Confusional states	8	—	5	11	16	14	8	3	3	16	9	6	6
Senile or arteriosclerotic dementia, organic cerebral conditions	31	29	32	25	45	30	43	33	59	33	29	50	45
Paranoid states (paraphrenia)	10	12	9	10	7	8	9	8	7	3	8	6	10
Miscellaneous disorders	3	5	13	9	5	14	19	—	—	22	—	—	10
TOTAL	101	100	101	100	101	100	100	100	100	100	100	99	100
Number	450	232	264	100	153	100	201	267	100	100	150	156	150

Sources.

(1) Roth (1955), pp. 286–301.
(2) Liddell et al., (1962), Table 5.
(3) Fish (1960), pp. 938–46.
(4) Gibson (1961), p. 921.
(5) Connolly (1962), p. 96.
(6) Kidd (1962), pp. 73–4.
(7) Macmillan (1962).
(8) Herbert and Jacobson (1966), p. 590.
(9) Morris (1962), p. 801.
(10) Haider (1968), p. 99.
(11) Roth and Morrissey (1952), p. 71.
(12) Post (1944), p. 559, Table vi.
(13) Woodside (1965), p. 286–302.

Table 10.13

Incidence of mental disorder and physical disability among
persons aged sixty-five and over admitted for the first
time during 1957–60 to three different kinds of unit from
five selected electoral wards in Newcastle upon Tyne

	Mental hospitals %	Geriatric wards %	Welfare homes %
1. *Mental disorder*			
Developed senile or arteriosclerotic dementia	49	42	29
Milder senile or arteriosclerotic dementia	0	18	11
Other psychotic states	51	8	4
Minor emotional disorders	0	16	11
Other miscellaneous conditions*	0	4	10
Mentally normal	0	12	35
TOTAL	100	100	100
Number	133	50	73
2. *Physical disability*			
Severe physical disability	28	48	12
Housebound (before admission)	34	30	40
Bedfast (before admission)	0	20	4
Not physically disabled	38	2	44
TOTAL	100	100	100
Number	133	50	73

Sources: 1. Kay *et al.* (1966, pp. 968, Table 11. 2. Kay *et al.* (1962) p. 181–2.
* Including lifelong mental subnormality, epilepsy, character disorder or mental confusion associated with serious physical illness.

crystallization for persons in this category roughly twelve times greater than in other local authority residential homes. Thus, although in terms of absolute numbers of beds separatist homes at present embrace only a tiny fraction of the total of confused old people resident in institutions, an increase in their provision on a significant scale would greatly intensify the degree of segregation for this group.

Influences over allocation

Given this distribution of the confused aged, what factors can be deduced as influencing this allocation? One approach to this question is to investigate significant differences that may exist between the elderly mentally infirm in the various institutonal populations. The most fruitful source of data here is the work by Kay and Roth and their colleagues concerning a sample of 838 old people in Newcastle upon Tyne.

They found (Table 10.13) that at least half of the geriatric patients in their sample exhibited mental symptoms severe enough for mental hospital care to be 'quite appropriate', while a quarter of mental hospital patients suffered from severe physical disability and more than a third were housebound so that geriatric ward care 'might equally have been recommended'. Nevertheless, while at least a fifth of elderly patients in geriatric wards were almost *wholly* incapacitated, in the sense of being bedfast or severely paralysed, none of the mental hospital patients was disabled to this degree. By the same criteria, only an eighth of welfare home residents were rated as severely disabled and almost half were free of physical handicap, in comparison with an incidence of 6 per cent severe disability and two-thirds in reasonable health among the general population over sixty-five.

Ideally, in order to answer the question posed, we also require full information about the socio-economic variables specifically applying to the confused elderly *within* each type of institution. Now it is known that the diagnostic pattern of mental hospital admissions of old people has altered in recent years to reveal a predominance of affective disorders over senile dementia and arteriosclerotic psychosis (C. B. Kidd, 1962c),[33] whilst among the latter group the most recent evidence (Registrar General's Statistical Review of England and Wales for the year 1960: Supplement on Mental Health, HMSO, 1964, p.19, table M.7) suggests a reduction in admissions since a peak in 1956 at the lower ages (below sixty-five) and a rise since that date in the higher age ranges (above sixty-five) for both sexes. But in the absence of more specialized data, we can only have recourse to such facts as are known concerning the more generalized institutional profiles. For the purposes of this approach, Kay, Beamish and Roth reveal that geriatric wards in Newcastle upon Tyne, in contrast to mental hospitals, took relatively more men, especially in the younger age groups, more very old people and more unmarried persons of both sexes and more widowers.[34] The mental hospital, on the other hand, not only took rather more elderly patients with no surviving children than the geriatric unit, but also attracted significantly (p $<\cdot$01) more middle-class persons than the welfare homes: for it absorbed 23 per cent of all admissions from the two predominantly middle-class wards in the city, while the welfare homes took only 13 per cent, a ratio almost exactly reversed by admissions from the two predominantly working-class wards in the sample.[35] Men who formerly held unskilled manual occupations were concentrated heavily in the geriatric wards and welfare homes, in both cases forming more than two-fifths of the male total.[36]

The welfare homes were characterized by a relatively very high proportion of unmarried persons, the very old (a quarter of residents over eighty-five), and residents with no surviving children (two-thirds), no surviving sibling (two-fifths) and a total absence of visitors (two-fifths). Admission rates were highest from areas of poor social integration and included many with previously poor work records as well as, significantly, 10 per cent who had had treatment in a psychiatric hospital at some time in their lives.[37] Whether the presence of mental infirmity or confusion remained allocatively neutral in the light of such differential factors as social isolation or severe physical disability, or whether it countermanded their influence in certain directions, can only be surmised on the existing evidence. It is only possible to report Bigot's finding that, among local authority residential establishments in Staffordshire, adapted homes relatively contained most transitorily confused persons who tended particularly to be younger (21 per cent under seventy-five) and either married or single rather than separated, while the former institutions accommodated disproportionately the permanently confused, most of whom were either divorced or separated and a quarter of whom had a marked physical incapacity (Bigot, 1967).

One final factor which should be mentioned here because of its alleged impact in distorting the pattern of allocation is section 29 of the Mental Health Act which permits compulsory admissions to a psychiatric hospital for a period of seventy-two hours on the basis of only one medical recommendation where urgent necessity arises. The possibility of misuse of this section derives from the failure to foresee in the early 'sixties, when a policy of reducing the number of psychiatric beds was strongly in the ascendant (Tooth and Brooke, 1961; Norton, 1961), the pressure on mental hospital beds that would arise from general hospitals and geriatric units. One commentator has described the effect of the ensuing bed shortage with the assertion that elderly patients 'tend to flow into any vacant bed, irrespective of administrative edict, and are usually labelled selectively from their multiple pathology with the diagnosis best calculated to gain admission by a particular hospital' (Parnell 1968). More specifically, Paterson and Dabbs, finding a significant excess of old people admitted to Oakwood Hospital in 1961 under section 29, contrary to expectations based on the age distribution of acute psychoses, concluded that the section was often used 'to enable a patient to bypass the waiting list for geriatric accommodation' (H. F. Paterson and Dabbs, 1963, p. 202.

Similarly, Enoch took the view that 'the truth is that mental hospitals have been used as dumping grounds because of the inadequacy of suitable accommodation for the elderly. In this process there has been an abuse of short-term orders – the previous three-day order and the present section 29' (Enoch, 1963). Indeed, the national figures for admissions to psychiatric hospitals in 1963 revealed that section 29 was used in 13 per cent of cases and section 26 on only 1 per cent (Enoch and Barker, 1965),[38] and at one hospital it was found that a third of section 29 admissions became informal after 72 hours (Paterson and Dabbs, 1963), which cast obvious doubt on the urgency of the original condition. Barton and Haider therefore concluded that, contrary to the spirit of the Mental Health Act,[39] 'some 5,000 people are now being admitted to psychiatric hospitals in England and Wales annually without adequate scrutiny of the need for compulsion' and 'without adequate scrutiny of the "troublesomeness" and proper prescription of their true needs to be at home or in hospital'. Defence of this disregard on the pretext that 'although technically we may be guilty of misusing the Act, it works well . . . because the "extramural doctor" (usually a GP but sometimes a consultant) only uses this section after the consultant has agreed to accept the patient for admission and therefore it is not possible to bypass the geriatric waiting list' (Kidd, 1963), or on grounds of 'the integrity of family doctors and mental welfare officers, most of whom use this section in a way that is calculated to serve the best interests of the patient' (Burowes, 1963), has been refuted by citation of Lord Chief Justice Goddard's judgment in the Rutty Case in 1956: 'The question is not whether the doctor thinks that it would be a good thing to have a patient in a hospital, but whether the Act of Parliament allows it' (Lowe, 1963).

In summary, therefore, it seems clear that even if a study of differences between institutional populations suggests some broad indicators of allocation, nevertheless the distortions of any rational system of assignment generated by section 29 in particular and by the fortuitous distribution of bed vacancies in general arising from differential turn-overs[40] was very considerable.

Appropriateness of care

What were the consequences in quality of care provided by the system of distribution revealed by this rather fragmentary picture, especially in the light of the overlap between institutions in allocation based on any single criterion? Here our information is even more meagre. How confused old people fare in such special units as mental hospital annexes converted from private houses, as at Gloucester, or in hostels for the mentally disordered, as at Bournemouth, or in homes catering predominantly for the elderly psychotic, as at Oldham, or in boarding out schemes in private or voluntary homes for old people or after-care hospitals, as in Somerset, has not yet been specifically investigated. All that can be stated is that one national survey which found that twenty hostels combined the mentally ill and the mentally subnormal, in some cases including persons with psychopathic disorder, behaviour disorders, social inadequacy and mental infirmity of old age, also reported that none of the sixteen county boroughs responsible indicated that any difficulties arose from such mixing.[41]

Our knowledge of the treatment of the elderly mentally infirm in private residential and nursing homes, former public assistance institutions or mental hospitals is as yet based on largely fortuitous data of an essentially episodal character. Thus the recent inquiry into conditions at Ely mental hospital, Cardiff, for example, which found general evidence of pilfering of patients' food, unprovoked violence against patients, overcrowding, an unduly casual attitude to death, lax and old-fashioned standards of nursing and excessive use of sedatives, also reported specifically an incident concerning one particular patient aged seventy-four suffering from senile dementia:

> When the wife of the late 'Dryden' was visiting him and wished to feed him a pear, she asked a female member of the nursing staff to obtain his dentures. The nurse returned with a bowl

containing a number of dentures, mixed up together, and proceeded, by trial and error, to fix some into the patient's mouth.
... We think it probable that, as the family alleged, the nurse in
question also tried to fit into the patient's mouth a set of teeth
which she had removed from the mouth of a sleeping patient, and
'rinsed under the tap'. It also seems likely that she did indeed
explain to the family that most of the dentures in the communal
bowl 'belonged to dead patients' (Howe Report, 1969, paras
51–3).

Though the Committee in their concluding judgment of 'insensitivity towards the family of the patient, Dryden, a laxity in the care,
provision and control of false teeth and toothbrushes' (para 47),
confined themselves to allegations which could be effectively substantiated, it is noteworthy that the patient's daughter 'complained
about several things' (para 50), and while this is reported as an
isolated instance, it is disquieting to observe the extent to which
other isolated incidents of an equally disturbing nature were
replicated in the subsequent publication of a national survey of
mental subnormality hospitals (P. Morris, 1969). More generally,
observation of the two mental hospital geriatric wards included in
the present investigations, one for women containing 19/35 patients
with a diagnosis of senile or arteriosclerotic psychosis and the other
for men with 19/32, a majority of the remainder being depressives,
chiefly gave an impression, apart from the employment of a high
proportion of foreign staff and occasional displays of forceful
handling,[42] of a complete breakdown in community inter-relations
among the patients such that social events seemed almost wholly
privatized for the manipulation of personal fantasies. Compared
with the welfare homes, whether ordinary or separatist, which
formed the centrepiece of the current study, it was true both that the
incidence of bizarre behaviour among patients on these wards was
higher and that the emphasis of staff supervision seemed more
rigidly directed towards the monotony of custodial control, whilst
partly because of staff shortages fewer opportunities for creative
activities were available to patients, the restraint of geriatric chairs
was much more in evidence, recourse was had more readily to the
expedient of keeping more enfeebled or incontinent patients in
pyjamas and towel dressing gowns all day, and more irritated outbursts of impatience or intolerance between patients was apparent.

However, the extent of relative responsibility for these problems as between the rather dispiriting routine, the subtle yet pervasive stigmatic overtones of the institution, the lack of sufficient trained staff, the possible inappropriateness of the psychiatric mix of patients or merely the greater severity of patients' confused state on admission, cannot be properly unravelled without a more precisely controlled study of this area than was attempted here.

On behalf of the care of the elderly mentally infirm in former public assistance institutions it has been claimed that the higher staff numbers together with the availability of space for wandering and the seclusion of personal idiosyncrasies offered a favourable environment. It is also true, however, that the standard of material amenities in these establishments is comparatively low, that they contain disproportionately a heterogeneous group of severely handicapped residents (P. Townsend, 1962, chapter 4), and that they have sometimes been used as dumping grounds for the antisocial.[43] Cavernous yet packed dayrooms, together with the higher incidence of physical infirmity and incontinence, minimize the opportunity for social activities and the development of community life: 'They absolutely want you to do nothing except keep yourself clean . . . in case you have an accident and fall over.' In the former PAI chosen for comparative investigation in this study,[44] one annexe possessed a huge dayroom containing seventy-five old people, of whom twenty-one were regarded by staff as confused, some being said to display very dirty habits.[45] Despite the greater space to hand, problems like wandering or incontinence could still be dealt with restrictively. 'One woman who wanders out to her former flat, wants to pay the rent, makes a nuisance of herself and abuses people for being in her flat, gets brought back by the police, so she's kept in bed now, to prevent her wandering.' Similarly, those with dirty social habits or disapproved eating manners were often segregated: 'For incontinents one room has been laid aside without carpets and mackintoshes put on the chairs . . . [though] five to ten are removed each year to mental hospital when they reach the animal stage – hygienically unclean.' A chief welfare officer in another county wrote about a former institution in his area: 'Two 38-bedded female blocks are used solely here for the very confused aged women and for younger women who are mentally backward. Many of these women are incontinent of urine, but as soon as they become doubly incontinent I find that the only way to cope with them is by keeping them in bed.' Nor, amid the pressure of numbers on a huge scale, were staff attitudes necessarily more enlightened on the question of residents' potential social initiatives. A sister in a former PAI suggested: 'I don't know that old people want to take decisions. They depend on sister for advice – they may want to go out on a cold day or to go to bed permanently. You *can't* let them have responsibility.'

The number of elderly confused in private nursing homes, as already indicated, is not known, but may be considerable. A survey of this population, embracing a classification of both their social and medical condition, is urgently needed since the most recent study in this field (Woodroffe and Townsend, 1961) concentrated rather on problems of public supervision of standards than on the incidence of physical or mental infirmity and social handicap of the patients. On the question of supervision the findings of the survey were disturbing:

A given establishment housing elderly people, a few of them bedfast and the others in varying degrees infirm, could easily be a convalescent, recuperative or rehabilitation Home, a private or a voluntary nursing home (and within either of these categories a mental nursing Home), a private old people's Home, or a 'Royal Charter' Voluntary Home. Depending on its status it could come under any one of six separate legislative requirements and be inspected or visited either by representatives of the Regional Hospital Board, the local authority Medical Officer of Health, the local authority Chief Welfare Officer, or by no one. Present legislation is pitted with anomalies (pp. 56–7).

Hill, herself a founder of a pioneer home for the elderly mentally infirm, has commented similarly on this matter: 'Nothing is easier than to collect a houseful of old people who are mentally weak and whose relatives want to get rid of them' (Hill, 1961, p. 101).[46] Moreover, such odd pieces of fragmentary evidence as were incidentally uncovered in the course of this study concerning treatment of the confused in private residential or nursing homes gave considerable cause for concern. An organizer of voluntary services for the aged in London noted that some private homes kept doors locked to keep in potential wanderers, and if, as often, they lacked night nursing, confused residents were 'sedated heavily'. A nursing home proprietor wrote: 'I think having a lounge for all up patients is difficult unless you have one for confused patients and one for normal patients, as the confused patients tend to get normal patients confused, if not annoyed' (Woodroffe and Townsend, 1961, p. 31). Indeed, commenting on the care of the elderly mentally infirm, the Ministry of Health recently declared that it now 'commanded general acceptance' that 'homes suitable for them are in no sense mental nursing homes' (Ministry of Health, 1963, p. 22). Nor did the revealed attitudes of some proprietors of private residential homes inspire much greater confidence:

> One such proprietor seemed to believe that resistance to infirmity was a matter of strength of will. 'Old habits die hard. People who have been slovenly all their lives are apt to give in and not bother. They make no fight against senility. I try to assess whether the people we take are independent-natured.' It was possible, she felt, to integrate the confused except for the incontinent and night wanderers. One of the latter, she said, she had kept up late watching TV and then administered sleeping drugs, but 'still she would not go to bed, even at 11 p.m., screaming and shouting on the stairs. One night she had a sleeping draught at 10 p.m., and I had to force her to sleep. She shook the banisters, though drooping with sleep: "I'll *not* go to sleep." Yet after bedtime at 11 p.m. she was up and into others' bedrooms at 3 a.m. So Hampton Royal [mental hospital] took her for two to three weeks, and she's now in a nursing home.'

Another proprietor of a private home for sixteen elderly women wrote:

> My husband and I charge eight to ten guineas per single room and for this reason we cannot afford to employ sufficient staff to supervise the wanderers. Getting up and dressing in the night and getting lost outside during the day and similar activities are time-devouring and very harassing. . . . We have sent away very few of our long-standing residents, but we try not to take new ones who may become confused. . . . The difficulty of dealing with the confused old person cannot be imagined; it has to be experienced. After twelve years in which we have had this home, it is, through bitter experience, the only difficulty which could make us give up.

Now such largely episodal evidence about the quality of care of elderly confused persons in different institutions, whilst *prima facie* disquieting in its implications, is clearly unsatisfactory without the backing of quantified comparison derived from a systematic enquiry. What can be asserted with greater confidence at this stage, however, concerning the care of the mentally infirm are the consequences of misplacement.

Misplacement

Now it is known from the work of Roth (1955, p.290, table 3) that old people admitted to psychiatric hospital, especially after the age of seventy, suffer a differentially high rate of mortality. Despite the fact that both Roth (1955) and Gibson (1961) have noted that such patients were a physically healthier group, Roth found that six months after admission, whilst 58 per cent of those with affective psychosis had been discharged and 76 per cent with late paraphrenia were still in-patients, 58 per cent of senile psychotics were dead.[47] After two years 82 per cent senile psychotics were dead, as also were 72 per cent of those with arteriosclerosis, though Post (Table 10.14) found more of the latter had been discharged.[48] Similarly, in another series C. B. Kidd (1962c) found that within a year more than half of those patients with senile psychosis were dead, most of them in the latter half of the year, reflecting the slow, progressive, downhill course of the disease. Again, the differential excess in mortality among elderly patients with organic brain disease was replicated in a more recent study by Herbert and Jacobson (1966, Table X), with a death rate after one year five times greater than in the case of affective disorder and eight times that for paraphrenia.

High though these mortality rates are, Kidd (1962a) has shown that they are actually significantly higher where misplacement occurs. Applying strict criteria – a patient was misplaced 'only if it was found that he manifested the sort of illness which could have been more suitably treated in the other [psychiatric or geriatric] hospital or that the condition for which he was admitted was clearly of secondary clinical importance to the major disability found' – he discovered that 24 per cent of the elderly patients in the mental hospital group in Belfast were misplaced, where the physical disability was predominant, and 34 per cent of the geriatric hospital group, where the psychiatric disability was predominant.[49] Factors associated with misplacement were higher age (seventy-five or more); single or widowed status[50]; low socio-economic status; admission

Table 10.14

Outcome of admission of demented persons over sixty to a psychiatric unit, 1937–43

Diagnosis	Discharged			Surviving in hospital	Deaths				All cases
	relieved	unchanged	Total		within one week	within one month	later	Total	
Arteriosclerosis	14	1	15	9	4	9	7	20	44
Senile dementia	4	1	5	10	3	7	29	39	54
Presenile dementia	—	1	1	4	—	—	1	1	6
Terminal confusional psychosis	—	—	—	—	5	2	—	7	7
TOTAL	18	3	21	23	12	18	37	67	111

Source. Post (1944), Table VII.

from welfare homes or lodgings (especially in the case of geriatric hospital); restlessness, disorientation and impaired ability to communicate; and (in the case of mental hospital) impaired physical mobility and incontinence of urine. The last three factors suggest that the elderly mentally infirm may as a group disproportionately suffer misplacement. The penalties of misallocation were severe. Not only did misplaced patients undergo a higher mortality than correctly placed patients in either hospital, but they also underwent a higher mortality than patients suffering from similar conditions who had been admitted correctly. Moreover, even of those who survived, significantly fewer misplaced patients were discharged (Kidd 1962b, table III).

The severity of the consequences of misplacement of elderly patients claimed in Kidd's study has, however, been challenged by Mezey, Hodkinson and Evans (1968) in their survey of the North London working-class boroughs of Tottenham and Edmonton. For, firstly, whilst he reported that of geriatric admissions 13 per cent were definitely misplaced and a further 11 per cent were probably misplaced in the psychiatric hospital, with corresponding figures for the geriatric hospital of 20 per cent and 14 per cent, they found that only 2·2 per cent were definitely misplaced in the geriatric unit and a further 6·0 per cent probably so, while in the psychiatric unit the numbers were 6·2 per cent and 8·4 per cent respectively. Secondly, their investigations suggested a much more qualified relationship between misplacement and mortality. For while mortality within six months among elderly patients with exclusively mental disorder was no higher (at one-fifth) where they had been misplaced than where they had been correctly allocated, and while the differentially excessive death rate among patients with solely physical illness misplaced in psychiatric units was explicable on other grounds,[51] those with mixed mental-physical symptoms offered contrary indications of the significance of misplacement. For of persons presenting with a mixed condition, where mental illness had mainly led to admission, misplacement in a geriatric unit appeared to double the mortality ratio (50·0 per cent compared to 24·5 per cent), yet where physical disorder was chiefly responsible for entry to hospital, apparently correct allocation to a geriatric unit also led a doubled mortality ratio (58·0 per cent compared to 27·3 per cent). A third qualification of Kidd's findings is necessary because he examined his sample three weeks after admission, by which time many deaths had already occurred. In the London study the much higher mortality in the geriatric unit, including the early peak of deaths within the first two weeks after admission, reflected less the possibility of misplacement than differences in the type of patient admitted, arising partly from structural factors such as the virtual absence of a waiting list for the geriatric unit which facilitated the reception of critically ill patients.

Misplacement, however, is not merely a matter of inappropriate allocation between psychiatric and geriatric units. It includes also admission to hospital of persons more suitably placed in residential care (including separatist homes) as well as admission to institutions of persons potentially fitted for community care. In this sense Boucher in his survey in 1955 gathered evidence which indicated that of 6,739 old patients in mental hospitals serving the London area, '952 could equally well have been tended in general hospitals and a further 1,920 in welfare accommodation' (Boucher, 1957, p. 47). Similarly, Kidd calculated that of 850 psychiatric patients aged sixty and over, 100 were suitable for care in a long-stay psycho-geriatric unit, eighty for care either at home or in part III accommodation, and eleven for geriatric hospital accommodation for the elderly chronic sick (H. B. Kidd, 1962). Again, Haider (1968) reviewing a hundred patients aged over sixty selected from admissions to a mental hospital, concluded not only that 5 per cent had merely social problems, but that also 17 per cent mainly needed the services of a home help and 15 per cent needed very little help at all. Altogether he judged that 28 per cent should definitely not have been admitted to a psychiatric hospital, but should have been maintained in the community, and a further 12 per cent cases were very marginal in this respect.[52] Indeed, Halsall and Lloyd (1961, table III) actually found that old people in need only of nursing care and with relatively unimportant medical symptoms were much *more* likely to be admitted to in-patient treatment and much *less* likely to receive general practitioner care than those with a specific and significant medical condition. While 62 per cent of the former did suffer from cerebrovascular disease, nevertheless many of them were demoralized and partly or completely rejected by their relatives largely because it was felt that 'nothing more could be done'. Yet many proved to suffer from conditions which could be alleviated sufficiently to allow them to return to 'some sort of life outside hospital'.

The key to proper placement must lie above all in replacing classification according to the nature of the disability by classification according to the kind of attention required. McKeown, the main proponent of this view, has long advocated the concept of a 'balanced hospital community' characterized by the acceptance of all types of patient on a common site, a centre consisting of multiple buildings of varied design, common staff, and an intimate relationship between hospital and domiciliary medical services (McKeown, 1958). Traditionally, however,

> the responsibilities placed on local public health and public assistance committees before 1948 were indirectly responsible for what amounted to a statutory division between the historical accidents of 'acute' and 'chronic', between technical medicine and custody, between the 'élite' and the 'under-labourer.' With the coming of the Health Service the dividing lines were redrawn and came to lie, not between 'acute' and 'chronic', but between those who needed a home and those who needed a hospital (Binks, 1968).

Thus, whilst part III of the National Assistance Act of 1948 defined a hospital as 'any institution for the reception and treatment of persons suffering from illness',[53] it also stated that local authorities should confine their provision of health services in residential accommodation to those 'not being specialist services or services of a kind normally provided only on admission to a hospital' (section 21). Rejecting this approach of tying particular services to certain institutions, McKeown has posited the alternative policy of estimating the prevalence of the demand for services to meet specified needs irrespective of institutional location. Thus, on the basis of a survey of all old people in institutions in Birmingham, McKeown and Cross calculated from their findings (Table 10.15) that 17·2 beds were needed per 1,000 population over sixty-five for residential care in welfare homes, 9·3 beds for mental nursing, 10·8 for basic nursing and rehabilitation, and 5·4 for the investigation or treatment of mental illness. Such a policy of allocation strictly by need would seem to put in jeopardy the independent *raison d'être* of the separatist homes.

Psychogeriatric assessment

The argument thus far has brought to light the substantial element of misplacement of elderly patients that was found to exist in several independent studies, though its consequential significance has been disputed. Thus the proportion of elderly patients admitted to geriatric units with psychiatric disorder of varying severity has been separately estimated at 30 per cent in North London (Mezey *et al.*, 1968),[54] 63 per cent in Belfast (C. B. Kidd, 1962a), 58 per cent in Newcastle (Kay *et al.*, 1962) and 40 per cent in south-west Scotland (Robinson and Isaacs, 1963), while the corresponding figures for those admitted to psychiatric units with physical illness or disability of various degrees are respectively 52, 47, 28, 50 and also 33 per cent in Brighton (Herbert and Jacobson, 1966). Furthermore, in the most thorough cross-institutional survey yet made of assessed needs for care, it was found in Birmingham that while 8·4 per cent of residents of homes had disabilities of a kind which would gain them admission to hospital, 16·8 per cent of patients in geriatric units had no disabilities or merely minor ones which required only simple personal attention from untrained staff, and 5·3 per cent of patients in acute hospitals had no disabilities for which it was necessary to stay in hospital (McKeown and Cross, 1969).

Clearly several drawbacks are inherent in this situation. Kidd has argued that misplacement may impair chances of recovery since, while conditions treated are largely similar, nevertheless the organization and accommodation, attitudes and training of medical and nursing staffs, ancillary services and staff-patient ratios in different types of unit are markedly dissimilar and the treatment regimens wholly different (C. B. Kidd, 1962b). It is also true that admission often tends to be delayed till a late stage and possibly until a medical or social emergency compels action to be taken, that the choice of unit may depend more on irrelevant factors than on the needs of the patient, that each type of unit is organized largely for the diagnosis and treatment of only one or other aspect of frequently complex conditions, that transfer to another more suitable type of unit may be difficult,[55] and that the special needs of the aged for the continuation of care after discharge from hospital are not always regarded. The solution most widely advocated in recent years for this set of problems has been the establishment of psycho-geriatric assessment units. Thus, Kay, Roth and Hall have cogently argued the case for such a unit which would be attached to a main district general or teaching hospital; with staffing by both physicians and psychiatrists supported by adjacent

Table 10.15

The Distribution of old people in Institutions in Birmingham, 1965, according to their assessed needs for care

Disability	Type of care required	Type of institution				
		Welfare homes %	Geriatric units %	Acute hospitals %	Mental* hospitals %	Total %
None requiring special accommodation or personal attention	Welfare home only	53 ⎫	⎫	⎫	⎫	⎫
Limited mobility; not requiring personal attention	Welfare home with ground floor accommodation or lifts	22 ⎬ 92	⎬ 17	⎬ 5	⎬ 16	⎬ 38
Infirm; requiring personal attention	Welfare home with personal assistance from untrained staff	17 ⎭	⎭	⎭	⎭	⎭
Incontinent, immobile or needing rehabilitation	Basic nursing and/or rehabilitation	4	59	16	60	37
Confused or disturbed to a degree requiring mental nursing	Mental nursing	4	18	0	19	11
Illness requiring hospital investigation and treatment	Investigation or treatment of acute illness	—	6	79	5	14
	TOTAL	100	100	100	100	100
	Number	1,394	1,210	607	1,333	4,544

Source. McKeown and Cross (1969), Tables I and II.

* The needs of patients in psychiatric hospitals were measured in an earlier (1958) assessment prior to the survey quoted.

out-patient and day hospital facilities it would be closely integrated, perhaps by joint appointments, with local authority health and welfare departments and with the general practitioner service (Kay *et al.*, 1966).

Several benefits are claimed for this arrangement. One is clearly the ready availability of joint consultation in cases of multiple disorder.[56] Thus Kidd has argued that as many as 30 per cent of elderly patients in mental hospital and 43 per cent in geriatric units would have gained from the provision of a unit where psychiatrists and general physicians worked together (C. B. Kidd, 1962a). Secondly, many welfare officers and matrons contacted in the national survey mentioned the submission of grossly misleading GP reports designed to secure admission, where the adverse consequences of abrupt transfer could only be obviated by full initial assessment:

Either the relatives 'play it cool' regarding their parents' real mental condition, or else the admissions officer cannot afford the necessary time or make another visit. But it has been one's frequent experience to admit a resident who has been described as 'mildly confused' and to find that it has been necessary to arrange for him to be seen by a consultant psychiatrist who has no hesitation in recommending the patient's immediate removal to the mental hospital. Also it is not unknown for a general practitioner to co-operate in describing a patient as 'mildly confused' in order to get a particularly awkward person off his hands.

Thirdly, such a unit would contribute to the integration of the various services for the elderly.[57] Indeed, some have insisted that its most important function would be, not avoiding misplacement, but 'to promote the cohesion of the relevant components of services for the elderly sick. It would, in addition, serve as a centre to give joint psychiatric and medical training to nurses and doctors working in all branches of the geriatric services.'[58] Fourthly, as an aspect of improved liaison, an assessment unit constitutes an integral part of a system of progressive patient care. The main original pioneer of this approach was Cosin (1956 and 1957, p. 110) at Oxford in the 1950s, since when it has been widely adopted elsewhere (e.g. Exton-Smith, 1962; Robinson, 1965; Irvine, 1963). Under Cosin's guidance the geriatric service at Oxford was based on the principle of quadruple assessment, embracing pathological, psychological, sociological and residual physical disability (Cosin, 1958, pp. 226–7). Several units were required deriving from the initial assessment executed by a team consisting of physician, nurse, biochemist, pathologist, electroencephalographer, dietician, occupational therapist, physiotherapist and various aides. Depending on the conclusions reached by this team, elderly patients were then transferred either to an active treatment unit, a very small nursing unit for the few permanently bedfast, or if infirm or frail ambulant, to rehabilitation and long-stay annexes or a joint residential home close to the geriatric unit.

Despite these substantial benefits afforded by an in-patient psychogeriatric unit, it is also true that a number of significant drawbacks attach to the idea. Not only may confusion be itself actually generated by a double transfer which may appear abrupt and bewildering,[59] but even the best hospital wards can tend towards a degree of depersonalization and sometimes offer as well a greater risk of bedsores and incontinence (Brocklehurst, 1966). Moreover, a recent study of an active geriatric unit revealed that 72 per cent of the patients admitted underwent complications during their illness in hospital, in half the cases not as a direct or indirect consequence of the illness which led to entry, but actually precipitated by the hospital stay itself, which was even judged to have caused a seventh of the deaths (Rosin and Boyd, 1966). Again, relevant to the post-admission assessment period, Newman has illustrated how the delay in waiting for bedpans and the inability to communicate their needs to nurses as easily as hitherto to their relatives both predispose old people to incontinence (Newman, 1962),[60] and the latter not only creates a 'shaming burden', but may also actually provide a self-fulfilling justification for their retention in hospital.

More positively, the advantages of domiciliary assessment require strong emphasis in their own right. Above all, the familiarity of the environment offers an opportunity for objectivity in appraisal which is necessarily reduced on an alien and possibly distressing hospital ward. Thus, Macmillan has declared that 'the whole situation can be examined in a home in a way which is superior to any other procedure in giving a complete picture and in determining the degree of true urgency' (Macmillan, 1967). Elsewhere he elaborates the social complexities which would only be brought fully to light by home visits.

Very often it turns out that the entire responsibility has been placed on the shoulders of one family member, the others having evaded their responsibilities by pleading illness, lack of accommodation, nervous strain on the married partner, etc. When a family conference is called by an impartial person [a social worker], it is often a potent factor in adjusting the load more fully (Macmillan, 1962b, p. 5).

Nevertheless, even with a strong policy towards domiciliary assessment, it is likely that in a small minority of cases the need for intensive in-patient appraisal will remain. To overcome the problem that the confused elderly patient may be incorrectly diagnosed at a single interview where variability of performance is suspected, prolonged observation for at least a minimum period may be necessary. Thus at Crichton Royal Hospital, for example, at weekly assessment meetings where all cases with diagnostic problems are reviewed, reports are made to an agreed formula not only by the doctor and psychiatrist, but also by the social worker and nurses with their sustained daily experience of the patients in question (Robinson, 1965, p. 195). Again, in-patient assessment may be used where dubious or overlapping responsibility exists between the medical, psychiatric and social spheres.[61]

Wherever exercised, however, the whole principle of assessment begs the question of what assessment is *for*? Are institutional functions so exclusively defined and the disabilities of old age so rigorously separate that classification for a single appropriate placement is even theoretically possible? The evidence suggests neither proposition applies. In a study in Birmingham, for example, Parnell, Cross and Wall (1968) concluded that because the geriatric service had become overstretched and under-organized, understaffed or under-capitalized, or all three, it was found expedient to admit the 'excess' of elderly patients to mental hospitals, unsatisfactory though such a solution was unless parts of these hospitals were radically re-equipped and appropriately staffed with persons properly trained for the change of duties.[62] Official acknowledgment of an inevitable overlap of function was contained in the 1965 circular:[63] 'Hospitals must be ready to retain people who do not at all times need full hospital care, and local authorities must be ready to retain people in residential homes who often need more than they normally expect to provide.' Equally, the multiple conjunction of disorders in old age has been clearly documented. Herridge found, in a study of 209 consecutive admissions of psychiatric in-patients, that in 5 per cent of cases major physical illness, first discovered on entry, was the principal diagnosis, while in 21 per cent of cases physical conditions contributed to the onset of psychiatric illness, in 8 per cent they resulted from it, and in 16 per cent they were unrelated to it (Herridge, 1960). Also, in addition to the evidence of Kidd and others already cited about multiple conditions among the elderly, Wilson, Lawson and Brass found from a study of 200 persons admitted to a geriatric unit in Aberdeen that the men had a mean of 6·4 disorders each and women 5·4 each (L. A. Wilson *et al.*, 1962).

What implications does this picture of overlapping functions and composite disorders hold for policy? It means that the scientific model of the hospital function – that it exists merely to give 'technical' treatment, rather than as part of a wider community structure to help people to live more satisfactorily – is inappropriate. Yet it has been argued that 'the hospital has evolved into a highly specialized medical factory or "disease plant" – a veritable power-house of scientific skills – which functions in terms of an un-complicated philosophy of "cure" ' (T. D. Hunter, 1967). This explains why geriatric hospitals and wards, where the average bed occupancy is 97 per cent and chronic staff shortages exist, are constantly being asked to take patients from 'acute' hospitals where the average bed occupancy is only 70 per cent and where there are no staff shortages (Binks, 1968).[64] It explains why the placement of confused, restless or incontinent elderly patients in general hospitals is seen as 'blocking medical beds', and why resort is had to custodial measures of less eligibility for those for whom science can do nothing. Nevertheless, full employment, the decreasing number of single women and the greater variety of opportunity for women generally constitute practical limiting factors which gradually but decisively are making the traditional solution of residual custody unworkable (D. Norton, 1967). For these reasons, if for no other, attention is forced towards the establishment of properly organized out-patient departments, day centres and work-rooms which are directed towards the development of the remaining physical function and personal response rather than being engrossed in the extent of structural disease. It is, therefore, only when the applicability and limitations of community care for the elderly mentally infirm have been fully surveyed that we can reliably and with confidence assess the place of separatist homes within the broad range of alternative policies. To this sphere then we must now turn.

NOTES

1. Though P. Townsend's (1962) finding that of a sample of 530 new residents from a cross-section of old people's homes 29·5 per cent of the men and 28·0 per cent of the women were drawn from hospital would not represent a significant departure from the pattern of admissions to separatist homes displayed here (p. 312, Table 66).

2. Data from other sources, however, indicates that policy could vary widely between authorities (Table 10.2), in particular in the proportion drawn from ordinary part III accommodation.

3. Discharges to private households are largely accounted for initially by the opportunity offered of short-stay beds while the intended population was being slowly assembled and thereafter by temporary admissions, particularly for holiday relief.

4. This suggests that the removal of Mrs L. might be at least in part the aim of taking up employment rather than an undesired side-effect.

5. Section 47, National Assistance Act 1948, covered the removal to suitable premises of persons in need of care and attention who '(*a*) are suffering from grave chronic disease or, being aged, infirm, or physically incapacitated, are living in insanitary conditions, and (*b*) are unable to devote to themselves, and are not receiving from other persons, proper care and attention'.

6. In the case of two of the separatist homes the initial assessment was made by a psychiatrist on a domiciliary visit, and in the other by a geriatrician, occasionally in conjunction with the general practitioner who was often originally responsible for the referral. In the case of the local authority home where psychiatric advice was sought (the other being a voluntary home), allocation was left to the Welfare Department once admission to mental hospital had been rejected.

7. Though some evidence was found that night wandering could precipitate transfer from ordinary homes without regular night staff.

8. Incontinence was not usually treated per se as a cause for transfer. In one of the ordinary homes studied here, for example, a rational resident who complained to staff on this account was told: 'Don't be fussy. They can't all be clean like you.' An Area Welfare Officer who was asked what were the criteria of selection for the local separatist home replied: 'If a resident is a disturbing influence to the other occupants – if he pokes round the possessions of others, takes others' clothing from drawers, or is dirty in the toilet and has dirty personal habits, like picking up faeces and putting them into a handbag.'

9. In the case of a sixth of residents in one of the separatist homes the note appeared in the record files: 'Would suit any home.'

10. For example 'At the time of her eviction the only strange things she's done are hang her washing in the kitchen and talk to herself' (case-record of widow, aged seventy-eight, score o); 'He lost his place in lodgings after his landlady's daughter had to go to London for a heart operation' (widower, aged seventy-one, score o). Thus P. Townsend (1962, chs. 11–12) in his national sample shows that the chief reasons for the admission of old people to residential homes are homelessness and economic insecurity in addition to social isolation and lack of domiciliary services.

11. That is, apart from removal from terminal care. The tendency has been noted in the past for old people with 'persistent senile confusion' frequently to be transferred to hospital during terminal phases of illness (Cook *et al.*, 1952, p. 377).

12. A review of the first year's experience at Llanerch, a purpose-built hostel at Bridgend, Glamorgan, containing 35 beds, showed that: 'Two residents have been transferred to the local psychiatric hospital, one, a woman, following suicidal behaviour while in a state of confusion and depression, and the other, a man, because of his constantly threatening attitude towards the staff' (Jones and Milne, 1966, p. 163).

13. Despite occasional positive (i.e. apart from sedation) efforts at accommodation, for instance by encouraging piano-playing as a release for aggressiveness and encouraging wanderers to use a confined area within the grounds for their perambulations.

14. The same principle could, of course, be applied to the separatist homes themselves. Thus one case record contained the following noteworthy comment: 'She treated other residents so spitefully that she had to be put at a table by herself for meals, though after she had been told that she was to be transferred to mental hospital, her behaviour improved considerably.'

15. For example, 'inability to feed themselves and incontinence are usually dealt with in one of the large homes, who employ more staff and have the facilities to cope' (letter in reply to the postal questionnaire).

16. P. Townsend (1962, p. 58, Table 17) notes that while the former public assistance institutions in his sample contained only 6 per cent of residents who were middle-class (RG classes I and II) and 60 per cent who were members of the semiskilled and un-skilled working classes IV and V), the post-1948 local authority homes contained respectively 14 per cent and 41 per cent.

17. Indeed, there is some evidence that the facilitation of discharge promoted by the establishment of separatist homes could be abused. Instances were recorded, for example, where (i) a hospital insisted that a patient be removed after recovery from a prolapsed rectum because of her confusion, though this was quickly revealed not to be endemic but rather the direct result of her physical disorder and anxiety; (ii) a woman who had been transferred from a mental hospital to a special home but was quickly returned because she did not settle there, was for a second time discharged by the hospital on the very dubious grounds that she had had a stroke and was now fully recovered from a cerebral catastrophe, yet again was immediately acutely unsettled and shouted continuously for a tablet till massively tranquillized and transported back to hospital.

18. These homes were extracted from a comprehensive list for England and Wales as at 1 January 1960, compiled by Professor Townsend, and from a similar list for Scotland as at 31 March 1965 supplied by the Scottish Home and Health Department.

19. Undertaken in Nov. 1967: see chapter 2.

20. No doubt partly as a result of the Ministry of Health's Building Note no. 2 (*Residential Accommodation for Elderly People*), 1962, which stated (p. 1): 'Where a large proportion of the residents will be mentally infirm or a home is planned specially for the elderly mentally disordered, it should not be for more than 35 residents. If it is necessary to exceed this figure, the residents' accommodation should be planned in self-contained units.'

21. For example, 'It is intended that the special home for the elderly mentally confused at present under construction will be used for the more difficult type of old person who is, or may be, causing disturbance or irritation in other small homes. There is no suggestion that the elderly mentally confused are to be segregated in this way as I anticipate a regular exchange of beds with Homes in the near vicinity.' 'One of our homes houses a rather larger proportion than the others of confused residents. This fact is largely fortuitous and we do not segregate the mentally infirm.'

22. The surveys showed that where night staff had already been recruited, they usually served in pairs, though occasionally singly, and that the day : night care staff ratio (on a whole-time-equivalent basis) was normally about 3/4 : 1 ranging up to 6/7 : 1 in the larger sixty-bed homes.

23. Failure to achieve this aim might be compensated for by resort to extensive medication. One Chief Welfare Officer wrote that: 'In a number of cases where old people are becoming difficult and awkward by reason of inevitable mental degeneration, tolerance, sympathetic understanding and competent medical care, particularly by way of heavy doses of sedating and tranquillizing drugs, will ensure that old people can be kept in a home although staff resources and the welfare of other residents would make it impossible to deal with any substantial numbers of such individuals.'

24. Section 6 of the Mental Health Act 1959.

25. That is 2,290 beds (Table 10.7) as a proportion of the total of 98,757 (*Dept. of Health and Social Security, Annual Report for 1968* (1969), p. 139).

26. P. Townsend and Wedderburn (1965, p. 23, Table 1) give a total of 280,000 persons age sixty-five and over in residential homes, psychiatric hospitals and nursing homes, and other hospitals and nursing homes in Britain, mid-1963.

27. If, however, the judgment of staff were accepted that 52·7 per cent of old people in institutions suffered from 'some or severe mental impairment', then separatist units would contain only 1·6 per cent of the total at present.

28. *Dept. of Health and Social Security Annual Report for 1968*, p. 139.

29. The definition of these terms as used by Roth and his colleagues has already been given in chapter 2.

30. The number of residents of pensionable age in former public assistance institutions at 1 January 1960 was 29,615, in adapted homes 27,334, and in purpose-built homes 6,343 (P. Townsend, 1962, p. 44, Table 7).

31. See p. 81.

32. It is interesting to note that some American data offers comparably high figures. G. Martin (1959, p. 11) found that 51·9 per cent of 1,350 residents in 100 licensed homes (nursing homes, adult boarding homes and homes for the aged) in Kansas were 'mentally disorientated or confused', though no criteria are offered. He reported that medical record diagnoses registered 10·7 per cent residents admitted with arteriosclerosis and other circulatory diseases, 5·1 per cent with cerebrovascular accidents (strokes), 11 per cent with senility (defined according to the International Statistical Classification), and 21·6 per cent with disorders of the brain, including 4·1 per cent with psychosis, 1 per cent with chronic brain syndromes, 1·7 per cent with cerebral arteriosclerosis, and 2·2 per cent with senile dementia. The apparent overlap in some of the categories is not explained.

33. The opposite was formerly the case (Robinson 1951).

34. A Birmingham study also indicated that old people needing the full facilities of a modern hospital were mainly to be found in chronic hospitals, while younger persons with similar needs were admitted to general or mental hospitals. Furthermore, those needing limited hospital facilities, with or without mental supervision, were distributed arbitrarily between chronic, mental and general hospitals according to age rather than the type of care needed. The survey made clear the importance of removing the traditional distinctions between the major classes of hospitals in place of emphasis on facilities appropriate to patient need (McKeown *et al.*, 1961).

35. Benson and Townsend however, postulated a class hierarchy of institutions whereby formerly unskilled manual workers among those admitted to institutions in old age appeared to be channelled disproportionately into mental hospitals: *Old People in Long-Stay Institutions*, Chapter 4.

36. In comparison with 16·6 per cent in the general population of all ages and 14·9 per cent in their field survey sample of old people.

37. In contrast to 1·3 per cent in the community sample and 4 per cent among geriatric ward patients.

38. H. B. Kidd (1961) even quotes a figure of 16 per cent section 29 admissions in Leicester as against 1 per cent admissions by section 26. It has, however, been stated

that a national survey on behalf of the Royal Medico-Psychological Association found that a significantly greater number of psychiatric hospitals showed a *decrease* in the percentage total intake admitted under section 29 over the two-year period 1964–66 (Markowe, 1967).

39. The Royal Commission on the Law Relating to Mental Illness and Mental Deficiency, 1957, para. 409, declared that 'it is important that emergency procedures should be used except in real emergencies when action to remove the patient must be taken before there is time for the two medical recommendations required under the normal procedure'.

40. In Newcastle it was found that whereas the duration of stay for two-thirds of elderly hospital patients was less than three months, the corresponding proportion among welfare home residents was only a sixth. Conversely, while two-thirds of residents stayed more than a year, only a tenth of hospital patients over sixty-five stayed as long. Over a four-year period, while only 10 per cent of welfare home residents were discharged home, the figure for geriatric wards was less than 30 per cent and for mental hospitals more than 40 per cent (Kay *et al.*, 1962, p. 186).

41. In one example, at High Wycombe, ten beds were reserved for mentally confused senile patients in a special unit for the mentally ill and subnormal, while in Staffordshire mental health hostels were designed for old people with 'a greater degree of psychiatric symptomatology than simple senile confusion' (Phillips, 1966, 115, 85–92).

42. One man, for example, who gripped the frame at the end of his bed while being undressed was seen to have his fingers forced off by a male nurse so that he could be pushed back and made to lie down, while another man (aged seventy-four, diagnosed with arteriosclerotic psychosis) who protested about being undressed was pushed round and placed in an armlock behind his back.

43. One welfare officer described them as repositories for 'tramps, casuals and persons without a settled way of life'.

44. A quarter of those regarded by staff as confused in seven rooms or wards were interviewed, together with at least one non-confused resident as a control, making a total of twenty-eight interviews with residents. Thirteen staff were also interviewed, and altogether a fortnight was spent on general observation.

45. One man, for example, was alleged to urinate on occasions in a mug and then to throw the contents over the floor and chairs. Repeated spitting in disapproved places was also cited.

46. The situation is reminiscent in some respects of the lack of regulation of the private madhouses in the eighteenth century.

47. Roth also interestingly reveals that among senile psychotics the mortality was consistently lower among women, while the proportion of in-patients who were women was consistently higher (significant at the $p = 0 \cdot 01$ level). He remarks that it is noteworthy that this difference 'should be so unequivocal in a group that is often regarded as a caricature of the process of normal senescence'.

48. In a study of 111 admissions of persons aged over sixty to a psychiatric unit (Table 10.14), Post found a much higher incidence of discharge of cerebral arteriosclerotics, though in conjunction with also a slightly higher initial death rate.

49. Apart from patients sent to mental hospitals when the sole psychiatric disorder is delirium due to severe physical disease, Sargant (1961) notes that in medical wards patients may be admitted for investigation of physical complaints which may not be recognized as hypochondriacal concomitants to primary depressive illness.

50. C. B. Kidd (1962b) notes that self-neglect is not uncommon here and may favour physical breakdown, or loneliness and social isolation may predispose to psychiatric disorder, so that the clinical picture is a mixed one.

51. Of the eight relevant persons in this category, of whom seven died, six had a very bad prognosis irrespective of place of admission.

52. In another presentation of his data a figure of 33 per cent suitable for community care is given (Haider, 1967).

53. Where illness included 'mental illness and any injury or disability requiring medical or dental treatment or nursing'.

54. Of the Scottish Hospital Centre conference on 'The Confused Elderly' it was reported that 'the availability of appropriate resources and not the designation of the unit determined whether or not the patient was correctly placed' (*Brit. Hosp. and Soc. Serv. J.*, 7 February 1969, p. 255).

55. It is interesting to note, however, the experience of Burnbank Home, Glasgow, opened in 1953 for fifty frail ambulant men and women, where regular exchanges were made between the local authority home and the nearby geriatric unit 'on a dispassionate assessment of suitability', though no criteria were stated (Nisbet, 1962).

56. Also, on grounds of the priority of medical care in acute cases, Fish has argued that psychiatric treatment should be tied to the geriatric unit. Because of the 'need for expert medical care and the dangers of misclassification, all acutely mentally ill old people should be admitted to a special psychiatric ward in a geriatric unit. The patient with an acute physical and psychological illness is more likely to die if he does not immediately receive adequate medical care than if he receives immediate psychiatric, but indifferent medical treatment' (Fish, 1963).

57. The WHO Expert Committee on Mental Health Aspects of Ageing and the Aged strongly recommended, for instance, that not only out-patient clinics and a day hospital, but also ancillary staff such as psychologists and social workers could be located on the same presmises, and that a club for old people and counselling services for patients and relatives alike, as well as a central records department, could be established there: *WHO Techn. Rep. Ser.*, no. 171, 1959.

58. Mezey *et al.* (1968). They argue further that ideally geriatrics and psychiatry should both be centred on the same general hospital, or otherwise to promote cooperation it may be necessary to allocate sessional time for geriatricians and psychiatrists to advise on the care of patients admitted to a parallel unit, especially where geriatric and psychiatric beds are separated from each other in specialized hospitals. Others have argued that the location of a psychiatric unit in a general hospital removes the stigma of mental illness, encourages inter-disciplinary research and brings psychiatry into the main-stream of medicine (Capoore and Nixon, 1961).

59. 'It is the initial move from well-known surroundings which is most likely to cause or aggravate the patient's confusion and therefore a move should not be made unless assessment cannot properly be carried out in the home', National Corporation for the Care of Old People, *Accommodation for the Mentally Infirm Aged*, 1963, p. 14. 'The referral of senile patients should be treated as acute rather than chronic situations, and first priority should be given to utilizing skilled, trained personnel in a social and medical assessment of the patient's and family's position before any move of the patient is contemplated' (P. Hunter, 1965, p. 739).

60. Newman has even drawn a parallel between some ward policies and the personality destruction aimed at in brain-washing techniques (cf. Sargant, 1957).

61. As at Nottingham (Fisher *et al.*, 1966).

62. They discovered that admissions of old people to both psychiatric and general hospitals had increased – by the end of 1967 some 43 per cent of all patients in the mental hospitals, including more than half the female patients, were over sixty-five – while in the geriatric hospital service the accommodation per head of population actually declined over the period 1961–67, as also did the total number of annual admissions and the rate of turnover.

63. LA 18/65; HM (65) 77; ECL 80/65; see further chapter 2.

64. Binks postulates two explanatory principles – 'imperative relegation' whereby it is assumed that certain people must be consigned to a somewhat less important sphere,

whether or not the person thus consigned naturally accepts this action or those to whom the old person is consigned accept total responsibility, and 'aggressive irresponsibility' whereby a critical situation is deliberately manufactured to force somebody else to act, including especially the discharge of a patient out of hospital to a situation known to be untenable and the refusal to help when disaster occurs.

11

Community care: policies for integration

How many mentally infirm elderly persons are at present living in private households in Britain? By what social or medical characteristics, if any, do they differ from confused old people admitted to institutions? What kind of propping mechanism sustains them in the community, and how satisfactory or otherwise is the relationship of reciprocity between them and their families, where are the latter available? These are some of the questions we must finally answer before turning to a policy review, with particular reference to the issue of segregation and the future of the separatist homes.

COMMUNITY CARE FOR THE ELDERLY MENTALLY INFIRM

Number of mentally infirm old people in private households

Such limited data as is available on the incidence of mental infirmity or mental disorder among old people living in the community appears irreconcilably divergent. Thus, a list of surveys carried out in various countries of the world in the last forty years concerning the prevalence of senile and arteriosclerotic psychoses (Table 11.1) reveals adjusted rates, which standardize for the varying proportions of old people in different populations, of between 0·2 per cent and 5·3 per cent. The much higher adjusted figures produced by Bremer in Norway and by Primose in North Scotland may be partly explained by the fact that they represent the sole general practitioner studies and that they include non-hospitalized cases. It is also possible that Primrose's recent study reflects the important advances in treatment that have enabled more of those of vulnerable disposition to survive into later life. Thus Malzberg, for example, has suggested that increases in the relative prevalence of senile and arteriosclerotic psychoses in the twenty years to 1940 in New York State (Table 11.2) came about 'because the individuals constituting

Prevalence of senile and arteriosclerotic psychoses as noted by recent surveys in various countries

Country	Area	Type of area	Size of population studied	Investigator	Date of investigation	Reference	Rates per 1,000	
							Raw data	Rates adjusted by Weinberg's method*
U.S.A.	Baltimore	Urban	55,129	Lemkau, Tietze and Cooper	1936	Ment. Hyg., 25, 1941, 624	0·7	—
	Tennessee	Rural	24,804	Roth and Luton	1938	Amer. J. Psychiat., 99, 1943, 662	0·9	—
	New Haven	Urban	236,940	Hollingshead and Redlich	1950	Social Class and Mental Illness, 1958	0·7	—
Japan	Hachijo Island	Rural	8,330	Uchimura	1940	—	0·2	2·2
	Komoro	Small-town	5,207	Akimoto	1941	—	2·3	6·3
	Tokyo	Urban	2,712	Tsugarva	1941	—	0·4	14·7
Sweden	Åbo	Rural	8,736	Sjögren	1944	Acta. Psychiat. et Neurol., Suppl, 52, 1948	0·6	—
Denmark	Bornholm	Rural	45,930	Strongren	1935		0·2	2·8
Germany	Thuringia	Rural	37,561	Brugger	1929	Z. ges. Neurol. Psychiat., 133, 1931, 352	0·5	9·3
	Bavaria	Rural	8,628	Brugger	1930–1	Z. ges. Neurol. Psychiat., 145, 1933, 516	0·6	10·9
China	Formosa	Rural, small town and Urban	19,931	Lin	1946–8	Psychiatry, 16, 1953, 313	0·3	10·7
Britain	S. Scotland	Small town and Rural	56,231	Mayer-Gross	1947	Eugenics Rev., 40, 1948, 3	6·0	—
	N. Scotland	Rural	1,701	Primrose	1959	Psychological Illness, 1962	4·7	53·3
Norway	North Coast	Rural	1,325	Bremer	1940–4	Acta Psychiat. et Neurol., suppl. 62, 1951	2·3	25·2

Source. Primrose (1962), pp. 34–5.
* A standardization technique to take account of the differing proportions of old people in the population. The rates are calculated on the basis of the aged group 60–100 years: see Reid (1960); cf. Lin's (1953) 'corrected expectancy' method.

Table 11.2

Expectation of psychoses with cerebral arteriosclerosis
per 10,000 population at given ages in New York State
1920, 1930 and 1940

Age	1920		1930		1940	
	men	*women*	*men*	*women*	*men*	*women*
0	51·2	37·4	113·9	95·4	191·6	186·3
60	83·2	49·7	172·6	119·8	262·9	226·1
65	75·3	41·6	168·6	111·5	256·6	210·5
70	56·3	34·8	157·3	97·0	234·3	184·7
75	44·9	28·6	135·2	82·6	206·0	154·2
80	33·9	18·0	103·5	59·9	160·5	105·6
85	26·7	13·7	68·8	37·9	129·7	77·8
90	28·6	12·6	40·1	21·7	125·0	50·1
95	—	—	—	—	129·3	28·4

Source. Malzberg (1945), p. 130.

the susceptible age groups today are probably not selected as
vigorously as were the corresponding age groups of an earlier
generation' (Malzberg, 1945, p. 130).

Nevertheless, even in recent English experience such variations
result from different investigations of the community incidence of
senile psychoses as to make numerical conclusions very hazardous
to draw. Roth and Kay, examining a sample of 297 persons aged
sixty-five and over in Newcastle upon Tyne in 1960–61, estimated
(Table 11.3) that senile psychosis was present in the case of 3 per
cent of the women, though virtually absent among the men, while
arteriosclerotic psychosis afflicted 5 per cent of the men and 1 per
cent of the women. Only slightly over two-thirds of both the men
and the women were regarded as being free of any kind of psychiatric
disorder.[1] Moreover, if *mild* forms of senile and arteriosclerotic
dementia were included together with other types of organic brain
syndrome, the figures would be higher still. Thus, Kay, Beamish
and Roth, in a further report on the on-going study of psychiatric
disorder in old age in Newcastle upon Tyne, judged (Table 11.4)
that, in addition to the figures already quoted, another $2\frac{1}{2}$ per cent
of men and 3 per cent of women suffered from a mild degree of
senile dementia, another $3\frac{1}{2}$ per cent of men (though no women)
exhibited mild arteriosclerotic dementia, and another 1 per cent of
men and $2\frac{1}{2}$ per cent of women demonstrated either severe or mild

Table 11.3

Incidence of psychiatric disorder among people aged
sixty-five or over in Newcastle upon Tyne

Diagnosis	Men %	Women %	Both sexes %
Senile psychosis	0	3	2
Arteriosclerotic psychosis	5	1	3
Manic – depressive	1	4	3
Paranoia or schizophrenia*	1	2	1
Neuroses†	18	16	17
Other disorder‡	5	4	4
No psychiatric disorder	70	70	70
TOTAL	100	100	100
Number			297

Source. Roth and Kay (1962).

* Refers to individuals who were markedly suspicious or deluded and withdrawn to an abnormal or at any rate unusual degree.

† Including the neurotic type of affective disorder, or predominantly anxious or phobic neuroses, but no case of hysteria or obsessive-compulsive neuroses was found.

‡ Including cases with toxic-confusional states associated with advanced physical illness.

stages of other kinds of organic brain syndrome. On this basis some 12 per cent of the men and 9 per cent of the women revealed the presence of some form of organic brain syndrome at varying stages of severity.

A national survey, however, carried out at the same time into the incidence of mental illness known to general practitioners among persons over sixty-five in Great Britain offers a very different picture. Extrapolating from figures produced by Watts, Cawte and Kuenssberg, it appears (Table 11.5) that only about ⅓ per cent of elderly men and ½ per cent of elderly women living in private households are known by their doctors to display symptoms of senile dementia. Furthermore, this was the commonest psychiatric disorder among their elderly patients known to general practitioners, slightly commoner even than depression.

Two problems need attention here. One is the conceptual difficulty of definition. The other is the technical question of reconciling divergent data. Concerning the former, Kay, Beamish and Roth have described the problem thus:

Difficulties in demarcation arise particularly when mild organic syndromes have to be distinguished from the normal mental

Table 11.4

Incidence of organic brain syndromes among persons
aged sixty-five and over living at home in Newcastle
upon Tyne

Organic brain syndromes*	Men %		Women %		Both sexes %	
Senile dementia: severe	0		2·1		1·3	
mild	2·6		3·1		2·9	
Arteriosclerotic dementia:						
severe	5·2		1·0		2·6	
mild	3·5		0		1·3	
Other organic brain syndromes:						
severe	0·9		1·0		1·0	
mild	0		1·5		1·0	
All organic brain syndromes:						
severe	6·1 ⎱	12·2	4·1 ⎱	8·8	4·9 ⎱	10·0
mild	6·1 ⎰	± 3·0	4·6 ⎰	± 2·0	5·2 ⎰	± 1·7
No organic brain syndrome	87·8		91·2		90·0	
TOTAL	100		100		100	
Number	115		194		309	

Source. Kay *et al.* (1964) Table 11. The symbol ± indicates the standard error.

* It is also noted (p. 148) that 'the clinical picture in the cases with severe mental deterioration was similar to that found among senile dements admitted to mental hospitals, i.e. there was evidence of disorganization of the personality and of failure in the common activities of everyday life. In the mild cases, these features were absent and the diagnosis rested on a clinical judgment, that the degree of deterioration exceeded that to be expected in a person of the subject's chronological age. The diagnosis was assisted by the use of a simple memory and information test' (as related by Roth and Hopkins, 1953).

changes of ageing, when anxiety and depression have to be evaluated in a chronically anxious and worrying person, or when mild and transient symptoms have arisen in response to some environmental or physical change. Our impression was that if specialist psychiatric treatment had been offered, it would have been considered unnecessary by many subjects. . . . [Secondly] the normal role of the aged person in the community is ill-defined. Several of the criteria of mental illness which are of help in arriving at a psychiatric formulation in the younger groups are no longer appropriate. Old people have usually retired, so that regular employment cannot be regarded as a criterion of health, and in the social sphere also no definite role seems to be expected of them. Nor can the pattern of sexual adjustment any longer provide useful information about their mental health. Thus

Community care: policies for integration

Table 11.5

Incidence of mental illness known to GPs in persons over sixty-five in Great Britain 1961-62, by sex

Mental illness	Men %	Women %	Both sexes %
Senile dementia	0·34	0·48	0·43
Manic-depressive depression	0·30	0·47	0·41 ⎫ 0·44
Manic-depression mania	0·02	0·03	0·03 ⎭
Schizophrenia without paranoid ideas	0·02	0·04	0·03
Schizophrenia with paranoid features	0·03	0·06	0·05
Anxiety states	0·07	0·17	0·13
Acute confusional states	0·05	0·04	0·05
Others	0·15	0·20	0·18
No mental illness	99·02	98·51	98·69
TOTAL	100·00	100·00	100·00
Number*	45,259	72,726	117,984

Source. Deduced from Watts, et al. (1964).

* These numbers were calculated as follows: the survey quoted drew on the experience of 261 practices in Great Britain between 1 November 1961 and 31 October 1962 and included a total of 1,001,720 persons at risk. This constitutes 1·9533 per cent of the population of Great Britain at the 1961 census (51,283,892). This fraction was then applied to the total male and female population in Great Britain aged sixty-five and over (respectively 2,317,061 and 3,728,344) at that date to provide a frame for the raw figures of the mentally ill in the table quoted.

diagnosis often has to depend on the subject's own account of his feelings and symptoms, and the disabilities attributed to them (Kay et al., 1964, pp. 151-3).

In addition to these already daunting obstacles, there remains the theoretical impasse that if the predominantly social aetiology expounded in Chapter 8 – that manifestations of 'confusion' are causally related to the institutional dynamics of segregation, isolation and powerlessness – is correct, then such behaviour is sui generis and its exact replication outside institutional boundaries should not be anticipated.

Quite apart from this analytic imponderable, there remains the technical problem of apparent data inconsistency. Reference has already been made to the prevalence rate for all types of 'severe brain syndrome' of 48·5 per 1,000 persons over sixty-five as estimated by Kay, Beamish and Roth in Newcastle which, if reproduced nationally, would provide a total of 300,700 elderly thus afflicted in

Britain (see p. 387). However, in view of the admitted inexplicitness of their criteria, it would be more salutary, at least from the point of view of this study, to adhere to the definitions discussed in Chapter 3 and to proceed thence on the basis of the ratio between institutional and community cases found in the Newcastle sample. In fact the authors of the latter survey discovered fourteen times more old people in private households than in welfare homes with senile or arteriosclerotic dementia on *their* definition, and if this ratio were transposed to those assessed as severely confused in the ordinary homes in this study, then with a proportion of 3·6 per cent in this group it would yield a figure of some 50,400 aged persons living in their own homes in Britain identifiable as 'severely confused' by the criteria of Chapter 3. Moreover, some support for this institution – community ratio is offered from another source. In a study of a sample of 228 persons aged sixty-five and over in Swansea in 1960–61, Parsons, defining dementia on the basis of an excessively high paired-associates learning test score which signified a degree of cognitive impairment such as to render self-care impossible (Table 11.6), found that 4·4 per cent of old people in this group were

Table 11.6

Clinical assessment of memory among a sample of
228 persons aged sixty-five and over in Swansea, 1960–61

Psychiatrist's assessment	Total number of cases	Number completing PALT*	PALT score	
			Mean	Median
Normal memory	146	141	17·4	13·6
Slightly impaired memory	50	48	23·1	18·0
Definitely forgetful	22	19	42·3	38·0
Demented (i.e. cognitive impairment of such a degree as to render self-care impossible)	10	6	81·2	93·0
TOTAL	228	214	—	—

Source. Parsons (1965), p. 44.

* A paired-associates learning test was administered (see Inglis, 1959). The scores represent the total number of times each of three pairs of words had to be presented to the subjects before they had learned them sufficiently well to give three consecutive correct responses for each stimulus word, or until each stimulus word had been presented 31 times. Thus the range of scores lies between 3 and 93, and the lower the score, the greater the learning ability. Cross-validation and cross-cultural validation of this test has been demonstrated (Caird, et al., 1962).

demented. This provides a ratio of 6·3 demented elderly living in private households for every one in hospital, which is very close to the Newcastle ratio of 6·5 with severe brain syndromes in the community for every one in any type of institution (Table 10.9).

Furthermore, a figure of about 50,000 'severely confused' elderly living in private households, which would represent a national incidence of 0·87 per cent in Britain, is reasonably compatible with two other pieces of evidence. One, a study of the incidence of physical and mental disorder among 200 elderly persons sampled from three general practices in and around Edinburgh in 1961–62, discovered thirty-nine with slight evidence of 'dementia', thirteen with moderate symptoms and three with severe manifestations (Table 11.7) – a rate for severe dementia of 1·5 per cent. Secondly,

Table 11.7

General practitioner knowledge of the incidence of dementia among a sample of 200 persons aged sixty-five and over in Edinburgh, by severity of the condition

Sex	Degree of dementia							
	Slight		Moderate		Severe		Total	
	Known	*Not known*	*Known*	*Not known*	*Known*	*Not Known*	*Known*	*Not known*
Males (N = 91)	2	19	1	5	1	1	4	25
Females (N = 109)	2	16	0	7	1	0	3	23

Source. Williamson *et al.* (1964), Table v.

an attempt was made to measure in one town the incidence of 'confusion' according to the criteria developed in the present study. Assessment of 300 randomly selected persons over eighty in York[2] by unqualified though carefully briefed interviewers yielded only two as definitely satisfying the conditions laid down – a rate of 0·7 per cent. If rates for confusion rise with age, perhaps this rate would have been even lower had a wider parameter embracing all persons over sixty-five been adopted, but this bias is probably countered by the greater likelihood for those of advanced age to be admitted to institutions.

The most precise conclusion which can therefore be reached on the available data concerning the incidence of mental infirmity among the elderly living in the Community is that the proportion displaying marked symptoms is rather less than 1 per cent. If more moderate signs of confusion were included, the Newcastle and Edinburgh surveys suggest that the total might be doubled or quadrupled. But the extreme difficulties of constructing comprehensive yet flexible criteria of the condition, let alone of applying them accurately in the deceptive context of a necessarily brief visit, as well as the problem of making valid comparisons between surveys based on differing premises and approaches, preclude closer refinement. The picture can, however, be rounded out in a few further respects. Firstly, the data confirms the well-recognized sex difference whereby women are twice as likely to suffer from senile dementia and men almost nine times more likely to exhibit arteriosclerotic symptoms (Table 11.4). Secondly, though more old people with marked confusion are to be found in private households than in all types of institution combined, the condition of the former was equally as severe as that of the latter. Roth and his colleagues judged that 'with regard to the severity of illness, patients living at home with severe brain syndromes were, in general, as severely ill as those under [institutional] care; but most of the severe and active cases of functional psychosis were found in hospital' (Kay *et al.*, 1964, p. 151). Thirdly, a substantial proportion of old people in the community even with severe dementia were not known by their doctors to be afflicted with the condition. The Edinburgh survey found that thirty-five out of thirty-nine old people with slight symptoms, twelve out of thirteen with moderate signs of this state and even one of the three severely affected (Table 11.7) did not have their condition recognized by their general practitioners. Parsons, in his intensive study of the physical and mental state of a similarly sized sample of the elderly population in Swansea, discovered that of the ten assessed as dements six were identified as having this diagnosis by their doctors, though two were not,[3] while in forty-six practices in Greater London embracing a total of 15,000 people the patient consulting rates for dementia per 1,000 at risk over the age of fifteen were only 1·2 for men and 1·6 for women (Shepherd *et al.*, 1964). Despite the very small numbers involved in the Edinburgh and Swansea surveys, some confirmation of the finding that a third or a quarter of cases of severe dementia were unknown to the general practitioners concerned is supplied by the discovery in a national investigation that only slightly over two-thirds of the elderly in the average general practice had been seen by the doctor in the last year.[4] Before the implications of this fact for community care are examined, we must first briefly review the data that exists concerning the social circumstances of this group of elderly mentally infirm in the community numbering at least 50,000.

Social and medical circumstances of the elderly mentally infirm living in private households

By far the most comprehensive social, familial, medical and environmental data concerning old people with 'organic brain syndromes' living in private households comes again from the Newcastle research programme. Comparing a small group of twenty-nine elderly identified on psychiatric criteria as 'organic' with a sample of 166 'normal' old people, Kay, Beamish and Roth found that the former were likely to be older (with a mean age for men of 75·9 years and for women 77·7, as against 71·6 and 72·1 respectively) and to be more isolated, though the data about civil state was conflicting (Kay *et al.*, 1964). Though three-quarters of the women with organic syndromes were widowed, compared with only half the control group, and very few (6 per cent) married, compared with a third of the 'normals', the position was almost exactly reversed among the men. Additional evidence about the relationship between mental infirmity and widowhood is also equivocal. Thus Agate noted an 'excessively high frequency of dementia amongst widowed persons'[5] and Trier (1966) found that 'organics' were significantly ($p < ·01$) more likely to be widowed than those with 'psychogenic' conditions.[6] On the other hand the figures produced by Stein and Susser for first-time referral rates of old people with diagnoses of organic and senile dementia (Table 11.8) indicated a greater proneness to dementia among the unmarried (except for women with organic dementia) (Stein and Susser, 1969).[7]

Domestically, the Newcastle study found that whilst men with organic disorders did not live alone, women were nearly twice as likely to be in this position if they exhibited an organic condition. This held true despite the fact that women as well as men in this latter category had larger families than their 'normal' counterparts in the control group. Furthermore, those with organic syndromes were significantly more likely to enjoy both restricted and decreasing

Table 11.8

Average annual rate of first-time referrals of persons with
diagnoses of organic and senile dementia per 100,000
population of Salford for the period 1959–63 by marital
status

Diagnosis	Sex	Marital Status		
		Single	Married	Widowed
Organic dementia	men	53	12	27
	women	17	15	39
Senile dementia	men	33	16	26
	women	57	34	49

Source. Stein and Susser (1969), Table 11.

daily contacts, to participate in no club membership, to have had no
holiday in the past year and to pursue no active hobby. They were
also more likely to have been unemployed for over five years and to
have a low income (less than £5 a week in 1961). Amenities in their
homes were significantly poorer and their homes were more
neglected.

The relationship between senile psychoses and domestic isolation
has been amply confirmed elsewhere. In his Swansea study Parsons
found that the main factors associated with cognitive impairment
were not only ageing itself (in excess of seventy-five years) and
peripheral arteriosclerosis (independent of age), but also residential
isolation. Conversely, the one social characteristic correlated with
lower paired – associates learning test scores was residence in multi-
generational households,[8] which seemed to imply that the stimulation of living with others might prevent, or at least postpone,
mental deterioration. In a survey carried out in Syracuse, New
York, Gruenberg discovered that areas with high institutional
admission rates due to senile or arteriosclerotic psychoses were
located near the centre of the town where most houses had been
isolated into a large number of small individual dwellings and where
a high proportion of inhabitants were living alone (Gruenberg,
1954).

Indeed, so strong was the connection between isolation and
psychosis in old age among a group of seventy-two elderly patients
subject to psychiatric referral over a three-year period (1961–64)
in Nottingham that Macmillan and Shaw (1966) postulated the

existence of a syndrome of senile breakdown. For of these persons who had been found living in filthy or verminous conditions, both in their persons and their surroundings, five-sevenths were living alone, and many of these were socially isolated. Slightly more than half were judged to be psychotic and of these almost two-thirds were diagnosed as suffering from senile dementia.[9] Half were widowed women, with a median age of seventy-eight, and a personality pattern characterized by an independent-minded, quarrelsome and domineering history was frequently reflected in a gradually developing rejection of the community and a resentment of any outside interference, even to the extent of permanently curtaining or papering the windows. In the case of the psychotics the condition seemed to have been precipitated especially by a rupture of the social contact with a younger supporting relative as the result of a quarrel. Accommodation was generally of low quality; half lived in old housing with a lack of hot water, old-fashioned grates and sometimes even a lack of electricity. The physical condition of the psychotic group was also poor: many had multiple disabilities especially a general frailty with or without anaemia and only 5 per cent were judged healthy. Cardiovascular degeneration was found in twenty cases and chronic bronchitis in five. Almost a third were known to be heavy drinkers though it was unclear whether alcoholism had preceded the breakdown or whether both had a common cause.[10] Ten were severely deaf, which exacerbated their isolation, and seven had poor vision or blindness. Nevertheless, more than half of the total sample were fully mobile and a further fifth could move freely about the house. Only 7 per cent were unable to climb stairs, though 15 per cent were severely immobilized, usually through heart failure or arthritis.

Further evidence seems to suggest that both personal isolation and social deprivation may be intensified in a large urban agglomeration. From a comparison of 200 cases selected from two general practices in Edinburgh and from one in the surrounding area, Williamson and his medical colleagues concluded that 'among the city patients with dementia,[11] more than two-thirds had some degree of social deprivation, and must therefore be regarded as being in a potentially dangerous predicament.[12] It is significant that none of the cases of dementia in the small town practice had social deprivation.' For only one person in the latter sample of fifty-two was found to be living in bad housing, compared to nearly a third of the 148 in the two city practices. In terms of financial need, which was taken to include special dietary requirements, exceptional laundry bills and the demand for extra heating – all related to medical factors – a fifth of those in the Edinburgh practices were assessed as being 'in need', in contrast to only 2 per cent in the outlying mining town. Similarly, about a third of the city patients were estimated to be deprived of sufficient human contact,[13] in comparison with only a tenth of the small town sample. The vulnerability of the former group was most dramatically illustrated by the one instance uncovered of a person subject to severe dementia which was nevertheless unknown to the doctor:

> He was aged eighty and had been bedridden at home for nine months, and he suffered from aortic incompetence, Paget's disease, neglect and subnutrition, and was frequently incontinent. He lived in a miserable old tenement with his son who was out at work all day. He had consulted his doctor twenty-two months previously when he was still mobile.

How far is the tendency for mental infirmity to be associated with social isolation influenced by social class differences? Little, if any, evidence is as yet available in Britain to answer this question. A hypothesis is, however, suggested by an American study of the social class incidence of psychosis which found that a significantly higher rate of hospitalized psychosis prevailed in a lower-middle-class community investigation than in an upper-middle or upper-class area (Kaplan *et al.*, 1956). Since this was associated with a significantly higher incidence of *non*-hospitalized psychosis in the latter, the authors theorized that the higher the socio-economic class, the greater might be the resistance to hospitalization for mentally ill family members. On this evidence it might be surmised that the elderly mentally infirm living in private households were both disproportionately of higher class status[14] and also to a large extent in regular and protective contact with other members of the family. No corroboration, however, exists for this view, and indeed it is somewhat at variance with data earlier presented here. All that can be said is that the social class distribution of one group of fifty old people with 'persistent senile confusion'[15] deviated from the national pattern chiefly in the disproportionately large group drawn from semi-skilled manual backgrounds balanced by the relatively smaller proportion drawn from lower professional/managerial levels (Table 11.9).

Table 11.9

Comparison between old people with persistent senile
confusion and the national population of old people by
social class

Social class (RG classifications)	(1) *Fifty old people with persistent senile confusion* (%)	(2) *All persons aged sixty-five and over in Britain, 1961* (%)
I	0	3
II	12	21
III	42	39
IV	36	25
V	10	13
TOTAL	100	101
Number	50	2,573,590

Sources. (1) Cosin (1957), p. 197. (2) Registrar General's Office, derived from the 1961 census for England and Wales, *Occupation Tables*, Table 20, p. 125; and for Scotland, vol. 6, *Occupation, Industry and Workplace*, Part I, *Occupation Tables*, Table 20, p. 120.

Family history and personality trends do not so far appear to yield much insight into the aetiology of senile confusion. According to the Newcastle survey, old people with 'organic' brain disorder were slightly less likely than their 'normal' counterparts to be members of a family containing mentally ill persons, though slightly more likely themselves to have been subject to mental illness. They were also characterized by lower sociability, narrower interests, a greater tendency to moodiness and a rather more marked concern about their health, though in no case were the differences between them and the normal control group particularly dramatic. On the point of attitudes, they were also to a significant extent more likely to express feelings of 'loneliness', 'self-pity', 'dissatisfaction' and 'poor health' (Kay *et al.*, 1964, pp. 672–3, Tables VI–VIII). More positive evidence of personality deviations was elicited by Post in a study of seventy-nine persons aged over sixty admitted to a mental hospital in Edinburgh with a diagnosis of senile or arteriosclerotic dementia over the period 1937–43. He found not only that no more than three-eighths exhibited a normal personality and satisfactory adjustment (Table 11.10), but also that there existed a 'strikingly

Table 11.10

Incidence of abnormalities in the previous personality of
seventy-nine persons with senile and arteriosclerotic
psychosis

Diagnosis	*Well-balanced personality*	*Some psychopathic traits present*	*Severe abnormalities of personality*	*Total cases*
Senile dementia with prominent psychotic symptoms*	5	7	8	20
Arteriosclerotic dementia with prominent psychotic symptoms*	3	5	8	16
Simple senile dementia	13	6	5	24
Simple arteriosclerotic dementia	9	4	6	19
TOTAL	30	22	27	79

Source. Post (1944), Table x.
* Especially paranoid delusions and affective disorders, mostly in a depressive direction.

high incidence of so-called "obsessional" trends, rigid outlook, obstinacy, narrowness of interests, over-conscientiousness and bigotry; many of the patients also had shown poor adaptability to social surroundings.' Whether these characteristics, however, were cause or effect phenomena is unclear. Later work in which Post was also involved concerning fifty old people admitted to a geriatric unit in Oxford presenting with 'persistent senile confusion' did confirm, nevertheless, that only eleven had possessed 'outgoing personalities' and that the build-up of the confusional state was usually lengthy: in 47 per cent of cases the duration was longer than two years, including 7 per cent in which it exceeded five years (Cosin *et al.*, 1957, p. 199).

Propping by relatives or friends

The distinguishing characteristics of old people with organic brain syndromes – reduced mobility and self-care capacity, more severe physical disability, feelings of poor health, fewer contacts, dissatisfaction with life, worse hearing and eyesight, poor amenities in the home, lower income and greater loneliness[16] – clearly involve a considerable problem of care for those living in private households. One attempt to measure this by a series of yardsticks graded according to the degree of severity was included in a recent survey of mental illness in general pratice. Among a sample constructed from medical records of 568 persons with senile dementia in 1961–62 it was found that, in the two categories of most severe disablement, two-fifths had been referred for psychiatric help and a similar proportion were assessed as 'helpless, but cared for at home'[17] (Table 11.11). Of the sixty-five persons included below the retirement age, about a third had been off work for a year or more continuously, while a further 8 per cent of the total were subject to continuous drug treatment for a year or more. In addition, 3 per cent overall, though up to 8 per cent among men in Scotland, had caused 'serious social upset' because of their symptoms and behaviour. Only 2 per cent were classified as psychotic persons living at home who could look after themselves without any treatment. Lastly, 3 per cent had at some point suffered from an acute confusional state of brief duration, though they could now be treated at home or at least outside a psychiatric unit.

How then is this burden of care undertaken in the community, bearing in mind, as has been argued (see Chapter 10), that at least as many old people, with at least as severe a degree of mental infirmity, live in private households as in all types of institutions combined? In particular, by whom was support chiefly provided, and what form did assistance normally take?

The concept of 'propping' of a mentally disabled and dependent relative was first chiefly developed by Whelan and Bree in their studies of community care of neurosyphilitics (GPI).[18] In a later detailed monograph Bree defined a 'prop' as: 'Someone who gives more support, and support of a different kind, than is normally given in his (or her) familial relationship to the patient, or than was in fact given in this particular case before the illness.' Also, 'in proportion to his mental weakness the degree of support the patient receives must be correspondingly greater and shown in more unusual ways in order to compensate for what is missing in himself' (Bree, 1960, p. 12). On this basis 61 per cent of the 275 dements with GPI in the sample were propped by their spouse, 6 per cent by parents, 5 per cent by siblings, 4 per cent by their children, 3 per cent by a friend living in the same house (though not known to be cohabiting), 1 per cent by an aunt, 1 per cent by neighbours and 1 per cent by a social agency; in 10 per cent of cases the prop had changed and in a further 9 per cent the position of support was mixed, with another relative or friend, other than the children or siblings, knowing the true situation and also acting as prop.

Using a similar approach in his study of 153 old people admitted to a mental hospital, Connolly (1962) concluded that in nineteen instances no prop had been required, while in twenty-one cases where it

Table 11.11

Degree of severity of mental disablement among a sample of 568 persons with senile dementia in Great Britain, 1961–62

Degree of severity (in descending order)*	England and Wales		Scotland		Total
	Men (%)	Women (%)	Men (%)	Women (%)	(%)
1. Persons referred to psychiatrist:					
incidence†	10 ⎫ 41	14 ⎫ 38	15 ⎫ 43	21 ⎫ 44	14 ⎫ 40
prevalence†	31 ⎭	24 ⎭	28 ⎭	23 ⎭	26 ⎭
2. Persons who were helpless but cared for at home	43	41	30	37	40
3. Persons off work for a year or more continuously‡	(6)	(4)	(7)	(3)	(4)
4. Persons who had to be maintained for a year or more on continuous drug treatment	6	8	5	12	8
5. Persons who had caused serious social upset because of psychiatric illness	2	4	8	1	3
6. Psychotic persons living at home who could look after themselves without any treatment	0	4	5	0	2
7. Persons who suffered from an acute confusional state which had lasted for 24 hours or more, but were treated at home or in a non-psychiatric hospital§	(2)	(3)	(3)	(3)	(3)
TOTAL	100	102	101	100	100
Number	125	279	61	103	568

Source. Extrapolated from Watts *et al.* (1964).

* Each person was placed in one category only, namely the highest category applicable to his case, from group 1 to group 7.

† The 'incidence' is the number of new cases occurring in a known population at risk in the course of the survey year, while the 'prevalence' is the number of persons ill at one point in time, in this instance when the survey began, on 1 Nov. 1961.

‡ Of the total 568 persons with senile dementia, 65 were aged less than sixty-five years.

§ This group differs from the others in being a syndrome and not explicitly definable in terms of its social implications.

was considered necessary it had not been available. Of the remainder, 88 per cent were propped by an individual and 12 per cent by a group of persons. Within the former category 25 per cent were supported by their wife and 12 per cent by their husband, while in sharp contrast to Bree's findings 33 per cent were propped by a daughter, though only 4 per cent by a son. A further 9 per cent were supported by a sister, 5 per cent by a niece, 3 per cent by a neighbour, 2 per cent by a sister-in-law, together with 1 per cent each by a step-daughter, grand-daughter, daughter-in-law, home help, female friend and female lodger. Where support was provided on a group basis, four persons were propped by two daughters, two by three daughters, two by two sons, and one each by various other combinations of relatives.[19] In these latter cases it was a frequent arrangement, especially where the person concerned was demented, for relatives to operate a rota system whereby care was regularly provided in each home for delimited periods of six to twelve weeks.

What was the nature of these propping relationships? In particular, what were the fundamental motivations of the prop, and how far did these attitudes change over the years? Again, the most systematic endeavour to explore such problems has been made by Bree. Thus she found that in 79 per cent of cases the basic drive behind propping was affection, in 9 per cent of cases it was loyalty, in 2 per cent pride, in 6 per cent emotional dependence (whether guilt, loneliness, or financial dependence, etc.), and in 4 per cent the motive was mixed. To a remarkable extent these attitudes were preserved over the long term. In almost three-quarters of cases (73 per cent) no change was registered in the basic motivation over periods of time ranging from five to fifteen years. In 8 per cent of relationships, however, the prop's initial concern had been replaced by indifference or even intolerance, in $2\frac{1}{2}$ per cent of instances love had become formalized into mere loyalty, and in 3 per cent of cases the position had been reached where further deterioration had become the last straw. In a further 4 per cent of cases the relative had himself or herself noticeably deteriorated in health.[20] Another indication of the prop's attitude lay in whether or not a façade was adopted to conceal the mental nature of the old person's disability. Of the 252 instances where this could be determined, no façade was discernible in almost two-thirds of the cases (62 per cent), while in exactly a quarter the facts were deliberately covered up, and in the remaining 13 per cent of cases the pretence was judged to be unconscious and designed to conceal the deep-seated tension arising from an acceptance of the truth. In half of these last instances the relatives attributed the symptoms of dementia to an accompanying physical handicap. Furthermore, in the twenty-one instances where the old person died in the course of this longitudinal study, the most common reaction of the prop (nine cases) was a feeling of 'loss of a permanent baby', while in three cases the main response was one of relief and in a further four cases a mixture of the two attitudes. In five instances the result was the restoration of the original partner in the prop's memory. Such details yield interesting insights into the motivations and emotions of supporting relatives, though of course the difference between senile psychosis and neurosyphilis necessarily inhibits any straightforward analogies.[21]

How many old people, however, with senile psychotic symptoms living in private households were deprived of regular social contact and the accompanying support? And how did such persons 'make out'? Of the seventy-two old people thoroughly investigated by Macmillan and Shaw in positing a breakdown syndrome, while three men and eighteen women had 'more or less effective visiting by members of their family', only two men and six women 'had no support or social contacts of any value' (Macmillan and Shaw, 1966). Yet Connolly, in examining the social circumstances of forty-two elderly persons who had been living alone, out of a total of 153 old people consecutively admitted to a mental hospital in 1960–61, found that without exception all with acute confusion, late paraphrenia, affective psychosis and senile or arteriosclerotic psychosis were technically 'isolated'[22] (Table 11.12). Indeed, evidence has abundantly accumulated in related fields that not only the absence or severance of close social contact, but even the degree of consanguineal propinquity of any relative in regular contact, is directly associated with the social consequences for the person concerned.[23]

Direct case histories of old people in a dementing condition, where such data exists in the literature, illustrate both the hazardous nature of the supportive framework in some instances as well as the dedication of close relatives, especially children, in others. Examples of the former demonstrate particularly the importance of a conscientious neighbour, whilst also inevitably implying the shakiness of unique reliance on the continuation of such aid or on its substitution in emergency:

438

Table 11.12

**Average social contacts per week of 42 elderly patients
living alone before admission to mental hospital**

Diagnosis	Number of patients	Average social contacts per week
Acute confusion	8	14
Late paraphrenia	7	15
Affective psychosis	10	18
Senile psychosis	9	20
Arteriosclerotic psychosis	6	21
Various	2	31

Source. J. Connolly, 'The social and medical circumstances of old people admitted to a psychiatric hospital', *loc. cit.*, p. 99.

Miss M, aged eighty-eight, a former seamstress, with a diagnosis of myxoedematous insanity and senile dementia with paranoid traits. Hospital stay of seven months, lives alone at the top of a tenement house and refuses to enter a welfare home. Now marooned in her flat as she cannot manage the three flights of steep winding stone stairs. At the time of the follow-up, she was kept going by daily visits from the district nurse, frequent supportive visits by the psychiatric social worker, fortnightly health visitor supervision and the good offices of an elderly neighbour who does her shopping and collects her pension and national assistance. Should this neighbour fall ill or decide not to continue, the whole precarious structure of the patient's independence would collapse (Woodside, 1965b).

Sometimes support might be shared in a rather arbitrary, unsystematic manner between neighbour and relative. An interviewer in a survey of the social needs of the over-eighties in York, undertaken by J. Bradshaw, 1969–70, reported the following details in one instance:

Mrs C, a former cook now aged eighty-two, lives alone, having been widowed in the last war, in an unfurnished privately rented flat. Her conversation centres incessantly round her health and her conviction that the neighbours want to get rid of her. All her rambling answers are pulled round to complaining about this point. Though the neighbours are rather noisy and the accommodation contains no fixed bath, piped hot water or inside WC,

439

she nevertheless shows great affection for the landlord. She receives neither mobile meals nor home help assistance, but her daughter, who lives not far away, pops in now and then, sometimes helping with her feet or having fish and chips sent round, while a visitor occasionally calls from the social club. Furthermore, despite her hostility to her neighbours, one of them is ready to be contacted, will lend her telephone when necessary and would assist in general if required.

Occasionally propping appeared to be balanced exclusively between certain of the medical and welfare services:

Miss W, aged eighty-seven, was reported as frequently wandering and had on one occasion been found far from her home dressed only in her nightgown. She came home very late and walked about her room through the night; sometimes she went repeatedly up and down the stairs, banged doors, and turned on gas taps. Apparently of very friendly disposition, the old lady engaged strangers in conversation. The other occupants of the house considered that she had lost weight over the previous twelve months. It was known that her teeth had deteriorated, but the old lady always failed to attend her dental appointments when these had been arranged for her.

A five-year history of disturbed behaviour was obtained from her doctor. He had visited regularly, but had never managed to persuade the patient to enter a hospital or residential accommodation for the aged. He had twice called in the mental welfare officer to interview her, but no action could be taken to remove her for observation. Prior to the second of these occasions, the doctor arranged for a domiciliary visit by a psychiatrist, who submitted a report on the patient to the mental welfare officer for his consideration. The psychiatrist considered that she had a progressive mental illness which would cause her to be an increasing danger to herself and the other tenants in the house. He recommended admission to an observation ward, and thought that she would be better looked after in hospital. The case was well known to the health visitor, who subsequently referred it to the local health authority.

The patient lived in a top flat on her own. She spoke of a sister living downstairs; in fact her sister had fallen ill the previous year and was in hospital. The patient was friendly and talkative, having a sharp memory for the details of distant events, but was obviously forgetful and disorientated as to the time and date of recent happenings. When questioned about wandering, the old lady said she was waiting to meet her sister. Offers to arrange admission to a home were refused.

The mental welfare officer was asked to call, and he arranged for the patient's removal to an observation ward; later she was certified and admitted to a mental hospital, where she died a few weeks later (Lowry, 1959, Case 2).

Apart from the vaguely unpremeditated and indeterminate structure of the support network, the available case histories also clearly reveal, even at advanced stages of confusion, the committed devotion of near relatives. It might be a spouse:

Mrs G, aged seventy-four, with a diagnosis of arteriosclerotic dementia, is looked after, following a hospital stay of three weeks, by her seventy-seven-year-old husband, a retired transport inspector, in their small flat up two flights of stairs. She needs help with dressing and the toilet, has difficulty in walking, and is unable to carry out any household duties. At her interview she answered questions in a vague rambling manner, but could not sustain a conversation. Mr G employs a woman to come in for two hours six mornings a week and does all the shopping himself. He has had to give up all his former social activities as he can never leave the patient alone (Woodside, 1965b).

Or it might be the children:

Mrs F, aged eighty-two, and widowed now thirty-four years, lives alone in an unfurnished privately rented house and, according to her daughter, has been mentally confused for the past six years.[24] She is effectively housebound, having difficulty even with assistance in walking indoors, climbing stairs and washing, bathing and dressing. Moreover, the housing amenities are poor, since they involve a ducket toilet and a lack of piped hot water and fixed bath. The children, however, were unstinting in their attentions. One daughter, the mainstay, comes in each morning and stays till after lunch, while her son visits in the evening and another daughter stays on Thursday nights. In the absence of any home help – 'mother wouldn't like a stranger in the house' – and also of meals on wheels, though her doctor suggested it, the first daughter has done the shopping regularly for five years and also cooks the meals, though the son provides tea. Indeed, her daughter would like her mother to move in with her, but the latter insists on staying in the house where she has lived for more than thirty years, and the children would never put her in a Home.[25]

A burden on family care?

The previous section, in examining what is known of or can be deduced about the care of mentally confused old people living in the community has indicated that the members of some families at least lavished a great deal of unremitting care on their dependent aged relatives. Since a balanced assessment of the possibilities and limitations of this familial type of care is so pivotal to social policy-making in this area, we must take this question further and systematically explore the whole range of data that would seem to bear on this important and perhaps emotive issue.

Several recent attempts have been made to assess the effects on family life of caring for persons in various dependent categories in the community[26] and to construct a grid of consequentially circumscribed or modified activities.[27] With regard to the impact of the mentally confused aged on those supporting them in private households, the relevant data is limited to the conclusions of three empirical surveys.

Hamilton and Hoenig, firstly, who investigated a representative sample of psychiatric patients over the age of sixty who had been incepted for the first time into the extra-mural psychiatric services of Manchester Regional Hospital Board, discovered that a more severe burden was felt by relatives concerning the over-sixties than in regard to other age groups of psychiatric patients. A fifth complained of a severe subjective burden, while of the remainder almost two-fifths (38 per cent) alleged no burden and another two-fifths (41 per cent) only some burden (Hamilton and Hoenig, 1966). Yet in no case were the relatives anxious to have the patient admitted to mental hospital, despite the fact that this age-group showed themselves to be very ill with a high degree of mental and physical morbidity throughout the four-year follow-up period. Perhaps even more surprisingly, only 4 per cent of the families felt (or admitted to feeling) that more could have been done for the patient by the social services (Hoenig and Hamilton, 1967b, p. 612).

Further light on factors affecting family reaction was shed by another carefully measured survey, again undertaken by Hoenig and Hamilton, comparing responses to psychiatric services based on a general hospital unit (Burnley) with reactions to a traditional mental hospital (Macclesfield). By relating assessments of subjective and objective burden, they discovered that of those households which carried any marked objective burden, fully a third in the area with general hospital psychiatric services recorded no subjective sense of hardship, compared to only an eighth (13 per cent) in the area more traditionally served. Secondly, of those households assessed as bearing no objective burden or only occasionally so, more than half (54 per cent) in the latter area complained of some subjective hardship, even sometimes of a severe kind, compared to none at all in the former district.

The greater efficacy of more community-oriented welfare policies in preventing potential family stress has not been confirmed so positively elsewhere – though not clearly disconfirmed either. Another study comparing family reactions to a framework of psychiatric services emphasizing community care (Chichester) with those to hospital-based services (Salisbury) concluded cautiously:

> The families of all patients over sixty-five . . . were not adversely affected to a significantly greater extent in the community care service after two years although there was an unmistakable trend in that direction (Grad and Sainsbury, 1968).

An earlier gloss on this finding by the same authors offered, however, a rather paradoxical conclusion:

> Families of patients who had more socially serious symptoms, nocturnal restlessness and dangerous, suicidal or peculiar behaviour, tended to be equally relieved in both services, but when the patient's behaviour was less socially conspicuous, families were relieved more in Salisbury. The families of patients with senile psychosis and the families of depressed patients also had their burden reduced more in Salisbury (Grad and Sainsbury, 1966).

A great deal more information is, of course, needed to supplement the picture. What types of household were particularly prone to stress from caring for a dependent member who might be difficult to manage? What kind of burdens were likely to prove too great for most, or at least some families and which could be more readily borne? How far did certain kinds of social service support ameliorate a burden that might otherwise have proved intolerable? On important questions such as the last no precise information is available, and on others such as the first data is derivable only by analogy. For a study of the effect on families of caring for a member with general paralysis of the insane revealed plainly that in the presence of children an adverse effect was much more likely (in 70% of cases) to be created, while in the absence of children the incidence of burden was diametrically the obverse (an adverse effect in only 30% of cases), and this applied for both male and female members who were demented.[28]

Regarding family reaction to particular types of burden, no survey has yet investigated the situation of households specifically with mentally infirm elderly members. Kidd, however, in a study of the main reasons for the admission of 170 old people to hospital, did elicit the fact that whilst in the case of more than half the families no burden[29] had been experienced, in a third of cases the burden had been heavy, to the extent of causing unemployment in a third of these latter instances. The economic hardship of managing the patient at home was nevertheless indicated as the main factor behind the admission in only a fifth to an eighth of cases (C. B. Kidd, 1962, p. 40) and among the old people admitted to psychiatric hospital much the commonest reason given (43 per cent) was that the patient was 'too difficult'. Examples of the meaning of this rather generalized classification were not provided, however, and can only here be illustrated piecemeal. Thus one married woman has described her difficulties caring for her arteriosclerotic father thus:

> The nights were the worst, and my husband had to sleep in a small box room to get any sleep at all. My daughters had to share a room with me, and I slept nearest the door to avoid disturbing them. . . . I might find my father's bed stripped, including the mattress, though he had lost the use of his right hand. Or he might wake and ask for tea at 4 a.m. Or with both legs failing he might fall to the floor, wedged between the wall and the bedstead. . . . The doctor's sedatives only made him livelier still (Kosmyryk, 1967).

In general, however, the precise effect of senile or arteriosclerotic psychosis on family life within private households has been very little documented and a topic urgently requiring careful research.[30] For the loss or decline of mental faculties has certainly been established as peculiarly hard to manage in the home. This was a central finding of a survey of a sample of 253 patients convalescing after a stroke, of whom two-thirds were aged fifty to sixty-nine (though none were over seventy):

> The greatest handicap from the social standpoint after a stroke is undoubtedly in the light of our experience the presence of mental deterioration. This frustrates attempts at physical rehabilitation, making the patient a greater physical burden. It renders the home atmosphere depressing as the patients are usually tearful, irritable or morose, rarely euphoric. But most of all it demands constant vigilance by relatives, by day and night. This interferes with necessary domestic tasks such as shopping, and leads to broken sleep because of patients getting out of bed. It seriously interferes with rest and recreation. Help was given by voluntary organiza- tions in the way of people who would spend some time with the patient when the relative went out, but this was the most difficult problem with which we had to cope (Collins *et al.*, 1960).

Despite these considerable disturbances, the available evidence nevertheless powerfully suggests there is no lack of zeal or deter- mination on the part of the vast majority of families to shoulder the burden, however arduous or sometimes distasteful, in support of handicapped members. An investigation of a sample of 460 old people admitted temporarily to a geriatric unit to give their relatives a rest concluded:

> A tremendous amount of extra laundering, often of a most un- pleasant sort, fell to the relatives. They all insisted on washing the patient's soiled linen by hand themselves, and would not allow anyone else to handle it. . . . Many patients were confused and disoriented, liable to get out of bed and fall, to turn on the gas, or to endanger themselves in other ways – a problem for the housewife where shopping or leisure was concerned. . . . Neigh- bours, friends and other members of the family were sometimes able to help. The person looking after the patient usually managed to go out on only one evening a week. A quarter of them said they never went out at all (Isaacs and Thompson, 1960).

The willingness of families to accept back an aged member after hospital convalescence, or a reluctance to part with them initially for institutional care, has been repeatedly confirmed by research.[31] Thus it was judged, in reviewing the discharge of 1,115 old people from one geriatric unit, that only 1·2 per cent of the relatives 'unreasonably' refused to provide home care (Lowther and Williamson, 1966), though of course the diagnosis of mental confusion in a patient might itself be taken to justify continued retention in hospital.[32]

A further sign of the same attitude derives from the comparative dilatoriness of relatives in calling medical attention to the senile decline of ageing members of the family. Thus Colwell and Post found, for example, that of thirty-three old people with organic mental symptoms admitted to the geriatric unit of Bethlem Royal and Maudsley Hospitals and later discharged, 73 per cent had been deteriorating for at least a year, including 55 per cent for longer than two years (Colwell and Post, 1959). Indeed, some data suggests that the community care of the elderly mentally infirm may actually enhance the climate of family relations. An Oxford study concluded that close, helpful and affectionate family ties were more likely to be found where an elderly member was demented than in the case of mentally healthy controls (Cosin *et al.*, 1957, p. 195). Cosin did however add one reservation: 'I have found that, if these [elderly mentally confused] patients are admitted temporarily for assessment, treatment of any organic disease and rehabilitation, their families are willing to take over their care provided that they are offered support [including] ... day hospital care' (Cosin, 1958, p. 230). How far, therefore, do local health and welfare services provide the range and continuity of care to enable families to maintain responsibility without undue burden for an elderly member who develops signs of mental infirmity? This is the final question we must ask in assessing the current position of community care for mentally confused old people in Britain at the present time.

The extent and adequacy of community care services

OVERALL COVERAGE

The variation in community provision by local authorities for the elderly mentally infirm is confirmed by two independent studies to be wide. One, undertaken by the mental health group of the Society of Medical Officers of Health in 1967–68, found that even the service most commonly provided in part for this category of old people, that of day hospital care, was confined to rather under a third of local authorities in England and Wales (Table 11.13).

Table 11.13

Community services for mentally infirm old people
provided by local authorities and voluntary bodies in
England and Wales, 1967–68

Community service	Local authorities themselves providing service (%)	Voluntary bodies in their area providing service (%)
Day centres	13	1
Day hospitals	31	—
Work centres	8	6
Welfare homes	26	3
Social clubs	12	4
TOTAL	100	100
Number	172	172

Source. G. Wigley, 'Community services for mentally infirm old people', *Lancet*, 1968, ii, 963.

Welfare homes in this survey were found to be available in a quarter of local authority areas, while day centres and social clubs were provided in only an eighth. Work centres were organized by only 8 per cent of local authorities, though this was the facility most commonly provided by voluntary bodies.

The other study, an exploration of different emphases in local authority community mental health policies by Rehin and Martin (1968b), strikingly reveals the very large differences in the day care of senile psychotics in the various towns compared. Thus in Oldham, organic psychotics and those afflicted with a 'senile state' formed 4 per cent of the whole referred population, yet 33 per cent of them received day care (*ibid.*, p. 77, Table 5.3). In Worthing, by contrast, they constituted 10 per cent of the referred population, but only 1 per cent were given day care. Underlying these discrepancies was a marked difference of interpretation as to the function of day care. In Oldham the typical day-patient was a very old woman who had been widowed and now displayed a senile organic psychosis or organic conditions without psychosis. In Worthing, on the other hand, it was a married women in her late middle or early old age suffering from psychotic depression. In Oldham day care was of a long-term nature and was not often employed as a method of caring for early, recoverable cases for whom extramural care was alleged to be most appropriate (*ibid.*, p. 84). For most of the day patients in Oldham began or ended as in-patients and many seemed to have day care as a 'short holiday between admissions'. It was not in fact a genuine alternative to hospitalization.

Rehin and Martin (1968b) also found that in several other respects there were significant differences in community care practices for the elderly mentally infirm between the three areas selected for their study. It was true that in each area the proportion of out-patients who were old people referred with 'organic or senile states' (3 per cent) was smaller than was the case for total referrals for mental health reasons which ranged between 6 per cent, 7 per cent and 11 per cent (p. 89). But the proportion of in-patients with senile states varied markedly by area, between 6 per cent only in Oldham to 11 per cent in east Middlesex and as high as 16 per cent in Worthing (p. 110, Table 6.20). Conversely, the proportion in this diagnostic category who were in-patients also diverged considerably, from about 38 per cent in Worthing to 54 per cent in Oldham and up to 62 per cent in east Middlesex (p. 60). This gives a prima facie impression that Worthing was comparatively successful with its community care policies, but the authors concluded that when the in-patient ratios were converted to index figures,[33] then relative to the overall risk of admission in each of the areas the degree to which elderly persons with organic states were admitted more than might be expected was far higher in Oldham and Worthing than in east Middlesex. This clearly shows that even areas with comparatively low in-patient ratios may not, within their own norms, be successful in treating senile states extramurally.

Quite apart from such differences in function and general approach to the main services, other data reveal marked variations in range of provision and use of particular services, though within the scope of small overall coverage. Reviewing the findings of a national survey, Wigley concluded 'that few community services are specifically provided for the elderly mentally infirm and that their distributon is very uneven. Very few authorities provide comprehensive services complementing community services provided by hospitals' (Wigley, 1968).[34] When asked the number of old people known to be receiving some community service by reason of their mental infirmity, local authorities gave extremely low figures, the highest being Plymouth with an estimate of 1·1 per cent among men and 1·8 per cent among women. However, most of these replies apparently represented merely the numbers of elderly mentally infirm on the current visiting list of the mental welfare officers, and from other evidence it is clear that these ratios vary considerably. Thus, Rehin and Martin (1968b) found that the proportion of persons referred with organic senile state who were referred to mental welfare officers ranged, for men, from 58 per cent in east Middlesex to as low as 14 per cent in Worthing, and for women from 61 per cent in Oldham to 13 per cent in Worthing. Elderly people in this condition composed a part of mental welfare officers' clienteles varying from 22 per cent in Worthing to 13 per cent in Oldham (pp. 117–18, Table 7.1). Clearly such discrepancies in practice may well be replicated elsewhere, and consequently the survey by the Society of Medical Officers of Health cannot be regarded as offering meaningful comparisons between different authorities in terms of the overall scope of services.

DAY CENTRES

The Society's study does, however, together with my own local authority survey,[35] offer some detailed insights into the operation of specific community services in particular places. Day centres were revealed by the former inquiry to be limited to only twenty-two authorities, less than an eighth of the total, and of these a third did not provide day centres exclusively for the elderly mentally infirm, but were prepared to accept them in centres run primarily for mentally ill adults.[36] One variant of this arrangement was the utilization for the confused elderly of a mental health hostel where the residents all went out to work during the day,[37] while in a few cases such were exclusively designed for the elderly mentally infirm under health service powers.[38] In five instances it was found that day centres were run in residential homes, the largest being at Leeds where thirty-five mentally infirm old people were admitted daily to a residential home. Most of the centres were open daily for several hours and provided a meal at midday (e.g. Booth *et al.*, 1963), though some were open only part-time, even for as little in one case as two hours a week (Wigley, 1968).

What is the function of day centres, and what do they achieve?

Several purposes have been claimed for them. They 'avoid any atmosphere of invalidism, and preventive measures can be taken' (Macmillan 1962a, p. 744). Nuffield House at Nottingham, a proto-type of its kind, was reserved for old people with 'some mental disturbance' in three distinct types of situation: where daytime care and attention proved necessary while the responsible relative was out at work;[39] where old people were living alone and deteriorating mentally because of their isolation; and where the home situation was so charged with emotional tension that the old person's future was in jeopardy (Shaw and Macmillan, 1961). The first of these purposes has, however, been challenged by Binks (1968) who, in rejecting the custodial function,[40] has insisted rather that day centres exist 'to help provide a reason for living for the old people themselves which their relatives alone could not give anyway'. Official sources have preferred not to commit themselves: in discussing the rise in the number of centres for the elderly, including the mentally infirm, from 115 in March 1965 to a projected 308 in 1971 and 429 in 1976, the Ministry remarked enigmatically that the increase 'reflects a revision in the light of growing experience of the nature and proper function of a centre properly so-called' (Ministry of Health, 1966, p. 18).

Whatever the unresolved doubts about function, much has been claimed for their achievement. At Nuffield House the main occupations were woodwork, seagrass stool-making and basketry for the men, and sewing and knitting for the women. The more disturbed men made window and car washers with offcuts from chamois leather gloves. A few men took pleasure in gardening in the good weather and a few women enjoyed helping in the kitchen. Though the conditions of those accepted were mostly senile psychosis, senile depression or paranoid states,[41] the conclusion was drawn that 'in some cases [unexpectedly] quite astonishing advances were made in techniques and handicrafts like embroidery and weaving': 'There is a subtle but unmistakable change in many individuals after they have attended for a few weeks. They often appear cleaner and better groomed; the men are shaved, and the women's hair is better cared for.[42] Usually they appear more alert and interested in their companions and their work (Shaw and Macmillan, 1961, p. 138), and elsewhere they assert that day centre care led to 'a more marked improvement in the patient's physical and emotional state and in morale' (Macmillan and Shaw, 1966, pp. 1032–7).

However, it should be added that attempts in an experimental situation to stimulate interest in craftwork and various social activities in occupational therapy sessions among groups of confused elderly have yielded more guarded conclusions:

> Their scores improved regarding activity, social contact and emotional state, but not their intellectual status and skill which remained relatively constant. This supports the widely held assumption that treatment is unlikely to reverse the process of intellectual deterioration, though it may enable patients to function at a better level (Cosin *et al.*, 1958).

DAY HOSPITALS

Though a third of local authorities provided day hospitals, few were specifically reserved for the elderly mentally infirm, and in most of them the numbers of the latter attending were 'quite small' (Wigley, 1968). Usually day hospitals started by the geriatric unit of a general hospital concentrated particularly on physical problems, while those started by psychiatric hospitals largely involved persons with a wide range of mental illness. Their functions, apart from offering social relief and support to patients' families, were basically either to prevent mental breakdown and give appropriate psychiatric treatment without recourse to hospital admission[43] or else to permit the earlier discharge of patients from hospital[44] by providing after-care following a period of in-patient treatment. Clearly the division of function between day hospital and day centre is a fine one, and indeed Brocklehurst, in a review of 180 day hospital patients,[45] considered that 19 per cent would have been more suitably accommodated at a social day centre.[46] The day hospital does of course offer facilities for patients who require more investigation and treatment than is available at a day centre, and also has the advantage of providing services seven days a week where necessary, while day centres close at the weekend. But discussion of their interlocking role must become academic when the two services have developed haphazardly and almost always without adequate consultation between the local authority and hospital services.

OTHER SERVICES

The number of work centres and social clubs provided specifically for the elderly mentally infirm is not known, though the Medical

Officers of Health survey did establish that seven local authorities (4 per cent) had social clubs for this group in their area run by voluntary bodies. Also a few local health authorities made available afternoon clubs for the mentally confused elderly; Bristol, for example, established such a club for twenty-five mentally infirm elderly men and women in 1960. But in general, coverage by other services, such as home visiting, remains completely unknown. All that can be said is that the local authority questionnaire of the present study indicated, as general principles, the greater likelihood that areas with separatist accommodation would also present a wider range of other specialist services, such as day hospitals and psychogeriatric assessment, and that those authorities most in favour of segregation would be least likely to have developed community care services.

If one takes into account, however, the full mosaic of other services required – including those of the home help, district nurse, health visitor, general practitioner, voluntary helpers, good neighbours, mobile meals, subsidized accommodation, home laundry, financial assistance for relatives, and unconsidered aid like daily delivery of bread and milk – a mass of irregularly scattered data suggests a very sizeable pool of unmet need. A follow-up during 1955–57 of thirty-four 'organic psychotics' discharged from psychiatric hospital revealed (Table 11.14) that at least six months'

Table 11.14

Number of months during which a sample of thirty-four elderly (over age sixty) organic psychotics had been ill, following discharge from a psychiatric hospital during 1955, though without receiving psychiatric treatment

Clinical status	Months ill without psychiatric treatment					
	0	<6	6<12	12<18	18<24	Total
Completely symptom-free throughout	2	—	—	—	—	2
Intermittent or continuous mild symptoms	1	1	2	1	—	5
Intermittently disabled	1	—	1	—	—	2
Continuously disabled	14	1	2	4	4	25
TOTAL	18	2	5	5	4	34

Source. Colwell and Post (1959), Table IV.

illness was endured without psychiatric treatment by two out of five with intermittent or continuous mild symptoms and, very disturbingly, by ten out of twenty-five who were continuously disabled.[47] Of the latter group, four had received no treatment for at least eight months. A depth survey of seventy-two old people identified by complete breakdown in standards of personal cleanliness, including twenty-three diagnosed with senile psychosis, demonstrated that the statutory services, especially home nurses and home helps, were in touch with only slightly over half (54 per cent), while also a significant amount of help from neighbours was received by less than a third (29 per cent). Of the third who refused help in any form, 'many were obviously lonely and tried to keep their visitor with them by many devices' (Macmillan and Shaw, 1966).

Most revealing of all, a review of a series of geriatric holiday admissions in 1959 documented the appalling lack even of simple household aids (Isaacs and Thompson, 1960). Of the forty-six old people in the sample, many of whom were confused, a quarter had been cared for for longer than ten years and more than a further third for between five and ten years. Two-sevenths were wholly confined to bed, a third had not been out of the house for a period in excess of five years, and two-thirds needed help in toileting. Yet more than a third of households lacked a bathroom, a third had no running water, and a seventh had no inside lavatory. Over a third of the patients were incontinent of urine and a third of faeces, yet in less than half the households were commodes, bedpans and urinals used.

> The common method of dealing with incontinence in bedfast patients was to tear up old sheets for draw-sheets and for wrapping between the patient's legs. These were washed and used again rather than destroyed. ... We were impressed by how much more could have been done to help their relatives by advice on disposable incontinence pads (which we found in use in only one household), by greater provision of commodes, urinals, rubber sheets and rubber urine bags, all of which are readily available, and by provision of a foul-laundry service (Isaacs and Thompson, 1966).

Only one family enjoyed the services of a local authority home help, though two others had private domestic help. But the authors concluded that 'the home help service could do little to help these households, for the problem was seldom one of home management, but rather of nursing care'.

Further data suggest a substantial extension of community services is required, not only because of the growing demand from old people,[48] but because by supporting families in the care of their mentally infirm elderly members, the impact on the scope for sustaining such persons in the community would be enhanced disproportionately to the extra expenditure. A medical specialist with long geriatric experience has asserted this view without qualification:

> There is no doubt that many old people with a considerable degree of dementia can be maintained in the community; and that even when they also have physical changes such as central arteriosclerosis, quiet myocardial infarction, respiratory infection and pulmonary collapse, or kidney failure. What is important is that the doctor should form a professional appreciation of these factors and deal with them before the social situation collapses; that is, before the family comes to regard the patient as incurable. Once they do this, they will be most unlikely to take him back again even after he has been treated in hospital and found fit to return home (Cosin, 1958, p. 225).

But more is required than merely early spotting of family strains. Transmission of the relevant expertise complementary to the family's existing skills is also crucially required. Commenting on the recovery of elderly patients from strokes, researchers noted that:

> A gratifying feature, and one contrary to the belief sometimes expressed, was the willingness with which relatives accepted the patient home and shouldered the burden of his care when they realized that a plan of rehabilitation and social help had been made. This they did even when it meant the bread-winner giving up his employment and the family accepting a lower standard of life, or when it meant a round-the-clock vigil by the family. When there was reluctance on the part of relatives to accept a patient home, it was usually associated with the fear that they might not be able to provide the degree of skilled care necessary, rather than because of an unwillingness to shoulder their responsibilities. The relatives were greatly helped to overcome this fear by being taught by nursing staff and physiotherapists before

the patient left hospital how to feed or dress him, how to help him out of bed, or how to assist his walking (Collins *et al.*, 1960).

The converse of such a policy of so deliberately involving and actively assisting the family in caring for a handicapped elderly member is that the eventual transfer to hospital or welfare accommodation, if later it does become necessary, may be attended by greater risks. Indeed, the rapid and marked deterioration of many old people soon after admission to psychiatric hospital, has been often noted (e.g. by Macmillan and Shaw, 1966), and despite the overlay of other social influences in these circumstances, it may be argued that over-commiment to domiciliary care may seriously prejudice the chances of later resettlement. However, this is to anticipate the policy issue of the appropriate balance between community and institutional care, and it is to such matters of policy evaluation, having completed the factual review, that we must now at last turn.

NOTES

1. Of the 30 per cent with some identifiable psychiatric disability, two-thirds were regarded as suffering from only minor disorder or less severe psychotic illness (*Report of the Medical Research Council for 1960–61*, HMSO, 1962). Similarly to this 10 per cent with severe disorder, Gruenberg, in an American study undertaken in 1952 found that among 1,592 old people interviewed 100 (or 6·3 per cent) had a psychosis of such a degree that they could not care for themselves or were in danger (Gruenberg, 1954).

2. The assessments required were specially added to a survey investigating the social needs of the over-eighties organized by J. Bradshaw, 1969.

3. In the remaining two cases no reply was received from the doctor concerned (Parsons, 1965).

4. Shanas *et al.* (1968) p. 87, Table IV/II reveals that 29 per cent of old people in Britain had not seen their doctor for more than a year, or had never seen him, the proportion being slightly higher for women (32 per cent) than for men (28 per cent).

5. See Agate (1968) p. 922.

6. 45 per cent of the organics were widowed, compared with only 30 per cent of the psychogenics, while 23 per cent of the latter were separated and 21 per cent single, compared with 15 per cent of the former in both categories.

7. A further refinement in the data is introduced by Bellin and Hardt (1958) who, in an investigation of a non-institutional population numbering 1,803 persons aged over sixty-five in New York, concluded that mental disorders rates for the widowed were significantly higher than those for the married, except for those aged sixty-five– seventy-four with low socio-economic status and good health, the latter qualification remaining true for both men and women.

8. By contrast, no significant correlation with test scores was found in the case of age, sex, mental state, social class, education, continued work, area of residence, mobility, physician's estimate of physical health, or physical disability score (Parsons, 1965, p. 45).

9. Of the remainder, one presented with presenile psychosis, two with schizophrenia, one with paraphrenia of long duration, five with senile paranoid psychosis, three with chronic alcoholism and three with manic-depressive psychosis.

10. It should be noted that on the point of alcoholism the Newcastle study did not discover a significant difference between normal old people and those with organic disorder (Kay *et al.*, 1962, Table VII).

11. The psychiatric examination 'took the form of a semi-structured interview with brief psychological testing incorporating the paired-associates learning test of Inglis' (1959). The breadth of the definition employed can be judged by the fact that 27·5 per cent of the sample were regarded as exhibiting dementia recognizable by the screening procedures used.

12. 'An old widowed man living alone and beginning to show signs of dementia is in an extremely precarious state with a high chance of self-neglect, malnutrition and danger from accidents' (Williamson, Stokoe *et al.*, 1964).

13. The criteria has related to family structure, the proximity of relations, the number of statutory and voluntary visitors, and outside social activities.

14. Significantly the Newcastle study found that Dene, the middle-class suburban area, had the lowest rate of admission to all three types of unit (geriatric wards, mental hospitals and welfare homes), while St Nicholas and Stephenson, the most working-class and least well integrated areas socially, had the highest overall rates of admission (Kay *et al.*, 1962, p. 178).

15. That is, all those persons aged sixty-five and over presenting with these symptoms who were found among 268 patients admitted consecutively to the Cowley Road geriatric unit between 1 February and 30 June 1955.

16. Kay *et al.*, (1964), Part II, Table IX, where significant differences between 'normal' old people and the organic and functional groups respectively are listed in order of T values.

17. In fact 85 per cent of all the mentally ill listed in GP records who fell into this latter category were diagnosed as suffering from senile dementia.

18. Whelan and Bree (1946) examined the contribution by friends and relatives to the patient's improvement, and ideas; 'Clinical outcome in General Paralysis of the Insane and Tabo Paresis', *Lancet*, 9 Jan. 1954, demonstrated that factors auxiliary to specific medical treatment played a part in the progress of patients with residual dementia. Predominant among such factors were a good pre-illness personality, a dependable and sympathetic prop (the key relative) and some occupation within their capacity.

19. Two sons and a daughter; wife and son; two sisters; a son and daughter-in-law; and a daughter and son-in-law plus daughter-in-law.

20. Various other modifications of the original motivation had occurred in another 4 per cent of the relationships, while in a further 5 per cent the data on possible changes was unobtainable.

21. Other evidence that exists, however, concerning the propping of another dependent group in the community, mental subnormals, suggests interesting parallels. Edgerton (1967), for example, found that discharged subnormals, within an IQ range of 47–85 coped chiefly by finding normal benefactors who helped them with practical problems, protected them from exploitation by the unscrupulous and provided them with reassurance. The benefactor was most likely to be a present or former employer, social worker, relative or the husband. The problems of 'making out' in the community were chiefly those of 'passing off' as normal and of 'denial' – the myth to explain the years spent in an institution.

22. The criterion here adopted is that devised by Townsend who assessed a person with 36 or more social contacts per week as 'not isolated', 22–35 as 'rather isolated', and 21 or less as 'isolated': P. Townsend, 1957. p. 167. The concept of 'social con-

tact is also discussed there. By Townsend's criterion, only 10 per cent of his sample in Bethnal Green were isolated.

23. Thus Sainsbury (1960), for example, found that an old person living with his spouse was less likely to come into hospital than one living with a relative not his spouse; see also Torrie (1960); and Roth (1960b).

24. Interviewers on this survey were trained in the criteria of confusion adopted in chapter 3 of this study and asked to apply them by personal observation and deduction during the interview.

25. York survey, *op. cit.*

26. For example, Tizard (1964); Moncrieff (1966); National Society for Mentally Handicapped Children (1967); Rehin and Martin (1968a). Other sources are quoted in the text below.

27. Thus Sainsbury and Grad, in assessing the impact of mental illness in the home in sixty cases at referral, judged that in 36 per cent of these cases family social activities were restricted, in 25 per cent the job of a family member was affected, in 20 per cent the patients presented severe problems of management, in 32 per cent the mental health of the informant suffered, and in 20 per cent family income was severely diminished (Sainsbury and Grad, 1962, p. 82). Crude though some of these measures are and requiring clarification as to degree, they do represent an effort to quantify some of the areas of potential conflict; cf. Atkin (1959 and 1963).

28. It is true that this study made no attempt to standardize for severity of neuro-syphilitic dementia, but the results remain strongly suggestive.

29. Unfortunately this term is not operationally defined by Kidd.

30. See Chapter 12: Conclusions for policy.

31. See especially Grad and Sainsbury (1968).

32. Thus the study of the discharge of 280 old people from mental hospital argued that chronically ill patients were detained through inability to walk (38 per cent of cases), mental confusion (25 per cent) and incontinence (22 per cent), while at the same time concluding that patients were unwanted by their relatives in only 1 per cent of cases: Howell (1967).

33. The in-patient ratios of all males referred being taken as 100 (p. 62).

34. Altogether, 163 out of 172 local health authorities in England and Wales supplied details of services (local authority and voluntary) provided for mentally infirm old people, who were defined as persons having 'serious loss of cerebral function resulting in abnormal inability to manage affairs without help'.

35. See Chapters 2 and 10.

36. Nottinghamshire, for example, runs a sixty-place centre which includes fifteen places reserved for the mentally infirm elderly.

37. As for example at the thirty-place purpose-built Park House Hostel at Barnet which was designed for the short-term rehabilitation of the mentally ill.

38. Ministry of Health, *The Development of Community Care* (1966), p. 8, in reviewing the increase in the numbers of places in local health authority hostels for the mentally ill from 323 at the end of 1962 to 1,084 at the end of 1964, comments: 'These figures include a few hostels specifically for the elderly mentally infirm provided under the National Health Service Act' (Section 6 of the Mental Health Act 1959 reflecting section 28 of the National Health Service Act 1946). It should be added that Apte, in a study of twenty-five halfway houses in England and Wales in 1963 found that the administrators had failed to collect a group of workers trained to think and act independently with a sound understanding of group and individual dynamics. Three-quarters of the wardens, he discovered, had gained most of their experience in institutions and so had developed preconceptions alien to the objectives of these houses (Apte, 1968).

39. A survey in 1957 on the effect of the Nuffield House centre at Nottingham on the

thirty families involved revealed that twenty individuals could go to work because an older relative was cared for during the day.

40. He quotes the opinion of one local authority that 'day accommodation and care enable members of the family who would normally provide this care to follow their occupation free of anxiety from leaving their aged relatives to fend for themselves during long periods of the day'.

41. A third had been recruited on discharge from psychiatric hospital and others had been accepted after pre-admission joint domiciliary visits.

42. This was thought to be partly due to improved nutrition, like the provision of a fresh orange juice drink each morning for vitamin C.

43. One study discovered that members of a treatment group who attended a geriatric day hospital one day a week were admitted to hospital more than the members of a control group in the first six months, and then the position reversed over the next six months, probably as a result of medical examination given and the effect of the subsequent treatment (Woodford-Williams *et al.*, 1962).

44. Cf. Droller (1958), concerning the earlier discharge of hemiplegics.

45. Including nineteen with cerebral ischaemia (which embraced muscular rigidity and dementia, but excluded Parkinsonism) and twelve with mental confusion as an associated condition.

46. Fifteen of the thirty-four were judged suitable for a day centre and not for a day hospital, and the remaining nineteen as fit to move on from the latter to the former (Brocklehurst, 1964).

47. Altogether, only seven of the total thirty-four received further out-patient and in-patient treatment, while thirteen received further in-patient treatment only, five further out-patient treatment only, and nine received no treatment at all (apart from the follow-up).

48. Thus, Sainsbury and Grad (1963), for example, found old people a major and still growing burden on comprehensive psychiatric services. But it should be added that a more localized study, in the Manchester area (Hoenig and Hamilton, 1967), detected a lower demand among old people than among under-sixty age groups.

12

Integration: a goal of social policy

Examination of such empirical evidence as exists concerning the community care of the mentally confused elderly has yielded certain tentative conclusions. The number displaying marked symptoms of mental infirmity would seem to be rather under 1 per cent of people aged over sixty-five, living in private households. The condition of a sizeable proportion in this group even with severe dementia is unknown to their doctors. Socially, they were likely to be characterized by isolation, poor living conditions in large urban areas and possibly also widowhood, though the data regarding the last is more equivocal. It is probable that they are sustained by a system of propping, in the sense of support beyond the normal expectations of the family relationship, and that this may be undertaken in perhaps a third of cases by the spouse, in a further third by a daughter and for the remainder by a variety of relatives or friends. Isolated case studies that have been individually reported suggest both the remarkable dedication of close relatives as well as the hazard of complete reliance on a unique source of assistance which might be irreplaceable in a sudden emergency. Systematic data, however, on the impact on the family of caring for an elderly confused member, with or without supportive social services, does not exist as such, though some evidence might indicate that community-oriented welfare policies may considerably reduce the subjective acknowledgement even of what was objectively assessed as a marked burden. Few social services are reserved exclusively for the elderly mentally infirm, though perhaps a third of local authorities run day centres for this group, however ambiguous their role. It would seem that both support at an earlier stage and the complementary provision of specialist skills by public services could considerably extend both the feasibility and scope of family care.

Given this brief picture of the state of community care for the confused elderly, juxtaposed by the earlier and much longer discussion of institutional services, we must now at last turn to the fundamental question of the most appropriate form of provision for these persons. Basically what balance should be aimed for between residential and community support? How far, weighing up administrative, economic and social costs, is some type of specialist provision required which is restricted, largely if not entirely, to mentally infirm old people, or how far is integration a viable goal? And if integration is entertained, what is the framework within which such an objective is realizable?

The model

Integration is a multi-faceted concept and for this reason it would be instructive quickly to review its applicability in related fields of social policy, in order that the range and complexity of the segregation–integration dimension can be more fully appreciated in the immediate context here.

If integration is scaled by the extent to which persons in particular contexts experience the same opportunities and reactions as others of the same age and sex, then Table 12.1 illustrates that types of segregation are categorized essentially by the factor producing this inhibition. Between extremes of physical coercion (imprisonment) on the one hand and positive utility (private schools and possibly general hospitals) on the other, segregation may be engendered by devices as complex and subtle as *ipso facto* govern the almost infinitely ramified channels of opportunity open to individuals in advanced societies. The operation of the price mechanism is only the crudest example here, though that too is often covered by an overlay of moral rationalization.

The table also reveals that segregation contains an essential *cui bono* component, and that it is in terms of the interests of these beneficiaries that its function must be interpreted. Since then segregation is by its nature manipulative, however indirectly, it follows that, except where it is exercised voluntarily and the beneficiaries of dissociation are identical to those to whom it is applied, its consequences are likely to be at best limiting and at worst punitive.

Functional variations: the consequences

RETRIBUTION

Where the purpose is retributive or deterrent and the segregation therefore strictly involuntary, as in the case par excellence of im-

Table 12.1

A typology of segregation and processes of social selection

Location of segregation	Category of persons	Technique of selection	Type of restriction	Degree of pressure towards segregation	Beneficiaries of dissociation	Function of segregation
Prison	lawbreakers	legal conviction	imprisonment	physical enforcement	remainder of society	retribution/ rehabilitation/ deterrence
Long-stay hospitals	mentally and physically handicapped	medical advice	indefinite hospital care	encouragement to relatives	healthy and able-bodied persons	custodial protection and relief to relatives
Council estates	working class	eligibility for rent subsidy	housing concentration	financial need	middle-class private estates	retention of 'select' neighbourhoods
Places of unwanted employment	coloured persons	job interview	employment discrimination	financial necessity	employers	exploitation of cheap labour
Public schools	children of high-income parents	private and unregulated choice of headmaster	fee charging (price mechanism)	voluntary and positive option	rich and powerful families	transmission of occupational elite
Acute hospitals	acutely ill persons	medical requirement	temporary in-patient care	voluntary concurrence	allegedly persons themselves	medical care

prisonment, several studies have attested that it is less the physical penalties of incarceration than the psychological deprivation of decision-making autonomy and personal autonomy which causes a damaging deterioration both of personality and relationships. The adjustment to this process, to which Merton's (1949) typology of conformity, innovation, ritualism, retreatism and rebellion can with small modifications be satisfactorily applied, is essentially of a pathological kind. Thus, Terence and Pauline Morris (1963, p. 169) have defined 'prisonization' as 'the continuous and systematic destruction of the psyche in consequence of the experience of imprisonment, and the adoption of new attitudes and ways of behaving which are not only unsuited to life in the outside world, but which may frequently make it impossible for the individual to act successfully in any normal social role'. To this extent it may be interpreted as the cumulative process of institutional neurosis in the specific moral context of a prison.

CUSTODIAL PROTECTION

The consequences of institutionalization are not readily disentangled from the effects of segregation *per se*, though the two are not of course identical. Institutions can retain greater or lesser degrees of residual contact with the outside world. Comparing matched groups of thirty-seven mentally subnormal adults in subnormality hospitals and local authority hostels, for example, Campbell found that the latter were significantly less isolated from family members not only geographically, but also socially since they 'regularly engaged in a variety of informal contacts with chance acquaintances and comparative or total strangers' (Campbell, 1968). Criteria for the measurement of segregation have, however, scarcely been applied at all over any range of residential or alternative social settings.[1] Such criteria would include scales of depersonalization of residents, degrees of social distance between staff and residents, measures of rigidity and block treatment, comparisons of residents' physical, cognitive and affective development, and approximation to the 'normal' network of social contacts experienced by persons of the same age and sex in the open community.

What conclusions have already been drawn along these lines are not clearly differentiated as between the effects of easier access and smaller size, since smaller hostels tend to be located nearer population centres than the more traditional institutions they often replace.

In the case of local hostels for the subnormal, for example, significantly greater IQ improvement, gains in self-confidence and greater sociability towards staff and each other may reflect either a more individualistic regime[2] related to smaller size, or closer access to the more sophisticated technical and medical services already available to children living in their own homes, or sheerly proximity for family visiting and the likelihood that child-rearing practices will assimilate to the norms set by the wider community (Lyle, 1959, 1960; Stedman and Eichorn, 1964; Bayley *et al.*, 1966).

Other consequences, however, may be more confidently attributed to the segregation implicit in long-stay institutions. One is that the classification which is the raison d'être of the establishment's existence will tend to become intensified. The official Working Party into the Special Hospitals (Ministry of Health, 1961), for example, which was investigating the security institutions at Broadmoor, Rampton and Moss Side, recommended *inter alia* greater specialization in the grouping of patients for treatment. In particular it urged that patients of normal or near-normal intelligence whose predominant abnormality was psychopathic behaviour should be treated as a special group. Subsidiary to this main point is the tendency for internal grading whereby the degree of deviance from normality, according to the terms of reference of the institution, is likely to be matched directly with living standards that are, however unwittingly, carefully calibrated. A documented instance of this is provided by Morris (1969) who, in her survey of subnormality hospitals, notes that 'there was a marked tendency for patients of lower intelligence to have much less satisfactory living conditions' (p. 90) and conversely 'many patients classified as "high grade" do live in the better conditions made available to them' (p. 82).

Secondly, an indirect consequence of segregation is that it may be used, whether consciously or not, as a means beneath the façade of apparently objective medical classification to secure the isolation of a not easily soluble social problem. Recently this has been most clearly demonstrated in the reaction to subnormality.

A local authority will claim, perhaps with justification, that a subnormal child is out of place and an embarrassment in an ordinary children's nursery or a children's home. Aberrations of behaviour are often used as the thin end of the wedge to have the child removed permanently to a hospital. . . . In hospital such children may be visited intermittently for a while by members of the staff of the nursery or children's home from which they came, but many of them receive no regular visits from the children's departments which have a responsibility towards them. ... Unfortunately, for as long as subnormal children can be placed out of sight and out of mind in hospitals provided by the NHS, local authorities will give little priority to accommodation for these children (Spencer, 1969).

A similar point has been made by Adams, that among the subnormal those admitted to institutions are not necessarily the more handicapped, but those who have failed in their social adjustment to adult life, a majority of whom have had adverse family backgrounds (Adams, 1960). A statistical gloss has been put on this phenomenon by Castell and Mittler who found, in a survey of IQ test results of a sample of 300 adult patients classified as subnormal and admitted to hospitals in 1961, that 57 per cent had an IQ over 70, which is regarded as defining the upper limit of subnormality of intelligence, while over a quarter had intelligence quotients in excess of 80 and 7 per cent actually within the normal range between 90 and 110 (Castell and Mittler, 1965). Similarly it has been found that the precipitating cause of admission to epileptic colonies is often of a social nature and that 24 per cent of residents in local authority colonies were 'attack-free' (Jones and Tillotson, 1964).

A third result of segregation is that nicety of causal attribution is sacrificed and all quirks of behaviour tend indiscriminately to be explained by the terms of reference of the institution. Thus it has been noted, for instance, in subnormality hospitals that physical disability is not readily differentiated from the underlying condition:

This may have arisen from a number of reasons: firstly because nurses seemed often ill-informed about physical symptoms, partly because so few appear to have had a general nurse training ... [also] from a tendency on the part of nursing staff to assume that physical disabilities were an intrinsic symptom of subnormality and they did not, therefore, consider the two factors independently. Thirdly, where patients had been looked after for many years by the same nurse (and those in charge of wards ... tended to stay on the same ward indefinitely, as did the patients) they seemed no longer to notice the patient's disability, they became adapted to it (P. Morris, 1969, p. 70).

464

Inevitably then conditions warranting alternative specialized treatment may be neglected.

A fourth consequence of long-term segregated care is that unwittingly it consolidates conventional beliefs in the essential differentness of those thus dissociated from the mainstream of community life (Rowland, 1939). Such beliefs and attitudes can then act as derivative justification for institutionalization as the expression of separatism. Through this logical circle segregative policies can be seen to feed on themselves, and the pattern is likely to be broken only by a publicly acknowledged acceptance that mental, physical or relational abnormalities are not qualitatively distinct, but only the extreme ends of a continuum of human abilities or range of human behaviour. This has important implications for the interpretation of mental infirmity among the old.

Fifthly, residential separateness, involving as it so often does denial of common rights and resources, can become a setting in which, because of sheer pressures of work and the perceived awkwardnesses of patients' responses, inhibitions against blunter and less sensitive handling are only weakly reinforced, depending partly on overall staff morale and the quality of communications within the staff hierarchy. Significantly, one reaction to the publication on 27 March 1969 of the report on conditions at the Ely Psychiatric Hospital, Cardiff, in 1966 and 1967 was not merely support for an appointment of an Ombudsman for the health or mental health services, but for the increasing absorption of mentally ill or subnormal patients into general hospitals.

Sixthly, in so far as the progress of patients' conditions is dependent on rational experiences, segregation, *qua* systematic confinement more or less exclusively with others similarly removed from society for largely identical behaviour or manifestations, must be prejudicial to their chances of regaining or achieving normality. This point has been noted in several different spheres, for example: 'Schizophrenic patients learn from normals by contact and example, not from one another. Living among normals promotes social values' (Hemphill, 1960); and in the field of child care: 'The policy of segregation – of institutional care from the cradle to the grave – is not only economically unsound, but also emotionally and psychologically wrong for the child, his parents and the community in which they live' (Ellis, 1958). Nor is a mixing of persons with varied yet still basically abnormal conditions more satisfactory in this respect. A Ministry of Health publication, for instance, whilst noting that the latest Health and Welfare Plan (para. 88) took the view that as a general rule the mentally ill should be accommodated separately from the mentally subnormal if their special needs were to be met, nevertheless added that 'experience shows that selectively one or two of one category of disorder may fit successfully into a hostel providing primarily for the other' (Min. of Health, 1967). The criteria of 'success' are not specified, but the comparative reference would seem not to be mixing with normals, but rather an unvarying homogeneity in residential selection.

A seventh consequence of a policy of secluding particular groups tends to be, indirectly, the aggravation of staff recruitment problems. A considerable body of evidence suggests that difficulties in achieving full staffing establishments derive partly from the physical isolation of many old institutions, partly from low pay associated with unqualified status and inadequate and unmilitant unionization deriving from disproportionate part-time female employment, and partly from the increasing demographic scarcity of single women.[3] But underlying all these factors lies the stigmatic nature of the institution generated by society's rejection of its residents and by the very act of physical and social separatism. But whatever the precise cause of the inadequate availability of personnel and physical resources the effects can be decisive. One such assessment about Special Hospitals was recently quoted: 'If every patient could have everything he needed, the average stay, doctors believe, might be reduced by three or four years' (Jacobs, 1969).

Above all, however, the segregating approach must be judged ultimately by the quality of life it offers to the residents concerned. Now a significant body of literature has stressed the *positive* role of institutions in isolating its inmates from the wider society in the interests of the former as well as the latter. This view has a long official history: the Radnor Report of the Royal Commission on the Care of the Feeble-Minded in 1908, for example, recommended segregation for the protection of mental defectives. A central thesis propounded by Stanton and Schwartz (1954) in their wide-ranging review of mental hospital sociology[4] argued that hospitalization represented 'a new beginning rather than the end' for at least a number of psychiatric patients, and the whole development of therapeutic communities throughout the last decade represents one attempt to give a positive expression to this approach (Rapoport,

1960; M. Jones, 1962; Martin, 1962; Clark, 1964; see also Belknap, 1956; Caudill, 1958). As opposed to the 'total push' philosophy, however, another trend in the same tradition has been the stress in the institutional setting as a positive sanctuary from exposure to the social demands of normal workaday pressures. (This idea has recently been chiefly developed by White *et al.*, 1955.)

Such arguments for temporary and limited seclusion, approximating to the pattern of admission to acute hospital for physical illness[5], clearly have much *prima facie* recommendation. But, putting this approach into a concrete context, to propose most existing old institutions as suitable settings is rather a rationalization for historical accident than a judgment of what is satisfactory, let alone the ideal. The inherent architectural disadvantages and sheer mass scale of many old establishments render them, despite often valiant efforts at modernization, practically unserviceable for the proper achievement of a positive sheltered asylum without intolerable offsetting drawbacks. Such arguments have been well rehearsed in the 1960s in several contexts (e.g. Barton, 1960; Goffman, 1961, especially Pt 1). Though institutionalization has been postulated to entail a positive content in certain circumstances,[6] most researchers have reported on segregation within the *existing* stock of old buildings as much more likely to impose crippling obstacles on personality development, especially since actual considerations of sanctuary are clearly often not applicable. The evidence relating to subnormal children is only the most dramatic of that recently discovered. Here it has been plainly shown that children who are restricted to unstimulating environments, typified by large secluded residences, have their development handicapped to a degree not explicable by any intellectual limitation, and that transfer to a more creative and richer environment can produce substantial changes in social maturity and verbal intelligence (Clarke and Clarke, 1966).

THE FOSTERING OF EXCLUSIVENESS

A very different set of objectives is served by segregation in the case of housing and educational separatism. Here the function is the preservation of selectness and élitism, and the chosen instrument is the price mechanism. The motive may however be rationalized. Just as the custodial function of long-stay institutions may be construed as creations for the self-protection of the most vulnerable and handicapped groups, so here the purpose may be interpreted as the provision of housing and education to reflect different needs and abilities.

Housing separatism is achieved not only financially through the cost of mortgages, but administratively too by policy decision. Two examples may be given of the implicit reinforcement of income inequalities by housing hierarchies even within the jurisdiction of local authorities where need might be expected to override financial differences. One is the recent finding that some local authorities have tried to maximize their rent income by refusing to allocate poor tenants to good quality dwellings when they would require large rebates, while other local authorities have excluded some of their modern properties from the scope of rent rebate schemes.[7] Similarly, many needy applicants for accommodation owned by housing associations have been rejected because the rent stop would be applied. Another example is the tendency of some local housing authorities to use a particular estate as the dumping ground for the segregation of 'problem families'.[8] Both policies, but particularly the latter, entail a self-fulfilling justification. By the concentration of those with limited resources in one place, standards are likely to fall below the threshold point beyond which even the scrupulous and conscientious will lose perseverance and where the dispersal and reabsorption of such families into the wider community is looked at askance.

Even more striking an illustration of housing separatism with apparent vindication inbuilt is that provided by the process of insulating coloured immigrants. With access to council tenancies denied them on any significant scale (Rex and Moore, 1967, p. 34) and with no small back-to-back cottages available for low cost purchase, they were forced to turn in Birmingham to multi-occupation lodging houses. Powers were then adopted by the local authority to ensure their isolation:

> The Birmingham Corporation Act . . . is based upon the principle of compulsory registration. Under this Act no-one is allowed to run a house let in lodgings without the permission of the City Council, and the Council may refuse on several grounds. The main grounds are that the setting up of lodging-houses would detract from the amenities of a particular area, or that the landlord is not thought to be a fit person to operate a lodging-house (Burney, 1967).

The ensuing confinement of multi-occupation to twilight zones inevitably produced racial ghettoes in the more deprived surroundings which then appeared to present an *ex post hoc* justification for the initial act of segregation.

Educational separatism, institutionalized in the 1944 Education Act, is unlikely to be eliminated so long as streaming survives the shift to comprehensives under the 10/65 circular (however amended) and this depends on the eventual outcome of the value conflict between meritocratic and egalitarian systems. Moreover, unevenness in standards between particular comprehensive schools reflects the homogeneous class structure associated with the neighbourhood catchment principle, so that housing and educational segregation are at this point intimately linked. The consequences of such systematic separatism have been lengthily discussed, but have perhaps been most authoritatively stated in a Unesco Institute of Education report:

There is strongly suggestive evidence that grouping based on distinctions such as measured ability, membership of a social class, racial group, or religious denomination helps to emphasize or even to exaggerate these distinctions. The gulf that separates able and less able children appears to widen if they are assigned to separate schools or to separate 'streams' or 'tracks' within a school. By the same token it would seem reasonable to suppose (although there is less direct evidence on this point) that fee-charging schools have a socially divisive effect and that to differentiate, for educational purposes, between members of different racial groups or religious denominations will increase the degree of mutual distrust and intolerance in these respects.

It is largely because grouping tends to sustain the difference on which it is based that it has been possible to claim success for some of the selective procedures that have been practised. To isolate an able minority of pupils at an early stage and to accord them preferential educational treatment – better facilities and equipment, more highly qualified teachers, and a longer period of schooling than are provided for their fellows – not unnaturally results in their producing superior levels of attainment. We are inclined to agree with those who have argued that to predict that they will do so in such circumstances is a self-fulfilling prophecy rather than a vindication of the practice (Unesco, 1966, p. 136).

Nor is it only that the expectations of teachers and the morale of pupils are both affected by those forms of grouping which can be interpreted as global judgments of ability, nor even that children are obliging creatures who are inclined to produce the standard of work regarded as appropriate for them by their elders. Perhaps more significant still is the development of a delinquent subculture in secondary modern schools as a compensation or rebuttal of perceived rejection as represented by the process of streaming (Hargreaves, 1967; Partridge, 1969).

Rather different arguments have been suggested to apply to children at either extreme end of the ability range. Special provision has been made by some LEAs for backwardness in every guise – remedial classes for the bright but backward, special schools for the 50–70 IQ group, tutorial classes for the emotionally disturbed, and remedial departments within ordinary schools for the 70+ IQ group. Segregation here is urged as offering a protective, encouraging atmosphere as well as slower, individualistic programmes,[9] with reduced hours. Integrationists, however, have argued that ESN children should be left in ordinary schools, provided they are not abnormal in temperament or behaviour, where they could be taught by trained interested teachers in small special classes. The balance of argument between considerations of social cohesion and the view that relatively homogeneous ability groups make for more efficient teaching, remains in the case of the slow learner undecided (Schonell *et al.*, 1963).

At the top end of the IQ distribution, special schools have sometimes been recommended.[10] Recent research, however, has tended to cast some doubt on their merits. A comparison, for example, of promise shown at 'O' level and actual achievement at 'A' level between five superselective élite schools and sixty-four other schools in the North and Midlands, as part of the research programme undertaken for the Public Schools Commission (1970), produced the tentative conclusion that pupils in highly selective schools who do not reach the very top may achieve worse 'A' level results than they would have attained at other schools. Underachievement by pupils at élite schools appeared most noticeable in arts subjects, and this aligns with other evidence that gifted children do not necessarily possess intellectual curiosity or creativity. Another recent report on exceptionally bright children concluded that 'special schools would no doubt turn them out better informed, but not well equipped for a life which would oblige them to work with all sorts and conditions of men' (Dept. of Education, 1968).

The lessons of segregation

Several points of significance for the present study emerge from this brief review. The most obvious is that while separatism offers a certain solution to a variety of social problems in the interests of the wider society, or the more influential sections of it, the experience of the minority on whom it is imposed is always restrictive and even positively damaging except where it is voluntarily chosen, for example for the purposes of meditation and worship in the case of religious orders, medical cure in the case of acute hospitals, and class exclusiveness and occupational aspirations in the case of private schools. Even in these instances the positive gains of segregation are earned at a certain social or psychological cost in the form respectively of monastic other-worldliness, emotional inhibitions on physical rehabilitation (Cartwright, 1964), and the repression of feelings and sexuality (Lambert, 1968). Where separation is involuntarily imposed, the effect is almost always stigmatic. What Myrdal has written specifically about race has much wider application: 'The Negro is segregated, and one deep idea behind segregation is that of quarantining what evil, shameful and feared in society' (Myrdal, 1944, p. 100).

Secondly, the analysis has shown that separatism, in so far as it exacerbates the problems of the minority group in question, is usually able to derive its justification from the self-fulfilment of expectations. In general it offers a salutary warning that social processes can rarely be properly understood if interpreted literally since so often the underlying dynamics have been structured to vindicate the interests and ideology of powerful groups in the background. Thus where separatism is claimed to be justified by the interests of the individuals concerned themselves, in terms of releasing them from unfair competition in the open world, or similar pretexts, such arguments on closer examination often take on the appearance of rationalizations. An authority on racial discrimination in employment, for example, has concluded: 'It seems

471

that the concentration of one group of recent immigrants in a factory does not in the long run lead to effective trade union organization; instead it may insulate that group from free association with other workers' (Hepple, 1968, p. 79). In another context, disabled persons cannot maintain their personal independence within flatlets reserved solely for the physically handicapped since it is precisely the daily proximity of a non-disabled person who can provide the range of small yet essential supportive services which others like themselves could not.

Thirdly, for these reasons the power of the forces in favour of dissociative policies should never be underestimated. Their strength can be measured by the resistance to desegregation. An example is offered by the notorious history of the Cutteslowe Walls, which were used in Oxford in 1934 to insulate a private housing estate for middle-class people which had been built immediately adjacent to a council estate housing working-class people. A long series of incidents, court actions, appeals, public enquiries, demolition and counter-construction intervened before the gradual ebbing of class hostility permitted their final removal twenty-five years later (Collison, 1963). Similarly in the educational sphere attempts to overcome housing divisions in the interests of truly comprehensive schooling through means such as 'bussing' or 'banding' have been bitterly resisted. Where the former device was used to integrate black children in Southall, black parents complained that the schools were then too far distant to allow them to take a close interest in them and that their children were separated from their school friends in after-school hours, while parents in suburbia threatened to withdraw their children to private schools. Furthermore, within the black community, because the Negroes could speak English and the Asian children could not, the former felt discriminated against. Equally, 'banding' as a technique to disperse white children in coloured areas was heavily resented in Haringey (Bourne, 1969). However, since class and race distinctions are so reinforced by emotive ideologies, desegregation of minority groups isolated by less contentious criteria may be expected not to involve welfare policy in such recriminatory retaliation.

Fourthly, any concerted endeavour towards unification requires a predetermined target of integrative balance. This is not always made explicit. The 'racial balance' clause in the Race Relations Act 1968, for example, permits employers to discriminate against immigrant workers 'if the act is done in good faith for the purpose of securing or preserving a balance of persons of differing racial groups which is reasonable in all circumstances' (Clause 8(2)). Yet balance in this context referred to particular sections of the workforce only, rather than to the whole factory, and nowhere within the Act was it defined. Equally, the target may be defined, though without supportive evidence. Thus the 1965 DES circular which recommended in the interests of racial integration and harmony that no more than a third of schoolchildren allocated per classroom should be coloured was not backed by any sociometric assessment of different racial balances on the quality of relationships.

Fifthly, even within a single context, integration may involve several facets, and unless the different dimensions are made explicit and disentangled, the objectives of positive discrimination programmes designed to promote integration may remain confused. A famous section of the Plowden Report (1967, chapter 5) outlined the criteria for selection of the educational priority areas, together with the techniques for remedy, but the policy goals were never clarified, at least in measurable terms. Is it a matter of improving reading comprehension or arithmetical achievement faster than would otherwise have been expected, or a question of liking school better or feeling greater confidence in native abilities, or a desire to stay on at school longer, or a tendency to commit fewer offences as teenagers, or a readiness amongst a higher proportion of the age-group to apply for further education, or the later capacity to earn more as adults, or indeed was there any still further objective or combination of objectives in mind? Similar problems underlie the current urban aid programme and community development projects. Again, attempts to construct a social conditions index to determine the regional allocation of resources[11] inevitably beg the questions of the choice of variables, the weighting between them and the precise aims in redressing the balance.

A sixth issue for integrationist policies concerns the nature of the ultimate check on the exercise of discretionary power. A long history exists of actions through the courts to limit preferential policies by central or local government designed to remedy unacceptable degrees of discrimination or inequality between particular areas, bodies, groups or persons (D. G. T. Williams, 1968). The usual basis for such actions, a counteremphasis on the fiduciary responsibility to ratepayers, has been notably applied against the introduction of a minimum wage irrespective of sex,[12] against efforts to alleviate the effects of the Rent Act 1957 by the councillors of St Pancras, and against the means-tested provision of free travel on municipal buses for the elderly.[13] But the same problem of influencing or moderating the ardour of positive counter-discriminatory policy arises at individual or group level as well as in institutional contexts, though the dynamics of reaction here have been little studied.

Related to this latter question is the apparent tendency towards polarization where opposed value systems are forced into coexistence. Some evidence of this is supplied by the incompatibility of rehabilitative goals superimposed on the essentially deterrent philosophy of the penal system, an inconsistency highlighted by the Mountbatten Report (1966).[14] But the most dramatic recent documentation derives from the pilot schemes aimed to integrate state pupils into the public schools, particularly at Marlborough. Reports from such schools which have experimented with 50 per cent or more integrants

> show that these schools tend to polarize; some move more rapidly towards an adjustment – open type which integrated children require, others move in the opposite direction towards greater rigidity and higher control as a means of meeting the manifold problems which children bring: and evoke a deep and widespread alienation in response. There are very few integrated schools which seem to be able to sustain a via media between these polar extremes (Lambert *et al.*, 1968, pp. 169–70).[15]

Exactly the same type of value conflict, between conformity to or rebellion against rigid middle-class grammar school hierarchies of closely prescribed behaviour and constant academic grading, has been posited as a central reason for high working-class dropout rates in secondary and higher education (Jackson and Marsden, 1962). Again, the point about polarization can be made in regard to the vertical dimension of social class opportunities since performance at each successive pivot of educational and occupational advancement disproportionately determines the outcome, whether for success or failure, at the next stage.

Lastly, it must be stressed that almost any problem in the field of social policy can be resolved in a manner which either promotes or obstructs the cause of integration. It is therefore not a specific goal as such, but a generalized value underpinning specific social processes of the widest variety. It is true not only of the forms and functions of giving that 'they may contribute to integrative processes in a society (binding together different ethnic, religious and generational groups) or they may spread, through separatist and segregationist acts, the reality and sense of alienation – as in South Africa and the Southern States of the United States (Titmuss, 1970, p. 71). Indeed, the consequences of political, economic and social acts, as well as of moral principles, in determining this balance can be truly described as one of the fundamental choices open to man. 'It is the explicit or implicit institutionalization of separateness, whether categorized in terms of income, class, race, colour or religion, rather than the recognition of the similarities between people and their needs which causes much of the world's suffering' (*ibid.*, p. 238).

CONCLUSIONS FOR POLICY

Most of these policy directions drawn from the wider ranges of social administrative experience do also apply directly or indirectly in the specific question of residential accommodation for the elderly mentally infirm, and points of parallel application have indeed been alluded to throughout the text of this study. Their implications in this limited field of residential policy must now therefore be spelt out, following only a first review of the consequences of separatism in this specific area of welfare as developed from time to time in the text.

CONSEQUENCES OF SEPARATIST POLICIES IN RESIDENTIAL ACCOMMODATION FOR THE MENTALLY CONFUSED ELDERLY

These effects as already discussed may be categorized as follows:

1. Positively, specialized homes ease problems of social disposal of a group among the elderly for whom medical or psychiatric relief appeared unavailing. In this role they protect small ordinary homes from the disturbances of disapproved or even repugnant behaviour and enable these homes to preserve their more select and exclusive

image by offering an alternative repository for the confused elderly discharged from former public assistance institutions as these are gradually run down and replaced,[16] and from psychiatric and geriatric hospitals as these increasingly refuse admissions of this type.[17] A complementary indirect function is that separatist homes fill the gap left in the network of services by the immature development of community care. The founding of Greenmount House in Bolton, for example, has been justified on the grounds that even if adequate supervision were available in a day hospital or from relatives in the daytime, confused old people are often alone at night and thus at some degree of risk, that other mentally infirm elderly could not manage at home even with help from relatives and friends, and that while doctors found the regulation of doses of sedatives difficult at home, medicines could be administered regularly and properly in hostels[18] (Nicholas and Johnson, 1966).

2. Separatist homes offer the advantages of administrative convenience by enabling, at least theoretically, scarce trained staff to be concentrated to the greatest effect. In practice, there is little evidence that this is normally achieved or even necessarily desirable.[19] Centralization does, however, permit the incorporation of architectural utilities such as mirror screens and 'spy-rooms'[20] as well as an enclosed walking circuit within the grounds.

3. Psychologically, the implications of separatism for both staff and residents are profound.[21] For staff what is signified is that there is something 'wrong' or abnormal about the residents: for why else should they be there, and how else is dissociation justified? Any quirk of behaviour is then naturally interpreted as derivative from the single underlying cause of admission, mental infirmity. Consequently a series of practices are adopted by administrative and care staff – such as dumping without explanation ("taking for a ride"), infantilizing procedures, heavy sedation, physical restrictions like the use of geriatric chairs, ritualised questions and similar devices[22] – the cumulative impact of which may generate the need for defensive psychological manoeuvres on the part of the residents. To the extent that the latter employ a strategy of compensation or dissociation (p. 304) or retreat negatively into paranoia or withdrawal[23] or even assume the ploys of punchy tactical defensiveness,[24] they expose themselves to the label of impression and provoke the rationalization that their condition is organic rather than reactive. A self-fulfilling prophecy is therefore built into the structure of

separatism via its determination of both the expectations and interpretations of both residents and staff.

4. More particularly, since separatism here has mental overtones and is involuntarily imposed, it carries stigmatic ramifications.[25] As a result it may inhibit the recruitment of staff, discourage the attentions of visitors, and even implicitly license the adoption of less sensitive and less considerate handling of residents by staff.[26] For separation other than for the purpose of cure and rehabilitation so often degenerates into second-class treatment.

5. Separatism as a philosphy tends not to be restricted to the single external decision that certain individuals shall be set apart in segregated accommodation, but to be applied *within* such establishments as well. Such a policy was found, however, to produce some bizarre groupings entirely devoid of community spirit,[27] and by extension to eating and sleeping arrangements[28] was significantly instrumental in generating that combination of segregation, isolation and decision-making impotence as a result of which confusion, it is argued, was spontaneously engendered or at least exacerbated. Certainly internal divisions are likely to polarize attitudes and to manufacture conflictful stereotypes.[29]

6. The quasi-medical foundation for separatist programmes may be paraded to conceal a system of control available for application to 'difficult' or aggressive elderly persons currently resident in other establishments.[30] This use of specialized homes as a repository for those considered to display non-conforming or disturbing behaviour may not even be disguised: one special home in Lancashire has been reported to bear the title 'Hostel for the Anti-Social' (Slaughter, 1970).

7. The association of separatism with mental disturbance can generate unhelpful presumptions. Such an association is created if the home is registered under mental health powers since in the completion of the necessary formalities documents have to be signed by relatives which make reference to the Mental Health Act.[31] But even in the absence of such indicators, the segregation of the confused elderly can easily produce an impression that the establishment is some latter-day lunatic asylum[32] – a stereotype which some have argued, rather dubiously, would be dissipated if specialist units for the elderly mentally infirm were built into existing homes as new or converted wings.[33] Even so, selection on explicit psychiatric criteria has been noted by some local authorities as likely to

cause the assimilation of separatist units to the role of the infirmary as attached to the older institutions, which the 1957 Royal Commission was so determined to prevent.[34]

8. In various indices of interrelationships the one measure clearly differentiating separatist from ordinary homes was the extent of visiting. In the latter, half the confused and two-thirds of the rational had weekly visits, while in the former a mere 2 per cent of the severely confused, 4 per cent of the rational and 8 per cent of the moderately confused received visits of this frequency.[35] Though this was partly accounted for by the paucity of special homes and their necessarily more distant geographical spread, it was seen distressingly by the confused as symbolic of their rejection,[36] and it certainly did involve a loss of protection and other services from relatives.[37] The effects of this isolation in special homes were reinforced in two other ways: the confused were less likely than in ordinary homes to venture beyond the grounds or to undertake any visits outside the home,[38] while the rational were inclined not to encourage visitors because of their anxieties concerning stigma.[39]

9. The fundamental question of the impact of segregation on the speed and extent of deterioration of the residents cannot be directly quantified from this survey. Certainly high morality rates were recorded in the separatist homes – a rate of 36 per cent over fifteen months in one and 21 per cent over twenty months at another – but this is less than the death rate of elderly patients admitted to many psychiatric hospitals (17 per cent within one month and 23 per cent within three months were recorded during this survey at one such hospital, and 24 per cent within three months have been noted at another hospital) (G. W. H. Townsend *et al.*, 1962, p. 12) and anyway the severity of the elderly persons' state on admission is not held constant as between these statistics. Since, therefore, comparative morality rates depend on a wide variety of factors other than environmental stimulus, such as the abruptness of transfer and misplacement as well as organic condition, they cannot properly be used to differentiate between the effects of alternative residential settings.

Another possible index is perhaps the degree of dissociation interwoven into the psychological fantasies of a proportion of the residents. By this measure there was undoubtedly a much more widespread and profound sense of alienation and craving for affection among residents of the separatist homes, though it may of course be argued that this merely represents their more deteriorated state at admission. Since however no baseline survey was undertaken of each resident's condition on arrival or, as was explained at the outset, was even methodologically practicable,[40] this point too remains unverifiable. Essentially the matter depends on whether the development of delusions and other confusional traits is seen as a pathological and morbid state, in which case their greater profusion in the special homes merely represents the contingent distribution of latent illness on admission, or whether such a development is seen as a struggle for compensatory survival, in which case it measures the penalties and ravages imposed by separatism. The consistently interpretable pattern of confusional manifestations as elucidated in Chapter 9 has been argued in this report to support the latter view, and by this criterion separatist homes are judged themselves productive of 'confusion', the more florid the more intense the concentration of the confused in one home. For if confusion is regarded as involving an adjustment function, then 89 per cent of the seventy-one confused residents in the special homes as compared to only 36 per cent of the twenty-two confused persons in the ordinary homes were observed to find such a compensatory device necessary.[41]

10. Criticism of confused behaviour occurred relatively less frequently in the separatist homes[42] and seemed to be minimized where the ratio between confused and rational roughly balanced.[43] For in the ordinary homes where confused residents were few, they tended to be exposed to criticism because they appeared exceptional, while in the one separatist home, where they numerically dominated, they made the rational feel unduly threatened and driven to retaliate. In the latter circumstances the confused could provide a target for scapegoating. In the ordinary homes the fact that the volume of criticism was similar though the incidence of confusion was much less is explained largely by adjustment to different norms and a greater objection to non-confusional irritations like gossiping; for it is also true of the ordinary homes that sympathy for confused residents was more commonly displayed here.[44] Yet in neither type of home could it be said that the assistance given to confused neighbours by the rational was systematic enough to constitute part of the regular social network.[45]

11. Participation rates for the confused varied significantly between the homes. Though they were inactive, as defined by certain

observed criteria, for three-fifths of the time in the separatist homes, their inactivity by the same standard amounted to seven-tenths of their time in the ordinary homes.[46] By another index they were also assessed as more reticent in the latter environment.[47] The meaning of this difference is however rather diluted by the fact that the greater activity and conversational participation of the confused in the separatist homes to a considerable extent reflected precisely their greater manifestation of confusional behaviour. It is not after all activity *per se* but integration that is socially meaningful and here it has been noted that assimilation is a function of dispersion of the confused rather than their concentration. Cosin, for example, has said that he 'found by experience that it is possible to maintain a feeling of family when two or three confused residents are together with five of six infirm or "frail ambulant" patients. But if there are more confused than this, the group becomes unstable and may disintegrate' (Cosin, 1958, p. 227).

12. Another facet of separatism is the restriction that concentrating confused residents together[48] imposes in different ways on the freedom of action of both them and their rational neighbours. They themselves were unduly limited in the special homes as regards, for example, smoking, exchanges of edibles like sweets or fruit, excursions or visits outside the home, or self-care like cutting toenails.[49] The larger their numbers, the more they seemed likely to be suffocated by staff anxieties for their safety. For the same reason the rational might also suffer restrictions in their access to, or use of, such instruments as scissors or knitting needles, lest the confused were to get hold of them.

13. Help to staff and the status deriving from the reciprocation of services appeared more likely to be monopolized by the rational in the separatist homes than in the ordinary establishments,[50] no doubt at least partly precisely to secure that dissociation from the confused which was observed as so marked a feature of that special home where the latter heavily predominated. Certainly it was noted that the confused in the specialized homes were significantly discouraged by staff from assisting by making beds or helping in the kitchen, and services were accepted from only a very few rational residents,[51] to whom such privileges as existed were largely confined.[52]

14. Separatism beyond a certain notional threshold could generate a polarized insularity between rational and confused residents from which the latter might be acutely harmed. If the confused appeared

too numerous,[53] the rational might retreat into self-imposed isolation in order to protect themselves from being swamped by what they regarded as a sea of unpredictable disorder.[54] The converse of this process is that the exclusive concentration together of numbers of confused elderly persons can, in the absence of constant available reference to conventional behaviour or normal standards, produce a complete breakdown in social organization and formal con-versational patterns.[55] As a consequence of this latter process, rational residents lose all expectations of reasonable normality or predictable reactions from their confused neighbours, and the barriers between them become increasingly consolidated.

15. Contentment and happiness among residents seem signi-ficantly less likely to be achieved in separatist homes. Nearly two-fifths (38 per cent) of thirty-nine confused persons in two of the separatist homes, together with half of the forty-four rational resi-dents, spontaneously at their interview expressed a desire to leave the home, whilst only 5 per cent of the confused and 2 per cent of the rational volunteered a positive wish to remain.[56] Indeed, much of the psychopathology of confusion appeared clearly traceable to patient manifestations of insecurity, shallowness of relationships and unrequited affection.[57] Insecurity seemed demonstrated by a constant harping on a happier past and by restlessness and hoarding; emptiness and superficiality of relationships were indicated by the outright sense of rejection and feelings of chronic self-abasement that were frequently manifested; and unreciprocated affection was apparent from the promiscuous desire for physical contact, some-times with undertones of sexual fantasy, by an inordinate eagerness for food, by the recalling of dead relatives (especially the spouse or mother), and by a host of attention-seeking devices.

16. Staff recruitment problems seem aggravated by separatist policies, at least at this stage of development of special homes. For there are still sufficiently few that their geographical isolation, combined with the often harder and more troublesome work involved in caring for sizeable concentrations of confused residents,[58] that employment prospects in separatist homes may well not compeet in attractiveness. In view of the greater work burden entailed, the special homes did not appear comparably staffed,[59] and workers for the night shifts, especially pairs as was often requested, were particularly difficult to find. Some administrators hoped that sep-aratism through the construction of special wings to existing homes

would ease staff recruitment problems by enabling a rotation of the work-load,[60] but no conclusive evidence was found in this survey to support such a view. Nor was the type of work so obviously demanding of professional skills that the concentration of confused residents acted as a natural focus for the attraction of trained personnel and scarce, expensive equipment, as in other instances of medical separatism.[61]

17. Separatism also appears to encourage discrimination, however this may be rationalized, in terms of access to amenities within the home. Not only did the rational monopolize the most advantageous chairs in the seating arrangements,[62] but the confused tended to be placed with others who were disabled, whether physically handicapped or mentally infirm, and also to be put to bed earlier and to be allocated larger bedrooms where less privacy was available.[63]

18. By definition separatism means, for those already ensconced in ordinary homes, another uprooting and transfer to another environment, with the anxiety, uncertainty and exacerbation of any underlying confusion that this necessarily entails. More insidiously the fact of segregation, of which most residents in ordinary homes were aware and which could be deliberately used by a matron, as a technique of social control over 'difficult' residents,[64] not only put a dubious power into the hands of authoritarian staff, but could give rise to a persisting degree of apprehension among the general body of residents which, however unjustified in practice, might badly affect morale and undermine feelings of integration and solidarity within the home.[65]

19. An often ignored though important point, given the aetiology of confusion posited in Chapter 9, is that in specialized homes confused persons, given to the systematic use of reminiscence as a means of ordering and harmonizing a disoriented perception of their role and situation,[66] are less likely to have at their disposal neighbours with the interest and skill to recognize the latent meanings of their speech and behaviour. To that extent separatism robs them of an aid for stabilization within bewildering surroundings.

It would seem clear from the accumulation of these various points that the balance of welfare advantage is decisively weighted against the separatist home. Is this therefore an equally decisive argument in favour of accommodating confused elderly persons entirely in ordinary homes, or if not, what alternative network of services can adequately undertake the functions at present served by separatist homes? If the latter are inherently unsatisfactory, what policy recommendations can be made for their supersession?

POLICIES FOR THE FUTURE

Policy considerations always relate to two separate dimensions, the short-term and the long-term, and since these involve entirely different perspectives, they must be distinguished here.

Short-term policy

Within the short term and irrespective of more radical and wide-ranging departures, several proposals for improvement of existing services can be suggested.

1. The use of former public assistance institutions and psychiatric or geriatric hospitals as repositories for confused elderly people should be rapidly phased out, and no further old people whose condition is purely confusional and free of specific and severe medical or psychiatric complications should in future be admitted to these institutions.[67] For the concentration of the confused in these establishments is often marked by symptoms of social disorganization and breakdown such as aimless wandering on a mass scale, loss of interest in territorial integrity, and a privatized and incoherent fragmentation of speech.[68]

2. Where separatist homes are built or ordinary homes in effect converted to this purpose by having a high proportion of confused persons concentrated in them, certain architectural features should usefully be incorporated. To avoid unnecessary locked doors, an enclosed courtyard or series of interconnected paths for walking round should be available for the purpose of combining apparent freedom of movement for the residents with security or care for the staff. An open design is preferable keeping doors and corners to a minimum, in order to reduce wandering among those disoriented on arrival by an unfamiliar layout. A consistent use of different colour patterns for doors to distinguish lavatories, bedrooms, sitting

rooms and dining rooms would also help to diminish initial bewilderment. A high proportion of single bedrooms to promote privacy and self-respect is desirable, even if ease of staff supervision is thereby hampered, and any compromise by subdividing large eight-bed or ten-bed rooms with glass partitions or curtaining, while it may facilitate night observation, is outweighed by the disadvantage of institutional appearance. Lastly, 'the frequency of incontinence makes an automatic sluicing apparatus an absolute necessity' (Jones and Milne, 1966, p. 163),[69] and urine-resistant coverings for the chairs, such as Vyanide plastic, should be plentifully available. A regular supply should also be available of disposable sheets, composed of cottonlike absorptive tissue underlaid by non-porous plastic.

3. Residents should above all be given every opportunity, consistent only with their safety and sometimes perhaps even at some small personal risk to exercise choice and self-determination (p. 227ff.) They should, including before arrival, be fully informed of any plans proposed for their future, especially where their interests are so centrally concerned as in questions of possible transfer, and their assent obtained. Exceptions should be strictly limited to instances where a relevant rational response is unequivocally excluded, however patiently sought, and apparent mild or spasmodic confusion should not be used as a convenient administrative means for sidestepping potential objections or expected recalcitrance. In general, residents should always have access to their clothing and be able to choose what to wear each day. They should have their due pocket-money regularly dispensed to them rather than its being stored for the paternalistic aim of purchasing on their behalf what it is thought they need or would like. Opportunities for involving them in daily tasks requiring some meaningful commiment should be assiduously cultivated.[70] They should be permitted, indeed encouraged, to bring with them on arrival, to promote continuity and self-identification, their own furniture and knick-knacks, and hence should also be given greater access to privacy, such as keys to drawers (with the matron retaining a set of master-keys in case of loss). Regular medical visits are desirable so that residents, whether rational or not, can more easily consult their doctor. Resort to the power of attorney[71] for obtaining decisions should be restricted to the absolute minimum. Like the rational, the confused should have the opportunity to go on holidays, celebrate birthdays, borrow

library books, and entertain guests in a special guest room.[72] The central goal should be to achieve a routine and an environment in which the capacity of confused persons to respond to occupational incentives[73] and to participate with awareness of social norms and conventions is stimulated to the maximum.

4. Segregation within the home, whether by sex, psychiatric condition or on any other grounds, should be carefully avoided, unless it is voluntarily wished by all or not merely by a dominant minority. Indeed, a rough numerical balance between confused and rational residents seemed, on the limited evidence of this study, most likely to avoid both the ostracism of a small number of the confused whose eccentricities are highlighted against the relative normality of the great majority, as well as on the other hand obviating a self-insulating rejection by a rational minority feeling psychologically threatened by the sea of insecurity around them.[74]

Short-term isolation in a special bedroom near the staff duty room may assist nursing supervision, but it can also severely undermine a resident's sense of security, with adverse effects on the prognosis, especially where the move is associated with transfer to the 'Death room' (P. Townsend, 1962, p. 147). Equally, transfers to obtain a specialized examination before entry to a home, as well as shifts within a home following an initial assessment, should be avoided because of their unsettling effect, and the same arguments apply against short-term holiday admissions[75] and the use of day hospital care for persons prone to disorientation. More seriously still, semi-permanent isolation in a particular room or wing of the home, can exacerbate, and perhaps even initiate, the spiral whereby exclusion from the main community may be interpreted as a reflection on eccentric or 'unsuitable' behaviour and the perceived rejection then prompts a compensatory or perhaps retaliatory response which is then regarded as justifying the original act of separation. The stereotyping process thereafter naturally and automatically intensifies.[76] Every effort should therefore be made to keep the confused in regular contact and interactive with the rational as a safeguard against the development of such isolationist spirals.

5. Though staff in separatist homes need no psychiatric training,[77] they should receive at least a brief preparation in the nature and possible aetiologies of confusion in old age. Such a course should stress the social dynamics of the condition and attempt some rational explanation of the kind of behaviour frequently observed. One aim

would be to obviate recourse later to the type of infantilizing practice earlier described,[78] but the main purpose would be to overcome subconscious staff hostility to confused residents and a natural tendency to favouritism towards the rational. The undesirable effects of resorting to mechanical restraints such as geriatric chairs,[79] would be stressed, and warnings would be given against an excess use of medication, particularly paraldehyde, barbituric acid derivatives and phenothiazines,[80] as well as against the use of such disciplinary curbs as the threat of transfer. More positively, the greatest value of training would lie in the opportunity to persuade matrons of the essential importance of integrating confused residents in a viable community and of their role as crucial to the success of such an aim. To this end it would be important to be able to assure matrons of the ready availability of support from associated services,[81] particularly those provided by mental welfare officers, local doctors and some voluntary organizations.

6. In so far as confused elderly residents are necessarily more susceptible to exploitation and less able to command resources for redress, a regional inspectorate should be instituted to supplement in the general field of daily welfare the legal safeguard already accorded in financial matters by the Court of Protection.[82] This is particularly needed in regard to private mental nursing homes,[83] as a check on the locking of doors, the degree of sedation and the suitability of the proprietor. Clear precedents for this exist both historically, with the Lunacy Commissioners who visited private madhouses in the nineteenth century, and internationally, for example with the Swedish Ombudsman who makes his visits unannounced and reports independently, and Scotland's Mental Health Commissioner who investigates on average more than a hundred cases a year. The need for a Health Service Commissioner in Britain has been plain since the revelations of the Ely Hospital report and reinforced by several later official enquiries. The case has been argued particularly by Brian Abel-Smith,[84] has been officially sanctioned in the recommendations of the Farleigh Hospital enquiry committee report,[85] and has now finally materialised after the Whittingham Hospital Report. Though the need for some protection against eruptions of staff authoritarianism is now virtually unchallengeable, opposition to this innovation derives not only from medical insistence that any complaints about clinical matters should be judged by doctors, but more seriously from Government

anxiety that repeated reports of low standards of care would inevitably be linked with inadequate training, understaffing, overcrowding, and badly located and outdated hospitals, with consequent demands for higher expenditure.[86] For there is no doubt that separatist homes, let alone geriatric units, are already seriously understaffed in relation to the greater requirements of care imposed on them.[87]

7. Psychogeriatric assessment of the confused elderly, to ensure proper placement, raises problems of location, but more acutely of institutional function.[88] Though correct placement remains crucial, as between psychiatric and geriatric units quite apart from the choice between residential and hospital admissions, in view of the higher mortality rates and lower discharge rates resulting from misplacement, nevertheless the precision of in-patient assessment involves definite disadvantages.[89] The emphasis should therefore shift to domiciliary assessment,[90] with in-patient examination strictly limited to cases of suspected complexity and unresolved doubt, and subject only to the proviso that where a hospital admission is undertaken, it should be to a special psychiatric ward in a geriatric unit. For as Fish (1963, p. 64) has pointed out, 'the patient with an acute physical and psychological illness is more likely to die if he does not immediately receive adequate medical care than if he receives immediate psychiatric, but indifferent medical treatment'.[91]

More fundamental to the question of placement and more difficult to resolve is the issue of the purpose of assessment. Are different hospitals and residential homes distinguishable by mutually exclusive functions which can thus serve as a clear guide for assignment? Empirical evidence tends to refute such neat categorizations,[92] and suggests that the role of separatist homes in particular must be defined residually by reference to gaps and problems inherent in the traditional nexus of institutional care.[93] Since this is so, it is clearly essential to return to the nature of confusion or mental infirmity in old age in order to determine, without presuppositions, the most appropriate form of care or support.

Longer-term objectives

THE NATURE AND AETIOLOGY OF CONFUSION

It is axiomatic that future policy be built on a proper understanding of the confusional condition.

Five main theories of causation must be considered:

(a) Inheritance

A genetic aetiology has been posited chiefly by Sjögren who has looked to conditioning by a major gene, inherited as a monohybrid autosomal dominant, as the relevant factor.[94] However, the evidence adduced for this theory appears equally explicable by sociocultural factors.[95] Further, if pathological cerebral change is regarded as a necessary medium for the transmission of a genetic inheritance, it must be taken into account that associations between senile behaviour and organic findings at autopsy[96] on the one hand, and between such behaviour and EEG recordings[97] on the other, appear far from conclusive.

Chromosome analysis has, however, been claimed to produce significant findings. One such investigation of ten women with senile dementia and ten controls of the same age group revealed a significantly higher proportion of hypodiploid cells in patients over the age of seventy diagnosed as senile dements ($P < \cdot 001$). It was concluded that 'it seems likely that an increased loss of chromosomes presumably mainly X chromosomes in females with senile dementia, is a basic part of the aetiology and pathogenesis in senile dementia' (Nielsen, 1968).

Other theorists have, however, suggested that the total group of senile dementias may be due to the effect of a dominant genetic factor of low penetrance, and Roth has noted that all dominant genes have the age of their manifestation pushed towards the end of reproductive life owing to the accumulation of genetic modifications (Roth and Morrissey, 1952). Notably, Meggendorfer (1939) has hypothesized that either one or two dominant genes are involved, one controlling longevity and one producing the pathological changes associated with senile dementia. He found, concerning sixty persons classified as senile dements, that there were eighteen cases of senile dementia occurring among blood relations, together with a high incidence of various forms of other mental disorders in the families of these patients (Meggendorfer, 1926). Similarly Sjögren *et al.* (1952) have provided data about Alzheimer's disease, a pathological process qualitatively similar to senile psychosis, which as Roth (1959) points out . . .

lend some support to the view which implicates multiple genes of small effect. The importance of the evidence in favour of this form of hereditary transmission is that environmental and exogenous factors usually play some part in deciding variations in such graded characteristics, and the corollary is that in mental ageing and its exaggerated versions in senile dementia, we are dealing with disabilities that may be potentially susceptible to mitigation within limits.[98]

Again, Weinberger (1926) found a positive family history of arteriosclerosis and senile psychosis in eleven out of fifty-one cases of senile dementia, plus a total of 135 instances where mental disorders had occurred in the case of direct or collateral members of the family. Post (1964) also discovered twelve cases (or 15·4 per cent) out of seventy-eight diagnosed as arteriosclerotic or senile psychotics where a positive family history of these disorders could be traced. Nevertheless, Kallman's (1953) twin family data indicated that it was unrealistic to search for a single mutant gene effect as the primary cause of psychotic phenomena in involutional and senile periods. His later conclusion went further: 'Biologically it may be inferred from observations on twins that prevention of a senile psychosis rests not only on adequate potentialities for emotional adjustment to functional losses in old age, but on the establishment of an adaptive stability before senescence (Kallman, 1961, p. 243).

(*b*) *Diet deficiencies*
The association between dementia and subnutrition, especially as revealed by vitamin B_{12} or folate deficiency, is well recognized.[99] Certainly nutritional deficiencies are known to be widespread among the elderly,[100] and this appears to be particularly true among those admitted to residential accommodation. One study, for example, found that, of fifty-one old people admitted to a residential home, folic acid deficiency was present in four-fifths and in two-thirds of those without severe anaemia (Read *et al.*, 1965), while other surveys have detected other deficiencies, including hypoprotanaemia and metabolic bone disease (Gough *et al.*, 1964). In Amsterdam the

pre-hospital food intake of 100 hospital in-patients over seventy was investigated and fifty-nine were found to have been consuming too little iron, fifty-one too little vitamin B_1 and thirty-nine too little vitamin B_2 (Brugand and Oldenbandring, 1962). Among a sample of sixty women over the age of seventy living in the London boroughs of Hornsey and Islington, it was found that though most consumed a varied diet and did not all live on the traditional bread and jam, nevertheless some diets were ill-balanced and provided too little vitamin C, vitamin D, calcium, iron or protein (Exton-Smith and Stanton, 1965). More seriously, another study concluded that 'vitamin deficiency was widespread among elderly people' (Griffiths *et al.*, 1966). Of those investigated, 41 per cent were assessed as deficient in ascorbic acid and 59 per cent as deficient in thiamine on admission to hospital, and among those living at home and not ill or not sufficiently ill for admission, 27 per cent were deficient in ascorbic acid and 22 per cent in thiamine.

It is true that malnutrition reduces not only the supply of glucose, but also that of the vitamins concerned in its effective oxidative processes, which underlie all cerebral activities (cf. Johnson, 1970). The result may often be mental confusion because the human brain, which is extremely vulnerable to anoxia, is completely dependent for its energy relations on the aerobic combustion of glucose and on those substances (namely electrolytes, water, enzymes and co-enzymes or vitamins) which take part in these reactions (Bedford, 1961). The need is clear therefore for a relatively high intake of both ascorbic acid (as stressed by Fine, 1961, and Ledermann, 1962), and also B–complex, especially where confusion is a complication of other illnesses (Blackadder, 1960) or where there are psychotic signs (Mayer-Gross *et al.*, 1960, p. 518). For 'there is clear-cut evidence that vitamin B deficiency can be associated with confusional states (in the elderly)' (Tunbridge, 1963). One study, reviewing the connection between dietary deficiency and various mental illnesses, concluded: 'The evidence that vitamin B_{12} deficiency may cause irreversible brain damage and dementia is more conclusive' (Shulman, 1967).

The data, however, are not entirely uniform. Post (1944) for example, has claimed that frank avitaminosis is rare, while an editorial of the *British Medical Journal* has taken the view that 'mental confusion in old age is thought by some to be evidence of deficiency of vitamins of the B–complex, but this is not conclusively proved, and the results of giving large doses of these vitamins have been unimpressive' (*Brit. Med. J.*, 1961, ii, 1486). One such experiment in treating ten senile patients with vitamin B complex, compared with ten control cases, for a period of two months led to no lessening of dementia as assessed by various psychometric tests, though the behaviour pattern appeared to be improved in the treated cases (Wadsworth, Quesnel *et al.*, 1943). Droller and Dossett (1959, p. 261) while estimating that 60 per cent of elderly patients admitted to geriatric units were more or less confused on admission, believed that only 10 per cent were chronically demented with a condition usually of more insidious onset which progressed in spite of treatment.

(*c*) *Drugs*

It is widely accepted now that among the variety of causes which may precipitate acute confusional states in the elderly is excessive sedation, and this is known to be widely employed in the case of senile and arteriosclerotic dementias (see e.g. Blackadder, 1960). But quite apart from such reversible conditions produced by heavy medication, there is also evidence that certain states often observed in association with confusion may also be generated by the excessive administration of particular drugs. One study noted that oral dyskinesias in elderly women in mental hospitals were associated with a high total intake of phenothiazines, possibly through the causing of structural damage to the basal ganglia (Pryce and Edwards, 1966). It must be taken into account, however, that several other explanations have been posited, including leucotomy (Hunter *et al.*, 1964a), brain damage from disease (Hunter *et al.*, 1964b), ECT (Uhrbrand and Faurbye, 1960) and even ill-fitting dentures (Joyston-Bechal, 1965), or a general edentulous state (Evans, 1965). On the basis of existing evidence therefore, it cannot be firmly concluded that excess medication is associated with more than particular manifestations of confusion, and even here a proven connection is not certainly established.

(*d*) *Organic deterioration*

The explanation for the condition traditionally defined as organic dementia has normally been seen in terms of cerebral deterioration. Originally Simchowicz was the first to conclude in 1910 that the intensity of plaque formation reflected the severity of the senile degenerative process (Simchowicz, 1910). Grünthal followed this in 1927 with an exhaustively painstaking comparative clinico-pathological study of senile dementia in which he found the correlation between cerebral atrophy and clinical state to be generally good, apart from certain notable exceptions, especially one of the two clinically normal patients in whom both cerebral atrophy and various senile changes were as marked as those in some states of senile dementia (Grünthal, 1927). He therefore concluded that there must be some qualitative as well as quantitative differences between the pathology of senile dementia and that of normal senescence. Similarly, Cerletti showed in 1925 that plaque formation could on occasion be as intense in normal subjects as in the demented elderly (Cerletti, 1925). Again, Gellerstedt (1933), in his exhaustive study into the cerebral changes of normal ageing, found various senile changes were frequently detectable in the brains of normal old people. Indeed he reported finding senile plaques in 84 per cent, neurofibrillary changes in 97 per cent and granulovacuolar degeneration in 40 per cent of the brains of normal elderly persons.

Rothschild in 1937 carried the argument further by claiming that senile dementia could occur without the presence of senile plaques and that there was a poor correlation between change found at post-mortem and the degree of intellectual impairment observed during life (Rothschild, 1937). He therefore hypothesized that the lack of correlation reflected the variable and unpredictable way in which different people compensate for cerebral change. Corsellis, however, contends that Rothschild did *not* fail to identify a correlation between histological change and a degree of intellectual deterioration since both were assessed crudely on a five-point scale ranging from 'none' to 'very severe', and when for example in senile dementia the severity of clinical deterioration was compared with the intensity of senile plaque formation, twenty out of twenty-four instances came within one point of agreement. Similarly for arteriosclerotic psychoses only four out of twenty-three cases showed more than one degree of difference between the severity of intellectual deterioration and that of cerebral damage (Corsellis, 1962, pp. 57–8). Clearly some of the discrepancies arose from incorrect diagnosis, such as the attribution of prominent, florid and depressive symptoms to an underlying organic basis. Roth considers that the reason why post-mortem neuropathological findings appear to support the non-correlation view is explained by such research as that of Newton in 1948 who discovered plaques and neurofibrillary changes in thirty-two of seventy-six cases of affective psychosis and in six out of twenty-four cases of schizophrenic and paranoid psychosis (Newton, 1948).

Corsellis, from a systematic study of the clinical records and pathological changes both in the body generally and in the brain found at 300 consecutive post-mortem examinations at Runwell Hospital between March 1953 and September 1957, concluded that 'the ways in which "organic" deterioration manifests itself during life are more often than not reflected in the ultimate appearance of the brain, even though the reflection may be crude and superficial' (Corsellis, 1962, p. 59). He found that only 25 per cent of those with functional disorders, but 75 per cent with organic psychosis, displayed moderate or severe degenerative changes, and surmised that the overlap was partly due to the development of organic changes at an advanced age in some subjects with an initial functional disorder.[101] In view of the highly significant correlation between mean plaque counts and scores given for dementia and performance in psychological tests, he concluded that the close relationship between pathological and psychological indices derived perhaps from a common association with underlying degenerative changes in the brain. At the same time, since in the case of six subjects out of sixty a dementia score of less than two (on a scale 0–28) was associated with a mean plaque count of six or more, the qualification was drawn that a certain amount of brain damage as assessed by plaque counts may be accommodated within the reserve capacity of the cerebrum without causing manifest intellectual damage.[102] A second broad conclusion developed by Corsellis was that among the severely demented and those clinically diagnosed as senile dements the correlation between psychological and pathological measures declines sharply, even though the pathological difference between normal, mildly demented and severly demented persons appears to be of a quantitative nature.

Corsellis's claims that a relatively close correlation exists have been largely supported by recent American work. Malamud (1963), who studied 411 patients inferred that the presence or absence of mental deterioration was quite closely linked to the extent of brain change. Again, from 505 consecutive autopsies of patients in several large mental hospitals who at death had a clinical diagnosis of either psychosis with cerebral arteriosclerosis or senile (including presenile) psychosis, Simon and Malamud found that psychiatrists diagnosed chronic brain disorder correctly in almost all cases, though they were less accurate in diagnosing the type, for example frequently diagnosing cerebral arteriosclerosis when the autopsy findings primarily showed senile brain disease or a mixed senile and arteriosclerotic picture (Simon and Malamud, 1953).

In summarizing this somewhat conflicting evidence Roth has taken the view that the 'possibility that there are qualitative differences in this group, inaccessible to present methods of detection, cannot be excluded' (Roth *et al.*, 1967). He notes that recent electron-microscopic studies have tended to confirm the association of senile plaques with an outfall of neurones (Liss, 1960; Kidd, 1964; and Terry et al., 1964), and concludes that the 'fixed cell population of the cerebrum would render it particularly susceptible to changes of senescence. . . . Differences between well-preserved and markedly demented old people may lie in the different rates of progression of one or more pathological processes they share in common. The stage reached by the pathological process appears to be measured, albeit in a crude manner, by plaque counts.' On the basis that intellectual performance and social behaviour declined as the number of senile plaques increased, Roth and his team have argued that the *intensity* of plaque formation is associated with the decline in intellectual ability (Roth *et al.*, 1969). In drawing attention to the fusion of plaques, the formation of plaques at the deepest cortical levels and the widespread ill-defined fibrillary change observed in the brains of severely demented patients they conclude that the differences between patients with senile dementia and other patients reflect a quantitative gradation of a pathological process common to old age rather than any qualitative difference.

Other researchers surveying the data have been struck more by the discrepancies than by the correlations and doubt if any significant association exists. Thus Wolf (1959) has asserted that 'no good correlation exists between the degree, distribution and character of various abnormal changes and the age and state of the neural function of the individual.' Sjögren has been even more emphatic: 'post-mortem findings do not show any deviations from common experience. It should be stressed that in spite of pronounced clinical symptoms, many of the cases did not display cerebral atrophy and cerebral arteriosclerosis' (Larsson, Sjögren and Jacobson, 1963, p. 221). Elsewhere he has doubted the role of plaques as a primary source in the pathogenesis of senile brain atrophy: 'there are more and more indications that at least the formation of plaques is associated with disturbed carbohydrate metabolism' (Sjögren, 1964). Kay and Roth conclude that follow-up-neuropathological studies have made untenable 'the view that cerebral disease has a ubiquitous aetiological role in old age mental disorder' (Kay and Roth, 1964).

To explain the variable clinical pictures seen, recourse has been had to the more subtle influences of personality and adaptive powers. As the Newcastle researchers have said, 'occasionally the brains of individuals who have never become demented have been found to show quite marked changes. The condition of the brain seems therefore to be only one of several factors determining the threshold at which dementia appears' (Kay, Beamish and Roth, 1964). Thus Kassel has hypothesized that the extent of psychosis might be considered in terms of the interaction of five factors: brain pathology, emotional responses to organic and functional changes and the diseases of ageing, the degree of abnormality of the underlying personality, the degree of interpersonal conflict, and the accumulated emotional traumata of living (Kassel, 1957). Such an unquantified congeries of factors, however, cannot readily be regarded as a theoretical formulation. An Oxford research team concluded that the 'deterioration of "communications" through declining mental and physical abilities is *not* the main source of senile failure, but that more basic personality functions described in terms like "drive" or "self-motivation" have become defective' (Cosin *et al.*, 1958). Elsewhere they stated that 'a tentative hypothesis putting forward the claim that preservation of motor function allows adjustment in the world in spite of irreversible cognitive decline, may help to explain why in spite of severe memory and intellectual impairment some people appear less "demented" than others' (Cosin *et al.*, 1937, p. 201). Post has developed an ingenious explanation by dis-distinguishing between Cattell's 'fluid' ability, defined as the capacity to manipulate unfamiliar concepts and perceive new relationships, and 'crystallized' mental ability which enables persons to adjust to situations and to solve tasks which require the combination and manipulation of skills and information accumulated throughout life:

Old people are rarely required to use fluid abilities especially when they are living within the family; their activities are largely of a routine type. Hence, senile confusion often manifests itself for the first time after loss of spouse or change of home. If a patient has remained in a protected environment, sooner or later the point will have been reached when crystallized ability sinks below the level required for most tasks involved in daily routine. Then, to everybody's surprise and over a few weeks or months, the patient has become persistently confused (Post, 1959a, p. 119).

Similarly, adopting a more interactional socio-psychological approach, Cameron points out that the patient may react to the perception of his own behaviour or to 'the reduced security and prestige [and] the neglect and prejudice that others show' as a result of the patient's diminished abilities (Cameron, 1947).

(e) Social influences

The ambiguities of the clinical picture have recently generated much closer attention to the possible relevance of various social factors. Macmillan in particular has argued that

> many cases present symptoms similar to those of organic conditions, but more and more one has the impression that initially the condition was essentially a functional reversible one, often associated with an underlying organic condition, either mental or physical, which in itself was not the sole basis of the illness, but was a predisposing factor . . . [since] cases diagnosed as irreversible and organic improve and symptoms disappear, necessitating a change of diagnosis to a functional one (Macmillan, 1967).

Elsewhere he has added:

> The attitudes of relatives and neighbours or the degree of isolation of the old person living in solitude can be the important factors and far outweigh the effect of the organic cerebral changes. The organic symptoms of impairment of memory, inability to recall recent events, and disorientation for time and place can be present and be quite compatible with continuation in the home environment if the relatives, friends or neighbours are desirous of retaining the old person in their midst, and if this desire outweighs the increased responsibility placed on them and the claims of their other commitments. Except when occurring in

confusional states and terminal conditions the symptoms of nocturnal restlessness, wandering and incontinence are usually reactive and not organic in origin, and are usually occasioned by the feeling of not being wanted which is caused by a loss of the desire on the part of the relatives to continue to care for the old person (Macmillan, 1962a, p. 740).

The precise contribution of different social factors, however, or their relative significance is difficult to determine. The Newcastle research failed to detect any relationship between organic brain syndromes and social class, ward or civil state.

But there is a more rapid rate of removal to geriatric wards and welfare homes from poor social areas than from prosperous areas, and of the single and widowed than of the married, and this may have concealed any relationship that actually existed. But whether the higher admission rates of certain groups are wholly due to social factors or do in fact reflect a higher incidence of psychiatric illness has yet to be determined (Kay, Beamish and Roth, 1964, p. 677).

The authors also found an association with poverty in the sense of low income, poor home amenities and unemployment, a connection obviously related to the advanced age of most of the sample (over half were aged over seventy-five, and most of these were over eighty). Poverty could not, however, they argued be regarded as a *major* cause of organic mental disorders, though 'in a few instances it seemed that an inadequate diet, partly the result of the mental failure itself, and partly due to economic stringencies, might have contributed to the development of the mental symptoms, and that in more favourable conditions the progress of the psychosis might have been delayed' (p. 676). Finally they suggest also that 'there was in fact, a small minority of cases in whom "isolation", and a consequent lack of stimulation from contacts with other people, did contribute to the apathy or depression that were quite commonly found. To this extent, these factors may have increased the tendency to self-neglect, and thus indirectly though dietary inadequacies or other physical causes, have aggravated the mental state' (p. 677).

Nevertheless there is a growing weight of evidence that what characterizes the recognized dement is the breakdown in the adopted pattern of adjustment for which social contingencies may be largely responsible. In the weaker form of this thesis the social adjustment is a secondary derivative factor created to deal with the primary mental breakdown. In this sense Kay has declared that 'while, as morbid anatomical studies have shown, senile brain disease is to be regarded as a quantitative rather than qualitative change, the outset of clinical dementia is a sign that a threshold has been reached at which adaptation even to familiar surroundings begins to break down' (Kay, 1962). The same viewpoint has been utilized to deny the traditional nihilistic association of mental enfeeblement with progressive and irreversible disease of the cerebral vessels and infarctive lesions of the brain. For in explaining why similar cerebrovascular lesions in younger persons did not necessarily lead to the overt psychological changes found in the elderly, it has been suggested that the compensatory mechanisms present in younger people have become increasingly impaired with the progressive systematic deterioration of advancing age (Wahal and Riggs, 1960). A slightly modified form of this weaker thesis assumes that the degree of deterioration depends on inter-personal skills and attitudes developed in early life. In this sense Roth has written that 'effort invested early in life in fostering interests, in helping the individual to cultivate friendships and social activities, would yield some dividends. Tolerance and flexibility in personal relations cannot be cultivated in old age' (Roth, 1960b, p. 1230).

The stronger thesis sees social breakdown as primary and originative. In this sense Macmillan and Shaw have posited a senile breakdown syndrome. 'Information obtained from neighbours and others suggested that these relatives had been the mainstay of the household, and the sudden loss of companionship allied to the necessity for the patients to fend for themselves had brought about social deterioration' (Macmillan and Shaw, 1966). Rapoport (1960, p. 26) has put the position more theoretically: 'there are obvious limitations to the extent to which reverse processes may be said to function (for example psychological intervention producing biophysiological and psychological change). But evidence is accumulating that such changes do occur under some circumstances, and that their manipulation may become a focal method of treatment.'

The nebulousness of social factors renders a dynamic theory based on these principles difficult to verify. Ecological surveys, such as that by Gruenberg in Syracuse, New York, have found that areas with high admission rates due to senile and arteriosclerotic psychoses were located near the centre of the town where most houses had been subdivided into large numbers of small individual dwellings and where a high proportion of the inhabitants were living alone (Gruenberg, 1954). On the other hand, while Post found that in the case of 100 consecutive patients he examined over the age of sixty, acute physical illness and then events like bereavement, serious illness of the spouse and the moving away of a close relative preceded the onset of (depressive) illness (Post, 1958b, p. 579), isolation appeared to be the result rather than the cause of mental disorder (Norris and Post, 1955). Equally it has been argued that senile mental changes may be hastened by depriving old people of many of their traditional roles (e.g. Albrecht, 1951, p. 380), yet comparative surveys have found that close, helpful and affectionate relationships, as opposed to weak family ties and interests, subsisted more frequently among demented patients than the mentally healthy (Cosin *et al.*, 1957, p. 195, cf. National Council of Social Service survey, 1954).

The most comprehensive statement of the social argument has been put by Macmillan from the observations of his professional experience, and is worth quoting at some length:

When an old person lives by himself, deterioration can easily set in because of lack of interest, solitude, antagonism, self-pity, or resentment on the part of relatives, neighbours and the community. Old people, except in very exceptional circumstances, are completely dependent on the feeling that they are still appreciated and that their existence is of value. If the feeling exists that they are of use and of some service to someone, deterioration and the development of senile psychosis seem to advance very slowly, if at all. Once this emotional link is lost, particularly when the person feels he has been 'rejected', senile psychosis develops very rapidly.

By 'rejection' I mean the feeling of determination by the relatives to be free from what has become an intolerable burden. This feeling takes time to develop. Initially many cases show a willing and unquestioning acceptance of the responsibility because of a sense of duty. With time this responsibility becomes more irksome, and the restriction of pleasures, social activities and holidays become more and more resented – usually subconsciously. These feelings seem to develop more rapidly if other people are affected, e.g. as children are deprived of holidays, or if there is grievance because other relatives are not bearing their fair share of the load. This state of 'partial rejection' lasts for a varying period, after which, if not relieved, it turns into complete 'rejection'. Usually one or more specific incidents bring it about, e.g. anxiety over wandering, sleeplessness at night, or resentment over paranoidal accusations. In other cases, denial of financial or some other benefit is responsible.

Once an attitude of rejection is fully established, it is my experience that nothing will alter it. Relief through hospital care, whether short or long, seems to be of no avail. The relatives are determined not to accept any further responsibility and will take extreme measures to avoid doing so.

The presence or absence of a rejection attitude is much more important than the duration of the senile psychosis, or the severity of the symptoms in deciding whether the patient requires hospital admission (Macmillan, 1962a).

It is the central thesis of this book that whether breakdown in old age occurs exclusively for reasons of organic deterioration or social rejection or from some combination or interaction between the two – and at this stage of our knowledge none of these possibilities is wholly precluded – then in accordance with the causes of dynamic psychology, a behavioural façade of social adjustment is super-imposed, the eccentricities and abnormalities of which afford the impression of 'confusion'. In Chapter 9 the development of an adaptation syndrome is traced with particular reference to the segregation, isolation and powerlessness to which residents are specially exposed in certain homes. But it is recognized of course that the theory has much wider application specific to the peculiarities of each individually different environment.

MODELS OF CONFUSION

A theoretical model of 'confusion' of this kind clearly has direct implications for the system of care proposed. Table 12.2 sets out some of the possible approaches and explores the follow-through of different systems.[103] It is of fundamental importance that the consequences of each approach are fully recognized, since care philosophies are normally totally pervasive and tend to unitary objectives.

Euthanasia is obviously not a positive approach so much as the rejection of any positive approach. For the other systems society

Table 12.2
Models of senility and dementia

Philosophy	Image of the elderly mentally infirm	Reaction of society	Management policy	Administrative procedures
1. Euthanasia	burden on charity/misery to themselves/ subhuman	total rejection	elmination	irrerversible medical deterioration best terminated
2. Warehousing	object of pity/helpless	segregation	paternalism	care to be restricted to physical nursing
3. Horticulture	mentally restricted	partial integration	develop-mental	independence and self-sufficiency to be encouraged as far as possible
4. Social deprivation	socially handicapped	full integration	normal-ization	expand social opportunities and prevent social rejection

imposes at least the minimum goal that the various institutions cater for the interval between social death on entry and physical death, inasmuch as 'to lack any actual or potential role that confers a positive social status in the wider society is tantamount to being socially dead' (Miller and Gwynne, 1968, chapter 5). The warehousing model takes the primary task to be the prolonging of the physical value of the person; the orientation is one of dependency. The horticultural model, on the other hand, is distinguished by the implementation of liberal as opposed to humanitarian values, inasmuch as its chief concern is to develop those capacities that remain to the person. Both models contain their inherent drawbacks: the patient in decline may feel as deprived by a horticultural climate as the active resident feels afflicted by the warehousing culture (*ibid*. chapter 7). In staff attitudes, warehousing institutions will tend to have a high proportion of qualified nursing staff who will be liable to overestimate physical and mental defects and to resist the pull of independence in those they look after. Evidence of these tendencies in certain special residential homes for the elderly mentally infirm has been documented in Chapter 8. But given the standpoint of the importance of the social aetiology, as has been argued here, it is clearly the social deprivation model that requires the closest attention.

FUTURE POLICY

If it is accepted that policies for old age should aim to recompense for disabilities in order to enable the elderly person to retain independence and normal functions so far as possible, and if it is recognized that the causation of mental confusion among the aged entails a strong social component, then certain prescriptions clearly follow:

1. Rather than increase residential accommodation, especially of a segregatively discriminatory kind, resources, both new and existing, should be decisively switched towards psychiatric community services which would give expert help with the causal situations at the earliest possible stage. It is vital to break the vicious circle whereby the obstinacy of seeking a physical or psychiatric aetiology for confusion[104] means in practice that release from an institution will not be contemplated till such symptoms are mitigated,[105] yet isolation, rejection and powerlessness are only too likely to intensify these characteristics. And once the appropriate social and physical responses are forthcoming, the apparent need for yet further specialized residential care becomes self-fulfilling.

2. The central emphasis should be placed on preventing family breakdown.

> Usually several factors had conspired in making admission necessary: medical reasons, breaking down of support from the family due to deaths, removals, etc., and mental deterioration causing unmanageable incontinence, wandering, danger from gas stoves, and fires. While in many cases hospitalization was inevitable in the long run, a review of all circumstances led us to believe that an earlier recognition of mental deterioration, more division of labour between relatives and the early deployment of social and medical services might have allowed many of these old people to spend most of their days in a happier state in their own homes. Referral of problem old people at an early state, and not at a time when 'disposal' dominates all other considerations, would also give doctors specializing in the geriatric field the experience from which preventive methods could be evolved (Cosin *et al.*, 1957, pp. 198–9).

3. In preventing social breakdown in the elderly, earlier ascertainment of incipient conditions is necessary than is usually achieved at present (Shaw, 1957). Post (1962), however, has noted that if dementia exists in elderly psychiatric patients, it is almost always well advanced by the time they are seen by psychiatrists, and that since mental difficulties do not manifest themselves until a certain threshold of cerebral deterioration is reached, psychological tests will also fail, sub-clinically, to indicate the presence of a dementing process (Post, 1959a). Nevertheless, research has pinpointed some of the known observable characteristics of psychiatrically disturbed old people in the community: poor health, looks older than age, physical disabilities more severe, mobility and capacity for self-care reduced, few personal contacts, secondary physical disabilities present, low income, lack of active hobbies, poor amenities in the home, age over seventy-five, admission to general hospital within the previous five years (all $P < 0.01$), together with failing eyesight and impaired hearing ($P < 0.02$) (Roth and Kay, 1962). Further research should refine these factors by their discriminating and predictive powers.

4. Assessment should be regularized on the basis of an annual medical and social check, as enabled by a comprehensive old people's community register, with more frequent contact with high-risk categories which should include the elderly mentally infirm as well as the severely incapacitated, those subject to extreme social isolation and the extreme aged (over eighty-five) (Agate and Meacher, 1969, p. 20). Investigation is preferable by domiciliary visit rather than examination in an out-patient clinic because of the greater opportunity provided for assessing the environment and the attitudes of all relevant parties.

The need for regular checks of this kind is amply revealed by research; for example, a study organized by the Royal College of Physicians (Edinburgh, 1963) found that a third of the disabilities of old people sampled were known to general practitioners, and other studies have discovered much higher proportions.[106] To cope with this problem, the attachment of nurses and health visitors to general practice has recently been rapidly proliferating,[107] to the reported mutual benefit of all the parties concerned.[108] Tests have revealed that health visitors can, with minimum training, efficiently detect physical disabilities, though they were less adequate at detecting psychiatric disability (Williamson *et al.*, 1966). (It should be added, however, that the health visitors had only had a few training sessions with psychiatrists and almost no practical instruction, so that their performance might be expected to improve considerably with training.)

Despite recent progress, ample scope for expansion is reported 'perhaps particularly in the direction of presymptomatic diagnosis by concentrating on high-risk practice patients' (Leiper and Warin, 1968). But even routine checks may yield salutary conclusions: it has, for example, been suggested that since 41 per cent of persons over sixty-five and known to be housebound in practices near Birmingham were found to have haemoglobin levels below 12·0 g/100 ml, periodic checks by a health visitor are warranted if the easy attribution of lassitude in old people to senile changes is to be avoided (Morgan, 1967).

In cases of doubt, referral to specialist consultative clinics will remain essential, for not only would early detection of unsuspected chronic illness appear to be the best means to prevent future ill-health (see, e.g., Beattie, 1963), but it has been shown that in the long term it avoids hospital admission (Anderson and Cowan, 1955). The best known of such preventive clinics was established in 1952 at Rutherglen (see *Brit. Med. J.*, 1964, ii, 1540) by the medical officer of health and a consultant physician, with the clinic located on local authority premises and patients referred by general practitioners. Other screening clinics set up recently include those at Twickenham, Dagenham and Paignton, but a much more comprehensive network of preventive care is required.

5. Once identified and assessed, the obligation should be clearly imposed on local authorities to ensure that all relevant services are made available, including mobile meals, laundry collection, home help or district nurse services, alternative housing, physiotherapy and occupational therapy. Since 1948 section 29(1) of the National Assistance Act has given the Minister powers to prescribe wider definitions of incapacity,[109] and section 29(4g) has given local authorities the power to compile and maintain registers. The need for very substantially widening the coverage of domiciliary services has been demonstrated by repeated surveys, such as Haider's (1968) findings that 46 per cent of a sample of old people admitted to psychiatric hopsital could have been maintained in the community by using the services of local authority and voluntary organizations supported by medical services. (He found that 15 per cent had

little or no infirmity, 17 per cent needed chiefly a home help, 14 per cent needed a home help in conjunction with nursing care and treatment, 34 per cent required psychiatric in-patient care and 20 per cent needed physical health care.) The most extensive recent documentation of the insufficiency of local authority services for the elderly – by Townsend and Wedderburn (1965), Harris and Clausen (1968) and Agate and Meacher (1969) – has abundantly illustrated not only the very high incidence of unsatisfied need, but also the substantial under-provision of existing services nationally as well as the asymmetry between measures of need and provision in the case of many individual authorities.

For specifically the mentally infirm aged, the evidence cited highlights the fragmentary present coverage of community services.[110] Day centres, for example, which could offer a valuable focus for confused persons, were run by only an eighth of local authorities,[111] and in a third of these cases not exclusively for the elderly mentally infirm, and even here their function was ambiguously understood.[112] Local authorities with separatist residential policies appeared less likely to develop community care facilities,[113] while great variations were seen in the use of mental welfare officers in the care of the confused elderly.[114] But apart from unexplained diversities, the overwhelming impression yielded is one of sheer inadequacy. Thus in a survey of seventy-two old people characterized by an extreme condition of senile breakdown, only half received such essential statutory services as those of the home nurse or home help, and only a third were helped by neighbours.[115]

What is therefore urgently required to universalize an adequate level of supportive care is, first, a legislative requirement that domiciliary services for the aged hitherto provided on a permissive basis, including especially dirty laundry collection, mobile meals and sheltered workshops, should be made mandatory; second, that specific health and welfare grants geared to at least minimum levels of provision of each individual service, which could be progressively raised over time, should replace the present rate support block grant which is inadequately discriminatory. In these respects the requirements of the elderly mentally infirm are no different, except in degree, from those of old people in need generally (see Agate and Meacher, 1969, pp. 27–30).

Where the mentally infirm to a disproportionate degree, like other handicapped groups in old age, have special needs unmet at the present time the solution lies in the availability of persisting personal assistance in an extended home help role. It has been suggested that such a function should comprehensively include the 'gamut of duties such as would be undertaken by a solicitous relative' (Wright and Roberts, 1958), and indeed the role of the social services in old age has been rightly construed as substituting for relatives, where these are absent or unable to assist, or alternatively supplementing their help with specialist skills. Yet it has already been indicated in this report (p. 364) that there was virtually no evidence in the case records of the six homes studied here of either statutory or voluntary assistance compensating for or supplementing relatives' efforts to support an elderly member in the community prior to admission. A regular and reliable home help able to devote several hours daily, or a team of home helps in total dispensing a similar time commitment, with duties including shopping, cooking, bathing and simple nursing duties as might be required, could transform the possibilities of community care for the isolated[116] and confused elderly if provided on a sufficient scale.[117]

6. Systematic home help of this kind might also be expected to offer a marked consolidation of both the extent and durability of family care of the elderly mentally infirm. Though near relatives often remain devoted even at advanced stages of confusion,[118] and reveal their dedication in washing soiled linen, accepting disruptions in shopping and sleeping, and in not calling medical attention to the senile decline of elderly members,[119] they are far more likely to retain the confused or to take back rehabilitated patients if given support,[120] especially in the provision of temporary holiday care[121] and night (or evening) sitting-in aid, and a sheet laundering service or substitute.[122]

The position of the unassisted family has been described succinctly by Barton (1966):

> After some months any housewife will come to the end of her tether if her life degenerates into endless washing of soiled sheets, poverty through additional expenditures, anxious rumination about what will have happened when she returns from shopping, the broken nights because the demented grannie starts wandering in the early hours of the morning. . . . Services such as home laundry, financial assistance (often such families are entitled to money but fail to realize it) and day hospital care two or three

days a week (during which period a bath can be given) can lighten the load. . . . Unrelenting and expert application of services like physiotherapy, walking exercises, chiropody, deaf aids (which are usually resisted and require an act in itself to persuade old people to use), and false teeth are essential, to enable a demented patient to make the most of his residual capacities (pp. 246–8).

Further valuable assistance in enabling a family to support an elderly mentally infirm relative should be given financially. As an extension of the present family allowance principle, special payments should be offered, subject to the confirmation of a medical certificate, for the long-term care in private households of old people who are either physically or mentally infirm. Such a payment should realistically cover the extra expenditures involved as well as to some extent potential earnings foregone, including the purchase of part-time services, if necessary for night attendance or a few hours' relief in the day. The same principle should also be extended to boarding-out arrangements[123] in the absence of a family, though subject to rigorous checks of suitability in view of the especial vulnerability of the confused.

The crucial importance of strengthening propping relationships[124] at an early stage is particularly demonstrated by Lieberman's findings concerning *pre-admission* family and group relations:

The common stereotype about the destructive influences on the aged of living in institutional settings is overdrawn. Many of the supposed psychological effects are characteristics of the person *prior* to his coming to an institution (and are related in part to the reasons for institutionalization) and some appear to be associated with aspects of *entering* the institution (making a radical change in the environment) which occurred before the individual actually entered the institution (Lieberman, 1969).

7. Since the evidence indicates not only an appalling lack of household aids for families caring for the confused elderly,[125] but also very poor quality accommodation in general, basic structural improvements in housing as well as adequate equipping with modern aids should be made a priority objective by local housing authorities. Also, sheltered housing should be enormously extended, and where local authorities have been dilatory under a permissive system,[126]

minimum levels of provision should be made mandatory. In order to facilitate the spread of such housing Government should offer a special subsidy for the provision of warden-supervised accommodation at prescribed adequate levels, and as a corresponding incentive to the laggards a local authority league table should be regularly (preferably annually) published by the Ministry.

Such solutions appear more desirable than the spread of temporary or longer-term hostels or group homes, which may not offer the same degree of integration in the community[127] and appear over time to be developing some of the 'dumping-ground' function of their larger institutional predecessors. Though it has been claimed that the half-way house which tests a patient's suitability to life either in his own home or a hostel 'has played an important role in diminishing the number of refused discharges' (Howell, 1967), Apte (1966, p. 158) and others have noted that transient hostels are increasingly becoming long-term and in the absence of any therapeutic role they have developed as places where former patients can live in rather closer contact with the community on a semi-permanent basis. It is significant here that no group homes, such as those started by Newport, Mon., in 1962, and by Colchester using a block of large council houses, have been found to contain any senile organic psychotics (D. Wilson, 1967).

8. Given a decisive switch from institutional to community care – with all that implies in terms of early and comprehensive assessment, more regular routine checks on those in high-risk categories, much wider provision of domiciliary services, improved housing and greater family aids – there would still remain the fundamental need to direct limited resources towards the yet earlier and logically prior goal of prevention. Clearly achievement here is dependent on a correct diagnosis of the (perhaps multiple) aetiology, but in so far as social influences have been plausibly revealed to play a significant contribution,[128] certain policy directives immediately follow. Perhaps the two most important are the need to preserve the family structure intact[129] as the natural care agency, and secondly to maintain and encourage work or other positive family commitments as long as possible.[130]

But if the deeper antecedents of confusion in old age are to be effectively pursued, a great deal more information must be uncovered by careful and systematic research. Such items must include seeking to answer the following questions:

(*a*) Given matched samples of old people according to sex, age, marital status and number of children, differentiated only by the presence or absence of confusional behaviour, what significant variations exist between the two groups in social history and psychological background?

(*b*) How many confused elderly persons, according to a standardized definition, are living in private households? How do they differ from the elderly population at large by age, sex, marital status, number of children, type of housing tenure, employment history, extent of social contacts, financial circumstances and so on?

(*c*) How do they cope? What family contacts do they maintain, and what statutory or voluntary services support them? How many are isolated, and what is the pattern of self-care in these cases, especially regarding nutrition?

(*d*) How many elderly mentally infirm persons are at present residing in geriatric wards, psychiatric hospitals, psychiatric units of general hospitals, nursing homes or other institutions? How do those allocated to each of these destinations differ from each of the other groups, and how do the various environments influence the course of their mental infirmity?

(*e*) What is the feasibility, in terms of both economic and social costs and gains, of switching to a largely, or even virtually exclusively, domiciliary pattern of care for the confused aged?

(*f*) What measures can be demonstrated to have the greatest prophylactic value in preventing or postponing the onset of confusion in old age? What events in the normal career sequence of old age, such as the loss of a close living companion in advanced age,[131] appear to be the most indicative signposts for the application of these measures?

Until these questions are answered, until the full provision of essential community services is systematized, the range and type of residential care required cannot be accurately gauged. Nor, most importantly of all, will we have begun to offer the growing numbers of confused elderly in our society the appropriate kind of social care that is their right, however it will involve the rest of us in extending to an as yet little understood group among us more of our time, commitment, patience and love.

NOTES

1. Attempts have certainly been made to devise scales appropriate to a single institutional system (for example, King and Raynes, 1968). A similar child management scale has been developed by Tizard *et al.* (1966).

2. See the Brooklands experiment (Tizard, 1964).

3. Identified as the key to the growing staff shortage in residential homes by the Williams Committee (National Council of Social Service, 1967). The Committee noted that single women formed fully two-thirds of existing staff, and took the view that when unmarried young women now represented only a third of their population proportion sixty years ago, a crisis was inevitable unless more men, more married couples and more older married women could be recruited.

4. See also Greenblatt *et al.* (1957).

5. A trend which for psychiatric patients has already advanced considerably further in some countries especially Sweden.

6. Where a patient's work has become so intimately associated with the routine for maintaining the satisfactory running of the hospital that he has (realistically?) formed a preference for hospital life rather than that outside, it has been suggested that the unconscious collusion between the hospital and the patient in thwarting the rehabilitative efforts of the psychiatrist may not necessarily be undesirable (Oram and Clark, 1966).

7. Fourth Report of the Estimates Committee, Session 1968–69, on *Housing Subsidies*.

8. 'Any applicant who, for whatever reason, is regarded (by the housing visitor) as undesirable as an occupant of the newer or better houses will be placed in slum property' (Rex and Moore, 1967, p. 26).

9. See Stein and Stores (1965) p. 379, for a discussion on IQ changes in ESN children at special schools.

10. See, for example, the recent proposal for 'super schools' for the top 2 per cent of the IQ range: *Sunday Times*, 29 March 1970.

11. For example, that compiled by the Labour Party, in *Labour's Social Strategy* (1969) p. 113, Table II, or by Davies (1968) p. 169, Table 23.

12. Roberts v. Hopwood, 1925, where it was held that Poplar councillors, who were surcharged, had been guided 'by some eccentric principles of socialistic philanthropy and by a feminist ambition to secure equality of the sexes in the matter of wages in the world of labour'. (D. G. T. Williams, 1968).

13. In Prescott v. Birmingham Corporation 1955, the Council's action was ruled as ultra vires on grounds of 'an excess of misplaced philanthropic zeal'.

14. See, for example, Klare 1967, pp. 286–7.

15. The report adds (pp. 169–70) that integrants were satisfied academically, had their outlook broadened by the diverse extracurricular life and found no substantial difficulties in social mixing, but 'persistently questioned, challenged and sometimes defied elements central to the public school system: its total control (and consequent cultural deprivation), its hierarchy and authority system'. Even if fundamental changes in the basic structure of the schools could hardly be made for an entry of 2 per cent, it is significant that even an entry of only 2 per cent caused problems of balance and blockage.

16. Former public assistance institutions continue to be used in part to perform the function of segregating the confused because of the room they provide for wandering and for the seclusion of private idiosyncrasies: see p. 400. But their generally much lower standard of amenities, despite substantial upgrading, renders them unsuitable, especially since they also disproportionately accommodate the more seriously physically handicapped and the avowedly anti-social.

17. See pp. 369–70. Separatist homes appear particularly to absorb elderly paranoics

from psychiatric hospitals and those described as displaying confusional or dementing symptoms from geriatric units: see p. 354.

18. Another reason given was isolation at home, though this does not of course justify explicitly separatist policies. A survey of Bolton reveals that 84 per cent of the old people sampled still had contact with and visits from relatives, though 'this contact was not always sufficient to meet the need of caring for elderly people in prolonged illness or diability'.

19. If mental confusion in old age has a strong social aetiology.

20. For example, see p. 112.

21. See *'The social and psychological implications of segregation . . .'*, Chapter 8, p. 378.

22. As described in Chapter 8. Again, the generally better physical appearance of the confused in the ordinary homes rather than in the special establishments may have resulted from the fact that where the confused were only relatively few, the staff devoted to them a level of attention which beyond a certain point of numerical balance between confused and rational residents, they gradually sacrificed as their standards of care declined: see p. 246.

23. p. 322ff.

24. p. 329ff.

25. Analogies involving stigma in other fields have been discussed above, under 'Integration: a goal of social policy, p. 459ff.

26. Some pointers to this conclusion are described at p. 258ff.

27. As described, for example, at p. 189–90.

28. See pp. 196–7.

29. See p. 192.

30. See pp. 360–2.

31. See p. 384.

32. See p. 213, n 18

33. See p. 379.

34. See p. 385.

35. See p. 199.

36. See p. 205.

37. See pp. 206–7.

38. See p. 207.

39. See p. 211.

40. See p. 8.

41. See p. 290.

42. See pp. 141–2.

43. See p. 152.

44. See pp. 152–3.

45. See p. 177ff.

46. See p. 174.

47. See p. 158, Table 7.2.

48. Though other factors such as the personality and ideology of the superintendent or matron are also clearly influential here: see pp. 214–15.

49. See p. 244.

50. See p. 226.

51. See p. 222.

52. See pp. 220–1.

53. For example in one separatist home where two-fifths of the residents were severely confused and a further third moderately so.

54. See pp. 188–90.

55. See, for example, pp. 166–9.

56. See p. 290.
57. See p. 294ff.
58. See p. 242ff.
59. See p. 241. Significantly the Chief Welfare Officer responsible for Warstone House, a twenty-seven-bed separatist home in West Bromwich, considered that in view of holidays and sickness the staff establishment was insufficient even though it comprised: chief male nurse, deputy charge nurse, six full-time and three part-time nurses, two full-time cooks and two part-time domestic assistants.
60. See p. 379.
61. See p. 7.
62. See p. 191.
63. See p. 194.
64. See p. 256.
65. See p. 383.
66. See p. 342, n. 7.
67. It is relevant to allude here to a directive in 1949 in the State of California to Boards of Supervisors; Superior Court Judges, Medical Examiners, District Attorneys, Welfare Directors and Health Officers. It discouraged the admission to mental hospitals of 'harmless seniles', the relevant symptoms regarded as not indicating state hospitalization being listed as physical infirmities, moderate memory loss, childishness, irritability or restlessness, careless toilet habits, feeding problems, and occasional periods of mild depression. As a result, within one year the admissions of persons aged sixty-five and over decreased from 22·7 per cent to 15·5 per cent of all admissions (Statistical Research Bureau, California, Department of Mental Hygiene, 23 July 1953). In 1958, despite the increasing proportion of elderly people in the general population, the percentage went down again (*ibid.*, 7 January 1959).
68. A psychiatrist has given his view – partly in exasperation at the mounting demands of the elderly on psychiatric beds – that 'patients with either senile or arteriosclerotic dementia die within two years, and they are more likely to be at peace at home than in a hospital': M. D. Enoch, 'The care of the elderly disturbed patient', *Lancet*, 1963, i, 1160.
69. A Local Authority Building Note no. 2, *Residential Accommodation for Elderly People*, Min. of Health, 1962, makes the explicit recommendation (p. 7): 'A sluice-room, fifty to sixty sq. ft, with a sink, slop hopper with drainer top and a slab for scrubbing mackintosh sheeting, is required for each floor with residents' bedrooms.'
70. Significantly, in the case of the mentally handicapped in one hospital, an occupational therapist noted that they were *never* incontinent when engaged in musical activities (P. Morris, 1970, p. 162).
71. See p. 232.
72. Indeed, Cumming, Clancy and Cumming (1956) argue that all mentally ill patients require a high level of interaction with other patients and with staff in order to improve.
73. See p. 287.
74. See p. 189.
75. See also Rudd *et al.* (1962), p. 1257.
76. See '*The social and psychological implication of segregation* . . .', Chapter 8, p. 270.
77. Some have, however, though without argument, suggested that psychiatric experience was required here. 'There is a need for accommodation for demented patients who require some degree of restraint, but who do not require all the services of a mental hospital. Their needs could be met largely by nurses trained in geriatrics if the nurse in charge had psychiatric training. Their medical officer need not be a psychiatrist so long as there is adequate psychiatric supervision' (1962), p. 100.

78. See p. 265.
79. See p. 249.
80. See p. 261. Goffman (1961, p. 381) interpreted medication as merely a method of keeping the ward quiet at night through the forced taking of drugs which permitted reduced night staffing.
81. See p. 248.
82. See p. 232.
83. See pp. 401-2. Woodroffe and Townsend similarly recommend, in order that a few individuals can develop an experienced knowledge in the enforcement of standards, that a regional inspectorate be established under a medical officer of health with powers to register and visit all types of voluntary and private homes for the sick and infirm (Woodroffe and Townsend, 1961, p. 58).
84. In Robb, ed. (1967), and Abel-Smith, 'A hospital ombudsman', *New Society*, 22 April 1971.
85. Cmnd 4557, HMSO 1971.
86. Indeed the official inquiry into Farleigh Mental Hospital, Somerset, recommended not only a code of conduct for nurses dealing with violent and difficult patients, but also more money and better staffing for wards having apparently intractable problems.
87. See p. 240.
88. See pp. 408-13.
89. See Agate and Meacher (1969), p. 18; also p. 411 of this report.
90. See below, 'Longer-term objectives', p. 488.
91. Fish adds: 'The nursing staff of mental hospitals do not have sufficient practice with such procedures as intravenous drip and are not well trained in the general care of acutely physically ill patients. Similarly the medical staff of such hospitals, although able to deal with life and death emergencies, have no special skill and interest in the physically sick old person.'
92. See pp. 412-13.
93. See p. 369.
94. See p. 43.
95. See p. 43.
96. See pp. 40.
97. See pp. 41-2.
98. M. Roth, 'Mental health problems of ageing and the aged', *Bull. Wld. Health Org.*, 1959, **21**, p. 534.
99. See for example Droller and Dorsett (1959), and Strachan and Henderson (1965 and 1967) 189. A *Brit. Med. J.* editorial argues: 'Dementia due to folate deficiency should be considered if an elderly mentally disturbed patient has a history suggestive of nutritional deficiency' *Brit. Med. J.* (1969, p. 608).
100. Dietary allowances recommended by the BMA committee (see *Brit. Med. J.*, 1950, i, 541) make no distinction between younger and older adults, but various surveys have suggested that the intake of nutrients among old people falls far short of the recommendations for 'adults with sedentary work and little travelling, in which category the groups of old people investigated most neatly fit' (*Brit. Med. J.*, 1961, ii, 1706).
101. It is known that of the two main types of cerebral degenerative process – vascular, affecting the large and small cerebral vessels, and senile, involving the nervous tissue more directly and including cerebral atrophy, formation of senile plaques and degeneration and loss of nerve cells – both are widely distributed through the elderly population and their intensity varies considerably from person to person (Foley, 1956; Botton, 1955).
102. Corsellis (1962, p. 259) argues that the correlation is not complete because (1) probably the disintegration and loss of nerve cells is the most important of the various changes known to occur in the senile brain, though it is not known whether the degree

of this loss is closely reflected in the extent to which senile plaques are formed; (2) the marked degree of small vessel degeneration which tends to occur as part of the degenerative process (see Surbek, 1961; Scholz, 1938) may have been underestimated in senile dementia; (3) the localization of the degenerative process in the brain may be more important at times than its severity.

103. Cf. Goffman (1961) ch. 4; Susser and Watson (1962), p. 293; Siegler and Osmond (1966); Scheff (1967); Nirje (1969); Wolfensberger (1969, 1970).

104. See p. 339.

105. See p. 340.

106. Of 486 old people selected by a records clerk from the age/sex register at the month they reached sixty-five, together with those over sixty-five referred by doctors, 3 to 7 per cent (of the two-thirds agreeing to examination) were found to be quite fit, 15 per cent had a single disability, and 77 to 82 per cent had multiple disabilities (Thomas, 1968).

107. Elliott (1969) estimated that 20 per cent of local authority nursing staff and 25 per cent of health visitors were then attached to general practitioners, and J. A. D. Anderson and Draper (1967) show that the rate of introduction of attachment schemes has trebled in the period 1964–67.

108. Abel (1969), in a study undertaken by the SSR Unit of DHSS, demonstrates the increase in work satisfactions. Other studies found that attached staff were much more satisfied about the information regarding patients supplied by doctors (Walker and McClure, 1969), and also that the majority of doctors have favoured such attachment schemes (Boddy, 1969).

109. Section 29(1) states: 'A local authority shall have power to make arrangements for promoting the welfare of persons ... who are blind, deaf or dumb and other persons who are substantially and permanently handicapped by illness, injury or congenital deformity *or such other disabilities as may be prescribed by the Minister*.' (Author's italics). This power has now been reinforced by the Chronically Sick and Disabled Persons Act 1970. Also, section 25 of the National Health Service Act 1948 states that it shall be the duty of every local authority to make such provision in their area ... for securing the attendance of nurses on persons who require nursing in their own homes.'

110. See pp. 447–9.

111. See p. 449.

112. See p. 450–1.

113. See pp. 451–2.

114. See p. 448.

115. See p. 453.

116. Connolly (see pp. 599–600) found that the elderly in his sample admitted to psychiatric hospital who were acutely confused were all technically 'isolated'.

117. Cf. regarding a severely physically disabled woman: 'One of the conditions of her being granted a council flat was that she would have a reliable companion living with her who would undertake the very considerable responsibilities involved' (letter from the National Campaign for the Young Chronic Sick to the Home Secretary, 1970).

118. See p. 441.

119. See p. 443.

120. See p. 446.

121. Short-term holiday admissions, however, unless restricted to careful selected cases, can produce very deleterious effects. In one such survey it was noted that those who fared worst were the very old, the confused and the incontinent, of whom a fifth under the age of seventy-four and fully a third over this age deteriorated or died, though 'some would have deteriorated or died even if they had not been admitted to hospital' (Isaacs and Thompson, 1960). Similar doubts, though on a lesser scale must be expressed about the effects of month-in/month-out care on a regular rota.

122. 'Incontinence was a large factor in determining whether relatives were able to cope with the [elderly] patient, and the suggestion is put forward that the more extensive use of disposable drawsheets might be useful in this connection' (Morris, 1962, p. 803).

123. Exeter Council of Social Service, *Mental Health – New Needs and Opportunities*, found (though on a small scale) that boarding-out could be achieved even with elderly persons who had been in mental hospital for twenty years. A scheme for subsidizing lodgings with sympathetic landladies is also put forward by Irvine (1967), pp. 34–5; see also National Council of Social Service (1970).

124. The evidence (p. 601) suggests these are often precarious in the extreme.

125. See p. 453.

126. The 1966 revised Blue Book (Cmnd 3022) *Health and Welfare: the Development of Community Care*, reveals that seventy-six of the 173 local authorities (42 per cent) were supplying less than 40 per cent of the national average and twenty-nine (16 per cent) had built no sheltered housing at all, of whom a quarter had still planned none even for 1971.

127. Doubts must be expressed on similar grounds about the AEGIS plan (Project 70) to rehouse old people from mental hospitals in supposedly integrated communities, in the vast acreage of land in the hospital grounds (Robb, ed., 1969, pp. 124–7).

128. See Chapter 9 and also p. 496ff.

129. 'In several cases widowhood and slum clearance shemes led to re-housing and this had a detrimental effect. Old ladies who had friends in the centre of the town were moved to very nice bungalows on the outskirts, where their friends had difficulty in visiting because of the distance involved and expense of the bus fares. The resultant isolation, combined with some confusion in the new surroundings, was sufficient to precipitate the necessity for admission' (Morris, 1962, p. 801).

130. The implications here for social policy are fully discussed in Agate and Meacher (1969), pp. 22–6.

131. As found in Nottingham by Shaw and Macmillan (1961).

Bibliography

ABEL, R. A. (1969) *Nursing Attachments to General Practice*, HMSO

ABEL-SMITH, B. (1971) 'A hospital ombudsman?', *New Society*, 672, 22 Apr.

ADAMS, M. (1960) *The Mentally Subnormal: the social casework approach*, Heinemann

AGATE, J. (1968) *Proc. Roy. Soc. Med.*, 61, 922

AGATE J. and MEACHER, M. (1969) *The Care of the Old*, Fabian Society

ALBRECHT, R. (1951) 'Social roles in the prevention of senility', *J. Gerontol.*, 6, 380–386

ALDERS, W. (1963) 'Senility: after the prognosis, what?', *Geriatrics*, 18, 315

ALLEN, E. B. (1955) 'The management of cerebral arteriosclerosis: psychiatric aspects', *Bull. N.Y. Acad. Med.*, 31, 366–475

ALLEN, R. M. (1947) 'Test performance of the brain injured', *J. Clin. Psychol.*, 3, 225–30

ALLISON, R. S. (1962) *The Senile Brain: a clinical study*, Arnold

ANDERSON, J. A. D. and DRAPER, P. A. (1967) *Med. Offr.*, 117, 111

ANDERSON, W. F. and COWAN, N. R. (1955) *Lancet*, ii, 239

ANDERSON, W. F. and COWAN, N. R. (1963) 'Preventive geriatric medicine', *Med. World, London*, 99, 553–5

ANDERSON, W. F. and ISAACS, B., eds (1964) *Current Achievements in Geriatrics*, Cassell

ANDREWS, J. D. B. and INSLEY, M. L. (1962) 'The long-stay psycho-geriatric unit: its role in the care of the ambulant confused elderly', *Geront. clin.*, 4, 94

APTE, R. Z. (1966) 'The transititional hostel', in *Problems and Progress in Medical Care*, 2nd series, Oxford University Press for Nuffield Provincial Hospitals Trust

APTE, R. Z. (1968) *Halfway Houses*, Bell

ARDREY, R. (1967) *The Territorial Imperative*, Collins

ATKIN, I. (1959) 'Community care of the mentally ill' (letter), *Brit. Med. J.*, ii, 1401

ATKIN, I. (1963) 'The demand for psychiatric beds', *Lancet*, i, 336

BABCOCK, H. (1930) 'An experiment in the measure of mental deterioration', *Arch. Psychol.*, 18, 117

BAILEY, P. (1967) *At the Jerusalem*, Cape

BAKER, A. A. and THORPE, J. G. (1956) *J. Ment. Sci.*, 102

BALINT, M. (1957) *The Doctor, His Patient and the Illness*, Pitman

BARKER, J. C. (1967) letter, *Brit. Med. J.*, iii, 245

BARKER, M. G. and LAWSON, J. S. (1968) 'Nominal aphasia in dementia', *Brit. J. Psychiat.*, 114, 1351–6

BARTON, R. (1959) *Institutional Neurosis*, Bristol, Wright

BARTON, R. (1963) 'Toxic side effects of drug usage', *Ment. Hosp.* Dec., 654–5

BARTON, R. (1966a) *Developing a Service for Elderly Demented Patients in Psychiatric Hospital Care*, ed. H. Freeman, Baillière, Tindall and Cassell

BARTON, R. (1966b) *Lancet*, ii, 1417

BARTON, R. and HAIDER, I. (1966) 'Unnecessary compulsory admissions to a psychatric hospital', *Med. Sci. Law*, 6, 147–50

BARTON, R. and HURST, L. (1966) 'Unnecessary use of tranquillisers in elderly patients', *Brit. J. Psychiat.*, 112, 989–90

BARTON, R. and WHITEHEAD, J. A. (1968) 'A psycho-geriatric domiciliary emergency service', *Brit. J. Psychiat.*, 114, 107–8

Bibliography

BAYLEY, N., RHODES, L. and GOOCH, B. (1966) 'A comparison of the growth and development of institutionalised and home-reared mongoloids – a follow-up study', *Amer. J. Ment. Defic.*, July

BEATTIE, J. W. (1963) *J. Coll. gen. Pract.*, 6, 20

BEDFORD, P. D. (1956a) *J. Amer. Geriat. Soc.*, 4, 1063

BEDFORD, P. D. (1956b) *Proc. Roy. Soc. Med.*, 49

BEDFORD, P. D. (1957) *Lancet*, ii, 505

BEDFORD, P. D. (1959) 'General medical aspects of confusional states in elderly people', *Brit. Med. J.*, ii, 185–8

BEDFORD, P. D. (1961) *Pakistan Med. J.*, i, 25

BELKNAP, I. (1956) *Human Problems of a State Medical Hospital*, McGraw-Hill

BELL, W. (1957) 'Anomie, social isolation and class structure', *Sociometry*, June

BELLIN, S. S. and HARDT, R. H. (1958) 'Marital status and mental disorders among the aged', *Amer. Soc. Rev.*, 23, 155–62

BENSON, S. and TOWNSEND, P. (forthcoming) *Old People in Long-Stay Institutions*

BIGOT, A. (1969) 'Apathy among elderly people living in residential homes: an interim report', August (unpublished)

BIGOT, A. (1967) 'Apathy: a preliminary report on Staffordshire local authority homes and some general characteristics of their residents', unpublished Ph.D. thesis, Keele, Sept.

BERK, N. G. (1958) 'The principles of sound nutrition in the aged', *Geriatrics*, 13, 334

BERESFORD-COOKE, K. (1965) 'Occupational therapy in the rehabilitation of the psychiatric geriatric patient at Crichton Royal, Dumfries', *J. Psychiat. Nursing, New Jersey*, 3, 160–73

BERESFORD, C. C. (1960) 'Senile dementia', *Practitioner*, 184, 712

BERESFORD, C. C. (1962) 'Senile dementia', *Nursing Times*, 58, 861

BINKS, F. A. (1968) 'An approach to disability and breakdown', *Brit. Med. J.*, i, 269–74

BINKS, J. K. and ROBERTSON, E. E. (1962) 'Pick's disease in old age', *J. Ment. Sci.*, 108, 804

BIRREN, J. E. (1959) *The Process of Ageing in the Nervous System*, Illinois, Springfield

BIRREN, J. E. (1963) *The Psychology of Ageing*, Prentice-Hall

BLACKADDER, E. S. (1960) *The Almoner*, 12, 469

BLACKER, C. P. (1959) *Mentally Infirm People over 65 : Need for Better Means of Support and Disposal*, Board of Governors of Bethlem and Maudsley Hospitals

BLUMENTHAL, H. T. ed. (1962) *Medical and Clinical Aspects of Ageing*, Columbia University Press

BODDY, F. A. (1969) 'The health of Cumberland: Report of County Medical Officer, Cumberland C.C.', *Brit. Med. J.*, ii, 438

BOOTH, W. G., SEPPALT, I. H. and TAYLOR, I. O. (1963) 'A day treatment centre for the elderly (at Ealing)', *Lancet*, i, 765–8

BOTTON, J. E. (1955) 'Arteriosclerose cérébrale: étude anatomo-clinique et statistique', *Encephale*, 44, 350–96

BOTWINICK, J. and BIRREN, J. E. (1951a) 'Differential decline in Wechsler–Bellevue sub-test in senile psychosis', *J. Geront.*, 6, 365–8

BOTWINICK, J. and BIRREN, J. E. (1951b) 'The measurement of intellectual decline in the senile psychoses', *J. Consult. Psychol.*, 15, 145–50

BOUCHER, C. A. (1957) *Survey of Services Available to the Chronic Sick and Elderly, 1954–5*, HMSO, ch. 7, 'Mental health'

BOURESTOM, N. C. and IVERSON, I. A. (1965) 'A rating scale for appraising the behavioural adjustment of elderly brain-damaged patients', paper read to 18th meeting of Gerontological Society, Los Angeles, November

BOURNE, R. (1969) ' "Fair" plan that angers parents', *Guardian*, 2 Apr.

BOZA, R., STOCKARD, J., WILDER, D. L. and CARMONA, N. (1969) 'Wandering away: a

Bibliography

major cause of psychiatric hospitalisation for the geriatric patient', paper read to the 8th International Congress of Gerontology, Washington

BREE, M. H. (1960) *The Dement in the Community*, Horton Group, HMC

BREMER, J. (1951) 'A social psychiatric investigation of a small community in northern Norway', *Acta psychiat. Scand.*, suppl. 62

BRITISH MEDICAL JOURNAL (1964) Editorial: 'Side effects of phenothiazine drugs', *Brit. Med. J.*, ii, 1412

BRITISH MEDICAL JOURNAL (1969) Editorial: 'Old age, nutrition and mental confusion', *Brit. Med. J.*, iii, 608–9

BROCKLEHURST, J. C. (1964) 'The work of a geriatric day hospital', *Geront. clin.*, 6, 151–66

BROCKLEHURST, J. C. (1966) 'Co-ordination in the care of the elderly', *Lancet*, i, 1363

BRODY, M. B. (1942) 'A psychometric study of dementia', *J. Ment. Sci.*, 88, 512–33

BROMLEY, D. B. (1966) *The Psychology of Human Ageing*, Pelican

BROWN, G. W. (1959) 'Social factors influencing length of stay of schizophrenic patients', *Brit. Med. J.*, ii, 1300

BROWN, G. W. (1960) 'Length of hospital stay and schizophrenia: a review of statistical studies', *Acta Psychiat. et Neurol. Scand.*, 35, 414

BURDOCK, E. I., HARDESTY, A. S., HAKEREM, G. and ZUBIN, J. (1960) 'A ward behaviour rating scale for mental patients', *J. Clin. Psychol.*, 16, 46–7

BURGMAN, J., OLDENBANDRING, G. H. and SCHRENDER, J. TH. R. (1962) *Geront. din. additamentum*, p. 179

BURNEY, E. (1967) *Housing on Trial: a Study of Immigrants and Local Government*, Institute of Race Relations

BUROWES, (1963) *Lancet*, i, 949

BURTON, L. (1965) Ph.D. thesis, Queen's University, Belfast

BUSSE, E. W., BARNES, R. H., SILVERMAN, A., THALER, M. and FROST, L. (1955) 'Studies of processes of ageing', *Amer. J. Psychiat.*, iii, 896–901

BUSSE, E. W. (1960) 'Psychiatric problems of the ageing: clinical principles underlying administrative practices', *Ment. Hosp.*, 11, 17

BUSSE, E. W. (1961) 'Psychoneurotic reactions and defence mechanisms in the aged', in *The Psychopathology of Ageing*, ed., Hoch and Zubin, q.v.

BUTLER, R. N. (1963) 'The life review: an interpretation of reminiscence in the aged', *Psychiat. J. for Study of Interpersonal Processes*, 26, 65–76

CAIRD, W. K., SANDERSON, R. E. and INGLIS, J. (1962) *J. Ment. Sci.*, 108, 368

CAMERON, N. (1947) *The Psychology of Behaviour Disorders*, Cambridge, Riverside Press

CAMPBELL, A. C. (1968) 'Comparison of family and community contacts of mentally subnormal adults in hospital and in local authority hostels', *Brit. J. prev. soc. Med.*, 22, 165–9

CAPOORE, H. S. and NIXON, J. W. G. (1961) 'Short-stay psychiatric unit in a general hospital', *Lancet*, ii, 1351–2

CARTWRIGHT, A. (1964) *Human Relations and Hospital Care*, Routledge

CASP, F. M. (1968) 'Some components of disengagement', *J. Gerontol.*, 23, 382–6

CASTELL, J. and MITTLER, P. (1965) 'The intelligence of patients in subnormality hospitals: a survey of admission in 1961', *Brit. J. Psychiat.*, iii, 219–25

CAUDILL, W. A. (1958) *The Psychiatric Hospital as a Small Community*, Harvard University Press

CERLETTI, U. (1925) *Atti. soc. lombardi Sci. med. biol.*, 14, 2

CHYNOWETH, R. and FOLEY, J. (1969) 'Treatment of pre-senile dementia by steroid therapy', *Brit. J. Psychiat.*, 115, 703–8

CICOUREL, A. V. and KITSUSE, J. I. (1963) *The Educational Decision-makers*, Bobbs-Merrill

CLARKE, A. and CLARKE, A. D. B. (1966) *Mental Deficiency: the Changing Outlook*, Methuen

CLARK, D. H. (1964) *Administrative Therapy: the Role of the Doctor in the Therapeutic Community*, Tavistock

CLARKE, P. R. F., WYKE, M. and ZANGWILL, O. L. (1958) *J. Neurol. Psychiat.*, **21**, 190

CLINARD, M. B., ed. (1964) *Anomie and Deviant Behaviour*, New York, Free Press

COLLINS, P., MARSHALL, J. and SHAW, D. A. (1960) 'Social rehabilitation following cerebrovascular accidents', *Geront. clin.*, **2**, 246–56

COLLISON, P. (1963) 'The Cutteslowe Saga', *New Society*, 25 Apr., pp. 18–20

COLWELL, C. and POST, F. (1959) 'Community needs of elderly psychiatric patients', *Brit. Med. J.*, ii, 214–17

COMFORT, A. (1967) 'Institutions without Sex', *New Society*, 5 Jan.

COMMITTEE OF ENQUIRY INTO ALLEGATIONS OF ILL-TREATMENT OF PATIENTS AND OTHER IRREGULARITIES AT THE ELY HOSPITAL, CARDIFF (1969), *Report*, Cmnd 3757, HMSO

COMMITTEE OF ENQUIRY INTO THE COST OF THE NATIONAL HEALTH SERVICE (Guillebaud Committee) (1956) *Report* Cmd 9663, HMSO, Jan.

COMMITTEE ON THE ECONOMIC AND FINANCIAL PROBLEMS OF THE PROVISION FOR OLD AGE (Phillips Committee) (1954), *Report*, Cmd 9333, HMSO

COMMITTEE ON LOCAL AUTHORITY AND ALLIED PERSONAL SERVICES (Seebohm Committee) (1968), *Report*, Cmnd 3703, HMSO

CONNOLLY, J. (1962) 'The social and medical circumstances of old people admitted to a psychiatric hospital', *Med. Offr.*, 10 Aug., 95–100

CONNOLLY, J., LUMSDEN, M. R. and ROSS, D. (1964) 'The care of old people six months after admission to a psychiatric hospital: a survey of 153 consecutive admissions of 60 years and over', *Med. Offr.*, **111**, 196

COOK, L. C., DAX, E. C. and MACLAY, W. S. (1952) 'The geriatric problem in mental hospitals', *Lancet*, i, 377–82

CORSELLIS, J. A. N. (1962) *Mental Illness and the Ageing Brain: the distribution of pathological change in a mental hospital population* (Maudsley Monograph no. 9) Oxford University Press

COR, M., FAURE, R. and RIDJANOVIC-LAIRY, G. C. (1963) 'EEG study of the sleep of normal and pathological elderly people', *Electroenceph. Clin. Neurophysiol.*, **15**

COPPLE, G. E. (1948) 'Senescent decline on the Wechsler–Bellevue Intelligence Scale', unpub. doctoral thesis, University of Pittsburgh

COOPER, D. (1967) *Psychiatry and Anti-psychiatry*, Tavistock

COSIN, L. Z. (1956) 'A new approach to the problem of geriatric care', *Kaiser Fedn. med. Bull.*, **4**, 321

COSIN, L. Z. (1954) 'The place of the day hospital in the geriatric unit', *Practitioner*, **172**, 552

COSIN, L. Z. (1957) *Progress in Psychotherapy*, New York, Grune & Stratton

COSIN, L. Z. (1958) 'The elderly' ch. 15 in *Bridging the Gap*, ed. R. F. Tredgold, q.v.

COSIN, L. Z. and MORT, M., *Occupational Therapy in a Geriatric Unit*, privately printed

COSIN, L. Z. and ROTH, M. (1956) 'Discussion on geriatric problems in psychiatry', *Proc. Roy. Soc. Med.*, **49**, 237

COSIN, L. Z., MORT, M., POST, F., WESTROPP, C. and WILLIAMS, M. (1957) 'Persistent senile confusion: a study of fifty consecutive cases', *Internat. J. Soc. Psychiat.*, **3**, 195ff.

COSIN, L. Z., MORT, M., POST, F., WESTROPP, C. and WILLIAMS, M. (1958) 'Experimental treatment of persistent senile confusion', *Internat. J. Soc. Psychiat.*, **4**, 24–42

CROSS, K. W. and YATES, J. (1961) 'Follow-up study of admission to mental hospitals', *Lancet*, May

CUMMING, E. and HENRY, W. E. (1961) *Growing Old : the process of disengagement*, New York, Basic Books

CUMMING, E., CLANCY, and CUMMING, J. (1956) *Psychiatry*, 19

CUMMING, E., DEAN, L. R., NEWELL, D. S. and MCCAFFREY, I. (1960) 'Disengagement: a tentative theory of ageing', *Sociometry*, 23, 23–35

DAVIES, B. (1968) *Social Needs and Resources in Local Services*, Michael Joseph

DAVISON, W. (1965) 'Drug hazards in the elderly', *Geront clin.*, 7, 257–64

DAX, E. C. and REITMAN, F. (1946) *Brit. Med. J.*, i, 736

DEJAIFFE, G. (1964) 'Electro-clinical correlations in senile dementia', *Acta Neurol. Belg.*, 64, 677

DELARGY, J. (1957) 'Six weeks in: six weeks out: a geriatric hospital scheme for rehabilitating the aged and relieving their relatives', *Lancet*, i, 418

DEWAN, J. G. and SPAULDING, W. B. (1958) *The Organic Psychosis*, Toronto University Press

DIETHELM, O. and ROCKWELL, F. V. (1943) 'Psychopathology of ageing', *Amer. J. Psychiat.*, 99, 553–6

DIXON, J. C. (1965) 'Cognitive structure in senile conditions with some suggestions for developing a brief screening test of mental status', *J. Gerontol.*, 20, 41–9

DONAHUE, W., HUNTER, W. H. and COONS, D. A. (1953) 'A study of the socialisation of old people', *Geriatrics*, 8, 656–66

DORKEN, H. (1954) 'Psychometric differences between senile dementia and normal senescent decline', *Canad. J. Psychol.*, 8, 187–94

DOUST, J. W., SCHNEIDER, R. A., TALLAND, G. A., WALSH, M. A. and BARKER, G. B. (1953) 'Studies of the physiology of awareness: the correlation between intelligence and anoxaemia in senile dementia', *J. Nerv. Ment. Dis.*, 117, 383–97

DROLLER, H. (1958) 'A geriatric out-patient department', *Lancet*, ii, 739–41

DROLLER, H. and DOSSETT, J. A. (1959) *Geront. clin.*, 1, 96

DUNHAM, H. W. (1956) 'Sociological aspects of mental disorders in later life', in O. J. Kaplan, ed., *q.v.*

EATON, M. T. and WITTSON, C. L. (1962) *Geriatrics*, 17, 229

EBAUGH, F. G. (1956) 'Age introduces stress into the family', *Geriatrics*, 11, 146–50

EDGERTON, R. B. (1967) *The Cloak of Competence*, California University Press

EDUCATION AND SCIENCE, DEPARTMENT OF (1967) *Children and their Primary Schools* (Plowden Report), HMSO

EDUCATION AND SCIENCE, DEPARTMENT OF (1968) *Educating Gifted Children*, Reports on Education, no. 48, HMSO

ELKINS, S. (1959) *Slavery: a problem in American Institutional and Intellectual Life*, University of Chicago Press

ELLIOTT, A. (1969) 'Nursing attachments to general practice', *Brit. Med. J.*, iv, 114

ELLIS, E. (1958) 'Responsibility in cerebral palsy', *Lancet*, 12 Apr.

ELLSWORTH, R. B. and CLAYTON, W. H. (1959) 'Measurement of improvement in mental illness', *J. Consult. Psychol.*, 23, 15–20

EMERY, R. (1965) 'The care of the elderly confused patient', *Brit. Med. J.*, ii, 643

ENOCH, M. D. (1963) 'The care of the elderly disturbed patient', *Lancet*, i, 1160

ENOCH, M. D. and BARKER, J. C. (1965) 'Misuse of Section 29, fact or fiction?', *Lancet*, i, 760–1

EPSTEIN, L. SIMON, A. and MOCK, R. (1963) *Proceedings of the 6th International Congress of Gerontology*, Copenhagen

ESSEN-MØLLER, E. (1956) 'Individual traits and morbidity in a Swedish rural population', *Acta psychiat. Scand.*, suppl. 100

Bibliography

EVANS, J. H. (1965) 'Persistent oral dyskinesia in treatment with phenothiazine derivatives', *Lancet*, i, 458–60

EXETER COUNCIL OF SOCIAL SERVICE *Mental Health – New Needs and Opportunities*

EXTON-SMITH, A. N. (1962) 'Progressive patient care in geriatrics', *Lancet*, i, 260

EXTON-SMITH, A. N. and STANTON, B. R. (1965) *Report of Investigation into the Dietary of Elderly Women Living Alone*, King Edward's Hospital Fund for London

EXTON-SMITH, A. N., NORTON, D. and MCLAREN, (1963) *An Investigation of Geriatric Nursing Problems in Hospitals*, National Corporation for the Care of Old People

EYSENCK, H. J. (1964) *Crime and Personality*, Routledge

EYSENCK, M. D. (1945) 'An exploratory study of mental organisation in senility', *J. Neurol. & Neurosurg. Psychiat.*, 8, 15

FALK, J. M. and LIEBERMAN, M. A. (1969) 'Effects of diverse social-psychological conditions on reminiscences of the elderly', University of Chicago

FARIS, R. E. and DUNHAM, H. W. (1939) *Mental Disorders in Urban Areas*, University of Chicago Press

FINE, W. (1961) *Med. Offr.*, 106, 286

FINE, W. (1963) 'Care of the elderly confused patient', *Lancet*, i, 557, 717

FINK, M., GREEN, M. A. and BENDER, M. B. (1952) 'Face-hand test', *Neurol.*, 2, 46

FISH, F. (1959) 'Senile paranoid states', *Geront. clin. (Basel)*, 1, 127–31

FISH, F. (1960) 'Senile schizophrenia', *J. Ment. Sci.*, 106, 938–46

FISH, F. (1963) 'The organisation of adequate care for the mentally sick old person', *Geront. clin.*, 5, 72–6

FISH, F. and WILLIAMSON, J. (1964) 'A delirium unit in an acute geriatric hospital', *Geront. clin. (Basel)*, 6, 71–80

FISHER, H., MORTON, E. V. B. and NOTLEY, B. (1966) 'Hospital services and the aged', *Brit. Med. J.*, ii, 1325

FISHER, J. and PIERCE, R. C. (1967) 'A typology of mental disorders in the aged', *J. Gerontol.*, 22, 478–84

FISHER, M. (1951) 'Senile dementia: a new explanation of its causation', *Canad. Med. Assoc. J.*, 65, 1–7

FLINT, F. J. and RICHARDS, S. M. (1956) *Brit. Med. J.*, ii, 1537

FOLEY, J. M. (1956) 'Hypertensive and arteriosclerotic vascular disease of the brain in the elderly: neurologic and psychiatric aspects of the disorders of ageing', *Res. Publ. Ass. Nerv. Ment. Dis.*, 35, 171–97

FOX, C. and BIRREN, J. E. (1950) 'Intellectual deterioration in the aged: agreement between the Wechsler–Bellevue and the Babcock–Levy', *J. Consult. Psychol.*, 14, 305–10

FREEMAN, H. E. and SIMMONS, O. G. (1963) *The Mental Patient Comes Home*, Wiley

FREEMAN, H. L. and FARNDALE, W. A. J., eds (1967) *New Aspects of the Mental Health Services*, Pergamon Press

FREEMAN, J. T. (1963) *Clinical Principles and Drugs in the Ageing*, Illinois

FREUD, S. (1900) *The Interpretation of Dreams*, trans. J. Strachey, Hogarth Press, 1952

FREYHAN, F. A., WOODFORD, R. B. and KETTY, S. S. (1951) 'Cerebral blood flow and metabolism in psychoses of senility', *J. nerv. ment. Dis.*, 113, 449

FRY, J. (1967) 'Five years of general practice: a study in simple epidemiology', *Brit. Med. J.*, ii, 1453–7

GARMANY, G. (1955) 'Mental infirmity in old age', *Social Services Quarterly*, Spring

GAWNE, S. C. (1961) in *Hostels and the Mental Health Act*, papers given at London and Leeds, Nat. Assoc. Mental Health

GELLERSTEDT, N. (1939) 'Zur Kenntnis der Hirnveränderungen bei der normalen Altersinvolution' (Our knowledge of cerebral changes in the normal involution of old age), *Upsala Läk.-Fören. Förh.*, 38, 193–408

GIBSON, A. C. (1961) 'Psychosis occurring in the senium', *J. Ment. Sci.*, **107**, 921

GLASSER, (1965) *Reality Therapy*, Harper

GOFFMAN, E. (1961) *Asylums: essays on the social situation of mental patients and other inmates*, Doubleday, Anchor Books

GOLDBERG, E. M. (1968) *The Families of Schizophrenic Patients*, Bedford Square Press

GOLDFARB, A. I. and BURR, H. T. (1969) *Mental Impairment in Homes for the Aged*, Mt Sinai Hospital School of Medicine, New York

GOLDSCHMIDT, L. (1953) 'Social causes for admission to a mental hospital for the aged', *Sociol. Rev.*, July/Oct.

GORDON, S., O'CONNOR, N. and TIZARD, J. (1955) 'Some effects of incentive on the performance of imbeciles on a repetitive task', *Amer. J. Ment. Defic.*, Oct.

GOSLING, R. H. (1955) 'The association of dementia with radiologically demonstrated cerebral atrophy', *J. Neurol. Neurosurg. Psychiat.*, **18**, 129

GOUGH, K. R., LLOYD, O. C. and WILLS, M. R. (1964) *Lancet*, ii, 1261

GRAD, J. and SAINSBURY, P. (1966) 'Problems of caring for the mentally ill at home', *Proc. Roy. Soc. Med.*, **59**, 20–3

GRAD, J. and SAINSBURY, P. (1968) 'The effects that patients have on their families in a community care and a control psychiatric service: a two-year follow-up', *Brit. J. Psychiat.*, **114**, 265–78

GRANICK, R. and NAHEMOW, L. (1961) 'Pre-admission isolation as a factor in adjustment to an old age home', in *The Psychopathology of Ageing*, ed. Hoch and Zubin, q.v.

GREENBLATT, M., LEVINSON, D. and WILLIAMS, R. (1957) eds, *The Patient and the Mental Hospital*, Free Press of Glencoe

GRIFFITHS, L. L., BROCKLEHURST, J. C., MacLEAN, R. and FRY, J. (1966) 'Diet in old age', *Brit. Med. J.*, i, 739

GRUENBERG, E. M. (1954) 'Community conditions and psychoses of the elderly', *Amer. J. Psychiat.*, **110**, 888

GRUENBERG, E. M. (1967) 'The social breakdown syndrome – some origins', *Amer. J. Psychiat.*, **123**, 12

GRUENBERG, E. M. and the staff of the Mental Health Research Unit, New York State Department of Mental Hygiene (1961) *A Mental Health Survey of Older People*, Utica, New York, State Hospitals Press

GRÜNTHAL, E. (1927) 'Klinisch – anatomisch vergleichende Untersuchungen über den Greisenblödsinn' (Clinical and anatomical investigations on senile dementia), *Z. ges. Neurol. Psychiat.*, iii, 763–817

GUILLEBAUD COMMITTEE, *see* Committee of Enquiry into the Cost of the National Health Service, 1956

HAASE, H-J. and JANSSEN, P. A. J. (1965) *The Action of Neuroleptic Drugs*, Amsterdam, North Holland Publishing Co.

HAIDER, I. (1967) 'Community care or hospitalisation: some observations on 100 senile patients', *Brit. J. Psychiat.*, **113**, 865–6

HAIDER, I. (1968) 'A social and clinical study of geriatric admission to a psychiatric hospital', *Internat. J. Soc. Psychiat.*, **14**, 95

HALL, M. R. P. (1965) *Lancet*, i, 1325

HALL, M. R. P., PEARSON, R. C. M. and ROTH, M. (1967) *Brit. Med. J.*, iii, 614

HALMOS, P. (1952) *Solitude and Privacy: a study of social isolation: its causes and therapy*, Routledge

HALSALL, R. W. and LLOYD, W. H. (1961) 'Admission of elderly people to hospital' *Brit. Med. J.*, ii, 1768

HALSTEAD, H. J. (1943) 'A psychometric study of senility', *J. Ment. Sci.*, **89**, 363–373

Bibliography

HAMILTON, M. W. and HOENIG, J. (1966) 'The elderly psychiatric patient and the medical social services', *Med. Offr.* 193–6, 7 Oct.

HARGREAVES, D. H. (1967) *Social Relations in a Secondary School*, Routledge

HARRIS, A. I. and CLAUSEN, R. (1968) *Social Welfare for the Elderly*, 2 vols, HMSO

HARVEY, A. (1965) 'The unknown prisoners', *Guardian*, 10 Aug.

HEALTH, MINISTER OF (1968) *Findings and Recommendations following Enquiries into Allegations concerning the Care of Elderly Patients in Certain Hospitals*, Cmnd 3687, HMSO

HEALTH, MINISTRY OF (1949) *Annual Report for 1948*, HMSO

HEALTH, MINISTRY OF (1950) *The Care of the Aged Suffering from Mental Disorder*, RHB (50) 26, HMSO, 1 Apr.

HEALTH, MINISTRY OF (1957a) *Annual Report* of the Chief Medical Officer

HEALTH, MINISTRY OF (1957b) *Local Authority Services for the Chronic Sick and Infirm*, Circular 14/57, HMSO

HEALTH, MINISTRY OF (1961) Working Party on Special Hospitals: *Report. Special Hospitals*, HMSO

HEALTH, MINISTRY OF (1962) *Residential Accommodation for Elderly People: Building Note*, no. 2, HMSO

HEALTH, MINISTRY OF (1963) *Health and Welfare: the development of community care*, Cmnd 1973, HMSO

HEALTH, MINISTRY OF (1965a) *Care of the Elderly in Hospitals and Residential Homes*, HM (65) 77

HEALTH, MINISTRY OF (1965b) Memorandum to local and hospital authorities, 15 Sept.

HEALTH, MINISTRY OF (1966) *The Development of Community Care*, Cmnd 3022, HMSO

HEALTH, MINISTRY OF (1967) *Residential Hostels for the Mentally Disordered*, Local Authority Building Note, no. 6

HEALTH, MINISTRY OF (1968) *Annual Report for the Year 1967*, Cmnd 3702, HMSO

HEALTH AND SOCIAL SECURITY, DEPARTMENT OF (1969) *Annual Report for the Year 1968*, Cmnd 4100, HMSO

HEMPHILL, R. E. (1960) 'Psychiatric half-way hostel', *Lancet*, 26 Mar.

HEPPLE, B. (1968) *Race, Jobs and the Law in Britain*, Allen Lane, Penguin Press

HERBERT, E. and JACOBSON, S. (1966) 'Geriatric admissions to a mental hospital', *Brit. J. Psychiat.*, 112, 592

HERRIDGE, C. F. (1960) 'Physical disorders in psychiatric illness,' *Lancet*, ii, 949–951

HETHERINGTON, R. J. (1965) 'The care of the elderly confused patient', (letter) *Brit. Med. J.*, ii, 879

HILL, M. N. (1961) *An Approach to Old Age and Its Problems*, Oliver & Boyd

HIMWICH, H. E. (1951) *Brain Metabolism and Cerebral Disorders*, Baltimore, Williams & Wilkins

HOCH, P. H. and ZUBIN, J. eds (1961) *The Psychopathology of Ageing*, Grune & Stratton

HOENIG, J. (1968) 'The de-segregation of the psychiatric patient', *Proc. Roy. Soc. Med.* (Section of Psychiatry), 61, 115–20

HOENIG, J. and HAMILTON, M. W. (1967a) 'The burden on the household in an extramural psychiatric service', in *New Aspects of the Mental Health Services*, ed. Freeman and Farndale, *q.v.*

HOENIG, J. and HAMILTON, M. W. (1967b) 'Extramural psychiatric care and the elderly', *Brit. J. Psychiat.*, 113, 435–43

HOPKINS, B. and POST, F. (1955) 'The significance of abstract and concrete behaviour in elderly psychiatric patients and control subjects', *J. Ment. Sci.*, 101, 841–50

HOPKINS, B. and ROTH, M. (1953) 'Psychological test performance in patients over 60;

II Paraphrenia, arteriosclerotic psychosis and acute confusion', *J. Ment. Sci.*, 99, 451–63

HOWELL, T. H. (1966) 'Trends in psychogeriatric care', *Brit. Hosp. J.*, 28 Oct.

HOWELL, T. H. (1967) *Lancet*, i, 110–11

HUGHES, J. C. and LITTLE, J. D. (1967) 'An appraisal of the continuing practice of prescribing tranquillizing drugs for long-stay psychiatric patients', *Brit. J. Psychiat.*, 113, 867–73

HUNTER, P. (1965) 'Dementia in the elderly', *Brit. Hosp. J. and Soc. Serv. Rev.*, 23 Apr.

HUNTER, R., EARL, C. J. and JANZ, D. (1964a) 'A syndrome of abnormal movements and dementia in leucotomized patients treated with phenothiazines', *J. Neurol. & Neurosurg. Psychiat.*, 27, 219–23

HUNTER, R., EARL, C. J. and THORNICROFT, S. (1964b) 'An apparently irreversible syndrome of abnormal movements following phenothiazine medications', *Brit. Med. J.*, 57, 758–62

HUNTER, T. D. (1967) 'Self-run hospitals', *New Society*, 9, 356

INGLIS, J. (1959) *J. Ment. Sci.*, 105, 440

IRVINE, E. D. (1967) 'Community care for the elderly mentally deteriorated', *District Nursing*, 34–5, May

IRVINE, R. E. (1963) 'Progressive patient care in the geriatric unit', *Postgrad. Med. J.*, 39, 401–7

IRVING, G., MCADAM, E. and ROBINSON, R. A. (1969) 'The validity of some cognitive tests in the assessment of dementia', *Brit. J. Psychiat.*, 115

ISAACS, B. and THOMPSON, J. (1960) 'Holiday admissions to a geriatric unit', *Lancet*, i, 969–71

JACKSON, B. and MARSDEN, D. (1962) *Education and the Working Class*, Routledge

JACOBS, E. (1969) 'Broadmoor: an institution based on risk', *Sunday Times*, 30 Mar.

JOHNSON, M. L. (1970) 'Sound factors in the health and nutrition of the elderly', *Med. Offr.*, 24 Apr.

JONES, K. S. and MILNE, V. M. (1966) 'Portrait of a psychogeriatric hostel', *Brit. Hosp. J. and Soc. Serv. Rev.*, 159–63, 28 Jan.

JONES, K. and TILLOTSON, A. (1967) 'The Adult Population of Epileptic Colonies', in *New Aspects of the Mental Health Service*, eds Freeman and Farndale, Pergamon Press

JONES, M. (1962) *Social Psychiatry*, Springfield, C. C. Thomas

JOYSTON-BECHAL, M. P. (1965) 'Persistent oral dyskinesia in treatment with phenothiazine derivatives', *Lancet*, i, 458–60

JUST, G., ed. (1939) *Handbuch der Erbbiologie des Menschen*, vol. 5, part 2, Berlin, Springer

KAHN, R. L., GOLDFARB, A. I., POLLACK, M. and PECK, A. (1960) 'Brief objective measures for the determination of mental status in the aged', *Amer. J. Psychiat.*, 117, 326–8

KAHN, R. L., GOLDFARB, A. I., POLLACK, M. and PECK, A. (1962) 'Factors in the selection of psychiatric treatment for institutionalized aged patients', *Amer. J. Psychiat.*, 118, 241

KALLMAN, F. J. (1953) *Heredity in Health and Mental Disorders*, New York, Norton

KALLMAN, F. J. (1961) 'Genetic factors in ageing', in *Psychopathology of Ageing*, ed. Hoch and Zubin, *q.v.*

KALZ, L., NEAL, M. W. and SIMON, A. (1961) 'Observations on psychic mechanisms in organic psychoses of the aged', in *The Psychopathology of Ageing*, ed. Hoch and Zubin, *q.v.*

KAPLAN, B., REED, R. B. and RICHARDSON, W. (1956) 'A comparison of the incidence of hospitalised and non-hospitalised cases of psychosis in two communities', *Amer. Soc. Rev.*, 21, 472–9

Bibliography

KAPLAN, O. J., ed. (1956) *Mental Disorders in Later Life*, Stanford University Press

KASS, W. (1949) 'Wechsler's Mental Deterioration Index in the diagnosis of organic brain damage', *Trans. Kansas Acad. Sci.*, 52, 66–70

KASSEL, V. (1957) 'Psychosis in the aged', *J. Amer. Geriat. Soc.*, 5, 319–37

KAY, D. W. K. (1959) 'Observations on the natural history and genetics of old age psychoses: A. Stockholm material, 1931–37', *Proc. Roy. Soc. Med.*, 52, 791–4

KAY, D. W. K. (1962) 'Outcome and cause of death in mental disorders of old age; a long-term follow-up of functional and organic psychoses', *Acta. psychiat. Scand.*, 38, 249–76

KAY, D. W. K. and ROTH, M. (1955) 'Physical accompaniments of mental disorder in old age', *Lancet*, ii, 740–5

KAY, D. W. K. and ROTH, M. (1961a) 'Environmental and hereditary factors in the schizophrenias of old age', *J. Ment. Sci.*, 107, 649

KAY, D. W. K. and ROTH, M. (1961b) 'Physical illness and social factors in the psychiatric disorders of old age', *Proc. of the Third World Congress of Psychiatry, Toronto*

KAY, D. W. K., BEAMISH, P. and ROTH, M. (1962) 'Some medical and social characteristrics of elderly people under state care: a comparison of geriatric wards, mental hospitals and welfare homes', Keele, *Sociol. Rev.* Monograph, no. 5, 173–93

KAY, D. W. K., BEAMISH, P. and ROTH, M. (1964) 'Old age mental disorders in Newcastle upon Tyne', *Brit. J. Psychiat.*, 110, 146 (part I, A survey of prevalence) and 668 (part II, A study of possible social and medical causes)

KAY, D. W. K., NORRIS, V. and POST, F. (1956) 'Prognosis in psychiatric disorders of the elderly: an attempt to define indicators of early death and early recovery', *J. Ment. Sci.*, 102, 129–40

KAY, D. W. K., ROTH, M. and HALL, M. R. P. (1966) 'Special problems of the aged and the organisation of hospital services', *Brit. Med. J.*, ii, 967–72

KEMP, R. (1962) 'Diagnosis of old age', *Lancet*, ii, 515

KENNEDY, A. (1959) 'Psychological factors in confusional states in the elderly', *Geront. clin. (Basel)*, 1, 71

KESSEL, W. I. N. (1960) 'Psychiatric morbidity in a London general practice', *Brit. J. prev. soc. Med.*, 14, 16–22

KIDD, C. B. (1962a) 'Criteria for the admission of the elderly to geriatric and psychiatric units', *J. Ment. Sci.*, 108, 68–74

KIDD, C. B. (1962b) 'Misplacement of the elderly in hospital', *Brit. Med. J.*, ii, 1491

KIDD, C. B. (1962c) 'Old people in mental hospitals', *Irish J. Med. Sci.*, 434, 72–8

KIDD, C. B. (1962d) 'Social attitudes to the elderly sick', *Geront. clin. (Basel)*, 4, 33–42

KIDD, H. B. (1961) *Brit. Med. J.*, i, suppl. 103 and 106

KIDD, H. B. (1962) 'Mental disorder in old age', *Brit. Med. J.*, ii, 857–8

KIDD, H. B. (1963a) 'The care of the elderly disturbed patient', *Lancet*, i, 442

KIDD, H. B. (1963b) [On the use of Section 29 of the Mental Health Act] *Lancet*, i, 997

KIDD, M. (1964) 'Alzheimer's Disease: an electron microscopical study', *Brain*, 87, 307

KING, P. D. (1960) 'A statistical comparison of senile brain disease and Alzheimer's Disease', *J. Clin. Exp. Psychopath.*, 21, 31

KING, R. D. and RAYNES, N. V. (1968) 'An operational measure of inmate management in residential institutions', *Soc. Science and Medicine*, 2(1) 41–53

KLARE, H. J. (1967) 'Prisons since the Mountbatten Report', *New Society*, 286–7, 31 Aug.

KOLB, L. (1956) 'Mental hospitalisation of the aged: is it being overdone?', *Amer. J. Psychiat.*, 112, 627–36

KOREY, S. R., SCHEINBERG, L., TERRY, R. and STEIN, A. (1961) 'Studies in presenile dementia', *Trans. Amer. Neurol. Ass.*, 86, 99

KOSMYRYK, R. (1967) 'Which homes for old people? Life with the daughter', *The Guardian*, 15 Aug., p. 14

KRAL, V. A. (1962) 'Senescent forgetfulness, benign and malignant', *Canad. med. Ass. J.*, 86, 257–60

KRAL, V. A. *et al.*, (1964) 'Biologic, psychologic and sociologic studies in normal aged persons and patients with senile psychosis', *J. Amer. Geriat. Soc.*, 12, 21

KUGEL, R. and WOLFENSBERGER, W., eds (1969) *Changing Patterns in Residential Services for the Mentally Retarded*, Washington, US Government Printing Office

KUSHLICK, A. (1967) 'A method of evaluating the effectiveness of a community health service', *Soc. Econ. Admin.*, 1(4)

KUTNER, B., ROSENSTOCK, F. and GOLDMAN, M. (1969) A Therapeutic Community for the Chronically Ill Ageing, unpublished paper, Centre for Social Research in Rehab. Med., New York

LABOUR PARTY (1969) *Labour's Social Strategy*

LAING, R. D. (1960) *The Divided Self*, Tavistock (Penguin 1965)

LAING, R. D. (1967) *The Politics of Experience and the Bird of Paradise*, Penguin

LAING, R. D. and COOPER, D. G. (1964) *Reason and Violence*, Tavistock

LAMBERT, R. (1968) *The Hothouse Society*, Weidenfeld & Nicolson

LAMBERT, R., HIPKIN, J. and STAGG, S. (1968) *New Wine in Old Bottles? Studies in integration within the public schools*, Occasional Paper 28, Bell

LARSSON, T. and SJÖGREN, T. (1954) 'A methodological, psychiatric and statistical study of a large Swedish population', *Acta. psychiat. Scand.*, suppl. 89

LARSSON, T., SJÖGREN, T. and JACOBSON, G. (1963) 'Senile dementia: a clinical, socio-medical and geriatric study', *Acta. psychiat. Scand.*, 39, suppl. 167, 1–259

LEAKE, C. D. (1964) 'Treating confused geriatric patients', *Geriatrics*, 19, 466–7

LEDERMANN, E. K. (1962) *Lancet*, ii, 1382

LEIPER, J. and WARIN, J. F. (1968) 'General practitioners and nursing staff: a complete attachment scheme in retrospect and prospect', *Brit. Med. J.*, ii, 41

LEMERT, E. (1967) *Human Deviance, Social Problems and Social Control*, Prentice-Hall

LEWANDOWSKI, T. (1962) 'Evaluation of patients in a geriatric rehabilitation unit of a state mental hospital: use of a rating scale system', *J. Amer. Geriat. Soc.*, 10, 526–31

LEWIS, A. J. (1946) 'Ageing and senility: a major problem of psychiatry', *J. Ment. Sci.*, 92, 150

LEWIS, A. J. and GOLDSCHMIDT, H. (1943) 'Social causes for admission to a mental hospital for the aged', *Sociol. Rev.*, 35, 86

LIDDELL, D. W., HERBERT, E. and CROTTY, I. (1962) 'Problem of the geriatric patient in the mental hospital', *Internat. J. Soc. Psychiat.*, 8, 253

LIEBERMAN, M. A. (1944) 'Symptomatology and management of acute grief', *Amer. J. Psychiat.*, 101, 141–8

LIEBERMAN, M. A. (1965a) 'Depressive affect and vulnerability to environmental change in the aged', paper presented at Duke University Council on Gerontology, 27 Apr., *Proceedings of Seminars, 1961–5*, 328–35

LIEBERMAN, M. A. (1965b) 'Factors in environmental change', in *Patterns of Living and Housing of Middle Aged and Older People*, US Dept. of Health, Education and Welfare, 117–25

LIEBERMAN, M. A. (1965c) 'Psychological correlates of impending death: some preliminary observations', *J. Gerontol.*, 20(2), 181–90

LIEBERMAN, M. A. (1965d) 'Observations on death and dying', paper presented to Gerontological Society meeting, Los Angeles, 12 Nov.

LIEBERMAN, M. A. (1969) 'Institutionalization of the aged: effects on behaviour', *J. Gerontol.*, 24, 336

LIEBERMAN, M. A. and LAKIN, M. (1963) 'On becoming an institutionalised aged person', in *Process of Ageing*, ed Williams, Tibbitts and Donahue, *q.v.*, i, 475–503

LIEBERMAN, M. A., PROCK, V. N. and TOBIN, S. S. (1968) 'Psychological effects of institutionalisation', *J. Gerontol.*, 23, 343–51

Bibliography

LIN, TSUNG-YI (1953) 'Mental disorder in Chinese and other cultures', *Psychiatry*, 16, 313–36

LIPMAN, A. (1967) 'Chairs as territory', *New Society* 20 Apr.

LISS, L. (1960) 'Senile brain changes: histopathology of the ganglion cells', *J. Neuropath. exp. Neurol.*, 19, 559

LLEWELLYN, A. (1961) 'Management of confusion and restlessness in the aged', *Brit. J. Clin. Pract.*, 15, 839

LORING, J., ed. (1965) *Teaching the Cerebral Palsied Child*, Heinemann

LOW, M., SINGER, M. and ZOBEL, H. (1951) 'Development of a record for the description of psychiatric patients', *Psychiat. Serv. Cent. J.*, 3, no. 3

LOWE, C. R. and MCKEOWN, T. (1950) 'Investigation of 393 patients seeking admission to a hospital for the chronic sick', *Brit. Med. J.*, ii, 699

LOWE, J. J. H. (1963) [On the use of section 29 of the Mental Health Act] *Lancet*, i, 997

LOWENTHAL, M. F. and TRIER, M. (1967) 'The elderly ex-mental patient', *Internat. J. Soc. Psychiat.*, Spring

LOWRY, D. M. O. (1959) 'The pursuit of mental ill-health: four cases in a London borough', *Med. Offr.*, 23 Oct.

LOWTHER, C. P. and WILLIAMSON, J. (1966) 'Old people and their relatives', *Lancet*, 31 Dec.

LUCE, G. and SEGAL, J. (1967) *Sleep*, Heinemann

LUCERO, R. J. and MEYER, B. T. (1951) 'A behavioural rating scale suitable for use in mental hospitals', *J. Clin. Psychol.*, 7, 250–4

LYLE, J. G. (1959) 'The effect of an institution environment upon verbal development of imbecile children, (1) Verbal intelligence', *J. Ment. Defic. Res.*, 3, 122–8

LYLE, J. G. (1960) 'Speech and language', *J. Ment. Defic. Res.*, 4, 1–13

MCADAM, W. and ROBINSON, R. A. (1956) 'Senile intellectual deterioration and the electroencephalogram: a quantitative correlation', *J. Ment. Sci.*, 102, 819–25

MCADAM, W. and ROBINSON, R. A. (1957) 'Prognosis in senile deterioration', *J. Ment. Sci.*, 103, 821–3

MCADAM, W. and ROBINSON, R. A. (1962) 'Diagnostic and prognostic value of the EEG in psychiatric geriatrics', in Blumenthal, ed., *q.v.*

MCDONALD, C. (1969) 'Clinical heterogeneity in senile dementia', *Brit. J. Psychiat.*, 115, 267–71

MCDONALD, J. (1964) 'Psychiatric nurse social worker', London, *Nursing Mirror*, 118 3084

MCKEOWN, T. (1958) *Lancet*, i, 701

MCKEOWN, T. and CROSS, K. W. (1969) 'Responsibilities of hospitals and local authorities for elderly patients', *Brit. J. prev. soc. Med.*, 23, 36

MCKEOWN, T., MACKINTOSH, J. M. and LOWE, C. R. (1961) 'The influence of age on the type of hospital to which patients are admitted', *Lancet*, i, 818–20

MCMAHON, A. W. and RHADICK, P. J. (1963) 'Reminiscing: its adaptational significance in the aged', paper at the World Congress of Gerontology, Copenhagen

MACMILLAN, D. (1957) 'Psychiatric aspects of social breakdown in the elderly', *Roy. Soc. Hlth J.*, 77, 830

MACMILLAN, D. (1960) 'Preventive geriatrics: opportunities of a community mental health service', *Lancet*, ii, 1439–41

MACMILLAN, D. (1962a) 'Mental deterioration in the elderly', *Practitioner*, 188, 739–45

MACMILLAN, D. (1962b) 'Mental health services for the aged – a British approach', Suppl. to *Canada's Mental Health*, June

MACMILLAN, D. (1967) 'Problems of a geriatric mental health service', *Brit. J. Psychiat.*, 113, 175–81

Bibliography

MACMILLAN, D. and SHAW, P. (1966) 'Senile breakdown in standards of personal and environmental cleanliness', *Brit. Med. J.*, ii, 1032–7

MALAMUD, N. (1963) *J. Amer. Geriat. Soc.*, **13**, 113

MALZBERG, B. (1945) 'Expectation of psychoses with cerebral arteriosclerosis in New York State, 1920, 1930, 1940', *Psychiat. Q.*, **19**, 122–38

MARKOWE, M. (1967) *Brit. Med. J.*, ii, 703

MARTIN, D. V. (1962) *Adventure in Psychiatry*, Cassirer

MARTIN, F. M. (1960) *Community Mental Health Services*, PEP, no. 447

MARTIN, F. M. (1966) *Trends in Psychogeriatric Care*, PEP, no. 497

MARTIN, G. (1959) *Characteristics of Residents in a Sample of Care Homes for the Ageing in Kansas*, Kansas State Board of Health

MAYER-GROSS, W. (1938) 'Discussion on the presenile dementia', *Proc. Roy. Soc. Med.*, **31**, 1443

MAYER-GROSS, W. (1948) 'Mental health survey in a rural area – a preliminary report', *Eugen. Rev.*, **40**, 142–8

MAYER-GROSS, W., SLATER, E. and ROTH, M. (1960) 'Ageing and the mental diseases of the aged', in *Clinical Psychiatry*, Cassell, ch. 11

MEACHER, M. H. (1967) 'Homes for the confused aged', *New Society*, 2 Mar.

MEACHER, M. H. (1968) 'Taken for a ride', *Guardian*, 27 Mar.

MEACHER, M. H. (1968) 'Not so confused anyway', *Soc. Serv. Q.*, **41**(4), 157–60

MEDICAL RESEARCH COUNCIL (1962) *Report for 1960–61*, HMSO

MEER, B. and BAKER, J. A. (1966) 'The Stockton geriatric rating scale', *J. Gerontol.*, **21**, 392–403

MEER, B. and KRAY, C. L. (1964) 'Correlates of disability in a population of hospitalised geriatric patients', *J. Gerontol.*, **19**, 440–6

MEGGENDORFER, F. (1926) Über die hereditare Disposition zur Dementia senilis, *Z. Neur.*, **101**, 387

MEGGENDORFER, F. (1939) 'Alterpsychosen' in *Handbuch der Erbbiologie*, ed. G. Just, *q.v.*, vol. 5, pp. 1021–37

MERTON, R. (1949) 'Social structure and anomie' in *Social Theory and Social Structure*, New York, Free Press of Glencoe

MEZEY, A. G., HODKINSON, H. M. and EVANS, G. J. (1968) 'The elderly in the wrong unit', *Brit. Med. J.*, iii, 17

MILES, H. L., LONDON, J. B. and RAWNSLEY, K. (1962) 'Attitudes of relatives of mental patients', *Brit. J. prev. soc. Med.*, 1

MILLER, E. J. and GWYNNE, G. V. (1968) *A Life Apart: A report on a pilot study of residential institutions for the physically handicapped and young chronic sick*, Tavistock

MITCHELL, J. (1958) 'Speech and language impairment in the older patient', *Geriatrics*, **13**, 467

MONCRIEFF, J. (1966) *Mental Sub-normality in London: a survey of community care*, PEP

MORGAN, R. H. (1967) *Brit. Med. J.*, iv, 171

MORRIS, P. A. (1962) 'A survey of 100 female senile admissions to a mental hospital', *J. Ment. Sci.*, **108**, 801ff.

MORRIS, P. (1969) *Put Away: a sociological study of institutions for the mentally retarded* Routledge

MORRIS, T. and MORRIS, P. (1963) *Pentonville: a sociological study of an English Prison*, Routledge

MOUNTBATTEN REPORT ON PRISON SECURITY (1966), Cmnd 3175, HMSO

MUNDY-CASTLE, A. C., HURST, L. A., BEERSTECHER, D. M. and PRINSLOO, T. (1954), 'The electroencephalogram in the senile psychoses', *Electroenceph. Clin. Neurophysiol.*, **6**, 245–52

MYRDAL, G. (1944) *The American Dilemma*, Harper

Bibliography

NATIONAL ASSOCIATION FOR MENTAL HEALTH (1961) *Hostels and the Mental Health Act*, Nat. Ass. Mental Health

NATIONAL COUNCIL OF SOCIAL SERVICE (1954) *Over Seventy* (Hammersmith Survey), London

NATIONAL COUNCIL OF SOCIAL SERVICE (1970) *Boarding-out Schemes for Elderly People*

NATIONAL COUNCIL OF SOCIAL SERVICE: Committee of Enquiry into the Staffing of Residential Homes (Williams Committee) (1967) *Report : Caring for People*, Allen & Unwin

NATIONAL COUNCIL OF WOMEN (1957) *Care of the Elderly Suffering from Mental Disorder in the London Area*

NATIONAL OLD PEOPLE'S WELFARE COUNCIL (1962) *Mental Frailty in the Elderly*

NATIONAL SOCIETY FOR MENTALLY HANDICAPPED CHILDREN (1967) *Stress in Families with a Mentally Handicapped Child*

NEWMAN, J. L. (1962) 'Old folk in wet beds', *Brit. Med. J.*, i, 1824

NEWMAN, J. L. (1969) *The Prevention of Incontinence*, Auckland, New Zealand

NEWTON, R. D. (1948) 'Identity of Alzheimer's Disease and senile dementia and their relationship to senility', *J. Ment. Sci.*, 94, 225–49

NICHOLAS, P. O. and JOHNSON, R. A. (1966) 'Greenmount House: a two-year study of a hostel for the elderly mentally infirm', *Brit. Med. J.*, ii, 999–1002

NIELSEN, J. M. (1948) *Agnosia, Apraxia, Aphasia : their value in cerebral localisation*, New York

NIELSEN, J. (1963) 'Geronto-psychiatric period-prevalence investigation in a geographically delimited population', *Acta. psychiat. Scand.*, 38, 307–30

NIELSEN, J. (1968) 'Chromosomes in senile dementia', *Brit. J. Psychiat.*, 114, 303–9

NIRJE, E. (1969) 'The normalisation principle and its human management implications', in *Changing Patterns in Residential Services*, ed. Kugel and Wolfensberger, *q.v.*

NISBET, N. H. (1962) 'Experiment in mutual aid between a geriatric unit and a local authority home', *Lancet*, i, 902–3

NOBBS, K. L. G. (1960) 'Confusion in the elderly – some common remediable causes', *Lancet*, ii, 888–9

NORDMAN, L. O. (1956) 'Reversible symptoms in senile psychosis', *Acta. psychiat. Scand.*, suppl. 106, 63–71

NORRIS, V. and POST, F. (1955) 'Outcome of mental breakdown in the elderly', *Brit. Med. J.*, i, 675

NORTON, A. (1961) *Brit. Med. J.*, i, 528

NORTON D. (1967) *The Hospital of the Long-Stay Patient*, Oxford University Press

OAKLEY, P. D. (1962) 'The aetiology of senile dementia', unpublished Ph.D. thesis, University of Manchester

OBRIST, W. D. and HENRY, C. E. (1958) 'Electroencephalographic findings in aged psychiatric patients', *J. nerv. ment. Dis.*, 126, 254–67

OBRIST, W. D., HENRY, C. E. and JUSTICE, W. A. (1961) 'Longitudinal study of EEG in old age', *Excerpts Med. Int. Congr. Series*, no. 37, 180–1

O'CONNELL, B. A. (1954) 'Psychiatric illness in the elderly: a follow-up study', *Brit. Med. J.*, ii, 1206

ØEDEGAARD, O. (1946) 'A statistical investigation of the incidence of mental disorder in Norway', *Psychiat. Q.*, 20, 381–99

ORAM, E. G. and CLARK, D. H. (1966) 'Working for the hospital', *Brit. J. Psychiat.*, 112, 997–1005

ORBACH, C. E., BARD, M. and SUTHERLAND, A. M. (1957) 'Fears and defensive adaptations to the loss of anal and sphincter control', *Psychoan. Rev.*, 44, 121

ORME, J. E. (1957) 'Non-verbal and verbal performance in normal old age, senile dementia and elderly depression', *J. Geront.*, 12, 408–13

Bibliography

PAMPIGLIONE, G. and POST, F. (1958) 'The value of electroencephalographic examinations in psychiatric disorders of old age', *Geriatrics*, 13, 725–32

PARKSIDE BEHAVIOURAL RATING SCALE (1957) *J. Ment. Sci.*, 103, 200–8

PARNELL, R. W. (1965) 'The care of the elderly confused patient', (letter) *Brit. Med. J.*, ii, 757, 1123

PARNELL, R. W. (1968) *Geront. clin.*, 10, 30

PARNELL, R. W., CROSS, K. W. and WALL, M. (1968) 'Changing use of hospital beds by the elderly', *Brit. Med. J.*, iv, 763–5

PARSONS, P. L. (1965) 'Mental health of Swansea's old folk', *Brit. J. prev. soc. Med.*, 19, 43ff.

PARTRIDGE, J. (1969) *Life in a Secondary Modern School*, Penguin

PATERSON, A. (1942) 'Emotional and cognitive changes in the post-traumatic concconfusional state', *Lancet*, ii, 717

PATERSON, H. F. and DABBS, A. R. (1963) 'Section 29', *Brit. J. Psychiat.*, 109

PATTERSON, O. (1967) *The Sociology of Slavery: an analysis of the origins, development and structure of Negro slave society in Jamaica*, MacGibbon & Kee

PHILLIPS REPORT, *see* Committee on the Economic and Financial Problems of the Provision for Old Age

PHILLIPS, H. T. (1966) 'Homes for the mentally disordered', *Med. Offr.*, 115, 85–92

PLOWDEN REPORT (1967) *see* Education and Science, Dept. of

POLLACK, B. (1956) 'The addition of chlorpromazine to the treatment program for emotional and behaviour disorders in ageing', *Geriatrics*, 11, 255–9

POST, F. (1944) 'Some problems arising from a study of mental patients over the age of sixty years', *J. Ment. Sci.*, 90, 554–65

POST, F. (1958a) 'Psychological disturbances of the elderly', *Public Health*, 231, Sept.

POST, F. (1958b) 'Social factors in old age psychiatry', *Geriatrics*, 13, 567–80

POST, F. (1959a) 'Early treatment of persistent senile confusion', *Geront. clin.*, 1, 114–21

POST, F. (1959b) 'Mental health in old age', *Public Health*, Sept.

POST, F. (1962) *The Significance of Affective Symptoms in Old Age*, Maudsley Monographs, 10, London

POST, F. (1965) *The Clinical Psychiatry of Late Life*, Pergamon Press

PRESSEY, G. L. and SIMCOE, E. (1950) 'Case study comparisons of successful and problem old people', *J. Gerontol.*, 5, 168

PRESTON-THOMAS, H. (1901) Report in 13th *Annual Report of the Local Government Board*, 122–3, quoted in S. Webb and B. Webb *English Poor Law History*, Cass, 1963, part II, i, 348

PRIMROSE, E. J. R. (1962) *Psychological Illness: a community study*, Tavistock

PRYCE, I. G. and EDWARDS, H. (1966) 'Persistent oral dyskinesia in female mental hospital patients', *Brit. J. Psychiat.*, 112, 983–7

PUBLIC SCHOOLS COMMISSION (1970) *Second Report*, HMSO, vol. ii

RABIN, A. I. (1945) 'Psychometric trends in senility and psychoses of the senium', *J. Gen. Psychol.*, 32, 149–62

RAPOPORT, R. N. (1960) *Community as Doctor: new perspectives on a therapeutic community*, Tavistock

RASKIN, N. and EHRENBERG, R. (1956) 'Senescence, senility and Alzheimer's Disease', *Amer. J. Psychiat.*, 113, 133–7

RAVEN, J. C. (1959) 'Changes in productive and reproductive intellectual capacity between sixty and ninety years of age', Symposium on old age at the British Psychological Society Conference, Cambridge

READ, A. E., GOUGH, K. R., PARDOE, J. L. and NICHOLAS, A. (1965) 'Nutritional studies on entrants to an old people's home', *Brit. Med. J.*, ii, 843–8

REGISTRAR-GENERAL (1964) *Statistical Review of England and Wales for the year 1960: Supplement on Mental Health*, HMSO

Bibliography

REHIN, G. F. and MARTIN, F. M. (1968a) *Carrying the Burden: a survey of community mental health services*, Oxford University Press

REHIN, G. F. and MARTIN, F. M. (1968b) *Patterns of Performance in Community Care*, Oxford University Press

REICHARD, S., LIVSON, F. and PETERSEN, P. G. (1962) *Ageing and Personality*, Wiley

REID, D. D. (1960) *Epidemiological Methods in the Study of Mental Disorders*, Public Health Papers, no. 2, Geneva, WHO

REX, J. and MOORE, R. (1967) *Race, Community and Conflict*, Oxford University Press

ROBB, B., ed. on behalf of AEGIS (1967) *Sans Everything: a case to answer*, Nelson

ROBERTS, N. (1961) *Not in My Perfect Mind*, Nat. Assoc. Mental Health

ROBERTSON, E. E. and MASON BROWN, N. L. (1952) 'Review of mental illness in the older age group', *Brit. Med. J.*, ii, 1076

ROBINSON, D. B. (1959) *Arch. gen. Psychiatry*, 1, 41

ROBINSON, K. (1961) '*Patterns of Care: a study of provisions for the mentally disordered in two continents*, Nat. Ass. for Mental Health

ROBINSON, R. A. (1951) *Ulster Med. J.*, 9, 2

ROBINSON, R. A. (1955) 'The correlation between EEG abnormality and senile/arterio-sclerotic organic deterioration', in *Old Age in the Modern World*, Edinburgh, Livingstone, pp. 433-7

ROBINSON, R. A. (1960) 'The practice of a psychiatric geriatric unit', *Geront. clin.*, additamentum 1-19

ROBINSON, R. A. (1962) 'Clinical therapy in the psychiatric geriatric unit', in *Geriatric '62*, ed. H. Le Compte, The Hague, Lannoo, Fielt

ROBINSON, R. A. (1965) 'The diagnosis and prognosis of dementia', in *Current Achievements in Geriatrics*, ed. Anderson and Isaacs, *q.v.*

ROBINSON, R. A. (1965) 'A psychiatric geriatric unit: progressive patient care system at Crichton Royal, Dumfries', pp. 184-9 in *Psychiatric Disorders in the Aged*, Report of symposium of the World Psychiatric Association, London, Geigy monograph

ROBINSON, R. A. and ISAACS, B. (1963) Report to Scottish Western RHB, unpublished

ROSE, A. M. and STUB, H. R. (1956) in *Mental Health and Mental Disorders*, ed. A. M. Rose, Routledge

ROSE, G. (1966) 'Anomie and deviation – a conceptual framework', *Brit. J. Soc.*, Mar.

ROSENMAYER, L. and KOCKEIS, E. (1963) 'Propositions for a sociological theory of ageing and the family', *Internat. Soc. Sci. J.*, 3, 423

ROSIN, A. J. and BOYD, R. V. (1966) *J. Chron. Dis.*, 19, 307

ROSOW, I. (1967) *Social Integration of the Aged*, New York, Free Press

ROTH, M. (1955) 'The natural history of mental disorder in old age', *J. Ment. Sci.*, 101, 281-301

ROTH, M. (1959) 'Mental health problems of ageing and the aged', *WHO Bull.*, 21, 527-61

ROTH, M. (1959) 'Some diagnostic and aetiological aspects of confusional states in the elderly', *Geront. clin. (Basel)*, 4, 83-95

ROTH, M. (1960a) *Conference on the Epidemiology of Mental Disorder*, London, Nuffield Provincial Hospitals Trust

ROTH, M. (1960b) 'Problems of an ageing population', *Brit. Med. J.*, i, 1226-30

ROTH, M. and HOPKINS, B. (1953) 'Psychological test performance in patients over sixty: (1) senile psychosis and the affective disorders of old age', *J. Ment. Sci.*, 99, 439-50

ROTH, M. and KAY, D. W. K. (1962) 'Social, medical and personality factors associated with vulnerability to psychiatric breakdown in old age', *Geront. clin.*, 4, 147-60

ROTH, M. and MORRISSEY, J. D. (1952) 'Problems in the diagnosis and classification of mental disorder in old age, with a study of case material', *J. Ment. Sci.*, 98, 66-80

ROTH, M., TOMLINSON, B. E. and BLESSED, G. (1967) 'The relationship between

531

quantitative measures of dementia and of degenerative changes in the cerebral grey matter of elderly subjects', *Proc. Roy. Soc. Med.*, **60**, 254–8

ROTH, M., TOMLINSON, B. E. and BLESSED, G. (1969) 'Quantitative measures of psychological impairment and cerebral damage (at post-mortem) in normal and demented elderly subjects, with a note on the significance of threshold effects', paper presented to the 8th International Congress of Gerontology at Washington

ROTHSCHILD, D. (1937) 'Pathologic changes in senile psychoses and their biologic significance', *Amer. J. Psychiat.*, **93**, 757–88

ROTHSCHILD, D. (1941) 'The clinical differentiation of senile and arteriosclerotic psychoses', *Amer. J. Psychiat.*, **98**, 324–33

ROTHSCHILD, D. (1956) 'Senile psychoses and psychoses with cerebral arteriosclerosis', in *Mental Disorders in Later Life*, ed. Kaplan, *q.v.*

ROWLAND, H. (1939) 'Segregated communities and mental health', in *Mental Health Publications of the American Association for the Advancement of Science*, ed. F. R. Moulton, no. 9

ROWNTREE, S. (1947) 'Old people', in Nuffield Foundation Report, Ministry of Health *Annual Report*, 1949, Appendix xi

ROYAL COLLEGE OF PHYSICIANS, EDINBURGH (1963) *The Care of the Elderly in Scotland*

ROYAL COMMISSION ON THE LAW RELATING TO MENTAL ILLNESS AND MENTAL DEFICIENCY, 1954–7 (1957) *Report*, Cmnd 169, and Minutes of Evidence, HMSO

RUDD, T. N. (1963) *Postgrad. Med. J.*, **39**, 394

RUDD, T. N., STRUTHERS, J. L. and WATERS, G. (1962) 'Holiday relief schemes: their difficulties and responsibilities', *Hosp. Soc. Serv. J.*, 1257

SAINSBURY, P. (1960) *Report to the Conference on the Epidemiology of Mental Disorders*, Nuffield Provincial Hospitals Trust

SAINSBURY, P. and GRAD, J. (1962) 'Evaluation of treatment and services', in *The Burden of the Community: the epidemiology of mental illness*, London, Oxford University Press for Nuffield Provincial Hospitals Trust

SAINSBURY, P. and GRAD, J. (1963) 'Community care and the elderly psychiatric patient', paper read at 6th International Congress of Gerontology

SARGANT, W. (1957) *Battle for the Mind*, Heinemann

SARGANT, W. (1961) *Brit. Med. J.*, i, 225

SCHEFF, T. J. (1967) 'Stereotypes of insanity', *New Society*, 348–50, 9 March

SCHEFF, T. J. (1967) *Mental Illness and Social Processes*, Harper

SCHEID, K. F. (1933) 'Über senile charakterentwicklung', *Z. Neur.*, **148**, 437

SCHOLZ, W. (1938) *Z. ges. Neurol. Psychiat.*, **162**, 694

SCHONELL, F. J., MCLEOD, J. and COCHRANE, R. G. eds (1963) 'The slow learner – segregation or integration', *Educational Research*, 146–50

SCHWARTZ, P., KURUCZ, J. and KURUCZ, A. (1964) 'Recent observations on senile cerebral changes and their pathogenesis', *J. Amer. Geriat. Soc.*, **12**, 908

SEEBOHM COMMITTEE, see Committee on Local Authority and Allied Personal Social Services

SEEMAN, M. (1959) 'On the meaning of alienation', *Amer. Soc. Rev.*, **24**, Dec.

SEMRAD, E. V. and MCKEON, C. C. (1941) Social factors in old age psychosis', *Dis. Nerv. Syst.*, **2**, 58–62

SHAH, K. V., BANKS, G. D. and MERSKEY, H. (1969) 'Survival in atherosclerotic and senile dementia', *Brit. J. Psychiat.*, **115**, 1283–6

SHANAS, E., TOWNSEND, P., WEDDERBURN, D., FRIIS, H., MILHOJ, P. and STEN-HOUWER, J. (1968) *Old People in Three Industrial Societies*, Routledge

SHAPIRO, M. B., POST, F., LÖFVING, B. and INGLIS, J. (1956) ' "Memory function" in psychiatric patients over sixty: some methodological and diagnostic implications', *J. Ment. Sci.*, **102**, 233–46

Bibliography

SHATIN, L. and FREED, E. X. (1955) 'A behavioural rating scale for mental patients', *J. Ment. Sci.*, 101, 644–53

SHAW, P. H. S. (1957) 'Evidence of social breakdown in the elderly', *Roy. Soc. Health J.*, 77

SHAW, P. and MACMILLAN, D. (1961) 'Nuffield House: a day centre for the psychiatric elderly', *Geront. clin. (Basel)*, 3, 133–45

SHAW, P. and STEVENS, S. (1964) 'Increasing frailty and the care of mentally infirm residents', unpublished, Feb.

SHELDON, J. H. (1948) *The Social Medicine of Old Age*, Oxford University Press

SHEPHERD, M., COOPER, B., BROWN, A. C. and KALTON, G. W. (1964) 'Minor mental illness in London: some aspects of a general practice survey', *Brit. Med. J.*, ii, 1359–63

SHIPLEY, W. C. and BURLINGAME, C. C. (1941) 'A convenient self-administering scale for measuring intellectual impairment in psychotics', *Amer. J. Psychiat.*, 97, 1313

SHOCK, N. W. (1963) *A Classified Bibliography of Gerontology and Geriatrics*, Sections in 3 vols: *to 1948, 1949–55, 1956–61*, Stanford University Press

SHULMAN, R. (1967) 'Vitamin B_{12} deficiency and psychiatric illness', *Brit. J. Psychiat.*, 113, 252–6

SIEGLER, M. and OSMOND, H. (1966) 'Models of Madness', *Brit. J. Psychiat.*, 112, 493, 1200

SIEGLER, M., OSMOND, H. and MANN, H. (1969) 'Laing's Model of Madness', *Brit. J. Psychiat.*, 115, 947–58

SILVER, J., HAMILTON, L. D. and BENNETT, J. L. (1963) 'Effects of personalised nursing care on psychotic geriatric patients', *J. Amer. Geriat. Soc.*, 11, 331

SIMCHOWICZ, T. (1910) 'Histologische Studien über die senile Demenz', *Histol. histopath. Arbeit*, 4, 267

SIMON, A. and CAHAN, R. B. (1963) 'The acute brain syndrome in geriatric patients', *Psychiat. res. Rep.*, 16, 8–21

SIMON, A. and MALAMUD, N. (1953) 'The inadequacy of clinical diagnosis in geriatric psychoses', paper presented at the Gerontological Society, San Francisco

SIMON, A. and MALAMUD, N. (1955) 'The inadequacy of clinical diagnosis in geriatric psychoses', paper presented before the Section on Psychiatry and Neurology, 84th Annual Session of the California Medical Association

SIMON, A. and NEAL, M. W. (1963) 'Patterns of geriatric and mental illness', in *Process of Ageing*, ed. Williams, Tibbitts and Donahue, *q.v.*, i, 449–71

SIMON, A., FISKE, M. and NEAL, M. W. (1959) 'An approach to the study of geriatric mental illness', paper delivered at First Annual Conference of Gerontology, Duke University Center for the Study of Ageing, Durham, North Carolina, Nov.

SIMONDS, W. H. and STEWART, A. (1954) 'Old people living in Dorset: a socio-medical survey of private households', *Brit. J. prev. soc. Med.*, 8, 139–46

SIMPSON, J. (1964) 'Special units for elderly people with mental confusion', *Brit. Hosp. J.*, 13 Nov.

SIMSON, M. R. F. (1965) 'Mentally infirm aged', *Brit. Hosp. J.*, 22 Jan.

SJÖGREN, T. (1948) 'Genetic – statistical and psychiatric investigation of a West Swedish population', *Acta. psychiat. Scand.*, suppl. 52

SJÖGREN, T. (1964) 'Paraphrenic, melancholic and psychoneurotic states in the presenile-senile period of life', *Acta. psychiat. Scand.*, 40, suppl. 176, 1–63

SJÖGREN, T., SJÖGREN, H. and LINDGREN, A. G. H. (1952) 'Morbus Alzheimer and Morbus Pick: a genetic, clinical and patho-anatomical study', *Acta. psychiat. Scand.*, suppl. 82

SLAUGHTER, J. (1970) 'The twilight queue', *Observer*, 10 May, p. 17

SLOTKIN, J. S. (1942) 'The nature and effects of social interaction in schizophrenia', *J. Abnorm. Soc. Psychol.*, 345

Bibliography

SNEDDON, R. (1967) 'Psychiatric geriatric assessment unit at Crichton Road Hospital', *Nursing Mirror*, 81, x–xv

SPENCER, A. D. (1969) letter, *Guardian*, 8 Apr.

SROLE, L. (1956) 'Social integration and certain corollaries', *Amer. Soc. Rev.*, December

STANTON, A. H. and SCHWARTZ, M. S. (1954) *The Mental Hospital*, New York, Basic Books

STEDMAN, D. J. and EICHORN, D. H. (1964) 'A comparison of growth and development of institutionalised and home-reared monogoloids during infancy and early childhood', *Amer. J. Ment. Defic.*, 69(3)

STEIN, Z. A. and STORES, G. (1965) Discussion of IQ changes in ESN children at special schools, *Brit. J. Educ. Psychol.*, 35, 379

STEIN, Z. and SUSSER, M. (1969) 'Widowhood and mental illness', *Brit. J. prev. soc. Med.*, 23, 108

STENGEL, E. (1944) 'Loss of spatial orientation, constructional apraxia and Gerstmann's Syndrome', *J. Ment. Sci.*, 90, 753

STENGEL, E. (1964) 'Psychopathology of dementia', *Proc. Roy. Soc. Med.*, 57, 911–14

STRATHAN, R. W. and HENDERSON, J. G. (1965) *Quart. J. Med.*, 34, 303

STRATHAN, R. W. and HENDERSON, J. G. (1967) *Quart. J. Med.*, 36, 189

SURBEK, B. (1961) Thesis no. 2755, Université de Génève, Fac. Med.

SUSSER, M. W. and WATSON, W. (1962) *Sociology in Medicine*, Oxford University Press

SYMONDS, C. P. (1953) 'Aphasia', *J. Neurol. Psychiat.*, 16, 1

SZASZ, T. S. (1962) *The Myth of Mental Illness*, Secker & Warburg

SZASZ, T. S. (1963) *Law, Liberty and Psychiatry*, New York, Macmillan

TEC, N. and GRANICK, R. (1960) 'Social isolation and difficulties in social interaction of residents of a home for the aged', *Social Problems*, 7, 226

TERRY, R. D., GONATAS, N. K. and WEISS, M. (1964) 'Ultrastructural studies in Alzheimer's Presenile Dementia', *Amer. J. Path.*, 44, 269

THOMAS, P. (1968) 'Experiences of two preventive clinics for the elderly', *Brit. Med. J.*, ii, 357–60

TIBBITTS, C., ed. (1960) *Handbook in Social Gerontology*, Chicago

TITMUSS, R. M. (1970) *The Gift Relationship : from Human Blood to Social Policy*, Allen & Unwin

TIZARD, J. (1964) *Community Services for the Mentally Handicapped*, London, Oxford Medical Publications

TIZARD, J., KING, R. D., RAYNES, N. V. and YULE, W. (1966) 'The care and treatment of subnormal children in residential institutions', paper read at the Association for Special Education, London

TOBIN, S. S. (1966) 'Childhood reminiscence and institutionalization in the aged', paper read at 7th Congress of International Association of Gerontology, Vienna, June

TOOTH, G. C. and BROOKE, E. (1961) 'Trends in the mental hospital population and their effect on future planning', *Lancet*, i, 710–13

TORRIE, G. (1960) 'Community Care of the Widow,' *Brit. Med. J.*, i 1267

TOWNSEND, G., EXTON-SMITH, A. N., NORMAN, (LADY), POST, F. and WILSON, T. S. (1963) *Accommodation for the Mentally Infirm Aged*, National Corporation for the Care of Old People, Oct.

TOWNSEND, P. (1957) *The Family Life of Old People*, Routledge

TOWNSEND, P. (1962) *The Last Refuge : a survey of residential institutions and homes for the aged in England and Wales*, Routledge

TOWNSEND, P. and WEDDERBURN, D. (1965) *The Aged in the Welfare State*, Bell

TOWNSEND, P. and WOODROFFE, C. (1961) *Nursing Homes in England and Wales: a study of public responsibility*, National Corporation for the Care of Old People

TREDGOLD, R. F., ed. (1958) *Bridging the Gap : from fear to understanding in mental illness*, Christopher Johnson

Bibliography

TRIER, T. R. (1966) 'Characteristics of the mentally-ill aged: a comparison of patients with psychogenic disorders and patients with organic brain syndrome', *J. Gerontol.*, 21, 354-64

TUCKMAN, J. and LORGE, I. (1954) 'Old people's appraisal of adjustment over the life span', *J. Personality*, 22, 417-22

TUNBRIDGE, R. E. (1963) *J. Coll. of GPs*, 6, 55, suppl. no. 2

TUNSTALL, J. (1966) *Old and Alone*, Routledge

TURTON, E. C. and WARREN, P. K. G. (1960) 'Dementia: a clinical and EEG study of 274 patients over the age of sixty', *J. Ment. Sci.*, 106, 1493-9

UHRBRAND, L. and FAURBYE, A. (1960) 'Reversible and irreversible dyskinesia after treatment with perphenazine, chlorpromazine, reserpine and electro-convulsive therapy', *Psychopharmacologia*, i, 408-18

WADSWORTH, G. L., QUESNEL, E., *et al.* (1943) 'An evaluation of treatment for senile psychosis with Vitamin B Complex', *Amer. J. Psychiat.*, 99, 807

WADSWORTH, W. V., SCOTT, R. F. and WELLS, B. W. P. (1961) 'Employability of long-stay schizophrenic patients', *Lancet*, 9 Sept., 593

WAHAL, K. M. and RIGGS, H. E. (1960) *Archs. Neurol.*, *Chicago*, 2, 151

WALKER, J. H. and MCCLURE, L. M. (1969) 'Community nurses' view of genera practice attachment', *Brit. Med. J.*, iii, 584-7

WALTON, H., BENNETT, R. G. and NAHEMOW, L. (1964) 'Psychiatric illness and adjustment in a home for the aged', *Ann. NY Acad. Sci.*, 105, 897-917

WATTS, C. A. H., CAWTE, E. C. and KUENSSBERG, E. V. (1964) 'A survey of mental illness in general practice', *Brit. Med. J.*, ii, 1351-9

WAYNE, G. J. (1960) 'The psychiatric problems of the elderly patient', *Mental Hygiene*, 44, 257

WEINBERGER, H. L. (1926) 'Über die hereditären Beziehungen der senilen Demenz', *Z. Neur.*, 106, 666

WEINER, H. and SCHUSTER, D. B. (1956) 'The electroencephalogram in dementia: some preliminary observations and conclusions', *Electroenceph. Clin. Neurophysiol.*, 8, 479-88

WEINSTEIN, E. A. and KAHN, R. L. (1952) 'Nonphasic misnaming (paraphasia) in organic brain disease', *Arch. Neurol. Psychiat.*, *Chicago*, 67, 72

WESTMORELAND, J. E. (1963) 'Special difficulties of mental welfare officers with the aged', *Mental Health*, Feb.

WEXBERG, L. E. (1942) 'Mental health in later maturity', *US Public Health Reports*, suppl. no. 168, 19-20

WHELAN, and BREE, M. H. (1946) 'Conducing to the cure', *Lancet*, Oct.

WHITE, R. B., MILLER, S. C. and POLANSKY, N. S. (1955) 'From sanctuary to social demand: dilemma of the therapeutic community', paper presented to the American Psychiatric Association, 12 May

WHITEHEAD, A. J. (1965) 'A comprehensive psychogeriatric service', *Lancet*, ii, 583-586

WIGLEY, G. (1968) 'Community services for mentally infirm old people', *Lancet*, ii, 963-6

WILLIAMS, D. G. T. (1968) 'Legal aspects of positive discrimination', *Soc. Econ. Admin.*, 2(4)

WILLIAMS, H. W., QUESNEL, E., FISH, V. W. and GOODMAN, L. (1942) 'Studies in senile and arteriosclerotic psychoses: I Relative significance of extrinsic factors in their development', *Amer. J. Psychiat.*, 98, 712-15

WILLIAMS, R. H. (1960) 'Changing status, roles and relationships', in *Handbook of Social Gerontology*, ed. Tibbitts, *q.v.*

WILLIAMS, R. H., TIBBITTS, C. and DONAHUE, W., eds (1963) *Processes of Ageing*, New York, Atherton Press, 2 vols.

535

Bibliography

WILLIAMSON, J., LOWTHER, C. P. and GRAY, S. (1966) 'The use of health visitors in preventive geriatrics', *Geront. clin.*, 8, 362–9

WILLIAMSON, J., STOKOE, I. H., GRAY, S., FISHER, M., SMITH, A., MCGHEE, A. and STEPHENSON, E. (1964) 'Old people at home: their unreported needs', *Lancet*, i, 1117–20

WILSON, D. (1967) 'Group homes for ex-psychiatric patients', MA thesis, University of Essex

WILSON, L. A., LAWSON, I. R. and BRASS, W. (1962) 'Multiple disorders in the elderly', *Lancet*, 27 Oct.

WILSON, T. S. (1965) 'Is there a better plan for the mentally frail?', unpublished paper delivered at Cambridge, 25 June

WING, J. K. and BROWN, G. W. (1961) 'Social treatment of chronic schizophrenia: a comparative survey of three mental hospitals', *J. Ment. Sci.*, 107, 847–61

WING, J. K. and FREUDENBERG, R. K. (1962) 'The response of severely ill chronic schizophrenic patients to social stimulation', *Amer. J. Psychiat.*, 118

WITTENBORN, R. J. (1955) *Psychiatric Rating Scales*, Psychological Corporation

WOLF, A. (1959) 'Clinical neuropathology in relation to the process of ageing', in *The Psychology of Ageing*, ed. Birren, q.v.

WOLFENSBERGER, W. (1969) 'The original nature of our institutional models', in Kugel and Wolfensberger, eds, q.v.

WOLFENSBERGER, W. (1970) 'Models of mental retardation', *New Society*, 51–3

WOLFF, K. (1962) 'Treatment of the confused geriatric patient', *Dis. Nerv. Syst.*, 23, 199–203

WOLFF, K. (1964) 'The confused geriatric patient', *J. Amer. Geriat. Soc.*, 12, 266–9

WOLLNER, L. (1964) *Geront. clin.*, 6, 65

WOODFORD-WILLIAMS, E., MCKEON, J. A., TROTTER, I. S., WATSON, D. and BUSHBY, C. (1962) 'The day hospital in the community care of the elderly', *Geront. clin.*, 4, 241–56

WOODROFFE, C. and TOWNSEND, P. (1961) *Nursing Homes in England and Wales: a study of public responsibility*, National Corporation for the Care of Old People

WOODSIDE, M. (1965a) 'Eventide homes', *New Society*, 21 Jan.

WOODSIDE, M. (1965b) 'Hospital and community experience of 150 psychogeriatric patients', *Geront. clin.*, 7, 286–302

WORLD HEALTH ORGANISATION (1959) *Report of Expert Committee on Mental Health Aspects of Ageing and the Aged*, WHO Techn. Rep. Serv., no. 171

WORTH, D. (1965) 'Not in their perfect mind', *Society of Housing Managers Quart. J.*, Jan.

WRIGHT, S. L. (1965) *Med. Offr.*, 114, 264

WRIGHT, C. H. and ROBERTS, C. (1958) 'The place of the Home Help Service in the care of the aged', *Lancet*, 1 Feb.

YARROW, M. R., SCHWARTZ, C. G., MURPHY, H. S. and DEASY, L. (1955) 'The psychological meaning of mental illness in the family', *J. Soc. Issues*, 11, 12–24

YATES, A., ed. (1966) *Grouping in Education*, Wiley

ZANGWILL, O. L. (1964) 'Psychopathology of dementia', *Proc. Roy. Soc. Med.*, 57, 914–17

Index